Malta
and Gozo

the Bradt Travel Guide

Juliet Rix

edition
4

www.bradtguides.com

Bradt Travel Guides Ltd, UK
The Globe Pequot Press Inc, USA

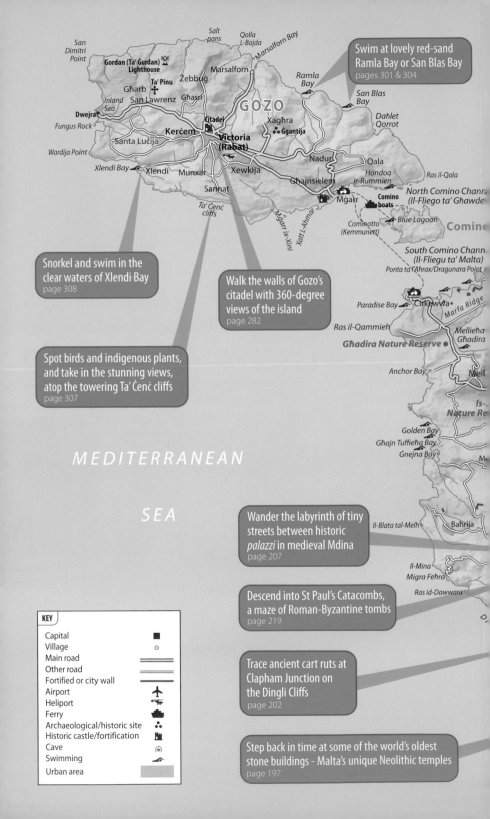

San Dimitri Point

Salt pans

Qolla L-Bajda

Marsalforn Bay

Swim at lovely red-sand Ramla Bay or San Blas Bay
pages 301 & 304

Gordan (Ta' Ġurdan) Lighthouse

Żebbuġ

Marsalforn

Ramla Bay

San Blas Bay

Dahlet Qorrot

Ta' Pinu

Gharb

Għasri

San Lawrenz

Inland Sea

GOZO

Dwejra

Citadel

Xagħra

Ġgantija

Kerċem

Fungus Rock

Victoria (Rabat)

Santa Luċija

Nadur

Qala

Ras il-Qala

Wardija Point

Xlendi Bay

Xlendi

Munxar

Xewkija

Għajnsielem

Hondoq ir-Rummien

North Comino Channel (Il-Fliego ta' Ghawde

Sannat

Mġarr

Comino boats

South Comino Channel (Il-Fliegu ta' Malta)

Ta' Ċenċ cliffs

Mġarr ix-Xini

Xatt L-Aħmar

Cominotto (Kemmunett)

Blue Lagoon

Comino

Ponta ta' l'Aħrax/Dragunara Point

Snorkel and swim in the clear waters of Xlendi Bay
page 308

Walk the walls of Gozo's citadel with 360-degree views of the island
page 282

Paradise Bay

Ċirkewwa

Marfa Ridge

Ras il-Qammieh

Mellieħa Ghadira

Spot birds and indigenous plants, and take in the stunning views, atop the towering Ta' Ċenċ cliffs
page 307

Għadira Nature Reserve

Anchor Bay

Meil

Is- Nature Re

Golden Bay

Għajn Tuffieħa Bay

Għejna Bay

MEDITERRANEAN

SEA

Wander the labyrinth of tiny streets between historic *palazzi* in medieval Mdina
page 207

Il-Blata tal-Melħ

Baħrija

Il-Mina

Migra Feħra

Descend into St Paul's Catacombs, a maze of Roman-Byzantine tombs
page 219

Ras id-Dawwara

Trace ancient cart ruts at Clapham Junction on the Dingli Cliffs
page 202

Step back in time at some of the world's oldest stone buildings - Malta's unique Neolithic temples
page 197

KEY

Capital	■
Village	○
Main road	
Other road	
Fortified or city wall	
Airport	✈
Heliport	⚓
Ferry	⛴
Archaeological/historic site	⁙
Historic castle/fortification	🏰
Cave	⌂
Swimming	🏊
Urban area	

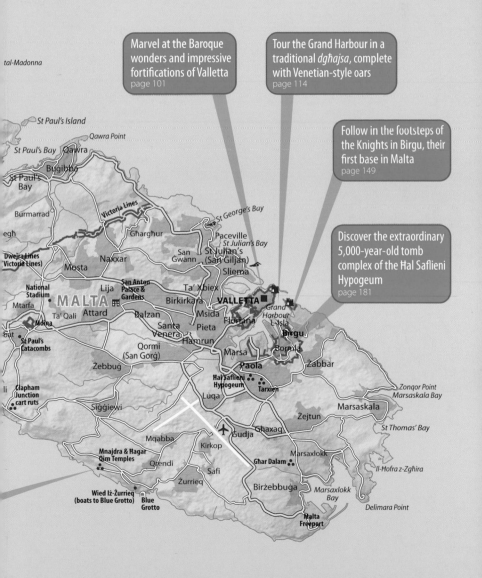

MEDITERRANEAN

SEA

N

0 _____ 4km
0 _____ 3 miles

tal-Madonna

Marvel at the Baroque
wonders and impressive
fortifications of Valletta
page 101

Tour the Grand Harbour in a
traditional *dgħajsa*, complete
with Venetian-style oars
page 114

Follow in the footsteps of
the Knights in Birgu, their
first base in Malta
page 149

Discover the extraordinary
5,000-year-old tomb
complex of the Ħal Saflieni
Hypogeum
page 181

St Paul's Island

Qawra Point

St Paul's Bay   Qawra

Bugibba

St Paul's
Bay

Burmarrad

St George's Bay

Victoria Lines

Gharghur   Paceville
                            St Julian's Bay
egh   San   St Julian's
Dwejra Lines   Gwann   (San Giljan)
Victoria Lines)   Naxxar   Sliema
Mosta
                  Lija   San Anten   Ta' Xbiex
National   Palace &
Stadium   Attard   Gardens   VALLETTA
         Ta' Qali   Birkirkara
Mtarfa   Msida   Floriana   Grand
     Mdina   Balzan   Pieta   Harbour
bat   Santa   L-Isla   Birgu
     St Paul's   Venera   Hamrun   Bormla
     Catacombs   Qormi   Marsa
li   (San Ġorġ)   Paola   Żabbar
     Żebbuġ   Ħal Saflieni
Clapham   Hypogeum
Junction   Siġġiewi   Tarxien   Zonqor Point
cart ruts   Luqa   Marsaskala Bay
                                              Żejtun   Marsaskala

Mqabba   Gudja   Għaxaq   St Thomas' Bay
         Kirkop
Mnajdra & Ħaġar   Safi   Marsaxlokk
Qim Temples   Qrendi   Għar Dalam   Il-Hofra z-Zghira
         Żurrieq
Wied Iż-Żurrieq   Birżebbuġa   Marsaxlokk
(boats to Blue Grotto)   Blue   Bay   Delimara Point
                         Grotto
                                              Malta
                                              Freeport

MALTA

Malta
Don't miss...

Medieval citadels
The walled town of Mdina has retained its medieval feel, with few cars allowed inside and narrow streets still lined with *palazzi* and religious buildings
(AT/S) page 207

Gozo
Ancient salt pans (pictured here; page 295) are just one of the remarkable coastal features of rural, laidback Gozo with its lovely beaches, charming villages and historic Citadel
(AT/S) page 263

Valletta
Malta's tiny capital, built by the Knights of St John, is almost completely surrounded by water (mR/S) page 101

Neolithic temples and carvings
The Ġgantija Temples (pictured here) are some of the oldest stone buildings in the world (VM) page 295

Snorkelling and diving
Malta's clear blue waters are ideal for snorkelling and diving (MJUB/S) page 89

Malta and Gozo in colour

top	St John's Co-Cathedral is a Baroque extravaganza, with a barrel-vaulted ceiling painted by Italian artist Mattia Preti (CW/VM) page 124
above left	Traditional Maltese enclosed balconies (*gallariji*) can be seen all over Valletta; their origin remains a mystery (PV/VM) page 131
below left	The Upper and Lower (pictured) Barrakka Gardens sit atop Valletta's extensive fortifications and offer panoramic views over the Grand Harbour (e/S) page 138
bottom	The imposing design of the Auberge de Castille testifies to the power of the Spanish and Portuguese Knights (CV/VM) page 117

right   The Manoel Theatre is one of the oldest theatres still in use in Europe (VM) page 135

below   Each day at noon in Valletta's Upper Barrakka Gardens the Saluting Battery cannons are fired to the accompaniment of British martial music (AK/S) page 118

bottom   The Grand Master's Palace was the seat of the Knights of Malta until Napoleon took over in 1798; today it contains the State Rooms used by the country's president (CV/VM) page 128

above   Malta's first purpose-built parliament, designed by the architect of the London Shard, Renzo Piano, opened in Valletta in 2015 (SS) page 115

below   The time of the Knights is regularly recreated in In Guardia with some 50 re-enactors parading before the Grand Master (VM) page 133

AUTHOR

Juliet Rix is an award-winning journalist, author and broadcaster for British national and international media in print, audio and online. She started her career at the BBC working in television then radio, including as a foreign correspondent, before going freelance. Travel – for pleasure and for work – has always played an important part in her life so travel writing was a natural development. Juliet writes for the *Telegraph*, *The Times* and the *Guardian*, as well as for BBC Radio and a wide range of other newspapers, magazines and websites. She lives in London.

FEEDBACK REQUEST AND UPDATES WEBSITE

At Bradt Travel Guides we're aware that guidebooks start to go out of date on the day they're published – and that you, our readers, are out there in the field doing research of your own. You'll find out before us when a fine new family-run hotel opens or a favourite restaurant changes hands and goes downhill. So why not write and tell us about your experiences? Contact us on ☏ 01753 893444 or e info@bradtguides.com. We will forward emails to the author, who may post updates on the Bradt website at w bradtupdates. com/maltaandgozo. Alternatively, you can add a review of the book to w bradtguides.com or Amazon.

PUBLISHER'S FOREWORD   *Adrian Phillips, Managing Director*

A few years ago, Hilary Bradt and I travelled to Malta to attend the AGM of the British Guild of Travel Writers. There were several stuffy hours to suffer in a conference room, of course, but when we were finally allowed out to explore we were met by a wind strong enough to pin boats against the harbour walls. It didn't matter; we enjoyed a happy time touring Valletta, with its beautiful monuments built by the Knights of St John and fortified reminders of the islanders' brave stand during World War II. Malta could have offered no clearer riposte to the sun-sand stereotype than it did that day. The perfect Bradt author was also on the trip – Juliet Rix, leading travel journalist and passionate advocate for Malta's historical attractions. And so it was that Bradt's *Malta* guidebook came to be, and – now into a fourth edition – it continues to cater for those visitors who want to learn more about the island's history and culture.

Fourth edition published March 2019
First published May 2010

Bradt Travel Guides Ltd
IDC House, The Vale, Chalfont St Peter, Bucks SL9 9RZ, England
www.bradtguides.com
Print edition published in the USA by The Globe Pequot Press Inc,
PO Box 480, Guilford, Connecticut 06437-0480

Text copyright © 2019 Juliet Rix
Maps copyright © 2019 Bradt Travel Guides Ltd. Includes map data © OpenStreetMap contributors
Illustrations copyright © 2019 Individual photographers and illustrators (see below and page v)
Project Manager: Susannah Lord
Cover research: Pepi Bluck, Perfect Picture

ISBN: 978 1 78477 070 9

British Library Cataloguing in Publication Data
A catalogue record for this book is available from the British Library

Photographs See page v

Maps David McCutcheon FBCart.S and Liezel Bohdanowicz; based on source material under licence from © RMF Publishing and Surveys Ltd (Malta). Temple plans based on site plans from Heritage Malta (all labelling is the author's own).

Illustrations Carole Vincer

Typeset by Ian Spick, Bradt Travel Guides Ltd; and www.dataworks.co.in
Production managed by Jellyfish Print Solutions; printed in India
Digital conversion by www.dataworks.co.in

When I first mentioned to people that I was writing a book on Malta, most looked a bit blank: they associated Malta with package holidays and not much else. Some would come up with 'The Knights of Malta' or the 'Grand Harbour and World War II'. Only very few knew more. This is not to be critical of my friends and colleagues – just a couple of years earlier I was in exactly the same position. It was almost by chance that I discovered just how much this tiny nation really has to offer and became a bit evangelical about it. So, when I was asked if I would write this book, I had to say yes.

Malta has spent many years hiding its light under the bushel of sun-and-sea mass tourism. This Mediterranean island nation certainly has plenty of glorious sunshine, and beautiful clear blue waters, and Gozo in particular is a great place for a relaxing holiday. But for the main island at least, Malta's USP is surely its extraordinary historic – and prehistoric – sites.

My first trip to Malta was actually to write about Gozo. My family and I walked the high Ta' Ċenċ cliffs, soaked up the autumn sun and swam at an almost deserted, red sandy Ramla Beach. And we visited the Ġgantija Temples, my introduction to one of the least-known and most intriguing aspects of Malta's past: the 'Temple Culture' that thrived here 5,500 years ago. It has left us the second-oldest stone buildings in the world, all of which now have UNESCO World Heritage status.

I did not get a chance to see any of the other temples on that trip. We had a mere half-day on the main island – a whirlwind press tour that did not include prehistory. In fact, as we drove past serried ranks of modern apartment blocks and hotels, our first impressions were not great. But then we reached Valletta, Malta's tiny, citadel capital surrounded on three sides by azure sea – a place of real historic charm. Across the Grand Harbour we saw Birgu, the Knights' first home in Malta, and, in the centre of the island, the walled medieval fortified city of Mdina. Historically, I realised, this tiny country punches well above its weight. I knew I would have to return.

And of course I have – criss-crossing the country exploring everything from underground tombs to towering cliffs, welcoming bays to forbidding fortifications, prehistoric temples to high-rise hotels, roadside kiosks to gourmet restaurants. This has only confirmed my view that Malta offers fascination and reward to the visitor way beyond mere sun and sea and far in excess of its size. I hope readers of this book will enjoy the sunshine and the coastline (as I do) but will also have the pleasure of discovering this country's extraordinary 7,000-year history.

Acknowledgements

So many people have helped with this book and I would like to thank them all! Specifically, it could not have happened without the support of the Malta Tourism Authority (MTA) both in London and in Malta. Over the years, Claude Zammit Trevisan, Rosanne Sciberras, Maryanne Portanier, Dominic Micallef, Angela Said and Peter Vella have been especially helpful.

Several members of staff at Heritage Malta have given invaluably of their precious time including Suzannah Depasquale and David Cardona of the Department of Phoenician, Roman and Medieval Sites; Sharon Sultana, Curator of the Museum of Archaeology; Russel Muscat; and in Gozo, Nicoline Sagona. Very special thanks go to Dr Reuben Grima, Senior Curator of Prehistoric Sites at the time of the first edition and now at the University of Malta, who has gone well beyond the call of duty to ensure that my material on the temples is accurate and up to date (if any inaccuracies have crept in, they are mine alone!). Malta guide Vince DeBono, introduced me to much of the history of his country, and checked almost all the first edition copy before it went to press. I am very grateful. And I have since also been kept in touch with developments by guide and Knight of the Order Dane Munro, and in Gozo by Cornil Wambergue of Gozo Adventures.

Dr Stephen Spiteri, world expert on Malta's fortifications, was kind enough both to brief me at the start and check almost all the first edition copy (again, he bears no responsibility for any errors). Joseph Mizzi of Midsea Books provided me with excellent reading material, as well as general advice. Many others took time to answer my questions, including Lorenzo Zahra of the Curia of Malta, Jennifer Wong of the British High Commission, nature guide Annalise Falzon, Petra Bianchi, Catherine Roe, Jay and Alan Jones in Gozo, historian Charles Galea Scannura, Emmanuel Magro Conti, Martin Morana, the staff at Din L-Art Ħelwa and, particularly during the preparation of the second and third editions, Konrad Buhagiar and Guillaume Dreyfus.

On the difficult issue of birds and hunting, I am most grateful to BirdLife Malta, particularly Ray Vella who has been unerring in his careful provision of information (and evidence). I am also grateful to Francis Albani for speaking to me at the time of my initial research when he was secretary to the government's ORNIS advisory committee on the protection of wild birds, hunting and trapping.

Back in the UK, I owe many thanks to Juliet Standing and Wendy Rix for reading the original manuscript and, of course, to the Bradt team who have handled everything with perfect good humour and an apparently genuine belief that, even with the very tight turnarounds we have often had to work with, all would come right in the end. Many thanks especially to Hilary Bradt and Adrian Phillips for believing I could write this book in the first place; and, across the various editions, to Anna Moores, Rachel Fielding, Maisie Fitzpatrick, Katie Wilding, Laura Pidgley, Deborah Gerrard, Hugh Brune, Anne-Marie McLeman, and for this edition particularly Susannah Lord.

Finally, many thanks to my husband, Rod, and sons Daniel and Luke, who put up with my absences (both while I was in Malta and while deep in the computer) and helped with initial research by contributing their own perspectives on Malta.

PHOTOGRAPHS

Alamy Stock Photo: robertharding (rh/A); Scott Bennett (SB); www.flpa.com: Rob Chittenden (RC/FLPA); Gillian Lloyd (GL); Juliet Rix (JR); Shutterstock: anyaivanova (a/S), eldeiv (e/S), Arsenie Krasnevsky (AK/S), Is Mildax (IM/S), Jaroslav Moravcik (JM/S), MJUB (MJUB/S), mRGB(mR/S), Petroos (P/S), Ralf Siemieniec (RS/S), Ildiko Szabo (IS/S), Anibal Trejo (AT/S), Pommeyrol Vincent (PV/S), ZGPhotography (ZGP/S); SuperStock(SS); Visit Malta (viewingmalta.com; VM): Carolina Crutchley (CC/VM), Cs California (C/W), Maysun Abu-Khdeir Granados (MG/VM), Markus Kirchgessner (MK/VM), Giovanni Maroni (GM/VM), ROLEX/Daniel Forster (R/DF/VM), Luke Scicluna (LS/VM), Peter Vanicsek (PV/VM), Clive Vella (CV/VM), Chen Wiezhong (CW/VM); Wikimedia Commons: Denis Barthel (DB/W), Jeffrey Scribberas (JS/W).

Front cover St Paul's Anglican Cathedral and Carmelite Church, Valletta (rh/A)
Back cover Street in Birgu (Three Cities) (LS/VM), Blue Grotto (JM/S)
Title page Gallariji – traditional Maltese balconies (SS), Jumping into a coral lagoon, Malta (VM), Architectural detail of St John's Co-Cathedral, Valletta (JR)

Contents

AUTHOR'S FAVOURITES Finding genuinely characterful accommodation or that unmissable off-the-beaten-track café can be difficult, so the author has chosen a few of her favourite places throughout the country to point you in the right direction. These 'author's favourites' are marked with a ✳.

LISTINGS Accommodation and restaurants are marked with price codes and, unless otherwise stated, are listed in descending price code order (**$$$$$–$**), and alphabetically in each price code.

MAPS

Keys Maps include alphabetical keys covering the locations of those places to stay, eat or drink that are featured in the book. Note that regional maps may not show all hotels and restaurants in the area: other establishments may be located in towns shown on the map.

Grids and grid references Several maps use gridlines to allow easy location of sites. Map grid references are listed in square brackets after the name of the place or site of interest in the text, with page number followed by grid number, eg: [103 C3].

NOTE ON WEBSITES Many Maltese organisations have websites, though some do not. Most use the usual www. prefix, but occasionally a site will just have an address with no prefix. Websites in this guide are indicated by a w, and the www. is omitted where it is not required.

Introduction

Malta offers a wonderful combination of sunshine holiday and fascinating sightseeing. In fact, this island nation has the greatest density of historic sites of any country in the world, and its gorgeous little capital, Valletta, is a UNESCO World Heritage city. There is always something happening in Malta and its year as European Capital of Culture 2018 was the catalyst for an even greater artistic, cultural and historic offering that will last for years to come.

Into an area smaller than the Isle of Wight Malta packs 7,000 years of history – and prehistory. The earliest of its Neolithic temples – strangely little-known beyond its shores – are 2,000 years older than Mycenae, 1,000 years older than the Great Pyramids and 500 years older than the famous standing stones at Stonehenge. They all have UNESCO World Heritage status, as does the Hal Saflieni Hypogeum, an extraordinary underground tomb complex, cut from solid rock, that echoes the architecture of the above-ground temples. And this is just the beginning of the story.

Malta's position in the middle of the Mediterranean and its perfect natural harbours have meant that anyone wishing to control or trade in the Mediterranean has needed access to this country. Almost every major European power in history (and some minor ones) has occupied these islands or tried very hard to do so. Each has left its mark on Malta's landscape and culture. So as well as megalithic temples, carved altars and dramatic underground rooms, Malta has colourful boats adorned with the 'Phoenician' eye of Osiris, Roman mosaics and Roman–Byzantine catacombs, and a still-inhabited medieval walled town of narrow lanes and heavy fortifications.

In the midst of the charming alleyways of today's diminutive capital, Valletta, is hidden the opulent St John's Co-Cathedral and many more examples of the Baroque art and architecture of the Knights of St John – the 'Knights of Malta' – who ruled these islands from 1530 to 1798.

They were followed (after a brief French occupation) by the British. There are still red letterboxes and phone booths all over Malta, and, in Valletta at noon each day, music of the Band of the Royal Marines is played and cannon fired beneath a public garden overlooking the vast expanse of the Grand Harbour.

This impressive harbour was at the centre of Malta's two famous sieges, both of them critical to the future of Europe. In the Great Siege of 1565 the Ottoman Turks very nearly took the island, and 1940–43 saw Hitler and Mussolini try to bomb and starve Malta into submission. The fortitude of the Maltese in holding out against the Axis powers was rewarded by King George VI with Britain's highest award for civilian bravery, the George Cross – the only one ever awarded to an entire nation.

This tiny country has absorbed so many influences over the centuries, and yet Malta is very much Maltese. Ninety-seven per cent of the population was born here and although English is widely spoken, Maltese (or Malti) remains the mother tongue of most of the population. The country has its own cuisine and its own culture. What's more the people of Gozo, Malta's smaller island, pride themselves on being different from the inhabitants of the main island – and Gozo does indeed have its own character.

Taking the 25-minute ferry from Malta to Gozo is like leaving the city for the countryside. Much less built up than its larger neighbour, Gozo has – besides a couple of lovely sandy beaches – a rugged coastal landscape described by a visiting Edward Lear as 'pomskizillious and gromphiberous'. It is thought by some to be the real Calypso's isle, where Homer's Odysseus (Ulysses) remained spellbound by the loving sea nymph for seven years. Gozo is the place to relax.

Malta is welcoming to visitors and nearly two million now come here each year (more than a quarter from the UK). The package-holiday image Malta lived with – and indeed promoted – for some three decades undersold this remarkable little country terribly and is fortunately now changing.

Malta has wonderful weather (with some 300 days of sunshine a year) and plenty of holiday facilities. There are excellent restaurants, and lots of outdoor activities to enjoy – swimming, snorkelling, diving, boating (of various kinds), walking, sports and spas. But there is also so much that is unique to Malta that has often been overlooked.

In the last few years, helped by the year with Valletta as Capital of Culture, Malta has begun to value and to capitalise on its superb historic sights. There has been a huge amount of restoration and refurbishment. Historic homes have risen from the dust, with quite a number becoming boutique hotels or visitor apartments, and cultural tourism is dramatically on the rise. A few cognoscenti have long known the hidden gem that was the real Malta; now the country is wide open for everyone to discover.

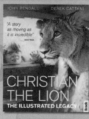

Part One

GENERAL INFORMATION

Location In the middle of the Mediterranean, 93km south of Sicily, 288km east of Tunisia, 355km north of Libya and 815km west of Crete.

Islands Three inhabited islands: Malta, Gozo and Comino. Three tiny uninhabited islands: Cominotto, Filfla and St Paul's Island, plus the semi-derelict Manoel Island in Marsamxett Harbour due for redevelopment.

Size Total area 316km^2 with 253km of coastline. Malta 30km (SE–NW) x 11km (SW–NE), area 245.7km^2; Gozo 14km x 5km, area 67.1km^2; Comino 2.5km x 1.5km, area 2.8km^2.

Population 475,000 and rising fast – of which Gozo about 32,700, Comino one family (approximately three people)

Status Independent republic. Member of the European Union, the Commonwealth and the United Nations.

Currency Euro

Exchange rate €1 = US$1.14, €1 = £0.89 (December 2018)

Climate Mediterranean island – hot dry summers and mild damp winters with chilly winds

Official languages Maltese and English

Capital Valletta

Religion Roman Catholic (98%)

Time GMT +2 hours in summer (from the last Sunday in March until the Saturday before the last Sunday in October), otherwise GMT +1 hour. Always UK +1 hour.

Economy 35% of GDP from tourism. Manufacturing strong in electronics and pharmaceuticals.

GDP US$26,900 per capita (an all-time high)

National airline Air Malta

Electricity 230–240V, 50Hz, with British-style three square-pin plugs (British visitors don't need adapters)

Telephone codes Into Malta +356, out of Malta 00. Within Malta, no area codes, just eight digits.

Weights and measures Mostly metric

Flag Half red (right side), half white, with the George Cross in the top left-hand corner. The cross was added in the 1940s after it was awarded to Malta by George VI for gallantry in World War II (page 18).

National anthem 'L'Innu Malti' ('The Maltese Hymn') 'Lil Din L-Art Ħelwa' ('To The Sweet Land'), music by Dr Robert Samut, words by Maltese national poet Dun Karm Psaila

National bird Il-Merrill, the blue rock thrush (*Monticola solitarius*)

National tree Għargħar/sandarac gum (*siġra ta' l-għargħar*) (*Tetraclinis articulata*) – a cypress tree

National sports Football, water polo

Public holidays 1 January (New Year's Day), 10 February (St Paul's Shipwreck), 19 March (St Joseph), 31 March (Freedom Day), Good Friday, 1 May (Workers' Day), 7 June (Sette Giugno), 29 June (St Peter and St Paul), 15 August (the Assumption), 8 September (Victory Day), 21 September (Independence Day), 8 December (the Immaculate Conception), 13 December (Republic Day), 25 December (Christmas Day)

1

History

OVERVIEW

Malta has had so many masters in its 7,000-year history that it can be useful to have a crib sheet of roughly who was in charge when.

Early settlers (Pre-temples)	6th–4th millennium BC
Temple period	3800–2350BC
Bronze Age	2350–8th century BC
Phoenician	8th–6th century BC
Carthaginian/Punic	6th century–218BC
Romans	218BC–AD535
Late Roman/Byzantine	AD535–870
Arab	870–1090
Norman	1090–1194
Hohenstaufen	1194–1268
Angevin	1268–84
Aragonese	1284–1412
Castillian	1412–1530
Knights of St John	1530–1798
Napoleonic	1798–1800
British	1800–1964
Independent Malta	1964–present
Republican Malta	1974–present

THE EARLY SETTLERS: 6th–4th MILLENNIUM BC

The first traces of humanity in Malta have been dated to more than seven millennia ago. The most recent research suggests the first people arrived on these islands by 5900BC, pushing the previous date back by hundreds of years. We know little about these early settlers except that they were farmers who almost certainly came from Sicily, just 93km across the sea. On a clear day, Malta can be seen from the south coast of Sicily, so early sailors knew where they were heading and, with a fair wind, could get there in a day. They seem to have brought livestock with them and initially set up home in caves including Għar Dalam, meaning 'Cave of Darkness', which gives the earliest period of Maltese habitation its name.

Later, villages of oval mud-brick houses were built. A few such huts have been excavated next to the prehistoric temples at Skorba. We know that contact with the outside world was maintained because, as well as tools made from local materials, these farmers had tools of obsidian (a volcanic glass whose exact source can be identified) and flint, which were imported, probably via Sicily.

3

The most recent research has suggested a decline in human activity on the Maltese islands during much of the 5th millennium BC, possibly caused by changes in the climate and environment. By the start of the 4th millennium BC intensive human activity is once again clearly visible in the archaeological record.

TEMPLE PERIOD: 4th MILLENNIUM–2350BC

In the early 4th millennium BC, the people of Malta seem to have started, quite suddenly, to construct large megalithic stone buildings – known to us as the temples. There is no evidence of earlier, simpler stone buildings, although there are rock-cut tombs (including at Xemxija; page 252) with a lobed pattern some see as possible forerunners to the design of the temples. The temple builders may have been partly descended from the earlier Neolithic people but it is also likely that a new wave of settlers and cultural influences arrived from Sicily.

The temple-builders lived in mud-brick houses like their predecessors. Their main community buildings – or temples – were stone. They continued to farm and lived without apparent conflict: their settlements show no concern for defence. Theirs seems to have been a relatively egalitarian society, too, without monarchs and based more on co-operation than coercion. They had no written language and crucially used no metal. Their stone-working and building skills, however, were exceptional and their temple design is unique in the archaeological record. There is no evidence of it having been learnt from elsewhere or copied by others.

CONTACT VERSUS ISOLATION It used to be thought that the temples were unique because the people who built them had become isolated from the outside world, but archaeological evidence suggests otherwise. The temple people owned imported alabaster, as well as obsidian from Lipari and Pantelleria (volcanic islands near Sicily). And their greenstone axe-shaped pendants came from various locations on the Italian peninsula.

The development of distinct cultures seems to have been a trend across the Mediterranean region at this time, a combination perhaps of the deliberate development of independent cultural identities and the fact that different peoples had different resources. Malta had vast deposits of limestone – so its people built megalithic limestone buildings.

More than 30 temple sites have been identified, some with more than one temple, as well as the remarkable underground tomb complex, the Ħal Saflieni Hypogeum – a kind of temple of the dead. A second hypogeum has been uncovered at Xagħra on Gozo suggesting there may be others yet to be found.

DATING THE TEMPLES Until the advent of carbon dating it was assumed that these temples were inspired by such famous centres of megalithic architecture as Mycenae and Knossos. It was only with the arrival of the more accurate chemical dating that it was revealed that the Maltese temples were far earlier. The earliest of them (including the oldest temples at Ġgantija on Gozo and the oldest temple at Mnajdra) were built some two millennia before Mycenae, nearly one millennium before the Egyptian pyramids and half a millennium before the famous stone circle at Stonehenge.

This dating made Malta's temples the oldest stone buildings in the world, until the mid 1990s when older stone structures were found at Göbekli Tepe in southeastern Turkey. Research into the Maltese temples is ongoing (see opposite) and the most recent work, including 300 new radiocarbon dates from nine different sites, has shifted the temple period to start in 3800BC and extend to around 2350BC.

BUILDING THE TEMPLES The temples were built of vast lumps of stone, megaliths of up to 50 tons in weight. The largest surviving block is at Ggantija, but there are huge stones of 20 tons or so at several sites. How they were moved has always been open to question. The 17th-century explanation was that the temples were created by a community of giants (obvious really!).

The reality is probably that the stone was found already broken into large chunks, or was cracked along natural fault lines using wedges. Some believe that the blocks were then transported by rolling them along on spherical stones about 30cm in diameter like those found in or just outside several of the temples. Others doubt these stone spheres, made of the same material as the megaliths, could have withstood the weight. We can only presume that some combination of sledges, rollers, ramps and levers was used – and, of course, a great deal of manpower, and perhaps animal power.

SOCIETY The society that built these temples must have been quite sophisticated. Several models and 'sketches' (on stone) have been identified as possible blueprints for the temples – leading to speculation about prehistoric architects. Certainly a degree of planning would have been needed, along with considerable teamwork, to create buildings of this size and complexity. And the craftsmanship of these people is remarkable. They had smart, decorated furniture and produced numerous stone statues and carvings for the temples (best seen in the National Museum of Archaeology in Valletta). They adorned the temples with spiral patterns as well as images of animals and plants, and the iconic 'Fat Ladies'. These rotund figures (some of which may not in fact be female) range in size from a few centimetres to over 2m tall, their vast hips and behinds often covered in fringed or pleated skirts. Their short conical legs peep out below. The most artistically impressive example is the small clay figurine known as the 'Sleeping Lady', found at the Hal Saflieni Hypogeum. She lies on a neat couch and was made at about the time that Stonehenge was begun.

It has been estimated that the prehistoric Maltese islands could have supported a population of up to 10,000, although 6,000–7,000 is considered more likely. Even so, this is a sufficient number of people to provide plenty of contributors to temple building. There is no suggestion of slave labour. More likely is a seasonal local labour force working outside harvest times, perhaps religiously motivated.

HOW WERE THE TEMPLES USED? Nobody really knows. The large forecourts typical of the temples may have acted as a communal gathering place and there is some evidence for ritual activity: equipment for animal sacrifice, holes into which libations (liquid offerings to the underworld) might have been poured, and the constant reappearance of statues of similar figures (the 'Fat Ladies') perhaps representing a deity or at least having some kind of cult status. What appear to be stone phalluses are also common, suggesting a possible fertility cult. There is also evidence of secular activity such as grinding corn. We can only make informed guesses. The word 'temple' is applied to the buildings as much because of the way in which monumental buildings were used elsewhere in the world (and at later dates) as because of direct evidence from Malta.

THE END In the second half of the 3rd millennium BC – more precisely in 2350BC according to the latest research – all evidence of the temple culture comes to an abrupt end. Not only were no more temples built, but the existing ones fell into disrepair. It seems that the whole temple culture collapsed.

1

Why this happened has long been a mystery. Many theories have been advanced, from invasion to priestly rivalry (but there is no evidence of conflict), disease (but it is rare for even the most vicious disease to kill off an entire population) to famine, perhaps brought on by overuse of the scarce agricultural land. The most recent research has found signs of soil erosion and drought during the early 3rd millennium which would have added to the stresses of living on a small archipelago. It now looks as if environmental factors may have played the greatest role in the fall of the temple culture.

FURTHER INFORMATION For more on the temples, key sites and a guide to interpreting the sites, see page 79. Though written some time ago, and long before the latest research, the seminal book on this period is probably still *Malta: Prehistory and Temples* by Dr David Trump (Midsea Books; w midseabooks.com; €25). There is also a series of podcasts about the temples available to download free from w visitmalta.com/en/podcasts and an excellent website with lots of photos at w web.infinito.it/utenti/m/malta_mega_temples/indxfram.html; the website of the latest research project (called FRAGSUS) is w qub.ac.uk/sites/FRAGSUS.

BRONZE AGE: 2350–8th CENTURY BC

Tarxien Cemetery phase 2350–1600BC, Borġ In-Nadur 1600–750BC.

The culture that dominated Malta for the next millennium was completely different from that of the temple people.

TARXIEN CEMETERY PEOPLE The new people did not bury their dead as the temple people had but cremated them, storing the ashes in pottery bowls or urns, sometimes with personal items including coloured beads. The urns were kept, perhaps in the islands' various dolmens of this period (structures consisting of a large horizontal stone on a couple of vertical slabs), and certainly at the Tarxien temple complex which was re-used in the Bronze Age as a crematorium. Most of the archaeological evidence for this time derives from this site so it has given the period its name.

The so-called Tarxien Cemetery People also brought metal to Malta for the first time. They used simple tools and weapons made of copper. They seem to have lived in mud-hut villages though their exact form is unclear. Where they came from remains unknown. Their culture does not accurately match that known anywhere else in the region and cremation has robbed us of much of the physical anthropological evidence.

BORĠ IN-NADUR PHASE By about 1600BC the picture had changed again. The islands are by now more heavily populated, with some well-defended cliff-top settlements of several hundred people. Remnants of one of these has survived at Borġ In-Nadur, which gives its name to the period. It is not clear who these communities were defending themselves from, but it could have been from each other.

They seem to have produced grain in considerable quantity and fished around Marsaxlokk Bay, still a centre of fishing today. They had looms for weaving and small quantities of imported bronze, possibly traded for textiles or grain. Malta certainly had contact with other nations at this time. Maltese-style pottery has been found in Sicilian tombs of the period and there is small but crucial evidence for contact (direct or indirect) with cultures further across the Mediterranean – a few little shards of Mycenaean pottery dated to about 1300BC.

This period is well covered in *Malta: Prehistory and Temples* by Dr David Trump; see page 314 for details.

PHOENICIANS AND CARTHAGINIANS: 8th CENTURY BC–218BC

Phoenician 8th–6th century BC, Punic/Carthaginian 6th century–218BC.

The Phoenicians (who came from the land of Canaan in modern-day Lebanon) were the great seafaring traders of the ancient world. Given Malta's position in the middle of the Mediterranean and its sheltered natural harbours it is hardly surprising that Phoenicians settled in Malta sometime around the 8th century BC, and may have visited considerably earlier. These ancient mariners stayed on the islands for over two centuries and the name Malta may come from the Phoenician *malat* meaning 'refuge' (though others source it to the Greek word *melita* meaning 'honey', which the island has long produced). Research has shown that some of the Maltese population still have a genetic marker linking them to the Phoenicians, and Malta's colourful fishing boats (which still carry

CLASSIC STORIES

In 73BC, **Gaius Verres** became Governor of Sicily, and therefore Malta, and began a two-year reign of corruption and plunder. Malta and Sicily got together and persuaded **Cicero**, one of Rome's greatest orators, to prosecute Verres. Cicero apparently stayed in Mdina while he wrote his extensive indictment of the corrupt governor. At his trial Verres quickly capitulated, but Cicero went on to publish his *Verrines* which tell us that Verres – without ever going to Malta – had amassed a considerable collection of Maltese booty including ivory from a temple to the goddess Juno, and large quantities of fine textiles.

Cicero is not the only classical writer to mention Malta. Homer's *Ogygia* where **Odysseus** (Ulysses) spends seven years under the spell of the sea nymph Calypso has been identified as Gozo and Ovid writes of Malta ('Melite' to him) as 'the fruitful isle'. The Maltese islanders' favourite story from Roman times, however, is that of the shipwreck of **St Paul** in AD60.

Paul was a prisoner on his way to stand trial before the Emperor Nero in Rome when his ship hit the rocks of Melite (Malta). Whilst warming himself by a bonfire after his ordeal, he was bitten by a viper but miraculously showed no ill effects, and it is said that he thus rid the islands of poisonous snakes. Malta certainly has no poisonous snakes, but the less pious amongst the population claim that the venom removed from the reptiles reappeared in the tongues of the nation's women (although Maltese men can be pretty fork-tongued too when they want to be!).

In his three months on the island, St Paul is meant to have converted the then governor Publius (later St Publius) to Christianity. Some say the rest of the population followed and Publius became the first Bishop of Malta. This still-devout Roman Catholic country likes the idea that it was one of the first Christian communities, but there is no archaeological or written evidence of Christianity on the islands before the 4th century AD. For the Bible story of St Paul's shipwreck, see the box on page 140.

the protective symbol of an eye on their bows) owe much to Phoenician trading vessels (see the boats in Marsaxlokk Harbour).

The Phoenicians brought the skill of making pottery on a wheel, and reintroduced the practice of burying the dead in rock-cut tombs (a practice that had disappeared through the Bronze Age). They ended Malta's relative isolation – and independence of culture – turning it into an outpost of the wider Mediterranean region, a position confirmed by the rise of the Phoenicians' prosperous colony on the Bay of Tunis, the city-state of Carthage.

The Carthaginians created Malta's first towns, a sophisticated civil administration and the islands' own coinage (some of their coins are in the Mdina Cathedral Museum). They planted vineyards and olive groves and stationed a garrison of some 2,000 men on the islands. They constructed temporal and sacred buildings of which, unfortunately, little remains other than a 5m-tall tower in a private garden in the village of Żurrieq (not open to the public). The Carthaginians also seem to have left behind two small carved pillars with dedications to the god Melqart written in both Phoenician and Greek, which in modern times helped in the decoding of the Phoenician alphabet (one is now in the National Museum of Archaeology, the other in the Louvre).

The rise of Rome inevitably brought conflict with the Carthaginians and by 264BC they were at war. There seems little doubt that Malta's harbours would have been used by the Carthaginian *quinquiremes* (boats with five banks of oars) for rest and repair as the two powers battled it out across the Mediterranean. Malta was raided and pillaged by Rome but by the end of the First Punic War (264–241BC), the islands remained a Carthaginian colony. During the Second Punic War (218–201BC), however, Malta fell to the Romans.

The most comprehensive book on this period is *Malta: Phoenician, Punic and Roman* by Anthony Bonanno (Midsea Books; w midseabooks.com; €25).

ROMANS AND BYZANTINES: 218BC–AD870

Romans 218BC–AD535, late Roman/Byzantine AD535–870.

Under the Romans, Malta was once again linked with Sicily as a *municipium* (a municipality with a fair degree of self-government), sharing the Italian island's Roman governor. Roman villas sprang up across Malta and Gozo (the well-preserved mosaic floor of one can still be seen in the Roman Domus in Rabat).

Vineyards and olive groves were tended, high-quality cloth produced and defences built around the main towns, including the largest, Melita. This stood on the hilltop that is now Mdina and spread to perhaps three times the size of the later medieval walled town. With a not unusual combination of Roman and local (Carthaginian) ways of life, the islands seem to have flourished.

For more on this period, see page 83. The main book on this period is *Malta: Phoenician, Punic and Roman* by Anthony Bonanno (Midsea Books; w midseabooks.com; €25).

DIVIDED EMPIRE In AD345, the Roman Empire was divided into east and west. Malta seems to have fallen into the eastern half. The period between this division and AD535 when Malta was clearly incorporated into the Byzantine Empire is a dark age in terms of Maltese historical evidence. During the 5th century, Malta may, like Sicily, have been occupied for a while by the Germanic Vandals, who had moved south through France and Spain to North Africa and were active in the Mediterranean (and yes, their behaviour gave us the word 'vandal'), and later by the Ostrogoths, the eastern Goths from the Black Sea area who went on to rule Italy.

There is some evidence that Byzantine emperor Justinian's top general, Belisarius, stopped off in Malta in AD533 on his way to take North Africa back from the Vandals, and again in AD535 en route to deal with the Ostrogoths in Sicily. After this both Sicily and Malta were directly incorporated into Justinian's empire.

Catacombs There may be little left on paper from the later Roman and Byzantine period but there is a remarkable legacy in stone, almost all of it religious (mainly Christian) underground tomb complexes ranging from large catacombs (St Paul's and St Agatha's) to small hypogea of a few individual burial chambers (such as Bingemma).

THE ARABS: 870–1090

The rise of Islam through the 8th century saw the Arabs conquer large parts of Africa, Asia and Europe. Malta was quite a late acquisition, taken in AD870. Interestingly, a plaque found in the Aghlabad Arab port of Sousse (in modern-day Tunisia) states that marble columns and dressed stones from Malta were shipped from the islands as booty after the invasion, which may help explain the lack of above-ground material remains from Malta's Roman and Byzantine periods.

Malta was once again ruled from Sicily, by an emir, with a military/naval governor stationed locally on the site of what is now Fort St Angelo. The Arabs retained the Roman capital, but instead of Melite, called it Mdina (meaning 'the fortress' in Arabic) and shrank its centre into the smaller, more defensible confines we see today. Rabat (meaning 'suburb') was left outside the walls.

There are few physical remains from this time, apart from some Arab tombstones (see the Roman Domus in Rabat and Gozo Archaeological Museum). There is an undoubted cultural legacy, however, in Malta's language, place names (though not the names for Malta and Gozo themselves) and surnames.

MEDIEVAL MALTA: 1090–1530

In 1091, Count Roger of Normandy invaded Malta and took over the islands. He seems to have had a very light touch, however, and Arab Muslim culture continued to predominate until 1127 when the count's son, Roger II (King of Sicily 1130–54), reconquered Malta and imposed an active European Christian administration. Trade (including burgeoning exports of cotton) began to shift from North Africa to Europe, particularly Genoa, and there is evidence of more Christians on the islands. Yet many Muslims remained and there appears to have been peaceful co-existence until the mid 13th century when the Muslim community seems to disappear.

By this time Malta was part of the Holy Roman Empire under Hohenstaufen emperor Frederick II (who inherited it along with the throne of Sicily from his mother Constance, daughter of Roger II). For the next 300 years, Malta was a European medieval Christian society (with a small but economically active Jewish population until Ferdinand of Aragon and Isabella of Castile expelled the Jews from all their territories in 1492). Most people worked the land, rearing animals and growing crops – the main cash crop being cotton, exported particularly through Sicily.

Local government was run from Mdina by the Università, a council dominated by a few Maltese noble families, and mostly kept in check by whichever overlord happened to be in charge at the time. As a minor part of the Kingdom of Sicily, the Maltese islands were passed around the royal houses of Europe – Hohenstaufen,

1

Angevin, Aragon and Castile – and, worse, these royal families repeatedly gave or rented Malta to a variety of nobles, despite repeated promises to the Maltese that they would never do so again.

In September 1429, Malta was invaded by a large Muslim force sent by Hafsid, ruler of Tunis. One account describes 70 ships and 18,000 fighting men. Mdina was besieged and may only have been saved by the invaders' fear of seasonal storms. But the Arabs did not leave empty-handed. Some 3,000 Maltese were taken into slavery, perhaps 30% of the island's population. This was a taste of things to come.

By the early 16th century, the Spanish had gained control over most of southern Europe and Malta was part of the dominion of the Holy Roman emperor Charles V. Once again, in 1530, he gave it away – to the Order of St John of Jerusalem (the Hospitallers). This time the deal stuck and opened a new and vital chapter in Malta's history.

The most comprehensive book on this period is *Malta: the Medieval Millennium* by Charles Dalli (Midsea Books; w midseabooks.com; €25).

THE KNIGHTS OF MALTA: 1530–1798

After losing their base in Rhodes in 1522–23 to the Ottoman Turks under Sultan Suleiman the Magnificent, the Hospitaller Knights of St John were homeless. Founded in about 1070, probably by Italian merchants from Amalfi, the Hospitallers were set up, as their name suggests, to care for the sick and give shelter to the poor amongst Christian pilgrims to Jerusalem. At first they did this with permission from the Egyptian caliph and then, after the First Crusade had taken Jerusalem (1099), under the Christian patriarch based in the Church of the Holy Sepulchre.

In 1113, Pope Paschal II (1099–1118) issued a papal bull (which is still in the National Library of Malta in Valletta) making the Hospitallers an Order of the Church under direct papal protection and control, but with the right to elect their own master. It is shortly after this that the order begins its military engagement with the Muslims, adding the physical protection of Christian pilgrims to its remit, and soon also the protection of Christian territory.

Those joining the order were obliged to take vows of chastity, obedience and poverty (often giving their property to the order). As monks and priests they were not allowed to shed blood, but the papacy found a way round this by creating a new class of knight – or warrior monk – who took the religious vows but was not allowed to take Mass. These knights were remarkably successful in their opposition to the Muslims and whilst the order continued to run hospitals, its primary purpose was soon military. The warrior knights became its undisputed leaders, the grand master always elected from within their ranks.

The renown of the order grew, as did its wealth as donations of money and land came in from across Europe. But when the Muslims retook the Holy Land in 1291, the Hospitallers were obliged to leave. By 1309, they had taken the island of Rhodes (keeping close to the east) and here they remained, built and prospered for 200 years. Surrounded by water, they developed into a formidable naval force and harried the Muslims by sea as well as by land. Needless to say, this did not best please the Ottoman Turks. Twice the Turks besieged Rhodes. The first time the Knights held out, but in 1522 the invaders took the island. After a six-month siege Grand Master Fra Philippe Villiers de L'Isle Adam was forced to seek a truce and Suleiman agreed to allow the Knights to leave. It was eight years before they were once again settled – this time in Malta.

1521–34	Philippe Villiers de L'Isle Adam (France)
1534–35	Pierino del Ponte (Italy)
1535–36	Didier de Saint Jaille (Provence)
1536–53	Juan de Homedes (Aragon)
1553–57	Claude de la Sengle (France)
1557–68	Jean Parisot de Valette (or Jean de Valette de Parisot) (Provence)
1568–72	Pietro del Monte (Italy)
1572–81	Jean L'Evêque de la Cassière (Auvergne)
1581–95	Hugues Loubenx de Verdale (Provence)
1595–1601	Martin Garzes (Aragon)
1601–22	Alof de Wignacourt (France)
1622–23	Luis Mendez de Vasconcellos (Castile)
1623–36	Antoine de Paule (Provence)
1636–57	Jean Paul de Lascaris Castellar (Provence)
1657–60	Martin de Redin (Aragon)
1660	Annet de Clermont de Chattes Gessan (Auvergne)
1660–63	Rafael Cotoner (Aragon)
1663–80	Nicolas Cotoner (Aragon)
1680–90	Gregorio Carafa (Italy)
1690–97	Adrien de Wignacourt (France)
1697–1720	Ramon Perellos y Roccaful (Aragon)
1720–22	Marc Antonio Zondadari (Italy)
1722–36	Antonio Manoel de Vilhena (Castile)
1736–41	Ramon Despuig (Aragon)
1741–73	Manoel Pinto de Fonseca (Castile)
1773–75	Francisco Ximenes de Texada (Aragon)
1775–97	Emmanuel de Rohan Polduc (France)
1797–1805	Ferdinand von Hompesch (German) – in Malta until 1798

1

The first contact with Malta came in 1524, when a commission of the order's *uomi saggi* (wise men) was sent to Malta to report on its suitability as a possible new headquarters. They were not impressed, reporting that the island was barren, with insufficient drinking water for its 12,000 inhabitants, poorly defended and with the one town (Mdina) in a dilapidated condition. It was also, however, an island at the eastern end of Europe and had excellent harbours. More to the point, there was nothing better on offer. So in 1530 – with agreement to pay a symbolic annual tribute of a Maltese falcon – the Knights took control of Malta. Initially, this certainly didn't please all Mdina's noble families, but the Knights brought wealth, organisation and protection from pirates and Turks, and put Malta back on the map of Europe.

The order's first priority was to strengthen the islands' defences particularly at Birgu (now Vittoriosa) on the south side of the Grand Harbour which they made their first capital. Here they built their *auberges* (usually translated as hostels, but more akin to university colleges) where members of the order lived and worked in communities of their own language. Each of the eight *langues* (literally, 'tongues') was designated certain jobs and areas to defend. A hospital (Sacra Infermeria) was built, the Knights settled in and the Maltese became used to their presence.

Almost from the start there was a desire on the part of the Knights to strengthen defences by building on Mount Sciberras, the rocky peninsula facing Birgu on the other side of the Grand Harbour (where Valletta now stands), but it seems there wasn't the money. The order's finances were not helped by Henry VIII appropriating the possessions of the English *langue* in 1540 as part of his break with Rome.

The Order of St John and the Turks continued to confront each other. The Knights' galleys harassed Turkish ships across the Mediterranean and the Ottomans made increasingly frequent raids on Malta and Gozo. In 1551, the most successful and feared corsair, Dragut (or Turgut) Reis, attacked Malta. Driven back, he cut his losses and led a devastating raid on Gozo, taking most of its able-bodied population into slavery. This made the Knights all too aware that a larger force might follow. A new fort, Fort St Elmo, was rapidly built on Mount Sciberras to provide crossfire with Birgu's Fort St Angelo but there was neither the time nor the resources to do much more.

THE GREAT SIEGE OF 1565 In May 1565, the Knights' old enemy, Suleiman the Magnificent, now in his 70s, sent a force of some 28,000 men in more than 180 ships to invade Malta. His intention was to oust the Knights from Malta as he had from Rhodes, secure the Mediterranean for Muslim shipping and push back the borders of Christendom.

His soldiers were led by one of his best generals, Mustapha Pasha, the fleet by Admiral Piali, and Dragut Reis – with yet more ships and perhaps another 10,000 to 12,000 men – was to join them as soon as he could get there from Tripoli. The defenders numbered no more than 9,000 spread across Malta and Gozo. In the harbour area Grand Master Jean Parisot de Valette had under his command some 500 Knights, 1,100 soldiers (400 of them mercenaries) and about 3,000 Maltese militiamen. He was heavily outnumbered and as soon as the invasion began, he sent word to Sicily requesting help.

The Turks landed first at Marsaxlokk Harbour. The men of St John went to meet them but were overwhelmed by the size of the Turkish force. The invaders' target was Birgu, the Knights' capital, so the colourful armoured column 'like a huge, lovely meadow in bloom' (according, oddly enough, to a Christian chronicler) moved inland and set up camp at the landward end of Mount Sciberras (today's Marsa). The siege began.

The Turks first attacked Fort St Elmo, expecting it to be easily taken. They underestimated the Knights. St Elmo held out for a month and by the time the Turks took possession 1,500 Christians had lost their lives, along with several thousand Turks – including Dragut Reis. Mustapha Pasha is reported to have cried, 'What will the parent cost, when the child was won at such expense?' In an attempt to terrify his opponents in Birgu, he mutilated the bodies of some Christians and floated them across the Grand Harbour. The Knights were not to be intimidated. The grand master's reply was to cut off the heads of Turkish prisoners and fire them back as cannonballs.

Battle was now joined for Birgu (Vittoriosa), L-Isla (Senglea) and Fort St Angelo. It was a long hard siege through a long hot summer. The Turks had problems supplying troops with sufficient food, and dysentery was rife (possibly caused by the deliberate poisoning of wells by the order just before the Turks arrived). The Knights held out – just. By early September, both sides seem to have been on their last legs.

Finally, on 7 September, reinforcements arrived for the Knights from Sicily under the command of Don Garcia de Toledo. Believing they had no chance against large numbers of fresh troops, and afraid of losing their ships, the Turks retreated to the sea. When they realised that the new force numbered only a few thousand the fleet returned, anchoring in St Paul's Bay. But the Knights had made good use of the intervening time and it was too late. The invaders finally fled Malta in disarray on 13 September 1565. The end of the siege on 8 September is still celebrated every year.

AFTER THE SIEGE Birgu, and the rest of what we now call the Three Cities, had been badly damaged, Malta's fortifications devastated and both the order and the Maltese population seriously depleted. Some Knights were in favour of abandoning Malta altogether, but Grand Master de Valette decided to stay and rebuild – in fact to build afresh, creating a new, defendable capital on Mount Sciberras, the city that would bear his name.

The Knights were the heroes of Christian Europe. They had held back 'the Infidel' and Christendom was willing to show its gratitude in financial support. The Pope sent his own military engineer, Francesco Laparelli (a pupil of Michelangelo), to design the city. The peninsula offered high ground with sea on three sides and a narrow entrance overland where Laparelli placed massive defences (mostly still in place).

The first stone of the new capital was laid in 1566. Neither the architect nor the grand master saw the city to completion. Laparelli returned to Italy leaving the project with a Maltese successor, Girolamo Cassar, and de Valette died in 1568. Building, however, moved quickly and by 1570 the Knights were able to start the move from Birgu to Valletta.

Valletta flourished and soon took over from Mdina as the Maltese capital as well as that of the Knights. The arts did well, with much embellishing of the new city, both in stone and paint. Another Turkish invasion (albeit much smaller than the Great Siege force) was defeated in 1614 and fortification of the islands continued apace. Coastal watchtowers and defences were built by successive grand masters along with additional fortification of the Three Cities, Floriana (on Valletta's landward side), Mdina and the Gozo Citadel (for more on fortifications, see page 84).

The power and determination of the Turks was now on the wane. The last Turkish raid on the Maltese islands took place in the early 18th century, though naval engagements and small-scale attacks on shipping continued. Both the Turks and the order now turned their minds more to trade than religious zealotry. The Ottomans began to make trade deals with Christian powers. Among the Knights, vows of poverty gave way to comfortable living and much of the fleet was given more to corsairing than crusading.

DECLINE AND FALL On the whole, Malta prospered under the Order of St John and its population rose from 15,000 in 1530 to 48,000 in 1798. By the mid 18th century, however, the Knights, and particularly Grand Master Manoel Pinto de Fonseca, were living a life of luxury and spending as if there were no tomorrow. Francisco Ximenes de Texada became grand master in 1773 promising to help the ordinary people, but on taking office he found that there was no money to pay for his plans. The financial situation only worsened with the French Revolution (from 1789) and the sequestration of the possessions of the French *langues* in France (1792). Resentment of the Knights grew both amongst the people and in the Church.

In 1775, a group of disaffected Maltese clergymen took advantage of the absence of the order's fleet (away raiding Algiers) to mount a surprise attack on the small garrison manning Fort St Elmo. The rebels took the fort and raised the red-and-white flag of the Maltese Università. They presumably hoped to trigger a popular uprising but none was forthcoming and the 'Priests' Revolt' was quickly and brutally put down with the ringleaders executed.

Tension, however, persisted. The Venetian representative in Malta reported in 1796 that he feared a revolution and in 1797 another plot was thwarted. So by 1798

1

it is fair to say that much of the population was no longer behind the Knights.

Add to this the fact that world politics was changing: Holy War was now seen as anomalous and small states were losing influence. Much larger powers – including France, Britain, Austria and Russia – were taking an interest in the Mediterranean, with Malta, as ever, at its centre.

On 9 June 1798, General Napoleon Bonaparte, en route to Egypt, dropped anchor off Malta and requested entry to the Grand Harbour to fill up with water. Rightly afraid that he was after more than liquid refreshment, the Knights refused, invoking an old rule that only four ships from a belligerent power might enter the harbour at once. Napoleon, with 29,000 men under his command, wasn't taking no for an answer. He met brave resistance in places, but within just a few days, Grand Master Ferdinand von Hompesch capitulated and signed the islands over to Napoleon, thus ending the rule of the Knights in Malta.

Why did he give up so easily? Perhaps he could not rely on the loyalty of the Maltese, or indeed of a few of his own in the French *langues*. Others were also ambivalent: they didn't like fighting Christians. Von Hompesch did send word to Lord Nelson requesting help from the British but the message was delayed by bad weather and the grand master seems to have had little confidence that it would bring the necessary relief. Napoleon had control of the sea and far superior numbers, so von Hompesch may have felt there was little point in sanctioning massive loss of life only to succumb a few weeks later.

Whatever his reasons, the grand master and the administration of the Order of St John left Malta on 17 June 1798, taking with them nothing but three relics: the icon of the Virgin of Philermos (brought with them from Rhodes), the hand of

THE KNIGHTS: WHERE ARE THEY NOW?

The end of the Knights in Malta was the end of the real power of the Order of St John. Their time had passed. But they do still exist. They have returned to their roots, predominantly doing charity work with the sick. Local branches run or help in hospitals, and take sick and disabled people on pilgrimages (for example to Lourdes). Their name today is the Sovereign Military Hospitaller Order of St John of Jerusalem, of Rhodes and of Malta, often shortened to SMOM (Sovereign Military Order of Malta).

The British order founded the St John Ambulance Brigade which provides first aid and training. There is a Museum of the Order of St John in Clerkenwell, London (℡ 020 7324 4005), based in the 16th-century gatehouse to the 11th-century priory that was the original home of the English *langue*.

Now based in Rome, the order itself remains a Catholic institution, closer than ever to the Vatican, under no secular government and answerable only to the Pope. Full Knights continue to be drawn from the upper echelons of European society, though there are now few of them. The great majority of the order's 12,500 members take only a vow of obedience and religious observance. They do not need to be of noble birth and may marry.

The current grand master, Fra Matthew Festing, is British – the second to hold the post after his immediate predecessor, Fra Andrew Bertie (1988–2008), a distant cousin of Queen Elizabeth II.

The order maintains embassies in more than 100 countries. In Malta it is based in St John's Cavalier in Valletta and, coming full circle, has also taken over the upper reaches of Fort St Angelo.

their patron saint John the Baptist, and a relic of the True Cross. Everything else – archives, treasure, paintings, the lot – they were obliged to leave in Malta.

There are many excellent books on the Knights (page 315). One good place to start is *Malta: The Order of St John* by Thomas Freller with photographs by Daniel Cilia (Midsea Books; w midseabooks.com; €25).

THE FRENCH: 1798–1800

Napoleon spent just six days in Malta before departing for the Egyptian campaign, leaving strict instructions and General Vaubois in charge. It took only three months for the French administration to so alienate the Maltese that they rose up against them. The reasons were financial and religious. The French administration had no budget for running Malta, so they raised taxes and refused to honour debts, wages or pensions owed by their predecessors. What really infuriated the Maltese, however, was the looting of churches. This united the most powerful institution left in Malta, the Church, with the populace in open rebellion.

Aware that they could not oust the French alone, the Maltese requested help from the British Royal Navy – by this time in Sicily en route to meet Napoleon in Egypt. Admiral Lord Nelson sent ships and men under the command of Sir Alexander Ball, whom the Maltese quickly made President of the National Assembly, de facto leader of the Maltese as well as the campaign against the French.

Soon Vaubois's men were holed up inside Malta's key fortifications and the Maltese (with British help) found themselves besieging and even bombarding their own forts and cities, including Valletta. Crucially, though, the British Royal Navy, with help from the Portuguese, prevented supplies from reaching the islands. This was not much fun for the Maltese, but instrumental in forcing the French into submission. On 5 September 1800, the French capitulation was signed. Napoleon's troops were given safe passage back to France but were obliged to leave their weapons behind.

THE BRITISH: 1800–1964

Who was now to rule Malta? For a while it looked as if – for the sake of good relations in Europe – the British would hand the islands back to the Order of St John. The Maltese were vehemently against this, but realised that they needed the protection of a larger state and so requested that the British remain. At first the British were not especially keen to stay, but Napoleon made it clear to them how much he wanted Malta and they soon discovered what a useful Mediterranean base they had acquired. Also, some of the Knights had gone to Russia when they left Malta and the British were concerned that their return might give the Russians a foothold in the Mediterranean. In 1814, the Treaty of Paris formally handed Malta to Britain and Sir Thomas Maitland became its first civilian and military governor.

Some Maltese felt they had got more than they bargained for with British governors ruling with little local input. In the first few decades of British rule, London was regularly petitioned with requests for greater self-government and in the 1830s, a partly elected council was created and freedom of the press granted. The powers of the Catholic Church, including that over education, were left largely undisturbed – the British knew better than to mess with this key institution.

Malta's importance for Britain was always primarily military. The British took over all Malta's defences, maintained them and made additions of their own (page 239). The Grand Harbour rapidly became a key naval base, home to the Royal

Navy's Mediterranean fleet, and important for merchant shipping too. Dockyards were built in the Three Cities and this was soon a hub of naval activity, employing large numbers of Maltese. In 1883 a steam railway was built from Valletta to Mdina (closed in 1931) and work on the construction of the breakwaters at the entrance to the Grand Harbour was opened in 1903 by King Edward VII.

In 1878, a Royal Commission recommended that English replace Italian as the language of education, culture and the courts, so as to better integrate Malta into the British Empire. The so-called 'language question' became the trigger for the creation of Malta's first political parties: the pro-British Reform Party whose supporters included merchants and dockyard workers, and the Partito Anti-Reformista (Anti-Reform Party) – in whose ranks local clergy and most of the middle class, especially lawyers, showed their support for tradition, Italy and Italian.

WORLD WAR I Politics was put aside as World War I hit Europe, and Malta became 'the Nurse of the Mediterranean'. Before the war, the country had 268 hospital beds. By January 1916, the number had rocketed to 20,000. At the height of the war 2,000 sick servicemen a week were arriving here, including the wounded of Gallipoli. A thousand nurses were required, some brought from Britain, some from the Maltese St John Ambulance, many with little training. Amongst the British contingent was Vera Brittain, who later wrote about her experiences in Malta in *Testament of Youth* (see box below). The French fleet used Malta as its base and so the dockyards too were kept extremely busy, employing some 10,000 men at their peak.

BETWEEN THE WARS The end of the war brought a drop in dockyard jobs and a rise in unemployment. Even those in work felt the pinch. The cost of living rose sharply (due to shortages resulting from the disruption of war) and wages failed

VERA BRITTAIN AND MALTA

Vera Brittain arrived in Malta in October 1916 sick and miserable. Her fiancé had been killed in France, and her beloved younger brother and two close friends were also in uniform. In 1915, she had abandoned her studies at Oxford to become a Voluntary Aid Detachment nurse, and on the dangerous voyage from Southampton to the Grand Harbour had become seriously ill. She was forced to spend several weeks in Imtarfa (Mtarfa) hospital before taking up her nursing duties at St George's Hospital, two miles west of Valletta, just above St George's Bay. But despite all this, she fell instantly and passionately in love with Malta.

> The place has become for me a shrine, the object of a pilgrimage, a fairy country which I know that I must see again before I die. Looking back through the years to sun-filled memory-pictures of golden stone buildings, of turquoise and sapphire seas, of jade and topaz and amethyst skies, of long stretches of dust-white road winding seaward over jagged black rocks older than history, I am filled with yearning and regret, and I cry in my heart: Come back, magic days!

From Vera Brittain's autobiography Testament of Youth *(Virago), included by permission of Mark Bostridge and T J Brittain-Catlin, literary executors for the Estate of Vera Brittain, 1970.*

to keep pace. Politics raised its head again with nationalists demanding a much greater say in the government of Malta – and showing some impatience about achieving their aims. All this came to a head in the Sette Giugno (7 June) riots in 1919. Thousands of people ransacked government buildings and the homes of those they thought were making money out of the situation. Soldiers were called in to help the police, some were attacked, and when a shot was heard from a building full of rioters, several soldiers opened fire. In total four Maltese were killed and tens of others injured. Since 1989, 7 June has been a public holiday in commemoration of these events.

Political reform, already under consideration before the riots, followed with a new constitution giving the Maltese control over local matters. Elections were held in 1921 and Malta's first prime minister, Joseph Howard of the Unione Politica Maltese (later part of the Nationalist Party), took office.

In the early 1930s, the 'language question' raised its head again – and again the dispute was about more than language. Italian was still widely spoken amongst Malta's upper and middle classes, English was on the rise and Malti remained the language of the working majority. The British decided to formally drop Italian as the official language of Malta and to replace it with English and Maltese. This alienated a few, who thought Malta should look towards Roman Catholic Italy rather than Protestant Britain, but allied the British with the mass of Maltese.

WORLD WAR II AND THE SECOND GREAT SIEGE
Mussolini had made it quite plain long before the war began that he believed Malta should be part of greater Italy. He even claimed that Malti was a dialect of Italian. British–Italian relations had also been soured by the Italian invasion of Abyssinia (Ethiopia) in 1935, which Britain opposed in the United Nations.

As tensions rose, some efforts were made to prepare Malta for war – the governor requested funds to build underground shelters (many of which remain), anti-aircraft guns and some radar were shipped in and details of food and fuel requirements drawn up. But these measures were little and late, partly because the military chiefs in London could not agree on whether Malta was defendable against the Italians, just 90km away in Sicily. The army and air force thought not, while the Navy argued that Malta was essential to the maintenance of a Mediterranean fleet.

Italy remained neutral for the first months of the war, but when Mussolini joined Hitler on 10 June 1940 Malta was ill prepared. It had only four aircraft, Gloster Gladiator biplanes, which came to be called *Faith, Hope* and *Charity* (plus an unnamed reserve) – even these were only in Malta by accident. The biplanes fought alone – and with remarkable effect – for three weeks before reinforcements arrived (what is left of *Faith* can be seen in the National War Museum in Valletta).

The first bombing raid on Malta came early on the day after Italy entered the war and the first casualties were taken at Fort St Elmo, though most of the damage was to the densely populated residential areas around the docks. The next day a single Italian reconnaissance aircraft flew over to see what the raid had achieved and was shot down. A few Italian sympathisers were interned but most of the population swung behind Britain and the Allies.

Malta suffered some of the heaviest bombing of the war. Air-raid sirens whined over 3,000 times between 1940 and 1943, tens of thousands of bombs fell and over a million incendiary devices hit the main island. Casualties were remarkably low considering the intensity of the bombardment. People rapidly evacuated the harbour areas or fled underground each time the sirens sounded, scurrying into ancient catacombs, tunnels and purpose-built shelters. The limestone rock of which

Malta and most of its buildings are made, was found to be resistant to incendiary bombs and to some extent to explosives as well.

It was no picnic, however. In the first months of 1942 Malta was pounded day after day for months on end – a period of bombing more intense than anything experienced elsewhere during World War II. Electricity failed, disease spread and food began to run short. Malta's importance was now very clear to both sides. Ships were repaired here and submarines made sorties from its harbours. It was from Malta that the Allies disrupted Axis supplies to their armies in North Africa – a crucial prerequisite to the key Allied victory at El Alamein later in the year.

In April 1942, King George VI awarded the George Cross to the nation of Malta. He wrote to the governor that, 'To honour her brave people, I award the George Cross to the Island Fortress of Malta to bear witness to a heroism and devotion that will long be famous in history.' The governor replied, 'By God's help Malta will not weaken but will endure until victory is won.'

Malta, however, was running out of food and fuel. In midsummer it was calculated that the islands could survive only another few weeks. The British sent a large convoy, Operation Pedestal, to relieve the besieged island. Running the gauntlet of minefields, E-boats and bombers, 400 lives were lost and only five of the original 14 merchant ships made it to their destination. But it was enough for Malta to survive. The last of the ships – the oil tanker *Ohio*, full of desperately needed fuel – limped into port on 15 August, the feast of Santa Marija (St Mary), leading the Maltese to call their 'miraculous' relief ships the Konvoj ta' Santa Marija (St Mary's Convoy).

In May 1943, the Axis forces in North Africa surrendered to the Allies and, in July, Malta acted as the base for Operation Husky, the successful invasion of Sicily. On 8 September (the same date that saw the lifting of the Great Siege of 1565) Italy surrendered. The Italian fleet, afraid of being destroyed by the Germans, gave itself up to the Allies in the Grand Harbour. Admiral Cunningham, Commander of the Royal Navy's Mediterranean Fleet, sent a cable to the Admiralty in London: 'Be pleased to inform their Lordships that the Italian Battle Fleet now lies at anchor under the guns of the fortress of Malta.' Malta's war was, to all intents and purposes, over.

There are several excellent books on Malta's World War II; see page 317.

POST-WAR POLITICS In July 1943, the British governor assured the beleaguered population of Malta that when hostilities ended, home rule would be reinstated. Sure enough, in 1947 a new constitution came into force with provision for universal suffrage over the age of 21, giving women and those without property or education the vote for the first time. The Labour Party won the election, Dr Paul Boffa became prime minister, and income tax and pensions were introduced. A split in the party in 1949 led to its fall from government. The new party leader was Dom Mintoff, Malta's best-known and most controversial politician (see box opposite).

Elections in 1950, 1951 and 1953 gave no party an overall majority, but in 1955 Mintoff fought the election on the promise of immediate negotiations with the British government to become part of Britain (in the same way as the Channel Islands), a move expected to significantly improve economic conditions in Malta. Labour won an overwhelming majority in the general election and the referendum on integration that followed. Britain, however, was wary of Mintoff's demand for Maltese MPs at Westminster and when it became clear that the UK (with post-war economic problems of its own) intended to reduce defence spending in Malta (risking the jobs of thousands of Labour voters in the dockyards) Mintoff changed tack. In 1958, he resigned and declared himself and his party for full independence from Britain.

This prompted a political crisis and a brief return to colonial administration, but by the early 1960s (with the Nationalist Party under Prime Minister Ġorġ Borg Olivier in power) both Labour and the Nationalists were backing independence. It was agreed that some British forces would stay for at least ten years and that London would provide tens of millions of pounds to help Malta rebuild. On 21 September 1964, Malta was declared an independent nation.

DOM MINTOFF

Malta's most famous and controversial politician, Dominic Mintoff, was a maverick socialist firebrand, rarely out of the European newspapers throughout the 1970s. He loved horseriding, reading, *boċċi* (Malta's version of boules) and swimming in the sea near his villa on the Delimara Peninsula. Born in Bormla/Cospicua (next to the docks) in 1916, he was educated at the University of Malta and then as a Rhodes scholar at Oxford. He was in Britain throughout Malta's war, returning to a devastated urban landscape In 1943.

By 1945 he was deputy leader of the Labour Party, led by Paul Boffa. Mintoff's outspoken character and overt ambition led to a split in the party in 1949. Boffa formed his own Malta Workers Party and Mintoff became leader of the (slightly renamed) Malta Labour Party (MLP). The Labour vote was thus split and it was not until 1955 that they regained power.

Mintoff's policy of full integration into the UK was deeply unpopular with the Catholic Church and created long-term enmity between Malta's most powerful man and its most powerful non-elected institution. The Church even declared at one point that it was a sin to vote for the MLP. Mintoff was equally vitriolic about the Church, and, after what he saw as Britain's rejection of his advances, also about the old colonial power he had initially so assiduously courted.

Mintoff's heyday was the 1970s: he was prime minister continuously from 1971 to 1984. A powerful orator with a genuine concern for working people, he made some controversial friends – most notably Colonel Gaddafi of Libya. Nobody in Malta was (or is) neutral on the subject of Mintoff – he has always evoked strong feelings.

In 1984, Mintoff chose to resign as prime minister, handing over to his chosen successor, Karmenu Mifsud Bonnici, who led the country until the next election in 1987. The old firebrand still retained his parliamentary seat and was sometimes accused of backseat driving. His outspokenness did not diminish – and was not always in his party's best interests.

The MLP and Mintoff himself were vehemently opposed to the Nationalists' policy of Malta joining the EU. In 1998, Labour was back in power under Dr Alfred Sant, but with a majority of only one. The government wanted to build a yacht marina on the Vittoriosa Waterfront to bring in income. Mintoff did not like the limitation this would place on access for local (less wealthy) people. Always one to act on his views – even at the age of 82 – he voted against his own party and brought down the government. In the resulting general election, the Nationalists won and reinstated Malta's application to join the European Union (as well as building the marina).

Mintoff did not return to parliament, although he continued to campaign (unsuccessfully) against EU membership until 2003.

He died in summer 2012 at the age of 96.

1

INDEPENDENT MALTA: 1964–ONGOING

Queen Elizabeth II remained Malta's head of state until 1974 when Dom Mintoff made Malta a republic headed by a president appointed by parliament. The last British forces left Malta on 31 March 1979. This was not only the end of a 180-year era; it also left a significant hole in Malta's economy. The British forces had been by far the largest employer in the country and Malta now needed to find other sources of income and employment fast.

Tourism was an obvious choice and the rush to attract as many visitors as possible began. Malta also needed manufacturing and trade. It was not self-sufficient in anything much and required the import of oil – most of which came from Libya – and (as ever) food. When the British departed, Mintoff declared Malta neutral and non-aligned and signed controversial agreements with North Korea, the Soviet Union and Libya.

Mintoff's Labour administration tried to control everything centrally and almost any significant economic activity required a government permit – a state of affairs that encouraged corruption. Tariffs were imposed on all imported goods, leading to the unseemly sight of Maltese families returning from abroad with suitcases containing just a thin layer of clothes covering electronics, foreign toiletries and a year's supply of chocolate – not a policy designed to increase the government's popularity.

In 1987, the Nationalist Party won the election, a feat they repeated in 1992 on a platform that included a commitment to begin negotiations to join the EU. Despite some ups and downs (see box, page 19), Malta became a full member of the European Union in May 2004 and joined the Eurozone on 1 January 2008.

For more on Malta's current politics, see page 28.

MALTA AND GOZO ONLINE

For additional online content, articles, photos and more on Malta and Gozo, why not visit **w** bradtguides.com/malta?

2

Background Information

GEOGRAPHY AND GEOLOGY

Malta's geography has been hugely important to its history. Its position in the middle of the Mediterranean and its natural harbours are what have made it desirable and put it on the international map. Malta lies 93km south of Sicily (just visible on a clear day and within a day's sailing) and 355km north of Libya. To the west is Tunisia,

MALTA IN CONTEXT

SLOVENIA
CROATIA
ROMANIA
BOSNIA &
HERZEGOVINA
SERBIA
Adriatic Sea
Corsica
ITALY
MONTENEGRO
KOSOVO
BULGARIA
MACEDONIA
Sardinia
ALBANIA
Tyrrhenian Sea
GREECE
Ionian Sea
Sicily
MEDITERRANEAN
Gozo MALTA
Malta
Crete
TUNISIA
N
Bradt
LIBYA
Gulf of Sirte
LIBYA
0 ——— 300km
0 ——— 200 miles
SEA

288km away, and to the east is Crete, 815km away. The Maltese islands are small (just 316km²), rocky and lack a good source of fresh water, but their harbours are a natural asset that have ensured the strategic importance of the country throughout its history.

GEOLOGY Geologically speaking Malta is young. Its oldest rock is less than 30 million years old – so no dinosaurs or dinosaur fossils here. The islands were formed by the buckling up of the seabed as the tectonic plates of Europe and Africa slowly collided – a process also responsible for the formation of the Etna and Vesuvius volcanoes. Malta has no volcanoes and no volcanic rock, although it does suffer occasional earthquakes.

Malta is basically made of limestone (calcium carbonate) and there are five main strata of rock. From the deepest (and oldest) upwards, they are lower coralline limestone, globigerina limestone, blue clay, greensand and upper coralline limestone.

Coralline limestone is, as its name suggests, formed from dead coral compressed on the seabed. It is hard and durable, relatively little affected by weather. **Globigerina limestone** was formed when the sea was deeper (100–150m). At this depth there is no sunlight or turbulence and fine dust and dead microorganisms (of which globigerina is one) form the sediment that becomes the limestone. This stone is a wonderful creamy yellow. It is soft and easily weathered, but also easily cut, and it is Malta's main building material.

Weather takes its toll even more readily on **blue clay**, but this is another useful layer, giving fertility to the soil. The **greensand** is in a very thin layer on top of the blue clay and is yet more easily weathered. The surface layer of rock is often **upper coralline**, the same type of rock as the bottom layer, resistant to the effects of weather. This can have a dramatic effect on cliffs where the clay and greensand layers weather faster than the rock above them. The upper coralline is left sitting on very little until eventually great boulders fall into the sea.

The southern sea cliffs of Malta and Gozo – such as at Dingli and Ta' Ċenċ – are lower coralline limestone, while those of the west and north of the main island have a strong clay element topped with upper coralline rock. Much of the interior, especially in the centre and east, is globigerina. Comino sits lower in the water than the other two islands and only the upper coralline is visible.

Gozo is made up of valley areas – mainly globigerina limestone – and flat-topped hills which have the full set of strata, topped with the upper coralline layer. Once you are aware of the five layers (which always come in the same order) you may start to spot them in the landscape.

Limestone Isles in a Crystal Sea by Martyn Pedley, Michael Hughes-Clarke and Pauline Galea (published by Maltese publisher PEG) summarises decades of research on Maltese geology, with colour illustrations, and includes a booklet of geological walks.

CLIMATE

Malta, unsurprisingly, has a Mediterranean-island climate: hot dry summers and mild damp winters with occasional chilly winds. The temperature rarely rises above the mid 30s (°C) or falls below the high single figures. It hasn't officially snowed here since 1962 (a few flakes were reported in 2014 but it wasn't regarded as a proper snowfall), and before that 1905, although in recent winters occasional dramatic hailstorms have occurred. Even frost tends not to touch Malta. Rain is extremely rare in summer, reasonably frequent in winter. Spring is drier than autumn but can be made colder by wind.

CLIMATE CHART

Month	Sunshine (hrs)	Rainfall (mm)	Minimum temp (°C)	Maximum temp (°C)	Sea surface temp (°C)	Relative humidity (%)
January	5.7	71.2	10.5	16.0	16.7	77.4
February	6.6	65.9	9.9	15.8	15.7	76.5
March	7.3	46.9	10.9	17.3	15.5	78.5
April	8.5	13.9	13.2	20.4	16.6	76.5
May	10.3	6.3	16	24.3	18.8	69.4
June	11.4	11.6	19.6	28.6	22.2	65.8
July	12.0	0.1	22.2	31.8	25.6	63
August	11.0	7.1	23	31.9	26.9	68.3
September	8.7	43.7	21.3	28.7	26.2	72.1
October	6.9	82.9	18.5	24.9	24.1	76.4
November	5.9	89.2	15.2	20.8	21.4	76.7
December	5.6	81.4	11.8	17.1	18.5	74.2

Figures provided by the Meteorological Office at Malta International Airport

MALTA'S WINDS

Wind is a common feature of Malta's weather. Even in summer only about one day a fortnight is windless. The Maltese have names for the winds:

MAJJISTRAL   Cool northwesterly, blows nearly one day in five all year round.

GRIGAL   Dry northeasterly, stirs up the sea so it batters the coast with waves, blows around 10% of days but especially in September and March.

TRAMONTANA   Meaning 'across the mountains' in Italian, this cold north wind from the Alps is the main wind of winter and also blows about one day in ten.

XLOKK   The Sirocco. Hot, humid, sometimes dust-laden and unpleasant southeasterly bringing heat from the Sahara and humidity picked up over the sea. May last several days. Strong Xlokks are most likely in March and November.

LBIC   Southwesterly, similar to the Xlokk.

RIH ISFEL   Warm wind from the south that, like the two above, brings sticky oppressive weather.

NATURAL HISTORY AND CONSERVATION

Nature and wildlife are under tremendous pressure on the main island of Malta, where human habitation has taken over most of the land. Despite this, there are some beautiful areas of countryside here and plenty more on Gozo. There is quite a range of plant life, with wild flowers plentiful in spring. Animals are more limited, with birdlife in particular not helped by the (albeit slowly declining) enthusiasm for hunting amongst some Maltese men.

FLORA Hard though it is to believe, experts say that before people arrived on Malta it had extensive tree cover. This has not been the case now for thousands of years and trees are a rarity, with most species introduced from other countries, including Aleppo pines, acacia, carob and fig trees, olive trees and a few palms. Tamarisk and oleander bushes add colour. Wild fennel, with its typical aniseed smell and tiny yellow flowers, is all over the place. Caper bushes are common and in spring you may see people harvesting the little green buds used in salads and cooking.

Malta's most typical habitat is the Mediterranean garigue, limestone rock with low shrubby vegetation. The tops of the Dingli and Ta' Ċenċ cliffs and Comino have good examples of coastal garigue with significant endemic flora (unique to the Maltese islands). Wild Mediterranean thyme is often the dominant species, and Malta's national plant, rock centaury, is usually to be seen. Golden samphire is common along with other hardy plants with fleshy fluid-retaining leaves. Other species include Maltese salt tree, sea chamomile and fleabane. More rarely you may find hoary rock-rose, wild artichoke and the scarce endemic Maltese pyramidal orchid.

Among Malta's more unusual plants is the Maltese everlasting (*Helichrystum melitense*), a rare bush up to 1m high, flowering yellow in May/June, found only on the western cliffs of Gozo and on Fungus Rock, Dwejra. Also on Fungus Rock (and occasionally on Ta' Ċenċ) is the once much-prized plant after which the rock was named (though it is not in fact a fungus), *Cynomorium coccineum* (page 288).

For more information, w maltawildplants.com has an index of over 1,000 plants found in Malta, many of them pictured.

FAUNA
Land fauna Besides rabbits, butterflies and birds, Malta's main animals are **reptiles**. Lizards are regularly seen: copious **geckos** camouflaged against the limestone or darting across the ground, as well as rounded stumpy **skinks**. There are four kinds of **snake** (two possibly accidentally introduced during World War I and limited to southeast Malta), but no poisonous species. This is credited by some to St Paul, who is meant to have miraculously remained unharmed by a viper biting him shortly after his shipwreck on Malta in AD60 (see box, page 7). The more scientifically minded suggest the snake that bit him was probably Malta's non-poisonous leopard snake.

The snake you are most likely to see is the black whip snake (*Coluber viridiflavus carbonarius*, or in Maltese, *serp*), found on Malta, Gozo and Comino. The adult has a black back, while the juvenile is dark green with grey and dark brown markings. It grows up to 2m long and lives in rock cracks and under rubble, coming out in the middle of the day to hunt for lizards, rodents and eggs. It hibernates in winter.

Marine fauna There have generally been plenty of fish in the sea around Malta, including some that have died out in more polluted parts of the Mediterranean. Fresh fish is a regular in Malta's restaurants and snorkelling usually brings several species into view very quickly. There is some concern, at the time of writing, that numbers may be declining, particularly of some of the sea life usually seen by divers such as grouper and octopus (see also page 71).

Turtles inhabit the seas around Malta and in summer 2012 one laid eggs on a crowded beach at Ġnejna Bay – an increasing occurrence along the Mediterranean coast. **Nature Trust Malta** (℡21313150; e info@naturetrustmalta.org) rescues turtles and patrols for eggs in summer. For more, see page 28.

There have long been stories that sharks breed around the tiny uninhabited island of Filfla off Malta's south coast. In fact, no dangerous sharks have been seen there, or anywhere else around Malta in a great many years. Small sharks, rays and

You are very unlikely to see a Maltese falcon in Malta but for the first time in many years there are a few on the islands. A subspecies of the peregrine falcon, the fastest bird in the world, the Maltese falcon was hunted to extinction here in the 1970s and 80s. It has recently re-colonised and a few pairs have bred successfully along the westerly cliffs, though their exact location is kept very quiet for their own protection.

From early in the 2nd millennium onwards, the leaders of Europe prized the Maltese falcon above all others for their sport of falconry. When Malta was ceded to the Order of St John by the Holy Roman emperor Charles V in 1530, the 'rent' was to be paid in falcons. More recently, Malta's *kaccaturi* (hunters) have ensured that birds of prey are an uncommon sight in Malta outside migration times. And some of the migratory ones are – illegally – shot down, too.

skate do exist in the area and Sharklab-Malta (w sharklab-malta.org) is trying to protect them. They organise a range of events (listed on their website) that visitors are welcome to attend.

There is a helpful section on Maltese marine life on the website w seastuff.com.

Birds Malta has very few permanently resident birds, with only 29 species breeding on the islands. This is partly due to destruction of habitat, but also to the continuing – though declining – popularity of bird hunting (page 50). The total species count to date, however, is nearly 400 because Malta is on the central Mediterranean migration, one of the three main routes used by birds to migrate between Africa, where they winter, and Europe, where they breed. Multitudes of birds fly over – and may stop for a rest – in spring and autumn. Unfortunately, some of these are also shot by Malta's bird hunters.

Hunting of certain species (mainly quail and turtle dove) is allowed in autumn. The rules in spring keep changing. Spring hunting was stopped in 2008 (under EU legislation) and although a few hunters broke the law, the positive impact of two consecutive closed spring seasons was clearly seen in summer 2009. Nine breeding species extended their distribution, three returned to breed after long absences – common kestrel, grey wagtail (the first breeding pair in nearly a century) and common cuckoo – and one new species, the pallid swift, colonised the islands.

Since then spring hunting has reopened for limited periods but illegal hunting is being better controlled and since 2010 several new species have bred in Malta including blackcaps and blackwing stilts.

The most common bird in Malta is the Spanish sparrow, which is abundant in towns and villages as well as the countryside. The national bird, the attractive blue rock thrush, is reasonably easily seen on coastal cliffs. Various warblers live in open country, garigue and valleys, and over the sea, Scopoli's shearwater, and in some places the much rarer and threatened Yelkouan shearwater, can be spotted on windy days or at dusk when they gather together like a raft on the water before flying into their cliff nests after dark. Malta has 10% of the world's population of Yelkouan shearwaters and a special conservation project reversed a decline in the population here and made valuable discoveries about the birds' habits (see box, page 251).

At migration times, Malta's bird population rises dramatically with songbirds such as finches as well as large birds of prey passing through. Unfortunately any spot that is good for birdwatching is also good for bird hunting.

For more information on birdwatching and related safety issues, see pages 50 and 72.

Hunting and trapping There are around 11,000 licensed bird hunters (*kaccaturi*) in Malta (not all of them active) and until recently. there were over 1,200 trapping licences too. Malta's membership of the EU has, however, changed the situation, as Malta is expected to comply with the EU Birds Directive. This rules out trapping and limits hunting to certain species, theoretically in the autumn season only. Hunting is, however, a political hot potato in Malta, so compliance with the regulations has been complicated.

Trapping The Maltese have long kept finches as pets. You can see their little cages hanging outside front doors in more traditional areas. Trapping of the seven main species of finch (including greenfinch, goldfinch and chaffinch) for this purpose was for many years a widespread hobby and until 2009 tens of thousands of finches were caught each year. Presumably as a result, Malta, despite once having had finches breeding here, is the only country in the Mediterranean that does not have a viable breeding population.

When Malta joined the EU it was given special dispensation to phase out rather than just stop the trapping of finches. That grace period ended at the close of 2008 and the trapping of finches became illegal. In 2012, a season of trapping song thrush and golden plover was allowed, even though the EU issued a letter saying that this did not comply with EU regulations. The government also strengthened the specialist police team that dealt with illegal hunting and trapping, however, and well over 80 trappers were caught illegally trapping finches.

In 2014, the autumn finch-trapping season was reinstated, allowing the trapping of 26,000 finches. The European Court of Justice found Malta guilty of breaching the Birds Directive in June 2018, saying trapping activities in Malta were a threat to the species. At time of writing it is unclear how the government will respond.

In the meantime you may still see trappers' huts on Malta's coast and in fertile valleys. Usually roughly built of stone, they may have poles or little stands outside to support cages containing captive finches used to sing their wild cousins into the traps.

Hunting Shooting birds has long been popular in Malta and there is a small but vocal minority that regards bird hunting as an inalienable right. They have even claimed that not being allowed to hunt was damaging to their mental health. In order to protect birds on their way to breed, the EU Birds Directive makes spring hunting illegal. Hunters may shoot certain named species during the autumn season only.

Since joining the EU in 2004, however, Malta has at times chosen to exempt itself from this regulation and allowed spring hunting to open. The Maltese government is perfectly entitled to do this under certain conditions and so long as it can justify its actions to the European Commission each year. In 2008, the European Court issued an interim measure ordering Malta not to open spring hunting. For two years this was complied with and, despite some illegal activity, had a very positive impact on Malta's birds. In September 2009, the issue was tested in the European Court of Justice and Malta was found *not* to have been justified in permitting spring hunting.

The hunters latched onto a small part of the ruling to claim that spring hunting should be reinstated, and this duly happened but for a while illegal hunting (outside permitted periods or of protected species within permitted times) was more actively policed. More illegal hunters were caught and they were dealt with more harshly. In autumn 2014 and spring 2015, the season was closed early in response to illegal activity.

The hunters have at times been quite aggressive about their 'rights'. In the past, BirdLife Malta has had not only its little reserve at Għadira attacked but one of its staff shot with a hunting gun (twice). When in spring 2012 a German group brought a drone to Birdlife Malta's Raptor Camp (aimed at preventing illegal activity, not at interfering with legitimate hunting), it was almost immediately shot down. These events are now a few years in the past and there has been no such behaviour recently.

The hunters remain adamant, however, that it is their right to hunt. On the other hand, there are many in Malta who would like year-round access to the country's limited areas of countryside without guns popping around them. A poll in 2007 indicated that some 85% of the population was against the government's decision to defy EU regulations and open spring hunting that year, and when the hunters' leader, Lino Farrugia (who has a conviction for illegal trapping) stood for the European Parliament in 2004 he gained just 3,308 votes.

However, in 2015, a referendum was held asking if spring hunting should be banned. The vote became politicised (so voting ended up being about more than hunting) and the hunters won by 50.44% to 49.56%.

Since then, spring hunting has continued to open and enforcement appears to have slackened. In 2017 a new Minister for Agriculture, Fisheries and Animal Rights (whose brief includes hunting) was appointed. He is a hunter and member of the Federation of Hunters.

For additional information, see also page 50.

CONSERVATION Despite rampant development, Malta does have some beautiful countryside – and much of Gozo remains unspoilt. Even in recent years, species of plant and insect new to science have been discovered on the islands and there are several NGOs working hard to try to protect and preserve the habitats and ecosystems of rural Malta. Most prominent amongst these are Nature Trust Malta, BirdLife Malta, Din L-Art Ħelwa (Malta's National Trust) and the GAIA Foundation.

A project known as PANACEA, working in partnership with Sicily, has designated two Marine Protected Areas in Malta: Dwejra (Gozo) and Rdum Majjiesa (near Għajn Tuffieħa on Malta). There is a small informative visitor education centre at Dwejra.

BirdLife Malta ☏ 21347646; e info@ birdlifemalta.org; w birdlifemalta.org. Affiliated to BirdLife International, this is Malta's equivalent of the UK's RSPB. It campaigns for the protection of birds & against poaching & illegal trapping, collects data & has a hugely informative website (including a section for kids) & multiple publications. It runs 2 small wetland reserves (Għadira & Is-Simar) as well as a reforestation project in conjunction with Din L-Art Ħelwa. BirdLife also organises data-gathering camps during autumn & spring migration & bird ringing on Comino.
Din L-Art Ħelwa ☏ 21225952; e info@ dinlarthelwa.org; w dinlarthelwa.org. Malta's National Trust is affiliated to the English National Trust. The primary purpose of Din L-Art Ħelwa is preservation of built heritage – they have renovated numerous sites & opened them to the public. Like their British counterpart they also work

to conserve the nation's natural heritage, usually in partnership with the other NGOs named here.
GAIA Foundation ☏ 21584473/4; e director@ projectgaia.org, elysium@projectgaia.org; ☐ thegaiafoundationmalta. Involved in a variety of projects including propagation of native & endemic plants, seabed protection, restoration of sand dunes at Ramla Bay on Gozo & coastal conservation at Għajn Tuffieħa Bay on Malta, as well as organic farming. They have a centre open to the public at Għajn Tuffieħa (near the Radisson Golden Bay Hotel) & a flexible volunteer programme that includes visitors (page 239).
Malta Nature Tours m 79546987; e info@ maltanaturetours.com; w maltanaturetours. com. Tailor-made outings for visitors led by people qualified in various areas of Malta's natural environment.

Nature Trust Malta ✆21313150; e info@
naturetrustmalta.org; w naturetrustmalta.org.
NGO involved in protection & promotion of Malta's
natural heritage. They help manage the Majjistral
National Park (w majjistral.org) – an area of

mainly rocky garigue in northwestern Malta –
as well as 2 forestation projects. They have been
involved in protecting the Dwejra region of Gozo
& the habitat of the rare freshwater crab. They run
occasional nature walks, including at Majjistral.

GOVERNMENT AND POLITICS

Malta is a democratic republic with high popular interest in politics: voter turnout
is usually over 90%. The president is the head of state while most executive powers
lie with the prime minister who is head of government. The president appoints the
cabinet (on the advice of the prime minister) from the ranks of the 65-seat House
of Representatives that sits in the Maltese Parliament in Valletta.

Elections to the House of Representatives take place at least every five years using
proportional representation by single transferable vote. Thirteen constituencies
each elect five MPs. Occasionally, as at present, 'bonus' MPs are elected in order
to ensure that a party gaining a majority of votes nationally has an appropriate
majority of seats. From 2008 to 2017 there were 69 MPs, and there are now 67.

Since independence in 1964, Maltese politics has been dominated by two
parties: the Nationalist Party (Partit Nazzjonalista) or PN, and the Malta Labour
Party (Partit Laburista) or MLP. MLP is a traditional labour movement with strong
support in the dock areas of the Three Cities, Marsaskala, Paola and Birżebbuġa.
The entrepreneurs, bankers and professionals of areas like Sliema tend to be
Nationalist (though there are obviously exceptions). Dom Mintoff, with his pro-
Arab policies and deals with the Chinese, did much to alienate the middle classes
from the Labour Party. The two parties now have very similar levels of support in
the country: the 2008 general election was won by the Nationalist Party with 49.3%
of the vote, just ahead of the Labour Party with 48.9%, giving the PN 35 seats, the
MLP 34.

The Alternativa Demokratika (AD), Malta's Green Party and Azzjoni Nazzjonaili
(National Action) (AN), won under 1.5% of the vote each and a handful of other
parties received fewer than 200 votes altogether. None of these smaller parties has
ever won a seat.

The leader of the majority party in the House of Representatives becomes prime
minister. Lawrence Gonzi, a lawyer, took the post in 2009 for the second time,
having been prime minister since March 2004. The president is separately chosen
by parliament every five years. In April 2009, George Abela (another lawyer, former
chairman of the Malta Football Association and recent contender for the leadership
of the opposition Labour Party) took the post. This was the first time a president
had been chosen from the opposition party, but Abela is a close friend of the prime
minister (going back to university days) and became president with the support of
the government.

In the 2013 general election, the Labour Party displaced the Nationalists after
15 years, taking 39 seats to the Nationalists' 30. Joseph Muscat became prime
minister. In April 2014, Marie Louise Coleiro Preca became president: the second
woman to hold the post. After accusations of corruption, Muscat called a snap
election in spring 2017 and was returned with 55% of the vote.

The Maltese are passionate about politics. Families are often firmly Labour or
Nationalist and debate can become heated. In a country as small and interconnected
as Malta, nepotism and back-scratching are common. The saying 'it is not what
you know, but who you know that matters', rings true here. Malta has never had

a Mafia like that in neighbouring Sicily, but the recent allegations of large-scale international corruption made by journalist Daphne Caruana Galizia, who was then murdered in a car bombing in October 2017, have shaken many Maltese and raised some very serious questions.

ECONOMY

From the early 16th century until the end of World War II, Malta did not have to stand on its own two feet economically. The Knights and then the British brought foreign money, trade and employment for over four centuries. When Dom Mintoff threw out the last of the British Navy in the 1970s, Malta had to fill the resulting economic gap. It has been fairly successful at doing so, though at a price – mass tourism has ruined significant stretches of the coast and countryside. The standard of living in Malta is somewhere in the middle of the EU range and there is universal free education and health care, and a life expectancy of 80.

Malta is dependent on imports for key supplies. It produces only 20% of its own food and has no local source of energy, so foreign trade is crucial. Key earners are manufacturing for export (especially electronics and pharmaceuticals), fish farming, internet betting companies and particularly tourism. The tourist industry accounts for some 35% of GDP and is the largest provider of employment.

In January 2008, Malta's currency became the euro and people complained that this led to a rise in prices. Malta was not as badly hit as some places in the 2008/09 credit crunch, however, and the economy has since been doing remarkably well.

There is, at the time of writing, something of a boom atmosphere in Malta. Tourism is rising fast, the government is making money from a scheme to sell Maltese passports, and there seems to be construction everywhere. Some worry that corruption is on the up and that boom is naturally followed by bust, but so far Malta seems to be sitting pretty.

PEOPLE AND MIGRATION

With a population of 475,000 (and rising) in an area of 316km², Malta has the fourth-highest population density in the world. Ninety-four per cent of the people live in urban areas – mainly in the large conglomeration that spreads inland from Valletta, Sliema and St Julian's. There are uncrowded places, however, especially on Gozo and Comino.

Ninety-seven per cent of Malta's permanent population was born in Malta. Emigration and working abroad have long been features of the country's history. Money earned in other countries has sustained many a family in hard economic times (there is a large Maltese population in Australia). Conversely Malta has absorbed Europeans of many nationalities over the centuries.

Yet the Maltese are not used to non-European, non-Christian immigrants from countries poorer than their own, so considerable disruption has been caused by the arrival over the last few years of several thousand destitute North African asylum seekers, many of whom are Muslim. The majority are trying to get to Italy but arrive in Maltese waters. This is a genuine problem for a small country, and has also brought to the surface an unattractive streak of racism.

On one level this is an odd place for colour-based racism as the Maltese themselves vary in colour enormously, from northern European white to quite dark. The deep-seated suspicion of anything Arab/Muslim/North African is not just a legacy of the Knights but also of the 1970s and Dom Mintoff's indiscriminate promotion of all things Libyan. At root, the current problem is the common fear homogenous communities frequently express at the arrival of a different culture.

That said, the Maltese are fundamentally a hospitable people. They can be quite unpleasant to each other at times and are not above bearing lengthy grudges, but to visitors they are generally charming, friendly and immensely helpful.

CULTURAL ATTITUDES Malta is changing fast. Until very recently it was a conservative Catholic country with attitudes to race, homosexuality, gender and disability you might have expected in non-metropolitan Britain several decades ago. However, in 2011 a referendum resulted, to the amazement even of the prime minister of the day, in a vote to allow divorce. In 2014 same-sex civil partnerships were legalised, giving gay couples the same rights as heterosexual married couples, including the right to adopt, and this was followed in 2017 by the introduction of gay marriage. Many in Malta itself are amazed by the speed with which this has happened and what it says about the loosening of the grip of the Catholic Church. The role of women is also changing with many more going out to work. The family, however, remains at the heart of Maltese society and grandmothers still do much of the childcare.

LANGUAGE

Maltese is a Semitic language (in the same family as Arabic and Hebrew), written in the Latin alphabet (the only one that is). However, much of its vocabulary – perhaps up to 50% – is derived from Italian and Sicilian, as well as some from English and a little from French. English words are increasingly incorporated, some of them with Italianised pronunciation; others retain their English pronunciation whilst being spelt the Maltese way; for example: *mowbajl* (as in 'mobile phone').

Maltese derives from Siculo-Arabic, the dialect of Arabic that developed in Sicily, Malta and southern Italy. The first documentary reference to Maltese comes in the mid 14th century followed in 1640 by the first dictionary, which was written by one of the Knights of St John, Frenchman François de Vion Thezan Court. The dictionary included phrases necessary for giving orders to soldiers. Most unusually for a European language, written Maltese was not standardised until the 19th century.

During the time of the Knights, Italian and French were the main languages of administration and Italian remained the lingua franca of the upper and middle classes well into the British period. In the 20th century, English took over and in 1934, Maltese (Malti) was formally recognised as an official language of the islands, alongside English. Maltese is also an official language of the European Union (the only Semitic language that is).

Most Maltese people now speak Maltese (Malti) and English. Many also speak Italian. In the 21st century, Maltese is increasingly spoken in offices and clubs where English would once have been *de rigueur*, although amongst the highly educated (particularly in Sliema) you will still find some Maltese using English as their primary language. One Maltese told me he speaks Malti with his parents but English with his siblings, friends and colleagues. Another said he generally speaks Malti at home unless he is arguing with his wife. This is done in English 'because it is more nuanced'!

As an English-speaker, you are unlikely to find yourself in any great linguistic difficulty. You are not going to need a phrasebook or a dictionary to get around. It is helpful to know how to pronounce Maltese, particularly place names – see page 310, which concentrates on this, as well as giving you a bit of very basic vocabulary, as it is always fun to be able to say hello.

In this guide place names are given in a mix of English and Maltese – sometimes in one, sometimes the other and sometimes both. This reflects how places are referred to in Malta.

RELIGION

Malta is 98% Catholic and religion remains an important part of both community life and the national sense of identity. Each parish runs a *festa*, the most important celebration of the year (page 32) and the Maltese are noticeably proud to be a Christian nation. Nearly three centuries of rule by a Christian religious order, whose *raison d'être* was opposing the Muslim 'infidel', has undoubtedly left its mark. A few old Maltese still remember their parents using the Turks like the bogeyman: 'Don't play in the street or the Turks will get you.'

Catholicism is the state religion (though the constitution guarantees freedom of worship) and is taught in all schools. The story goes that from anywhere in Malta you can see a church (not quite) and that you could go to a different church every day of the year (very nearly). The power of the Church is, however, undoubtedly waning. Only about half the population now goes to Mass every Sunday (well down on a decade ago) and the Church is losing control of social issues.

The Church canvassed hard against the legalisation of divorce in Malta, which was nonetheless voted through following a referendum in summer 2011. Abortion remains illegal, but the Church seems to be losing the battle against sex outside marriage: about a quarter of babies born in Malta are now born out of wedlock.

There are a handful of Protestant churches in Malta, including the Anglican cathedral in Valletta, and there is one synagogue and one mosque.

EDUCATION

The Church has historically had control over education in Malta and many private schools are still Church-run, though there are also some non-religious independent schools. Education is compulsory for children aged 5–16 and state schools are free and open to all. Under the British, most teaching was done in English and in some schools this is still the case, though most now teach in Maltese/Malti with English as the second language.

Secondary education is divided by academic ability into selective junior lyceums (like UK grammar schools) and area secondary schools (for those not passing the 11+ exam). Most schools are single sex and pupils sit O levels at 16 and A levels at 18. There is one university, the University of Malta in Msida, at the head of Marsamxett Harbour, where the number of women graduating recently overtook that of men.

The literacy rate in Malta has risen dramatically in the last 50 years. Before World War II nearly three-quarters of the population was illiterate. Now 94% can read and write, 99% amongst 15–24-year-olds.

ARTS AND CRAFTS

MUSIC Malta has a strong musical tradition and a remarkable proportion of the population participates in music making. Each parish has at least one **wind band** and some have a small **orchestra** as well. The main musical events of the year are the *festi* (page 32), but there are plenty of other concerts and events too. Pop music is also plentiful, both live and recorded, and the Eurovision Song Contest is a national event (w eurovisionmalta.com).

Malta's traditional folk music is *ghana*. Sung mostly by men it is peasant music with an Eastern root. There are various forms including one with improvised words in which the song is batted back and forth between two singers, and another in which the song is high-pitched, well above the normal male range. An annual festival of *ghana* takes place in July (page 37).

LITERATURE For many centuries Maltese was the language of the uneducated and so not of literature. The languages of writing were Latin, French, Italian and then English. The earliest known work of literature in Malti is an isolated example: Pietro Caxaro's 15th-century poem, *Cantilena* (also known as *Xidew il-Qada*). The next – a sonnet in praise of Grand Master Nicolas Cotoner by Gian Francesco Bonamico – wasn't written until 1672.

Writing in Maltese only really took hold with the beginnings of nationalist feeling in the 19th century. The first history of Malta in Maltese was not written until 1862 (by Gan Anton Vassallo, who was also a nationalist poet) and the first novel, Anton Manwel Caruana's *Inez Farrug* – modelled on Italian historical novels – not until 1889. Maltese writers today often write in English or in both Maltese and English.

Dun Karm Psaila (1871–1961) is considered the national poet and he wrote the words to the national anthem as well as poetry documenting the emotional landscape of World War II. Owing partly to his influence, poetry was the favourite genre for Maltese writers in the first half of the 20th century. Now there is greater diversity and the most influential contemporary writer, and commentator on matters literary, is Oliver Friggieri, novelist, poet and professor of Maltese at the University of Malta.

VISUAL ART The Knights left Malta with a strong artistic heritage and churches full of paintings, some of real quality. There is a lot of work by Malta's top 'Old Master', Mattia Preti (see box, page 126) and a couple of paintings by Caravaggio in the oratory museum of St John's Co-Cathedral in Valletta. The new MUŻA National Art Museum (page 121) has a broad collection and there is a thriving contemporary art scene too. New private galleries keep popping up in Valletta, and several historic sites and restaurants/bars exhibit changing displays of contemporary art. A useful source of information is the Malta Council for Culture and the Arts.

CRAFTS Lacemaking seems to have become established in Malta – and particularly amongst the women of Gozo – in the 16th and 17th centuries. It was given a boost in the 19th century when Genoese lacemakers were brought to Malta to help revive the industry; Maltese lace is therefore a variation on Genoese style. Lace made in Malta, however, often contains the Maltese cross somewhere in the design (see box opposite). In Gozo you may still occasionally see older women sitting on their doorsteps making lace.

The Knights brought the art of **silverwork** to Malta and there are some very fine examples in museums and churches. Many small workshops still produce fine silver filigree and a classic tourist souvenir is a filigree Maltese cross. Other crafts include weaving, knitting and glassblowing. Maltese blown glassware – often in very bright colours – is marketed extensively to tourists, although it is in fact a relatively new addition to Malta's crafts.

FESTA

The *festa* is a hugely important part of Maltese culture – both religious and secular – and the high point of the local community year. Every parish has its *festa* and money

THE MALTESE CROSS

The 'Maltese cross' has become a symbol of Malta, though it really belongs to the Order of St John. However, it is correctly 'Maltese' in that, contrary to popular belief, it did not (in its current form) become the universal symbol of the Hospitallers until the mid 16th century, when the Knights were firmly established in Malta.

It has long been believed that the cross was the order's symbol from the start because it is also a symbol of Amalfi, the city-state thought to be the home of the merchants who started the Hospitallers way back in the 11th century. The 'Maltese' cross still appears on the coat of arms of the city (as well as on the flag of the Italian Navy).

A recent survey of the evidence by a British knight, however, suggests that the current design evolved over the first few hundred years of the order's existence. Early on, the Hospitallers used a variety of crosses, shared with other Christians and crusaders, and particularly a simple Greek cross (with splayed arms but without the V-shaped ends). Only in Rhodes (1309–1522) does the eight-pointed cross emerge as predominant, but still in a less sharp-cornered, thicker-set, design than today's.

It is only in the immediate aftermath of the Great Siege of Malta (1565) that the modern version of the Maltese cross, with its four arrowhead arms coming to a point in the middle, displaces all other designs and starts to appear all over the coinage, art and architecture of the order (see St John's Co-Cathedral for example). It was even used when depicting scenes from earlier times, helping to plant the idea that it had always been the Knights' emblem.

The symbolism of the cross is certainly Christian. It is a cross as in the Crucifixion and the four arms stand for the four cardinal virtues of prudence, temperance, justice and fortitude. The meaning of the eight points is less clear. They were generally understood to stand for the eight beatitudes but may also have come to represent the eight obligations of the knight: truth, faith, sincerity, humility, justice, mercy, endurance of persecution and repentance of sin.

is raised and preparations made for it throughout the year. *Festa* is theoretically celebrated on the feast day of the saint to whom the parish church is dedicated, but most are in fact held on summer weekends. From late May to mid-September there is hardly a weekend without at least one *festa* and many weekends with several.

Several days before the big day, the church is decorated with red damask, and the *festa* statue – a more-than-life-size painted figure of the saint – is brought out of its shrine (usually behind glass) to stand in the main body of the church. Other statues are set up on pedestals outside the church and the exterior of the building is decorated with strings of lights. Bunting, flags and more lights are hung along nearby streets – you can tell as soon as you enter a town or village if it is *festa* time.

Festa eve – usually a Saturday – is firework time. Most parishes have their own tiny firework factory (with between one and five firework makers) and there is vehement competition for who can put on the best show. Lija used to have the reputation for the best *festa* fireworks, but Mqabba is challenging for the crown. Fireworks are usually accompanied by music, food stalls and a general festival atmosphere.

On Sunday, the *festa* itself, the day starts with High Mass, usually with an invited preacher and sacred music played by local musicians. Some parishes traditionally play the music of a particular Maltese or Italian composer (or composers). Works may be new or old, on occasion played from handwritten manuscripts dating back as far as the 18th century.

This is followed by the *festa* procession around the local streets. Often accompanied by the setting off of bangers, the procession is led by representatives of local confraternities (like guilds but attached to the Church). Next comes the statue of the saint carried shoulder-high by six or eight men, accompanied by priests bearing church relics, altar boys (still mostly boys in Malta) and members of the public who also line the streets.

As well as, or as part of, the religious processions, there are band marches. Each parish has at least one wind band. These evolved from simple fife and drums in the 18th century under the influence of British military music – and this is the high point of their year. The band marches are usually accompanied by considerable secular celebration and often quite a lot of alcohol; they can occasionally become raucous.

The day after the *festa*, usually a Monday, many people take the day off work and go to the beach for a picnic.

ATTENDING A *FESTA* Tourists are always welcome at these feast-day celebrations with their processions, religious services, music, fireworks, food and general jollity. The exact date of each *festa* varies from year to year so check what is happening during your visit by going to w visitmalta.com/en/village-festas or by contacting the Malta Tourism Authority – see page 42 for a list of MTA offices.

There are a few *festi* in **winter**, but the main *festa* season opens with the feast of St Publius in Floriana in the last week of April. After that (with a brief gap in mid-May) there are *festi* almost every weekend until the end of September. The biggest are public holidays). Other particularly popular *festi* include St Nicholas in Siġġiewi (last Sunday of June), St George in Qormi (same day), St Philip in Żebbuġ (second Sunday of June) and St George in Victoria, Gozo (mid-July), which includes horse and *sulky* (horse cart) races up the main street.

SPORTS AND ACTIVITIES

FOOTBALL Football is a big thing in Malta. There are more than 50 local clubs (w maltafootball.com) and most Maltese males support at least two teams – a Maltese team, of the Malta Football Association (w mfa.com.mt) and a British or Italian team. Leagues are followed assiduously and with great passion. The main games in Malta are played at the Ta' Qali National Stadium, while many bars show live international football. The most popular foreign teams – including Manchester United and Liverpool – have their own clubhouses.

WATER POLO Water polo is the next most popular sport, played throughout the summer (in football's close season). There are lidos in many coastal towns and important matches take place at the Olympic-sized National Swimming Pool (Maria Teresa Spinelli St, Gżira GZR 06; ☏ 21322884; w asaofmalta.org).

HORSE RACING A popular spectator sport, horse racing here is often more like Roman chariot racing: the driver sits on a *sulky*, a lightweight two-wheeled cart, behind the horse which trots the course. You will occasionally see these vehicles on the street, and in Gozo's capital Victoria they race along the main road during the July and August *festi*. The national racecourse is at the Marsa Sports Complex near Valletta (Marsa Grounds, Aldo Moro St; ☏ 21233851; e info@ marsasportsclub.com).

BOĊĊI Similar to boules, this traditional game is played on local pitches, mostly by the older generation (rather like bowls in England); see box, page 305.

NATIONAL/PUBLIC HOLIDAYS AND OTHER EVENTS

Malta has more national holidays than any other EU country:

New Year's Day	1 January
Feast of St Paul's Shipwreck	10 February. A national winter *festa* commemorating the day when St Paul, Malta's patron saint, is thought to have been shipwrecked on the rocks of St Paul's Bay in AD60 (see box, page 7).
The feast day of St Joseph	19 March. Celebrated with Mass in the morning and picnicking in the countryside in the afternoon. Rabat hosts a (San Ġużepp) full *festa* procession in the evening.
Freedom Day	31 March. Commemorates the final withdrawal of the British forces from Malta in 1979. A monument on the Vittoriosa Waterfront commemorates the event.
Good Friday	Churches are decorated and there are processions through the streets.
George Cross Ceremony	15 April, St George Square. Celebrates the awarding of the George Cross for bravery to the whole nation by George VI in 1942.
Workers' Day	1 May. Celebrations mainly by the General Workers Union and Labour Party in Valletta.
Sette Giugno	7 June. In commemoration of serious riots and four deaths that occurred on this day in 1919 (page 17).
Feast of St Peter and St Paul (L-Imnarja)	29 June. Celebrated particularly in Buskett Gardens with music and rabbit stew.
Feast of the Assumption of Our Lady (Santa Marija)	15 August. An important *festa* celebrated in many parishes, particularly Victoria and Żebbuġ on Gozo and on Malta in Mqabba, Qrendi, Mosta, Gudja, Attard and Għaxaq. Good view of fireworks from the bastion walls of Mdina.
Victory Day	8 September. Celebrating the victory at the end of the Great Siege of 1565 (page 12) as well as the Italian surrender in World War II (8 September 1943; page 18). Also the religious feast of Marija Bambina, the birth of the Holy Virgin, centred on Senglea. Regatta in the Grand Harbour with six harbour towns competing and feasts in Naxxar, Mellieħa and Xagħra (Gozo).
Independence Day	21 September. Celebrating this day in 1964 when Malta became an independent state.
Feast of the Immaculate Conception	8 December. Particularly celebrated in Bormla and well attended because it is the only *festa* at this time of year.
Republic Day	13 December. Malta became a republic on this day in 1974.
Christmas Day	25 December

OTHER EVENTS Besides the national holidays and many *festi*, there are a number of other annual events. For up-to-date event listings, see w visitmalta.com/en/events; or contact the MTA (page 42; ☎23397000; w maltaculture.com).

January

Baroque Music Festival (w vallettabaroquefestival.com.mt) Valletta's annual Baroque Music Festival sees concerts by leading international as well as national Baroque musicians performed in Valletta's Baroque Manoel Theatre and many Baroque churches. UK tour operators including ACE Cultural Tours, Kirker Holidays and Martin Randall run tours to the festival (page 44).

February

Carnival Malta's carnival has existed since at least the 1530s (the time of the Knights) and possibly much earlier. For five days before the start of Lent (usually, but not always, in February), Malta, and particularly Valletta, goes a little crazy. Colourful floats roll through the capital and people in wild costumes populate the streets, cafés and bars. On Gozo, Victoria plays host to the floats while Nadur's carnival, sometimes called the Silent Carnival, is celebrated in stranger fashion. Here there is no organising committee; the whole thing is spontaneous. Costumes are simple (sacks, wigs) and designed for disguise rather than show. Many participants do not speak in order to keep their identities secret (hence the nickname) and some carry placards hand-painted with veiled insults to public (and private) personalities.

Malta Marathon and Half-Marathon (w maltamarathon.com) Run from Mdina, via Ta' Qali, Attard and Mosta to finish in Sliema. There is also a walkers' half-marathon, the Walkathon. Specialist holiday operator Sports Tours International offers trips to this event (page 44).

March

Opera Festival Based in the historic Manoel Theatre in Valletta, the festival usually consists of two fully staged operas and an opera-related concert. Specialist tour operator Travel for the Arts offers packages to this festival (page 44).

Easter The Maltese take Easter week very seriously and many processions take place as well as devotional church visits. On Easter Sunday, church is followed by a large family lunch. Children are given Easter eggs and a *figolla*, a pastry filled with almond paste and topped with icing.

Tour Ta' Malta Maltese version of the Tour de France held over four days towards the end of March. Organised by the Malta Cycling Federation (m 79471935; w tourtamalta.com).

April/May

Fireworks Festival Annual competition held in early May or sometimes late April with a vast display of foreign and local fireworks over the Grand Harbour.

Mother's Day (Variable date) A great excuse for a large long lunch in a restaurant with all the family. If you want to eat out on this day, book well in advance.

P1 Powerboat Race (w powerboatp1.com) A weekend of roaring engines as powerboats race along the Grand Harbour.

June
Malta Music Week and Isle of MTV (w isleofmtv.com) A week of club nights, concerts and parties leading up to the isle of MTV, said to be the largest open-air free concert in Europe with international pop stars. Performers have included Lady Gaga, Rod Stewart, Flo Rida and Will.i.am.

July
Għanafest (w festivalsmalta.com/ghanafest) A national folk festival of *għana* singing (page 32) held in the Argotti Gardens, Floriana.

Malta Arts Festival (↖ 21245168; w maltaartsfestival.org) Concerts, opera, theatre, visual arts, food and wine, mainly in Valletta. Also includes the Malta Jazz Festival.

Malta Jazz Festival (w maltajazzfestival.org) Concerts around the Grand Harbour by Maltese and international jazz artists.

September/October
Notte Bianca ✳ (White Night;↖ 21232515; w nottebiancamalta.com) Date varies, but usually in September or October. Shops and museums stay open all evening and some into the early hours. Historic buildings not normally open to the public welcome visitors and there is a variety of entertainment.

Festival Mediterranea (↖ 21550985; w mediterranea.com.mt) Gozo's annual arts festival, based in Victoria. Dominated by concerts and opera but also including talks, walks, art exhibitions, etc.

Malta Military Tattoo (w maltamilitarytattoo.org) At Ta' Qali Stadium. Precision marching, gymnastics and lots of military music.

Rolex Middle Sea Race Around 70–80 boats take part in this sailing race of 606 nautical miles starting and ending in Valletta's Marsamxett Harbour. Hosted by the Royal Malta Yacht Club (↖ 21333109; w rolexmiddlesearace.com).

Malta Classic Mdina Grand Prix (↖ 21339165; m 99477735, 99473377; UK contact: ↖ 01243 263364; e mdinagp4uk@gmail.com; w maltaclassic.com) Classic cars race along a 2.2km track below the bastions of Mdina. Plenty of social events and sightseeing for the international participants too.

Three Palaces Festival (↖ 23397000; w 3palacesfestival.com) Concerts in Malta's three presidential palaces (The Grand Master's, San Anton and Verdala).

November
International Choir Competition and Festival (↖ 22915136; w maltachoirfest.com) Five days of concerts and choral get-togethers in some of Malta's many churches.

December
Christmas Richly celebrated in this Catholic country, Christmas brings nativity scenes all over the place, decorated churches and lots of carol singing.

3

Practical Information

WHEN TO VISIT

Malta enjoys some 300 days of sunshine a year and doesn't have a closed season (except in Comino), so you can visit at any time. The weather does, of course, vary through the year and can get wet and windy, and occasionally chilly, in winter. The best time to visit depends largely on what you want to do.

Summer (which in Malta runs to mid-September) is dry, hot and quite busy. July and August are driest, hottest and busiest. The summer – especially August – is also dramatically more expensive in many areas with accommodation prices often double the winter rates. On the other hand there is very rarely any rain from early July to mid-September and the average peak temperature during the day is 30°C. Temperatures can go higher, but on the coast there is usually a breeze to stop it becoming oppressive.

Watersports – swimming, snorkelling, diving, windsurfing, etc – are most reliable in summer when the water is warm and more likely to be calm. Summer is also *festa* time when each parish has its colourful religious feast day (page 32). There are feasts almost every weekend in summer and many other events besides (page 35).

Winter is generally mild and can be warm, sunny T-shirt weather. Even in January (the coldest month) average daylight temperatures are 9–14°C and winter days still average 5 hours of sunshine. There are, however, significant patches of wind and rain when it can feel chilly. When it is very windy and the sea boils up (which can be great to watch), ferries may stop running, though rarely for more than a few hours. The cooler months are generally OK for sightseeing, but not, of course, for swimming. Accommodation is much cheaper than in summer, except over Christmas and New Year, when – although Malta is not busy – prices rise dramatically and during the January Baroque Music Festival when Valletta accommodation fills up.

Spring and **autumn** (April–June/late September–November) are ideal if you would like some sun and are primarily interested in the sights and the countryside rather than lying on the beach. Swimming can, however, be very pleasant from June until the end of October (with the water warmer in the autumn) and on weekdays at least you are quite likely to have the beach to yourself. See also page 49.

There are some differences between spring and autumn besides water temperature: spring generally has a lower rainfall than autumn and the countryside is greener and full of wild flowers, making it the nicest time for walking. Also, in spring, the season for bird hunting is shorter and less intense than in autumn, when you are more likely to have to share rural and coastal areas with men taking potshots at migrating birds (pages 50 and 72). This is a particular issue for birdwatchers, who may find the hunters less than accommodating.

What makes Malta different from other parts of southern Europe is its history – and its prehistory. Malta's **prehistoric temples**, built 3800–2350BC, are unique. There is nothing like them anywhere else in the world and nothing built this early comes close to their sophistication (page 79). If you would visit Stonehenge or Mycenae, then don't miss the temples of Malta.

Malta's other main claim to fame – and far better known – is the art, architecture and fortifications of the **Knights of St John**. A walk around Malta's tiny capital, **Valletta**, is a must, and **St John's Co-Cathedral** is the artistic and decorative highlight. The best way to see fortified Valletta as the Knights and their enemies saw it is from the water (see box, page 114). This is also the most congenial way to get between Valletta and Sliema, and Valletta and the Three Cities.

In the island's interior is the medieval walled town of **Mdina**. Take a walk around, by day if you plan to go into the museums, otherwise in the evening when the tour groups have gone. **Rabat** (around Mdina) is often ignored, but it is a pleasant place with some amazing late **Roman catacombs**, of which St Paul's is the largest and most accessible.

The other period of European history that stands out in Malta is World War II, when 'Fortress Malta' played a significant (and locally devastating) role in the Allied victory. There are several underground shelters that can be visited, the **Malta at War Museum** being the most organised.

Beyond history, many people come to Malta, and especially to Gozo, for the **diving, snorkelling** and **swimming**. **Walking** is great, especially in spring, along the coasts of northeastern Malta and on Gozo.

If you are interested in **churches**, there are hundreds! See page 88 for details on those most worth a visit. The churches and villages come particularly alive during the *festa* season (mostly May to September but with a few outside these dates; page 32). Bunting and lights decorate the church and streets, and the whole parish, as well as outside visitors, gathers to make music, worship, parade, party, eat, drink and watch fireworks.

Finally, don't miss **Gozo**. It is completely different from the main island, much greener and much more relaxed. The **Citadel** is well worth a visit, there is plenty else to see and the swimming is excellent. A day trip is better than nothing, but really this is a place to stop for a few days and chill out.

For a list of highlights and suggestions for ways to amuse **children**, see page 51. For a list of **public holidays** and **cultural events**, see page 35.

SUGGESTED ITINERARIES

Malta in a day Most one-day visitors are cruise passengers, who arrive at the Grand Harbour's purpose-built waterfront (w vallettawaterfront.com) in Floriana, just outside the walls of Valletta. If you organise it in advance, you could step straight off your huge modern ship onto a tiny traditional boat, a *dgħajsa*, for a 30-minute tour of the Grand Harbour.

If you want to see the historic sights and do not want to do so in a large unwieldy group, then book a guide for the day (page 42) and ask him/her to arrange a car (or minibus) and driver for the afternoon. Grab a sandwich, so you don't have to stop for lunch, and request something like the following whistlestop tour (obviously adapted to your interests and time available):

- Walk around Valletta (1hr)
- Highlights of the National Museum of Archaeology (30mins)

- St John's Co-Cathedral (30mins)
- *Dgħajsa* boat tour around the Grand Harbour (30mins)
- If you have time (for instance, if you are unable to book a slot at the hypogeum – page 181) then take a walk around Birgu (1hr)

Pick up car and driver and head to:

- Mnajdra and Ħaġar Qim temples (1½hrs inc travelling time) – if you don't have time for this then replace it with the less attractive but still very interesting Tarxien Temples which are close to the hypogeum
- Mdina and Rabat – including St Paul's Catacombs (1½hrs inc driving time)
- The hypogeum (1hr) – you will not need a guide for this but do need to book well in advance. If few slots are available, you may have to adapt the day's programme to fit in with the slot you are allotted.
- Back to Valletta (20mins' drive)

Malta in five days

Day 1 Wander around Valletta's narrow streets and seafront fortifications, taking in whatever grabs your interest (1–2hrs). Visit the National Museum of Archaeology (1hr) and arrive at the Upper Barrakka Gardens at 11.45 for the firing of the noonday gun. Bring *pastizzi* (page 64) or similar for a quick lunch or grab something at the Barrakka café. Take the Barrakka lift down to the harbourside and hop in a traditional *dgħajsa* water taxi for a tour of the Grand Harbour (30mins) ending at the Vittoriosa Waterfront (Birgu). Go inside Fort St Angelo and wander around Birgu and the Knights' area, the Collachio, before visiting the Malta at War Musuem. Either eat supper early in Birgu or take the ferry or water taxi (or bus or car) back to Valletta and its many excellent restaurants.

Day 2 Start at Mnajdra and Ħaġar Qim temples (1hr), then (in summer) perhaps a swim and lunch at nearby Għar Lapsi, or a stroll along Marsaxlokk Harbour and a fish lunch at any time of year.

Head inland to Rabat to see St Paul's Catacombs and take a stroll around Mdina, perhaps including the interior of the cathedral and its museum. Hop on the bus (if you're not driving) to Dingli Cliffs to explore 'Clapham Junction' with its mysterious ancient cart ruts and troglodyte caves. Maybe have a walk and watch the sunset.

If you have a car, you could reverse the order of the last two visits and follow an evening walk at Dingli Cliffs with an atmospheric supper in a historic building along one of Mdina's medieval alleyways.

Day 3 At 09.00 (before the tour groups arrive) head to the Tarxien Temples, then walk to the not-to-be-missed underground tomb complex, the Ħal Saflieni Hypogeum (book well ahead). In the afternoon head back into Valletta to visit St John's Co-Cathedral (with the audio guide, 1–1½hrs) and Fort St Elmo including the National War Museum. Finish the touring day with a visit to Casa Rocca Piccola, then catch a show at the Manoel Theatre or Pjazza Teatru Rjal.

Day 4 Take the ferry to Gozo (page 264) and check into your accommodation before taking a walk around the Citadel before a lunch of fresh Gozitan food at Ta' Rikardu (page 272). Once lunch has gone down, head for Ramla Bay for a swim and a visit to Calypso's Cave for the view. If it isn't swimming weather, explore the salt pans outside Marsalforn and walk along the north coast (page 276) towards Żebbuġ.

Day 5 Visit the Ġgantija Temples and then have a swim or a snorkel at rocky inlet Mġarr ix-Xini and visit the Knights-period tower (check opening times) or take a walk (and maybe a boat ride) around Dwejra before heading for the ferry.

Longer stays If you have longer than five days, all the better. Take your time and spread the sights out so that you can do them more thoroughly and in a more relaxed way. And go to some of the more minor ones too. Leave yourself time to sit over your lunch as the Maltese do and, if it's summer, take a break on the beach or by the swimming pool.

When you have had your fill of the main island, head to Gozo. Leave yourself as much time here as you can. Gozo is not a place to be rushed; it is somewhere to really let your hair down and relax. Walk the remarkable coastal landscape, climb the flat-topped hills and laze by the crystal-clear water.

You can cram the highlights into a few days but if you really want to chill out and enjoy the country, the longer the better. And there is plenty to do, as I hope you will discover in the rest of this book!

CHOOSING A BASE

Malta is not a large place, so if you plan to have your own transport you can visit almost any part of the islands from almost any base. If you want to do a lot of sightseeing and especially if you will be using public transport, the ideal place to stay is Valletta. The sights of the capital are then within walking distance, with water transport to Sliema and the Three Cities, and easy access to the island's main bus station from which you can get almost anywhere on Malta.

Malta often sells itself as 'sun and sea', but the word 'beach' in the tourist brochures can mean anything from a decent stretch of golden sand to a patch of rock from which to enter the water. Rock swimming can be just as good as (or, for some, better than) sandy beaches but it helps to know what to expect. Ask your operator or hotel; see also *Chapter 4* (page 89).

Chapter 4 also shows the whereabouts of the main sights for a variety of other special interests, from the historic to the active, which may help you choose where to base yourself. If you are looking for nightclubs, then the place to be is St Julian's, or neighbouring Sliema. If you don't like night-time noise and karaoke bars, stay away from Paceville. Valletta has recently developed a lively but civilised bar-café culture alongside its excellent restaurants. Buġibba and Qawra (which often feature in cheaper package deals) are the Blackpool of Malta.

Malta works well as a city break, with plenty to see and do and good places to eat, or you can have a more classic holiday with a mix of sunbathing and swimming (pool or sea), outdoor activities and sightseeing. My personal favourite is to spend a few days based in Valletta visiting the historic and prehistoric sights of the main island, followed by some laid-back time for relaxed exploring, sun, swimming and snorkelling in Gozo.

TOURIST INFORMATION

The **Malta Tourism Authority** (MTA; e info@visitmalta.com; w visitmalta.com) has lots of general information as well as a useful list of tour operators that can be searched by requirements, weather forecasts, events listings and contacts for guides who speak a variety of languages. The website can be accessed in ten languages (English, Dutch, Swedish, Italian, German, French, Spanish, Russian, Hungarian and Japanese); to go direct to the English website, use w visitmalta.com/en. A series of MTA themed trails

– maps on specific subjects (eg: bars, diving) can also be found at **w** maltauk.com/trails. You can also contact MTA direct by email or via the offices listed below (for a list of MTA offices, see also **w** visitmalta.com/en/info-offices).

The MTA keeps a list of **licensed guides** and the languages they speak at **w** visitmalta.com/en/guides. If you are interested in history, then start by contacting Vince DeBono, known locally as 'the Walking Encyclopaedia' (**m** 79448771; **e** v_debono@maltanet.net) or Dane Munro (**m** 99471318; **e** info@danemunro.com), who is also a Knight of St John.

The MTA has also produced **podcast guides** that can be used online or downloaded to a computer, MP3 or smartphone from **w** visitmalta.com/en/podcasts or **w** visitmalta.com/en/mobile-apps. There are numerous podcasts on Malta's UNESCO World Heritage sites (particularly the temples and Valletta) with input from leading experts. There are also cultural guides (like Music in Malta) and a Mattia Preti and Caravaggio itinerary.

MTA OFFICES ABROAD

For a full list of overseas offices, visit **w** mta.com.mt/overseas-network.

𝒊 Austria ☎+43 1 585 37 70; **e** wien@urlaubmalta.com

𝒊 France ☎+33 1 47 58 12 61; **e** thierry.durand@visitemalte.com

𝒊 Germany ☎+49 69 2475 03135; **e** info@urlaubmalta.com

𝒊 Italy ☎+39 06 6500 2437; **e** info@visitmalta.it, claude.zammittrevisan@visitmalta.com

𝒊 Netherlands ☎+31 206 541 565; **e** MLeeuwen@aviareps.com

𝒊 Nordic countries ☎+45 7023 3577; **e** tra@related.dk

𝒊 Spain ☎+34 91 781 3987; **e** ana.martin@newlink-group.com

𝒊 UK ☎+44 20 8877 6990; **e** office.uk@visitmalta.com

𝒊 USA ☎+1 212 213 0944; **e** michelle-margaret.buttigieg@visitmalta.com

TOURIST INFORMATION IN MALTA

There are also tourist information offices in Mdina, Mellieħa, on the Valletta Waterfront, in Marsaxlokk, Birgu & Gozo. These are listed in the relevant chapters.

𝒊 Malta International Airport [map, page 176] Arrivals; ☎23696073/4; ⏲ 10.00–21.00 daily*

𝒊 Valletta [106 D5] Auberge d'Italie, 229 Merchants St; ☎22915440/41/42; ⏲ 09.00–17.30 Mon–Sat, 09.00–13.00 Sun & public hols*. Malta's main tourist information office. Well-informed staff, lots of leaflets & maps.
*Open most public holidays but closed on Christmas Day, New Year's Day, Good Friday & Easter Sunday.

USEFUL WEBSITES

For websites dealing specifically with Gozo, see page 266.

w heritagemalta.org The government's heritage department. Information both historical & practical about many of Malta's most important historic & prehistoric sites.

w maltabookers.com Independent commercial website for information & online bookings.
w maltaweather.com Forecasts & general weather/climate information.

w starwebmalta.com 'Malta's first online concierge' with listings (for locals & foreigners) of restaurants, accommodation, attractions, etc.

BOOKS A few key books are recommended within the text of this guide, and a much broader list can be found on page 314. Most books on Malta are available from Amazon and from general bookshops in Malta and abroad, but some are harder to find so you may want to try the websites listed below.

Once **in Malta**, all bookshops have English-language sections and many of the sights have an interesting selection of relevant books in English. The **Agenda bookshops** in Valletta (26 Republic St, opposite the National Museum of Archaeology; ☏ 21233621) and Sliema (The Point shopping centre; ☏ 20601051/2) have a particularly good range of books on Malta. Agenda (**w** agendamalta.com) also has other shops including at the airport and on the Gozo ferry. The **Aquilina Bookshop** (58 Republic St, St Elmo end of St George Sq; ☏ 21233774) also has a good range of Malta books, as does the tiny **Maltese bookshop**. Officially called Dar il-Ktieb Malti' (literally 'The Home of the Maltese Book') it is at 6 Strait Street (between South St & Melita St; ☏ 21239039; ⊕ 09.00–13.00 Mon–Sat). This is the bookshop of Midsea Books, publisher of, among others, the Insight Heritage guides and Malta Living Heritage series, as well as many more specialist books on all things Maltese.

w maltabook.com
w maltaonlinebookshop.com
w midseabooks.com

w pen-and-sword.co.uk Search 'Malta' for a large selection of this British publisher's books on Maltese military history.

MAPS It is, of course, hoped that the maps in this guidebook will give you most of what you need to get around and sightsee, and Google maps now covers Malta too. But if you are planning to drive around the islands or to do extensive walking and would like more detailed paper maps, the best road map I have found is the Freytag and Berndt *Malta and Gozo*. Miller's *Gozo & Comino*, and AA *Malta & Gozo* are also quite good. These are available from bookshops in Malta as well as online. The MTA's A4 coloured city maps are easy to read and easy to use. They are available free from tourist information offices. If it is detail of topography you're after, the specialist Malta Survey maps produced by MEPA (the Maltese planning authority) are the ones for you – but they aren't cheap.

TOUR OPERATORS

Some 200 companies provide travel packages to Malta and most of the large cruise operators stop here. The following is inevitably a small selection of operators. A full list with a useful search facility (by country and specialism) is available at **w** visitmalta.com/en/tour-operators. If you are looking for a 'sustainable' holiday in Malta, there are lots listed on **w** responsibletravel.com.

MALTA SPECIALISTS IN THE UK
Chevron Air Holidays ☏ 0800 640 9011; **w** chevron.co.uk. A real Malta specialist covering only Malta & Gozo, offering over 50 different hotels on the islands.

Choice Holidays Direct ☏ 0800 091 8888; **w** choiceholidaysdirect.co.uk. Malta & Italy.
Malta Direct ☏ 0330 838 1424; **w** maltadirect.com
Mercury Holidays ☏ 0800 781 4893; **w** mercuryholidays.co.uk

Sunspot Tours ✆0800 408 0506;
w sunspottours.com

OTHER UK OPERATORS OFFERING TRAVEL TO MALTA

Cox & Kings ✆020 3797 8471; w coxandkings.co.uk

The Discovery Collection ✆01371 859733; w discovery-collection.com

First Choice/Tui ✆020 3451 2720; w firstchoice.co.uk

James Villa Holidays ✆0808 273 3627; w jamesvillas.co.uk

Jet2 Holidays ✆0800 408 0778; w jet2holidays.com

Kirker Holidays ✆020 7593 1899; w kirkerholidays.com

Olympic Holidays ✆020 8492 6868; w olympicholidays.com

Prestige Holidays ✆01425 480400; w prestigeholidays.co.uk

Saga ✆0808 252 4316; w travel.saga.co.uk/holidays

Sovereign Luxury Travel ✆01293 839566; w sovereign.com

Thomas Cook ✆01733 224808; w thomascook.com

CULTURAL AND HISTORICAL HOLIDAYS

The following are led by specialist lecturers/guides.

ACE Cultural Tours ✆01223 841055; w aceculturaltours.co.uk. Musical expert-led tours to the Baroque Music Festival.

Andante Travel ✆01722 569409; w andantetravels.co.uk. Archaeology tours led by leading archaeological experts.

Authentic Adventures ✆01453 823328; w authenticadventures.co.uk. Cultural activity holidays (such as painting & singing).

Martin Randall ✆020 8742 3355; w martinrandall.com. Lecturer-led history & culture tours & the Baroque Music Festival.

Travel for the Arts ✆020 8799 8350; w travelforthearts.co.uk. Escorted tours to Malta's opera festival.

Voyage Jules Verne ✆020 3553 9341; w vjv.com. Short cultural tours.

ACTIVE HOLIDAYS

For cycling holidays, see page 61; for companies running other activity-based trips, see page 74.

Activities Abroad ✆01670 789991; w activitiesabroad.com. Family activity holidays in Gozo.

Dive Worldwide ✆01962 302087; w diveworldwide.com

Exodus ✆020 8712 9260; w exodus.co.uk. Including family holidays.

Explore ✆01252 883619; w explore.co.uk. Cycling & family tours.

Headwater ✆01606 369811; w headwater.com. Walking & cycling holidays in Gozo.

InnTravel ✆01653 617001; w inntravel.co.uk. Self-guided walking holidays in Gozo.

Ramblers Holidays ✆01707 817332; w www.ramblersholidays.co.uk

Running Crazy ✆02392 255033; w runningcrazy.co.uk. Packages to the Malta Marathon (page 36).

Sports Tours International ✆0161 703 8161; w sportstoursinternational.co.uk/running. Packages to the Malta Marathon.

TOURS WITHIN MALTA There are coach tours available to the main sites of Malta and for day trips to Gozo. These are usually booked through the hotels or your tour-operator representative. If a tour is being offered cheaply (ie: less than about €24 per half day or €45 for a whole day) check the details: will you have a separate guide and driver, for instance? You may not want your driver to be holding a microphone with one hand and pointing out sights with the other!

You can, of course, create your own tour by booking a guide (page 42) and a car (page 60, or ask the guide to book a car), giving you much greater flexibility and avoiding any risk of being herded. If you feel like splashing out, **Exclusively Malta** (✆35505953; w exclusivelymalta.com; see ad, page 78) provides private tailor-made tours including exclusive access to private *palazzi* and out-of-hours visits to sights. If you are on a tight budget, the hop-on-hop-off sightseeing buses can be very useful. They cover all the main sights and many minor ones (see box, page 58).

As well as a few Catholic pilgrimage sites, including St Paul's Grotto in Rabat and Ta' Pinu on Gozo, there are a number of **retreat houses** in Malta. The first dedicated retreat house on the islands, built in 1957 by the Franciscans, was **Porziuncola Retreat House** in Baħar iċ-Ċagħaq (↘21375711; w ofm.org.mt/ ofm/?page_id=1264). With 35 en-suite guest rooms, Porziuncola offers guests the chance to spend time in quiet prayer and contemplation, either alone or in a directed retreat with preaching, counselling and spiritual direction from the friars. The Franciscans run the **Padova Retreat House** overlooking Mġarr on Gozo (↘21556095) with six en-suite rooms and a slightly more relaxed regime. All retreat houses in Gozo are listed at w gozodiocese.org/ institutions/retreat-houses.

Further information on the Catholic religious life of Malta can be found at w thechurchinmalta.org/en/ and for Gozo at w gozodiocese.org. There is a free downloadable **Pilgrimage Travel Itinerary** at w visitmalta.com/en/ religious-sites.

British tour operator **Tangney Travel** (↘01732 886666; w tangney-tours. com) runs pilgrimage tours to Malta, and guide Dane Munro (page 42) can organise one-day (and longer) religious tours.

RED TAPE

TRAVEL DOCUMENTS Visitors from the UK and Ireland need a valid passport but do not need a visa. Nationals of EU countries with national identity cards may travel on these instead of a passport. There is no limit on how long an EU national may stay in Malta so long as he/she is economically self-sufficient. After the first 90 days, however, residence documents are issued.

Malta is a member of the EU Schengen area, giving it the same entry rules as other EU counties (except the UK and Ireland) for visitors **from outside the EU**. No visa is required for a stay of less than three months by those from the USA, Canada, Australia, New Zealand, Japan or most non-EU European countries (with the exception of Russia).

Other nationalities need to contact a Maltese embassy, consulate or high commission or, where none exists, the embassy or consulate that looks after Malta (often the Italian or Austrian). Further information can be found on the Maltese Ministry for Home Affairs website at w homeaffairs.gov.mt/en.

Maltese embassies and consulates are listed on the Ministry for Foreign Affairs website (w foreignaffairs.gov.mt). The full list is at w bit.ly/1E4mscY.

EMBASSIES, HIGH COMMISSIONS AND CONSULATES IN MALTA A full list of the foreign embassies and consulates in Malta can be found on the Foreign Ministry website (w foreignaffairs.gov.mt) at w bit.ly/1JHq8aR. The following list includes contact details for consular assistance (where they exist) for nationalities most likely to be using this guidebook.

ⓔ Australia Ta' Xbiex Terrace, Ta' Xbiex, MSD 11; ↘21338201, +61 2 6261 3305; w malta. highcommission.gov.au. 24hr consular assistance.

ⓔ Denmark & Sweden Honorary Consul General: 19 Zachary St, Valletta, VLT 1133; ↘25691790; e consulategeneral@gollcher.com

E Finland 63/64 Graham St, Sliema, SLM 1711; ☏ 21343790/3; e info@oswaldarrigoltd.com; w embassypages.com/missions/embassy3939

E Ireland Whitehall Mansions, Ta' Xbiex Seafront, Ta' Xbiex, XBX 1026; ☏ 21334744; w dfa.ie/irish-embassy/malta

E Netherlands Whitehall Mansions, 3rd Floor, Ta' Xbiex Seafront, Ta' Xbiex, MSD 11; ☏ 21313980/1; f.

E New Zealand Honorary Consul: Jill Camilleri, 'Villa Hampstead', Oliver Agius St, Attard, ATD 3102; ☏ 21435025; e jill.camilleri@nzcmalta.com

E Norway Anthony Zammit Cutajar, Capital Business Centre, Triq Taz-Zwejt, San Gwann Industrial Estate, San Gwann, SGN 3000; ☏ 21448466, 21448596; e tzcutajar@pcutajar.com.mt

E UK Whitehall Mansions, Ta' Xbiex Seafront, Ta' Xbiex, XBX 1026; ☏ 23230000; w gov.uk/government/world/organisations/british-high-commission-malta

E USA Ta' Qali National Park, Attard, ATD 4000; ☏ 25614000; w mt.usembassy.gov

CUSTOMS AND DUTY-FREE Malta is a member of the European Union. There are no limits on what can be carried between EU countries for personal use. There are guidelines as to what the receiving country considers reasonable for personal use. Within the EU you are likely to be questioned if carrying more than 110 litres beer, 90 litres wine, 20 litres fortified wine and 10 litres spirits, 800 cigarettes and 1kg of tobacco. Those entering from outside the EU may bring up to 200 cigarettes, 1 litre of spirits and €430 worth of gifts or goods for personal use.

GETTING THERE AND AWAY

BY AIR There is one international airport in Malta, in the southeast of the main island [map, page 176]. It is just 3 hours' flying time from the UK – less from southern Europe. There are numerous direct flights, on low-cost airlines and national carriers, scheduled and charter, including from many regional airports.

EasyJet (☏ 0843 104 5000; w easyjet.com) flies to Malta from Gatwick, Manchester, Newcastle and Southend; and **Ryanair** (☏ 0871 246 0000; w ryanair.com) goes from Luton, Stansted, Bristol, Birmingham, Belfast, Manchester, Leeds-Bradford, East Midlands, Liverpool, Edinburgh, Glasgow Prestwick and Dublin, plus, in summer, Aberdeen; and from summer 2019 Exeter, Cardiff and Cork. **Jet2** (☏ 0800 408 1350, 0333 300 0042; w jet2.com) operates to Malta out of Leeds-Bradford, Manchester, Birmingham and Glasgow Prestwick, while in summer it adds Stansted, Newcastle, Glasgow, East Midlands and Belfast.

British Airways (☏ 0344 493 0787; w ba.com) flies from Gatwick, while Malta's national carrier, **Air Malta** (☏ 020 7660 0543 (UK), 21662211 (Malta); w airmalta.com), has year-round scheduled services from Heathrow and Gatwick, as well as summer services from Birmingham, Bristol, Manchester and Southend. Air Malta also flies from many European capitals, other Italian and German cities and parts of North Africa.

In addition to the scheduled flights, in the summer there are regular **charter flights** out of London and regional airports. The largest charter operators are **Thomas Cook** (☏ 0871 895 0055; w thomascook.com/holidays/malta) and **Tui Fly** (☏ 020 3451 2695; w en.tuifly.com), both of which offer flights from Gatwick, Bristol, Birmingham and Manchester. Air Malta also runs charters.

Getting to and from the airport It doesn't take long to get from the airport to anywhere on Malta (unless it is a rainy rush hour). No part of the main island is more than 50 minutes away by car (a little longer by bus). It takes 15–20 minutes to get to Valletta, 25 minutes to St Julian's.

Buses Buses run between the airport and all the main tourist centres (and many much smaller places) across the main island. Most airport bus numbers start with an X, but always check. There are direct buses not only to Valletta, but also to St Julian's, Sliema, Marsaskala, Buġibba, Qawra, St Paul's Bay, Mellieħa and Ċirkewwa for the Gozo ferry. Buses into Valletta are the most frequent and take as little as 20 minutes (outside the busiest times). Valletta buses stop just outside the city walls near City Gate where the main bus station provides buses to almost everywhere on the island. To get to your accommodation in the capital without walking, you will need a taxi or, if you are staying on a pedestrianised street then one of the golf-buggy-style electric Smart Cabs (page 103). If in doubt, talk to your accommodation provider – they may send a member of staff to help you from the nearest place a cab can stop.

Taxis These are readily available at the airport and Malta's Public Transport Directorate fixes taxi fares from the airport to each town in Malta (w maltairport. com/passenger/getting-here/taxi-service). As a guide, at the time of writing the cost between the airport and Valletta is €15, to Sliema or St Julian's €20, and to Ċirkewwa (the Gozo ferry terminal) €32. Despite set fares, it is worth agreeing the price before you get in.

Malta Transfer (☎ 21332016; m 79646481; w maltatransfer.com) is a tailor-made bus service that will take you from/to the airport more cheaply than a taxi and without the hassle of having to drag your luggage to the public bus stop. You need to book at least 24 hours in advance. Trips can be slow because the bus picks up from/ drops off at multiple places.

Some hotels and self-catering accommodation will arrange airport transfer for you (usually for a fee, though sometimes free) and hire cars are also available at the airport. It is best to book ahead (page 60).

BY SEA Ferries operate to Malta from Sicily, arriving at the Sea Passenger Terminal on the Valletta Waterfront. They take as little as 1½ hours to cross from Pozzallo on Sicily or 3–4 hours including a coach transfer from Catania. The ferries are fast catamarans that also carry cars and are run by **Virtu Ferries** (☎ (UK) 020 8206 3420, (Malta) 22069022, 23491000, (Catania) 095 535711, (Pozzallo) 0932 954062; w virtuferries.com).

HEALTH *With Dr Felicity Nicholson*

POTENTIAL HEALTH PROBLEMS Malta is a European Mediterranean country with no specific health problems. It is hot in summer, so be sure to drink enough water, have a little extra salt if you are sweating more than usual, and protect yourself from sunburn and the glare of the sun's rays. A hat is a very good idea and sunglasses are essential on water, and also in town where the sun comes off the creamy yellow limestone like a mirror.

Sandfly bites and leishmaniasis
Leishmaniasis is caused by a protozoan parasite *Leishmania donovani* sp. and is spread by the bite of an infected sandfly during the warmer months. They bite mainly at night and are most common in forested areas but can also exist on sandy beaches. This disease, which can affect the skin or organs, is rare in travellers but still worth thinking about.

DEET-containing insect repellents may help to prevent sand-fly bites, and a concentration of 50–55% DEET is recommended. It should not be applied to broken skin or used on infants under two months old. If you need to wear it when also requiring sunscreen, then apply the sunscreen first and the repellent second.

Ticks should ideally be removed complete, and as soon as possible, to reduce the chance of infection. You can use special tick tweezers, which can be bought in good travel shops, or failing this with your finger nails, grasping the tick as close to your body as possible, and pulling it away steadily and firmly at right angles to your skin without jerking or twisting. If possible, douse the wound with alcohol (any spirit will do), soap and water, or iodine. Irritants (eg: Olbas oil) or lit cigarettes are to be discouraged since they can cause the ticks to regurgitate and therefore increase the risk of disease. If you are travelling with small children, remember to check their heads, and particularly behind the ears, for ticks. Spreading redness around the bite and/or fever and/or aching joints after a tick bite imply that you have an infection that requires antibiotic treatment. In this case seek medical advice.

Tick bites In Malta as in the UK, ticks can cause a variety of diseases such as Lyme disease, tick-borne encephalitis and Crimean Congo Haemorrhagic fever. Whilst these diseases seem to be rare in Malta, it is always best to check for ticks if you have been walking in forested or grassy areas – though these are limited to a small area of the island. Ticks like to hide in the creases of the body, such as the groin, armpits, behind the ears, etc. They are about the size of a sesame seed until they start to feed so are easy to miss. See box above.

Rabies There is no rabies in terrestrial mammals in Malta but there is bat rabies (Lyssavirus). Most travellers do not need to be vaccinated before travel to Malta but should be aware that, if they are bitten by a bat or if bat saliva gets into their eyes, nose or mouth, then they need to seek treatment as soon as possible.

VACCINATIONS Travellers should, as is advised even at home, be up to date with routine vaccination courses, for example measles, mumps and rubella and tetanus, diphtheria and polio. Although there is no yellow fever in Malta, there is, however, a certificate requirement for anyone over the age of nine months travelling from a yellow fever endemic country or who has transited an airport in one of these countries for more than 12 hours. These travellers must be able to show a certificate of yellow fever vaccination.

Other vaccinations may occasionally be advised in specific circumstances. Please check current advice at w travelhealthpro.org.uk.

TRAVEL CLINICS AND HEALTH INFORMATION A full list of current travel clinic websites worldwide is available on w istm.org. For other journey preparation information, consult w travelhealthpro.org.uk (UK) or w wwwnc.cdc.gov/travel (USA). Information about various medications may be found on w netdoctor. co.uk/travel. All advice found online should be used in conjunction with expert advice received prior to or during travel.

THE HEALTH SERVICE IN MALTA Malta's public health-care system is free to EU citizens carrying an EHIC (European Health Insurance Card; w ehic. org.uk) and a passport or EU ID document, and the UK also has a reciprocal arrangement that makes most public health care free. Travel insurance is, however, still recommended.

Emergency hospital treatment and consultations at health centres are covered by the EHIC. Medicines (other than in-patient medication and that prescribed for the first three days after discharge from hospital) and non-urgent treatment and repatriation are not. There are eight primary care health centres on Malta and one on Gozo (w deputyprimeminister.gov.mt/en/phc/Pages/Home.aspx) and there are also inexpensive private GPs (not covered by EHIC). The out-of-hours pharmacy roster is listed at: w health.gov.mt/en/PharmacyRoster.

The **main hospital** in Malta is the modern 825-bed Mater Dei Hospital in Msida (℡ 25450000; w health.gov.mt/en/MDH/Pages/Home.aspx). Gozo has its own general hospital in Victoria (℡ 21561600, 21562700). There are also numerous **private medical facilities** which are not covered by the EHIC and may or may not be covered by your travel insurance. There are no private beds in public hospitals.

DRINKING WATER The tap water is theoretically drinkable, but it is very heavily chlorinated and you are likely to be advised – by middle-class locals, as well as hotels – to drink bottled water. This is sensible advice. The tap water is not dangerous, however, so you do not need to worry about salad washed in it, ice, ice cream, cleaning your teeth, etc.

SAFETY

SWIMMING There are only two things likely to keep you out of the water in Malta: bad weather and jellyfish. It is highly inadvisable to swim off rocks when there are waves or even a significant swell – you might find yourself bashed against sharp edges or unable to get out of the water. Many beaches also have occasional rip currents. These usually occur during or for a day or so after windy weather and can be difficult to detect. Some Maltese beaches have flags to indicate water conditions in summer (see box below); others do not. Here you need to take local advice. In summer the Maltese will swim almost anywhere where they can get safely into and out of the water (as well as off boats), so if there is nobody swimming, you might want to find out why before doing so yourself. If you like to swim out of your depth, do take this advice seriously: several tourists have drowned in recent years including two British men.

There is little marine wildlife in Malta likely to do a swimmer harm. A huge shark was caught off Filfla by a fisherman in 1987, but the last shark attack on a person was over half a century ago and this was some way out from the shore. Recent research has found no evidence of dangerous sharks in the area. The main problem is **jellyfish**, purple stingers with see-through bodies patterned with purple and tentacles perhaps 10–15cm long. A bay may be clear one day and the next these irritating creatures will be floating around. They are quite pretty to look at but do not make good swimming companions. Being stung by one jellyfish hurts but will do you no lasting damage (though it may take kids a while to go back in the water);

BEACH FLAGS – WHAT DO THEY MEAN?	
Green	All fine
Yellow	OK, but could be choppy
Red	Take care
Double red	Do not swim
Purple	Pests; in Malta this usually means jellyfish

jump into a mass of them and you could end up in hospital. So when you arrive at a beach, take a look around. If there is a gaggle of people on the shore and few in the water, it may signal jellies. Ask.

If there are only one or two jellyfish you may want to remove them from the water (with a net or bucket) and leave them in a marked spot on the sand to dry out. Do not damage them in the water, or you may leave stinging tentacles behind. If one beach is plagued with jellyfish, try another, preferably one facing in a different direction. There is almost always somewhere that is not infested.

Jumping into the water off rocks is a favourite summer pastime of the local youth and can be great fun. Just make sure you know what is beneath you – even in deep water there may be rocks sticking up.

The greatest danger to swimmers and snorkellers, however, is **boats**. Almost every year someone is hit and seriously injured or killed. Just remember: boats can't see snorkellers and swimmers. Stay inside the buoys that mark the swimming areas where boats are not allowed, or take an **inflatable buoy** to mark your presence, as divers should also do. These can be bought from dive shops. If swimming from a boat, stay close, swim in a group or be aware of what is around you (which is hard as a snorkeller, head down in the underwater world!).

On a more trivial note (but one that may make a significant difference to enjoyment), Maltese **rocks** can be very sharp and many beaches are stony – it is worth having something to cover your feet when you swim if you don't want to discover of an evening that you have a host of random cuts. Shoes will protect you from sea urchins as well.

For more information, see page 89.

ROAD SAFETY When it comes to Malta's roads the key is to expect the unexpected. Like the UK, Malta drives on the left and most of its road rules are the same as in the UK – officially. What drivers actually do varies widely. The local joke is that the Maltese drive in the shade. The reality is even less predictable – they drive to avoid the many pot-holes. The bottom line is that as a pedestrian or a driver, you need to look in all directions. See also page 59.

FIREWORK FACTORIES Most parishes in Malta have a firework factory making *festa* fireworks (page 33). These are usually small buildings standing alone on the outskirts of villages. If a red flag is flying, it means keep away; they are working with explosive material. Accidents do happen – an average of one person a year over the last century has been killed making fireworks. These are, of course, manufacturing accidents, not accidents at displays!

BIRD HUNTING Though this is less of an issue than it used to be, if you are out in the Maltese countryside in the autumn – particularly early in the morning or from mid afternoon – you may come across men popping guns at passing birdlife. This may also be true for a week or two in spring. Malta has a significant but declining group of dedicated (licensed) bird hunters. Accidents involving people other than the hunters themselves are very rare, but it is obviously worth being aware of what is going on around you.

If you are a birdwatcher with binoculars or a camera with a long lens around your neck, be conscious too that some hardcore hunters have a deep antipathy to your hobby. Though less militant than a few years ago, some hunters see birders as a threat to their own pastime, and a few are willing to go to some lengths to defend their patch. You may see signs, often hand painted, saying 'RTO', meaning 'reserved to owner'. The land may or may not be genuinely private, but it is best to treat it as such. You are extremely unlikely to be the subject of anything worse than shouting, but confrontation is best avoided. If you see anything illegal, don't try to deal with it yourself; call the police on ☏119, or regarding anything threatening, call the emergency number ☏112.

CRIME AND TERRORISM Crime-wise, Malta is an ordinary European destination. Crime against tourists is rare. Simply take the same common-sense precautions you would at home or in any western European country: don't leave valuables visible in parked cars; keep an eye on your belongings; and if you plan to wander the streets in the early hours, take advice from locals or hotel reception as to where is safe and where might not be (most places are safe).

There have, at the time of writing, been no recent terrorist attacks in Malta and there are no particular conflicts or unrest. For up-to-date travel advice, see the FCO website (w gov.uk/foreign-travel-advice/malta).

In the unlikely event that you have problems, call the police on the international emergency number: ☏112.

MALTA FOR FAMILIES

Malta is a great place for a family holiday, especially with older children. Flying time is short (under 3hrs from London), there are no long transfers, it is a safe and easy place to be with no particular health or hygiene problems, the Maltese like children, English is very widely spoken and there is plenty to see and do.

This is not, however, an ideal country for toddlers. There are too many cobbles, steps and areas of rough ground to want to be pushing a buggy, and too many sheer drops (off fortifications, as well as cliffs) around the tourist sites for toddlers to be safe without constant supervision. And only a few beaches are suitable for the very young. Ideally, bring the baby and a papoose or backpack baby-carrier or wait for a trip to Malta until children are old enough to walk, talk and understand what they are seeing.

If travelling with kids in summer, try to have access to a swimming pool. Sightseeing can be hot and bothersome for children and a nice cool pool to plunge into when you get back makes all the difference. Check with the hotel that youngsters are welcome and their activities not too restricted – you don't want to be hushing your children all the time. Gozo is a particularly good place for a relaxed family break, being more laid-back than Malta and with plenty of places to swim and lots of good-quality self-catering accommodation. Restaurants tend to be relaxed and family-friendly too.

A set of large-format **children's books** on Malta can make sightseeing more fun for kids. The *Exploring Malta* series includes *1565: The Great Siege of Malta*, *World War II* and *The Knights of St John* as well as several **activity books**, one general and one each on Birgu (Vittoriosa) and St John's Co-Cathedral. All are published by Peg (Miller Malta) and cost a few euros.

There is also a website (w maltababyandkids.com). Though aimed primarily at those living in Malta, it lists activities (and summer schools) for kids up to about the age of 14.

WHERE TO GO AND WHAT TO DO WITH KIDS IN MALTA
Valletta A child-sized capital, Valletta is great to wander around and explore, with narrow alleys and few cars. Stop for an ice cream at Caffe Cordina in the

3

middle of town (page 67); admire the fortifications (Valletta is one big castle!); and hear the cannons fired at the Upper Barrakka Gardens. Take a horse-and-carriage ride and visit the Malta Experience for an accessible 45-minute filmic introduction to the country and its history.

Boat trips Most kids like boat trips and Malta has plenty to offer: try a crossing of the Grand Harbour in a traditional *dgħajsa* (see box, page 186), the Two Harbours Tour to admire the fortifications (page 170) or simply hop on the Sliema and Three Cities ferries. A boat round Gozo and Comino with swimming stops can also be a lot of fun (page 275).

Beaches Children may prefer sandy beaches where they can dig, build and play as well as laze and swim and where there is a slope into the sea. The best beach on Malta for young children is Mellieħa Bay, all sand with plentiful shallows. On Gozo, head for Ramla Bay. Be aware that some beaches (including Golden Bay and Ramla) can have nasty undertows, especially during or after bad or windy weather, so keep children near the beach and pay attention to flags.

Malta at War Museum, Birgu Descend into the subterranean world of this large World War II shelter. Excellent guides bring it all to life for children (it's even relevant to the British National Curriculum!). Take a look at the fortifications of Birgu on the way out (more castles).

Il-Barri and the Mġarr Shelter Take the kids for a good, inexpensive Maltese lunch in this family-friendly restaurant then take them downstairs (maybe without telling them why) and they will find themselves in the long underground corridors of a World War II shelter.

The temples Mnajdra and Ħaġar Qim are the most child-friendly of the main island's temple sites with lots of space, three temples, a watchtower and a visitor centre with information and loos. On Gozo, Ġgantija is also child-friendly with interesting, self-explanatory displays in the visitor centre (including about what temple people ate and a temple period fashion show) and plenty of space to explore the temples.

Ħal Saflieni Hypogeum Extraordinary underground tomb complex, which should intrigue older kids. No children under six.

Clapham Junction and the troglodyte caves Cliff-top area with loads of space. Seek out and follow the mysterious cart ruts then take a look at caves with rock-cut shelving. People lived here until a couple of centuries ago.

Mdina The ancient capital of the Romans, Arabs and medieval Maltese, smaller than Valletta. A maze of narrow alleys to get lost in. Very few cars during the day. Another castle city.

St Paul's Catacombs An underground labyrinth of late Roman tombs. Great for those with an interest in history or who just like exploring!

Fort St Elmo Many kids like castles and St Elmo is a good one. If you or your child have played 'Age of Empires', you may have defended this fort against the Turks.

Fort St Angelo Another good castle to explore, with broad parade grounds, battlements and cannons.

Birding Kids are welcome at BirdLife Malta's reserves (pages 245 and 252) and staff will make an effort to interest them. Those accustomed to bird reserves in the UK or elsewhere in Europe may, however, find them unimpressive. For children happy to view birds in aviaries, there is also BirdPark Malta.

On Gozo The best beach for youngsters here is **Ramla Bay**. Take older kids up to **Calypso's Cave** for the stunning view and spot the Knights' underwater fortification (hidden protection from Turkish pirates). In the middle of Gozo's capital, the **Citadel** is another massive fort (or very small city) with high, fortified walls and narrow car-free streets. Pop into the **cathedral** for a surprise.

Get **snorkels** for older children, or just **paddle** and look with the very young. There can be fish within a few feet of the shore. Mġarr ix-Xini and Xlendi are good places to try (Xlendi is easier with the youngest kids).

Restaurants Most restaurants in Malta are at least tolerant of children and many very welcoming, offering special menus, high chairs, etc. There are a few that are particularly family-friendly: **Ta' Nenu** in Valletta serves Maltese pizzas and other traditional dishes and has a very relaxed atmosphere and computer games for kids. **The Avenue** in Paceville is always packed with families, and **Ta' Karolina** in Xlendi, Gozo, is right next to a very shallow and contained patch of sea perfect for kids to paddle in and feed fish while parents enjoy their meal (book ahead for a waterside table).

INFORMATION ON TRAVELLING WITH A DISABILITY

The UK's **gov.uk** website (w gov.uk/guidance/foreign-travel-for-disabled-people) provides general advice and practical information for travellers with disabilities preparing for overseas travel. **Accessible Journeys** (w disabilitytravel.com) is a comprehensive US site written by wheelchair users who have been researching wheelchair-accessible travel full-time since 1985. There are many tips and useful contacts (including lists of travel agents on request) for slow walkers, wheelchair travellers and their families, plus informative articles, including pieces on disabled travelling worldwide. The company also organises group tours. **Global Access News** (w globalaccessnews.com/index.htm) provides general travel information, reviews and tips for travelling with a disability. The **Society for Accessible Travel and Hospitality** (w sath.org) also provides some general information.

SPECIALIST TOUR OPERATORS Specialist UK-based tour operators that offer trips to Malta include: **Enable Holidays** (w enableholidays.com; including accessible holidays for children with specialist needs), **Disabled Holidays** (w disabledholidays.com), and **Disabled Access Holidays** (w disabledaccessholidays.com).

FURTHER INFORMATION
Malta Tourism Authority (MTA) London; ℡ 020 8877 6990; e info@visitmalta.com
National Commission for People with Disabilities Malta; ℡ 22788555; w knpd.org

TRAVELLING WITH A DISABILITY *With Mark Davidson*

Malta has made great strides in recent years to improve conditions for those with disabilities and many hotels and restaurants are now wheelchair-accessible. The nature of the country's towns, villages and countryside, however, does not make it an easy place for those with limited mobility or a wheelchair and getting around and historic sightseeing can be a problem.

GETTING THERE AND AROUND Assistance is on offer with facilities for getting on/off the **aircraft** (book in advance) and there are disabled toilets at the airport. Contact the airline you are travelling with directly for any service needed on the aircraft. For further information, contact Malta International Airport (✆ +356 21249600; w maltairport.com). Buses are of the low-door accessible type, and the **Gozo ferry** is fully accessible with lifts from the car to passenger decks (✆ +356 22109000; e admin@gozochannel.com). If driving (or being driven), you can use your blue badge to park in designated disabled bays. These are listed in the *mAZe* map book (Uptrend Publishing). Wheelchairs can be rented from w maltabookers.com.

ACCOMMODATION It is required of almost all new accommodation providers that they have at least one accessible room and many now do. Unfortunately this does not always mean that the street outside is accessible. The situation is undoubtedly improving, however, and many more hotels and B&Bs are able to receive guests with disabilities.

The main resort hotels have ramps and wide doorways, as well as adapted rooms. Examples include: the **Hilton** (page 163) and **Westin Dragonara** (page 164) in Paceville; **Radisson Golden Sands** (page 238) on the beach in Golden Bay; **Seabank** all-inclusive Hotel in Mellieħa Bay (page 243); and the **Phoenicia** and **Excelsior** in Valletta (page 104), where many of the new boutique hotels also have provision for disabled visitors. The boutique **Juliani Hotel** (page 165) in St Julian's has one adapted room and lifts to all facilities, and there are also cheaper options including bungalows at the **Mellieħa Holiday Village** (page 243). In Gozo the **Kempinski** (page 267), the **Ta' Ċenċ** (page 267) and the less expensive **Calypso** (page 268) offer access to all facilities and at least one wheelchair-accessible room.

EATING OUT There are many restaurants that are easily accessible, though it is worth checking beforehand. The website w restaurantsmalta.com gives a comprehensive guide to restaurants and allows you to search for those that are wheelchair-accessible.

SIGHTSEEING Malta's buses mostly have access for people with disabilities and the Valletta Waterfront is wheelchair-accessible. The authorities in Malta are trying to make more sites accessible but this isn't easy in some of the historic buildings. Valletta is a city of cobbles, hills and steps. Similarly, the Three Cities are full of stone staircases. The streets of Mdina and the Gozo Citadel are also uneven, narrow and sometimes steep, although when the lift is working at least parts of the Gozo Citadel are accessible.

TRAVEL INSURANCE AND HOSPITALS There are a few specialist companies that deal with travel to Malta. Some will accept pre-existing medical conditions, for example **Travelbility** (✆ 0845 338 1638).

If you need **hospital treatment**, the main hospital the Mater Dei Hospital in Msida (Triq Dun Karm, Msida; ✆ 25450000), is fully accessible to wheelchair users, with ramps and lifts.

FOR THE ADVENTUROUS A couple of **dive centres** in Malta offer scuba diving for the disabled; contact the **International Association for Handicapped Divers** (w iahd. org) for information.

LGBTQ MALTA

By Maltese – British Art Director Gattaldo, owner of boutique rental Indulgence Divine (w indulgencedivine.com)

Malta topped the Europe Rainbow Index for LGBTQ-friendliness in 2018 for the third year running, representing an extraordinarily rapid shift in attitudes and law in the last few years. Civil unions were introduced in April 2014, followed by gay marriage in July 2017, and some of Europe's most advanced gender identity and intersex protection laws. In 2016 Malta also became the first European country to ban 'gay conversion therapy'. The island has even had its first transgender politician, Alex Mangion of the Nationalist (conservative) party. The LGBTQ scene in Malta is changing as a result of all this, with less need for exclusively gay places of entertainment. Young gay men and women now rub shoulders confidently with their hetero peers in public.

BEACH

Gnejna Bay [map, page 242] Bus 41 to Mellieħa, then 101 or 102 to Gnejna, then walk. Stunning rocky bay with rugged natural beauty, just secluded enough for private encounters. Take refreshments with you as the walk itself makes for thirsty work.

ENTERTAINMENT AND NIGHTLIFE

The Birdcage Lounge [map, page 217] Triq il-Kbira, Rabat; m 79782243; f. If Paceville is not your cup of tea, here's a relaxed cocktail bar in one of the older, more beautiful villages of the island. Live music, cabaret shows, karaoke.

Festa m 99443792; f. Annual LGBTQ+ Festival in Jul organised by 3 promoters featuring Outdoor Party by Lollipop, Gay Pride Party by S2S & a Boat Party by Beatbears.

Lollipop Tigullio, Paceville; w lollipopnight.com; f. Gay club events playing camp, bubblegum pop with a mix of disco & house. Young & creative atmosphere.

Malta Pride w maltapride.org. The annual Malta Pride Parade & Celebration, organised by Allied Rainbow Communities (ARC), is gaining bigger

crowds each year. It's a great way of meeting a wider spectrum of local LGBTQA+s.

Michelangelo Club Lounge [173 B2] Triq Santa Rita, Paceville; m 79772017; f; ⊙ 10.00–02.00 Mon, Wed, Thu & Sun, 10.00–04.00 Fri & Sat. 2 floors of fun with lounge, dance & private areas.

Station2Station Events m 79272601; f. Events organised in various venues around the island by the S2S duo Frankie & James. Dancers, fire eaters, drag artists, the lot – these people know how to party.

FURTHER INFORMATION

Malta Gay Rights Movement 32 Parish St, Mosta; m 99255559; mgrm@maltagayrights.org; w maltagayrights.org. Young NGO started in 2001 & has been instrumental in the vital changes in law. Runs the Rainbow Support Service (m 79430006; f).

A Seat at the Table Malta's colourful gay history is brought to life in Simon Bartolo's book (available from w shop.maltagayrights.org), which documents the history of the LGBTQA+ movement in Malta through interviews with movers & shakers.

WHAT TO TAKE

British travellers will *not* need to pack **electric plug adapters** as Malta uses plugs with three square pins as in the UK, and a similar voltage. Those from continental Europe will need to use adapters, and American devices require adapters and transformers.

Walking in Malta is best done in sturdy **shoes**. Trainers will do for short walks, but if you plan to spend hours stomping over rough rock (and the most beautiful walking spots in Malta and Gozo have rough rock underfoot), you might like to bring something with a tougher sole and some ankle support, preferably walking **boots**. Swimming (often off rocks or with stones in the sand) can be more comfortable if you have something to wear on your feet in the water.

Sunglasses, sunhat and sunscreen are a must (except in winter, though you'll need sunglasses even then), and a small pack each of **tissues and wipes** can be handy as public loos are sometimes not fully equipped. A **torch** is an important item if you intend to explore caves, tombs or catacombs. Don't panic if you forget something – you can buy almost all standard items in Malta.

If you are planning to take part in any specialist activities, it might be worth checking what equipment is available and what to bring with you. In most cases Malta will be able to provide, but rock-climbing equipment, for instance, may be less easily available (page 74).

MONEY

Malta joined the euro on 1 January 2008. There are no limits on the money that can be brought in or out of countries within the EU. If crossing the EU border, however, anyone lucky enough to be in possession of more than €10,000 (in any form – including cheques, money orders, etc) must declare it.

BANKS, ATMS AND CHANGING MONEY Banks in Malta usually open 08.30–13.30 Monday to Friday (later on Fridays) and Saturday mornings. A few larger branches open again from 16.30 to about 19.00. There is an HSBC or Bank of Valletta (often both), usually with an ATM, in every town and many villages. On Gozo, banks and ATMs are less widespread but are available in Victoria and Xagħra and in tourist centres like Xlendi and Marsalforn, as well as a few of the villages. At the airport, you will find 24-hour banking.

CREDIT CARDS Most places take credit cards, but some restaurants, smaller guesthouses and village shops do not.

BUDGETING

The cost of living as a visitor in Malta depends on when you go because costs vary so much between high and low season. Even within a season it is well worth shopping around as most hotel prices rise and fall by the day according to occupancy.

The cost of eating in Malta is less variable – but the quality varies a great deal. Other than at the two extremes of price, you can eat very well indeed or not very well at all for the same money – so do take a look at the restaurant sections of this guide.

DAILY LIVING COSTS The costs shown opposite are based on per-day rates for two people and are broken down so that you can take out or add parts (for instance, swapping buses for car hire in the comfortable, middle-of-the-road budget, or hiring a car for a day in the shoestring option) and adjust for the prices you actually find. These are, of course, only examples.

COST OF COMMON ITEMS

Note: Prices will vary from shop to shop, and from town to village, so all of these are rough guides only.

Loaf of Maltese bread	€0.60–0.80
Six-pack of large bottles of water	€2.50
33cl can of Cisk lager (in a supermarket)	€0.90
1 litre of milk	€0.85
Postcard	€0.50
Margherita pizza (take-away)	€4.50–7.50
Petrol (regulated by government)	€1.40/litre

Top whack

Junior suite in a top five-star hotel	€350
Large car with driver	€120
Lunch in a very good restaurant (two courses and coffee)	€80
Three-course supper in a top restaurant with a bottle of good wine	€160
Sundries (museum entry, water, tips, snacks, etc)	€30
Total	**€740**

Comfortable, middle-of-the-road

Accommodation (five-star low season/special offer, or three–four-star summer/full price)	€150
Small car, self-drive	€40
Petrol	€10
Light lunch out	€30
Restaurant supper with a glass of wine	€60
Sundries (museum entry, postcards, snack, water, etc)	€15
Total	**€305**

Shoestring

Accommodation (hostel)	€30
Public transport	€5
Bread and cheese lunch	€6
Supper out (pizza/pasta/single dish and wine)	€30
Sundries (as above)	€15
Total	**€86**

TIPPING Tipping is usual practice in Malta and a tip of 10–15% is appreciated when reasonable service has been received, for instance in a restaurant or taxi. Service will sometimes be added to bills, in which case nothing additional is required. Hotel porters in four- and five-star hotels expect a few euros (depending on the number of bags) and most people will tip parking attendants at makeshift car parks around €1.

GETTING AROUND

Public transport in Malta is good. There are no trains but you can get buses to almost everywhere and there are plenty of taxis. The ferry between Malta and Gozo is frequent and takes under half an hour. It goes from Ċirkewwa in the very north of Malta, about 45 minutes by car from Valletta (unless it is raining or rush hour, in which case it will take longer).

BY BUS Gone are Malta's iconic brightly painted 1950s Leyland 'boneshakers' that lasted until 2011. They have been replaced with boring modern single-decker buses with air conditioning (usually, and sometimes too much!). The main bus station is just outside the city walls of Valletta at City Gate where you will find a long row of bus stops and an information kiosk which also sells tickets. Unless you are in a huge hurry or going somewhere really off the beaten track, buses are a great way to get around. Most stops (other than bus stations/termini) are request stops so you need to stick your arm out to board the bus and push the button to get off.

Generally, bus numbers below 100 start in Valletta and buses with an X go to the airport, but there are exceptions so do check. No buses run inside the capital, as most streets are s pedestrianised and even those that aren't are narrow. The bus station is only a few minutes' walk from the centre of town, however, and buses do run around the outside of the city walls, so you can get within a few minutes' walk of anywhere in the city.

Gozo also has a good network of bus routes (page 265). The service has greatly improved in the last few years but is still less frequent than on Malta. The main bus station is in the centre of Victoria, a couple of minutes' walk from the main square (Independence Square/It-Tokk). Tickets cost €1.50 (in winter), €2 (in summer) for a 2-hour multi-ride ticket (adults and children alike). Twelve 2-hour tickets cost €15 while a seven-day pass is €21 for adults/€15 for children). After 23.00 tickets cost €3 (unless you have the seven-day pass, which includes night travel). All tickets are limited to one island – Malta or Gozo; you can't cross the water and use the same ticket.

Bus routes and timetables are available from the Public Transport website (w publictransport.com.mt) or by phoning ✆ 21222000. For a map of the main tourist routes, drop by a tourist information office for a leaflet.

OPEN-TOP BUS TOURS

Two companies run hop-on-hop-off open-topped bus tours taking in most of the country on three tours – North, South (both on the main island) and Gozo. Tours last about 3 hours if you stay on the bus. Get off, and another bus will be along every half an hour. Malta Sightseeing also do a 4-hour (not hop-on-hop-off) summer-night tour with a 45-minute stop in Mdina.

Most tours cost €15 for adults, €9 for children aged five–15 and under-fives go free. Book more than one tour and the price may fall. Malta Sightseeing usually offer a free harbour cruise when you book a bus tour. Both companies also pick up (at no extra charge) from most tourist centres to take you to Sliema Ferries, from where tours leave on the half-hour from 09.00 to 15.00 Monday–Saturday and 10.00 to 13.00 Sundays and public holidays.

City Sightseeing Malta ✆ 20102090; m (out of office hours) 99822416; w citysightseeing.com.mt

Malta Sightseeing ✆ 21694967; w maltasightseeing.com. Commentary in a choice of 16 languages.

Sightseeing flights in a five-passenger Cessna plane are available from the airport. The plane has high wings so there is nothing to obstruct the fabulous views of the islands of Malta.

Malta Wings ☎ 21647888; m 79705877; w maltaflying.com

BY TAXI Taxi fares from the airport are regulated (see w maltairport.com/passenger/getting-here/taxi-service), but it is still worth agreeing the fare before getting in, as it is on all other trips in taxis, water taxis and horse-drawn cabs.

The main island's official white taxis (☎ 21823017), sometimes known as 'the white sharks', gather at strategic points, often by tourist sites and bus stations, and ply the streets. They can also be ordered by phone. If booking a cab in advance many Maltese use private taxi firms, which will do short journeys, as well as offering hourly/day rates.

For taxis on Gozo, see page 265; and for water taxis, Valletta Smart Cabs and horse-drawn carriages, see page 103.

ECabs ☎ 21383838. 24hr service with fixed prices.

Wembley Cars [173 B4] ☎ 21374141, 27374242; m 79374141, 79374242; w wembleys.com. 24hr taxi service based in Paceville close to St Julian's.

BY BOAT Travelling between Malta and Gozo is easy, with regular ferries taking less than half an hour. Boats also operate to the tiny island of Comino from both Malta and Gozo – see page 259. There are ferries across the harbours either side of Valletta to Sliema (page 103) and the Three Cities (page 103). Plenty of day cruises are on offer too, including around Malta, around Gozo, harbour tours and day trips to Comino.

Captain Morgan Cruises ☎ 23463333; w captainmorgan.com.mt. For harbour tours.

Hera Cruises ☎ 21330583, 21347483; m 79445448; w heracruises.com

SELF-DRIVE The Maltese love their cars. They will always drive rather than walk – even if it's just a few hundred metres – and there is lots of interest in the best new model. There are therefore far too many cars on the roads, with some of them going rather faster than they should. Malta drives on the left (like the UK) – at least in theory. As one local put it: 'We drive on the left… or on the right, or in the middle of the road.' The standard of driving in Malta is described by the British Foreign Office as 'poor' and it can certainly be erratic. If you hire a car, make sure you will not be stung for some massive excess if someone 'eases' past you. Should you have an accident, call the police on the international emergency number: ☎ 112. Anyone driving in Malta needs to be aware that the Maltese do not like to give way – even at roundabouts. They are not generally inattentive drivers, but they aren't keen on slowing down, let alone stopping. Overtaking happens on all sides and in almost any place so it may be worth beeping on blind bends.

The speed limits are 80km/h on highways and 50km/h in urban areas – and they are enforced. Perhaps unfortunately, the locals mostly know where the cameras are and only slow down accordingly. Seatbelts are mandatory except

Practical Information GETTING AROUND

3

where there are none available in the back seat. Crash helmets on mopeds and motorbikes are also required.

Malta's main roads are in reasonable condition, but side roads are often pot-holed. When it rains, some roads flood and main routes are frequently jammed. Getting into Valletta in the morning rush hour when it is raining can be very slow indeed.

The price of petrol in Malta is set by the government. It is therefore the same at all petrol stations, so there is no point in shopping around.

Driving on **Gozo** is easier and less hair-raising, although the road surfaces are equally variable and minor roads worse than on Malta (page 266).

Car hire Many car-hire companies in Malta require you to be aged 25 or over, although a few will hire to over-21s. If you are 70+, you may be asked for a medical certificate to prove fitness to drive. Prices can vary considerably from company to company, as can the insurance excess (and the cost of removing it), so it is worth shopping around. Some companies also charge extra for a second driver or out-of-hours pickup.

🚗 **Avis Rent-a-Car** UK office: ☎ 0808 284 0014, Malta airport office: ☎ 25677550; w avis.co.uk. 24hr office at Malta International Airport, plus several other offices in Malta.
🚗 **Europcar** ☎ 25761000; w europcar.com. Several offices including an airport branch.

🚗 **Sixt** Branches at Malta International Airport, & in St Julian's & Gozo; ☎ 21861416; w sixt.co.uk
🚗 **Supercar Hire** ☎ 21446004; m 79446004; w supercarhire.com. Local company with about 200 vehicles.

Parking Parking can be difficult on Malta but tends not to be a problem in Gozo except occasionally in Victoria. The usual yellow lines and driveway restrictions apply and some towns have restricted parking areas where you can only stay for a certain length of time. These are signed with a blue clock and require you to place a cardboard clock on the dashboard showing the time of arrival. Make sure you are given one of these when hiring a car. There is no charge but fines apply if you overstay or fail to display your arrival time. If you have to park and don't have the necessary clock, you could try writing a note to the parking attendant with the time of arrival on it – this is sometimes accepted (but no guarantees).

Sliema and Floriana (just outside Valletta) each have a large multi-storey car park, and there is a big open car park at the airport. Otherwise it is a matter of using car parks attached to tourist sites (where they exist) and the small, less formal, open car-parking spaces (where attendants expect a small fee) or finding unrestricted areas.

BY BICYCLE I would not recommend cycling as a way of getting around the main island of Malta (for Gozo, see page 276). Not only are some roads very pot-holed, but the traffic can also be fast and unpredictable (page 59). There are an increasing number of cycle lanes, but don't expect them to contain only bikes or to necessarily extend the whole length of the road. In Malta's main towns there are charming metal stands shaped like small bicycles especially for locking up your two-wheeler; I have only once seen a bike attached to one. It is rare to see anyone riding a bike as transport, though there are a growing number of sports cycling enthusiasts, particularly tourists, in the full cycling kit and there are some quieter rural roads in northern Malta and Gozo where cycling is more of a pleasure.

If you want to cycle in Malta, there is an excellent little book, *Cycle Malta & Gozo* by Joseph Montebello (hard copy or download from w cyclemaltandgozo.

com); and two e-books, *Cycling Malta* and *Cycling Gozo* by Jonathan Henwood and Emmet McMahon (w greatwalksmalta.com/cycling-malta-gozo). Guided cycling tours and bike hire are available from w maltabookers.com and on Gozo with Gozo Adventures (page 275). **Bike hire** is also available from **EcoBikesMalta** (℘ 27500022; m 99471627; w bikerentalmalta.com). The sports cycling body in Malta is the **Malta Cycling Federation** (m 79471935; ∎) which organises the annual four-day Tour Ta' Malta (as in Tour de France; w tourtamalta.com), usually in March.

Headwater (℘ 01606 720099 (UK); w headwater.com) offers cycling holiday package deals.

ACCOMMODATION

Malta has well over 200 hotels and other forms of accommodation ranging from large five-star resort hotels to four-room B&Bs, luxury designer boutiques to hostel dorms. The options have expanded dramatically over the last few years, especially in Valletta, with the opening of a multitude of small hotels and B&Bs, many with contemporary interiors and all mod cons inside restored historic buildings. Each with its own individual style, these are a welcome addition to the more conventional hotels.

Star ratings can be a little unreliable. There are three-star hotels that could be four stars and fives that should be four. For standard hotels ratings are perhaps a little more generous than in the UK and may not be updated when a hotel becomes a bit tired. The stars don't always work for the new breed of boutique hotels either; some are certainly luxury but may not qualify for five stars because they lack some specific facility.

Malta has a couple of hotels embedded in its history. **The Phoenicia**, just outside City Gate, was the nation's first luxury hotel built by the British in the 1930s. It retains its 1930s charm – and its place in Maltese government and British Royal favour. The **Xara Palace** is a classic luxury 17th-century Mdina palazzo and the only hotel inside the walls of the old capital.

Self-catering options for all budgets are available around the country – ranging from modern apartments to Gozitan farmhouses. For the shallowest pockets there are a few inexpensive guesthouses and B&Bs and a couple of excellent hostels like **Inhawi** in St Julian's which even has its own swimming pool. There is little provision for camping: just one campsite in the far north of Malta (page 249) and a small patch of land for pitching tents on Comino (page 259).

For information on **religious retreat houses**, see the box on page 45, and for details on **spa hotels**, page 96.

PRICES AND DISCOUNTS Many of the hotels' published room rates are way above what you should expect to pay, particularly in low season. On the whole, the more

---

ACCOMMODATION PRICE CODES

Standard double room B&B (unless self-catering or all-inclusive) in peak season (NB: may be half the price in low season). See also page 57.

€€€€	€200+
€€€	€130–199
€€	€80–129
€	under €80

expensive the hotel, the more dramatic the reductions can be (though there are exceptions to this). Some establishments are more straightforward about this than others, admitting that rates rise and fall daily according to occupancy. It is always worth checking third-party websites, the hotel's own website, and emailing or phoning for the best available rate.

Booking in advance can also gain you substantial discounts, and low-season prices may be less than half the August highs. Hotels vary as to when they consider high season to begin, so if you are visiting in the shoulder months, shop around.

Given all this, the price ratings for accommodation in this book are inevitably rough and ready and categories more flexible than you might expect. Particularly outside the summer it is well worth contacting establishments directly to see what they can offer you.

SEA VIEWS Many hotels in Malta charge extra for a sea view. It is often worth paying if you can. When considering a non-sea-view room ask in detail about how much window you will have, what it will look over and how noisy it is likely to be. If you say you are trying to choose between sea view and non-sea view (rather than between hotels) they may give you the truth about the non-sea views!

SMOKING Smoking is not allowed in public buildings including restaurants and the communal areas of hotels (as in the UK) and this is generally adhered to. Of course, many people do smoke and some hotels (especially the larger ones) designate certain bedrooms or whole floors to smokers. These rooms may occasionally stink of tobacco, so make clear when booking whether you want a smoking or a non-smoking room.

AIR CONDITIONING AND CENTRAL HEATING Summers in Malta are hot. Most hotels have air conditioning, but budget accommodation and self-catering properties (especially in old buildings) may not and a few budget establishments charge extra for it. Winters are generally mild so central heating is rare. There are, however, times when it is wet and cold and being in an unheated room, especially one designed to stay cool in summer (as most Maltese buildings are), can be damp and miserable. It is worth asking what heating and bedding will be provided.

SWIMMING POOLS If travelling in winter, especially with children, you may want to check the size and warmth of indoor pools, and whether children are allowed. Indoor pools are sometimes part of the spa and under-16s may be barred from entering. If you want your children to be able to relax and play in the pool, it is also worth checking whether balls and inflatables are allowed and how many families use the hotel.

EATING AND DRINKING

FOOD The Maltese love to eat almost as much as they hate to exercise. This unfortunate combination makes Malta a European record-breaker for both obesity and diabetes. Yet their love of food has a positive effect – Malta has a substantial number of very good restaurants, almost all serving locals and visitors alike.

Maltese food is heavily influenced by Italy. Pasta – usually fresh – is omnipresent as a starter or 'light' lunch. Mains are mostly meat or fish. Few people in Malta are vegetarian, although understanding of the idea of vegetarianism and veganism has spread rapidly in the last few years and restaurants are beginning to get it.

Many restaurants in Malta offer local specialities. Here are a few to look out for.

SOUPS Traditional soups include:

Aljotta Fish soup with a thin base rather like a fish minestrone with lots of bits of fish.
Minestra Vegetable soup much thicker than Italian minestrone and often including one or more pulses.
Soppa ta l-armla ('widow's soup') Meant to be cheap to make: a mix of potatoes, cauliflower and onion with a fresh *gbejna* (or a lump of ricotta) and sometimes an egg dropped in at the end.

MAIN COURSES
Fenek Rabbit in almost any form (fried, stewed, in wine, with tomato, as pasta sauce).
Braġioli Slices of beef wrapped around a mix of minced beef and herbs. Sometimes called 'beef olives' because of the shape (there are no olives in it).
Laħam taż-żiemel Horse meat, usually steamed or fried.
Zalzett tal-Malti Maltese sausage. Short, fat, rough-cut pork sausage.
Lampuka The national favourite among the many fresh fish served in Malta (see box, page 188). *Lampuki* pie is particularly popular when *lampuki* are most plentiful. Chopped *lampuki* fillet is mixed with tomato, onion, spinach and olives.
Sawrell Mimli il-forn Baked stuffed mackerel. Mackerel, breadcrumbs, anchovies, olives and parsley between layers of potato and onion.
Laħam il-forn Baked meat. Slices of pork or beef between layers of onion and potato, often with fennel seeds.

PASTA AND OTHER BAKES Pasta, in all the usual forms, comes with sauces ranging from octopus and sea urchin to rabbit.

Ravjul Ravioli. Fresh homemade ravioli are widely available with fillings from rabbit to ricotta, spinach to minced meat and, in Gozo, local cheese. Usually large and priced by the dozen.
Għaġin il-forn Baked pasta, usually macaroni, with cheese, tomato sauce and minced meat.
Ross il-forn Similar to the above, but made with rice.
Għaġin bl-inċova Crispy spaghetti with anchovy sauce.

VEGETABLES The Maltese for vegetables is *ħaxix* (pronounced *hashish* – not to be confused!)

Patata il-Forn Literally baked potato, but actually layers of potato and onion with fennel or caraway seeds baked in the oven. Meat is often cooked underneath this.
Ħaxix Mimli Stuffed vegetables. Courgette, aubergine, peppers, tomatoes, cabbage leaves, etc, filled with ricotta, local cheese, minced meat and herbs, or fish of various kinds.

Malta's cuisine is Mediterranean, so it is no good being shy of olive oil or garlic, unless you are eating the excellent and copious fresh fish, in which case you can ask for it simply grilled or steamed. Meat is mostly pork, beef and rabbit (the national favourite). After World War II Malta was advised to reduce the number of sheep and goats on the islands. The result has been less lamb, but more vegetation in the countryside.

Homemade cakes and puddings are very popular, often delicious and rarely sickly sweet. There is excellent local ice cream (try fig or passion fruit), which is widely available. Meals are generally accompanied by fresh Maltese bread (*ħobż Malti*; see box, page 303), a crusty loaf rather like a French *pain de campagne* or an Italian *ciabatta*.

Many Maltese cannot get through the morning without a **pastizza** (confusingly translated as 'cheesecake'), a traditional mini pasty filled with local cheese (or ricotta) or mushy peas. These are sold in almost all cafés and tiny shopfronts known as *pastizzeria*.

Snacks and fast food The most Maltese snack you can get is *pastizzi* (see above), but there is also the delicious traditional sweet snack **imqaret** (pronounced *im-aart*), which is a pastry filled with date paste and fennel seeds, and deep fried. For fast food, **pizza** is readily available, and even the street-side slice is usually a cut above its northern European counterpart. Malta does not escape McDonald's and Burger King either.

Vegetarian food Malta is just discovering the pleasures of good vegetarian and vegan food. In some restaurants vegetarian options may still be few and rather dull, but others, such as the Harbour Club in Valletta (page 111) offer delicious imaginative vegetarian options, and there are increasing numbers of outlets catering particularly for the health-food market. Traditional Maltese food includes some excellent vegetarian appetisers and antipasti and you can ask for vegetarian pasta sauces and pizza, too. Common local vegetarian dishes include *bigilla* – a tasty rough paste made from crushed beans and garlic, usually served with *galletti* (thin crackers sometimes with herbs); and *ħobż Malti,* which literally means 'Maltese bread', but in this case comes with fresh tomato, local olive oil, salt and pepper.

Local **cheese** – often called Gozitan cheese although it is also made on Malta – is usually made from sheep's and goat's milk, and comes in three main forms: fresh (soft, like an extra-smooth ricotta, with which it is sometimes mixed or replaced in recipes); peppered (dried hard with pepper on the outside); and semi-dried (in between, without pepper). The dried may also come unpeppered or 'pickled' in vinegar. The cheese is usually produced in small roundels an inch or two across known as *ġbejna* (usually translated as 'cheeselets').

DRINK The drinking age in Malta is 17, but adherence to it is distinctly variable, particularly in Paceville.

Malta produces its own wine and beer – most popularly **Cisk lager** (pronounced *chisk*). There is also a national soft drink, **Kinnie** (pronounced *keeny*), which is a little like Coke but less sickly sweet (more like the traditional English dandelion and burdock). Kinnie is drunk by kids and adults alike and is sometimes used as a mixer with spirits. Malta's favourite local **liqueurs** are limoncello – lemon zest, alcohol, water and sugar – and Bajtra, a very sweet liqueur made from prickly pears.

Wine There are a number of wineries in Malta. Many make wine both from their own grapes and from grapes imported, usually from Italy. Until recently it was difficult to know which was which but wine made from foreign grapes bottled after 2007 has to be clearly labelled as such. A form of quality control, similar to that in Italy, has also been introduced. DOK is the equivalent of the French

appellation contrôlée, while IGT is like a *vin de pays*. Both must be made from grapes grown in Malta.

Five wineries produce wine with DOK and IGT certification: **Delicata** (w delicata. com) – the largest and oldest, drawing grapes from 650 small independent vineyards; **Marsovin** (w marsovin.com.mt), the largest until a few years ago, has some vineyards of its own, produces a broad range of wines and seems to have the widest distribution; **Camilleri** (w camilleriwines.com); **Montekristo** (w montekristo. com); and **Meridiana** (w meridiana.com.mt), which has a small winery next to its single vineyard near Mdina and makes some of Malta's best wines. On Gozo there are an increasing number of small artisan wineries (page 278).

Meridiana Winery (Ta' Qali, ATD 4000; ✆ 21413550; w meridiana.com.mt; ⊕ 09.00–16.00 Mon–Fri but book ahead) is open to visitors and offers tastings of its wines.

In August each year, the **Delicata Classic Wine Festival** (✆ 21825199; e info@ delicata.com; w delicata.com) is held first in Valletta and, later in the month, on Gozo. Buy a wine glass for €12, then taste (and drink) as many wines as you like all evening while enjoying the atmosphere and entertainment – and keep the glass.

RESTAURANTS Malta has some excellent restaurants and you can eat extremely well here. Many restaurants are closed on Mondays or Sundays and some do only lunch or only dinner. Outside the main tourist areas, restaurants often do not stay open late, so if you need to eat after 22.00 check ahead. Portions tend to be generous. Even top-end restaurants with nouvelle-cuisine-style presentation don't usually have nouvelle-cuisine-sized portions ('our local clients would not

3

DINNER IN THE SKY

Eating a five-course meal from one of Malta's best restaurants 40m above the ground with the island laid out in a 360° panorama beneath you is definitely a treat. A specially designed table with 22 comfortable chairs (with harnesses) arrayed around it is lifted smoothly into the air by a dedicated crane (you can wave to the driver). Staff stand in a gap in the middle of the table and prep, heat, and serve the food – and top up the wine glasses – chatting as they go. It's different, it's fun (and inevitably it isn't cheap). The food is from Tarragon (page 251), which won Malta's Best Restaurant award 2018, and the wine flows freely. Dinner in the Sky runs from mid-May to the end of September, Friday to Sunday, and the location changes each year. There are two sessions a night, the best is undoubtedly the sunset sitting.

For reservations contact m 99988835; w dinnerintheskymalta.com.

Ftira is a low-rise ring-shaped loaf usually eaten with fillings (a Maltese sandwich). Gozitan *ftira* is more like pizza and comes open (like normal pizza) or folded over (like calzone but the folding is from all edges so it stays round). Unlike pizza, Gozitan *ftira* has thin slices of potato directly on top of the crust. One traditional version is topped with sardine (or tuna if you don't like sardine), potato, fresh tomato, onion, capers and olives. The most traditional (and delicious) closed Gozitan *ftira* is filled with Gozitan cheese which puffs up so it is almost like a crusty savoury cheesecake.

All the usual pizzas are also readily available.

stand for it'). Be warned though: restaurateurs have got wise to people ordering starters as main courses and some will slap an extra couple of euros on the bill.

The restaurants recommended in this guide are mostly establishments that offer at least some Maltese or Mediterranean food on the grounds that most people do not come to Malta to eat Asian or Chinese (although Chinese food is popular with the Maltese). If you are desperate to escape the Mediterranean diet, you can find other good places on Malta's restaurant website (see below). The listings in this guide also concentrate on independent restaurants; hotel restaurants are included only if there is a particular reason to do so. Those Maltese who can afford it love to eat at the restaurants of the five-star hotels, but for visitors the independent restaurants tend to be more interesting and better value for money.

The price categorisation is inevitably only a guideline and you may be able to eat more cheaply than the category suggests by ordering carefully or eating pasta rather than a meat or fish dish. Equally, if you order steak or the most expensive fresh fish you may find yourself in the price bracket above that listed. Occasionally you may come across a restaurant with a range of price rating (eg: €–€€€). This is where, for instance, the restaurant serves pizzas at €6 and fresh fish dishes at €25.

The Definitive(ly) Good Guide to Restaurants in Malta and Gozo is published annually both as a book and online (**w** restaurantsmalta.com). Based on votes from Maltese restaurant-goers, it rates food, ambience and service and has useful indexes/searches by location, opening times, type of food, child-friendliness and even wheelchair access.

SHOPPING

Most shops are open from 09.00 to noon and about 16.00 to 19.00. In tourist areas shops often do not close in the middle of the day and may stay open later than 19.00 in summer and close considerably earlier in winter. Most shops are shut on Sundays, though in tourist resorts and in Valletta some are open, particularly in peak season. You can buy almost anything you need (or want) in Valletta and Sliema and most things in Victoria, Gozo, too. Chains here range from Body Shop and Marks & Spencer to Next and Tommy Hilfiger. Few people from other European countries would come to Malta primarily to shop, however. Prices are not particularly low and variety is similar to elsewhere. Specifically Maltese items and souvenirs are, of course, exceptions.

There have recently been a few cases of tourists being overcharged, not massively but enough to be annoying. So keep an eye on bills/receipts and particularly in markets make sure you know the price (and are happy with it) before you commit to buying.

Local crafts include gold and particularly silver filigree, lace, glass and pottery (see page 32 for additional information). These can be found at the official 'craft villages': Ta' Dbiegi on Gozo and Ta' Qali in Malta. The Artisans Centre in Valletta also has a reasonable selection. There is a little row of jewellers on Valletta's St Lucy Street with a range of silver, while glass specialist Mdina Glass has several retail outlets, as well as an online shop. An **Artisans Market** pops up monthly at different locations around Malta, usually in a historic site, selling everything Maltese from jewellery to artisan beer, crafted household items to fine art. Dates and locations are listed on w maltaartisanmarkets.com.

Some of Malta's **specialist foods** – including jams, honeys, liqueurs, capers, mini cheeses, and antipasti – can be purchased packed for long-distance travel, mostly produced by Cordina (Malta) or Savina (Gozo).

For the kids, small 'pocket money' items – including miniature versions of the colourful painted wooden **Eye of Osiris** seen on the traditional boats – can be found at Marsaxlokk Market (especially on Sundays; page 185) and other markets and small shops. For something completely different, the Early Learning Centre on Merchants Street in Valletta sells **Malta Monopoly** (but it is very expensive at up to €60).

For shopping on Gozo, see page 274. For books, see page 43.

CRAFTS
For crafts on Gozo, see page 274.

Artisans Centre [106 C5] 284 Republic St; ☎21221563, 21224166; ⊕ 09.00–19.00 Mon–Fri, 09.00–14.00 Sat, 11.00–14.00 Sun

Mdina Glass Various locations including Mdina, Valletta, Ta' Qali Craft Village (see below) & Victoria (Gozo). You can also order direct from the factory (☎ 21415786; w mdinaglass.com. mt).

Ta' Qali Craft Village [map, page 224] On the old airfield at Ta' Qali; ⊕ 09.00–16.00 Mon–Fri, until 13.00 Sat

SOUVENIRS
Souvenirs That Don't Suck [169 C3] 108 Triq Manwel Dimech, Sliema, SLM 1055 (near Sliema ferries; m 79072313; w souvenirsthatdontsuck. com. For fun, original, modern souvenirs (including some great T-shirts).

FOOD
For food shops on Gozo, see page 274.

Caffe Cordina [106 D4] Republic Sq, 244–5 Republic St, Valletta; ☎21234385; e info@ caffecordina.com; w caffecordina.com

Jubilee Foods [281 B2] ☎21558921; w jubileefoods.net. Sold in various food shops in Malta (as well as in their own shop on Gozo) & via their website.

Malta International Airport [map, page 176] There is a good selection in the departures area.

Marsaxlokk Market Page 185.

ARTS AND ENTERTAINMENT

The Maltese love **music** and there are concerts and festivals of all kinds of music in churches, historic buildings, and outdoors in summer (page 36), as well as at the **Manoel Theatre** and **St James Cavalier Centre for Creativity** in Valletta. There are two **opera festivals** each year (one in March at the Manoel Theatre, and one in Gozo, in the autumn) as well as a summer **jazz festival** and a **festival of traditional music**. Valletta's popular **Baroque Music Festival** takes place each January. Music – classical and popular – also plays a major part in the Maltese *festa*, a mix of religious and secular celebration held at least once a year by each parish in the islands.

The Manoel Theatre is one of the oldest theatres still in use in Europe, having been founded by the Knights of St John. It has performances most days. From May to October there is a programme of performances at the **Pjazza Teatru Rjal**, the open-air theatre in the ruins of the old Opera House near Valletta's City Gate.

There are occasional theatrical performances too at **St James Cavalier** – a modern arts centre in a historic building – which also houses an arts cinema and a large, interesting gallery space with changing exhibitions.

Contemporary art is displayed and sold in some public buildings, restaurants and wine bars including the Trabuxu wine bar and bistro (pages 111 and 112). The number of commercial galleries is growing, and Gozo has quite a thriving little community of working artists (page 274).

There are three commercial **cinemas** showing the usual Hollywood fare: the Embassy Complex in Valletta [106 D4] (St Lucy St (Triq Santa Luċija); 21222225, 21227436; w embassycomplex.com.mt); the Empire in Buġibba [250 E3] (Pioneer Rd; 21581787,21581909; w empirecinema.com.mt); and The Eden in Paceville [173 A2] (23710400; w edencinemas.com.mt), which is next to the Intercontinental near the Bay Street shopping centre and opposite the Eden Superbowl. The **Eden Superbowl** is Malta's only public bowling venue [173 A2] (23710777; w edensuperbowl.com; ⊕ 10.00–midnight daily).

THE CLUBS No, not nightclubs, **band clubs**. Every parish in Malta has at least one band (of the wind-instrument variety) and usually an associated band club. These clubhouses are often in the main church square, and may have an interesting façade. They frequently include an inexpensive bar, café or restaurant – of variable quality – as well as a snooker table and a television, which seems to perpetually show live English Premier League and Italian Serie A football. In Valletta, two central band clubs have large restaurants that do a roaring trade (page 112).

Many towns also have **political clubs** – Nationalist and Labour, the latter often being the more prominent. Here again there are usually cheap bars and restaurants, often occupied by semi-resident groups of older men smoking, chatting and drinking (and watching football). The Labour Party Club on Republic Street in Valletta (page 112) has a sign saying tourists are welcome. At other clubs, check that they are open to non-members before settling in. **Football clubs** offer a similar atmosphere and facilities but are dedicated to sport – some even have a sign prohibiting discussion of politics!

The clubs vary hugely in their congeniality, and – outside the capital at least – they are a side of Malta most tourists never see.

NIGHTLIFE Most of Malta goes pretty quiet after about 21.00 – though less of it than was the case a decade ago. There are lots of excellent restaurants (page 65), but outside the main towns and tourist areas don't expect to be served at midnight, or in some cases after 22.00. Even in **Valletta** most restaurants close by 23.00 although there are now cafés and bars staying open into the early hours, especially at weekends. There is plenty of nightlife in **St Julian's** and particularly in neighbouring **Paceville**. Here streets full of fast-food joints, pubs, bars, restaurants and clubs boom with thudding bass until four in the morning.

Paceville tends to attract a very young crowd (many under the official drinking age of 17). It can, particularly on summer weekends, become rowdy and fractious. Around midnight the age may rise into the 20s; St Julian's has an older clientele.

Recently, in summer, hip 20-something Maltese have been abandoning Paceville for Gianpula, Café Del Mar and pop-up events and festivals like British DJ Annie Mac's Lost & Found (w lostandfoundfestival.com). **Gianpula** [map, page 208] (the limits of Rabat, RBT 5032; m 99472133; w gianpula.com)

– a rooftop nightclub between Rabat and Ta' Qali – holds huge public parties at weekends. **Café Del Mar** (page 253) combines a contemporary daytime beach club with evening nightclub on the water's edge in the National Aquarium complex in Qawra; by day it is all about sunbathing and swimming (there is even a children's pool) while by night it takes on a laid-back party vibe and is Malta's home of 'chill out' music. Other bars in Qawra and Buġibba also stay open late, but Brits run a significant risk here of bumping into embarrassing groups of alcohol-fuelled compatriots.

The large hotels of course have their own bars and restaurants, some of which stay open well into the night.

Far more fun and more interesting than most of these venues is to get involved in a *festa*: eat Maltese snacks, watch fireworks and enjoy congenial local nightlife under the stars.

MUSEUMS AND HISTORIC SITES

Malta has a remarkable range of museums and historic sites ranging across its 7,000-year history. The temple sites and many of the key museums are run by the government body **Heritage Malta** (♦ 22954000; w heritagemalta.org). They offer a 30-day pass (see box, page 42) to all their sites except the Ħal Saflieni Hypogeum. The **hypogeum** – the extraordinary 5,500-year-old underground temple of the dead – must be booked through Heritage Malta preferably well in advance, but at all other sites you can pay for entry on arrival. Independent museums each have their own ways of doing things and these are covered in the relevant chapters.

FILM LOCATIONS

Malta has created quite a niche for itself as a location for film-makers looking for an inexpensive, accessible, English-speaking European location. Blockbusters *Troy* (2004) starring Brad Pitt and Orlando Bloom, and Ridley Scott's *Gladiator* (2000) were both shot here. Remains of their sets can still be seen by looking over the wall of the Mediterranean Film Studios in Kalkara (next to the Three Cities, *Chapter 6*).

Comino Tower took the role of Château d'If in *The Count of Monte Cristo* (2002) and parts of the *Da Vinci Code* (2006) and *Captain Philips* (2013) were also shot in Malta. Brad Pitt returned with Angelina Jolie to shoot *By the Sea* in Gozo, particularly at Mġarr ix-Xini (and many regard the scenery as the best bit of the film).

For television, the most famous drama with locations in Malta is undoubtedly *Game of Thrones*. In episode 101, 'Winter is Coming', Daenerys and Khal Drogo marry in front of Gozo's now collapsed Azure Window, while Malta's Verdala Palace becomes Illyrio's Mansion. San Anton Palace features in both episodes 105 and 108 while its gardens are seen in episode 104. Catelyn and Ser Rodrik ride into King's Landing through the Main Gate of Mdina (page 211) in episode 103 while The King's Gate in the same episode was filmed at Fort Ricasoli (page 161, not open to the public). Fort St Angelo provides the location for the Red Keep Dungeon in episode 105 and Red Keep Garden was filmed at the Dominican Monastery in Rabat. More details of these locations and the roles they played can be found at w moviemaps. org/movies/aa.

SWIMMING Malta has no shortage of places to swim in beautiful clear blue waters. Beware of finding your own secluded spots – there are hidden currents in some areas and getting out of the water onto rocks is not nearly as easy as getting in. Be guided by what the locals do. See also page 49.

'Beach' in Malta merely means a place to swim. It may be sandy, rocky or even concrete. The most common is rocky and, as long as you are all competent swimmers, these can be the pleasantest places, and good for snorkelling too. With young children you may want sand, a gentle slope into the water and shallows to paddle in (see page 89, for swimming locations).

Having had only one blue-flag beach for many years, Malta now has a wealth of these awards (w blueflag.org) including for Mellieħa Bay, Għajn Tuffieħa, Qawra Point, St George's Bay (Paceville), Fond Għadir (Sliema Waterfront), Buġibba Perched Beach, Paradise Bay, Reef Club in the Westin Dragonara (Paceville) and on Gozo, Ramla Beach, Hondoq and Marsalforn.

Some beaches, including most of the above-mentioned blue-flag beaches, along with Golden Bay, are managed from June to at least mid-September with lifeguards and flags to indicate water conditions (see box, page 49).

The website/app whichbeach.com.mt gives excellent guidance on which beach is best on any given day, taking into account weather and jellyfish.

Topless and nude sunbathing and swimming are illegal. You may see it, but if someone complains, you could find yourself in trouble.

SNORKELLING With some of the clearest waters in the Mediterranean, Malta is a great place to snorkel, whether casually off a beach or more formally as an easier alternative to diving. Basic equipment is sold in hotels and shops and snorkelling gear can be hired from many dive centres (see opposite). The Majjistral National Park also runs guided snorkelling trips along the coast near Golden Bay (minimum age 9). Equipment can be provided and details are on the website at w majjistral.org.

DIVING Some 50,000 people a year visit the Maltese islands for diving. The water is warm in summer and autumn and diveable even in spring and winter; it is known for its clarity, with visibility of up to 30m in undisturbed sea. The water is also cleaner than in some other parts of the Mediterranean. There are nearly 100 dive sites around the Maltese coast, about half of them accessible from the shore. There are sites suitable for beginners as well as deep-water challenges for the very experienced. Seasoned divers tend to come here for the underwater landscape of dramatic rock formations and caves, as well as for the wrecks (including nine deliberately scuttled), more than for the fish, but there is plenty of marine wildlife too. Night dives are also popular and many local divers are involved in underwater photography. Advice on this is available through dive centres and also in Peter Lemon's excellent dive guide (see opposite).

Malta's islands are small and offer a wide variety of dives quite close together. If one site is too windy, there is almost always an alternative not far away. Established dive companies offer instruction ranging from children's taster sessions (age 8+) through beginners' Open Water Diving courses right up to specialist and instructor qualifications. If you have PADI Advanced, BSAC Sports Diver or equivalent qualification – and can show your certificate – you can also hire equipment to dive independently, though if it is your first time in Malta it may be wise to take a guide, at least to begin with. When diving, please always leave wildlife and underwater heritage as you find them.

Choosing a dive centre There are around 50 approved dive centres in Malta, a dozen in Gozo, and one on Comino. They are licensed by the Malta Tourism Authority and listed at w visitmalta.com/en/dive-centres. It is important to dive with one of these; any other company is acting illegally. Malta's Professional Diving Schools Association (w pdsa.org.mt) admits only licensed operators and many of the top Maltese dive centres are also registered with PADI International (w padi.com) and/or with the British Sub-Aqua Club (BSAC; w bsac.com).

Exactly which dive centre you choose will depend on where you want to stay, your level of experience and what kind of diving you wish to do. Gozo is a particularly good place for diving and there are several well-established dive centres there (page 276).

Diver safety During the summer the number of motorboats around the coast of Malta can be considerable and they are a real danger to divers and snorkellers, so do make your presence obvious with a surface marker buoy, or an 'A' flag if diving from a boat.

The Mediterranean is almost tideless but there can be currents around the coast of Malta, particularly during or after windy weather (and note that the currents may go in the opposite direction to the wind). Seek local advice.

There is little in the water to present a serious danger to divers, but there are a few species that should not be touched, including scorpion fish, bristle worm (fireworm), jellyfish, snakelock anemone, weaver fish and stingray.

Finally, if despite your best efforts the worst should happen, there is a decompression chamber at Malta's main hospital and one on Gozo. Helicopter airlift is also available if necessary.

Marine wildlife Malta does not offer the rainbow kaleidoscope of the tropics, but there is plenty to see at all levels of diving – and indeed snorkelling. Species that divers are likely to see include barracuda, wrasse and bream (of various kinds), damsel fish, parrot fish, cardinal fish, painted combers, groupers, bogue, amberjack, octopus (especially on night dives), red mullet, meagre, stingrays, flying gurnard and squid. Conger eel and moray eel are often found around wrecks and John Dory is sometimes spotted, usually in winter.

You are very unlikely to see 'big game'. Dolphin, tuna and turtles are rare and dangerous sharks almost unheard of. Sea horses can occasionally be seen, usually in July, but they are shy and well camouflaged and once a location is known may be taken by locals to sell. Malta has a small minority of people who enjoy hunting marine wildlife, so if you find anything rare, be careful who you tell.

Two Marine Protected Areas have recently been designated in a project called PANACEA. They are Dwejra (Gozo) and Rdum Majjiesa (near Għajn Tuffieħa, Malta). Short films about the marine landscape, flora and fauna of these areas can be found at w youtube.com/watch?v=ArJOWrwwz98 (Dwejra) and w youtube.com/watch?v=xzpPK1pAlLA (Rdum Majjiesa).

The website w seastuff.com has an excellent section on the marine wildlife you are likely to see in Malta's waters.

Dive guide *Scuba Diving Malta, Gozo, Comino* by Peter G Lemon (third edition) is an excellent guide to diving in Malta with details and maps of more than 90

3

dive sites, as well as photographs and general information. It is available from w scubadivingmalta.co.uk, Amazon, dive centres and possibly the airport in Malta. For more on diving see page 90; and for diving on Gozo, page 276.

BIRDWATCHING Malta should be an excellent place for birdwatching in spring and autumn. With few resident birds there is little to see in summer, but Malta sits on one of the main migration routes between Africa and Europe and whilst the birds are not quite as abundant as in Israel or Sicily, some 170 species are reliably seen during migration. There is one significant drawback to birding here, however, especially in autumn: bird hunters. See also pages 25, 38 and 50.

In autumn it is legal for hunters to shoot certain species (most notably quail and turtle dove). Spring hunting is theoretically outlawed by the EU Birds Directive but Malta has recently been pleading special circumstances and opening hunting for a limited period each spring. If you see hunters shooting birds of prey or other protected species at any time of year, they are breaking the law and should be reported to the police on ✆ 119 and BirdLife Malta on ✆ 21347644.

There are two tiny bird reserves on Malta: Għadira and Is-Simar, both run by BirdLife Malta. The whole of Comino is classed as a bird reserve with no hunting allowed and a BirdLife ringing station set up there during migration. The other best places to bird are mainly on the top of cliffs on Malta and Gozo where tired birds make landfall, and high points in fertile valleys. For more on exactly what to see when and a **map** of some of the best birding spots, see page 95.

Both organisations listed below are happy to help visiting birders and would be interested to know about your sightings. BirdLife Malta produces a *Checklist of the Birds of Malta* (€1), which lists all 381 species seen in Malta with their English, Maltese and scientific names, their local status and a tick-box. For more information, see page 78.

BirdLife Malta ✆ 21347646, 21347644; w birdlifemalta.org. Malta's branch of the international birding organisation. Detailed, informative website.

Birding in Malta w birdinginmalta.com. Excellent website run by 2 birdwatching Maltese.

SAILING
Yachting with your own boat Malta has been a stopping place for people sailing around the Mediterranean for many hundreds of years – the only difference now being that most are leisure sailors. The country's natural harbours are as good today as they were for the Phoenicians and the Knights of St John, and the facilities are a little more modern.

Grand Harbour Marina on Vittoriosa Waterfront [map, page 150] (✆ 21800700; w ghm.com.mt) is a thriving yacht and super-yacht marina in a great location.

The largest yacht marina on Malta is **Msida** [map, page 100] (Ta' Xbiex Waterfront on Marsamxett Harbour, the other side of Valletta; ✆ 21337049; 24hr m 7933724; w marinamalta.com), while there is also **Portomaso Marina** [173 C4] (St Julian's; ✆ 21387803, 21489656; w portomasomarina.com) which is next to the Hilton in St Julian's/Paceville. The Excelsior Hotel also has a small private marina on Marsamxett Harbour next to Valletta.

In Gozo, the marina is at **Mġarr** next to where the Gozo ferry arrives [map, page 262] (Mġarr Marina; ✆ 20992501; m 99242501; w gozomarina.net).

The **Online Maritime Directory** (w maritimedirectory.com.mt) covers everything from navigational rules to a list of chandlers. The old established **Royal Malta**

Yacht Club in Marsamxett Harbour [map, page 100] (Ta' Xbiex Seafront, Ta' Xbiex; ✆21333109; w rmyc.org) has reciprocal arrangements with many other yacht clubs around the world and organises the annual **Rolex Middle Sea Race** in October.

Sailing courses, boat hire and charter You can of course sail without having your own boat. Dinghies can be hired and yachts chartered for day trips or longer – including sailing to Sicily. Tuition is also available. Charters, particularly in peak season, should be booked well in advance.

⚠ **BoatLink** [map, page 100] Msida Marina; m 99882615; w boatlinkmalta.com. Courses in sailing dinghies & yachts, small boat hire & yacht charters with skipper.

⚠ **Fairwind Sailing** Portomaso Marina & St George's Bay (near St Julian's); ✆21459398; m 79552222; w fairwindsailing.com.mt. A sailing school offering adults & children instruction in dinghy sailing, windsurfing & yachting as well as boat hire to the experienced.

⚠ **Malta Sailing Academy & Malta Yacht Charters** 10 St Lawrence St, Sliema (but boats based at Msida); ✆21378586; m 79432526; w msa.maltasailingacademy.com, myc.

maltayachtcharters.com. RYA yachting courses, from Start Yachting to Yachtmaster, & tailor-made yachting trips/charters.

⚠ **Royal Malta Yacht Club** [map, page 100] Ta' Xbiex; ✆21333109; w rmyc.org. All things sailing in Malta including events, racing & their own sailing school with courses for adults & children.

⚠ **S&D Yachts** Sea Breeze, Triq Giuseppe Calì, Ta' Xbiex; ✆21320577, 21331515; w sdyachts.com. Acts as a broker for chartering yachts – access to a great many.

⚠ **Yachting Malta** James Dowling: m 99821460; w yachtingmalta.com. A small British–Maltese yacht charter company.

WALKING Many people – even in Malta – think there is so little countryside left that walking is not a realistic pastime. This is not true. There are some lovely walks, especially in the north/northwestern part of the main island, and on Gozo (for which see page 275). Most of the best walks are coastal, although there are inland walks as well – including along the Victoria Lines on Malta (see box, page 239) and up some of Gozo's flat-topped hills.

The MTA produces a series of walks booklets, each detailing a long walk. These can be picked up from the larger tourist offices or downloaded free (w visitmalta. com/en/walks). They are well mapped out with lots of information and all start and end at public transport. With your own car, you can cherry pick the best bits (although you will either need a driver or have to backtrack to fetch the car). A series of walking books/e-books/apps has been produced by a Brit and an Irishman. *The Malta Coastal Walk* and *The Gozo Coastal Walk* guide you through circumnavigating the islands, or there are *10 Great Walks* for each island and *Nature Walks in Malta and Gozo*. The books and apps can be bought or downloaded at w greatwalksmalta.com. The **Ramblers Association of Malta** (w ramblersmalta.org) runs a regular programme of walks and is happy to help visiting walkers. It can also organise a whole programme for rambling groups visiting Malta.

The **Majjistral Nature and History Park** (w majjistral.org) covers the coast from Golden Bay (Ir-Ramla tal-Mixquqa) to Anchor Bay (Il-Prajjet) along the west coast towards the north of the island – an area of rocky garigue, cliffs and clay with some rare plants. Anyone can walk here and a leaflet with a map and recommended routes is available from the Gaia Foundation in Golden Bay, from some tourist information offices and from their website (click on Downloads, then New Welcome Board). Guided walks and other events are also listed on the website. British companies **Ramblers Holidays** (✆01707 331133; w ramblersholidays.co.uk),

Headwater (✆ 01606 720099; w headwater.com) and **InnTravel** (✆ 01653 617002; w inntravel.co.uk) offer walking holidays to Malta and/or Gozo.

FISHING Malta is naturally an ideal place for coastal and deep-water fishing from boats. Tuna, swordfish, barracuda, dorado, bream, wrasse, grouper and snapper can be caught, amongst others – depending, of course, on how far from the shore you go and on the season. Many of the boating companies will hire out a boat and boatman for fishing trips. Those listed here set out to provide a specialist service including all the fishing gear you will need and an experienced skipper. It is advisable to book well in advance.

To share information with other fishermen in Malta, you can join the Facebook group **f** Malta Fishing Forum.

↬ Fishing Mania m 99959028; **f**. Sport-fishing charters, day or night.

↬ Malta Sport Fishing Charters m 79063462; w fishingmalta.com. Tailor-made fishing trips for up to 4 people, offshore & coastal.

ROCK CLIMBING Rock climbing is increasingly popular and Malta certainly has plenty of rock to climb! There are some 1,500 routes on the islands in about 30 locations ranging from fairly straightforward to very challenging. The adventurous will find plenty of scope for bouldering, deep-water soloing and sea-level traversing. Not all equipment is easily found in Malta, so do bring your own.

The Malta rock-climbers' bible is *Malta Rock Climbing: The Comprehensive Guide* by John Codling, Andrew Warrington and Richard Abela (available from w maltaclimbingguide.com/buy-the-guide-online), which has details of 1,200 routes. The main source of information online is w climbmalta.com, home of Malta's **Climbing Club**. For climbing on Gozo see w gozo-climbing.com, and **Gozo Adventures** (page 275) offers rock-climbing days and half days.

British company **Rock and Sun** (✆ 020 3390 0391; w rockandsun.com) also runs climbing holidays to Malta.

OTHER SPORTS AND OUTDOOR ACTIVITIES Malta Tourism Authority lists companies and clubs offering sporting and outdoor activities of all kinds at w visitmalta.com/en/sport-contacts. For **cycling**, see page 60, and for cycling on Gozo, page 276.

Besides sporting facilities in hotels, there are various local sports and leisure centres around the country. By far the largest centre for land-based sporting activity is the **Marsa Sports Club** [map, page 100] (about 4km from Valletta; ✆ 21233851, 21232842; w marsasportsclub.com; visitor membership available), which began life as the British colonial club. Here you will find plenty of tennis courts, squash courts, a gym and sauna, polo and cricket pitches, several football pitches, a racetrack and a swimming pool. It is also home to the **Royal Malta Golf Club** (Aldo Moro Rd, Marsa; ✆ 21227019; w royalmaltagolfclub.com) with its 18-hole course (no beginners) and mini golf.

Watersports Watersports – including windsurfing, waterskiing and jetskiing – are catered for on many of Malta's beaches, particularly the main sandy ones like Golden Bay and Mellieħa Beach, as well as by most large hotels. **Windsurfers** favour Mellieħa Bay and St Thomas's Bay. More information can be found at w windsurfmalta.com. **Fairwind Sailing** (page 73) also runs various windsurfing courses.

Gozo Adventures offers sea kayaking in Gozo (page 275), and **Sun & Fun Watersports and Yacht Charter** (✆ 21373822, 23702780; w sunfunmalta.com) caters for a wide range of watersports and boat hire, as does **Pembroke Watersports** (☎ 21389401; w pembrokewatersports.com).

Horseriding This is available from **Golden Bay Horseriding** (☎ 21573360; m 99856862; w goldenbayhorseriding.com) and **Bidnija Riding School** (m 79992326; w bidnijahorseriding.com; note: no public transport but they will collect you if you are staying in northern Malta). Rides are usually 1 or 2 hours accompanied by instructors. All equipment is provided and no prior experience is required.

PHOTOGRAPHY

Most of the time Malta has marvellous light for photographs. The only problem can be that the sun is very bright and therefore contrast is generally high. Most sights and museums allow photography so long as the flash is switched off (the bright light can damage some exhibits). Tempting though it is, please don't climb over ropes at prehistoric and ancient sites to get a better picture: the ropes are there to protect the fabric of the site and the archaeological evidence it holds.

MEDIA AND COMMUNICATIONS

PHONE To **phone Malta from abroad** you need the exit code for your country ('00' from the UK) plus '356' for Malta, followed by the number. Within Malta, there are no area codes, just the phone number, which usually has eight digits. The first two numbers are geographically indicative but are always used. To **dial out of Malta**, the code is '00'.

The Malta **phone book** is online at w go.com.mt/personal/phone-directory or **directory enquiries** can be called on ☎ 1182 or 1187. The **emergency number** is ☎ 112.

MOBILE PHONES Mobile numbers start with a 7 or 9. EU mobiles can now be used as you would use them at home and at the same price. Note, though, that for someone phoning you from your home country this is (bizarrely) not always the case.

INTERNET Wi-Fi is now widespread in Malta. Most accommodation has free Wi-Fi as do many cafés, restaurants, fast-food joints, entertainment centres and even some street corners.

POST Post is reasonably reliable in Malta and there are small post offices dotted across the country. All are open in the morning, usually Monday to Saturday, and some also open in the afternoon on weekdays. Full details can be found at w maltapost.com.

NEWSPAPERS Malta has several English-language newspapers, which are produced in print, as well as having a strong presence online.

Independent & Independent on Sunday
w independent.com.mt. Much smaller daily paper than the *Times of Malta* with fewer resources & a weaker link to the establishment.
Malta Today w maltatoday.com.mt. A midweek & a Sun edition. Fiercely independent & critical.

Times of Malta & Malta Sunday Times
w timesofmalta.com. By far the most comprehensive daily coverage. The useful website features its own articles with blog comments on them (which can be quite revealing about the mood in the country). In the run-up to elections it tends to support the Nationalist Party.

3

TELEVISION Maltese television has a mix of programmes, mostly in Maltese but some in English. There are two public service (PBS) stations. The main station, **TVM**, is primarily in Maltese but also airs a few undubbed British programmes from the BBC and ITV as well as American shows and news in English. A second channel, TVM², launched in autumn 2012, shows documentaries (in Maltese and English) and sport. There are two private political channels. **One TV** (w one.com. mt) is affiliated to the Labour Party and **Net TV** (w nettv.com.mt) to the Nationalists. Cable is also widely available and includes a wide range of international, American, British and Italian channels including BBC World, CNN, al-Jazeera, Discovery UK and several sports channels.

RADIO There are numerous radio stations in Malta, some in English and most based around popular music, much of it fairly easy listening. Some have names you might recognise, such as **Malta's Magic** (91.7MHz, 'more music, less talk') and **Kiss FM** (91.3MHz). **Bay** (89.7MHz) is a popular music and entertainment station and **Vibe FM** (88.7MHz) specialises in dance and R&B. The national public service channel, **Radio Malta** (93.7MHz), is mainly in Maltese but takes news in English from the BBC three or four times a day (usually 06.00, 09.00, 11.00 and 15.00), and **Campus Radio** (103.7MHz) is a 24-hour station run by Malta University which includes content from the BBC World Service and the UK's Classic FM.

BUSINESS

Nearly 5% of foreign visitors to Malta are conference delegates. Many of Malta's four- and five-star hotels (including those that are part of international chains like Intercontinental, Corinthia Hotels, Radisson and Kempinski) have meeting and conference facilities, some extensive. The **Hilton Malta Conference Centre** in St Julian's (✆ 21383383; w hilton.co.uk/malta) is particularly large with a capacity of 1,400.

There are also non-hotel conference centres including the grand historic **Mediterranean Conference Centre** in Valletta within the hospital of the Knights of St John [107 G3] (✆ 21243840/3; w mcc.com.mt).

Destination management companies (DMCs) can organise team-building and incentive activities from film-making to historic treasure hunts, beach Olympics to walking, as well as the more common sports.

The **Malta Tourism Authority** (✆ 020 8877 6993; e office.uk@visitmalta.com) has a dedicated unit in London to help anyone wanting to organise a conference or incentive trip in Malta.

The world of business in Malta is male-dominated, although there are increasing numbers of working women. Some 60% of recent graduates are female, and there are more women in senior positions than ever before.

Although Malta has none of the Mafia problems of its nearest neighbour to the north (Sicily), nor is bribery a regular part of daily life as it is in its next nearest neighbours to the south (in North Africa), favours are part of business in Malta and who you know can be as important as what you know.

Most offices are full of educated people used to working in English, but government offices in particular are run more and more in Maltese. Everyone you are likely to deal with will, however, speak English, so there is no actual language barrier. Office hours are generally from 08.00 (sometimes 09.00) until about 17.00. Most people do not work late into the evening and in summer the working day may end significantly earlier.

BUYING PROPERTY

Malta is increasingly seen, mostly by Brits, as a potential place for a holiday or retirement home, as well as being something of a tax haven. Ex-Manchester United footballer Gary Neville has a house here and Billy Connolly spends much of his time on Gozo, but it's not just the mega-rich and famous who are getting into Maltese property. You do need a reasonable sum, however. Property prices here have risen dramatically in recent years, particularly in Valletta.

EU nationals may freely buy property in Malta if they are planning to make it their primary residence. If the property is to be a second or holiday home then, unless the individual has resided in Malta for five years, an AIP permit is required and the price paid for the property must be above a set minimum (at the time of writing this is €17,972 for apartments and €195,120 for houses). The property must be for personal/family use. Renting it out requires an additional permit.

Further information can be found on the websites of two of the most established estate agents in Malta: **Frank Salt** (✎ 23794554; w franksalt.com.mt) and **Perry's** (✎ 21310800; w perry.com.mt). Permits are obtained from the government Office of Acquisition of Immovable Property (w cfr.gov.mt).

CULTURAL ETIQUETTE

Malta is conservative, but not formal – and getting less conservative all the time (page 30). The Maltese don't much like to see people in **swimwear** on the streets of Valletta or Mdina (let alone in restaurants), but bikinis on the beach are fine. **Topless bathing** is (despite what you might occasionally see) illegal. Smart casual, including jeans (with a shirt), is perfectly acceptable in almost all **restaurants**, even the top ones, and shorts are fine by day. In **churches**, however, you need to cover knees and shoulders. A few churches provide wraps for this purpose, but most do not. Suitably dressed, you are always welcome to attend services, but this is obviously not the time to wander around the interior of the church sightseeing.

Greeting is usually by handshake – or a kiss on each cheek if you know someone better. **Public displays of affection** are frowned upon by older people, though walking arm in arm or holding hands is common. The age of consent (heterosexual and homosexual) is 18.

TRAVELLING POSITIVELY

Malta is a moderately well-off European country, so not a place where you can help by stuffing your rucksack with pencils or hard-to-get foods. What you can do, though, is support its efforts to care for its remarkable historic heritage and its environment. Join, or donate to, one of the NGOs active in the renovation and care of historic properties (see below), and in opening them to the public. These organisations also act as lobby groups with government for the protection of places of historic importance. If you are going to be in Malta for a long time, offer to help at one of their sites. There are many foreigners, mainly Brits, already volunteering with these organisations.

For more on natural history and conservation issues, see page 27.

HERITAGE
Din L-Art Helwa ✎ 21220358, 21225952; w dinlarthelwa.org. Malta's National Trust, with annual membership €20, youth €5 & life €200.

Responsible for quite a few small properties including Knights-period towers on Malta, Gozo & Comino. Reciprocal arrangements with the English National Trust.

Fondazzjoni Wirt Artna 📞21800992, 21803091; w wirtartna.org. The Malta Heritage Trust. Join for €35/year, €50 for a couple (also gives free entry to their sites). Covers several military properties including key World War II sites.
Wirt Għawdex 📞21562666; m 79771981; w wirtghawdex.org. Gozo Heritage, with annual membership fees of adult €11.50, senior €7, student/child €4.50, family €23 & life €115. Projects from Knights' fortifications to an old Gozo ferry.

ENVIRONMENT
BirdLife Malta 📞21347646; w birdlifemalta.org. Malta's equivalent of the British RSPB. Runs 2 small nature reserves & a reforestation project as well as working to protect birds. Overseas membership is €28 for up to 2 adults at the same address. If you go birdwatching in Malta, BirdLife would be pleased to have a copy of your sightings & to hear immediately of anything unusual (rarities, large flocks, injured bird). For these there is also an out-of-hours number: m 79255697. You can also volunteer for the Raptor Camp (e raptorcamp@birdlifemalta. org), which runs for a couple of weeks each spring & autumn. Birders from across Europe gather to observe & note sightings of migratory birds & to help keep illegal hunting in check.

GAIA Foundation 📞21584473/4; f thegaiafoundationmalta. Donate or volunteer to help protect environments Gaia manages. Placements can be short or long & may be on any of the NGO's projects. You could help with tree planting, organic farming, designing visitor information, seed gathering or helping wardens on beach watch in summer. Sign up for 4 weeks or more at 32hrs/week & the foundation can provide free accommodation & a bike for getting to work.
Nature Trust Malta 📞21313150; w naturetrustmalta.org. Manages several nature reserves & has a 24hr animal rescue service. Donate or help with beach clean-up & patrols, turtle rescue & rehabilitation, work in the tree nursery, etc.
Sharklab-Malta w sharklab-malta.org. Sharklab exists to protect sharks, rays & skates through research & education. They also collect the egg sacs of dead sharks in the fish market, nurture them at the National Aquarium (page 254) & release them into the sea. These are not dangerous sharks. You can volunteer to help them with their research, attend events (listed on the website) or adopt a shark (e adoptashark@shaklab-malta. org), as well as attend a shark release.

4

Planning for Your Interests

This chapter aims to help you organise your trip to suit your particular interests. The idea is to provide a bit of extra information, highlight top locations (each section is accompanied by a map with relevant sites plotted) and make it easier to find relevant material elsewhere in the book. It is, of course, worth reading any general material in *Chapters 2* and *3* first.

PREHISTORIC MALTA AND THE TEMPLES

Malta's temples are unique. They are some of the oldest stone buildings in the world and exceptionally sophisticated for their time (the 4th and 3rd millennium BC). Despite having UNESCO World Heritage status, the sites were for many years not highly valued in Malta and there was little or no visitor information. This has now changed and continues to change. With help from EU funding, there are now visitor centres at two temple sites: Mnajdra and Ħaġar Qim and Ġgantija. The one at Ġgantija has a particularly good exhibition and museum. Mnajdra and Ħaġar Qim and the Tarxien temples are also now protected by vast canopies keeping off the sun and rain that previously damaged the stone. These sites have been chosen for covers because they are constructed of the softer globigerina limestone that is most prone to erosion.

INTERPRETING THE TEMPLES
Location and orientation The temples are generally located on south-facing slopes in areas favourable to agriculture and with access to the sea. You don't find them on the top of Malta's many high rocky cliffs, but in the rare places where the coastline dips down closer to sea level and boats might feasibly land nearby. They may face south in order to bring in light and to keep out the prevalent northerly winds.

Often two or more temples are found together. The reason for building additional temples on the same site remains a mystery but we do know that they were usually built at different times and the new ones were additional rather than replacements for the older ones. Older temples continued to be used alongside new ones.

Construction, exteriors and doorways Temple construction is sophisticated and follows a roughly similar pattern – though with many variations. Typically the temple has an **oval forecourt**, big enough perhaps to gather the whole community. The substantial **concave façades** usually face south or southwest.

The **doorways** are interesting. Some are made of a single stone with its centre cut out to allow passage through. Such '**porthole' doorways** are found at main entrances (as at Mnajdra) and internal doorways as well as connecting apses to side chambers. Smaller portholes (more like windows) are also found in many temples and are often known as 'oracle holes'. Portholes are not easy to make so it seems likely that the space behind them was important in some way.

Many of the temple doorways are not portholes but constructed of **slabs of stone**. Most appear to be simple trilithons, two uprights with a lintel or capstone. They are, however, often more sophisticated than this. Most have a 'box within a box' construction with the lintel also touching (and occasionally even rebated into) two further, taller, uprights. This ingenious system helps to support the megalithic walls that are pushing in on the doorway space and makes the whole construction much stronger and able to support the immense weight of the roofed apses either side.

In temple doorways you will also often see large '**hinge holes**' indicating that there would have been a closing door of some kind, as well as occasional larger holes that look as though they were meant to house 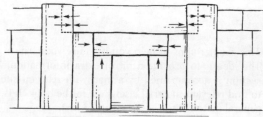 the end of some kind of bar that would have blocked the doorway or carried a drape or curtain.

Holes may also be found in the threshold stones at your feet and just inside or outside entranceways. These have become known as **libation holes** (where liquid offerings are poured into the underworld) because they have been identified as such in ancient architecture elsewhere in the world (though in all cases less ancient than this). There is, however, no direct evidence as to what they were for.

At each corner of the façade (where the corners survive) you will usually find a particularly **tall upright stone**. The outer walls of the temples are built of large close-fitting stone slabs known as **orthostats**, topped with smaller blocks. Often there is a bench-like structure along the base of the façade. Where you see part of a wall built from a mass of small stones or capped with concrete this is usually reconstruction (mostly from the 1950s).

Building materials The temples are all built of local limestone. Malta has little wood, but plenty of stone. There are two main types of limestone used in temple building: **globigerina**, which is soft, workable and smooth – the better for creating decoration but easily weathered; and **coralline**, which is harder and weathers better, but is rougher looking and harder to carve.

Most temples are built of the stone most locally available – although some built on coralline deposits still have a few internal features of the more attractive globigerina limestone. It was clearly thought worth the effort to transport relatively small quantities of the smoother stone for decorative purposes.

Ta' Ħaġrat is constructed from coralline, likewise Skorba and Ġgantija are mainly so. Mnajdra South has the perfect combination – its outside is coralline, the inside globigerina. Meanwhile, Ħaġar Qim, which is a mere 500m from Mnajdra, is constructed entirely from globigerina, the rock on which it sits. It seems even 500m was considered a long way to drag 20 tons of stone!

For the formation of these limestones, see page 22.

Temple roofs There are no surviving temple roofs, but archaeologists believe they must have existed because the plaster (sometimes painted with ochre) known to have covered many internal walls, and indeed internal globigerina stone carvings, would not have survived being open to the weather. Carved decorations at both Ġgantija and Mnajdra weathered badly even in the few decades they were left open to the skies following excavation in the early 19th century. Most carvings are now inside: in the National Museum of Archaeology in Valletta and the Ġgantija visitor centre in Gozo.

Nobody is quite sure how the roofs would have been constructed; the likelihood is that there were several techniques. It seems probable that some temples were roofed with flat slabs of stone or possibly wood. Another technique was more sophisticated: a corbelled stone roof with concentric circles of stone blocks getting smaller and higher towards the centre. The ceiling of the 'Holy of Holies' – an inner room of the Ħal Saflieni Hypogeum – is carved to look like a corbelled roof. Since there are many other architectural echoes of the above-ground temples in this underground tomb complex, it seems logical to conclude that the roof is another. It is also possible to see the beginnings of corbelling (stones starting to lean in) at the top of some temple walls, particularly at Mnajdra. Roofs could of course have been a mix of corbelling and slabs, with a few layers of corbelled stones topped by slabs closing the remaining, smaller, hole.

Inside the temples Inside the temple entrance there is usually a **corridor or central space** off which are internal chambers, D-shaped or oval rooms known as **apses**. These are laid out in pairs, usually with a trefoil to finish. The apse floors were usually made of **torba** – crushed and pounded limestone that could be smoothed and, confusingly for archaeologists, sometimes looks like bedrock.

The temples are constructed with an outer and inner wall. The gap between the two is generally filled with earth and rubble, although in a few places there are small subsidiary 'rooms' between the walls.

Altars, reliefs and statuary Inside, most of the temples have what are known as **altars**. Some are solid blocks of stone, others constructed of trilithons (three megaliths, two uprights supporting one horizontally across the top creating a door or table-like construction) or groups of trilithons. Still others consist of a single slab on a pedestal or are smaller and mushroom-shaped. Some of the larger slab altars are so tall that a person can hardly reach the top, which makes it seem more likely that the inside was used rather than the top surface. One at Tarxien is a likely candidate for animal sacrifice as it has a cubbyhole with a carved door that was found to contain animal bones and a flint knife.

Some experts have identified stone 'rings' (holes going right through the corner piece of stone often seen at entrances) as tethering points for animals. Others think the holes may have been used to attach ropes when hauling the stones to the temple site. They could of course have been used for both.

Some altars are **decorated** with pitting (creating a dotted pattern) and/or with carvings of spirals and occasionally animals and plants. The remarkable **temple statuary** is usually found close by. Most of these statues are of some version of the 'Fat Lady', with huge hips and rear ends, conical legs, and variable upper bodies (some of which may even be male). There are also many phallic symbols in stone and clay. These two together suggest a possible fertility cult, perhaps with the fat figures as a deity or deities.

Most of the carvings and statues seen at the temple sites are copies, the originals having been removed to the safety of the National Museum of Archaeology in Valletta, a real must-see for anyone interested in the temples. On Gozo, the best finds are on site in the visitor centre at the Ġgantija Temples.

WHERE TO VISIT *Map, right*
The key temple-period sites are as follows:

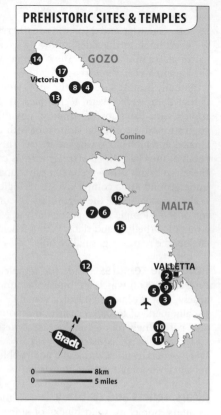

PREHISTORIC SITES & TEMPLES

❶ **Mnajdra and Ħaġar Qim** (on one site; page 197) The most scenic on Malta, two of the best preserved and with interesting contrasts in design, in the visitor centre with some information about the temples.

❷ **The National Museum of Archaeology in Valletta: Neolithic Galleries** (page 122) Home to most of the best statuary and carvings and some useful information.

❸ **The Tarxien Temples** (page 176) The latest, most complex site with the greatest decoration. Not the loveliest location.

❹ **Ġgantija Temples** (Xagħra, Gozo; page 295) This is the oldest of the well-preserved temples, and has the largest megalith. Set in a pleasant location and with an excellent visitor exhibition and museum.

❺ **Ħal Saflieni Hypogeum** (page 181) An extraordinary underground tomb complex in Paola whose design echoes the above-ground temples. Book well in advance to be sure of getting in, although some (slightly more expensive) tickets are sold the day before.

If you see the sites above, you have seen the best and most interesting of the prehistoric temples, and anything else is a plus. Three other, smaller, temple-period sites are open to the public:

❻ **Skorba** (page 236)
❼ **Ta' Ħaġrat** (page 235)
❽ **Xagħra Hypogeum** (page 299)

Other important prehistoric sites include:

❾ **Kordin III Temples** (page 182) An overgrown site with two hard-to-interpret remnants of temples.

❿ **Għar Dalam** (page 188) This is the cave where some of the first people in Malta settled in about 5000BC.

⓫ **Borġ In-Nadur** (page 190) Bronze Age site (and cart ruts; see box, page 204).

⓬ **Clapham Junction** (page 203) At Dingli Cliffs you will find the greatest concentration of Malta's mysterious cart ruts (see also box, page 204).

⓭ **Ta' Ċenċ** (Gozo; page 307) Cart ruts and dolmens.

⓮ **Dwejra** (Gozo; page 288) Cart ruts.

⓯ **San Pawl Tat-Tarġa** (Naxxar; page 231) Cart ruts.

⑯ Xemxija graves (page 252) Early rock tombs that may have been models for the temples.

⑰ Gozo Archaeological Museum (page 285) Within Victoria's Citadel, this has a few prehistoric displays, though the best finds have been moved to the Ġgantija visitor centre.

ROMAN/BYZANTINE MALTA

The most interesting sites of this period are underground – the late Roman/ Byzantine catacombs that lie beneath several areas of Malta – although there are also a few places to see above ground. All the tomb complexes are referred to as 'catacombs' even though strictly speaking the smaller ones are 'hypogea' (a collection of individual tombs, or those of a single family or guild, rather than of a whole community). They are particularly interesting because they have surviving stone agape tables – the tables at which the funeral feast took place. These are not seen in Rome's catacombs or other continental catacombs (where they were perhaps made of wood). Other stone examples exist in North Africa.

Some sites – including the largest and most impressive – are regularly open to the public; others are opened only on request and with an extra payment to **Heritage Malta** (✆ 22954000; w heritagemalta.org; €20–30/hr to open the sites plus normal entry fees of €5 adult, €3.50 student/senior/child 12–17, €2.50 child 6–12).

The main public catacombs are St Paul's in Rabat, with St Agatha's up the road. St Augustine's Catacombs are only about 100m beyond St Paul's Catacombs but these are a request site. There is one Roman house to visit, and Roman Baths at Għajn Tuffieħa have long been earmarked for restoration but at the time of writing are still closed.

Also see the box text, page 220, for an introduction to Roman burial practices in Malta. For more information on open sites see the page numbers below. Request sites are also listed here.

WHERE TO VISIT *Map, right*
Open to the public
① **St Paul's Catacombs** (page 219) The largest and most accessible; a must-see.

② **St Agatha's Catacombs** (page 222) Large, with frescoes.

③ **Wignacourt Museum Catacombs** (page 218) Originally part of the same catacombs as St Paul's, but accessed from the museum.

④ **Binġemma** (page 237) Always open, hillside tombs.

⑤ **Dingli Cliffs** (page 202) Three punic graves; always open.

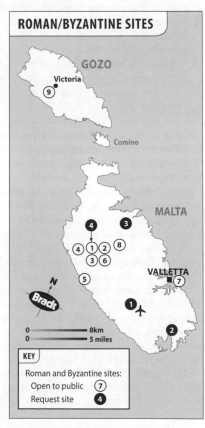

ROMAN/BYZANTINE SITES

KEY
Roman and Byzantine sites:
Open to public ⑦
Request site ④

⑥ **Roman Domus** (page 217) Mosaics and statuary on site of 1st-century house.

⑦ **National Museum of Archaeology, Valletta** (page 122) Galleries devoted to Phoenician times (just pre-dating the Roman period). A Roman gallery is planned.

⑧ **Ta' Bistra Catacombs** (page 233) Extensive catacombs in the side of a ridge in central Malta.

⑨ **Gozo Archaeological Museum** (page 285) A few unusual Roman artefacts.

Request sites

❶ **Tal-Mintna Catacombs** Located beneath Pjazza Tal-Gublew Tad-Djamanti (Diamond Jubilee Square) in Mqabba (near the airport). Under an ordinary, modern street lie these three Roman hypogea (early for Malta, possibly AD4–6). They are small but particularly well preserved. Here are excellent examples of window tombs, scalloped decoration, an exceptionally well-preserved triclinium (agape table), triangular lamp holes and arched and pointed doorways.

❷ **Tas-Silġ** Just northeast of Marsaxlokk is a multi-period site, running from the prehistoric to the medieval via Phoenician, Roman and Byzantine. Tas-Silġ is a modern name taken from the nearby Church of Our Lady of the Snows. It's a very important site for archaeology (excavation is ongoing every summer), but laymen will need an expert to point things out so when booking ask for a well-informed member of Heritage Malta to open it up for you. The most striking feature here is obvious – the red Roman flooring – *opus signinam* – made from crushed pottery and lime and white marble mini tiles.

❸ **San Pawl Milqi** Just west of Burmarrad you will find the sparse remains of a large Roman 'villa' occupied from the 2nd century BC to the 4th century AD, now partly beneath a 17th-century church. Evidence of olive pressing was found here.

❹ **St Augustine's Catacombs** A closely packed maze of canopy tombs and loculi and well-preserved agape tables neighbouring and akin to those in St Paul's Catacombs.

FORTIFICATIONS

For anyone interested in fortifications, Malta is a dream destination, with a tremendous concentration of remarkable fortifications in a very small area. Although the name 'Fortress Malta' came to prominence only during World War II, it applies equally well from the late 16th century onwards. Malta has four dramatically **defended historic capitals**: **Valletta**, a small, fully fortified coastal city; the hilltop Citadels of **Mdina** (the old capital of Malta) and **Gozo**; and **Birgu**, first capital of the 'Knights of Malta', divided (along with its neighbours Senglea and Bormla) from the surrounding countryside by a monumental set of defensive walls (the Santa Margarita and Cottonera lines). Add to these the 19th-century wall that runs the full width of the country (the Victoria Lines) and the system of watchtowers and smaller defensive installations that dot the coast and you have a veritable feast of fortifications.

There are fragments of defensive structures dating back to as early as the Roman and Arab administration of the islands (mainly remnants of Mdina walls), medieval defensive systems (including the street layout of Mdina and parts of Fort St Angelo) and British-built 19th-century installations, including the Victoria Lines, which divide the main island into north and south. But the great majority of fortifications – and by far the most interesting to look at – date from the period of the Knights of St John (1530–1798).

The Fortress Builders: Fortifications Interpretation Centre in Valletta, created by the world expert on Malta's fortifications, Stephen Spiteri, offers an excellent place to start – and to return to. It introduces Fortress Malta in its widest sense and offers as much depth of information as you want (page 136).

THE KNIGHTS' FORTIFICATIONS The Knights were in a semi-permanent state of war with the Ottoman Turks and so in almost constant fear of being attacked and besieged. They very nearly lost the islands in the Great Siege of 1565 (page 12) and were determined thereafter never to come close to defeat again.

The Order of St John drew its members from the aristocracy of Europe and, after the Great Siege, Malta was seen as Christianity's bulwark against Islam. So when fortifications were built here, they were the best and most up to date. Malta's defences were designed by the top military architects in Europe. The Italians dominated the field through the 16th and 17th centuries (Francesco Laparelli da Cortona, for instance, produced the blueprints for Valletta); by the 18th century the top men were from France – like François de Mondion who, in the early part of the century, reshaped (and redecorated) many of Malta's defences, as well as renovating Mdina.

Many of Malta's fortifications make use of its natural landscape, digging down into the bedrock to create defensive ditches, and using the stone quarried there to build upwards. In some places, including the landward fortifications of Valletta and Fort Manoel, a large percentage of the very walls themselves is carved out of bedrock, making them far stronger than anything that could be built. It is worth remembering in this context that the Knights' workmen used no machinery: pickaxe marks can still be seen on the surface of the stone.

The defences were designed not only to be strong but to *look* strong. Stephen Spiteri describes Fort St Elmo – at the entrance to the Grand Harbour – as 'propaganda as well as physical defence'. Fortifications that deterred the enemy and never had to be used were the most successful fortifications of all. Walk, drive or take a boat around Valletta and the deterrent effect is obvious.

The Knights' coastal towers
Fortifying the Grand Harbour and the main cities was all very well, but the rest of the coast needed protection too. From the start of the 17th century, a series of coastal towers were constructed. Thanks to four grand masters – Alof de Wignacourt (1601–22), Jean Paul de Lascaris (1636–57), Martin de Redin (1657–60) and Nicolas Cotoner (1663–80), after whom the towers are often known – Malta had, by the end of the century, an interlinked system of towers right around the coast of the archipelago. These provided both an effective early warning system as well as small-scale physical defence to ward off enemy landings. They communicated by means of flags and fire and if you travel the North Coast Road it is easy to see how it was possible to pass messages from one tower to the next.

These towers remain a feature of the Maltese coast and some have been renovated and opened to the public. The most rewarding to visit are the **Wignacourt Tower**, the **Red Tower**, **Comino Tower** and, on Gozo, the **Dwejra Tower** and **Mġarr ix-Xini Tower**.

Until 1715, the Knights' policy was to place lookouts around the coast but to reserve fighting for its stronger fortresses. In 1715, the strategy changed to trying to repel invaders at the point of landing. This led to the creation of sea walls, redoubts and batteries – a 'one island, one fortress' approach that attempted to secure every bay around the islands. Resources were running short, however, and the project was not completed by the time Napoleon arrived in 1798 and ended the rule of the Knights in Malta.

Spiteri points out that, ironically, all the order's amazing fortifications could not in the end protect it. Napoleon was the catalyst, but the order had lost the confidence of the Maltese population and had run out of money as well as morals. High walls could not defend them from themselves (page 13).

The best book on the Knights' fortifications is *The Art of Fortress Building in Hospitaller Malta* by Stephen C Spiteri (BDL, Malta).

WHERE TO VISIT *Map, right*

① Valletta key sites

- The walls from outside: City Gate and Great Siege Road (pages 114 and 137) and Hastings Gardens (page 136).
- The walls from above: Upper Barrakka Gardens (page 118).
- Walk the walls: walk right round the edge of Valletta (page 114).
- The walls from the water (as the enemy saw them): the Two Harbours Tour (see box, page 114) and Fort St Elmo (page 132).
- Fortifications Interpretation Centre (page 136).
- Fort St Elmo (page 132).

② Three Cities key sites

- Fort St Angelo (page 156).
- Walk the fortifications of Birgu and Senglea (pages 149 and 158).
- Take a look at the Margarita Lines and the Cottonera Lines (page 161 for both).

③ Mdina key sites

- See it from a distance, straight-sided above the surrounding countryside.
- The gates and the walls to either side of the gates (page 210).
- Bastion Square (page 215).

④ Gozo Citadel key sites

- See it from a distance dominating the land around it.
- Walk the walls (page 282).
- The Knights' gunpowder store (page 286).

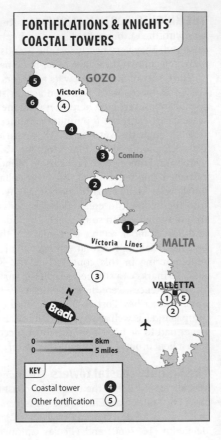

FORTIFICATIONS & KNIGHTS' COASTAL TOWERS

KEY
Coastal tower ④
Other fortification ⑤

Coastal towers key sites The following are all open to the public, but do check opening times as they are mostly opened by volunteers and so may vary. Travel the North Coast Road to see how the towers could communicate along the coast (page 85).

❶ Wignacourt Tower (page 253)
❷ The Red Tower (page 246)
❸ Comino Tower (page 260)
❹ Mġarr ix-Xini Tower, Gozo (page 307)
❺ Dwejra Tower, Gozo (page 289)

Also worth a look, but for now only viewable from the outside, is ❻ Xlendi Tower, Gozo (page 308).

BRITISH FORTIFICATIONS In the 19th century, new technology completely changed what was required of fortifications. Monumental walls were little use against 100-ton guns, and defensive installations became all about weaponry rather than strongholds. It was the guns that now defended the island rather than the walls.

The **Victoria Lines** (see box, page 239) – the 12km barrier built along a natural ridge across the entire width of the main island in 1870–97 – were the last gasp of the old defensive style, and within a few years they fell into disuse. They remain interesting to look at, and the infantry walkway that runs along the top of the walls makes a scenic footpath. The British took over many of the Knights' fortifications, maintaining them to a varying degree, and using them, though not always for the original purpose. The colonial administration also built a few new forts and batteries, mostly for coastal artillery. The best surviving example is ⑨ **Fort Rinella** with its 100-ton gun.

The *Glossary* on page 312 explains key terms you may come across in relation to fortifications. For more on Malta's (and other) fortifications see w militaryarchitecture.com, which is edited by world expert in the field, Stephen Spiteri, who has also written a number of books on the subject.

WORLD WAR II

Malta's greatest moment on the modern world stage was its part in World War II for which the whole country was awarded the George Cross. 'Fortress Malta' hung on through some of the heaviest bombing of the war (by some reckonings, the heaviest) and through siege conditions leading to shortages of food and fuel, to make a genuine difference to the Allied campaign. The **Grand Harbour** was of course the star location. Here, mostly in the Three Cities, British naval vessels were hidden, resupplied and repaired, the wounded were brought ashore and healthy servicemen given a break. And here too 'Operation Pedestal' broke the siege of Malta in August 1942.

Besides the harbour itself, which is best seen from the Upper Barrakka Gardens in Valletta and from the water (see box, page 114), the most interesting World War II sites are listed below.

WHERE TO VISIT *Map, right*
Underground shelters (see box, page 151)

① **Malta at War Museum** (page 149)
In Birgu, the most organised and informative visit to a World War II shelter.
② **Mġarr Shelter** (page 234) The most surprising and personal shelter visit – you may be shown round by a man who was born there.

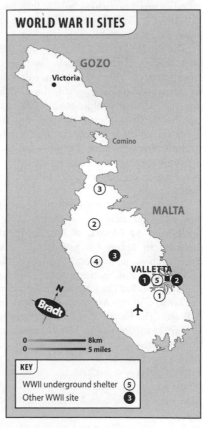

WORLD WAR II SITES

GOZO

Victoria

Comino

MALTA

VALLETTA

Bradt

0 — 8km
0 — 5 miles

KEY
WWII underground shelter ⑤
Other WWII site ❸

③ **Mellieħa Wartime Shelter** (page 245) Extensive shelter under Mellieħa Village.
④ **Wignacourt Museum and Underground Shelter** (page 218) Situated in Rabat, there is a shelter under the museum (as well as a Roman catacomb).
⑤ **Casa Rocca Piccola** (page 131) Regular tours of the house also take you underground to see the first World War II shelter built in Valletta, by the far-sighted grandfather of the present owner. The only World War II shelter in the capital.

Other World War II sites
❶ **Lascaris War Rooms** (page 119) Secret Allied HQ from where the Allies controlled the Mediterranean fleet and the invasion of Sicily.
❷ **National War Museum, Fort St Elmo** (page 132) In Valletta.
❸ **Malta Aviation Museum** (page 233) In Ta' Qali.

CHURCHES

Anyone interested in churches is spoilt for choice in Malta. There are more than 350 of them, ranging in age from the little medieval chapel of Ħal Millieri built in the mid 15th century, to cavernous 20th-century constructions. Yet the majority of Malta's churches, from tiny wayside chapels to lavish cathedrals, were built during the reign of the Catholic Order of St John, the Knights Hospitaller, who ruled here from 1530–1798. A few were built by the order itself, most notably St John's Co-Cathedral in Valletta, but most were the work of the local diocese and often paid for by public subscription.

The Knights' earliest churches and the first chapels of their *langues* (language groups; page 11) were plain, almost brutal in style, often designed, along with the rest of their buildings, by military architects. The advent of the Italian Renaissance left some imprint on church architecture in Malta, but it was the Baroque that became the dominant style, resulting in the many opulent churches still seen today.

The 19th and 20th centuries saw a few churches built in neogothic style, including the **Church of Our Lady of Lourdes** in Mġarr on Gozo, and the construction of several neoclassical buildings, most famously the **Mosta Dome** on Malta, **The Rotunda** in Xewkija on Gozo and the **Anglican cathedral** in Valletta. The most conspicuous attempt at a truly modern style – **St Theresa's** in Birkirkara – is sadly hideous, although **Manikata Church** by Malta's leading contemporary architect, Richard England, is an interesting Modernist take on the design of Malta's Neolithic temples.

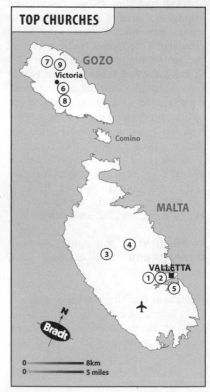

TOP CHURCHES

Some of the most important churches are geared up for tourists, opening throughout the day. Others open only for worship, usually first thing in the morning and in the early evening. Rural chapels are often kept closed except on special occasions. Visitors are always welcome in Malta's churches so long as respect is shown for services, and knees and shoulders are covered. Mass times and contact numbers for each parish can be found at w thechurchinmalta.org/en. For more on the Anglican Church in Malta, see w anglicanmalta.org.

WHERE TO VISIT *Map, opposite*
The top churches for visitors are as follows:

On Malta
① **St John's Co-Cathedral** (page 124) In Valletta, the Knights' main church.
② **Church of St Paul's Shipwreck** (page 139) Celebrating St Paul's miraculous stay on Malta. Also in Valletta.
③ **Mdina Cathedral** (page 213)
④ **Mosta Dome** (page 232) One of the largest domes in Europe.
⑤ **Church of St Lawrence** (page 154) In Birgu, on the site of, and with remnants of, the Knights' first church in Malta.

On Gozo
⑥ **Gozo Cathedral** (page 284)
⑦ **Ta' Pinu** (page 291) Malta's most famous and favourite shrine.
⑧ **The Rotunda** (page 306) In Xewkija – another of Europe's largest domes.
⑨ **Church of St Mary** (page 293) In Żebbuġ; for its onyx interior.

SWIMMING, SNORKELLING AND DIVING

There are some wonderful places to swim in Malta, but the brochures do not always give a very honest impression of what to expect. You may be promised a 'private beach' and find a rocky foreshore. Nothing wrong with swimming from rocks – unless you were expecting to build sandcastles. The following should help you choose where to go and key sites are plotted on the map on page 90.

The main tourist centres of **St Julian's**, **Paceville** and **Sliema** (page 163), as well as **Buġibba** and **Qawra** (page 253) are basically rocky coasts. Many Maltese prefer swimming off rocks because the water is usually clearest here, much clearer than around sandy shores. This makes it ideal for snorkelling, but swimming from rocks may not be so good for young children or those nervous of deep water. **Marsalforn** and **Xlendi** (pages 293 and 308), the two bays where Gozo's tourist accommodation is concentrated, are also rocky, although each has a tiny sandy beach along the head of the bay to complement the long stretches of flat rocks where most people base themselves.

There are several good sandy beaches in Malta. On the main island, the three largest are **Golden Bay**, **Għajn Tuffieħa** and **Mellieħa Bay**. **Golden Bay** (page 239) is dominated by a five-star hotel, but is broad and pleasant. Early and late in the season there is plenty of sand to play on. In summer it can get crowded. Neighbouring red-sand **Għajn Tuffieħa** (page 239) is usually quieter due to the long flight of stone steps leading down to the beach. The longest beach on Malta is on **Mellieħa Bay** (Għadira Bay; page 241). It has a main road running along behind it but offers great sand and sea and plenty of beach facilities and watersports. **St George's Bay** (page 174) at Paceville is sandy due to annual artificial top-ups. This is beach party central and sardine-like on summer weekends. There are also several bays with

4

some sand along the northwestern coast by the Gozo ferry. **Paradise Bay** (page 248) is by far the best of them.

On Gozo, **Ramla Bay** (page 301) is the largest and most popular sandy beach – probably not just Gozo's but Malta's best beach. Easily reached by car or bus, it is backed by protected sand dunes and has two large cafés well tucked away. There are remnants of Knights' fortifications and rocks to explore at either end. Nearby is the usually less populous **San Blas Bay** (page 304), a beautiful red-sandy cove surrounded by cliffs and greenery. If you are looking for **swimming** and snorkelling rather than sand and sunbathing, **Mġarr ix-Xini** (page 307), a long, secluded inlet on the south coast of Gozo, is the perfect spot. It gets a bit more crowded than it used to be – mainly on summer weekends – since main-islanders discovered its fish restaurant and Angelina Jolie filmed here, but it remains a lovely place to swim and snorkel.

Peter's Pool (page 187) on the Delimara Peninsula (near Marsaxlokk on Malta) has insalubrious wider surroundings, but is itself a delightful rocky cove, rarely crowded because it is not on a bus route and is a few minutes' walk from the nearest available parking. If you prefer somewhere less remote, with parking space, people and somewhere to eat, **Għar Lapsi** (page 195) is a popular place to swim on the south coast, close to the temple sites of Mnajdra and Ħaġar Qim.

Malta's most sought-after swimming spot – the target of flocks of tourists each day in summer – is the **Blue Lagoon** (page 259) on the coast of Comino. This is a glorious area of clear blue sea over white sand perfect for swimming and neighbouring a stretch of fish-filled seaweed ideal for snorkelling, all surrounded by picturesque caves. Note that it has little shore and what there is gets horrendously crowded in summer.

There are a number of bays around the islands with rock and concrete shorelines and sometimes a little sand where the Maltese congregate to swim on summer weekends. These places are not always beautiful to look at, but the water is generally clear and inviting. Not necessarily places to seek out, they may be useful swim-stops between sights (sightseeing in summer can get very hot and sweaty!) so they are mentioned in the relevant chapters of the text.

For additional information on swimming and important swimming safety information, see pages 49 and 89.

DIVING Even if you are a very experienced diver, you will need to find a good dive centre, hire equipment and take much more advice than can be provided here. So this is just to give you an idea of some of the more interesting dive sites available, and where they are on the islands.

TOP SWIMMING & SNORKELLING SITES

Ghasri Valley
Dwejra
Marsalforn
Victoria
Xlendi
GOZO
Ramla Bay
San Blas
Ta' Ċenċ
Mġarr ix-Xini
Blue Lagoon
San Niklaw Bay
Comino

Golden Bay
Għajn Tuffieħa Bay

MALTA
VALLETTA

Għar Lapsi

N

Bradt

Peter's Pool

0 ——— 8km
0 ——— 5 miles

You will notice that there is a concentration of good shore dive sites around Gozo. This is a very congenial place to be based while diving, with short travelling times between accommodation, dive centres and dive sites. (More on Gozo diving on page 276.) See also page 70, and importantly, the safety information. The dives listed below can be accessed from the shore unless otherwise stated.

Dive sites *Map, below*

Here is a selection of some of the top dive sites on Malta and Gozo:

① **Dwejra** (page 288) Several key dives attracting more divers than anywhere else on Gozo. Spectacular underwater landscape, plus fish (including grouper and perhaps barracuda), corals and marine flora. The famous **Blue Hole** drops 16m to the seabed where there is a cave and a 'window' letting you look out into the open water of **Dwejra Point** and where the great rock column of the **Azure Window** (page 288) once stood. From the **Inland Sea** you can dive through the 80m tunnel that connects it to the open sea (beware of the shoals of motorboats carrying tourists) emerging through a cliff face falling 40m to the seabed. Other rocks, including **Crocodile Rock** (best accessed by boat) also offer a focus. **Fungus Rock** (always a boat dive) falls 45m to the seabed and is surrounded by boulders where groupers may hide. The rock itself is covered with coloured corals and other marine life. The dives here are mainly deep dives for experienced divers.

② **Xlendi Bay** (page 308) An easily accessed reef, 50m-long underwater tunnel, barracuda, octopuses and moray eels and abundant other fish. The bay is also used for training beginners.

③ **Mġarr ix-Xini** (page 307) Two caves at 10m and 16m and a chance in summer of spotting sea horses.

④ **Fessej Rock** A boat dive: about 400m from the entrance to Mġarr ix-Xini a column rises 15m out of the water and drops some 50m below. The column is full of holes inhabited by corals, tube worms and octopuses and there are plenty of fish passing by.

⑤ **Xatt l-Aħmar** A protected bay with a shallow reef, a drop-off and a couple of caves as well as three deliberately scuttled wrecks at about 45m – **MV Xlendi**, an old Gozo ferry (do not enter); and **MV Karwela** and **MV Cominoland**, 1940s and 1950s passenger ferries once owned by Captain Morgan Cruises.

⑥ **Xwejni Bay near Marsalforn** (page 295) There are several dives here: **Double Arch**, a very unusual double stone arch some 200m offshore (NB: local divers call the entry point for this dive 'the washing machine' – for the very experienced only); **Anchor**

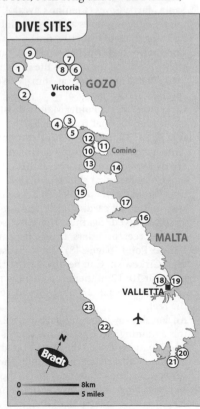

DIVE SITES

Reef, a reef, but no anchor – deep, with possible groupers; **Reqqa Point** with a spectacular drop-off, reef, boulders and lots of fish at depths up to 50m; and in the shallows by the **salt pans** the less experienced can have fun following a maze of channels in 5–7m of water. Beginners can also dive directly into the bay.

⑦ **Billinghurst Cave** (near Marsalforn) A boat dive: 120–130m tunnel with two caverns (maximum depth 27m). Plentiful coloured corals, anemones and sponges but no light after 30m. Torch and experience required. Just outside the cave a P33 patrol boat has been newly scuttled to create a **wreck dive** at a depth of about 40m.

⑧ **Cathedral Cave, Għasri Valley** (Wied il-Għasri) (page 293) Nearly 100 stone steps must be descended to get to the starting point for this dive in a deep ravine. In calm weather only, the Cathedral Cave or Blue Dome dive takes you into a vast cave with a dome (in which it is possible to surface) as big as that of St Paul's Cathedral with luminous blues created by sunlight entering via a crack in the rock.

⑨ **San Dimitri Point (Barracuda Point)** A boat dive: at Gozo's westernmost point with vast boulders creating a remarkable underwater landscape with plenty of wildlife possibly including grouper, barracuda and passing tuna. Can be adapted to varying levels of experience and even snorkellers.

⑩ **Lantern Point Comino** Boat dive: a dramatic and popular dive down a steep drop-off with a reef, chimney (4–18m) and massive boulders (at 30–50m) with plenty of wildlife, which can include groupers, bream, barracuda, moray eels, cuttlefish and octopus.

⑪ **Santa Marija Caves (Comino Caves)** A Comino boat dive: much enjoyed for its interconnecting caves and large numbers of bream that divers feed creating a writhing mass of fish (10–16m).

⑫ **Cominotto Reef (Anchor Reef)** A Comino boat dive: a drop-off and long wall with plenty of marine life in its nooks and crannies. This Anchor Reef actually has an anchor (at 38m), a World War II relic now taken over by sponges and corals.

⑬ **Ċirkewwa (Marfa Point)** Malta's most-dived location has five different dives, but beware of boat traffic including dive boats anchoring. **Ċirkewwa Arch** is at about 12m (seabed 20m), some distance – via a cave – from the shore. Amberjack are sometimes seen here as well as groupers and moray eel. There are two wrecks in the area: at 30m there's *Tugboat Rozi* (at a maximum depth of 34m) which was scuttled in 1992 as an artificial reef and is much dived; likewise *Patrol Boat P29* (38m down). The **Madonna Statue** (at 18m), often surrounded by cardinal fish, and the **Sugar Loaf**, an 8m rock on the seabed, are often dived together. There is also plenty of underwater scenery to explore: reef, boulders, drop-offs, caves, etc, including around **Paradise Bay**.

⑭ **L'Aħrax Point** (page 248) Malta's most northerly point and much less crowded than Ċirkewwa. Can be dived from the shore, but is often a boat dive. The reef is at 10–12m, there is a curving tunnel at 8m, and over the edge depths reach 23–30m. Best dived in the morning when sunlight colours the reef.

⑮ **Anchor Bay** (by Popeye Village; page 246) Depths of 2–12m within the bay make this a training site. Further out, depths fall to 20m. Named after the anchor to which barges moored during the building of Popeye Village, the heavy anchor chain now attracts marine wildlife. There's a cavern at 10m inside which you can surface to admire its domed shape; there's a sunken barge at 20m.

⑯ *Imperial Eagle* A boat dive: about 38m down lies this 45m 1930s British boat that served as a Gozo ferry from the 1950s to the 1970s. Deliberately scuttled in 1999.

⑰ **St Paul's Island** This is where St Paul is thought to have been shipwrecked in AD60. There is nothing of this period, but there is a valley to explore between the two above-sea parts of the island, a reef and the scuttled wreck of a small ferry.

⑱ **X127 *Water Lighter*/Carolita Barge** Built for the Gallipoli campaign in World War I and sunk during World War II, the wreck lies with its bows in 5m and its stern in 22m of water. Interesting to explore, but do not enter.

⑲ **HMS *Maori*** Half a British Navy destroyer, which was involved in Malta convoys in 1941 and 1942. Sunk in 1942 in the Grand Harbour, it was cut in half and moved to deeper water in 1945.

⑳ **Blenheim Bomber** This is the wreck of a British World War II bomber that ditched in the sea after attack by an Italian plane in 1941 (the crew were rescued); it now lies, with wings intact, in 42m of water. An interesting dive beloved of underwater photographers. Experienced divers only.

㉑ **Delimara Point** Two main reefs and plenty of underwater landscape, flora and fauna down to 30m and deeper. Currents can be a problem here.

㉒ **Wied Iż-Żurrieq** The tanker *Um el Faroud*, scuttled here in 1998 to a depth of 38m, is regarded by some as the best wreck dive in Malta. An explosion on board the 110m tanker in the Grand Harbour killed nine dockyard workers to whom there is a brass plaque in the centre of the bridge. There is also a reef near the ship. Experienced divers only. There are two other **reefs** at Wied Iż-Żurrieq with drop-offs, ledges, boulders and, of course, fish. These are considered good night- as well as daytime dive sites. Beware of boats taking tourists to the Blue Grotto (page 197), fishermen's lines and currents.

㉓ **Għar Lapsi** (page 195) There are several dives around this popular summer swimming spot including **Finger Reef**, shaped as you would expect, and **Crib Reef**, home to an almost life-size metal nativity scene (at 22m), both of which lead to a narrow entrance to a substantial cave system.

BIRDWATCHING

As noted in *Chapters 2* and *3* (from pages 25 and 72 respectively), Malta has great potential for birdwatching. This section will give you a more detailed guide to what to look out for and when – as well as highlighting the best spots from which to do it. Please be sure, though, to also read the information on hunting (pages 26 and 50) as anyone birding in Malta, certainly in the autumn, is likely to come across hunters.

MIGRATION BIRDWATCHING IN MALTA *By Ray Vella (BirdLife Malta)*

Situated between Europe and North Africa, Malta is on the migratory route for many species and, being quite small, it acts as a magnet for birds crossing the Mediterranean in both spring and autumn seasons. Some 397 bird species have been recorded, including vagrants from as far away as North America, Africa and Asia.

Spring The first spring migrants sometimes appear as early as **late January**. These are usually house martins and barn swallows already heading north. In February the first marsh harriers can be encountered usually quartering the wheat fields and the airport vicinity (to its south side or even opposite the terminal building), while hoopoes are also quite frequent.

It is in **March**, however, that the migration starts in earnest. Hirundines are passing in good numbers while herons and waders can be spotted feeding and resting at the small wetland areas of Għadira, Salina and Is-Simar, all located in the north of the island. Keep an eye out for falcons, as lesser kestrels are frequent in spring.

Usually around the **full moon phase of March** very good numbers of pintail and garganey, together with ferruginous ducks and northern shovelers, can be seen resting in the Gozo Channel just off the Ċirkewwa ferry terminals. These usually congregate in the sea during the day, waiting for the evening when they then fly off through the channel in flocks, comprising sometimes hundreds of birds. Since hunting in spring has been largely banned, the flocks tend to remain unmolested and can now be seen quite easily from the ferry landing. In some years, upwards of 15,000 birds may pass through the channel.

Around this time, expect to see small numbers of waders, common cranes, slender-billed gulls and glossy ibises, which are found migrating in the same area. Strong northwesterlies also bring large numbers of Scopoli's and Yelkouan shearwaters close to land, the latter already feeding their chicks while the former are just arriving to nest on the western cliffs of the islands.

April is the month that brings the largest number of passerines to the islands, especially with southeasterlies and rainy weather. Turtle doves – although far fewer in number than 30 years ago – are still seen regularly, while golden orioles are encountered frequently feeding in valleys, together with common whitethroats, subalpine, wood and willow warblers. Barn swallows, house martins, red-rumped swallows, as well as common, alpine and pallid swifts can be seen hawking insects in the calm skies during April. In the open areas whinchat and northern wheatears are common. Woodchat shrikes are seen regularly in shrubs and low trees as well as all flycatcher species – including collared, pied, semi-collared and spotted.

A trip to the island of Comino is well worth the effort at this time of the year as it sometimes acts as a bottleneck for many of the passerines, which seem to take cover in every tree and shrub on the island.

In **May** there are still many passerines migrating while small numbers of red-footed falcons and honey-buzzards soar over the hillsides. Waders, especially curlew sandpipers, are frequently seen feeding at Għadira and Salina, together with little and Temminck's stints, and the calls of European bee-eaters overhead herald approaching hotter weather.

Autumn Autumn migration in Malta starts early, with **late June** bringing the first common redshanks already migrating south. While the beaches are packed solid with locals and tourists soaking up the hot rays, waders are already winging their way towards Africa. **July and August** bring wood, common and green sandpipers, while little ringed plovers, ringed plovers, curlew sandpipers and black-winged stilts are all common migrants at the Salina salt pans and Għadira.

Subalpine warblers are already heading south in early August, while hoopoe and common kingfisher arrive throughout the month. By the **end of August** the first marsh, Montagu's and pallid harriers are soaring over Buskett in the afternoons, while large flocks of little egrets and grey, purple and night herons are seen migrating high up in formation.

September at Buskett Gardens (where shooting is not allowed) is highly rewarding for honey-buzzards, ospreys and Eleonora's falcons. The birds can be seen quite close here and the hunting ban in Buskett is mostly obeyed. Occasional poaching unfortunately continues, especially of the larger and rarer birds prized by the poachers for their taxidermy collections. Up to 3,000 birds are usually seen around this time at Buskett. These include almost all species of medium-sized birds of prey. In recent years, lesser spotted eagles have been sighted more regularly, along with black storks.

At least two **Raptor Camps** run during the month of September, one organised by BirdLife Malta (page 78) and another, parallel camp run by Animal Rescue and a German organisation named CABS (Committee Against Bird Slaughter) (w komitee.de/en). These camps keep an eye on the migrating raptors and make sure that any infringements of the law are dealt with by ALE (Administrative Law Enforcement), a specialist unit of the Maltese police.

In **October** the first of the seven finch species migrating south pass through in flocks. These were trapped in huge numbers until the end of 2008; since then a complete ban on finch trapping has come into force following pressure from the European Union. It is hoped that this will bring more birds to winter on the islands and lead to an increase in breeding birds, although the first years may be difficult as some people might not wish to change their habits overnight.

It is in October, too, that vagrants are normally seen. Yellow-browed warblers are spotted annually while red-breasted flycatchers are also regulars. In this period, sea watching can bring some surprises as many species may be encountered, especially on the east coast of the islands. Great crested grebes are sometimes seen in the bays with black-necked grebes. Some numbers of the latter species winter at BirdLife Malta's nature reserves at Għadira and Is-Simar. A few duck species also winter regularly in the reserves, including common shelduck, common pochard, mallard, Eurasian wigeon and pintail.

The wintering species, such as black redstart, meadow pipit, grey and white wagtails, common stonechats and very large numbers of robins, arrive at this time. Song thrush, skylark and golden plover are common at this time of the year, together with woodcock and these are the main target species for the hunters in the autumn season.

There's an interesting roost of white wagtails in Valletta, in front of the Law Courts, which attracts up to 5,000 birds from 17.00 onwards. These may be seen approaching the city from a westerly direction, heading into town to roost in the ficus trees, to shelter from the cold and windy nights which can be typical of Maltese winters.

TOP BIRDWATCHING SITES *Map, page 96*

① **Qammieh** (by the Red Tower; page 247) Coastal garigue, cliffs and clay slopes. Qammieh Point offers views of the channel between Malta and Comino.

② **Għadira Nature Reserve** (page 245)

③ **Ta' Biskra and Cumnija** Typical garigue with cliffs at the coast, next to Għadira Nature Reserve (the part directly around the reserve is a buffer zone where hunting is not allowed).

④ **Is-Simar Nature Reserve** (page 252)

⑤ **Salina** (page 253) Salt pans with degraded marshland (hunting prohibited).

⑥ **Dwejra** (Malta; page 288) and **Binġemma** (page 237) Natural ridge surrounded by fields, garigue and some planted trees. Particularly good for migrating birds of prey September to mid-October.

⑦ **Buskett** (page 201) Mature, semi-natural woodland park (hunting prohibited).

⑧ **Għar Lapsi** (page 195) Coastal cliffs with low vegetation and caves.

⑨ **Comino** (page 257) The whole island is a bird sanctuary (hunting prohibited).

⑩ **Ta' Ċenċ** (page 307) Sheer cliffs topped by typical garigue – privately owned but open to the public. The owners do not allow hunting.

⑪ **Ċirkewwa** (page 92) Near the Gozo ferry.

⑫ **Nadur** (Malta; page 237) High point offering good views of migrating birds of prey in autumn.

⑬ **Dingli Cliffs** (page 202) Cliff-top coastal garigue. Popular with hunters.

⑭ **The Qawra–Għallis–Baħar iċ-Ċagħaq coast** (page 253) Good place for watching seabirds flying along the coast. A telescope is helpful.

⑮ **Delimara Peninsula** (page 187)

⑯ **Ramla Valley** (page 301) Winding valley of terraced fields leading down to Ramla Bay in Gozo. Migrants funnel through the valley.

⑰ **Dwejra** (Gozo; page 288) Coastal garigue, cliffs and Inland Sea. Breeding blue rock thrush and warblers plus migrants including seabirds.

⑱ **Lunzjata Valley** (page 277) Running south from Fontana, here is a reedbed, fields and year-round stream (unusual in Malta). Rarities have been seen here. The land is private, however, and birdwatching has to be done from the road.

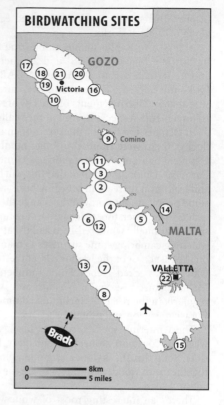

⑲ **Xlendi Valley** (page 308) Inland from Xlendi Bay, this is a deep valley with rocky heights and fertile base.

⑳ **Marsalforn Valley** (page 293) One of Gozo's largest valleys running from the heart of the island down to Marsalforn. Good for migrants during southeasterly, southerly and northeasterly winds.

㉑ **The Gozo Citadel** (page 282) High point from which to watch for migratory birds, especially birds of prey. Also good for blue rock thrush.

㉒ **Valletta** (page 101) A roost of white wagtails gathers in front of the Law Courts.

SPAS

Among Malta's many hotels are a number with spas attached. The hotels listed opposite are all five-star unless otherwise stated and all are also included in the hotel listings, where you will find more general information about them.

Most spas in Malta include treatments aimed specifically at men. Some do not admit children under 16. Note also that many hotels claim to have a spa, but it's worth asking what facilities are actually included; they vary from a couple of treatment rooms with therapists brought in ad hoc to full expert-run spa facilities.

At the time of writing, two established spas – at the Fortina and the Meridien – are closed. The Fortina is due to reopen in 2020 and the Meridien to reopen as a Marriott towards the end of 2019. Also due to open by the end of 2019 are a brand-new spa at the Phoenicia Hotel and the spa of the new Iniala Hotel.

🏠 **Aquamarine Spa & Fitness** [map, page 244] Seabank Hotel & Spa, Marfa Rd, Mellieħa Bay; ☎22891330, 22891000; w dbhotelsresorts.com/dbseabank/the-resort/spa. Beneath the glass-walled indoor swimming pool is a fake cave with sauna & steam room. Treatments offered include massages from sports to Thai, facials, thalasso bath & thinning wraps.

🏠 **Athenaeum Spa** [map, page 224] Corinthia Palace Hotel, De Paul Av, Attard, BZN 9023; ☎21440301; w corinthia.com. See also page 227. In a building of its own in the hotel garden, the Athenaeum Spa offers a very warm indoor pool, steam bath, solarium, sauna garden, gym & comfortable treatment room. A wide range of massages & beauty therapies is available.

🏠 **Fortina Spa** [169 F4] Tigné Seafront, Sliema SLM15; ☎(UK) 0800 917 3001, (Malta) 23462149; w fortinasparesort.com. See also page 165. Once claiming to be 'the largest hotel spa in Europe', the spa as well as the hotel is closed at time of writing. Due to reopen in 2020, it is likely to retain its extensive spa facilities including swimming pools, wet & dry therapy rooms, & a menu of 250 different treatments from around the world: Balinese body scrub to thalasso, Le Stone therapy to Thai massage – & 'Cleopatra's bath' (yes, in asses' milk – well, horses').

🏠 **Le Grand Spa** [map, page 142] Grand Hotel Excelsior, Great Siege Rd, Floriana, FRN 1810; w excelsior.com.mt/thespa. Le Grand Spa direct; ☎23192115. See also page 104. Le Grand Spa next to the terrace overlooking Marsamxett Harbour has a large indoor swimming pool, sauna & steam room, as well as a candlelit maze of treatment rooms offering a variety of beauty & massage therapies – Swedish, Balinese, Thai, deep tissue & aromatherapy. Their signature Maharlika massage is a thorough whole-body mix of all of these therapies plus a bit of reflexology & Indian head massage thrown in.

🏠 **Kempinski San Lawrenz Spa** [map, page 262] Kempinski Hotel, Triq ir-Rokon, San Lawrenz, SLZ 1040, Gozo; ☎22115800; w kempinski-gozo.com. See also page 267. A relaxing & professionally run spa with a very warm indoor swimming pool & many & varied treatments from algae wraps to 'the aphrodisiac'! This spa also boasts of being the only Ayurveda & Marine Cure Centre in the Mediterranean. Ayurvedic treatments are overseen by the resident Indian Ayurvedic doctor & include everything from one-offs to a full 3-week detox programme of treatments & a prescribed Ayurvedic diet cooked up by the hotel kitchens.

🏠 **Lotus Spa** [173 C6] Malta Marriott, 39 Main St, St Julian's, STJ 1017; ☎21370163. See also page 164. The hotel's Lotus Spa (a Myoka spa: w myoka.com) is due to reopen – enlarged – along with the hotel by the end of 2019. A large heated, well-landscaped, indoor swimming pool takes centre stage here. There are a couple of jacuzzis, cold tub, sauna & steam room. Treatment rooms are staffed by well-trained therapists offering a wide range of massages, facials, Ayurvedic treatments, & even facial ultrasound.

🏠 **Myoka Five Senses Spa** [173 C3] The Hilton, Portomaso, St Julian's, PTM 01; ☎21383383, 21386386; w hilton.co.uk/malta, myoka.com. See also page 163. The multi-national team of therapists in this smart spa treat rather than merely relax you (or if necessary instead of relaxing you). Over 80 treatments from hot-stone massage to full-body wraps, algae baths to Botox. There's a couple's duet massage in the same room with its own jacuzzi bath. Downstairs is a steam room & sauna along with a large indoor swimming pool, naturally lit through huge windows.

🏠 **Myoka Spa, Radisson Golden Sands** [map, page 224] Golden Bay MLH 5510; ☎23561000; w radissonblu.com/goldensandsresort-malta/spa. See also page 238. 1,000m² spa & leisure centre. Several swimming pools & plentiful sports facilities accompany the Myoka Spa (w myoka.com), which has glass walls overlooking the bay, wet & dry scented therapy rooms & a wide range of massage & beauty treatments by trained international therapists. From Ayurveda to aromatherapy, lava shell massage to dermal filling.

🏠 **Ta' Ċenċ Hotel Wellness Spa** [map, page 262] Sannat, SNT 9049, Gozo; ☎22191000; w tacenc.com. See also page 267. Swimming pool (part inside, part out), jacuzzi, steam room, sauna & a selection of massages, facials, wraps, peels, pedicures & manicures.

Part Two

THE GUIDE

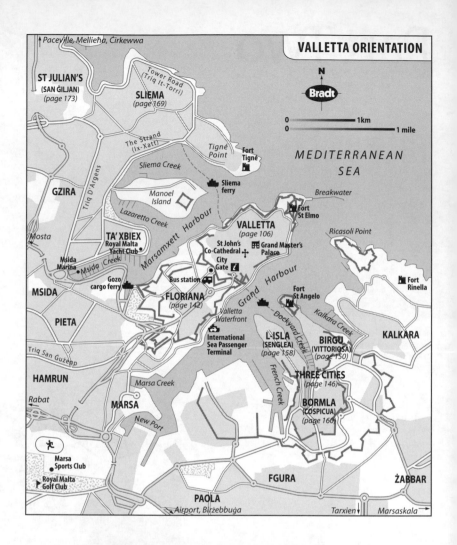

VALLETTA ORIENTATION

N

Bradt

0 ————————— 1km
0 ————————— 1 mile

Paceville, Mellieħa, Ċirkewwa

ST JULIAN'S
(SAN ĠILJAN)
(page 173)

Tower Road
(Triq It-Torri)

SLIEMA
(page 169)

The Strand
(Ix-Xatt)

Tigné
Point

Fort
Tigné

MEDITERRANEAN
SEA

Sliema Creek

Sliema
ferry

Breakwater

Fort
St Elmo

GZIRA

Manoel
Island

Lazaretto Creek

Marsamxett Harbour

VALLETTA
(page 106)

Ricasoli Point

Mosta

TA' XBIEX
Royal Malta
Yacht Club

Triq D'Argens

St John's
Co-Cathedral
City
Gate

Grand Master's
Palace

Msida
Marina

Msida Creek

Bus station

Fort
Rinella

MSIDA

Gozo
cargo ferry

FLORIANA
(page 142)

Grand Harbour

Fort
St Angelo

Kalkara Creek

KALKARA

PIETA

Valletta
Waterfront

Dockyard Creek

Triq San Ġużepp

International
Sea Passenger
Terminal

L-ISLA
(SENGLEA)
(page 158)

BIRGU
(VITTORIOSA)
(page 150)

HAMRUN

Marsa Creek

French Creek

THREE CITIES
(page 146)

Rabat

MARSA

New Port

BORMLA
(COSPICUA)
(page 160)

Marsa
Sports Club

Royal Malta
Golf Club

FGURA

ŻABBAR

PAOLA

Airport, Birżebbuġa

Tarxien

Marsaskala

5

Valletta

Valletta must be the easiest capital city in the world to explore and is probably the most charming. A UNESCO World Heritage Site and European Capital of Culture in 2018, it is just 1,000m by 600m and sits on a peninsula surrounded on three sides by the sea and on the fourth by the suburb of Floriana. On all sides it is enclosed by massive 16th- and 17th-century bastion walls.

Initiated by, and named after, Grand Master of the Order of St John, Jean Parisot de Valette, who led the Knights to victory in the Great Siege of 1565 (page 12), the city was begun in 1566 with the clear intent that it should withstand any future attack by the Ottoman Turks. It was designed by military engineers, the first city since Roman times to be built from scratch on a grid system.

Valletta's main entrance, City Gate, and the area just inside it have received a very 21st-century facelift. Nothing 16th century has been destroyed; a rather scruffy bit of 1960s reconstruction has made way for a controversial but thoughtful redesign by contemporary architect Renzo Piano (creator of the London Shard). Nonetheless, Valletta remains fundamentally the Knights' city. The layout is little changed and many of their buildings – the *auberges* where the Knights lived and worked in their eight *langues* (language groups; see box, page 117), the churches and fortifications, and the Grand Master's Palace – are still standing.

The grid layout makes the city easy to navigate and offers glimpses of bright blue water at many crossroads. The warm limestone of the old buildings is set off by painted wooden *gallariji* (closed balconies) that overhang the narrow streets. Much of Valletta is pedestrianised and even some of the shabbier streets towards the edge of town have real charm.

Republic Street (Triq Ir-Repubblika) runs right down the middle from City Gate at the landward end to Fort St Elmo on the seaward tip. It passes along the brow of the rock (Mount Sceberras/Sciberras) on which the city is built, making it the easiest route to walk, free from the dipping and rising of the streets on the hill's slopes. Republic Street is also the busiest and when a large cruise ship pours out 1,000 people, you may want to escape to a parallel street (a mere 10m or so either side). The hordes rarely venture beyond the main drag.

At one time or another, it is worth taking all the main routes through Valletta (there aren't very many), as well as the diminutive side streets, some of which are little more than a stone staircase. Circling the city just inside the fortifications (sometimes on their top) is also a pleasant and enlightening walk.

Valletta is admittedly not the easiest place for wheelchairs or buggies (though it can be done). For anyone able and willing to walk (even a few hundred metres), though, it is a simple and hugely rewarding place to explore, packed with things to see and do.

For **multi-site tickets** that include Valletta sights, see the box on page 42.

After the 1565 siege, the Knights and the Maltese were seen as heroes across Christian Europe for holding back the Turks. The order had long wanted to build a fortified city on the Mount Sciberras Peninsula (where Valletta now stands) but had not had the money. Now funds flowed in from many Christian quarters and Pope Pius IV sent not only cash but also his favourite military engineer and architect Francesco Laparelli da Cortona. It was he who conceived the design for Valletta and its defences before departing Malta in 1569 leaving the project in the hands of Maltese architect Girolamo Cassar.

The first stone was laid – at the Church of Our Lady of Victory – by Grand Master de Valette on 28 March 1566. He did not live to see his city completed (dying, aged 74, in 1568), but he made sure his connection with the city lived on by officially naming it Humilissima Civitas Valletta – 'The Most Humble City of Valletta'. Needless to say the 'humble' bit was never used!

Much of the work was done by labourers brought over from Sicily (including many Maltese) with promises of good pay, as well as by the order's slaves who served on the galleys in summer and worked on the construction sites in winter. The Knights built fast; they never wanted to leave a fortress unfinished through the summer fighting season in case it was taken, completed and used against them. Initially the architecture was plain, even severe; elegant, but military rather than decorative. The almost omnipresent Baroque embellishments were added later, as were the *gallariji* (painted wooden balconies).

Despite heavy bombing in World War II, a remarkable amount of the original city remains. Valletta was famously described in the 18th or 19th century (though by whom is contested) as 'a city built by gentlemen for gentlemen' and it still has a refined and elegant air. Some areas are faded but an increasing number of historic buildings is being renovated and renewed, both by government and private owners.

The resident population of the capital is small. During World War II, when the Grand Harbour was being heavily bombed, most residents moved out (the wealthy to summer houses in Sliema, the rest to the villages) and many never returned. Until recently Valletta had a thriving working population but emptied at night. This is now changing. Young Maltese, often in the creative industries, as well as foreigners, are moving in and rediscovering the delights of Malta's tiny capital. Valletta is revitalising and, particularly at weekends, now has a nightlife for the first time in decades.

GETTING THERE AND AWAY

BY BUS Valletta is the easiest place to get to and from on Malta. Just outside its main gate (City Gate) is the island's public transport hub – the central bus station [106 B6] with regular buses to and from almost everywhere on the island including the airport and the Gozo ferry terminal. There is an information kiosk too with bus maps and people to help. When travelling to the capital from elsewhere, bus numbers below 100 go to Valletta (but it is always worth checking with the driver).

BY CAR Coming towards Valletta in the morning rush hour (approx 07.00–09.00) can be slow – if it rains it can be very slow indeed. You cannot drive far into Valletta as much of it is pedestrianised. You can, however, get quite close to most places by driving along the main road just outside the walls and into the outer streets. You will almost certainly need to park outside the city. One option is the

CT car park opposite the Phoenicia Hotel; another is to leave the car at the free park and ride car park (Horn Works Ditch/Crown Works Ditch, National Rd, Blata l-Bajda) and take the free minibus. This car park is open 24 hours a day and the bus runs 06.00–01.00.

For a list of car-hire firms operating on the island, see page 60.

BY TAXI The island's official white taxis gather at most of Valletta's entrance/exit points, or you can book a car from one of the private firms that many Maltese themselves use (page 47), asking it to meet you outside the pedestrian zone.

BY WATER Ferries run across the harbours either side of Valletta to Sliema and the Three Cities (✆ 23463862; w vallettaferryservices.com; €1.50/2.80 adult single/return, €0.50/0.90 children). Ferries run every half-hour from about 07.00 until at least 18.00, usually 19.00 on weekdays in winter and 23.30/ midnight in summer. The ferries take 5 minutes to/from Sliema, 10 minutes to the Three Cities. This is much quicker than the half-hour bus ride, and a lot more fun. The Sliema ferry leaves from next to the water polo pool at the bottom of St Mark Street, while the Three Cities ferry goes from Customs House on the Valletta Waterfront at the bottom of the Barrakka lift (which is included in the ticket price).

If you prefer a private boat, **water taxis** using the traditional *dgħajsa* (open, painted, harbour boats) also ply the Grand Harbour between Customs House and the Vittoriosa Waterfront (Three Cities) and will take you straight across for a couple of euros or on a half-hour tour of the Grand Harbour en route (usually €10 pp but agree with the boatman). In the mid 19th century there were more than 1,000 of these boats in the Grand Harbour. They are now down to a handful.

Ferries from Sicily and cruise ships arrive just outside the walls of Valletta, at the Sea Passenger Terminal on **Valletta Waterfront** (technically in Floriana; see page 145 for details). The Barrakka lift (€1) takes you from the waterfront straight up the side of the bastion walls to Valletta's Upper Barrakka Gardens.

GETTING AROUND

The best way to get around Valletta is **on foot**. Should you need wheels, though, there are **Smart Cabs** (m 77414177; e smartcabsmalta@gmail.com; ⊕ until 20.00 in summer, until 19.00 in winter). These little electric taxis, like golf buggies carrying up to three passengers, gather in St John Square and charge €3–5 to take you anywhere within the city walls. There are also **horse-drawn cabs** (*karrozin*) offering tourist transport around the streets. They can usually be found at City Gate, outside the Knights' Infirmary by the Malta Experience and plying the non-pedestrianised streets. Expect to pay perhaps €10 each for a drive around Valletta. Always agree a fare before boarding.

For information on **harbour cruises**, which are a great way to view Valletta's fortifications, see the box on page 114.

TOURIST INFORMATION

Valletta's main tourist information office is in the Auberge d'Italie [106 D5] (Merchants Street; ✆ 22915440/41/42; ⊕ 09.00–17.30 Mon–Sat, 09.00–13.00 Sun & public holidays). Staff here are very well informed and have lots of good maps and leaflets.

VALLETTA AUDIO GUIDE AND PODCASTS An informative 55-minute audio guide can be downloaded from **w** myguide.com.mt for €5 or collected in traditional form (€8) from the National Museum of Archaeology. It comes with an excellent map that guides you around the main buildings of Valletta.

Alternatively, the Malta Tourism Authority has recently produced a series of podcasts covering many aspects of Valletta's history and culture. These can be downloaded free from **w** visitmalta.com/en/podcasts or as mobile apps from **w** visitmalta.com/en/mobile-apps.

🏠 WHERE TO STAY

The accommodation options in Valletta have burgeoned in the last few years with the opening of numerous small boutique hotels, bed-and-breakfasts and self-catering properties, mostly in refurbished historic buildings. There are two large five-star hotels just outside the bastions of the city if you are looking for extensive facilities and full-scale swimming pools. Otherwise there is now plenty on offer inside the city. Given the difficulty of comparing a boutique hotel with a few rooms with a 300-room hotel, the top boutique hotels are listed separately here. All Valletta accommodation is listed alphabetically within each category.

TOP END

🏠 **Grand Hotel Excelsior***** [map, page 142] (429 rooms) Great Siege Rd, Floriana, FRN 1810; ☎21250520; **w** excelsior.com.mt. Large modern business-style hotel right up against the bastion walls of Valletta overlooking Marsamxett Harbour. Expansive public areas (some with psychedelic carpets), spacious rooms, large indoor & outdoor swimming pools, rocky 'beach' for harbour swimming, private yacht marina, car park & huge buffets. See page 97 for spa details. Variable service. €€€€

🏠 **Iniala** [107 E5] (23 rooms) St Barbara Bastion; ☎21661111. Due to open 2019. Splash-out luxury boutique hotel on the most sought-after street in Valletta overlooking the Grand Harbour. Rooftop restaurant, 2 bars, spa, gym, indoor pool, hotel yacht, fabulous harbour-view penthouse suite. €€€€

🏠 **Phoenicia Hotel***** [map, page 142] (136 rooms) The Mall, Floriana, FRN 1478; ☎21225241, 22911024, freephone from UK ☎0800 862 0025; **w** phoeniciamalta.com. Malta's 1st top-flight hotel, built by the British. Still true to its 1930s roots & still Maltese government & British royalty's hotel of choice. Perfect location next to gateway into Valletta & the island's main bus station. Fully refurbished in 2017/18. Free car park, pleasant gardens & lovely heated infinity pool with harbour views beneath Valletta's bastion walls. Spa & indoor pool due to open in 2019. €€€€

🏠 **Rosseli** [107 F4] (25 rooms) 167 Merchants St (cnr St Christopher St); ☎23312345; **w** palazzomerkantimalta.com. A new luxury boutique hotel due to open before the end of 2019. Opposite the Jesuit church that was paid for by the same wealthy Knight as once owned this 17th-century *palazzo*, now modernised with designer rooms in midnight blue & several individually designed suites. Roof terrace with small pool, and own restaurant serving all day. €€€€

LUXURY BOUTIQUE HOTELS

✳ 🏠 **66 Saint Paul** [107 E5] (18 rooms) **w** 66saintpaulsmalta.com. Smart, contemporary boutique hotel in 17th-century limestone *palazzo*. Courtyard with retracting roof. Terrace with small pool, sunbeds & adjoining bar. Wonderful penthouse suite with own terrace & Grand Harbour views. Excellent, imaginative b/fast. €€€

✳ 🏠 **Casa Ellul** [106 D3] (8 rooms) 81 Old Theatre St, VLT 1429; ☎21224821; **w** casaellul. com. Luxury boutique hotel in a historic Valletta house. Large contemporary designer rooms, some with open-plan bathrooms. Several have a *gallarija* or stone balcony over the street. Small but fancy restaurant on the ground floor. €€€€

🏠 **Casa Rocca Piccola** [107 F3] (5 rooms) Inside the family home of the noble Maltese de Piro family (page 131). 4 colourful spacious rooms & 1 suite with handpainted ceilings & doors (by the Marquis's grandson & grand-daughter, descendants of one of Malta's top artists, Giuseppe Calì). Traditional courtyard & little b/fast room with coffee machine & simple b/fast. €€€–€€€€

🏠 **The Coleridge** [107 E3] (6 rooms) 89 Old Bakery St, VLT 1456; ✆20105511; w thecoleridgehotel.com. Elegant antique-furnished luxury boutique hotel in a traditional historic townhouse in the heart of Valletta. 4 suites with at least 2 rooms, except penthouse with harbour-view terrace. €€€

🏠 **Cumberland** [106 D5] (22 rooms) 111 St John St; ✆20165100; w cumberlandhotel.com. Modern boutique hotel just round the corner from St John's Co-Cathedral. Roof terrace with jacuzzi & harbour views. Good 64 Gun Mediterranean restaurant. €€€

🏠 **Domus Zamittello** [106 C5] (21 rooms) 7 Republic St; ✆21227700; w domuszamittello. com. An original 16th-century Valletta *palazzo* lovingly restored by its aristocratic owner. Very traditional but with all mod cons. Superb location, roof terrace overlooking Republic St, parliament & City Gate. Courtyard lounge with retractable roof. Small spa. Restaurant. €€€

🏠 **Palais Le Brun** [107 E3] (28 rooms) 101 Old Bakery St (just St Elmo side of St Christopher St); ✆22260300; w palaislebrun.com. Modern but in very traditional style in a converted 16th-century *palazzo* built for a Grand Master of the Knights, & later the childhood home of Malta's first prime minister. Marble floors, wood panel/neutral walls, tiny limestone courtyard, roof terrace with plunge pool & views of Fort St Elmo. Small fitness room. Patakka Restaurant in the cellar serves b/fast & excellent à la carte dinner daily, lunch at w/ends. €€€

🏠 **Palazzo Consiglia** [107 F4] (13 rooms) 102 St Ursula St, VLT 1234; ✆21244222; w palazzoconsiglia.com. Clever conversion of a historic building into luxury boutique hotel. Covered stone courtyard lounge/bar, roof terrace with plunge pool & cellar mini- spa. Rooms are a modern take on traditional décor. Helpful staff. €€€

🏠 **Palazzo Prince D'Orange** [106 D5] (5 suites) 316 St Paul St, VLT 1211; m 99125200; w palazzoprincemalta.com. Beautifully converted 400-year-old *palazzo* in the heart of Valletta. Luxury self-catering/boutique B&B. Wonderful contemporary b/fast room with terrace overlooking the Grand Harbour. Guests also have use of the brand-new kitchen, roof-terrace

barbecue, & ultra-traditional *palazzo* sitting room (with open fire in winter). Lift to all floors. €€€

🏠 **The Saint John** [107 E4] (21 rooms) 176 Merchants St, VLT 1174; ✆21243243; m 79377190; w thesaintjohnmalta.com. Urban boutique hotel in heart of historic Valletta. Some fun retro design touches, with gastropub & crêperie. €€€€

✳ 🏠 **SU29** [106 D6] (8 rooms) 29 St Ursula St, VLT 1230; ✆21242929; m 99994377; w su29hotel. com. Fun contemporary luxury designer boutique hotel on historic street. Each room unique, from Classic Maltese to Fitness (with boxing bag!). €€€

🏠 **The Vincent** [107 F3] (9 rooms) 84 Hospital St, VLT 1643; ✆21240408; w thevincenthotelmalta. com. Colourful, eclectic, bohemian conversion of a 400-year-old building. Fun design with touches of humour. Rooms all different & include suites & a loft apt. Inner courtyard. €€€

MID-RANGE

🏠 **19 Rooms** [106 D2] (19 rooms) 87 St Christopher St; ✆20106029; m 19rooms.com.mt. From smaller 'modpods' to dbls, duplexes & 2 self-catering apts, this modern mélange of boutique accommodation & self-catering offers croissant & coffee each morning but no actual meals. Modern steel & wood inside typical 300-year-old Valletta limestone. €€€

🏠 **De Vilhena** [106 D3] (22 rooms) 55 Old Theatre St; ✆21242020; w devilhena.com. In the heart of Valletta's small but lively bar-café area, this well-run modern hotel has a pleasant limestone rooftop (& church dome) views & a friendly pizzeria/trattoria at street level. €€€

🏠 **Falconeria** [106 C4] (43 rooms) 62 Melita St; ✆22476600; w lafalconeria.com. This tardis-like hotel crams 43 rooms into an old Valletta building. Modern urban décor. Excellent L'Artiglio restaurant (page 110) on ground floor. €€€

🏠 **Merchant Suites** [107 E4] (19 rooms) 191 Merchants St; ✆21242696; m merchant-suites. valletta.hotels-mt.com/en. Right in the heart of Valletta, almost opposite Is-Suq tal-Belt food hall, 2mins from St John's. Modern hotel tucked into an 18th-century Valletta townhouse. Couple of rooms with own *gallarija*, attractive penthouse suite with jacuzzi on small terrace, but most standard rooms have no window at all & are perhaps a little pricey. €€€

🏠 **The Osborne Hotel***** [106 B4] (60 rooms) 50 South St, VLT 1101; ✆21243656/7,

5

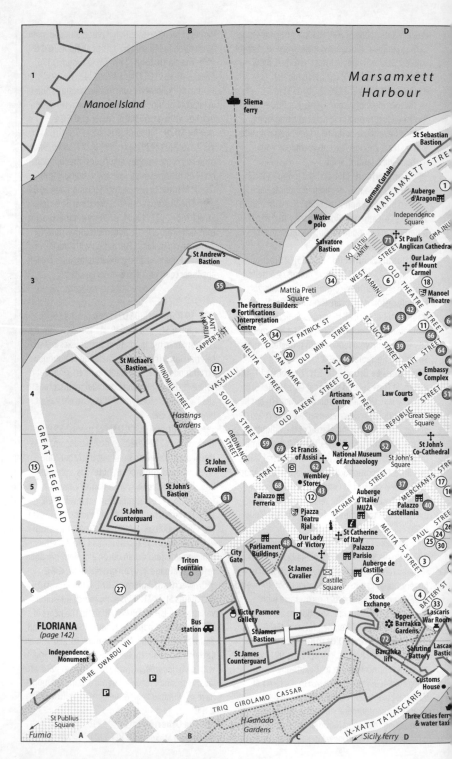

Manoel Island

Marsamxett Harbour

Sliema ferry

German Curtain

MARSAMXETT STREET

St Sebastian Bastion

Water polo

Salvatore Bastion

St Andrew's Bastion

SQ TEATRU L-ANTIK

Auberge d'Aragon (1)

Independence Square

(71) St Paul's Anglican Cathedral

Our Lady of Mount Carmel

GHAJNU

WEST KARMNU

OLD THEATRE STREET

(6)

(18)

Manoel Theatre

Mattia Preti Square

(55)

(34)

The Fortress Builders: Fortifications Interpretation Centre

(34)

TRIQ SAN MARK

ST LUCY STREET

(63) (42)

(54)

(39)

(11) (66)

(64)

SANT'ANDRIJA

SAPPER'S ST

St Michael's Bastion

VASSALLI

(21)

ST PATRICK ST

MELITA STREET

OLD MINT STREET

(20)

ST JOHN STREET

(46)

STRAIT STREET

Embassy Complex

(51)

WINDMILL STREET

Hastings Gardens

SOUTH STREET

(13)

OLD BAKERY STREET

Artisans Centre

Law Courts

Great Siege Square

(4)

ORDINANCE STREET

St John Cavalier

STRAIT ST

(59) (69)

St Francis of Assisi

(70)

(50)

National Museum of Archaeology

(52)

St John's Square

REPUBLIC STREET

St John's Co-Cathedral

GREAT SIEGE ROAD

(15)

(62)

Wembley Stores

Auberge d'Italie/ MUŻA

(37)

MERCHANTS STREET

(17) (10)

St John's Bastion

(61)

(68)

Palazzo Ferreria

(12) (43)

ZACHARY STREET

Palazzo Castellania

(40)

(26)

St John Counterguard

Pjazza Teatru Rjal

St Catherine of Italy

Palazzo Parisio

PAUL STREET

(25) (24) (30)

(3)

St John Cavalier

Our Lady of Victory

Parliament Buildings

(48)

Auberge de Castille

(8)

MELITA ST STREET

Triton Fountain

City Gate

St James Cavalier

Castille Square

Stock Exchange

(4)

BATTERY ST

(33)

Lascaris War Room

FLORIANA (page 142)

(27)

Bus station

Victor Pasmore Gallery

St James Bastion

Upper Barrakka Gardens

(72)

Lascaris

Independence Monument

IR-RE DWARDU VII

St James Counterguard

Barrakka lift

Saluting Battery

Lascaris Bastion

(P)

Customs House

(P)

St Publius Square

TRIQ GIROLAMO CASSAR

H Ganado Gardens

IX-XATT TA'LASCARIS

Three Cities ferry & water taxi

Fumia

Sicily ferry

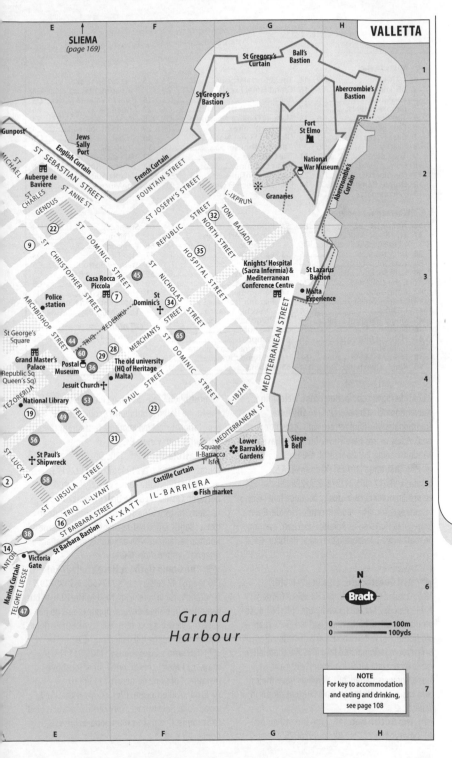

SLIEMA
(page 169)

St Gregory's
Curtain

Ball's
Bastion

St Gregory's
Bastion

Abercrombie's
Bastion

Gunpost

Jews
Sally
Port

English Curtain

ST SEBASTIAN STREET

French Curtain

Fort
St Elmo

National
War Museum

Auberge de
Bavière

ST
MICHAEL

ST
CHARLES

ST ANNE ST

GENDUS

FOUNTAIN STREET

ST JOSEPH'S STREET

L-IXPRUN

Granaries

Abercrombie's
Curtain

22

9

ST DOMINIC STREET

ST CHRISTOPHER STREET

REPUBLIC STREET

NORTH STREET

TONI BAJADA

32

35

HOSPITAL STREET

Knights' Hospital
(Sacra Infermia) &
Mediterranean
Conference Centre

St Lazarus
Bastion

Casa Rocca
Piccola

45

7

ST NICHOLAS STREET

St
Dominic's

34

ST DOMINIC STREET

Malta
Experience

Police
station

ARCHBISHOP STREET

TRIQ FEDERHKU

MERCHANTS STREET

65

MEDITERRANEAN STREET

St George's
Square

44

60

29

28

Grand Master's
Palace

Postal
Museum

36

The old university
(HQ of Heritage
Malta)

ST PAUL STREET

Republic Sq
Queen's Sq)

Jesuit Church

TEZORERIJA

National Library

53

23

L-IBJAR

MEDITERRANEAN ST

19

49

FELIX

56

31

St Paul's
Shipwreck

Square
Il-Barracca
T' Isfel

Lower
Barrakka
Gardens

Siege
Bell

ST LUCY ST

2

58

ST URSULA STREET

TRIQ IL-LVANT

Castille Curtain

IX-XATT IL-BARRIERA

Fish market

38

16

ST BARBARA STREET

St Barbara Bastion

14

ANTON

Victoria
Gate

Marina Curtain

TELGHET LIESSE

47

Grand
Harbour

N

Bradt

0 ———— 100m
0 ———— 100yds

NOTE
For key to accommodation
and eating and drinking,
see page 108

Valletta WHERE TO STAY

5

VALLETTA

For listings, see from page 104

21241854/5; w osbornehotel.com. Welcoming, conventional 3-star hotel close to City Gate. Traditional-style. Roof terrace with little plunge pool. A few rooms have views, but a few have no window or only 1 at floor level. €€

✳🏠 **Ursulino** [107 F5] (7 rooms) 82A St Ursula St, VLT 1234; 🕿21227860, 21228024; w ursulinovalletta.com. Luxury boutique hotel with historic exterior, ultra-modern comfort inside. Rooms from dbl to triplex suite. Aperitifs (inc) each evening on roof terrace overlooking the Grand Harbour. €€€

BUDGET

🏠 **Asti Guesthouse** [106 D6] (9 rooms) 18 St Ursula St, close to Upper Barrakka Gardens; 🕿21239506, 21227483. Run by the elderly, house-proud Mrs Galea. Immaculately clean, 350-year-old traditional Valletta house in a great location. B/fast room is dominated by a massive chandelier made by the late Mr Galea. Rooms are basic & loos & showers shared, but all rooms have their own basin. Usually the cheapest decent rooms in Valletta. €

🏠 **The British Hotel** [106 D6] (40 rooms) 40 Battery St; 🕿21224730; m 99768250;

w britishhotel.com. Stunning location overlooking the Grand Harbour but rooms in dire need of renovation. B/fast in Panorama Restaurant (page 110) with 180° views. €€

🏠 **Castille Hotel**★★★ [106 D6] (38 rooms) Castille Sq; 🕿21243677/8, 21220173; w hotelcastillemalta.com. Perfectly located between Castille Sq & the Upper Barrakka Gardens. Historic atmosphere with rooms rather like a slightly faded old-fashioned English home. Rooftop restaurant with panoramic view, cellar pizzeria & coffee shop. €€

🏠 **The Grand Harbour Hotel**★★ [107 E6] (30 rooms) 47 Battery St; 🕿21246003, 21237197; w grandharbourhotel.com. Next to The British, but recently refurbished. Foyer & public rooms do not have the view but roof terrace & some upper-floor bedrooms have the full panorama. €€

🏠 **Luciano's Guesthouse** [106 D5] (13 rooms) 21 Merchants St, on St John Sq, above restaurant of same name; m 77111110; w lucianovalletta.com. Tiles, plants & coloured woodwork. Roof terrace. Very central location next to St John's. Room sizes from good-value sgls to a duplex for 4. €

SELF-CATERING ACCOMMODATION

🏠 **Barrakka Suites** [106 D6] Battery St; m 99828017, 99471406; w barrakkasuites. com. 4 modern studio apts each sleeping 2–4 in a traditional limestone Valletta house. Great location with views over the Upper Barrakka Gardens. Kitchenette; AC; laundry service; lift from 1st floor up. €–€€

🏠 **Manoel Theatre Apartments** [106 D3] Enter through stage door of Manoel Theatre; 21246389; w teatrumanoel.com.mt. 3 plain modern apts in the Manoel Theatre building. Each has a dbl bedroom, 2 'day beds', TV, phone. Electricity & water on a meter. Inexpensive accommodation in the heart of Valletta. Min 1 week. €

🏠 **Old Mint Street Nos 1, 2 & the Penthouse** (top of no 2) [106 C4] UK: 020 8133 5775 (diverts to Malta); m 77400900; w thehouseinoldmintstreet.com. Stylish ultra-modern interiors in traditional Valletta townhouses, each with 2 bedrooms sleeping a total of 4. €€

🏠 **Palazzo San Pawl Apartments** [106 D6] 318 St Paul St, VLT 1211; m 99331621; w livinginvalletta.com. 4 1-bedroom apts in recently restored Palazzo San Pawl. Old building, modern facilities. Central heating, fans, open walkways. Sofa bed can take up to 2 extra people (extra charge). Min 3-night stay. €€

🏠 **Palazzo Valletta Suites** [106 D5] 314 St Paul St, VLT 1211; m 99434323; w palazzovallettasuites.com. 6 suites in a traditional Valletta home. Narrow balconies around a small plant-filled courtyard. Stylishly homely with a living room & harbour-view roof terrace for all guests. €€

🏠 **Valletta G-House** [107 F2] North St & Republic St; m (call Aldo) 79815145; w vallettahouse.com. Part of a 16th-century house at the rapidly gentrifying residential end of town (plenty of local food shops) & set over 2 levels with stone walls & floors. The apt is airy & cool (if a little dark) with its own *gallarija*, interesting wooden furniture, modern kitchen, low ceilings. Fans, not AC. Shower only 1.8m high. Helpful owner. Guests must be aged 20 or over. €€

🏠 **Valletta Studios** [106 D6] 60A Battery St; 21251748; m 99895827; w vallettastudios. com. 4 studios (1 dbl bed in each), just below the Upper Barrakka Gardens. Wonderful views over the Grand Harbour. Modern interiors. 1 studio has its own wooden *gallarija*, another an open balcony. €–€€

🏠 **Valletta Suites** [106 C3/4] & [107 F3] m 79488047; w vallettasuites.com. 3 self-contained rental properties in historic Valletta houses near St Elmo. Stylishly decorated in a mix of preserved old & designer new. All mod cons (inc Wi-Fi). 1–2 bedroom: Valletta Nobile (a 2nd-floor apt with a *gallarija* overlooking Merchants St), Maison La Vallette (in the Mandragg) & Lucia Nova (on St Lucy St, with its own roof terrace). €€

🏠 **Valletta Vintage** [not mapped] (5 studio apts) various locations in Valletta & 1 in Birgu (HQ 179 Republic St); m 79718083; w vallettavintage. com. Stylish, contemporary studios in houses over a century old, converted & individually designed by well-known Maltese architect Chris Briffa. €€–€€€

✗ WHERE TO EAT AND DRINK

Valletta has some excellent restaurants. Most are in the middle expense brackets and they compare well with other places in Europe in terms of value for money. There are also places – like Trabuxu Wine Bar, No. 43, and the clubs (page 112) – where you can eat well for relatively little. Booking is advisable at most Valletta restaurants.

A new addition to the scene, opened in 2018 is Is-Suq tal-Belt on Merchants Street. Valletta's Victorian covered market has been imaginatively redesigned and turned into a modern food hall with outlets serving a wide range of cuisines (eat in and take-away) – and it's open usefully late at weekends too.

It is also possible to do a **Valletta Food Trail** (21802383; w offbeatmaltafoodtrails. com; €65) run by Restaurants Malta which produces the *Definitively Good Restaurant Guide*. Running 10.00–13.00 most Saturday mornings, the tour covers

Maltese gastronomic history and food today with good-sized tasters of Maltese specialities at each of five stops.

If you need a quick pick-me-up, there are plenty of places for a *pastizzi*, or if you fancy something sweet and different try *imqaret* (see page 64 for more information on both). Apart from **Wembley Stores** and **Is-Suq Tal Belt** (page 113), most of the food shops are towards the St Elmo end of Valletta where more people live. Vans also park in this area selling fresh fruit and vegetables.

The main Valletta **market** is open each morning on Ordnance Street (opposite the open-air theatre/parliament). If you like to cook fish and are an early riser, there is a wholesale **fish market** on the harbourside below the Lower Barrakka Gardens (⊕ approx 04.30–06.30).

RESTAURANTS

✗ **Fumia** [map, page 142] La Vecchia Dogana, Sa Maison Rd, Pietà (a 5min taxi ride from City Gate or walk or bus); ☏21317053; w fumiarestaurant.eu; ⊕ 12.30–14.30 & 19.30–22.30/23.00 Tue–Sun. Excellent food, especially fish. Unpretentiously elegant restaurant in a Knights-period customs house on the edge of Pietà Harbour just outside Valletta. Sit inside by picture windows or out on the terrace. €€€–€€€€

✗ **Ambrosia** [107 E4] 137 Archbishop St; ☏21225923; m 99801348; ⊕ 12.30–14.30 & 19.30–22.00 Mon–Sat. Friendly place on a narrow Valletta side street. Busy at lunchtimes, quieter in the evenings. Great for a winter dinner. Decorated with old wooden dressers & their mirrors. Imaginative, changing, menu of 'Food for the Gods' listed on a large wood-framed blackboard. The Mediterranean & Maltese food is indeed exceptionally flavoursome. No fussy explanations on the menu but plenty of little extras on the plate. €€€

✗ **D'Office** [107 E4] 132 Archbishop St; ☏27221475; m 99441120; w d-officevalletta.com; ⊕11.30–23.30 daily. Excellent Mediterranean dining in the casual interior or out on the street beneath the walls of Grand Master's Palace. Same owner as Rampila. €€€

✗ **Is-Suq Tal-Belt** [107 E4] ☏22103500; w issuqtalbelt.com; ⊕ 09.00–at least 22.00 daily (until midnight Fri & Sat; outlets vary. Valletta's Victorian covered market converted into a stylish contemporary food hall. The ground floor is full of restaurant outlets (several of them well known for their full-scale restaurants elsewhere on the islands), as well as top-quality international coffee, chocolate, ice cream & drinks. There is seating in the middle so you can sit together with friends all eating different cuisines. Choices include fresh fish,

Turkish kebabs, tapas, burgers, pizza & Gululu's award-winning Maltese food. *Prices vary*.

✗ **L'Artiglio** [106 C4] 64 Melita St; ☏22476601; w lartiglio.com.mt; ⊕ noon–14.30 & 19.00–22.30 daily. Excellent female Maltese chef serves up foodie international cuisine in this little modern restaurant next to the Falconeria hotel. Short, constantly changing menu all freshly prepared in the open kitchen. €€€

✗ **La Sfoglia** [107 E4] 67–68 Merchants Street; m 79919966, 99834105; w lasfogliarestaurant.com; ⊕ noon–23.00 daily. Mediterranean/French restaurant run by Maltese brothers. Sit inside, or out in the middle of pedestrianised Merchants St, Valletta's alfresco dining centre. There is plenty of choice on the menu but this place is particularly known for its fish. Try tender calamari & ask about fish of the day. €€€

✳ ✗ **Panorama** [106 D6] 267 St Ursula St (stepped street) or via British Hotel (lift); m 79877980; w panorama.com.mt; ⊕ 12.30–15.00 & 19.00–22.00 daily (until 22.30 Fri–Sun), in summer the bar opens for longer: 17.00–23.00+. Bar & restaurant with, yup, panoramic views of the Grand Harbour. Book in advance for a table on the balcony terrace in warm weather or right by the picture window in winter. Mediterranean cuisine. €€€

✳ ✗ **Rampila** [106 B5] St John Cavalier St; ☏21226625; m 99441120; e info@rampila.com; w rampila.com; ⊕ noon–22.30 daily. Built into a sloping tunnel inside 400-year-old fortifications. Smart but relaxed with excellent Mediterranean food. Atmospheric outside terrace tucked in between the bastion walls. Sunlit by day, floodlit by night, it overlooks the defensive ditch of Valletta & the City Gate. Byzantine hemispheric catapult boulders (found inside the *cavalier*) sit on the terrace, & inside is the 'Traditions & Crafts of Malta' exhibition – a life-size Victorian Valletta street scene with sound effects. €€–€€€

✳ ✘ Guzé [106 C4] 22 Old Bakery St, VLT 1459 (cnr St John St); ☏21239686; w guzevalletta. com; ⏰ 17.45–22.00 Mon–Sat, noon–14.30 Thu–Sat. Lovely family-run Mediterreanean/ European restaurant in cosy old Valletta house, thought once to have been part of the home & workshop of Valletta's main Maltese architect. Food is beautifully presented with taste to match. €€–€€€

✳ ✘ Harbour Club [107 E6] 4/5 Quarry Wharf; ☏21222332; e info@theharbourclubmalta.com; ✚; ⏰ noon–15.00 & 18.30–23.00 Tue–Sat & 11.00–19.00 Sun lunch. Terrace beneath Valletta's bastion walls overlooking the Grand Harbour, & elegant dining room with white linen, glass wall & the remains of a Knights-era shop downstairs. Service is usually excellent, as is the food. Perfectly cooked fish & delectable signature vegetarian dish: asparagus & parmesan millefeuille. €€–€€€

✘ Capistrano [106 D3] 61 Old Bakery St, VLT 1454; ☏21225329; m 99487226; w capistranorestaurant.com; ⏰ noon–15.00 & 18.00–22.00 daily (23.00 at w/ends). Well-cooked traditional Maltese & Italian cuisine in a tiny modern interior done out in natural colours, wood & bamboo. Good puds too. €€

✳ ✘ Legligin [106 D3] 119 St Lucy St/Triq Santa Luċija; ☏21221699; m 79932985; ⏰ around 19.30 onwards Wed–Mon; lunch usually 13.00 onwards Fri. This small, cosy cellar with pillar-box red doors has a gently bohemian feel. Though you are welcome to come in just for the wine (of which there is a great-value selection), it seems a shame when the food is so good. Chris serves a 'Maltese Mezze' (€27.50) using many of his mother's recipes, a magical mystery tour of at least 9 items. He also sells his homemade wine (rough around the edges but earthy & flavoursome) & great homemade limoncello (the best I've had). This place is a favourite of mine – & unusually usefully it's open Sun evenings. €€

✳ ✘ Rubino [106 D3] 53 Old Bakery St/Triq Il-Fran; ☏21224656; m 99493579; w rubinomalta. com; ⏰ 12.30–14.30 Mon–Fri, 19.30–22.30 Tue–Sat, closed for 1 week mid-Aug. A tiny old-fashioned black-&-gold shopfront leads into this charming Valletta favourite. Excellent traditional Maltese & Mediterranean food, including slow-

cooked lamb, cheesy risotto & their traditional *cassata siciliana* (made with real ricotta), which is rightly famous. Intimate, friendly atmosphere. Book in advance. €€

✘ StrEat [106 D4] (often known as the Whisky Bar for its attached bar – see page 113) Strait St near the corner with Old Theatre St; ☏21228347; ✚ StrEat Whisky; ⏰ noon–midnight daily. Bistro in a plain stone cellar & out on the street corner. Serves pasta, burgers, etc & delicious 'home-cured fresh salmon in 10-year-old Talisker whisky'. €€

✘ Trabuxu Bistro [106 C5] 8/9 South St; ☏21220357; e info@trabuxu.com.mt; w trabuxu. com.mt; ⏰ noon–15.00 & 19.00–23.00 Mon–Sat, closed for 1–2 weeks each Aug. Owned by the same couple as Trabuxu Wine Bar (page 112) just around the corner. Friendly restaurant with a few outside tables & a cosy interior with contemporary art (for sale) on the dark red walls. Serves delicious freshly cooked Mediterranean food at reasonable prices. The fresh tuna salad (with slabs of tuna steak) is excellent. €€

✘ Trattoria da Pippo [106 C5] 136 Melita St; ☏21248029; ⏰ 11.30–15.00 Mon–Sat. Cosy, busy, popular lunch-only restaurant just off Republic St. Serves large portions of fresh fish, traditional pasta & other Italian/Sicilian dishes that change daily according to what is fresh on the market. The lobster ravioli is delicious. Booking essential. €€

✘ Ta' Nenu [107 F4] 143 St Dominic St, just off Merchants St; ☏22581535; w nenuthebaker.com; ⏰ 11.00–23.00 Tue–Sat, 11.00–14.30 Sun. This is a popular family restaurant specialising in Maltese pizza (*ftira*; €) & traditional dishes. Walk in across a glass floor looking down on a tableau of the traditional bakery this establishment once was. The *ftira* are cooked in the original 80-year-old oven. Bright modern furnishings. Relaxed & child-friendly. There are even 3 computers with games to keep the children happy while you wait for the cooked-to-order food. €–€€

✘ No. 43 [107 E5] 43 Merchants St; ☏27032294; ✚; ⏰ 08.00–17.00 Mon–Sat. A great lunch spot for salad lovers. Tiny shop-in-the-wall offers pick 'n' mix of 20–30 different salads a day for a few euros per bowl (€1 less to take away). Seats outside on Merchants St. €

✘ Pizzeria Trattoria La Vecchia Taranto [107 E5] St Paul St (opposite the Church of St Paul Shipwreck); ☏21221783; m 79944904; ⏰ noon–

15.00 & 19.00–about 23.30 daily. Best pizzeria in town – & it's really great value too. You walk past the little kitchen (or maybe stop to watch) & up a narrow spiral staircase to the 1st floor to the chequered-tablecloth dining room. Also offers a take-away service. €

✗ Trabuxu Wine Bar [106 C5] 1 Strait St (at the South St end); ☎21223036; w trabuxu.com. mt; ⏰ from 19.00–late Tue–Sun. A small, friendly little wine bar in a traditional 300-year-old stone barrel-vaulted cellar decorated with brass musical instruments & contemporary paintings (for sale). Small blackboard menu of excellent, inexpensive & beautifully presented home-cooked dishes. Over 300 wines, both local & international. €

CLUBS

There are 2 band clubs (page 68) in Valletta that both serve decent inexpensive food. There are also a couple of other clubs.

✗ The Anglo-Maltese League/Club [106 D5] 221 Merchants St. Founded 1935, this club serves a 2-course daily set menu. €

✗ King's Own Band Club [106 D4] 247 Republic St. More a restaurant these days than a traditional band club eatery (though the décor is still the band club). Good fresh fish & other Maltese & Mediterranean dishes. €€

✗ Labour Party Club [106 D5] Republic St. Very male 'Old Labour'. Full-English b/fast to omelette & chips or Maltese mains. English Premier League & Italian Serie A football on TV. €

✗ Restaurant La Vallette & Band Club [106 C5] Occupies the traditional building of the San Pawl band club towards the City Gate end of Republic St. It has snooker tables & a large canteen-style dining room (⏰ 09.00–22.00) serving sandwiches on Maltese bread & ravioli by the dozen. €

CAFÉS & BARS

☕ Café Jubilee [106 D4] 125 St Lucy St (Triq Santa Luċija); ☎21252332; w cafejubilee.com; ⏰ 08.00–01.00 daily (until 03.00 w/ends) food until midnight. Fun café/bar, decorated with old newspapers, adverts & wonky posters, & an upside-down table & chairs on the ceiling. Perfect for an inexpensive drink, snack or meal – b/fast, lunch or supper. Cosy in winter. Free Wi-Fi.

☕ Caffe Cordina [106 D4] 244–5 Republic St (Republic Sq/Queen's Sq); ☎21234385, 21238661; w caffecordina.com; ⏰ 08.00–19.00 Mon–Sat, 08.00–15.00 Sun. A Valletta institution founded in 1837, perfectly located in the heart of the city next to the Grand Master's Palace & just off the city's main square. This is the place to meet & watch the Vallettan world go by over coffee, homemade pastries, large filling (& inexpensive) *pastizzi*, light meals or very good ice cream. Sit outside under the watchful gaze of Queen Victoria & her ever-present pigeons or in the bustling Viennese-style coffee-shop interior.

☕ Charles Grech [106 C5] 10 Republic St; ☎21228848; w charlesgrech.com; ⏰ 08.00–21.00 Mon–Thu (food until 16.30), 08.00–late Fri & Sat. Smart little café at the City Gate end of Republic St. Popular by day & night. Coffees, light lunches, including good salads (at reasonable prices), beer, wine & cocktails. Charles Grech is one of the largest importers of spirits to Malta so there is plenty of choice. Spills out onto Republic St when the shops have closed.

☕ Inspirations [106 C6] St James Cavalier; ☎21241224; w inspirations.com.mt; ⏰ 09.30–20.00 daily & until 23.00 Thu–Sun. Inside St James Cavalier & on a pleasant outside terrace overlooking the new parliament & open-air theatre. Snacks, light meals, wine & smoothies. Also has a bistro attached serving more substantial meals.

☕ Prego [106 C5] 58 South St; ☎21224062. A traditional Maltese coffee bar, little changed since the 1950s, or indeed since its 60s role as literary café to the emerging Maltese literati in newly independent Malta. A place for a coffee & a *pastizzi*.

☕ The Undercroft [106 D3] Under St Paul's Anglican Cathedral, Old Theatre St; ☎27075876; w theundercroftcafe.com; ⏰ 10.00–16.00 Mon–Sat. Opened by Prince Charles in 2017, this daytime café occupies the 16th-century cellar beneath the 20th-century cathedral. Cakes, salads, & English afternoon tea.

☕ Upper Barrakka Kiosk [106 D7] Upper Barrakka Gardens; ⏰ 08.00–19.00 daily. Open-air café serving drinks & snacks inside these iconic gardens atop Valletta's bastion walls.

✳ ♀ Bridge Bar [107 E5] 258 St Ursula St; m 79474227; f; ⏰ claims to be 'always open', actually until about 02.30. Best known for its Fri-night live jazz on the bridge when people settle all over the limestone steps to drink, eat & listen. Great atmosphere. Inexpensive cocktails, wine & beer.

✳ ♀**Café Society** [106 D5] 13 St John St; ☎27137991; **f**; ⊕ 17.30–01.00 Mon–Sat. Friendly little place with a snug at the far end, copper bar & tiled floor. Good music, mixed-age clientele, spills out onto the limestone steps outside. Interesting cocktails.

♀**Gugar Hangout & Bar** [107 F3] 89A Republic St; ☎27032837; **f** gugarmalta; ⊕ 10.00–01.00 Wed–Sat, 18.00–01.00 Tue & Sun. Tiny, trendy, arty & friendly shabby-chic café-bar serving drinks from coffee to beer, dishes (all veggie) from falafel to halva & chocolate balls.

♀**Kingsway** [106 D4] 57 Republic St; ☎20995757; **w** kingswayvalletta.com; ⊕ 08.00–23.00 Mon–Sat. Excellent cocktails & coffee under the arches on Valletta's main drag or in the tiny interior of this new, already popular, bar-café.

♀**Legligin Wine Bar** See page 111.

♀**Monaliza** [106 B3] 222 Great Siege Rd, VLT 1811; ☎21242303; **m** 77382303/05; **w** monaliza. com.mt; **f**; ⊕ noon–02.00 Sun–Thu, noon–04.00 Fri & Sat. A remarkable piece of architecture, this bar is reversibly built into Valletta's bastion walls. Inside it is strikingly modern. The arched glass window looks out on the spires & domes of Valletta while the outside terrace is tucked between the towering fortifications & the road along the harbourside.

♀**The Pub** [107 E4] 136 Archbishop St; ☎21223086; **m** 79052522; ⊕ noon–22.00 Mon–Fri (much later at w/ends). A throwback to the days when the Royal Navy frequented the bars of Valletta. The ceiling of this tiny pub is decorated with Navy flags. BBC News plays on the TV – but the soundtrack is mostly 80s rock. You'd swear tattooed publican Nathan was British but he's Maltese.

♀**Taproom** [106 D3] 53A Old Theatre; ☎27491316; **f**; ⊕ noon–01.00. Trendy café-bar with great cocktails & good food (especially the glazed pork belly). Sit at a small 'private' table or go communal at the big wooden table at the back.

♀**Tico Tico** [106 D3] 61 Strait St, between Old Theatre St & Archbishop St; **m** 99797269; **f**; ⊕ 10.00–late. This quirky little bar was at the forefront of the revival of Strait St (formerly Valletta's red-light district, now trendy rather than seedy). Reflecting on its past as a true Strait St bar, its walls are hung with photos of Strait St's insalubrious heyday, film posters, & a model *gallarija* with women's underwear hung out to dry. Furniture ranges from the plain to glam pink velvet armchairs on the narrow (pedestrian) street outside. Age 21+. Small menu of home-cooked food.

♀**Trabuxu Wine Bar** See page 112.

♀**The Whisky Bar** Details as for StrEat (page 111); ⊕ 12.30–15.00 & 19.00–22.30 Mon–Thu, 12.30–late Fri, 18.00–late Sat. Enjoyably crowded from about 22.00 at w/ends. Around 70 different kinds of whisky, as well as wines, beers & other spirits. Relaxed & friendly, reminiscent of a (good, clean) student bar but with a much greater mix of ages.

SNACKS & SELF-CATERING SUPPLIES

Is-Suq Tal Belt [107 E4] Merchants St; ☎22103500; **w** issuqtalbelt.com; ⊕ 07.00–22.00 daily. Down the escalator, beneath the food hall, are a few deli outlets for local food (fresh cheeses, meat, breads) & a selection of Waitrose products.

Wembley Stores [106 C5] Cnr Republic & South sts; ☎21225147; ⊕ 07.15–19.00 Mon–Fri, 07.45–19.00 Sat, 10.00–13.00 Sun. Upmarket grocers – some basics plus local specialities & treats (both Maltese & imported).

OTHER PRACTICALITIES

The **main post office** [106 C6] is in Castille Square (**w** maltapost.com; ⊕ 08.15–15.45 Mon–Fri, 08.15–12.30 Sat) and there are banks – with ATMs – along Republic Street. Wi-Fi is now common in bars, cafés and restaurants, as well as in accommodation. For arts and entertainment, see page 67.

WHAT TO SEE AND DO

WANDER AND WONDER ✳ Valletta is a lovely place to wander. You will happen upon many of the main sights – *auberges*, churches and museums – as well as historic buildings marked with plaques which, happily for tourists, the Maltese love. Nothing is far away so you can always double back to take in anything you miss. If you are following the text below, be sure not to have your nose too firmly in the book or map. It is worth looking up and around, both at the architecture and to allow for chance encounters: a woman lowering a basket from her *gallarija* for a pint of milk, perhaps, or a silversmith at work by an open door.

If you have time, walk the streets at different hours of the day and you will see at least three different Vallettas. First thing in the morning (around 06.30–08.00) all the church doors are open as people drop in for early Mass, often audible from the street. You can drop in too as long as you are quiet. Small workshops and bakeries are just opening up (and you will notice them, which you may not in the midday bustle) and the market will be setting up too.

In the middle of the day, everyone is out and about, and, of course, the museums, cafés, sights and shops are all open. Evenings are calmer, at least during the week. At weekends a wander through Valletta will find happy people sipping beers and cocktails on pedestrianised streets or lolling on flights of limestone stairs listening to live music.

SEEING THE SIGHTS If you follow the text below it will take you – albeit with a bit of inevitable zigzagging and doubling back – to all the main sites of Valletta, as well as many minor ones. This is just one way of seeing the sights, however, and there are many other ways of walking around Valletta. As Valletta is so small and since opening times vary, you may find yourself viewing things in a different order. The way this is laid out, therefore, is to give a list of sights by type (see box, page 116), each with a map reference and page numbers and then to provide a description and navigation/orientation for each small area before going into more detail about key sites.

CITY GATE AREA City Gate [106 B6] is and always has been Valletta's main entrance. The original Porta San Giorgio was locked each night and the drawbridge over the (still present) deep defensive ditch was raised. However, the 16th-century gate is long

---

VALLETTA'S FORTIFICATIONS FROM THE INVADER'S POINT OF VIEW

To see Valletta's fortifications in their full glory – as they would have been seen by a potential invader – you need to be outside the city. Walk from City Gate down **Great Siege Road** and turn right into the ditch in front of St Michael's Bastion. You'll be left in no doubt about the difficulty of scaling these walls.

To see the whole of the city walls, follow the road all the way round Valletta. This can be walked (though it is quite a main road) or driven, or you can take bus 133, which does the full circuit.

HARBOUR CRUISES ✳ The other great way to see Valletta's bastions and its harbours is from the water. Tours of the Grand Harbour and the creeks of the Three Cities in a *dgħajsa*, a traditional harbour boat, can be arranged by just turning up at Customs House and hiring a water taxi (usually €10 pp for a half-hour tour but agree with the boatman before setting off). An old-fashioned pair of Venetian-style oars is still used to manoeuvre the *dgħajsa* into and away from land, while an engine speeds things up around the harbour.

These boats are, however, too small to take outside the harbour so if you want to cruise both the Grand Harbour and Marsamxett Harbour, you need a tourist boat. Two-harbour cruises start from Sliema (page 103), which is just a cheap, 5-minute ferry ride from Valletta.

gone. Until very recently the gate was a 1960s replacement with no architectural merit (even in its time) and the area inside the gate was a mess of 1960s construction, car parking and the bombed-out ruins of the National Opera House.

This all changed with the arrival of an ambitious redesign by Italian architect **Renzo Piano** (creator of the London Shard). He has taken the bridge back to its 1633 proportions and created a new gate – a towering entranceway that locals complain is not a gate because it cannot be shut. This was actually part of Piano's thinking; that Valletta now wished to welcome visitors rather than keep them out. The bastion walls themselves are unchanged except for much-needed restoration and conservation. Just inside the entrance, to either side, two broad limestone stairways lead up onto the fortifications, providing access not available for decades.

In the square inside City Gate Piano has designed Malta's first purpose-built **parliament**, inaugurated in 2015. It is an ultra-modern building, but look carefully at the texture of the walls outside the gate then at the geometric pattern of the parliament's façade (made from the same local stone) and you will see that he was very aware of the building's setting. It is controversial of course. Some locals refer to the building dismissively as 'the cheese-grater' or 'the pigeon roost' and a proportion of them resent the €80 million it cost. However, even some of its critics are coming round now that it has been in use for a while. The parliament stands on stilts so that there remains a piazza beneath it. Open space has also been created on the other side of the square at the top of Zacchary Street where there now stands a statue of Grand Master de Valette, the city's founder (until now without a public likeness).

Between the parliament and Zachary Street lies the **Pjazza Teatru Rjal** [106 C5] (Royal Piazza Theatre; ✆ 21223366; w pjazzateatrurjal.com), usually referred to just as the Open-Air Theatre (though there is a move afoot to roof it) or The Opera House. This last name comes from the fact that the theatre has been built inside the ruins of Valletta's much-loved **Royal Opera House**. Designed by Edward Middleton Barry (architect of the Royal Opera House, Covent Garden), it was built in 1866 but irreparably damaged by German bombing in 1942. Something of a national icon, nobody could bear to tear it down; nor could they agree what to do with it. So it sat ruined and untouched for nearly 60 years until the current redevelopment. Renzo Piano has created a modern open-air performance space within the ruins. Entry is through what remains of the original opera house façade while remnants of neoclassical columns fringe the building. The theatre operates from about May to October with performances from orchestral concerts to plays, bands to opera, and often free events too.

Castille Square (Misraħ Kastilja)/Pjazza Kastilja [106 C6] If you turn right after the parliament and walk up South Street/Triq Nofs In-Nhar you will come to **Castille Square,** which can also be reached directly from outside Valletta, including by car. The square has just been completely renovated and resurfaced, limiting cars to a single route and opening it up to pedestrians. Just before you enter the square you will have the small, but historically important, **Church of Our Lady of Victory** on your right, and on your left, the main church of the Italian Knights of St John, the **Church of St Catherine of Italy.**

Along the city side of the square (on your left as you enter from the direction of the open-air theatre) is the **Auberge de Castille**, while along the side closest to City Gate are the main **post office** and the entrance to **St James Cavalier**. On the other side is the former British garrison church, now the Malta Stock Exchange, and to its left just beyond the square is the entrance to the **Upper Barrakka Gardens**.

CHURCHES AND CATHEDRALS
Church of Our Lady of Victory [106 C6] See below.
Church of St Catherine of Italy [106 C5] See opposite.
Church of St Francis of Assisi [106 C5] Page 122.
Church of St Paul's Shipwreck [107 E5] Page 139.
Old Jesuit church [107 E4] Page 140.
Sanctuary Basilica of Our Lady of Mount Carmel [106 D3] Page 135.
St Dominic's Basilica [107 F3] Page 121.
St John's Co-Cathedral [106 D5] Page 124.
St Paul's Anglican Cathedral [106 D3] Page 135.

MUSEUMS AND GALLERIES
The Fortress Builders – Fortifications Interpretation Centre [106 B3] Page 136.
Malta Postal Museum [107 E4] Page 130.
National Museum of Archaeology and the Auberge de Provence [106 C5] Page 122.
MUŻA – National Museum of Fine Art [106 D5] Page 121.
National War Museum [107 G2] Page 133.
St John's Co-Cathedral Museum [106 D5] Page 127.
Victor Pasmore Gallery [106 B6] Page 118.

PARKS AND GARDENS
Hastings Gardens [106 B4] Page 136.
Lower Barrakka Gardens [107 G5] Page 138.
Upper Barrakka Gardens [106 D6] Page 118.

OTHER PLACES OF INTEREST
Casa Rocca Piccola [107 F3] Page 131.
Fort St Elmo [107 G2] Page 132.
Grand Master's Palace [107 E4] Page 128.
Knights' *auberges* See box, page 153.
Lascaris War Rooms [106 D6] Page 119.
Manoel Theatre [106 D3] Page 135.
National Library/Biblioteca [107 E4] Page 127.
Sacra Infermeria – the Knights' Hospital [107 G3] Page 138.
St James Cavalier [106 C6] Page 118.
The Malta Experience [107 G3] Page 138.

If you follow **Girolamo Cassar Street** away from Castille Square, a little track on the right leads down through the bastion walls to Malta's Central Bank Annexe and the small **Victor Pasmore Gallery**. This can also be reached via a narrow pedestrian tunnel by the kiosks between City Gate and the bus station.

Church of Our Lady of Victory [106 C6] (↖ Din L'Art Ħelwa, Malta's National Trust; ✎ 21225952, 21220358; w ourladyofvictory.org.mt; ⊕ by volunteers, usually 09.00–16.00 Mon–Fri, but may vary) This delightful, peaceful little chapel was the very first public building in Valletta – dedicated in thanks for the newly won victory in the Great Siege. Built in 1566 to the design of Girolamo Cassar it served as the Knights' church until the completion of St John's in 1577. This chapel was also the

above   Colourful wooden *luzzus*, traditional Maltese fishing boats, gather in the harbour at Marsaxlokk, Malta's main fishing village (SS) page 185

right   *Pastizzi*, Malta's most popular traditional snack, come filled with local cheese or peas (VM) page 64

below left   A traditional game, *bocci* is a close relative of boules or bowls, but the Maltese versions are played a little differently (GL) page 305

below right   Lacemaking became established in Malta in the 16th and 17th centuries, with designs often featuring the Maltese cross (JR) pages 32 & 274

above The Roman Domus in Rabat is the best preserved of Malta's Roman dwellings, and contains some 1st-century AD statuary (MG/VM) page 217

above right St Agatha's Catacombs contain colourful frescoes and a number of different tomb types (MG/VM) page 222

right On the Marfa Peninsula, the Red Tower was built by the Knights to defend the Straits of Comino; from the top there are excellent views over northern Malta and across to Gozo (PV/VM) page 246

below The British first built the Victoria Lines across the entire width of the island to defend against potential invasion from the north (SS) page 239

above left Small shrines in niches embedded in house walls can be seen all over the country (JR)

above right Malta's oldest fortress, Fort St Angelo, is a microcosm of Maltese history (JR) page 156

left & below Mdina's labyrinthine alleyways, fortified walls and medieval monuments make it ideal for exploring on foot or by horse-drawn carriage (CV/VM and MG/VM) page 207

above   St Julian's is one of Malta's modern resort towns, with abundant waterside restaurants, bars and clubs (VM) page 171

right   The Mosta Dome (Church of Santa Marija Assunta) has arguably the third largest unsupported church dome in Europe (ZGP/S) page 232

below   The attractive little town of Mellieħa perches high above Malta's longest sandy beach (IM/S) page 241

above   During Notte Bianca, which takes place every autumn in Valletta, historical buildings and museums stay open into the night and streets are filled with food stalls and performances (VM) page 37

below   Malta's many Baroque churches feature gilded carvings that require intensive upkeep (GM/VM) page 88

above A Maltese *festa* is a joyful occasion complete with impressive fireworks. Lija has traditionally held the crown for the best displays, but competition is fierce (VM) page 33

below Every parish has a band which plays for the annual *festa* — and, of course, always better than the band from the next village! (GL) page 34

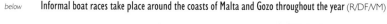

above left Kayaking around the coast of Gozo is a great way to see the landscape Edward Lear described as 'pomskizillious and gromphiberous' (VM) page 74

above right Gozo is popular with sports enthusiasts and offers a range of activities, including rock climbing (MK/VM) page 74

below Informal boat races take place around the coasts of Malta and Gozo throughout the year (R/DF/VM)

first burial place of Grand Master de Valette, until his body was moved to the crypt of St John's (now the Co-Cathedral). The recently restored interior paintings by Alessio Erardi and the Baroque façade, including the bust of Pope Innocent XI (1676–89) above the door, are 18th-century additions.

Church of St Catherine of Italy [106 C5] (⊕ 08.30–12.15 Mon–Sat, Mass in Italian 11.00 Sun) Recently refurbished, this is the 16th-century work of Girolamo Cassar, with a Baroque façade added in the early 18th century. The octagonal interior has a dome, luminously painted. There is a fine altarpiece by Mattia Preti (1613–99), the distinguished Italian artist who spent four decades in Malta and is represented in many of its main churches (see box, page 126). This was the Church of the Italian *langue* of the Knights and was originally attached to the Auberge d'Italie behind it on Merchants Street (page 120).

Auberge de Castille [106 D6] (Castille Sq (Pjazza Kastilja), only visible from the outside except on Notte Bianca; w nottebiancamalta.com) Now the office of the prime minister, the Auberge de Castille with its cannons, broad steps and imposing Baroque stone façade testifies to the power of this *langue* of the Spanish and Portuguese. The

---

THE KNIGHTS, *LANGUES* AND THEIR *AUBERGES*

The order was divided into eight *langues* (literally 'tongues') within which the Knights lived and worked with others who spoke the same language. Each *langue* took responsibility for certain areas of administration and defence. The Italian-, German- and English-speaking knights had one *langue* each. There were two from what is now Spain: Aragon, which included Catalonia and Navarre; and Castile, which shared its *langue* with Portugal. What is now France was divided into three: Provence, France and Auvergne (central-eastern modern France). Traditionally named in French, each *langue* had its own *auberge* (usually translated as 'hostel', but perhaps more like a university college) and many of these buildings remain. The earliest are in Birgu, where they are mostly concentrated into a small defensible area of town known as the Collachio. The later (post-1570) *auberges* in Valletta – where the defensive walls go all around the city – are much more spread out.

THE VALLETTA *AUBERGES*
Auberge d'Aragon [106 D2] On Independence Sq, this is now the Ministry of Justice (page 134).
Auberge d'Auvergne [106 D4] Destroyed in World War II, this *auberge* stood where you now see the law courts in Great Siege Sq.
Auberge de Castille [106 D6] In Castille Sq, now the prime minister's office (see above).
Auberge d'Italie [106 D5] On Merchants St, now home to the new national art museum, MUŻA, & Valletta's main tourist information office (page 121).
Auberge de Provence [106 C5] Situated on Republic St, now the National Museum of Archaeology (page 122).
English None after Birgu until 1783 when the English joined with Bavaria in a shared *auberge* (the Auberge de Bavière [107 E2]), now government offices (page 137).
French Destroyed by World War II bombing, it was on the corner of South St & Bakery St where the General Workers Union now stands.
German Demolished to make way for the Anglican cathedral.

Valletta WHAT TO SEE AND DO

5

main doorway is topped with a bust of Portuguese grand master Manoel Pinto de Fonseca (grand master from 1741 to 1773) – who was responsible for the Baroque embellishment of the building – and surrounded by symbolic stonework and coats of arms. This site (at the high point of Valletta) was originally intended for the palace of the grand master, but Grand Master Pietro de Ponte (who succeeded de Valette) became impatient to move to Valletta and so took over a house in the centre of the city, later extended into the Grand Master's Palace we see today.

St James Cavalier [106 C6] (Castille Sq; ☎21223200; w sjcav.org) This most solid of buildings formed a major part of Valletta's original landward defences. Along with its twin – St John Cavalier, the other side of City Gate – it was designed by Francesco Laparelli da Cortona. The *cavaliers* were raised gun emplacements that guarded the city's main entrance and, should the enemy somehow get in, also had guns that could shoot down into the town. Walk around the outside to get a feel for the strength of the building. This was built just after the Great Siege and the Knights were not taking any chances.

When the British arrived, the building became first an officers' mess, then a water tower fed from the Wignacourt Aqueduct and finally the forces' shop, the NAAFI. The building has now been imaginatively converted by Maltese architect Richard England into the **Centre for Creativity**, focusing on contemporary arts. You enter up a long stone stairway in an original limestone tunnel (well floodlit) to find an art-house cinema, a theatre and plenty of exhibition space – including stone-vaulted galleries and a central cylinder (once a water cistern) with a cylindrical lift to match. It is a great space with regularly changing art to view. The **Inspirations Café**, with a stone-vaulted ceiling inside and a stone terrace outside, is pleasant and reasonably priced (page 112).

Victor Pasmore Gallery [106 B6] (Central Bank Annexe, St James Counterguard; w centralbankmalta.org/victor-pasmore-gallery; ⊕ 11.00–15.00 Tue, Thu, Fri; admission free) Victor Pasmore, one of the UK's leading abstract artists, and his wife Wendy, bought a house in Gudja, southern Malta (near the airport) in 1965. They spent more and more time at the house until they were living there almost full-time. He died in Malta in 1998. This small, modern, air-conditioned gallery has 11 of the works he created in Malta.

UPPER BARRAKKA GARDENS, THE GRAND HARBOUR AND THE SALUTING BATTERY (⊕ 07.00–22.00 daily) Just off Castille Square on the opposite side from City Gate is the Upper Barrakka Gardens [106 D6]. This arcaded public garden stands at Valletta's highest point, offering stunning panoramic views of the Grand Harbour and the Three Cities. It is also the setting for the daily firing of the noonday gun – accompanied by rousing British military music.

At the Floriana end of the gardens you get a vertiginous sense of the strength of Valletta's defences, even though the view is now partly blocked by a modern outdoor lift – built in the same place as an earlier one – that joins the gardens to sea level at Lascaris Wharf, between the Valletta Waterfront and Customs House. The waterfront has been developed from the Knights' old warehouses into the landing stage for cruise ships and in the warehouses are now bars, restaurants and souvenir shops. Customs House is the departure and arrival point for the Three Cities ferry and water taxis (page 103).

Looking straight out from the main wall of the Upper Barrakka Gardens, you can take in the full sweep of the Grand Harbour. It is primarily this harbour and its natural hidden creeks that have made Malta so attractive to any power that wished to control the Mediterranean, and so have dictated Malta's history.

From the breakwater (built in 1903) at the harbour mouth and Fort Ricasoli [147 F2] guarding the entrance (opposite Fort St Elmo), moving right you see several peninsulas: Kalkara (not part of the Three Cities but part of the same district) dominated from here by Bighi Hospital, a grand old British-era building, now offices; Vittoriosa/Birgu with Fort St Angelo on its tip; then Senglea/Isla, with Cospicua/Bormla at the head of the creek.

High up here on the bastion walls, there is usually a breeze freshening the gardens' walkways, flower beds and fountain. Built in 1661 (to the design of Italian knight Flaminio Balbiani) the arcades were once roofed. The story goes that Spanish grand master Ximenes de Texada (1773–75) suspected shady goings on and ordered that the roofs be removed.

There is a little snack bar with tables out in the gardens.

Monuments The gardens are dotted with monuments, mostly to Maltese and British military men – including Churchill and Battle of Trafalgar hero Sir Thomas Fremantle – along with others, bizarrely including Albert Einstein, who has no link with Malta other than the admiration of a Maltese influential and wealthy enough to commission the memorial!

Taking centre stage is **Lord Strickland** (1861–1940), an Anglo-Maltese politician, UK peer and Malta's fourth prime minister. At the landward side stands the Malta Stock Exchange and in front of it a statue of painter **Giuseppe Calì** (1846–1930) whose work features in many of Malta's churches. Finally, the sculpture, *Les Gavroches* (*The Urchins*), is by Antonio Sciortino (1879–1947), Malta's most famous modern sculptor. This is in fact a copy; the original is in the national art museum (MUŻA).

Saluting Battery [106 D7] (✆ 21800992, 21803091; w salutingbattery.com; ⏰ 10.00–17.00 Mon–Sat. Cannon firings at noon & 16.00; view from the gardens for free or go in & take an audio guide for €3 adults, €1 children) Directly beneath the public gardens and visible from them, is the Saluting Battery, reached by steps down in front of the fountain. The battery, its guns overlooking the Grand Harbour, was part of Valletta's original defences and the terrace would at first have held bronze cannon firing stone cannonballs. The battery was in continuous use (with 21 different kinds of cannon over the years) until 1960, although in its last 100 years its use was primarily ceremonial.

The battery also acted as the city clock. It fired at sunrise, noon and sunset, signalling the opening and closing of the gates of this fortified city as well as the start and end of the military day (reveille and retreat). From the second half of the 18th century, the noon gun provided the all-important marker by which ships set their chronometers (crucial for navigation).

The battery now consists of eight renovated two-ton 1807 British cannons looked after by an NGO, Fondazzjoni Wirt Artna. **Guided tours** in English – with great detail about the weaponry – are available for the enthusiast or just turn up at 11.45 for a short briefing through loudspeakers before the noon salute.

Lascaris War Rooms ✳ [106 D6] (Lascaris Bastion, almost beneath the Upper Barrakka Gardens – enter via Saluting Battery or go down Battery St to the left of the entrance to the gardens then right down steps signed to the war rooms; run by Fondazzjoni Wirt Artna; ✆ 21234717; w lascariswarrooms.com; ⏰ 10.00–17.00

Mon–Sat; €10 adults, €5 children under 16, inc audio guide &/or guided tour) Dug deep into the rock under the Upper Barrakka Gardens and the Saluting Battery lies the once-secret World War II control centre of the British and Allied Mediterranean forces. Officially called the Lascaris War Rooms it was known to troops as 'The Hole'. Named after French grand master Jean Paul de Lascaris Castellar (1636–57), the tunnels were originally built by the Knights as living quarters for their galley slaves. These dank corridors became the nerve centre of successful campaigns to disrupt the Axis powers in North Africa and to invade Sicily, achieving the surrender of Italy. They were also an important listening post for military intelligence.

The services had begun the war in a range of locations from Fort St Angelo to the Auberge de Castille, but these all became too dangerous once serious bombing got underway and they withdrew to the depths of the Lascaris Bastion. There are bunk rooms and mess rooms and, most interestingly, operations rooms for the army, navy and air force. Vast maps, plotting tables and ancient communications equipment give a real sense of the work that went on here. Overlooking one of the map rooms is a little room once part of the office of General Dwight Eisenhower (Supreme Commander of the Allied forces in the Mediterranean). From here he directed the invasion of Sicily.

MERCHANTS STREET (TRIQ IL-MERKANTI) [106 D5] (Back on the City Gate side of Castille Sq, Merchants St leads off into the city) Although Republic Street is Valletta's backbone, Merchants Street also runs almost the entire length of town from the Church of St Catherine of Italy and the **Auberge d'Italie** to the edge of Fort St Elmo. It is a pleasant place to walk with little trees, benches to sit on and plenty of cafés and restaurants.

Merchants Street is one of the few roads in Valletta to retain the name given to it by Napoleon in 1798 (though he said it in French, of course) in his mass renaming of Valletta's streets. For most of his few days in Malta he stayed here, opposite the Auberge d'Italie at **Palazzo Parisio** [106 C6], now the foreign ministry (not to be confused with Palazzo Parisio in Naxxar, which belonged to the same family). When offices are open you can see into the central courtyard; the interior is only open to the public during Notte Bianca each autumn (w nottebianca.com).

A little further down Merchants Street is **Palazzo Castellania** [106 D5] (1760) once the Law Courts of the Order of St John – hence the allegorical figures of Justice, Truth and Fame on its façade. It is now the Ministry for Health.

Where Old Theatre Street crosses Merchants Street, is Valletta's Victorian **covered market** (Is-Suq Tal Belt) [107 E4] now converted into a contemporary food hall with restaurant outlets and shops. The daily morning market is now held on Ordnance Street.

On the corner of St Dominic Street is **St Dominic's Basilica** [107 F3], originally built in 1571 and dedicated to the Madonna of Porto Salvo ('safe haven') by whose name it is often still known. The church was made the mother church of Valletta by Pope Pius V (1566–72), infuriating the other monastic orders. It is still Valletta's largest parish. The present richly decorated building dates from 1815 and contains a 17th-century wooden polychrome statue of St Dominic that is a fine example of the genre. In Holy Week, the church's oratory is turned into a tableau of the Last Supper.

MUŻA and the Auberge d'Italie [106 D5] (Merchants St; ☎ 22915000) The
Auberge d'Italie on Merchants Street, with a British red letterbox just outside, was built in 1574, and enlarged in 1683. The bust above the door is of Italian grand master Gregorio Carafa (1680–90). Italy was responsible for the Knights' ships and their leader was always the Admiral of the Fleet. In the former meeting room of the Order's Congregation of the Galleys (the fleet's ruling body) there is an inscription dating to 1655. The text is in praise of Carafa for leading seven Maltese galleys that helped Venice to victory in the Battle of the Dardanelles. It states proudly that he took 360 Turks as slaves and rescued 2,600 Christians. The *auberge* centres on a courtyard] – newly open to the public – with a Knights-period triumphal arch at its heart.

At the time of writing, Malta's new national art museum, MUŻA (w muza. heritagemalta.org; ⊕ 09.00–17.00, last entry 16.30; admission €7 adults), is just about to open in the *auberge*. MUŻA is both an acronym for Mużew Nazzjonali Tal-Arti (National Art Museum) and the Maltese word for inspiration. A thoroughly modern museum, with interactive and digital elements, MUŻA has four main permanent galleries – The Mediterranean, Europe, Empire, and Twentieth Century – as well as space for temporary exhibitions.

The displays include a significant body of work by baroque master Mattia Preti (see box, page 126), complementing his work in Malta's churches. His large Martyrdom of St Catherine is particularly impressive. St Catherine was the patron saint of the Italian Knights, and the order was keen on themes of martyrdom since its own warrior knights were expected to be willing to die for their religion.

British artists are represented by a handful of evocative watercolour sketches by Edward Lear (1812–88), who spent time on Malta and Gozo in the 1860s, and a single watercolour by J M W Turner. Turner's only painting of Malta, a country he never visited, this picture of Valletta was done from a view by another artist, probably George Philip Reinagle (1802–35). It was made for a series of engravings of places visited by Lord Byron (who was in Malta in 1809 and 1811). Perhaps for this reason, the picture is precise and lacks any sign of Turner's more impressionistic work.

Also in the collection is Les Gavroches, a sculpture of street urchins by Malta's most famous 20th-century sculptor, Antonio Sciortino (1879–1947), which used to stand in the Upper Barrakka Gardens and was moved inside for conservation reasons. A copy stands in its original place. In a sense Malta's art collection is coming home as the Auberge d'Italie was the site of the first Museum of Malta, opened in 1924.

The Museum has its own café, restaurant and shop, and the *auberge* is also home to Valletta's main tourist office (page 103).

REPUBLIC STREET – UPPER (CITY GATE) END [106 C5] Republic Street is Valletta's
main street – and its backbone: it runs straight down the middle of the city from just south of City Gate to Fort St Elmo; see page 130 for the lower end. Coming from the City Gate end you will first pass **Palazzo Ferreria** [106 C5] on the corner

of Ordnance Street (Triq L-Ordinanza), with shops on the ground floor and the Ministry for Social Policy above. This fine 19th-century Valletta building was the largest to be built as a private palace other than the grand master's, and the first to integrate *gallariji* fully into the design of its stone façade. A few metres further on is the **Church of St Francis of Assisi** [106 C5]. Built in 1598–1607 but altered in 1681 with the dome added in the 1920s, it has one of the earliest Baroque interiors.

About 200m down the road from City Gate is one of Malta's most important – and under-visited – sights, the **National Museum of Archaeology** [106 C5], housed in the **Auberge de Provence**, home of de Valette's *langue* (see box, page 117).

The road then opens out into Valletta's three central squares: the narrow Great Siege Square, the slightly larger Republic Square and the true centre of Valletta, A tiny detour along the side of the Grand Master's Palace (at the St Elmo end) on Archbishop Street takes you to the little Malta Postal Museum (page 130), before returning to Republic Street, St George Square or Palace Square (page 128).

A tiny detour along the side of the Grand Master's Palace (at the St Elmo end) on Archbishop Street takes you to the little Malta Postal Museum, before returning to Republic Street.

National Museum of Archaeology ✳ and the Auberge de Provence [106
C5] (Republic St, VLT 1112, between Melita St & St John St (Triq San Gwann); ☏ 1221623; w heritagemalta.org/museums-sites/national-museum-of-archaeology; ⊕ 08.00–19.00 daily, last admission 18.15; €5 adults, €3.50 over-60s/children aged 12–17/students, €2.50 child (6–11), children under 6 free; combined ticket available inc entry to other Heritage Malta sites (see box, page 42); informative audio guide) The National Museum of Archaeology is a must for anyone remotely interested in Malta's unique prehistoric temples as this is where all the most important finds from the temples reside – including the iconic 'Sleeping Lady'. Even before you pay to go in, there are two monumental upright panels with polished surfaces decorated with pitting and spirals that certainly do not look five millennia old. There is plenty more inside, as well as galleries devoted to the Maltese Bronze Age and Phoenician periods. Roman galleries are set to follow.

Auberge de Provence The museum building was the Auberge of the Knights of Provence – de Valette's *langue* – built in 1571 and probably designed by Girolamo Cassar. The original *auberge* took up the whole block and included stables and a bakery and was almost self-sufficient in the event of a siege. Upstairs is the **Grand Salon** – the Knights' banqueting hall – with an unusual wooden ceiling and richly painted walls. The room was painted in the Knights' time and it is unclear how close the present Victorian paintings are to the originals. The **minstrels' gallery** is a British addition. The room is open to the public and temporary exhibitions are held here.

Neolithic Galleries The ground floor of the museum is given over to the period from **first settlement** of the Maltese islands by around 5900BC to the end of the temple period in 2350BC (NB These dates are the result of the latest research; some museum labels may still be on the old timeline putting first settlement around 5200BC and the temples 3600–2500BC).

The exhibition begins with the time when people lived in caves, including at Għar Dalam. It shows the changes in style of pottery over the first 1½ millennia of settlement and includes shell pendants, biconical limestone 'sling stones', and a few very early animal and human figures including one with a triangular head, like those in Cycladic art but around a millennium older.

The real highlights, however, are architectural and artistic artefacts from the **temples** (3800–2350BC) – which are likely to be more evocative to those who also visit the temple sites. **Don't miss**: the highly decorated little altar from Ħaġar Qim; the stone slab carved with low-relief fish from Buġibba; friezes of animals from Tarxien; several monumental stone blocks decorated with a variety of spirals and geometric patterns; and the extraordinary huge 'bowls'. There is also a little model of a temple found at Ta' Ħaġrat (ie: made at the time the temples were built) and interesting displays on the debate about how the temples were built and roofed.

Here too is the place to see Malta's '**Fat Ladies**'. The largest – now reduced to the lower body and fringed skirt – would once have stood 2m or more in height. It was found at Tarxien, as was the smallest 'fat lady'. The 'ladies' come in a variety of styles (some very obviously female, others less so). There are eight seated figures from Ħaġar Qim, one with traces of paint, another with exceptionally delicate hands, all with vast bums and thighs. (A well-rounded local woman once pointed out to me that it is only in the last 20 years that the Maltese have begun to move away from seeing the 'very well fed' female as the most attractive.)

In a smaller side room is the lovely **Sleeping Lady**, a delicate naturalistic little clay model of a fat lady asleep on a couch (even the base of which is rendered in detail). She was found in the Ħal Saflieni Hypogeum and is thought to be a personification of death (if so, a very peaceful death) or a deity, but nobody actually knows.

A variety of **phallic symbols** has also been found in the temples (and several are displayed here), adding support to the theory that the fat ladies may have been the central figures or deities of a fertility cult. Other female figures (not always obese) are shown with one hand on their (sometimes rounded) bellies. The so-called **Venus of Malta**, a 15cm headless clay figure, is the most famous of these.

Pieces of obsidian and greenstone axe-head pendants demonstrate the temple people's contacts with Sicily and Italy, and there are beads and a few other pieces of personal ornamentation.

Bronze Age Galleries These galleries cover the Maltese Bronze Age from the mid 3rd millennium BC when, following the end of the Temple Culture, the islands were inhabited by the so-called Tarxien Cemetery People. The Bronze Age here ended around 700BC. The case is clearly made for Malta's connectedness to its neighbours during this time – particularly to Sicily – through materials and objects that have to have been imported. There is even a shard of **Mycenaean pottery** (though it did not necessarily come directly from Mycenae).

Malta's mysterious **cart ruts** are explored here too with a reconstruction and an interesting video by one of the world experts, Dr David Trump. You will find it much easier to spot the ruts in the countryside once you have seen them here (for more on the cart ruts, see the box on page 204).

Phoenician Gallery This gallery is largely self-explanatory, presenting the Phoenicians in general and their role in Malta in particular. Exhibits include pottery and other tomb goods including a terracotta sarcophagus and a few stone carvings of the human form. There is a reconstructed Phoenician tomb and a little bronze figure of Egyptian god Horus discovered in a tomb on the outskirts of Rabat with a fragment of papyrus found within it. The papyrus is a Phoenician prayer from the dead person asking for divine help in making the treacherous sea journey to the underworld.

Further information In addition to the museum's very good audio guide, there is an excellent short **guidebook** to the Neolithic Galleries by the curator, Sharon

Sultana: *The National Museum of Archaeology: The Neolithic Period* (Insight Heritage Guides; €7). A **podcast** on the museum's highlights by Senior Curator of Prehistoric Sites, Reuben Grima, can be downloaded free from w visitmalta.com/en/podcasts. There is also a variety of free **children's activity sheets** and a children's room where kids can draw and read books connected with the periods covered by the museum.

GREAT SIEGE SQUARE (MISRAH L-ASSEDJU L-KBIR)

A short way down Republic Street from the Museum of Archaeology, the road opens out into **Great Siege Square** – which looks more like a widening of the road than a real square. Along one side is the columned façade of the **law courts**, built on the site of the Auberge d'Auvergne, which was destroyed during World War II. Opposite is the **Great Siege Monument** (1927) designed by Malta's most respected 20th-century sculptor, Antonio Sciortino, and behind that is the side wall of **St John's Co-Cathedral** where you will find the tourist entrance (see below). The façade and main doors of the church (used to enter for Mass) are in St John Square (Misrah San Gwann) round the corner along St John Street (Triq San Gwann).

St John's Co-Cathedral [106 D5]

(St John Sq (Misrah San Gwann); ☏ 21220536; w stjohnscocathedral.com; ◷ 09.30–16.30 Mon–Fri, 09.30–12.30 Sat (last admission 30mins before closing), open only for Mass on Sun; no narrow-heeled shoes (they damage the floor); €10 adults, €7.50 seniors & students, children under 12 free; admission inc audio guide – in English, French, Italian, Spanish, German & Maltese – which is well worth having) This was the order's church in Valletta, with a chapel for each *langue*. Begun in 1572 by Girolamo Cassar (a military architect by training), it started life as a large, plain limestone building completed in 1577 and consecrated in 1578. The oratory and sacristy were added in 1604 under Grand Master de Wignacourt, who was also responsible for handing the chapels over to the individual *langues* to decorate. As Baroque fashion took hold in the second half of the 17th century, the serious aggrandising of the interior began with Italian artist Mattia Preti's redesigns and his painting of the six-section barrel-vaulted ceiling (1661–66). The Knights continued to lavish artistic attention (and money) on their church and the *langues* competed for superiority until St John's became what it is today – the most opulent church you could imagine, every inch covered in gold, paint or marble. In 1816 (after the Knights had left Malta), Pope Pius VII gave the church cathedral status so that the single diocese of Malta had two cathedrals (the other being St Paul's in Mdina) – hence the term 'co-cathedral'.

Church The **façade**, flanked by two bell towers, has a balcony, used by the grand master to address the people, and a copy of a bronze Christ by Alessandro Algardi (1598–1654), the remarkable original of which will be on display in the cathedral museum when it reopens in its new building in 2020/21. The sculpture was brought here from a church on the Grand Harbour in 1853.

Inside, the **cathedral floor** consists entirely of colourful inlaid marble tombs (though many are covered for protection). They date from the early 17th century to the end of the Knights' time in Malta in 1798. Symbolic images recur, particularly a sickle-wielding skeleton (Death) and the angel of fame blowing a trumpet. The Knights blew their own trumpet right enough and this image appears on the memorial monuments of a number of grand masters – most of whom are buried here.

Preti's ceiling paintings, done with great skill, start from the lunette over the main door and represent (unsurprisingly) scenes from the life of St John the Baptist, patron saint of the order. They are not frescoes but painted with oils direct onto the stone. Notice the *trompe l'oeil* of the figures at the base of the ceiling vaults. They are so three-dimensional that they look like sculptures, and with some figures, like the one opposite the main tourist entrance to the church, Preti has actually painted their shadows onto the gold stone carvings next to them. The ceiling decoration was paid for by Raphael and Nicolas Cotoner – brothers who were both grand

CARAVAGGIO AND MALTA

Born Michelangelo Merisi in 1571, a middle-class boy in the town of Caravaggio, the artist-to-be lost his father to the plague at the age of five and his mother in his teens. He took his inheritance and departed for Rome, never to return. This brilliant but hotheaded young man was soon making waves with his painting and with his violence. In 1606, things came to a head when he killed a well-connected Roman in a duel. He fled south, a wanted man, and a year later boarded a galley belonging to the Order of St John heading for Malta. En route, word came of Turkish ships lying in wait off Gozo and all men were armed and made ready, but it was a false alarm and Caravaggio arrived safely in the Grand Harbour in July 1607.

On the same voyage to Malta was knight Ippolito Malaspina (a personal friend of the grand master). He soon became the owner of Caravaggio's *St Jerome*, which now hangs in St John's Oratory. Grand Master de Wignacourt too recognised Caravaggio's talent and commissioned him to paint his portrait (now in the Louvre). He also accepted him as an unlikely novice of the Order of St John. Caravaggio was neither noble-born, nor of good character, but Wignacourt petitioned the Pope for special dispensation and received it. While a novice, Caravaggio painted the powerful *Beheading of St John*, now the highlight of the co-cathedral's art collection.

Caravaggio was formally admitted to the order as a knight on 14 July 1608. His studies over, he left the confines of the church and within weeks was involved in a brawl with six other Italian knights in the house of the church organist. A high-ranking knight was shot and seriously wounded and Caravaggio was imprisoned in Fort St Angelo. A risky escape (perhaps aided by powerful friends) using ropes to scale the fort's massive walls saw the artist on a boat to Sicily. This was a bridge too far for the order and on 1 December 1608, in the oratory of St John's with the artist's painting hanging on the wall, Caravaggio was, 'like a rotten and fetid limb', cut off from the Hospitallers.

From Sicily he returned to Naples, and by early 1610, after more than a year on the run, he was in a bad way. He painted *Salome with the Head of John the Baptist* showing his own head on the platter and sent it to Wignacourt. With hopes that powerful friends in Rome might succeed in extracting a pardon from the Pope, Caravaggio took a boat north but died mysteriously, probably from a fever, a few days before the pardon was forthcoming.

His effect on European painting is hard to overestimate and, despite the fact that he spent little over a year in Malta, his effect on painting here is clear to see in the friezes in the State Rooms of the Palace of the Grand Master (completed shortly after his departure) and in the work of many of his admirers, including Mattia Preti.

A podcast on Caravaggio in Malta by a local art historian and a Mattia Preti and Caravaggio itinerary can be downloaded free (w visitmalta.com/en/podcasts) or as a mobile app (w visitmalta.com/en/mobile-apps).

Although Italian, Mattia Preti is arguably Malta's most important painter. He spent 40 years here and is represented in numerous churches – particularly St John's Co-Cathedral where he painted the vast vaulted ceiling. Born in Calabria in 1613 and later known as Il Cavalier Calabrese, he trained in Naples and Rome (where he was influenced by the work of Caravaggio) before travelling to Venice and all over Italy absorbing the work of many of Europe's greatest painters. He developed an eclectic style, carried out numerous commissions and made influential friends before being admitted as a Knight of the Order of St John in 1642.

A few years later he received a commission from Grand Master de Redin for a painting depicting St Francis Xavier. The following year, 1659, he travelled to Malta where he spent most of the rest of his life. Art historian Nikolaus Pevsner credits Preti with the creation of High Baroque art, identifying as seminal works his altarpiece in the Church of St Catherine of Italy and his decoration of St John's (Preti went on to paint numerous other altarpieces and private commissions, mostly of a religious nature). He died in Malta in 1699 and is buried in St John's. His memorial plaque of coloured marble can be seen on the floor of the side chapel to the left of the main door (looking from inside) that leads to the sacristy. The plaque is by the wall on the side closest to the tourist entrance.

A Mattia Preti itinerary, created for the artist's 400th anniversary in 2013, can be downloaded free from w visitmalta.com/en/podcasts or as a mobile app from w visitmalta.com/en/mobile-apps. For those who prefer a printed book, Malta's National Trust (Din L'Art Ħelwa) publishes *Mattia Preti: A Guide to His Paintings in the Churches of Malta and Gozo* by Giuseppe Mantella and Sante Guido.

masters – who can be seen at either end of the broad lunette above the main door. You can get closer to these paintings by climbing up to the **gallery** above the main door, which also affords a fabulous view the length of the church.

The **chapels of the *langues*** are all richly decorated – with altarpiece paintings (several by Mattia Preti), carvings and monuments, some of real artistic merit. Most have been recently restored and are well worth a good look round.

The **Chapel of Our Lady of Philermos** used to house the Knights' most precious icon, carried with them since their time in Jerusalem. In preparation for battle they would pray before this painting and, if victorious, bring the keys of the captured fortress to the chapel. A few keys still hang here (though they are not easy to see). The icon left Malta with the Knights, and was taken to St Petersburg. After the Russian Revolution, it disappeared for some years. It now hangs in the Museum of Fine Arts in Montenegro and St John's has a copy.

Oratory The highlight of a visit to the oratory is **Caravaggio**'s ✳ vast *Beheading of St John* (1608) – his largest painting and only signed work ('Fra Michaelangelo' scrawled in the Baptist's blood). It is worth noting that when Caravaggio was here the church was still in its original austere, unembellished state (Mattia Preti and the Baroque came later) and the oratory was newly built. The painting was commissioned by Grand Master de Wignacourt who wanted a devotional picture for the order's novices who used the oratory.

Although already in his mid 30s, Caravaggio was one of these novices, training to become a knight, hoping to escape his violent past in Italy (see box, page 125).

The painting is a powerfully realistic portrayal of the story with a total absence of religious iconography (no angels, God, etc). The spare composition is painted in a limited palette, lending extra power to the splash of red that is St John's mantle.

Also in the oratory is Caravaggio's *St Jerome*, another very human image, this one of an old man writing (St Jerome translated the Bible from Hebrew into Latin). The painting was a private possession of the knight who commissioned it (you can see his coat of arms on the work). After his death, his property passed to the order (as was usual) and the painting was placed in the Italian chapel. When the painting was moved to the oratory, a copy was put in its place and still hangs in the chapel.

Cathedral museum (⊕ Closed for the creation of a new museum, not expected to open before 2020) The museum's most treasured possession is a set of 29 **Flemish tapestries** (1697–1700), the largest such complete set in the world. Made by Jodicus de Vos from cartoons, many of which were by Peter Paul Rubens, the tapestries were Spanish grand master Ramon Perellos y Roccaful's contribution to St John's and they used to be hung in the church on feast days. The new museum is expected to allow all the tapestries to be displayed.

The museum also has some huge **illuminated choral books** (16th- and 17th-century) and a silver-and-gilt monstrance (sacred receptacle, 1686–89), which once held a relic believed to be part of St John's forearm – the arm that baptised Christ. Napoleon pinched the gold from it and the Knights took the relic with them when they left Malta.

Richly embroidered vestments that once belonged to several grand masters are followed by a picture gallery which includes the original altarpiece of the church by Matteo Perez d'Aleccio, a pupil of Michelangelo, paintings by Mattia Preti and an interesting portrait by Antoine de Favray of Grand Master Manuel Pinto de Fonseca (1747) in an ermine cape which is meant to be reserved for royalty.

Mass Mass is said at 07.30 and 08.30 each weekday. On Sundays at 09.15 there is High Mass in Latin with organ and full choir – quite an experience. There is no charge for entering the church for Mass, but you cannot wander around and sightsee while the service is on.

Further information There's an informative official guidebook to St John's by the curator, Cynthia de Giorgio (Insight Heritage Guides; €7) available at the cathedral.

REPUBLIC SQUARE (MISRAH IR-REPUBLIKA) [107 E4] A few metres from Great Siege Square is Republic Square, also known as 'Queen's Square' because of the statue of Queen Victoria that stands at its centre looking down on the denizens of Valletta sipping coffee at the capital's most famous café. **Caffe Cordina** (page 67) has attracted locals and visitors alike since the 19th century. Locals will often suggest meeting here as a central Valletta landmark – as well as for a coffee. In the arcade behind the café tables is the **National Library**.

National Library (Biblioteca) [107 E4] ☏ 21243297, 21236585, 21232691; e customercare.nlm@gov.mt; w maltalibraries.gov.mt; ⬛; ⊕ to the public on production of ID 1 Oct–15 Jun 08.15–17.00 Mon–Fri, 08.15–13.15 Sat, 16 Jun–30 Sep 08.15–13.15 Mon–Sat; accessing books & documents requires a research ticket – contact the library in advance) This was the last important building to be constructed by the order in 1796, two years before Napoleon arrived. They needed a new home for the massive collection of papers and books accumulated through the order's statute that forbade the sale of any of a deceased knight's books. Napoleon

ordered that the contents of the library be destroyed. Fortunately, he was not obeyed and today the library houses over 300,000 books and 10,000 manuscripts, some dating back to the 12th century. These include the written records of the order from 1107 to 1798 as well as a letter from Henry VIII proclaiming himself head of the Church of England, the Act of Donation in which Charles V gave Malta to the Knights and the papal bull of 1113 that first recognised the Order of St John. Convincing copies of these last three can sometimes be seen in a polished wooden showcase in the atmospheric old library, but at times they are removed to make way for temporary exhibitions of varying interest to the visitor.

ST GEORGE SQUARE (MISRAH SAN ĠORĠ)/PALACE SQUARE [107 E4] Right next to Republic Square is St George Square, also known as Palace Square because one side of it is taken up with the **Grand Master's Palace**. For many years the car park for Malta's MPs, since their move to the new parliament the renovated square has become a pleasant place to sit, use the free Wi-Fi, and watch people and the fountains. Recently refurbished, the water spurts straight from the ground so the square remains flat for the many national ceremonies and events that take place here. These include the changing of the guard with full military band (dates from tourist information), as well as the annual celebration of the awarding of the George Cross to the nation of Malta. This originally took place here in 1942 and is a moment of which the nation is still proud. Visiting dignitaries are also often officially received in the square and impromptu events are not unusual.

A see-through slab covers a maypole base, found during the refurbishment works. This was where the maypole was set up in the time of the Knights.

Grand Master's Palace [107 E4] (St George Sq; ✆ 21249349; w heritagemalta.org; ⊕ see below for details; joint admission to the State Rooms & Armoury €10 adults (€15 with audio guide), €7 over-60s/children aged 12–17/students, €5 child aged 6–11. If the State Rooms are closed, admission to the armoury alone costs €6/4.50/3; combined ticket available inc admission to other Heritage Malta museums; see box page 42) At time of writing, major restoration works are planned at the palace, so there may be significant disruption to visits and eventual changes, including the armoury moving back to its original location. The first building on this site was built under Grand Master Jean de la Cassière (1572–81) and designed by Girolamo Cassar along with much of the rest of Valletta at the time. It had a simple, almost severe, exterior, now a little softened by some ornamentation and the long corner *gallarija* (a real gallery this one), which may have been responsible for starting the craze for these closed balconies across the city and the country (see box, page 131). With numerous grand-masterly extensions and additions, the palace reached its present shape in the mid 18th century.

Grand masters were based here until Napoleon took over in 1798. The palace subsequently became the headquarters of the British Governors of Malta and is now the office of the president. Until 2015 it was also home to Malta's parliament, based in the Knights' original armoury (the armoury moved to the old stable block). The MPs have, however, now moved to the new parliament building at City Gate. In due course the armoury may move back here reopening this room to the public.

State Rooms [107 E4] (Grand Master's Palace; ⊕ 10.00–16.30 Mon–Wed & Fri, 09.00–17.00 Sat & Sun; last admission 30mins before closing; may be closed if the president is using the rooms) The audio guide is good, but if you prefer not to use it, you may wish to use the short guide below while in the state rooms since (at the time of writing) there is little written on-site information for visitors.

Up a modern staircase clamped onto the side of the palace (or the lift) you enter a **painted gallery**, with a 19th-century coloured-marble floor, which runs round three sides of **Neptune's Courtyard**. The courtyard is named after the statue at its centre, moved here during British rule from its original position below the Upper Barrakka Gardens (now a road) where it was part of a fountain installed in 1615 by Grand Master de Wignacourt to celebrate the completion of his aqueduct (see box, page 226). Beneath the statue, known locally as Il-Ggant ('The Giant') and said to resemble Wignacourt, was a waterspout from which the Knights' ships could fill up with water (page 155).

The gallery is flanked by suits of armour and adorned with portraits of grand masters – quite telling as to what they thought of themselves. Nicolas Cotoner, for instance, sits severely in tall black hat and robes of the order pointing at a map of his fortifications and looking thoroughly imperious. Doors off the gallery lead to the five State Rooms.

Room 1: Tapestry Room Named after the set of French Gobelins tapestries that hangs here. Known as the *Tentures des Indes,* they were made for the room in 1708–10 to exotic designs originating in a gift from a Dutch prince to Louis XIV of France. This is the only surviving full set of its kind.

The room itself – with its original coffered ceiling and paintings of naval battles against the Ottoman Turks – was the centre of the Government of Malta for some four centuries. It was the meeting place first of the Council of the Order of St John, then of the Legislative Council under British rule and finally of Malta's Parliamentary Assembly (which began under British rule in 1921). The parliament continued to meet here after independence until it outgrew the room and moved in 1976 to the Knights' Armoury (the arms being removed to their present location; page 130).

Room 2: Dining Room Rebuilt after a bomb hit it during World War II, this room now houses portraits of Malta's heads of state since independence in 1964 – including Queen Elizabeth II who was Queen of Malta until it became a republic in 1974.

Room 3: Throne Room The grand master's ceremonial chamber was built in the reign of French grand master de la Cassière (1572–81). The coffered ceiling is original and the wall paintings showing scenes from the Great Siege of 1565 are by Italian artist Matteo Perez d'Aleccio (1547–1616), a pupil of Michelangelo, whom he assisted at the Sistine Chapel.

Under the British the room became known as the 'Hall of St Michael and St George' after the chivalric order created for the Maltese and Ionian islands. The minstrels' gallery is not original to the room and was probably moved here from the palace chapel. Like the Tapestry Room, the Throne Room has long retained its original function and is today still used by the President of Malta on state occasions.

Room 4: Pages Room (Also known as the 'Yellow Room') This room originally linked the grand master's private quarters with the Throne Room and here the grand master's many young pages would await their orders. These boys of noble birth worked from age 12 on the promise that at 18 they could apply to be Knights. Around the top of the walls are scenes from the history of the order prior to its arrival in Malta. The narrative of the frieze can be followed through the Ambassadors' Room to link with the images of the Great Siege in the Throne Room.

Room 5: Ambassadors' Room (Also known as the 'Red Room') This was the grand master's audience room, used for meeting and greeting visiting ambassadors and other dignitaries. It serves a similar purpose today for the President of Malta.

The portraits (which are sometimes hard to see) are of 17th- and 18th-century monarchs and dignitaries.

Armoury [107 E4] (Grand Master's Palace; ☉ 09.00–17.00 daily (last admission 16.30); joint ticket with State Rooms; if the State Rooms are closed, admission to the armoury alone costs €6 adults, €4.50 seniors/students/children over 12, €3 children 6–12) If you are interested in period weaponry, this place ranks high. It was a working armoury, intended to keep the Knights and their militias kitted out with the best European equipment, until Napoleon arrived in 1798. In fact, the Knights had just bought a whole batch of state-of-the-art weaponry for their militias in the 1780s, which Napoleon no doubt found very useful. Certainly he depleted the collection, as did his British successors, but much remains.

One of the two rooms is dominated by armour, mainly European but with a little Ottoman as well. There is a fabulous black suit embossed with gold made for Grand Master de Wignacourt (1601–22), as well as a very fancy 16th-century cuirass engraved to look like a buttoned waistcoat.

The order's militiamen were issued with a helmet, a back plate and a breastplate (all on view here). A leather or quilted jacket was worn underneath for comfort, though with most campaigns fought in summer they must have been horrendously hot. If you were fat, your sides were left exposed – unless you were wealthy enough to order a made-to-measure suit of armour like the one at the end of the gallery on the left.

In the Ottoman showcase you can see that the Turks wore much less armour than the Christians, particularly the Knights themselves. The Ottomans wore just a few pieces of protection and were undoubtedly more vulnerable, but also much less encumbered. In the same showcase are some vast cannonballs (perhaps 45cm across). These were fired from a Turkish Great Siege battery in the area that is now Castille Square. At the end of the siege the Turks tipped their bronze cannons into the sea. The Knights recovered them and melted them down to cast the bells of St John's Co-Cathedral.

The other room is mostly weapons. Since Napoleon and the British took many of the war weapons, there is a preponderance of hunting equipment in the remaining collection. There are still some interesting and impressive items, from huge cannon to spears, swords, muskets and crossbows, thin guns that could be poked through defensive walls, and a flintlock rocket launcher (that looks like a mere rifle). There is a matchlock gun that could have been used in the Great Siege and a vast weighing machine for cannons, as well as some beautifully engraved horn powder flasks.

MALTA POSTAL MUSEUM [107 E4] (135 Archbishop St, VLT 1444; ☏ 25961750; w maltapostalmuseum.com; ☉ 10.00–16.00 Mon–Fri, 10.00–14.00 Sat; adults €5, children €3) This museum follows Malta's history through its postal service from 1530 when the Knights arrived and letters were carried by sailing masters for a fee between Malta and Sicily, via the first fixed prices for sending letters set by the Knights in 1708 and the first stamps (issued by the British) in 1860. The collection includes a letter from Lord Nelson dated 1799 requesting support from Naples in the blockade of Malta against the French, lots of stamps (up to 2010) and even a functioning post office from which to send your postcards.

REPUBLIC STREET – LOWER (FORT ST ELMO) END [107 F3] Below St George Square and the Grand Master's Palace, Republic Street continues down towards the tip of the peninsula. Here you will find the unobtrusive entrance to Casa Rocca Piccola, the remaining section of a traditional 16th-century Maltese aristocratic townhouse open to the public, before reaching Fort St Elmo.

The Maltese *gallarija* is the enclosed painted wooden balcony with glass windows that is such a prominent feature of Malta's towns and villages. Yet, despite now being so closely associated with traditional Maltese architecture, when Valletta was first built in the 16th century, there were almost certainly no *gallariji* at all, only open stone balconies.

The origins of the *gallariji* are obscure. People used to think they were an Arab phenomenon pre-dating the Knights, but Maltese historian Judge Giovanni Bonnello points out that not only are all the names for the various parts of the balcony derived from Italian rather than any Semitic language, but the first evidence of a *gallarija* in Valletta is not until 1675, the date of the earliest known painting of the long *gallarija* of the Grand Master's Palace.

It seems quite likely that this was the first *gallarija* in Malta, which would explain the name; *gallarija* means 'gallery' not 'balcony' (Italian for 'balcony' is *balcone*) and the *gallarija* of the Grand Master's Palace is indeed a gallery – a long wooden walkway linking several of the palace rooms (page 128). The grand master apparently strolled up and down here keeping an eye on the goings on in the streets and squares below.

This might also explain the sudden popularity of the enclosed wooden structures. If the palace has one, naturally everyone else wants one too! They might not be able to manage a whole gallery – but a shorter version, perhaps superimposed on an old stone balcony, is better than nothing. The craze lasted. While there are enclosed wooden balconies elsewhere in the world, the Maltese have made the *gallarija* their own.

Casa Rocca Piccola [107 F3] (74 Republic St, VLT 05, between St Christopher & St Dominic sts; ☏ 21221499; w casaroccapiccola.com; ⊕ 10.00–16.00 Mon–Sat for guided tours in English on the hour; written translations of the main points available in Italian, French, German, Spanish, Japanese & Hungarian; €9 adults, €5 students/children (under 14) free) A treasure trove of Maltese history, the house is part of an original Valletta *palazzo* built around 1580 for Don Pietro La Rocca, Italian admiral of the order. He left it to the Langue of Italy, from where it passed into private hands and in 1918, it was bought by the grandfather of the present owner and became the home of a distinguished Maltese noble family. If you can afford it, book a private tour (€200 for up to 8 people then €25 per additonal person) and ask if you could possibly be shown round by the 9th Marquis Nicholas de Piro (9th Baron Budach and a Knight of St John) – an impeccable guide who describes the house as representing Maltese aristocratic 'aspiration, ambition and pretension' – or by his English marchioness, Frances. Both are wonderfully well informed and full of good stories. You can also stay here (page 104).

House Highlights include a set of silver surgical instruments from the Knights' **Sacra Infermeria** (page 138), dated to around 1780, and possibly the only remaining set; a Maltese **Knights-period chess set** with a grand master as king and a crownless queen to mark the order's celibacy; and an almost new-looking golden **sedan chair** belonging to a French knight and former Captain of the Galleys, Fra Nicholas de Vachon Belmont. The knight was old and unwilling to leave Malta in 1798; the British found him penniless, having sold his belongings (probably including this chair) to continue his charity work. He was given a small pension and eventually buried in the French chapel of St John's.

Among the **furniture** are a beautifully inlaid bureau constructed in 1640 and marked with the double-headed eagle of Grand Master Lascaris; a painted portable chapel; and a wooden chest decorated with the cross of St John (the 'Maltese cross'; see box, page 33), which is reputed to be the oldest piece of Maltese domestic furniture in existence. Among the smallest items on display, don't miss the earrings given to the family by the Bishop of Gozo after they donated land for the building of the pilgrimage church at Ta' Pinu.

There are some important **paintings** including interesting portraits and works by Mattia Preti (see box, page 126) and Antoine de Favray, and an exhibition of **Maltese costumes**. The *gallarija* is worth a visit too. It is one of the very few that still has the covered hole in the floor through which to check on who is arriving at the front door (do you wish to be in or are you diplomatically 'out'?) as well as a little shuttered window at a child's eye level.

'Quarry', 'wells' and World War II shelters   When Valletta was built, the stone for its buildings was mostly quarried on the spot – creating foundations as the stone for the house was removed. At Casa Rocca Piccola, beneath the house you can see part of the area from which stones were cut. Valletta was always short of water, so every house had to have a 'well' – actually a cistern or stone tank where rainwater collected from the roof was stored underground. Visitors can now walk down into Casa Rocca Piccola's largest cistern – a vast conical stone room – which was later used as part of a World War II shelter.

Nicholas de Piro's grandfather was convinced as early as 1935 that war was inevitable and built for his family the first shelter in Malta, a zigzag corridor (to protect from bomb blasts), and a tiny room with steps up into the house's garden. Later, two larger shelters were added, offering protection to some 150 people.

Further information and souvenirs   Nicholas de Piro has written an excellent short **guidebook** to the house and his family: *Casa Rocca Piccola* (Insight Heritage Guides; €7). He is also the author/editor of several books on Maltese art, crafts and history (page 319).

Fort St Elmo   [107 G2] (VLT 1741; ✆ 21233088; w heritagemalta.org/museums-sites; ☉ 09.00–18.00 in summer, 09.00–17.00 in winter, daily; last admission 30mins before closing; you can walk round much of the fort for free – if you ask at reception, they may give access to the outer fort for great views. Access to the National War Museum is ticketed: €10 adults, €7.50 students/seniors/children 12–17, €5.50 children 6–11, aged under 6 free. A combined ticket with other Heritage Malta sites is also available; see box, page 42.) At the bottom of Republic Street on the tip of the Sciberras Peninsula is Fort St Elmo. A watchtower and a chapel (dedicated to St Elmo) stood on this point from 1488 (before the Knights arrived). Following the Turkish assault of 1551, in 1552 the solid star-shaped fort at the centre of today's complex was built in anticipation of further attack by the Turks. The fort was indeed the Ottomans' first target at the start of the Great Siege in 1565 and despite heavy bombardment from three sides it held out for a month.

Fort St Elmo fell on 23 June with the loss of 1,500 men including all the defending Knights. Nine Maltese swam across the Grand Harbour to safety. The Turks suffered far heavier losses including their greatest corsair and strategist, Dragut Reis, apparently killed by what we would now call 'friendly fire'. After the siege, Fort St Elmo was rebuilt and incorporated into the fortifications of the new capital, Valletta.

In the Priest's Uprising of 1775 the fort was seized by the rebels. The Maltese flag flew briefly over Fort St Elmo and St James Cavalier, but the Knights' reaction was swift and the flags were soon replaced with the heads of three of the conspirators. Napoleon turned the place into a French prison but the British returned it to its defensive purpose. Malta's first victims of World War II fell here, casualties of the first Italian bombing raid. The fort was instrumental in repelling an attack by E-boats (small fast enemy gunboats) on the Grand Harbour in 1941.

Fort St Elmo recently served as the Maltese police academy and had fallen into considerable disrepair before it was the subject of a massive restoration project. It now looks splendid. The 1552 gateway, the Chapel of St Anne and the parade ground surrounded by the Knights-period (and later) barracks are free to access.

A ticket to the National War Museum gives access to the battlements. Here there are stunning views over the city, both Valletta's harbours and the open sea – indeed, you can see many of the locations of the events described in the National War Museum, which is spread through the upper fort.

Just outside the fortress gates is a large flat forecourt. The substantial round slabs of stone raised from the ground here are openings to the Knights' granaries or fosse – stores for the crucial grain that Malta has, since at least Roman times, had to import for its staple diet of bread.

For the media-minded, the lower bastion was used as the Turkish prison in the 1970s film *Midnight Express*, and in the strategic computer game *Age of Empires III* you can defend Fort St Elmo against the Ottoman Turks.

Knights-period re-enactments: In Guardia (⏰ 11.00 most Sun, tourist infomation can confirm exact dates; 📞 22915440/1/2; w visitmalta.com/en/event-details/2018-10/in-guardia-parade-12059; tickets on the gate €7/3 adults/children) A 45-minute re-enactment of an inspection by the Grand Bailiff of the Order of St John to ensure the fort was battle-ready. Some 50 re-enactors in Knights-period costumes – pikemen, swordsmen and musketeers with ensigns of the various *langues* – take over the parade ground to drill and demonstrate their weapons. It starts off a bit slowly but the cannon-fire towards the end is impressive.

National War Museum [107 G2] (See Fort St Elmo, opposite, for contact & opening information) Starting with a brief nod to Malta's earliest history from the Neolithic to the Romans, the museum really gets into its stride with the Great Siege (1565) which Grand Master de Valette called 'the great battle of the cross and the Quran'. From here the story of Malta's military history is informatively and engagingly told through a combination of audiovisual and interactive digital displays, archive footage and original objects. This is a museum for those with a general interest in Malta's history as well as for the military historian and takes you right up to the 21st century. Among the key exhibits are Great Siege-period armour, cannonballs and a 16th-century hand grenade as well as the table on which the armistice was signed between Napoleon's French and the British in 1800. From World War II, we have 'Husky' – the jeep used by General Eisenhower when he was based in Malta (with the same name as the invasion of Sicily he was here to command) – and the Gloster Sea Gladiator plane *Faith* (minus wings). This was

From Strait Street you can of course choose to explore the sites next to Fort St Elmo on the Grand Harbour side (the Malta Experience, Knights' Hospital, etc; page 138) and indeed walk along the fortifications beyond them (page 139) back towards City Gate. You could, of course, also turn the other way and follow the fortifications overlooking Marsamxett Harbour (page 136; although they are listed from the other end coming towards Fort St Elmo). If you take the Grand Harbour side first, you could do a full circuit of the fortifications following the text down the Marsamxett side, returning to this point to pick up the next part of the route into the middle of town.

one of only four planes in Malta when Italy declared war in June 1940. They were nicknamed *Faith*, *Hope* and *Charity* (plus an unnamed reserve) and by February 1941 only *Faith* survived. It lost its wings in the bombing of a nearby hangar.

Here, too, is Malta's proudest World War II souvenir: the George Cross medal along with the letter from George VI that came with it.

STRAIT STREET (TRIQ ID-DEJQA) [106 D4] Running on the other side from Merchants Street, parallel with Republic Street, is narrow Strait Street. Known in the days of the British Navy in Malta as 'The Gut', this is the back alley to Republic Street. Strait Street had a dubious reputation even in the days of the Knights when it was the favourite place for a duel, but it really came into its insalubrious own as the place where British sailors went to relax. At the lower end (nearest Fort St Elmo), it was Valletta's red-light district full of bars, dance halls and establishments of ill repute. The life of The Gut came to an end with the departure of the Royal Navy, the last of whom left in 1979. Some of the prostitutes moved to Gżira (next to Sliema) and Strait Street fell into disuse and disrepair. It has now, however, risen phoenix-like and is at the heart of Valletta's small but lively and burgeoning (and not seedy) bar-café culture. There is also a programme of arts and cultural events centred on the street.

Strait Street by John Schofield and Emily Morrissey (Midsea, 2012) gives a building-by-building account of 'The Gut' as well as bringing together memories of the street with lots of historic photos.

Turning off Strait Street into **Archbishop Street** (towards Marsamxett Harbour) you pass the **Archbishop's Palace** (the building with two large columns taking up the pavement), designed by Tommaso Dingli in 1622 (with the second storey added in the 1950s), before you reach Independence Square.

INDEPENDENCE SQUARE (MISRAĦ INDEPENDENZA) [106 D2] This square is dominated by St Paul's Anglican Cathedral, built on the site of the Auberge d'Allemagne (home of the German Knights), which was pulled down to make way for it in 1839. Directly opposite stands the Auberge d'Aragon, which, of all the surviving *auberges*, has remained closest to its original 16th-century state.

Auberge d'Aragon [106 D2] The Auberge of Aragon, Catalonia and Navarre to give it its full name, is the only surviving *auberge* not to have received the Baroque treatment. It is largely untouched and its plain façade and simple courtyard give you an idea of what all the *auberges* would originally have looked like. The building is now the Ministry of Justice and during office hours you can go into the front hall and look into the central courtyard.

This used to be the office of the prime minister (1921–72) before he moved to the Auberge de Castille, and there is a plaque listing all of Malta's prime ministers up to that point, as well as one naming the Knights' 'venerable drapers' (1539–1796) – always members of the Langue D'Aragon.

St Paul's Anglican Cathedral [106 D3] (St Paul's Pro-Cathedral, Independence Sq, VLT 1535; ☎ 21225714; w anglicanmalta.org; ⊕ 08.30–12.30 primarily for 'prayer & contemplation') This neoclassical cathedral was built in 1839–44 after the Dowager Queen Adelaide, widow of William IV (and Queen Victoria's aunt), visited Malta and was horrified to find no proper Anglican church. The Anglican congregation (or those who could fit in) met in a room in the Grand Master's Palace. Queen Adelaide put up £20,000 and work began immediately – the old *auberge* of the German *langue* being knocked down to make way for the new church. Its 200ft spire can now be seen from all over Valletta.

In the very plain interior are memorial plaques naming all the units of British and Commonwealth forces that took part in World War II in Malta. Army, navy and air force are listed on oak panels around the sanctuary, Merchant Navy on the north wall and submariners on a plaque outside facing northwest towards Manoel Island, where the submarines were based.

The cathedral is in dire need of restoration, and an appeal is underway to raise several million euros to secure its fabric and its future. More information can be found at w savethecathedral.com.

There is **sung Eucharist** in English every Sunday at 11.00 as well as other services (details on the website). The Undercroft café is beneath the cathedral (page 112).

OLD THEATRE STREET (TRIQ IL-TEATRU L-ANTIK) [106 D3] If you walk one block up West Street (Triq Il-Punent; towards City Gate) from Independence Square and turn left into Old Theatre Street you will come to the Sanctuary Basilica of Our Lady of Mount Carmel, an odd combination of old and new, and then to the Manoel Theatre, one of Europe's oldest functioning theatres.

Sanctuary Basilica of Our Lady of Mount Carmel [106 D3] (Old Theatre St, between Old Mint & West sts; ☎ 21233808; ⊕ usually 06.30–noon & 16.00–19.00) This is Valletta's newest church, built between 1958 and 1981, but its history goes back 400 years. The first church on this site dated from 1570, but it was so badly damaged in World War II that total reconstruction was needed. The new church, with its 42m-high elliptical dome, was designed to ensure that the spire of a Protestant church (the Anglican cathedral) did not alone dominate the skyline of Valletta. The façade is very unassuming and the interior cavernous and quite plain. The church contains several paintings by Mattia Preti (see box, page 126) and the 17th-century picture of *Our Lady of Mount Carmel* above the high altar (curtained off except when the church is open to visitors and on special occasions) is considered to have miraculous powers.

Manoel Theatre [106 D3] (115 Old Theatre St, between Old Mint & Old Bakery sts; ☎ (box office) 21246389; w teatrumanoel.com.mt; ⊕ 10.00–noon Mon–Fri subject to performance & rehearsal schedules; €5 inc audio guide; free podcast about the theatre at w visitmalta.com/podcasts) One of the oldest theatres still in use in Europe, the delightful Baroque Manoel Theatre was commissioned by Grand Master Antonio Manoel de Vilhena in 1731 and run by the Knights for their own and the population's 'honest entertainment'. The interior, with tiers of

gilded boxes, has legendarily accurate acoustics and is perhaps best enjoyed at a performance. A tour, however, is also worthwhile providing history and anecdotes and access to the small **museum** displaying costumes, old sound-effects machines and early programmes (some painted on silk). The theatre hosts an opera festival in March and Valletta's Baroque Music Festival in January. Following recent renovations including a climate-control system, the performance season has been extended into the summer.

OLD MINT STREET (TRIQ IZ-ZEKKA) [106 C4] Walk 200–300m up Old Mint Street and at the end you will find **St John Cavalier**, twin to St James Cavalier (on the other side of City Gate). St John Cavalier is smaller and now houses the Embassy of the Knights of St John in Malta (not open to the public). Beyond the *cavalier*, and a little to the right between St John's and St Michael's bastions, is **Hastings Gardens** and about 100m toward St Elmo from here on Biagio Steps is the **Fortifications Interpretation Centre**.

Hastings Gardens [106 B4] (Entrance on Ordnance St (Triq L-Ordinanza)) A pleasant public garden, recently refurbished and reconnected to the rest of the city by Renzo Piano's broad stairway up from City Gate. Perched on top of the bastion walls, this is a great place to get a sense of Valletta's defences: look back towards Valletta at the twin *cavaliers* (St James and St John) guarding its landward side, then stand looking away from the city for the view of the defender. Note how thick the walls are and the several large cannons that still point out through their own firing channels (embrasures) towards Floriana. Further along (away from City Gate) are views of Marsamxett Harbour.

At the centre of the garden is a colonnaded **monument** with a reclining figure of the first Marquis of Hastings, a distinguished British soldier, Governor General of India and Governor of Malta 1824–26 who died at sea in the Mediterranean and is buried here.

The Fortress Builders: Fortifications Interpretation Centre [106 B3]
(Biagio Steps, St Mark St; ✆ 21228594; w thefortressbuilders.weebly.com; ⊕ summer 09.00–13.00 Mon–Fri, until 16.00 Tue & Thu, winter 10.00–16.00 Mon–Fri, until 19.00 Tue & Thu, Sat 09.30–13.00; admission free) This conversion of a 16th-century Knights' warehouse attached to the bastion walls just above Marsamxett Harbour won a top architectural award from Malta's National Trust before it was even open. The warehouse has been turned into an interpretation centre, a learned but accessible introduction to Malta's fortifications from the Bronze Age to World War II, with special emphasis on the period of the Knights of St John. The idea is that you can visit this exhibition, then head out and see the fortifications with renewed understanding of their construction and purpose.

An introductory video starts off a chronological journey through the creation of Fortress Malta. Information boards, touch-screens, 3D virtual modelling and actual physical models show how defence changed through the ages and how Malta's remarkable defensive structures were built. There is a sizeable children's area, with building blocks and child-friendly touch-screens, as well as some more basic information (good for the uninitiated adult too). There is also a café, and a library for those with a special interest.

FORTIFICATIONS ON THE MARSAMXETT HARBOUR SIDE From Hastings Gardens you can follow the fortifications round past **St Michael's Bastion** [106 A4] (in the equivalent position to the Upper Barrakka Gardens on the other side of town) to **St Andrew's Bastion** [106 B3]. Just inland from here, in the 1580s Biagio Steps Building, on St Mark Street and Melita Street, is **The Fortress Builders: Fortifications Interpretation Centre** (see opposite). An **MTA podcast** on Valletta's fortifications, with Stephen Spiteri, the top expert on the subject, can be downloaded free (w visitmalta. com/podcasts) or as a mobile app (w visitmalta.com/en/mobile-apps).

The main road that starts as **Great Siege Road** running round the outside of the city walls from Floriana, enters Valletta here through the fortifications (inside which is Monaliza Bar; page 113), becoming **Marsamxett Street (Triq Marsamxett)**. A steep slope leads down from here to the **Sliema ferry** (page 170) and a **water polo lido**.

This area, around today's **Mattia Preti Square** [106 C3], used to be known as **The Mandragg** and sometimes still is. The Knights planned to dig a vast hole here to create a sheltered harbour (a *manderaggio*) to serve the same function for Valletta as the natural creeks of the Three Cities had served in Birgu (Vittoriosa). The project was soon abandoned and the semi-sunken area became a slum. At the start of the 20th century, some 2,500 people were living here in a space the size of 2½ football pitches. It was cleared and redeveloped into social housing in the 1950s and is now slowly gentrifying.

Continuing, you pass along the **German Curtain** [106 D2] (the part of the fortifications that were the responsibility of the German *langue* whose *auberge* was nearby in Independence Square) to **St Sebastian Bastion** and the **gunpost**, a World War II gun tower.

There are clear views of **Marsamxett Harbour**, **Manoel Island** and the ugly modern developments on the Sliema Waterfront, as well as **Fort Tigné**, a late Knights' fort built in 1792. The fort sits on the tip of Sliema known as **Dragut Point** after its use by Turkish leader Dragut Reis to position cannons to attack Fort St Elmo during the Great Siege.

The walls now become the **English Curtain** [107 E2], breached by the **Jews Sally Port**, an unobtrusive way through the fortifications for Knights' sorties. It is unclear why the Jewish connection – the gateway has had this name since at least the 1580s and although some people say it was so called because it was the only entrance through which Jews visiting Valletta were allowed to pass, there is no documentary evidence to support this.

Opposite the English Curtain is the **Auberge de Bavière** – a late addition to the Knights' *auberges*. Past the English Curtain the French took over responsibility for defence and the **French Curtain** [107 F2] leads to **Fort St Elmo**.

Auberge de Bavière [107 E2] (31 Marsamxetto Rd, cnr West St opposite the

English Curtain, can only be viewed from outside) The Bavarians had long wanted their own *langue* (separate from the rest of the Germans) when in 1782 the grand master finally gave his permission. However, the Knights did not want to raise the number of *langues* above the existing eight. Since there were hardly any English Knights, the Bavarian king persuaded the Hanoverian King George III to combine forces and, in 1783, Palazzo Carnerio, built as a private house in 1696, became the *auberge* of the Anglo-Bavarian Langue. The English continued to defend the English Curtain and the Bavarians were put in charge of the St Lazarus Bastion just the other side of Fort St Elmo. The *palazzo* is now government offices.

MEDITERRANEAN STREET (TRIQ IL-MEDITERRAN) [107 G4] If you walk away

from Fort St Elmo towards the **Grand Harbour** you pass the **St Lazarus Bastion** [107 G3] (on your left overlooking the harbour) before reaching a small clutch of other sights right next to each other.

The Malta Experience and Sacra Infermeria – the Knights' Hospital [107 G3]

(St Elmo Bastions, Mediterranean St (Triq Il-Mediterran), VLT 1253; ⬙ 5524000; w themaltaexperience.com; shows on the hour: 11.00–16.00 Mon–Fri, 11.00–13.00 w/ends (Oct–Jun closes at 14.00) followed by a tour of the Sacra Infermeria; €16 adults, €11.50 students, €6 children 5–14, under 5s free; commentary available in 17 languages) The Malta Experience is the best of the various audiovisual shows around the country. It offers a very good 45-minute introduction to the country, a romp through Malta's 7,000-year history and some great photography. The cinema is actually part of the Sacra Infermeria and guided tours of the Knights' Hospital are offered after each show.

Now the **Mediterranean Conference Centre** (⬙ 21243840/3; w mcc.com.mt), the **Sacra Infermeria** was built in 1574. The hospital was central to the order and known throughout Europe for its quality of care. In the early days, all Knights – even the Grand Master – took a turn caring for the sick. All medical instruments and dishes were silver because the Knights knew it had anti-infection properties, patients had a bed each (unusual at the time) and a lavatory each (unusual even today!).

The 155m **Long Ward** is one of the longest halls in Europe, its unsupported roof recognised at the time of its construction in the 16th century as a serious architectural feat.

In winter the ward used to be hung with 131 (insulating) tapestries, in summer with paintings by Mattia Preti. All classes and nationalities were treated – though in different wards – but no women. Non-Catholics wishing to stay on the Long Ward (the best ward) for more than three days had to accept religious instruction, though there is no record of any conversions.

Off the Long Ward is a small **chapel** (1712) next to the **Sallette** – the ward for the dying. The **central courtyard** of the *infermeria* has been roofed over and is now the 1,400-seat **Republic Hall** – the main venue of the conference centre – but you can still see some of the original arches. The vaulted **Magazine Ward** in the basement is used for dinners as well as housing **Knights Hospitallers**, a missable 'heritage attraction' consisting of recreated scenes from the time of the Knights.

When the Knights were thrown out by Napoleon in 1798, the hospital was declared to be for French troops only and when the British took over it became the British Military Hospital. So it remained until after World War I, in which it played a significant role. It was badly bombed in World War II and stayed largely unusable until its award-winning renovation and conversion in the 1970s.

There is a **café** at the entrance to the Malta Experience. Go through to the terrace to avoid the crowds and enjoy marvellous views over the Grand Harbour.

Siege Bell Memorial [107 G5]

At the far end of the Sacra Infermeria, overlooking the Grand Harbour, is the Siege Bell Memorial that honours the 7,000 service personnel and civilians who died during the 'Siege of Malta' that took place from 1940 to 1943. A neoclassical cupola containing a 12-ton bell that tolls daily at noon (mind your ears), the memorial was unveiled by Queen Elizabeth II in 1992 – the 50th anniversary of the award of the George Cross by her father to the people of Malta. Between the bell and the water is a **monument to World War II sailors** lost at sea – a bronze statue of a sailor being prepared for water burial. On the other side is a *bočċi* club. *Bočċi* is a traditional Maltese game a little like boules (see box, page 305).

Lower Barrakka Gardens [107 G5]

Just beyond the Siege Bell monument is the Lower Barrakka Gardens, a colonnaded public garden smaller than the Upper Barrakka Gardens and – funnily enough – a little lower, but still affording good views of the Grand Harbour, as does much of this side of the bastion walls of

Valletta. The central **monument** is to Sir Alexander Ball, the British captain, later admiral, who was instrumental in taking Malta from the French. He went on to become Malta's hugely popular first governor.

Below the Lower Barrakka Gardens (outside the city walls on the harbour side) is Valletta's wholesale **fish market** (⊕ approx 04.30–06.30).

GRAND HARBOUR FORTIFICATIONS: LOWER BARRAKKA TO UPPER BARRAKKA Continuing up **Mediterranean Street (Triq Il-Mediterran)**, you follow the **Castille Curtain** [107 F5] (the part of the bastions defended by the Langue of Castille). Stay next to the Grand Harbour and you will find yourself on **St Barbara Street (Triq Santa Barbara)** [107 E5] and **St Barbara Bastion** [107 E6], a lovely row of 19th-century houses looking straight out over the Grand Harbour – one of the most sought-after addresses in Valletta. The fortifications continue up to meet the high walls supporting the Saluting Battery and the Upper Barrakka Gardens. If you have already been here, however, turn inland up St Lucy Street (Triq Santa Luċija) to find one of Malta's most important churches.

Church of St Paul's Shipwreck [107 E5] (74 St Paul St, VLT 1212, tourist entrance from St Lucy St (Triq Santa Luċija); ✆ 21236013; ⊕ officially 09.30– noon & 15.30–17.30 but may vary) The Church of St Paul's Shipwreck celebrates the stormy arrival of St Paul on Malta in AD60 – an event many Maltese see as the foundation of the nation's Christianity (page 7). First built in the 1570s, the present church dates to later in the 16th century. It is large and richly painted with coloured marble tombstones along the nave, marble columns and multiple domes.

The polychrome wood and gilt **statue of St Paul** (in the niche to your left as you enter the church from the sacristy) was carved in about 1657 by Maltese sculptor Melchiorre Gafà (brother of Lorenzo Gafà who redesigned the church in 1680, as well as designing Mdina Cathedral). It is carried in procession for the feast of St Paul's Shipwreck on 10 February – when tradition has it that it always rains!

To the right of the high altar in and by the **Chapel of St Joseph** are two important relics: 'the right wrist-bone of St Paul' contained in a golden forearm; and a piece of marble column topped with the severed head of St Paul in silver. The stone is said to be part of the 'pillar of St Paul' on which the saint was executed. It was given to the church by Pope Pius VII in 1817 in recognition of its work during the plague of 1813. There are various **paintings** of the life of St Paul. The most important, the altarpiece from the original church by Matteo Perez d'Aleccio (1580), is unfortunately ill lit and quite hard to see. The **side chapels** are interesting: each belongs to a particular confraternity (guild) and there are signs explaining their roles and their contributions to the church. The cobblers, for instance, made an annual donation of one pair of shoes to the rector.

ST PAUL STREET (TRIQ SAN PAWL) AND BACK TO CITY GATE Running most of the length of the city just to the Grand Harbour side of Merchants Street is St Paul Street, the only street in Valletta to have retained its 16th-century name and quite a traditional area with several *palazzi* – some now converted into tourist accommodation – and a few workshops. It is home to the **Old University**, now housing government offices (the public entrance is round the corner in Merchants Street). It began as a Jesuit college (Collegium Melitense) in 1595–1602 offering the first higher education in Malta (albeit, of course, primarily religious). During the carnival of 1639 some overexcited knights attacked the building, which led to

Paul is a prisoner on a ship en route to Rome where he is to be judged by Caesar, and this account is said to be by his travelling companion St Luke:

ACTS 27: 20–24, 36–39, 41–44

And when neither sun nor stars in many days appeared, and no small tempest lay on us, all hope that we should be saved was then taken away.

But after long abstinence Paul stood forth in the midst of them, and said, 'Sirs, ye should have hearkened unto me, and not have loosed from Crete, and to have gained this harm and loss.

'And now I exhort you to be of good cheer: for there shall be no loss of any man's life among you, but of the ship.

'For there stood by me this night the angel of God, whose I am, and whom I serve.

Saying "Fear not, Paul; thou must be brought before Caesar: and, lo, God hath given thee all them that sail with thee."'

[…]

Then they were all of good cheer, and they also took some meat.

And we were in all in the ship two hundred threescore and sixteen souls.

And when they had eaten enough, they lightened the ship, and cast out the wheat into the sea.

And when it was day, they knew not the land: but they discovered a certain creek with a shore, into the which they were minded if it were possible, to thrust the ship.

[…]

And falling into a place where two seas met, they ran the ship aground; and the forepart stuck fast, and remained unmoveable, but the hinder part was broken with the violence of the waves.

And the soldiers counsel was to kill the prisoners, lest any of them should swim out, and escape.

But the centurion, willing to save Paul, kept them from their purpose; and commanded that they which could swim should cast themselves first into the sea, and get to land:

Grand Master Lascaris making himself and the Jesuits very unpopular by severely limiting future carnival celebrations. In 1676, Grand Master Cotoner founded Malta's first medical school here and in 1769, after the Jesuits had been expelled from the country for political interference, it became Malta's first university.

Next door is the old **Jesuit church** [107 E4] (☉ 09.00–noon & sometimes early evening). Originally 16th century, the church was rebuilt in the 1630s and 40s after an explosion at a nearby powder store damaged both it and the college. It was designed by Italian military engineer Francesco Buonamici to echo the plan of the Jesuit church in Rome. In the fourth side chapel on the left are an altarpiece and lunettes by Mattia Preti.

From here, to get back to the City Gate area, you can either walk towards the Grand Harbour and up the steps past some lovely (if faded) old buildings on **Ursula Street (Triq Sant'Orsla)**, or simply follow St Paul Street or Merchants Street back to Castille Square, South Street and City Gate.

FLORIANA

Floriana is Valletta's suburb sitting just outside City Gate, filling the gap between the defensive walls of Valletta and the later fortifications, the **Floriana**

And the rest, some on boards and some on broken pieces of the ship. And so it came to pass, that they escaped all safe to land.

ACTS 28: 1–11

And when they were escaped, then they knew that the island was called Melita.

And the barbarous people showed us no little kindness: for they kindled a fire, and received us every one, because of the present rain, and because of the cold.

And when Paul had gathered a bundle of sticks, and laid them on the fire, there came a viper out of the heat, and fastened on his hand.

And when the barbarians saw the venomous beast hang on his hand, they said among themselves, 'No doubt this man is a murderer, whom, though he hath escaped the sea, yet vengeance suffereth not to live.'

And he shook off the beast into the fire, and felt no harm.

Howbeit they looked when he should have swollen, or fallen down dead suddenly: but after they had looked a great while, and saw no harm come to him, they changed their minds, and said that he was a god.

In the same quarters were possessions of the chief man of the island, whose name was Publius; who received us, and lodged us three days courteously.

And it came to pass, that the father of Publius lay sick of a fever and a bloody flux: to whom Paul entered in, and prayed, and laid his hands on him, and healed him.

So when this was done, others also, which had diseases in the island, came, and were healed:

Who also honoured us with many honours; and when we departed, they laded us with such things as were necessary.

And after three months we departed in a ship of Alexandria which had wintered in the isle...

From the Authorised King James version of The Bible.

Lines. It is not a must for visitors but there are a few places of interest. Places to stay in Floriana are detailed along with Valletta accommodation. Strictly speaking, both of 'Valletta's' large five-star hotels are in Floriana, along with the Valletta Waterfront where the Sicily ferry and cruise ships dock, the Three Cities ferry and the base of the Barrakka lift. In practical terms, all are integral parts of Valletta.

WHAT TO SEE AND DO

Floriana Lines In 1634, Grand Master Antoine de Paule became convinced that the Turks were planning another attack on Malta and appealed to the Pope for help to strengthen Malta's defences. Pope Urban VIII sent Italian military engineer, Pietro Paolo Floriani, to help. Floriani designed a hugely ambitious plan for a defensive system spanning the Sciberras Peninsula on Valletta's landward flank – and set to cost more than all of Valletta's existing fortifications put together. Work began in 1636, but by 1638 Floriani was fed up with constant criticism of his expensive plans and returned to Italy, where he promptly died.

His successor, Vincenzo da Firenzuola, was more concerned with the defence of the south side of the harbour and work shifted to the **Margarita Lines**. Progress on the Floriana Lines resumed in 1640 after a visit from Giovanni

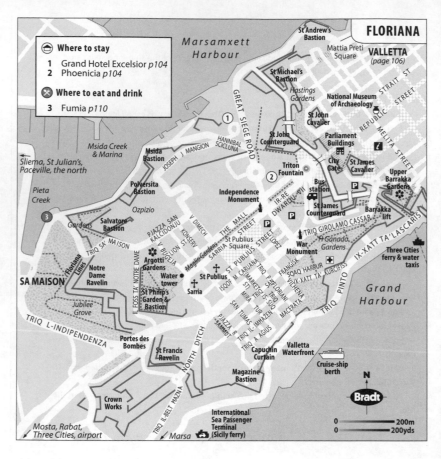

de' Medici; the defences were eventually completed with the help of French military engineer de Tigné. There is a good view of them from **St Philip's Garden** (see opposite).

The town The little town of Floriana was planned in 1724 under the rule of Grand Master de Vilhena. Although it suffered enormous damage during World War II, the layout remains largely original. It is centred on two parallel streets, **The Mall** and **Sarria Street**, which run straight from the Triton Fountain by City Gate bus station to the defensive walls at the other end of town, a few hundred metres away. The narrow strip of garden between them is **Maglio Gardens**, originally created by Grand Master de Lascaris (1636–57) as a place for young Knights to exercise. He had this inscribed in Latin on the wall:

> Here perish sloth, here perish cupid's darts
> Knights, on you this place I now bestow
> Here play your games and harden your warrior hearts
> Let not wine, women or dice bring you low.

The closest thing to his games ground remaining is the neighbouring (and much used) football pitch on what was once the British parade ground.

St Publius Square Also running almost the length of Floriana, on the other side of Sarria Street, is St Publius Square, or 'Il-Fosos' ('The Granaries'). It is dotted with raised circular stones (like the ones outside Fort St Elmo), which cover the openings into the Knights' stores for the island's precious grain. Some 5,000 tons of grain could be stored in the conical pits beneath this square. They were re-used during World War II and are still in good repair.

The huge Floriana parish **Church of St Publius** dominates one end of the square. It was built in 1733–68, but substantially restructured after sustaining bomb damage in World War II. St Publius was the Roman governor of Malta at the time of St Paul's shipwreck and was said to have been converted by Paul to Christianity, becoming the first Bishop of Malta (see box, page 7). This church's *festa* opens the summer *festa* season (page 32). Behind St Publius's Church is the much smaller, circular **Church of Sarria** (1676), probably designed by Mattia Preti (see box, page 126) who, at the very least, decorated the interior.

The far end of Floriana Beyond this, at the end of The Mall and Sarria Street, is the 19th-century botanical **Argotti Gardens** (w um.edu.mt/science/biology/argotti; ⊕ usually 09.00–15.00 Mon–Fri) and a 17th-century **water tower**, carved with the emblem of Grand Master de Wignacourt, to whose Mdina–Valletta aqueduct it was once attached (see box, page 226). In neighbouring **St Philip's Garden** is the **Wignacourt Fountain**, originally created in St George Square in 1615 to celebrate the arrival of the first water along the aqueduct. The gardens sit atop **St Philip Bastion** with a great view of the Floriana Lines and the **Portes des Bombes**, through (and now around) which all road traffic must pass to get into Floriana and thence Valletta. The gate was built in 1697–1720 as a single arch with a drawbridge, but was extended in the 19th century when the defensive walls around it were dismantled to improve traffic flow.

6

The Three Cities

Across the Grand Harbour from Valletta are the Three Cities. They lie around Dockyard Creek (called Galley Creek by the Knights), one of the natural hideaways that have made Malta so attractive to maritime powers through the ages. Behind Fort St Angelo lies **Birgu** (pronounced *beergoo*), the Knights' first capital in Malta which still oozes history from its narrow streets. It was renamed Vittoriosa after the Great Siege victory of 1565, but locals have never really taken to the 'new' name. On the other side of the creek is **Senglea** (pronounced *sengleea*), originally called L-Isla (pronounced *leezla*). Between Senglea and Birgu at the head of the creek is the relative newcomer, **Cospicua** or Bormla. Cospicua has long been the poor relation, but ongoing renovation of the waterfront and some historic buildings is making a big difference.

The three 'cities' are actually three very small towns, each only a few hundred metres across, with little other than an occasional length of military ditch to divide them. The three really became one when they were enclosed together within the Knights' improved 17th-century defences, the Santa Margarita Lines and the massive Cottonera Lines, which still run 5km around the landward side of the cities. This enclosure led to the area being known as the Cottonera District. The name the 'Three Cities' was coined much later by Napoleon's general Vaubois in 1798.

The Three Cities were at the centre of both Malta's historic sieges. In 1565, the Knights resupplied Fort St Elmo from Birgu and L-Isla and held out against the Turks. In World War II, the cities' proximity to the Grand Harbour meant that they bore the brunt of the bombing (it has been estimated that in one month – April 1942 – over 3,156 tons of bombs fell on the Three Cities). It is amazing how much of Birgu has survived, whilst, in each of the sieges, Bormla/Cospicua was more or less destroyed.

For the rest of the 20th century, the Three Cities deteriorated, not helped by the departure of the Royal Navy in the late 1970s and the closure of the dockyards. By the 1990s, the area was in a sad state. Revitalisation of Birgu began some years ago with the renovation of some of the Knights-period buildings, a thriving yacht marina and the Vittoriosa Waterfront full of cafés and restaurants. This revitalisation is now spreading to the rest of the area, integrating the Three Cities and their waterfronts all the way from Fort St Angelo (on the tip of Birgu) right round the creek to Senglea Point.

GETTING THERE AND AWAY

BY BUS There are buses to all three cities and to Kalkara.

BY CAR For Birgu, cars can be parked outside the Three Gates or driven into town via the Gate of Provence (a modern addition) though parking can be tricky. There is free parking on the streets in Senglea and Cospicua.

BY WATER The best way to get here is by ferry or water taxi from Valletta. Both leave from Customs House on the Valletta Waterfront at the bottom of the Barrakka lift (which is included in the ferry fare). The ferry runs every half-hour from 07.00 to about 18.00 or until around midnight in summer. It lands at Cospicua Waterfront on the Birgu side (✆ 23463862; w vallettaferryservices.com; fares are €1.50 single, €2.80 return, €0.50/€0.90 for children). The ferry takes 10–15 minutes and in good weather is a thoroughly pleasant journey.

If you prefer your own boat (and perhaps a tour of the harbour en route), take a water taxi, a traditional *dgħajsa*. They gather around the ferry stop on the Valletta side and by the archway to the Vittoriosa Waterfront on the Three Cities side.

GETTING AROUND

The main way to get around the Three Cities is on foot, but there is an alternative if you want a techie tour: a talking car. **Rolling Geeks** (Vittoriosa Waterfront; ✆ 21805339; m 79950695; w rolling-geeks.com; ⊕ 09.30–18.30 daily, except noon–18.30 Tue; €75 per car for a 2½hr tour) are little golf-buggy-style vehicles with built-in tablets and internet connectivity. Drive around, triggering commentary (in a choice of eight languages). You can stop whenever you like and the office keeps track of you and is always at the end of the tablet communication system should you need help. The GPS-led tour covers the whole Cottonera area, from Kalkara to Senglea, but perhaps the most fun is driving the medieval alleys of Birgu where no other car can go. One Rolling Geek can take up to two adults and two children – and it helps to have a driver and a navigator.

TOURIST INFORMATION

There is a small official tourist office in the Inquisitor's Palace, Main Gate Street (just off the main square; ✆ 21800145; ⊕ 09.00–16.45 Mon–Sat, 09.00–12.45 Sun & public holidays).

WHERE TO STAY

From no hotels a few years ago, the Three Cities have jumped rapidly to having several boutique hotels and bed and breakfasts with contemporary interiors in renovated old buildings.

Locanda La Gelsomina [map, page 150] (4 rooms) 3 Triq il-Kunsill Popolari, Vittoriosa 1131; ✆ 21807897; w locandalagelsomina.com. Stylish East-meets-West family-run converted townhouse in heart of Birgu. Large characterful rooms. Tailored itineraries offered. €€€–€€€€

✳ **Boco Boutique** [map, page 160] (6 rooms) 65 Triq I-Oratorju, Cospicua; ✆ 20341578; w bocoboutique.com. Wonderfully arty fun boutique hotel in 400-year-old house minutes from sights of Birgu & ferry to Valletta. Full of original art by local artists. €€€

Cugó Gran Macina Grand Harbour [map, page 158] (21 rooms) Triq Il-31 ta'Marzu, Senglea;

ISL 1040; ✆ 27112711; w ibbhotels.com. Luxury boutique hotel built into a waterside Knights-period bastion (the *macina* is the old crane once used in ship maintenance). Creamy limestone & black slate décor. Lovely roof terrace with swimming pool. Excellent Hammett's restaurant (page 148). €€€

Julesy's B&B [map, page 160] 105 Triq San Gorg, Cospicua; m 99953465, 99939007; w julesysbnb.com. A luxury B&B with 2 spacious rooms in an 18th-century house. Run by Aussies, Glen (whose mother is Maltese) & Julie, an ex-restaurateur who also offers cookery courses. They can organise any of 45 different tours & excursions. Price includes full 'gourmet' cooked b/fast. €€€

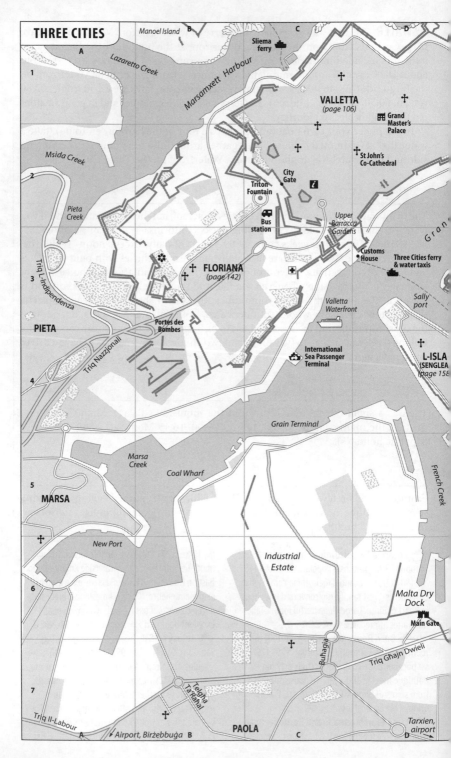

THREE CITIES

A · B · C · D

Manoel Island

Sliema ferry

Lazaretto Creek

1

VALLETTA
(page 106)

Grand Master's Palace

Marsamxett Harbour

St John's Co-Cathedral

Msida Creek

2

City Gate

Triton Fountain

Pieta Creek

Bus station

Upper Barracca Gardens

Grand

Customs House

Three Cities ferry & water taxis

FLORIANA
(page 142)

3

PIETA

Sally port

Valletta Waterfront

L-ISLA
(SENGLEA
(page 158)

Portes des Bombes

International Sea Passenger Terminal

4

Grain Terminal

Marsa Creek

Coal Wharf

French Creek

5

MARSA

New Port

Industrial Estate

6

Malta Dry Dock

Main Gate

Buhagia

Triq Għajn Dwieli

7

Telgha Ta' Raħal

Tarxien, airport

Triq Il-Labour

PAOLA

A · B · Airport, Birżebbuġa · C · D

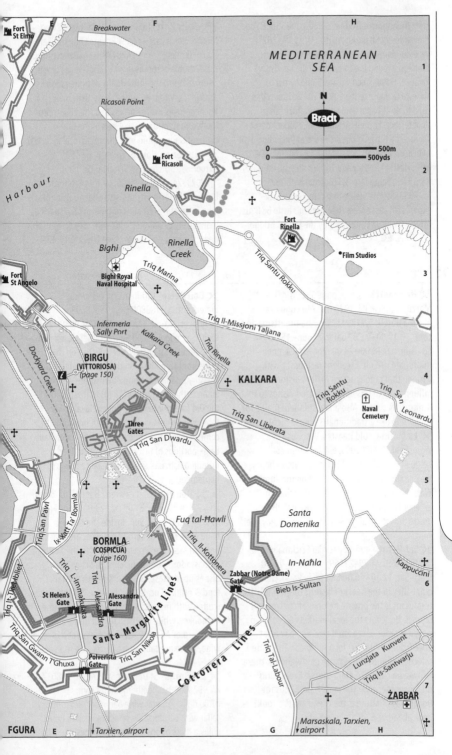

MEDITERRANEAN
SEA

Bradt

N

0   500m
0   500yds

Fort
St Elmo

Breakwater

Ricasoli Point

Fort
Ricasoli

Rinella

Harbour

Bighi

Rinella
Creek

Fort
Rinella

Triq Santu Rokku

•Film Studios

Bighi Royal
Naval Hospital

Triq Marina

Fort
St Angelo

Infermeria
Sally Port

Triq Il-Missjoni Taljana

Kalkara Creek

Triq Rinella

BIRGU
(VITTORIOSA)
(page 150)

KALKARA

Triq Santu
Rokku

Triq San Leonardu

Dockyard Creek

Three
Gates

Triq San Liberata

Naval
Cemetery

Triq San Dwardu

Fuq tal-Ħawli

Santa
Domenika

Triq San Pawl

Ix-Xatt Ta' Bormla

BORMLA
(COSPICUA)
(page 160)

Triq Il-Kottonera

In-Naħla

Kappuċċini

Triq L-Immakulata

Triq
Alessandra

Zabbar (Notre Dame)
Gate

Bieb Is-Sultan

Triq Ik-Tlett Ibliet

St Helen's
Gate

Alessandra
Gate

Triq San Nikola

Santa Margarita Lines

Lunzjata Kunvent

Triq San Gwann T'Għuxa

Polverista
Gate

Cottonera Lines

Triq Tal-Labour

Triq Is-Santwarju

ŻABBAR

FGURA   E   F

↓ Tarxien, airport

G

↓ Marsaskala, Tarxien,
↓ airport

H

147

Indulgence Divine [map, page 150] 6 Pope Alexander VII St, Birgu; **m** (UK) 0781 398 8827; **w** indulgencedivine.com. A converted historic house just round the corner from the Inquisitor's Palace & Birgu's main square. Same owner as Valletta G-House (page 109). 1 dbl bedroom that used to be a chapel with votive graffiti of ships. Roof terrace, kitchen, sitting room. Modern décor themed on the religious & the secret (including a bit of historic erotica). Not suitable for children. €€

Nelli's [map, page 160] (4 dbls, all en suite) 36/37 Triq Santa Teresa, Cospicua, BML 1821; **m** 79588897; **w** nellis-bnb.com. Belgian ex-superyacht stewardess Nele runs this little B&B just off the Cospicua Waterfront by the Dock 1 bridge. AC, Wi-Fi. €€

Sally Port [map, page 158] Triq Ix-Zweg Mini, Senglea (between St Philip's Church & Safe Haven Gardens); **m** 99478778; **w** sallyport.com. mt. A couple of rooms in a historic house close to Senglea Point. The individually designed rooms are fully serviced, en suite & have their own kitchenette as well as access to a shared kitchen/lounge/roof terrace with views of the Grand Harbour & Birgu. Run by a charming local lady. €€

The Snop House [map, page 158] (6 rooms) 23 Victory St, Senglea, ISL 1164; **℡** 27029324; **m** 99454825; **w** thesnophouse.com. Boutique hotel in un-touristy residential Senglea with interesting (& calm) original art & 6 spacious, individually designed rooms with very comfortable beds. A 10min walk from Three Cities ferry. €€

WHERE TO EAT AND DRINK *Map, page 150, unless otherwise stated*

Hammett's [map, page 158] Triq il-31 ta' Marzu, Senglea, ISL 1040 (next to Cugó Gran Macina Hotel); **℡** 27794171; **w** hammettsmacina.com; ⏲ 19.00–22.00 daily & noon–15.00 Fri–Sun, bar 18.00–23.00 Mon–Thu & noon–midnight Fri–Sun. Excellent restaurant with a menu that ranges across Malta's history & influences with lots of starter-sized dishes to mix & match (& share). Also a few standard mains for those who like a traditional 3-course meal. €€€

La Marina Old Treasury, Vittoriosa Waterfront; **℡** 21809909; **f**; ⏲ summer 10.00–15.00 & 18.00–22.00 daily, winter hours may be shorter. Lots of tables out on the Vittoriosa Waterfront. Very good Italian food, including excellent fresh fish & salads. Service not always quick (though willing). Sit back, relax & enjoy the view. €€

Tal-Petut 20 Triq Pacifiku Scicluna, Birgu; **℡** 21891169; **m** 79421169; ⏲ 19.30–22.00 Mon–Sat, 12.30–16.00 Sun (may vary). On a quiet alley in the heart of historic Birgu this little restaurant is the private fiefdom of chef-owner Donald. He scours the local markets & cooks up a mystery tour of seasonal fare. You pay a set price (usually €28/29) for a full meal. The wide selection of antipasti is particularly good & there is always a choice of main course. Everything is homemade, even the jams & pork sausage. Donald says, 'nature is the chef, I am the cook'. Book ahead. €€

Don Berto Old Treasury, Vittoriosa Waterfront; **℡** 21808008; **m** 79808008; **w** donberto.com; ⏲ noon–15.30 & 18.30–23.00 Mon–Sat, noon–23.00 Sun, summer closed Mon lunchtime. For a different perspective on the waterfront sit up here on the balcony of the Old Treasury building looking down at the water & along to the clock tower (1810) that separates the Old Treasury from the British Naval Bakery (now Maritime Museum). Modern interior with comfortable sofas. Lift for buggies & wheelchairs. Large portions of tasty Mediterranean food including fish, pasta & pizzas & large bowls of homemade soup. €–€€€

✱ Bebirgu San Lawrenz Band Club, Birgu; **m** 77220077; **f**; ⏲ 09.00–23.00 Mon–Fri, 07.00–23.00 Sat & Sun. Inside the historic band club, right on Birgu's main square & at the heart of local life. Previously chef to the Maltese ambassador in Belgium, chef Ed Schoebben dishes up Maltese, Belgian & international food & drinks. Locals drop by for a *kafe bil-halib* (coffee with milk & sugar in a glass) & a game of snooker, while tourists cool off in the shady courtyard or AC bar with an espresso or a glass of wine. There are tables on a terrace on the square too. €–€€

Del Borgo St Dominic St, Birgu; **℡** 21803710; **m** 99280000; **w** delborgomalta.com; ⏲ 17.00–01.00 daily. Popular wine bar in an 18th-century cellar with comfortable sofas in which to flop & enjoy a glass of one of their 300 wines. €–€€

✗ Il-Hnejja [map, page 158] Sengela Waterfront, 14 Xatt Juan B Azzopardo; m 79603564; ▯; ⊕ 09.00–16.00 daily & 19.00– 23.00 Fri–Sun. Local restaurant right on the creek serving pasta & other Maltese/Mediterranean/ European home cooking. €–€€

BIRGU/VITTORIOSA

The oldest of the Three Cities, Birgu or Vittoriosa is a wonderful place to wander and has a few significant sights around which to plan a visit. When the Knights arrived in Malta in 1530, Birgu (or Il Borgo, meaning 'the town') was a fishing settlement and mercantile port with a fortress, Fort St Angelo, which the Knights regarded as thoroughly inadequate. It was, however, the main centre of population outside Mdina and its position next to the Grand Harbour made it the natural place for the maritime Knights to settle, particularly as the Sciberras Peninsula on the other side of the harbour (where Valletta now stands) was at the time a barren hillside.

The Hospitallers enlarged, embellished and fortified Birgu into their capital. Its layout remains largely unchanged with narrow streets radiating out from the central Victory Square, and there are many old buildings dating from the period between the arrival of the order (1530) and their post-Siege move to Valletta (1570s).

WHAT TO SEE AND DO

The Three Gates This is the original fortified entrance to Birgu/Vittoriosa, and until the building of the modern road it was the only way into the city. The **Advanced Gate** with its carved crossed cannons was rebuilt in 1722. Within the gate is the entrance to the Malta at War Museum and beyond it a courtyard. Spanish Knights once lived in the buildings, which were later converted into a British police station. On the far side of the courtyard is a defensive ditch, now a little public garden, which was used as a location for the film *Gladiator* featuring Russell Crowe.

Crossing the bridge over the ditch (which would originally have been a drawbridge) you pass through the second gate, the **Couvre Porte**. Steps lead up onto the ramparts, the **Porte de France** (the area manned by the French Knights), with great views of the fortifications. Go back down the steps and through the **Gate of Provence** to join the road into Birgu.

Malta at War Museum ✳ (Couvre Porte; ☏ 21896617; w maltaatwarmuseum. com; ⊕ 10.00–17.00 Mon–Sat; €12 adults, €10 seniors, €5 children under 16, €25 family (2 adults, 3 children), inc tour in English or audio guide in English & several other languages; for a combined ticket, see the box on j155 page 42) The visit starts in a museum of World War II, but the main reason to come here is the guided tour of one of Malta's largest World War II underground shelters ✳ (see box, page 151), plus a remarkable historic film.

The museum covers the period from the Abyssinian crisis in 1935 to the end of the war in Malta in 1943, displaying uniforms, weaponry, documents, touch-screens and archive footage, as well as a marvellous old Maltese bread cart, milestones (both defaced for security and – probably mistakenly – intact) and a reconstruction of an underground tunnel with the noise of bombing as it would have sounded to the people sheltering in it. At the end of the exhibition, you are led through a (replica) gas curtain down into the real hand-dug tunnels of the World War II shelter deep in the rock.

Being right next to the Grand Harbour, the Three Cities were heavily bombed and this shelter regularly held 500 people overnight. There was theoretically electricity down here but by the time the Luftwaffe had bombed the power system a few times,

6

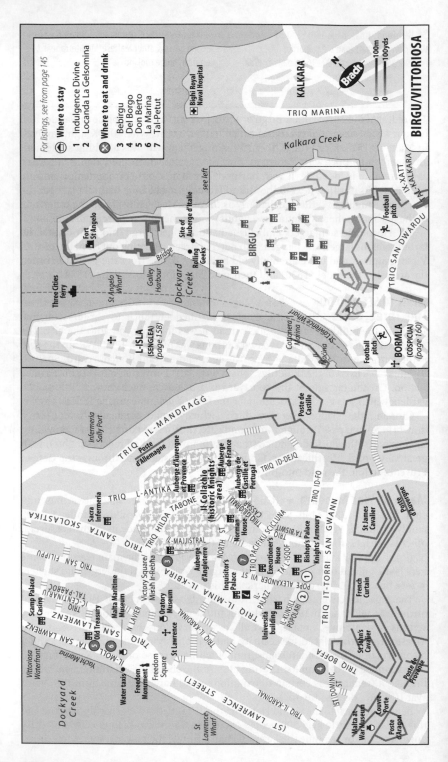

BIRGU/VITTORIOSA

Until 1944, Malta was the most bombed place in Europe, hit by some 16,000 tons of bombs (see box, page 120). Underground shelters were obviously essential. At the start of the war there were only five (including part of the Malta at War Museum shelter) but by the time it was over the entire population could be housed underground – albeit in far from ideal conditions.

Some people sheltered in old wells (cisterns), catacombs or tunnels but many of these needed to be extended and plenty of shelters were dug fresh from the rock. All the work was done by hand and the walls are lined with chisel marks. Fortunately Malta was a nation of quarrymen and stonemasons skilled in techniques that had been in use here for centuries if not millennia. Two parallel channels were cut, then the stone between broken up with sledgehammers. During the war everyone, from the Royal Engineers to local children, was involved.

The standard pattern for a shelter is long corridors with rooms off to the sides. The corridors were the public shelter, where most people waited out the air-raid alert and, when necessary, slept. The rooms were 'private'. Better-off families paid for a stretch of wall 6ft long into which to build a family shelter. These rooms offered some privacy and elbow room but little protection from the diseases that spread in the crowded corridors (tuberculosis, scabies and dysentery) and they were as rough, damp and dark as the rest of the shelter. If conditions became too overcrowded, even the private rooms had to be shared.

When it rained, water seeped quickly through the porous limestone, and in the deeper corridors people were sometimes knee-deep in water. Some shelters had electricity but enemy bombing often interfered with supply. Candles were used briefly, but Malta imported its candles from Italy, so the Maltese were soon reduced to burning olive oil in hollowed-out bowls in niches in the shelter walls (much as the Romans did in the catacombs 1,000 years earlier). The oil was smoky but effective: 500ml of olive oil would burn for two days. This, like much else about the shelters, was not ideal – but it worked.

only one bulb was kept functioning – the one in the tiled birth room. As you walk the hundreds of metres of corridors, the guide brings Malta's extraordinary wartime experience to life.

The audiovisual presentation is not to be missed. It includes an original 20-minute film, *Malta G.C.*, made in 1942 on the orders of King George VI, who had just awarded Malta the George Cross (page 18). Voiced by Laurence Olivier, it is rousing stuff: a marvellous example of wartime propaganda and, through the archive footage, a real insight into the destruction that Malta suffered between June 1940 and September 1943.

The Inquisitor's Palace (Main Gate St; ☏ 21827006; w heritagemalta.org; ⏲ 09.00–17.00 daily, last admission 16.30; €6 adults, €4.50 over-60s/children aged 12–17/students, €3 children 6–11, children under 6 free) This is one of very few inquisitor's palaces to survive anywhere and the only one regularly open to the public. Recent excavations suggest the building began life before the Knights arrived in Malta, probably as a late medieval private home. In the 1530s, it became the law courts of the Order of St John until the courts moved to Valletta in 1571, soon after which the first inquisitor arrived on the island and made his base here.

The Three Cities BIRGU/VITTORIOSA

6

The Inquisition remained here for over 220 years, through at least 62 inquisitors, until Napoleon kicked out both the Knights and the Inquisition in 1798.

The basement houses the prison cells, the ground floor the inquisitor's domestic rooms (and ticket office and shop), and the first floor was the official working area of the Inquisition. All can be visited.

The **cells** were rebuilt for greater security in 1698 after a prisoner managed to dig his way out eight times in one year. On the walls, prisoners have carved graffiti including names, a boat and a beautiful rose. The occupants were a very mixed bunch, among them a newly Christian slave who told his wine-merchant owner he would have been better off staying Muslim, a Sicilian priest (and convicted murderer) who was tortured and found guilty of 'satanic magic', a couple of female British Quakers (in the 1650s) and various prostitutes and bigamists.

The civilian warden, sworn to secrecy about the workings of the Inquisition, was responsible for the prisoners' routine. His room can be visited and just outside it on the exterior wall of the building is a little **sundial**, carved in 1730 by a warden (Leonardo Polombo) who needed a clock.

The accused who did not immediately admit his or her 'crime' risked torture in the chamber on the back stairs (between the prison and the Tribunal Room). **Torture** was usually by stretching and here you can see the hooks, ropes and pulleys designed for the purpose. Records show that those tortured included a Flemish member of the order accused of keeping prohibited books (1573), a Maltese person 'with a love of magic', a Sicilian 'blasphemer' and a French sailor who had converted to Islam (1641).

On the first floor a low door connects the stairs to the **Tribunal Room**. This ensured that prisoners always arrived in front of the inquisitor looking suitably supplicant. The flimsy little stool for the accused contrasts sharply with the heavy, carved dark-wood bank of thrones on which the inquisitor and his officials sat.

The rest of the first floor is now the **Museum of Ethnography** (focusing particularly on objects of domestic religious devotion), but the rooms remain little changed. In the chancery there is a frieze around the top of the walls with the coats of arms of Malta's inquisitors, two of whom became Pope: Fabio Chigi (Pope Alexander VII; 1655–67) and Antonio Pignatelli (Pope Innocent XII; 1691–1700). The neighbouring **audience hall** has pink walls and *trompe l'oeil* windows.

The museum shop sells three short but detailed **guidebooks** by Kenneth Gambin: *The Inquisitor's Palace, Torture and the Roman Inquisition* and *The Prison Experience at the Inquisitor's Palace* (Insight Heritage Guides; €7.99 each).

Victory Square (Misraħ ir-Rebħa)

Victory Square (Misraħ ir-Rebħa) This was originally two squares with lower buildings than today's and a watchtower from which Grand Master Jean Parisot de Valette directed some of the battles of the Great Siege. The square was the rallying point for the Knights' troops and de Valette is said to have moved out of his palace into a tavern on the square to be closer to the centre of operations. Bomb damage in World War II meant that the tower had to be knocked down and the two squares were merged into one.

At the centre of today's square are two monuments: a white statue of Birgu's patron saint **St Lawrence** (1880) and the **Victory Monument**, erected in 1705 to commemorate the defeat of the Turks in the Great Siege 150 years earlier. The railings make the order's position very clear with a repeated pattern of the cross of St John atop a sword that points down on the crescent of the Ottoman Empire. At the corner with La Vallette Street is a wall-mounted lamp and small **shrine** by which is a plaque marking the spot where **public executions** took place in the 16th century.

The wonderfully ornate building with a splendid *gallarija* and intricate white wrought-iron balconies is the **San Lawrenz Band Club** (in British times, the Duke of Edinburgh Band Club). Still at the heart of local life, it contains a snooker room, and a bar-café-restaurant (page 148), as well as a shady courtyard. Almost next door is the site of the **German Auberge** (7 Victory Sq, marked with a plaque), which was (ironically) destroyed by Axis bombing in World War II and is now a modern building. This was on the edge of the Collachio and the granite bollard marks the start of the Knights' private area of the capital.

The Collachio✱ and the Knights' *auberges* Just off the square are the narrow

stone-paved streets which were Il Collachio, the area reserved for the Knights. Here their *auberges* were concentrated, the idea being that keeping them close together made them easier to defend in times of trouble. A surprising number have survived. The interiors are not open to the public but the buildings are marked with marble plaques.

Triq Hilda Tabone (which the Knights called Strada della Castiglia) was the main street of the Collachio. Here you will find four of the Knights' first *auberges*:

- 17–23: shared **Auberge d'Auvergne et Provence** – structurally changed by subdivision of the middle of the façade into smaller houses.
- 24–7: **Auberge de France** – larger and a little grander than the others because at this time the French were the largest and most influential group. Grand Master de L'Isle Adam (grand master at the time the Knights arrived in Malta) was a Frenchman and the French *langue* ran the Sacra Infermeria. The Knights continued to use this *auberge* up until 1586 in addition to their new *auberge* in Valletta which was destroyed in World War II.
- 28–30: **Auberge d'Aragon** – almost unrecognisable due to modern alterations.
- 57–9: (on the corner of Triq Gilormu Cassar) **Auberge de Castille et Portugal** – a large portion of the building was destroyed in World War II but the corner is original.

The **Auberge d'Angleterre** is round the corner in Mistral Street (Triq Il-Majjistral) (numbers 39–40). This is the only true English *auberge* in Malta. Henry VIII broke with Rome shortly after the Knights' arrival here and seized their property in England in 1540. This left the English Knights in an awkward, and financially compromised, position. Mary Tudor reinstated the order in 1557 but the *langue* never really recovered and when the order moved to Valletta no English *auberge* was built. The few English Knights that remained (and at times there were none) had to find other accommodation until the late 18th century and the creation of the shared Auberge of Bavaria and England (Auberge de Bavière; page 137). Even in Birgu the relationship between the German and English *langues* was close, with their *auberges* connected at the back.

The site of the **Auberge d'Italie** is a couple of hundred metres away towards Fort St Angelo at 1–6 St Lawrence Street (Triq San Lawrenz). The head of the Italian *langue* was also the Admiral of the Fleet so the *auberge* was built closer to the ships and the naval headquarters at Fort St Angelo.

Other historic buildings you might pass Like the *auberges*, the following

buildings are of historical interest, but can only be viewed from the outside.

Sacra Infermeria (Santa Scholastica St (Triq Santa Skolastica), overlooking Kalkara (Calcaara) Creek) This large early Renaissance building was the Knights' first hospital in Malta, built in 1532, and as Hospitallers it was central to their mission. Part of the building (on Saint Scholastica Street) was pulled down to make way for modern housing. When the order moved into its new hospital in Valletta in 1604 this building became a Benedictine convent and so it remains today. Next door is the small **Benedictine Church of St Anne** (1679) designed by Lorenzo Gafà with an altarpiece by Mattia Preti. Close by at 19 Observer Street is an old house that was the residence of the chief medical superintendent of the hospital.

The Norman House (10–11 North St; e Charlie.bugeja@hvassallo.com) Almost all that is left to be seen of pre-1530 Birgu, this house was reputedly built in the 13th century. The first-floor window and façade frieze are 15th century. It has been restored by its present owner and is now open Mondays, Wednesdays, Fridays and Saturdays, usually from about 08.30 to 17.00 by donation.

The Executioner's House (6 Pope Alexander VII St, cnr 17 Pacifico Scicluna St) This was the grace and favour home of the Knights' official executioner. It is on the corner and identifiable by the pair of axes carved above the upper window.

Palace of the Conventual Chaplains (7–9 Pope Alexander VII St) Home of the order's chaplains of St Lawrence Church until the move to Valletta.

The Università building (36–7 Popular Council St) Built in 1538, this was home to the Birgu Università – local council – until the British took over.

The Bishop's Palace (26–9 Bishop's Palace St) Built in 1542 and enlarged in 1620 by the last bishop to be based in Vittoriosa. When the order moved to Valletta they did not want the bishop to move with them, so this palace and St Lawrence Church remained his second base after Mdina.

St Lawrence Church (San Lawrenz) (St Lawrence St; ⊕ mornings early for prayer & usually 09.30–noon for visitors except on Sun; reopens around 16.30/17.00 for prayer prior to 18.00 Mass (you can pop in if you are quiet), 09.15–11.00 Sun; *festa* in Aug) Immediately to the left inside the visitors' door to the church is a red-and-grey **monument** with the cross of the Order of St John and a Maltese flag. It commemorates the 900th anniversary of the parish (1090–1990) for which Pope John Paul II made a visit. The first church here is believed to have been built in the time of Roger the Norman, and whilst the Knights were based in Birgu (1530–71), the church on this site was the main religious centre of the order. It was here that Grand Master de Valette gathered his Knights and the people of Birgu on the eve of the Great Siege in May 1565, and here that those who survived met again in September when victory was finally theirs.

The present building, built in 1681–97, was designed by Baroque architect Lorenzo Gafà (also responsible for the cathedrals of Mdina and Gozo). The left tower was added in the 18th century, the right only in 1930. The church – including Gafà's dome – was badly damaged in World War II, but has been faithfully restored. The huge altarpiece of *The Martyrdom of St Lawrence* is thought to be Mattia Preti's largest painting. The detail is, as so often in churches, frustratingly hard to see. If the painting is unlit, ask the warden if he could switch on the lights for a short while (and perhaps make a small contribution to the church in exchange).

In front of the church on the waterfront is the **Freedom Monument**, which was unveiled on the eve of 31 March 1979 when the British armed forces departed from

Malta. The **precincts** to the side of the church were once a burial ground for people killed during the Turkish insurgency of 1551, as well as a few of the dead from the Great Siege. Here too is the entrance to the oratory dedicated to St Joseph which houses a small but interesting **museum** (see below) including items rescued from the church and other parts of Birgu after they suffered serious bomb damage in 1942.

St Lawrence Oratory Museum (⊕ approx 09.30–noon Mon–Sat; admission free)

An Aladdin's cave of historic documents and objects. Most famous among them are the hat and sword of Grand Master de Valette which hang in the chapel, originally a small Greek parish church. The hat is black and wide-brimmed and the functional sword is said to be the one de Valette wore during the victory ceremonies after the Great Siege. He apparently left them in the church in pious thanks for victory and was given a richly decorated replacement sword by Catholic king Philip II of Spain in gratitude for the body blow his order had dealt the Turks. Only a picture of this ornate sword hangs on the wall here; the original was taken by Napoleon and is now in the Louvre in Paris.

Among other items in the museum are a 15th-century Gutenberg incunabulum (a book printed before 1501 in Europe), a 1777 bill of lading for a Knights' galley (in Italian), the Grand Inquisitor's Pectoral Cross, a copy of the first newspaper ever published in Malta (1804, after the British took over, although the paper is in Italian and French), a cap from an SS uniform (hidden among other World War II memorabilia 'so as not to offend German visitors'), and a rare early atlas published in Venice in 1598 using the maps of ancient Greek geographer Ptolemy (AD90–168), a copy of which Christopher Columbus is assumed to have used on his famous voyage.

Malta Maritime Museum (Ex-Naval Bakery; ✆ 21660052; w heritagemalta.org; ⊕ 09.00–17.00 daily; €5 adults, €3.50 over-60s/children aged 12–17/students, €2.50 children aged 6–11, children under 6 free)

This building, next to the Freedom Monument on the Vittoriosa Waterfront, is the old **British Naval Bakery** in which steam-driven machinery produced 30,000lb of bread and biscuits a day for the Mediterranean Fleet. The building was designed by William Scamp and built in 1842–45 in place of the order's Galley Arsenal. Its façade was apparently inspired by Windsor Castle (I can't see it).

The highlight of the museum for most people will be a large (about 3.5m long) mid 18th-century model of a ship of the line of the Order of St John. The model was probably used by the order's nautical school and gives a good idea of the sort of vessels that once dominated the creeks and harbour outside the museum. There is also a variety of smaller contemporary models of the Knights' ships, as well as of a couple of opulent grand masters' barges.

All sorts of objects take you through Malta's maritime history: cannons, anchors – including the largest known **Roman anchor** in the world weighing four tons – hand-held weapons, manuals, documents, paintings and uniforms including the order's extremely smart 18th-century naval garb of knickerbockers and long red jackets. The old dark-wood Customs cupboard is here too, full of weights and measures, some still marked with the coats of arms of grand masters. A marble waterspout in the shape of a cannon barrel used to be part of a harbourside fountain fed by the Wignacourt Aqueduct (see box, page 226) from which the Knights' galleys filled up with water. Its Latin inscription reads: 'Why are you afraid little boat? There is no fire here, but water instead of shot.'

An extensive gallery is devoted to 200 years of the British Royal Navy in Malta: from a portrait of Sir Alexander Ball (one of Nelson's admirals who helped the

Maltese see off the French in 1798–1800 and became first British governor of Malta) to a uniform, documents and photographs of Admiral Sir Nigel Cecil, last Commander of the British forces in Malta (1975–79).

There is a brightly painted figurehead from HMS *Hibernia* (1805) and for ship buffs a case of over 250 tiny models showing the evolution of Royal Navy warships from HMS *Victory* through to today. There are also four barmaids' (for which read prostitutes') licences – like large coins – probably used in the notorious Valletta street nicknamed 'The Gut' (page 134). The final gallery covers the arrival of steam and modern ship propulsion, displaying a variety of machinery including a working triple expansion steam engine.

Vittoriosa Waterfront

The wharf that faces Dockyard Creek (Galley Creek) has always been at the centre of Birgu's activities. It was the first place to be inhabited on the Grand Harbour (as far back as Phoenician times) before becoming the Grand Marina of the Order and then the Royal Navy's base in Malta. It is now a modern yacht marina and its old buildings have been renovated and turned into cafés and restaurants. Vittoriosa Waterfront offers the best views of **Senglea** – from its tip in the Grand Harbour, along its fortifications and Dock Number 1 to the start of Cospicua. This is also the best place to look at Il-Maċina, a large crane once used to turn ships over for cleaning and repair. **Dock 1** has been recently renovated to create a pleasant walkway along the water's edge from Birgu to Senglea. There are patches of grass, seats made from old wooden docksides and some children's play equipment. There is also a new bridge crossing the dock from the Birgu end of Cospicua to Senglea. The atmospheric old warehouses are now being redeveloped.

During the Great Siege a pontoon bridge was laid across the water to speed up resupply of Fort St Michael (which then stood on the Senglea side towards the head of the creek), and a great chain linked Fort St Angelo to Senglea Point to prevent enemy ships from entering the creek.

The wharf (with very limited access for motor vehicles) starts at the Malta Maritime Museum, which abuts the order's **Old Treasury**. After the move to Valletta, this became a centre for the manufacture of galley rigging and sails. Its arched arcade has now been sympathetically converted into restaurants with waterfront terraces.

A little further along the waterfront towards Fort St Angelo is **Scamp Palace**, once the residence of the order's Captain General of the Galleys and later the office of the British Admiralty. It was named after the architect of the British Naval Bakery who was based here during its construction. Next along is a patch of wasteland. Here stood the palace of the head of the order's arsenal until it was bombed in World War II. By St Angelo Bridge (leading to the fort) is a modern apartment block, St Angelo Mansions, built on the site of the order's slave cells.

Fort St Angelo

(✆ 22954000; w heritagemalta.org; ☉ summer 09.00–18.00 daily, winter until 17.00; €8 adults, €5 seniors/students, €3 children 6–11, free for ages 5 & under) Cut off from the rest of Birgu by a moat, Fort St Angelo is a dominating presence at the tip of the Vittoriosa Peninsula. The oldest extant fort in Malta, it is first mentioned as early as 1223 and documented as the Castrum Maris ('Castle by the Sea') in 1274. The site was probably used for centuries before that. The medieval *castellan* (governor of the fort) lived here, representative of his overlord in Sicily, and his late medieval house still stands at the high point of the castle. The first grand master of the Order of St John in Malta, Phillippe Villiers de L'Isle Adam, converted the house into a palace for himself.

Expanded and strengthened by the Knights to withstand cannon-fire, the fort was the order's military HQ from their arrival in Malta in 1530 until 1571. After this, when the Knights had moved to Valletta, the order used it as their own high-security prison, with prisoners including the deposed grand master's artist Caravaggio. St Angelo played a crucial role in the Great Siege of 1565, though it was never itself besieged by the Turks.

After the order's move to Valletta and the strengthening of the Cottonera fortifications around the Three Cities, the fort was sidelined until 1691 when a senior Knight, who was also a military engineer, Carlos Grunenburgh, reshaped it to its present form. So determined was he to modernise the castle that he paid for the work himself and his contribution is recognised by the presence of his coat of arms (where the grand master's would usually be) above St Angelo's main entrance.

The 19th century saw St Angelo – still guardian of the Grand Harbour – in the hands of the British army, before in 1906 it became the headquarters of the Royal Navy in Malta. In 1912, the fort was renamed as if it were a ship: HMS *Egmont*, and in 1933 HMS *St Angelo*. In World War II, Fort St Angelo withstood 69 direct hits. One of the bombs can be seen in the old Naval Bakery, now the National Maritime Museum, a few doors away on the Vittoriosa Waterfront.

When the remaining British troops left Malta in 1979, this fort was the last to be vacated, before becoming (in a move characteristic of the time) briefly a tourist hotel with a swimming pool destructively built into the walls. In the 1990s, it fell into disrepair and suffered from vandalism.

In 1998, the Maltese government signed a 99-year lease, handing over the upper layer of the fortress to the modern Sovereign Military Hospitaller Order of St John of Jerusalem, of Rhodes and of Malta (to give it its full name). Two hundred years after its expulsion, the order returned. One of Malta's most senior Knights now occupies a house inside the fortress.

Following a €13 million restoration programme, the fort was opened to the public in 2016. Inside are Knights- and British-period barracks, a historic chapel, parade grounds overlooking the Grand Harbour, battlements and stunning 360° views from the top of the *cavalier*. It is also possible to visit the otherwise-private Upper St Angelo on a 1-hour tour that runs once a day (times vary, costs an extra €5). Book ahead to be sure of a place.

The fortifications From Fort St Angelo the fortifications of Birgu/Vittoriosa run right along the water's edge on the Kalkara Creek side and then along the landward flank of the town back to the Three Gates. Much of this stretch of wall has been recently restored and is an interesting route to walk.

Each *langue* took responsibility for a stretch (a *poste* or post) of Birgu's defences as they did later in Valletta. The first length of fortifications along Triq Il-Mandragg is the **Poste d'Angleterre**, which runs as far as the **Bighi Sally Port**, also called the **Infermeria Sally Port**. Originally the bastion walls on this side of Birgu rose straight from the water. The only way to land or leave was through small sally ports (hidden entrances/exits from which the order's troops could 'sally forth').

From here there are good views across the creek to Kalkara and the **Bighi Royal Naval Hospital** [147 F3] with its tall tower containing a lift that carried the sick directly to the hospital from the ship below. The building now houses a government Restoration Centre.

The next stretch of wall is the **German Post** (Poste d'Allemagne), which seems to be a favourite dog-walking spot, so watch where you tread. Where the fortifications turn the corner is the **Poste de Castille**. During the Great Siege, the Turks stormed the ramparts here (spawning its nickname, Il-breccja – 'the breach'). It looked as though the day was lost for the Knights until Grand Master Jean Parisot de Valette arrived personally leading reinforcements. A plaque marks the spot where he was wounded in the leg in the subsequent fighting. The need to reinforce the defences at this corner was clear and the outer fortifications you now see are mainly 18th century.

The landward fortifications centre on **two** *cavaliers* (massive raised gun platforms) – called, as in Valletta, St James and St John. Both were the responsibility of the French *langue* and are joined by the French Curtain Wall. The present structures are post-Siege. **St James Cavalier** was planned in 1588 but only built in 1723–30. It is uncared for but always open. The tunnel underneath was a World War II shelter. **St John's** (also 1723–30) is closed to the public. It is hoped that both *cavaliers* will be restored in the not too distant future.

Next to St James Cavalier is the Knights' **Old Armoury** on Triq L'Arċisqof Mikiel Gonzi (Archbishop Michael Gonzi St) at the top of Triq Il-Palazz tal-Isqof (Bishop's Palace St). Probably originally dating from the mid 16th century, this was the Knights' main weapons store in Birgu and served as a makeshift hospital during the Great Siege. The first floor was added in 1636 and under the British it was a military hospital and residential quarters (gaining it the name Il-Kwartier). It is now government offices.

L-ISLA/SENGLEA

The hunting grounds of L-Isla became the village of Senglea in the 1550s when Grand Master Claude de la Sengle offered a plot of land to anyone willing to build a house. He also strengthened its fortifications, which proved to have been a prudent move when the Turks attacked a decade later. Senglea's main fort, Fort St Michael, was demolished in 1922 so the British could expand the

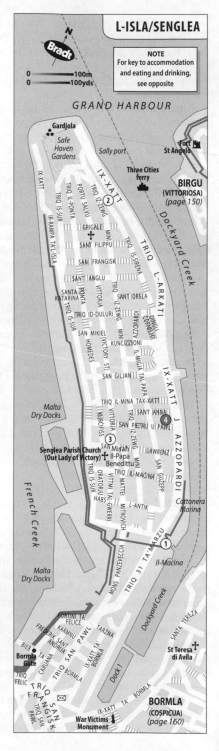

L-ISLA/SENGLEA
For listings, see from page 145

 Where to stay
1 Cugó Gran Macina Grand Harbour
2 Sally Port
3 The Snop House

Where to eat and drink
Hammett's (see 1)
4 Il-Hnejja

docks, but the fortifications at Senglea Point and along the side of French Creek remain. Whilst it has fewer specific sights than Birgu/Vittoriosa, Senglea is well worth wandering around. You can circle the peninsula along the water's edge, with views across the creeks and the Grand Harbour, then duck inland to see the parish church and a few of the older streets and soak up local life.

WHAT TO SEE AND DO
Safe Haven Gardens (Gardjola Gardens) (Senglea Point, end of Victory St)
Right at the tip of the peninsula is Senglea Point and a small public garden with spectacular views over the Grand Harbour and across to Valletta. The Upper Barrakka Gardens are clearly visible atop the bastion walls of the capital. There are great views too of Fort St Angelo and Birgu/Vittoriosa.

On the wall of the gardens overlooking the Grand Harbour is a stone *gardjola*, rebuilt Knights-period sentry box, carved with an eye and an ear to remind the guards to be vigilant. It was from just below here that the Great Chain (page 156) ran across the mouth of the creek to Fort St Angelo.

Senglea Parish Church (⊕ usually early until noon & then 16.00–19.00)
The substantial **Church of Our Lady of Victory** was built in 1743 but had to be reconstructed in the 1950s after it was severely damaged in 1941 by bombs meant for the British aircraft carrier HMS *Illustrious* anchored in Dockyard Creek. The church is chiefly known for its statue of **Christ the Redeemer (Gesu Redentur)** – in the chapel to the right of the altar. This unusually emotional polychrome statue of Christ on his hands and knees under the weight of the Cross is believed to have miraculous powers. The parish has two feast days – in March and June.

BORMLA/COSPICUA

Bormla was given the title Città Cospicua (Italian for the 'conspicuous' or 'distinguished one') in the early 18th century on account of its then recently completed massive, eye-catching fortifications (page 161).

Bormla suffered terribly in both of Malta's sieges. Just before the start of the Great Siege, Grand Master de Valette ordered that the few homes in the area (then outside any fortifications) be razed to the ground so that they could not be used by the invading Turks. Bormla was largely destroyed again in World War II, this time by enemy bombing. One of the few buildings to survive was the vast, ornate **Church of the Immaculate Conception** (built in 1584, enlarged 1637), which sits at the top of a long flight of steps staring down at the dock. It is at the centre of a large *festa* in December. The **monument** at the bottom of the steps is to the fallen of World War II and there are a few old streets around the church that are worth exploring. Narrow **Nelson Street** is possibly the oldest of many streets around the world named after the British admiral – in this case in thanks for his efforts to free Bormla and Malta from Napoleon's troops.

To add to Bormla's woes, it suffered disproportionately from loss of employment in the second half of the 20th century as the British Navy departed and ship-repair yards closed. Bormla's narrow, stepped streets became among the poorest urban

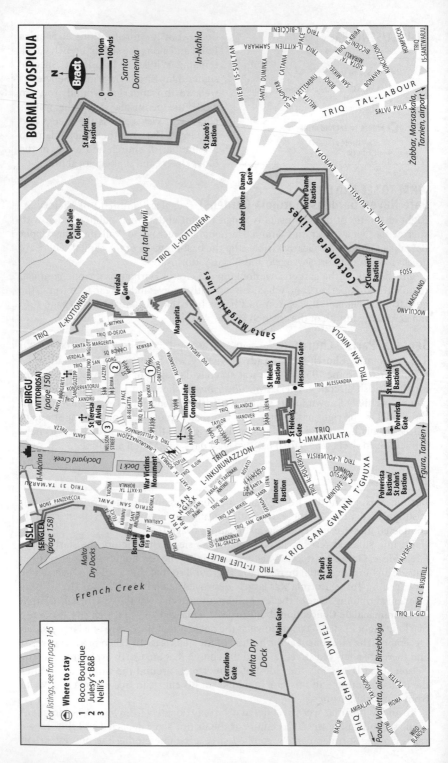

BORMLA/COSPICUA

For listings, see from page 145

Where to stay
1 Boco Boutique
2 Julesy's B&B
3 Nelli's

N

0   100m
0   100yds

Bradt

Santa Domenika

BIRGU
(VITTORIOSA)
(page 150)

L-ISLA
(SENGLEA)
(page 158)

areas in Malta. They are now well on their way to regeneration with old buildings being restored and employment rising.

WHAT TO SEE AND DO
The Santa Margarita/Firenzuola Lines
Bormla/Cospicua is surrounded on the landward side by the Santa Margarita Lines – four bastions joined by curtain walls breached by two gates. Begun in 1638 to designs by military engineer Vincenzo Maculano da Firenzuola, these were intended to protect the rear of the Three Cities. Even after the move to Valletta, the creeks here remained home to the Knights' ships as the new capital had no such harbours. Protecting the landward side of the Three Cities was therefore very important at a time when fear of Turkish invasion remained high. The order's concern was not without reason: Turkish raids took place in 1641 and 1645, though never with the force of 1565.

Work on the Santa Margarita Lines stopped before the project was finished and although additions continued to be made into the 18th century, they were never fully completed. The attention of the Knights' defence teams had moved to the creation of an even larger, more all-encompassing line of defence, the **Cottonera Lines**. St Helen's Gate, with its stone mortars, carved scroll and decorative columns, is a good place to start to see a stretch of the Santa Margarita Lines. Note that although this is the main gate through the Santa Margarita Lines, its Latin inscription commemorates the completion of the Cottonera defences.

AROUND THE THREE CITIES

THE COTTONERA LINES [147 F7–G6] In 1669, the Venetian city of Candia (modern-day Heraklion on Crete), then the easternmost outpost of Christianity, fell to the Ottoman Turks, leaving Malta next in line. The Knights put the nation on a war footing, expecting a repeat of the Great Siege. Italian military engineer Antonio Maurizio Valperga was loaned to the order by the Duke of Savoy and in 1670 he created an ambitious master plan for the defence of the Grand Harbour area. The only parts that were actually built were the Cottonera Lines (named after Grand Master Nicolas Cotoner), Fort Ricasoli [147 F2] (which languishes, battered by the sea at the entrance to the Grand Harbour) and some additions to the Floriana Lines.

The Cottonera Lines still stand – a massive 5km defensive barrier around the landward side of the Three Cities. There are eight bastions and two demi-bastions. The monumental Baroque **Żabbar Gate/Notre Dame Gate** is still the tallest building in Bormla and still one of the main routes into town. It now houses the headquarters of the **Fondazzjoni Wirt Artna** (Malta Heritage Trust; ✎ 21800992, 21803091; w wirtartna.org) and tours of the building can be arranged with them (€5 pp). If driving (or walking, though on foot you might want to be aware this is not the most salubrious spot in Malta), turn left inside the gate and follow the walls along for a good sense of the Cottonera Lines.

FORT RINELLA [147 G3] (St Rocco Rd, Kalkara; ✎ 21800992; w fortrinella.com, wirtartna.org; ⊙ 10.00–17.00 Mon–Sat; €12 adults, €5 children under 16, €10 seniors/students, €25 family (2 adults, 3 children) or for multi-site pass see the box on page 42, inc guided tour in English (or audio guide in other languages), film & demonstrations; main tour & demos daily ⊙ 14.00; to get there take bus 3 from Valletta which stops right outside) Fort Rinella, the world's first fully mechanised fort, was built by the British in 1878 to house the new 100-ton gun, then the largest cannon available. This monster gun with its bizarre (but authentic) pink camouflage, still stands pointing menacingly out to sea. With a range of eight miles, it could penetrate 65cm into steel armour and was so heavy that it had to be turned, cleaned and loaded by steam-powered hydraulic machinery.

There were originally two such guns in Malta, the other at Fort Cambridge (page 171), now largely demolished. The guns were intended to fire alternately, keeping up a devastating bombardment of the sea at the entrances to Valletta's harbours. They were never used in anger.

An interesting film explains why this gun was needed. The short version is that its British inventor sold it to the Italian Navy so the British Navy then had to have it too! Some 135 men were stationed here: 100 to guard the landward side of the fort, 35 to operate the gun.

Demonstrations include various 19th-century British military skills, firing of historic artillery, sometimes including the only six-ton howitzer cannon left in the world. This was the sort of gun that defended the Victoria Lines (see box, page 239).

7

Sliema, St Julian's and Paceville

Most of Malta's better chain resort hotels (and many others) are in this built-up area along the northern coast on the other side of Marsamxett Harbour from Valletta. The rocky shoreline is backed with apartment blocks and hotels and, particularly in summer, life goes on into the early hours.

Sliema is the area closest to Valletta (with the Sliema ferry linking the two). At Balluta Bay, Sliema seamlessly blends into St Julian's, which itself morphs unnoticeably into Paceville on the other side of Spinola Bay. Despite this lack of clear borders between the three areas, they each have a distinct character. Sliema is upmarket, with Malta's most prestigious shopping and expensive residential areas as well as the popular seafront promenades (and some cheaper tourist accommodation). St Julian's is the main centre of upmarket mass tourism on the island with lots of seafront restaurants, and Paceville is its brasher, noisier, younger and cheaper neighbour.

PRACTICALITIES

There are plenty of **shops** (standard European fare), **banks** and **ATMs** in this built-up part of Malta. There is a **post office** in St Julian's (Lombard Bank bldg, Triq, Paceville; ⊕ w/day mornings) and a **sub-post office** in Sliema (7 Triq Ċensu Xerri, Tigné; ⊕ 07.30–12.45 Mon–Sat).

⌂ WHERE TO STAY

In addition to the hotels listed here, there are a variety of two- to four-star modern hotels, particularly along the Sliema Waterfront which have little character and are used mostly by package-holiday operators, though they can now be booked direct online.

TOP END

⌂ **Corinthia St George's Bay******* [173 B1] (250 rooms) St George's Bay; ✆ 21374114; w corinthia.com. A conventional 5-star resort hotel on the edge of St George's Bay, Paceville, but secluded enough to avoid the noise. Shares facilities with neighbouring 4-star Marina Hotel. 4 swimming pools (1 indoor, 1 adults only), kids' pool (tucked away), gym, spa (inc outdoor massage), rocky private beach, watersports, 9 restaurants/cafés/bars from American diner to

fusion fine dining, including 2 smart restaurants, Buddhaman & Caviar & Bull, that regularly win Malta's main restaurant awards based on public voting. €€€€

⌂ **The Hilton******* [173 C3] (410 rooms, 6 apts/suites) Portomaso; ✆ 21383383; w malta. hilton.com. On the edge of Paceville in the expensive, modern Portomaso complex: 98m tower, private yacht marina, cafés & restaurants. The hotel has 4 outdoor & 1 indoor swimming pools, 2 children's paddling pools, a small rocky

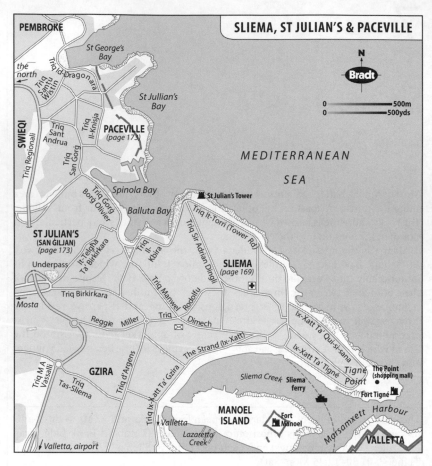

N

Bradt

0 — 500m
0 — 500yds

PEMBROKE

the north

St George's Bay

St Jullian's Bay

Triq Santu Wistin

Triq Id-Dragonara

SWIEQI

Triq Regionali

Triq Sant Andrua

Triq Il-Knisja

Triq San Gorg

PACEVILLE
(page 173)

MEDITERRANEAN

SEA

Triq Gorg Borg Olivier

Spinola Bay

Balluta Bay

St Julian's Tower

Triq It-Torri (Tower Rd)

ST JULIAN'S
(SAN ĠILJAN)
(page 173)

It-Telgha Ta' Birkirkara

Triq Il-Kbira

Triq Sir Adrian Dingli

Underpass

Triq Manwel Rodolfu

SLIEMA
(page 169)

Mosta

Triq Birkirkara

Reggie Miller Triq

Dimech

Ix-Xatt Ta' Qui-si-sana

GZIRA

Triq M A Vassali

Triq Tas-Sliema

Triq d'Argens

Triq Ix-Xatt Ta' Gzira

The Strand (Ix-Xatt)

Ix-Xatt Ta' Tigné

Sliema Creek

Sliema ferry

Tigné Point

The Point
(shopping mall)

Fort Tigné

Valletta

MANOEL ISLAND

Fort Manoel

Lazaretto Creek

Marsamxett Harbour

VALLETTA

'beach' (summer only), jacuzzi, fitness centre, spa (page 97), tennis & squash. Choice of classic or contemporary décor in rooms (the contemporary are newer), all with balconies overlooking the sea, swimming pools or yacht marina. Also 6 new studio apts/family suites (sleeping up to 4), which can be quite a good deal if you need extended high-end hotel accommodation (over 1 month). The hotel has its own desalination plant so the tap water is drinkable & 99% of water is recycled. €€€€

Malta Marriott (formerly Le Meridien) ***** [173 C6] 39 Main St, St Julian's; \23110000/1, 23112810; due to (re)open 2nd half 2019. Modern 5-star hotel on Balluta Bay, with lovely views of St Julian's & the sea. Indoor & outdoor pools, spa (page 97), terraces & restaurants. €€€€

Westin Dragonara Resort*** [173 C2] (340 rooms) Dragonara Rd, St Julian's;

\21381000, 21381347; e westin.dragonara@ westin.com; w westinmalta.com. Pompous exterior, but spacious, recently renovated rooms with attractive bathrooms, good-sized balconies & sea views. Although on the edge of Paceville, rooms are quiet as they all face away from the town. Family rooms, kids' club & small outdoor children's play area. Private rocky 'beach'. Large sea-view terrace. Indoor, 2 outdoor & children's pools. Watersports. €€€€

Intercontinental*** [173 B2] (451 rooms) St George's Bay; \UK reservations: 0871 423 4949, Malta: 21377600, 21372222; w intercontinental.com. Good hotel in a neon location – opposite the Bay Street shopping centre, Paceville. Extensive paved 'garden', large indoor & outdoor pools. Private area of St George's Bay Beach. €€€–€€€€

Radisson Blu St Julian's*** [173 B1] (252 rooms, 9 apts) St George's Bay; ☎21374894; w radissonblu.com/stjuliansresort-malta. Large resort hotel just north of St George's Bay, Paceville. 3 outdoor pools, 1 indoor pool (heated in winter) & a children's pool, sauna, tennis, watersports, courtesy minibus. 3 restaurants (4 in summer), families welcome. €€€–€€€€

Fortina Spa*** [169 F4] (150 rooms) Tigné Seafront, Sliema; ☎23462149; w fortinasparesort. com. 17-storey skyscraper next to the Tigné Point shopping centre. Gorgeous views of Valletta from upper-floor sea-view rooms especially at night. Spa bedrooms, several restaurants, pools & a large fitness centre. Closed due to major works next door. Should reopen in 2020. €€€

Marina Hotel** [173 B1] (189 rooms) Corinthia Beach Resort, St George's Bay, Paceville; ☎23702000, 23702370; w marinahotel.com.mt. Bright modern hotel sharing all the facilities of the 5-star Corinthia St George's Bay. The difference is interior décor & rooms, which are fresher here, & atmosphere, which is more relaxed. €€€

The Palace*** [169 D2] (150 rooms) High St, Sliema; ☎21333444; w thepalacemalta. com. Tucked into the quiet residential heart of Sliema, this smart urban hotel has a designer lobby & modern rooms, well-heated indoor pool & unheated rooftop infinity pool, gym & small spa. Full refurbishment of rooms is planned during the 1st quarter of 2019. Excellent b/fasts & buffet dinners on ground floor & popular Asian fusion rooftop restaurant. Easy walk to both seafronts & Sliema Ferries. Helpful staff. Avoid rooms just beneath the 9th-floor restaurant. €€€

MID-RANGE

The George** [173 C3] (126 rooms) Paceville Av, Paceville, STJ 3103; ☎20111000; w thegeorgemalta.com. Modern hotel in the heart of Paceville, with vast foyer & spacious rooms. Pleasant rooftop terrace with good-sized pool, spa including indoor pool. Front rooms quieter than back. Prices change daily with occupancy & are good value in winter. €€€

Golden Tulip Vivaldi** [173 C2] (263 rooms) Dragonara Rd, St Julian's; ☎21378100; w goldentulipvivaldi.com. On the edge of Paceville opposite the Westin Dragonara. Typical modern, high-ceilinged, marble-clad, wannabe 5-star-hotel lobby. No character but pleasant

rooms (no views) & good service. Indoor & rooftop pools, sauna & gym. €€€

✳ **Juliani**** [173 B4] (47 rooms) 25 St George's Rd, St Julian's; ☎21388000; w hoteljuliani. com; see ad, 3rd colour section. Overlooking Spinola Bay in the centre of St Julian's. Contemporary city boutique hotel with smart public areas full of comfortable seating. Lobby café, gym, pleasant blue-&-white-tiled roof terrace with small swimming pool, & good b/fasts with fresh juice. Friendly, personal service. The hotel's Asian restaurant, Zest, is very popular with locals. €€€

The Victoria** [169 D2] (137 rooms) Ġorġ Borġ Olivier St, Sliema; ☎21334711; w victoriahotel.com. The Palace's older & more traditional neighbouring sister hotel shares its spa, gym & pool facilities. A little faded in places, but most rooms are fine & the staff friendly & helpful. There may be special offers. €€€

Pebbles Apartments [169 D3] (36 studios/apts) 89 The Strand, Sliema; ☎21311889; w pebbleshotelmalta.com. Bright, clean self-catering studio rooms & apts on the Sliema promenade. €€

Preluna** [169 E2] (280 rooms) 124 Tower Rd, Sliema; ☎21334001; w preluna. com. Large high-rise seafront hotel spread over 3 buildings. Rooms mostly bright & clean with good-sized windows even on the town side. Indoor spa & pool. Outdoor pool by the sea across the road. €€

Hotel Valentina* [173 C3] (94 rooms) Dobbie St, Paceville; ☎21382232, 21382407; w hotelvalentina.com. Contemporary urban hotel with high-ceilinged foyer full of natural light & modern art. Glass-walled b/fast room overlooks foyer. Other meals at 10% discount at nearby restaurant, The Avenue (page 167), which will also deliver to your room. Small, attractive rooftop pool. Library area. Rooms sleep 1–4. Front rooms have French windows/balcony, back rooms quieter. As good as many 4-stars in Malta. €–€€

BUDGET

Hostel Malti [173 B7] (4 dorms) 41 Birkakara Hill, Ta' Ġiorni, St Julian's; ☎27302758; m 79491648, 79361599; w hostelmalti.com/ en/home.htm. Sociable hostel a few mins' walk up a steep hill behind Balluta Bay. Roof terrace where evening barbecues are held. 4 mixed dorms sleeping 6–12. Guests must be 18+. €

🏠 **Inhawi Boutique Hostel** [173 C7] (20 rooms, 134 beds) Triq It-Telghet, St Julian's; ↘21382554; w inhawi.com. A friendly modern hostel with great facilities including a terrace with swimming pool & a large eat-in kitchen with retractable roof. Comfortable bunks in dorms of 2–12 (mixed or women only) & twin rooms. €

🏠 **NSTS Hibernia Hostel** [169 C2] (40 rooms) De Piro St, Sliema; ↘25588340 (mornings), other times call NSTS HQ on ↘2558000; w nsts.org. Excellent location just off the seafront near Balluta

Bay where Sliema meets St Julian's. Decent-sized bright, clean rooms (though older showers & loos) with 2–8 beds & kitchenette. Communal lounge, TV, & canteen serving a good cold b/fast buffet. NSTS also has a branch in Msida. €

🏠 **Two Pillows Boutique Hostel** [169 D3] 49 Triq San Piju V, Sliema; ↘21317070; w twopillowsmalta.com. Very popular hostel with everything from dorms to studio apts. Not a 'party hostel'. All ages welcome. Mins from the waterfront & Sliema Ferries. €

✖ WHERE TO EAT AND DRINK

SLIEMA

✖ **Charles Grech Bistro** [169 C1] 59 Sir Adrian Dingli St (cnr Tower Rd, nr St Julian's Tower); ↘ 21320926; w charlesgrech.com; ⊕ noon–22.30 Mon–Sat. Delicious food with Mediterranean in the ascendant. Smart but relaxed modern setting just off the Sliema Waterfront. Wide selection of drinks, too. €€€

✖ **The Chophouse** [169 G4] Tigné Point, Sliema; ↘20603355; w chophouse.com.mt; ⊕ 19.00–23.00 daily & 12.30–15.00 Sun lunch. In the Tigné Point development, this modern steakhouse with large wood-charcoal grill has a terrace & glass-fronted interior with wonderful views of Valletta. €€€

✖ **Fish Restaurant by Fumia** [169 F4] Tigné Point, Sliema (next to Chophouse); ↘21337694; ⏸; ⊕ noon–14.30 & 19.00–22.30 daily, closed Tue. Excellent fish restaurant (run by the same people as Fumia just outside Valletta; page 110) with conservatory in winter, open-sided terrace in summer. Lovely views of Valletta across the harbour (especially good at night). The mixed grilled fish is excellent (& large). €€€

✖ **Pearl Beach Club** [169 F3] Qui-si-sana Seafront, Sliema ; ↘21338341; w pearlbeachmalta.com; ⊕ Jun–mid-Oct 10.00 daily until clients leave; admission fee €15–20/day (inc swimming pool, sunbeds, DJ music), Fri–Sun over-18s only. Sometimes has special offer giving entrance price off food. Owned by Charles Grech (as in the bistro at the other end of Sliema & the café in Valletta) so food is a good notch above the usual beachclub burger – & there's a decent wine list too. €€–€€€

✖ **Ta' Kris** [169 E3] 80 Fawwara La, Sliema; ↘21337367; m 99847713; w takrisrestaurant.

com; ⊕ 12.30–15.30 & 19.30–23.00 daily. On a tiny alley off Bisazza St (one of Sliema's main shopping streets). Converted from a traditional Maltese bakery, the oven is still here & the warm orange walls are decorated with baking implements. Service can be a touch slow, but chef Kris produces excellent Maltese/Mediterranean food artistically presented. Relaxed atmosphere. Families welcome. Highchairs available. Book in advance, it's popular. €€

✖ **Mint** [169 E2] 30-9 Luzio Junction/ Stella Maris St, Sliema Waterfront (Tower Rd); ↘21337177; w mintmalta.com; ⊕ 08.00–16.00 Tue–Sun. Bright modern café with seats inside & out, run by New Zealanders. Choose fresh food from the glass cabinets. International dishes from Mexican beancakes to Thai fishcakes & Spanish omelette all cooked on site. Good coffee & cake. Excellent for vegetarians. €

✖ **Vecchia Napoli** [169 C2] Tower Rd, Sliema; ↘ 21343434; w vecchianapoli.com; ⊕ 18.00–23.00 Mon–Fri, noon–23.00 Sat & Sun. Neapolitan pizza directly across the road from Balluta Bay. Plain wood interior. Cheap & cheerful. €

ST JULIAN'S & PACEVILLE

✖ **Barracuda** [173 D6] 194–5 Censu Tabone St (better known as Main St), St Julian's, SLM 05; ↘21331817; w barracudarestaurant.com; ⊕ 19.00–22.45 daily & noon–14.30 Sun. Elegant restaurant in an early 18th-century seaside villa with wonderful views of Balluta Bay from inside & from the summer dining terrace. The restaurant is centred on the villa's drawing room & the conversion won an award from Din L-Art Helwa (Malta's National Trust). Excellent Mediterranean cuisine specialising in *carpaccio* & fresh fish. €€€

✖ Rocksalt [173 C7] Telghet San Ġiljan, Balluta Bay, St Julian's; ☎21336226; w shoprocksalt.com; ⏰ 17.30–late Tue–Sun & 12.30–14.30-ish Sat & Sun. In a modern conservatory & on a limestone terrace just off the Sliema seafront (in the same building as Inhawi Hostel but in a different price bracket), this little restaurant serves excellent interesting modern Mediterranean/European food & wine. Along with an à la carte menu is a popular foodie tasting menu of 5 or 9 courses. €€€

✖ Wigi's Kitchen [173 C6] Censu Tabone St (better known as Main St), Balluta Bay, St Julian's; ☎21377504; w wigiskitchen.com; ⏰ 19.00–22.45 Mon–Sat & 12.30–14.45 Tue–Fri. Small 1st-floor family-run restaurant overlooking Balluta Bay serving very good Mediterranean food popular with locals. Menu changes daily. €€€

✖ Gululu [173 C4] Spinola Bay, St Julian's; ☎21444431, 21333431; w gululu.com.mt; ⏰ noon–17.00 & 18.00–23.00 daily. Winner of the best Maltese food category in Malta's main restaurant awards in 2018, so this is the locals' top choice for their own cuisine. With colourful modern décor & a terrace by the water's edge. Brings traditional specialities into the 21st century – successfully. Maltese pizza, pasta, rabbit dishes, local cheeses, soups, *pulpetti* (patties). €€–€€€€

✖ Fresco's [173 D6] Tower Rd; ☎27344763; w frescomalta.com; ⏰ 11.00–23.00 daily. Lovely Italian right on the waterfront, serving excellent pizzas, seafood & salads. Pasta & risotto starters are big enough for a main meal. Nice place to watch the sunset over St Julian's Bay – if you can see past the bright lights of the bars. €€

✖ La Maltija [173 C3] Church St, Paceville; ☎21359602; w lamaltija.com; ⏰ 18.00–23.00 daily. Traditional Maltese fare (*bigilla*, *aljotta*, rabbit, fresh fish). Run by the voluble Charlie (in his youth chef to the Governor of Malta, then to its first president) & his daughters. Sit in the stone interior of an ex-British officer's house or out on the wide balcony over the street. €€

✖ Naar [173 C6] Ġorġ Borġ Olivier St, Balluta Bay, St Julian's; ☎21373412; w naarmalta.com; ⏰ 11.00–23.00 Mon–Fri, 10.00–midnight Sat, 10.00–17.00 Sun. With a lovely terrace over the water of Balluta Bay (largely enclosed in bad weather) this place won Malta's restaurant award for the best vegetarian food (2018), though it serves meat too. Pizza, pasta, interesting salads & veggie & vegan snacks. €€

✖ The Avenue [173 B3] Gort St, Paceville, STJ 3063; ☎21351753, 21378731; w theavenuemalta. com; ⏰ noon–14.30 & 18.00–23.30 daily. Always buzzing, this popular family restaurant is 'cheap & cheerful' with plenty of choice. Kids' menu & highchairs available. Somewhere locals consider comfortable to dine alone, as well as *à deux* or *en famille*. €–€€

✖ Bianco's [173 B4] St George Rd, St Julian's; ☎21359865, 21383030; w biancos.info; ⏰ noon–23.00 daily. Large tasty pizzas & calzone, as well as other Mediterranean food (also good) made in the open kitchen of this relaxed modern indoor restaurant on the St Julian's seafront. €–€€

✖ 1927 [173 B4] St Julian's Band Club (Banda San Ġiljan), St George St, Spinola Bay; ☎21354361; m 99251459; ⏰ 18.00–22.30 Tue–Sat, noon–15.30/16.00 Sun lunch. Cosy, traditional, inexpensive restaurant in the local band club with football on TV & a few tables outside. Local specialities, fresh fish & daily specials. €

✖ Piccolo Padre [173 D6] 195 Censu Tabone St (better known as Main St); ☎21344875; w www. piccolopadre.com; ⏰ 18.15–23.00 daily & noon–15.00 Sat & Sun. Descend as if to go underground, but emerge into an attractive family-run pizzeria with uninterrupted views of the bay. For seats on the edge of the terrace or by the large windows, book or arrive early. Same ownership as elegant Barracuda upstairs. Tasty thin-crust pizzas, pasta & seafood. Great for families. Highchairs available. €

ENTERTAINMENT AND NIGHTLIFE

A lot of the venues in Paceville change hands and names so regularly that there is little point in listing them. That said, there are some which have survived long enough to suggest they may still be there when you get there! The clubs of Paceville tend to have no entry fee and basic drinks mostly cost €2.50–3.50 (unless otherwise stated); cocktails a bit more. There are quite a few 'pubs' – styled as English, Irish and Scottish – and a cinema and a bowling alley in St George's Bay, Paceville.

BARS AND CLUBS

⏻ Tapaz [173 A2] St George's Bay, Paceville; ☏21383634; w tapazmalta.com; ⏲ for food noon–23.45 daily & until 00.45 Fri & Sat; drinks until at least 02.00 daily. A rare Paceville café-bar where you can actually hold a conversation. Modern interior with large chandeliers, but low light. €€

✩ **Havana** [173 B2] St George St, Paceville; ☏21374500; f Havana808; ⏲ 20.00–04.00 daily. Large soul & R&B club with 6 bars on 2 floors & loads of room to dance. Also here is Flashback, playing music from the 1960s to the 90s. Keep hold of your phones.

✩ **Hugo's Passion** [173 B2] St George Rd, Paceville; ☏21382264; ⏲ 20.00–04.00 daily. In the heart of Paceville, Hugo's Passion is a nightclub playing chart toppers, disco & other commercial music appealing to a largely teenage clientele. There is a small outside terrace where you can get some air, watch the party that spills out on to the road at w/ends, & maybe even hear yourself speak (maybe). Beneath the club is Hugo's Lounge Sushi restaurant.

✩ **Hugo's Terrace** [173 B1] St George's Bay, Paceville; ☏21376767; f; ⏲ noon–04.00 daily. Beside the beach at St George's Bay, this relaxed beach club plays chilled-out music – 80s to current – all afternoon & half the night. A place for a drink &/or a dance by the sea surrounded by all the action of Malta's party town.

✩ **Twenty Two** [173 C3] Top floor of Portomaso Tower; ⏲ 21.30–04.00 Wed–Sun (may close early on quiet nights), lounge bar Wed, Thu & Sun; club with DJ Fri & Sat. Upmarket venue on the 22nd floor of the tower next to the Hilton hotel with fantastic views & a large screen showing music videos (rather than the usual football). On lounge-bar nights it is candlelit, comfortable & the music is quiet enough to allow conversation. On DJ nights the dance floor is used. A bit pricier than the rest of Paceville.

PUBS

🛢 **Cork's Irish Pub** [173 B4] Next door to the Scotsman & equally busy.

🛢 **The Scotsman** [173 B3] St George St, Paceville; ⏲ 11.00–late daily. Traditional Scottish-themed pub – a long survivor.

SLIEMA

Sliema isn't just a place, it's a type (like 'Sloane' in London). If you are 'Slimiz' you are likely to be a well-educated, English-speaking member of the professional classes with a cosmopolitan outlook and, although not necessarily rich, certainly not poor. Sliema is the place where Maltese families can still be heard speaking English in preference to Maltese, or unselfconsciously mixing the two into 'Manglish'.

Sliema began as a fishing village and by the 19th century was the place for well-off Vallettans to have a summer house (there is good swimming off the rocks). During World War II, many of these people left Valletta to escape the bombing and based themselves full-time in Sliema. With the capital a mere 5-minute ferry ride away, most didn't bother to return to Valletta when the war ended. The population duly shrank and that of Sliema swelled towards its present 14,000.

The once-elegant 3km seafront promenades along The Strand and Tower Road are now lined with unattractive modern apartment blocks and hotels. Tower Road is still *the* place in Malta to stroll of a summer evening and you will find Maltese of all ages promenading here as the heat of the day subsides.

The coast may have been overtaken by development but the interior of Sliema is largely untouched – a quietly elegant residential area with some lovely old buildings, colourful *gallariji*, churches and pretty squares.

Sliema is Malta's premier shopping area. It has most of the European high-street chains plus a few independent shops of its own, occasionally elegant, rarely cheap. And it boasts Malta's newest and largest shopping centre, The Point, on Tigné Point.

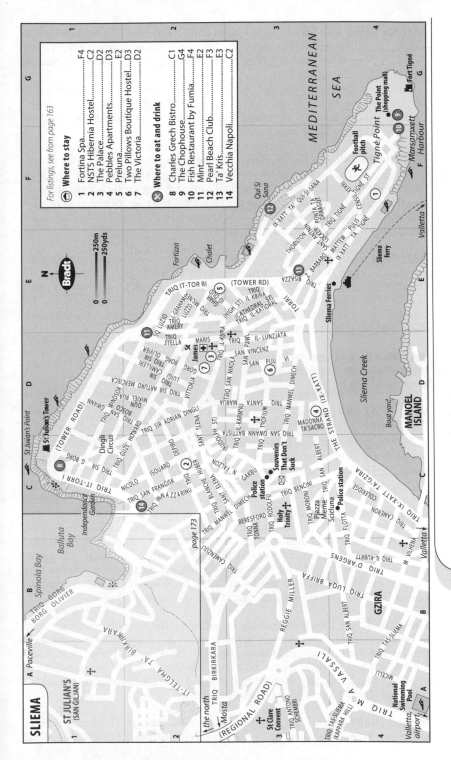

SLIEMA

ST JULIAN'S
(SAN ĠILJAN)

MEDITERRANEAN SEA

page 173

For listings, see from page 163

Where to stay

1	Fortina Spa.............................F4
2	NSTS Hibernia Hostel............C2
3	The Palace...............................D2
4	Pebbles Apartments...............D3
5	Preluna...................................E2
6	Two Pillows Boutique Hostel....D3
7	The Victoria.............................D2

Where to eat and drink

8	Charles Grech Bistro................C1
9	The Chophouse.......................G4
10	Fish Restaurant by Fumia........F4
11	Mint..E2
12	Pearl Beach Club....................F3
13	Ta' Kris...................................E3
14	Vecchia Napoli.......................C2

GZIRA

MANOEL ISLAND

GETTING THERE AND AWAY Lots of **buses** run to and from Sliema, linking it to Valletta, the airport and further afield. The best option for getting here from Valletta though (as long as the weather is reasonable) is to take the **Sliema ferry** – a pleasant 5–10-minute crossing (page 103).

Parking on the streets in Sliema requires a parking clock (page 266) and can be very difficult, but there is a multi-storey car park (113 High St, SLM 16; ❧21335800, 21339541; w cccp.com.mt) just inland from the Sliema ferry and one at The Point shopping centre on Tigné Point.

GETTING AROUND The key thing to remember with Sliema is that if you want to cross town quickly, cut through the middle rather than taking the coast road. This is obvious on the map but not so obvious on the ground. The Sliema ferry to St Julian's is perhaps a 15-minute walk through the centre but can take 45 minutes along the seafront. There are, however, plenty of buses running the length of Tower Road if you want to ride along the coast to St Julian's.

Boat trips Sliema is the starting point for numerous boat trips, including the excellent 1½-hour **Two Harbours Cruise** which offers full English commentary on a circuit of the Grand Harbour and Marsamxett Harbour with great views of Valletta and the Three Cities. There is also a range of coastal cruises, sunset outings and day trips to Comino and the Blue Lagoon. Boats may leave from slightly different points along the Sliema Waterfront.

🚢**Captain Morgan Cruises** ❧23463333; w captainmorgan.com.mt. Good for harbour cruises, less so for the rest.

🚢**Luzzu Cruises** m 79064489; w luzzucruises.com

WHAT TO SEE AND DO

Tigné Point [169 E3–G4] Sliema has two waterfronts: The Strand (facing Valletta) and Tower Road, which leads up to St Julian's. Between them is Tigné Point, with Malta's largest and newest shopping centre, The Point (w thepointmalta.com), surrounded by luxury flats. You can walk through or around this new development to **Dragut Point** [169 G4], named after the fearsome Turkish corsair who harried Malta through the middle of the 16th century. Some accounts say that this is where he was mortally wounded during the Great Siege of 1565. On the point is Fort Tigné.

Fort Tigné [169 G4], constructed in 1792–95, was the last of the Knights' defences and one of the first truly polygonal forts in the world. It was intended (rather belatedly) to partner Fort St Elmo in the defence of Marsamxett Harbour. Just six years after it was built, Napoleon arrived, expelled the Knights and took Valletta. The Maltese rebelled and (with British help) found themselves firing the cannons of Fort Tigné at Fort St Elmo and their own capital.

The Strand [169 C4–D3] The main attraction of The Strand is the great views of Valletta, especially impressive at night when the bastion walls of the capital are floodlit. The Strand also leads to **Sliema Ferries** [169 E4], not only the landing stage for the ferry and for many tourist boat trips, but also an area of shops, banks and other facilities. If you keep going along The Strand you come into Gżira, a less classy version of Sliema and the bridge to Manoel Island.

Manoel Island [map, page 164] This island in Marsamxett Harbour was home to the **quarantine hospital** set up by the Knights in 1643 after bubonic plague had hit Malta twice, in 1592 and 1623. By the middle of the 18th century, 1,000 people could be processed here at one time and ships could be quarantined for several weeks. The maximum penalty for breaking quarantine was death. This strictness seems to have paid off: Malta didn't suffer another serious outbreak of plague until 1813 and that was its last.

Fort Manoel was built on the orders of Grand Master António Manoel de Vilhena (1722–36) to protect Marsamxett Harbour (this was before Fort Tigné was built). Some French troops were held here after their defeat in 1800 before signing away any rights to Malta and being sent back to France aboard ships of the British Royal Navy.

You can cross the bridge from Gżira to visit the island. There is not a great deal to see that is not better viewed from across the water, but locals swim off the rocks at the far end of the island with views across to Valletta.

Tower Road [169 C1–E3] Tower Road runs right along the northwest coast of Sliema to St Julian's, with a promenade along the seafront next to the rocks and the sea. There are few specific sights. This is a place for **strolling**, **swimming** and watching or joining the Maltese at play. There are cafés and bars varying from the brash and noisy to the calm and peaceful, as well as several 'beach clubs' and lidos (with changing rooms and showers). Free to access is a vast swathe of flattish rocks on which to picnic, sunbathe (if you can find a comfortable patch) and swim. The swimming is directly into deep clear water, so best for competent swimmers and ideal for **snorkellers**. Be guided on exactly where to swim by where the locals choose.

There are two small historic forts, one at each end of the main stretch of promenade: Il-Fortizza at the Tigné Point end, and St Julian's Tower on the border with St Julian's. **Il-Fortizza** [169 E2], also known as Sliema Point Battery or Għar Id-Dud, and now Fortizza Pizzeria, was built by the British in 1872–76 though in a Gothic style that makes it look much older. The observation tower was added in 1905. Originally equipped with artillery guns, these were replaced with searchlights after the 100-ton guns came into service at Fort Rinella and at Fort Cambridge. Fort Cambridge faced out to sea from the Sliema end of Tigné Point, but has given way to later buildings, most recently the Tigné Point development.

St Julian's Tower [169 C1] is one of a system of coastal watchtowers built by Grand Master Martin de Redin in 1658–59 (page 255) – later turned into a coastal battery in 1715. Its seafront terrace is now a bar-café. Next to the tower is a colourful little **children's playground** and below, the laid-back trendy beach-bar-style Paradise Exiles Bar and Café with steps down from the rocks for **swimming** in deep water at the mouth of Balluta Bay.

ST JULIAN'S (SAN ĠILJAN) AND PACEVILLE

St Julian's covers the area from Balluta Bay to Spinola Bay, including both bays. Walk 100m up St George Street (Triq San Ġorġ) from Spinola Bay to Spinola Gardens and you are in Paceville. On your right here is the shiny, modern and expensive Portomaso/Hilton complex. Keep going along St George Street and you come to the heart of Paceville – full of bars, pubs, clubs (page 168), fast food and pounding bass: brasher, louder and cheaper.

GETTING THERE AND AROUND
Buses Plenty of buses run to both St Julian's and Paceville.

Parking It can be difficult to find a parking space in St Julian's and Paceville, particularly at weekends, but there is a large underground car park in the Portomaso complex (in front of the Hilton hotel) and another by the Westin Dragonara Resort, where you can park for a few euros. Some, but by no means all, hotels have parking for their guests (and it may be charged as an extra) so if you are planning to stay here and hire a car it is worth checking.

Taxis Taxis are readily available in St Julian's and in Paceville; they gather both at Spinola Gardens next to the Portomaso complex and in St George's Bay by the shopping centre. By Spinola Gardens, you will find a white taxi kiosk (✆ 21353838) with a price list. Private cab company Wembley Cars (✆ 21374141, 21374242; m 79374141, 79374242; w wembleys.com) is also based on St George Street opposite the bus stop by Spinola Gardens.

ST JULIAN'S Not so long ago St Julian's was a delightful little seaside fishing town. Unsympathetic development has changed all that, although if you look carefully at the two bays (Balluta Bay and Spinola Bay) – especially on a quiet night and with your back to the vast Malta Marriott – you can still see what they once were. The 19th-century Carmelite church and priory (with 'Gothic' windows added in the 20th century) look particularly impressive lit up after dark. During the *festa* of **Our Lady of Mount Carmel** in late July you can get a great view of the fireworks from the Twenty Two bar in Portomaso Tower (page 168).

So long as you are expecting a modern resort town, St Julian's is quite pleasant and, along with neighbouring Paceville, it has several of the island's top modern five-star hotels and some excellent restaurants. You can swim in Balluta Bay and Spinola Bay, but there is little beach. A water polo lido sits to one side of this and many of the hotels have swimming pools as well as 'private' rocky 'beaches' from which to get into the sea. The nearest full-scale sandy beach is at St George's Bay the other side of Paceville.

Historically, the coast around St Julian's was largely uninhabited because of the fear of Turkish invasion. It was here that Dragut Reis anchored 15 ships when he arrived to join the Great Siege of 1565 and indeed here that Napoleon's general Vaubois disembarked in 1798. When the Royal Navy came to help remove the French, St Julian's became a British ship-repair yard and supply base. Development began later under the British, with the construction of a few seaside residences, but it went mad only in the 1970s with Malta's headlong plunge into mass tourism.

PACEVILLE The heart of Paceville (pronounced *pachéville*) is one of Malta's least peaceful areas with all the downsides of St Julian's and none of the

---

ST JULIAN'S & PACEVILLE
For listings, see from page 163

⊖ **Where to stay**

1	Corinthia St George's Bay	B1
2	The George	C3
3	Golden Tulip Vivaldi	C2
4	The Hilton	C3
5	Hostel Malti	B7
6	Hotel Valentina	C3
7	Inhawi Boutique Hostel	C7
8	Intercontinental	B2
9	Juliani	B4
10	Malta Marriott	C6
11	Marina	B1
12	Westin Dragonara Resort	C2

Off map

	Radisson Blu St Julian's	B1

✖ **Where to eat and drink**

13	1927	B4
14	The Avenue	B3
15	Barracuda	D6
16	Bianco's	B4
17	Fresco's	D6
18	Gululu	C4
19	La Maltija	C3
20	Naar	C6
	Piccolo Padre	(see 15)
21	Rocksalt	C7
22	Wigi's Kitchen	C6

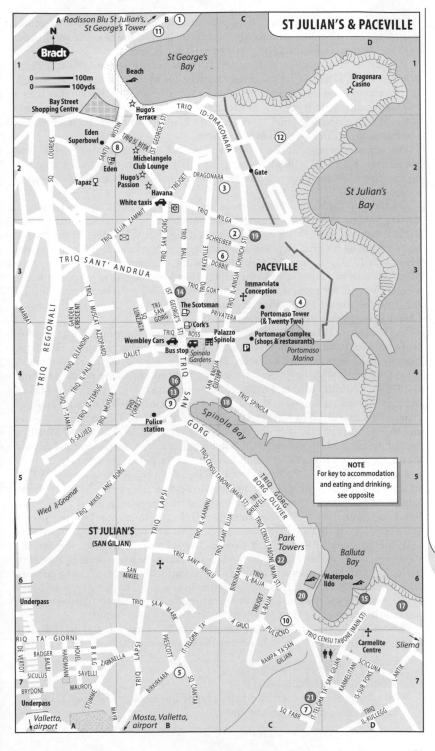

St George's
Bay

Dragonara
Casino

Radisson Blu St Julian's,
St George's Tower

Beach

Bay Street
Shopping Centre

Hugo's
Terrace

Eden
Superbowl

TRIQ ID-DRAGONARA

Eden

Michelangelo
Club Lounge

Gate

St Julian's
Bay

Tapaz

Hugo's
Passion

Havana

White taxis

TRIQ ELIJA ZAMMIT

TRIQ WILGA

SCHREIBER

TRIQ SANT' ANDRUA

DOBBIE

PACEVILLE

Immaculate
Conception

The Scotsman

Portomaso Tower
(& Twenty Two)

Cork's

Palazzo
Spinola

Portomaso Complex
(shops & restaurants)

Wembley Cars

Bus stop

Spinola
Gardens

Portomaso
Marina

Police
station

Spinola Bay

TRIQ SPINOLA

NOTE
For key to accommodation
and eating and drinking,
see opposite

Wied il-Gnomar

ST JULIAN'S
(SAN ĠILJAN)

Park
Towers

Balluta
Bay

Waterpolo
lido

Sliema

Underpass

Carmelite
Centre

Underpass

Valletta,
airport

Mosta, Valletta,
airport

residual charm. This is an area of bars, pubs, discos, clubs, hotels, fast-food outlets and restaurants all crammed together with the noise and the clientele spilling out onto the narrow (and fortunately part-pedestrianised) streets.

Paceville is most popular with teenagers (some certainly below Malta's official drinking age of 17), though the age rises into the 20s after about midnight. There is little to recommend this area to anyone older (or younger, or calmer) other than a few of the restaurants. It might also attract a football addict in need of a fix as many of the bars show live television coverage of the English and Italian premier leagues – although these can also be found elsewhere.

On summer weekends Paceville can get not only busy, but rowdy and occasionally violent. It is illegal to carry open glass bottles here or to drink alcohol on the streets although notice is not always taken of this. Bars are legally required to close by 04.00.

On the St Julian's side of town, there are a few older buildings worth noting. **Palazzo Spinola** (Spinola Palace) [173 B4] was built by an Italian knight, Paola Raffaele Spinola, in 1688 when it was the first significant building in the area. It was enlarged by his great-nephew, another high-ranking knight, Giovanni Battista Spinola, in 1733. It is now the Malta home of the Parliamentary Assembly of the Mediterranean and is not open to the public. The former stables of the palace house a Pizza Hut and the *loggia* that was originally boathouses built by Spinola for local fishermen is home to a number of restaurants. Spinola Sr also built the nearby **Church of the Immaculate Conception** (1688) [173 C3].

The **Dragonara Palace** [173 D1] – now a casino – holds a commanding position on Dragonara Point. The point is named for the legend that the roars emanating from its rocks were those of a dragon. They were, of course, the roar of the sea. A colonnaded folly with Egyptian-style statues at its entrance, the palace was built in 1870 by a wealthy banker, Emanuele Scicluna, who five years later was made a marquis for lending money to the Pope. His nephew inherited the palace and also created Palazzo Parisio in Naxxar. During World War I, the Dragonara Palace was an officers' hospital taking in the wounded of Gallipoli, and in World War II it housed people made homeless in the bombing. The casino opened in 1964 and the Westin Dragonara Resort now stands in what was the palace gardens.

Paceville is home to Malta's tallest building, the Portomaso Tower [173 C3], which at the time of writing is expected soon to be overtaken by the Mercury Tower, a dramatic 31-storey, 112m skyscraper designed by superstar architect Zaha Hadid before her death in 2016. It will eventually contain apartments in the lower storeys and a hotel above, with a striking twist and an open-air swimming pool in between.

At the far side of Paceville is **St George's Bay** [173 B1] where you will find the Superbowl, cinema, shopping centre, and the only **sandy beach** in the area, a smallish stretch next to the road that is regularly topped up with imported coarse-grained sand. The Intercontinental Hotel keeps it clean in return for having its private beach at one end. This was the first beach in Malta to gain a Blue Flag (w blueflag.org), an accolade it retains at the time of writing. It gets very busy in summer.

The bay has the Westin Dragonara Resort on the St Julian's side and the Corinthia hotels on the other. A promenade runs all the way around the bay.

8

Southeast Malta

Outside the Cottonera Lines that enclose the Three Cities (page 161), urbanisation has now claimed an area far larger than that within the fortifications and consumed a number of historic villages along the way. In most of these suburban areas there is little to draw the visitor, but hidden among the houses are two of the most important sites in Malta – the **Tarxien temple** complex and the **Ħal Saflieni Hypogeum**. Further southeast is a site that takes you back even further – **Għar Dalam**, the cave occupied by Malta's first known settlers. On the other half of the same large bay is **Marsaxlokk**, long the centre of fishing in Malta and now also of fish restaurants. Less on the tourist map, but with their own interest and historical importance if you are in the area, are Żejtun and Żabbar.

ŻABBAR

Żabbar lies just outside the Three Cities, the other side of the Żabbar Gate. During the Great Siege, rural Żabbar had little protection and it was in the fields around here that the Turks established themselves to besiege Birgu. Only after the building of the huge Cottonera fortifications and the lessening of the threat from the Turks in the late 17th century did the population of Żabbar begin to grow. Today it is the fourth-largest population centre in Malta with some 15,000 people.

In the middle of a roundabout along the road from the Żabbar Gate stands the rather forgotten-looking **Hompesch Arch**, once the main entrance to Żabbar. It was built to celebrate the elevation of the village into a town by Grand Master Hompesch (1797–98), the order's last Grand Master in Malta. Żabbar is still officially known as 'Citta Hompesch'.

In the centre of town is the heavily decorated parish church, the **Sanctuary of Our Lady of Divine Grace** (tal-Grazzja, *festa* in September). Originally built between 1641 and 1696, it has been subjected to copious later adjustments and additions. The altarpiece of Our Lady is crowned (making it particularly sacred in Catholic eyes) and has long been the object of pilgrimage and requests for intercession. There is a significant collection of ex-voto paintings (see box, page 291) in the small purpose-built **Sanctuary Museum** (✆21824383; ⊕ usually 09.00–noon daily). Most are connected with seafaring at the time of the Knights. Also in the museum are sedan chairs, an 18th-century model of a ship of the line, a plague hearse (1813), silverware, coins and religious paintings by Mattia Preti and Giuseppe Calì among others. A small exhibition recalls the explosion of an RAF Vulcan bomber over Żabbar in 1975. Some locals regard the fact that only one resident died, despite the debris landing around a packed school, as a veritable miracle.

GETTING THERE AND AWAY Several **buses** stop in Żabbar. **Parking** is possible on the streets but be aware of the usual restrictions.

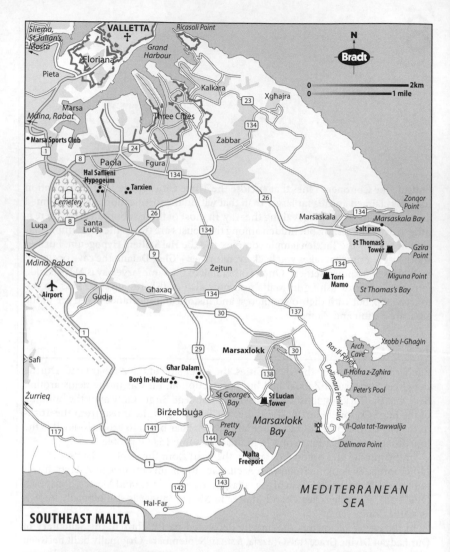

SOUTHEAST MALTA

TARXIEN TEMPLES

(Neolithic Temples St, Tarxien, TXN 1063; ✆ 21695578; w heritagemalta.org; ⊕ 09.00–17.00 daily (last entry 16.30); €6 adults, €4.50 over-60s/children aged 12–17/students, €3 children aged 6–12, children under 6 free) This is the most complex of the temple sites, and was the most decorated. Tarxien is the source of many of the outstanding carved reliefs and statues now in the National Museum of Archaeology in Valletta, represented on site by copies.

The Tarxien site is not picturesque, walled around as it is by a modern suburb, but it is of huge archaeological importance and there is plenty to see.

The temple site here was probably originally larger than it is now and is likely to have served a significant Neolithic community. Other prehistoric structures have been found nearby, including the Ħal Saflieni Hypogeum and the Kordin Temples.

Rediscovered by local farmers in 1913–14 when their ploughs kept hitting large lumps of stone, the site was excavated by 'the father of Maltese archaeology' Temi Zammit (see box, page 180) in 1915–19. The remains of four temples were revealed, the earliest (Tarxien Far East) dating from the first phase of temple building (from 3800BC), with the South and East temples added in the period named after them, Tarxien phase (3000BC+), and the Central one slotted in between them. Changes and embellishments seem to have continued until the temple culture disappeared in 2350BC.

The South Temple at Tarxien (the first temple you reach) was re-used as a crematorium/cemetery in the early Bronze Age (2350–1500BC) – leaving evidence of a very different culture from that of the temple builders. The Tarxien Cemetery People burnt their dead, storing the ashes in urns, and made use of copper weapons. The Romans also re-used the site, and a medieval oven was constructed in front of the East Temple before soil covered the area until the 20th century.

GETTING THERE AND AWAY Several buses come to Tarxien from Valletta. Buses to Paola also get you within walking distance of the temples. The temples are less than 10 minutes' walk from the hypogeum and the ticket offices at both the Tarxien Temples and the hypogeum should be able to give you a little map showing how to get between the two. There is free **parking** on the street outside though it is not always easy to find a space.

OTHER PRACTICALITIES The official route takes you round the outside of the temples first, but you are not obliged to follow the signs – I tend to go the other way seeing the temples from inside first. The Tarxien Temples are now covered by a canopy designed to protect the site and ancient stones from damaging rain and sunlight (see box, page 199). The ticket office sells a few souvenirs and a guidebook, *The Tarxien Temples* by Anthony Pace (Insight Heritage Guides; €7.99), which contains quite detailed information and an excellent aerial photo. There are loos here but no other facilities. If you are in need of snacks or water, there are shops close by.

EXPLORING THE TEMPLES
Tarxien South Built in the early 4th millennium and 2500BC, Tarxien South was probably the most richly decorated temple on the islands. It was first built as a four-apse temple but had various structural changes made during prehistory as well as after. Entering the Tarxien site, you walk along the front of the South Temple to the **monumental entrance** rebuilt in 1960 (thank goodness they don't do that anymore!). There is nothing left of the façade except the 'benches' but these allow you to see how the façade would have been a concave shape with the entrance at its centre.

In front of the temple are some **stone spheres** (about the size of cannonballs) that may have been used as rollers to transport building blocks, though opinions differ, with other experts believing these rollers may have been used to level the paving slabs or may have had some ritual significance, perhaps as votive offerings.

To the right of the doorway, at the far end of the large stones of the façade 'bench' is a massive stone with its centre carved out to create a kind of three-sided box. You can see it from the walkway by the main entrance to this temple but will see it again from above on the walkway on the other side of the temples. Its floor is punctured by five holes. This may have been a **shrine** and the holes could have been libation holes through which to pour offerings to the underworld. There are two more similar holes in front of the entrance to the temple.

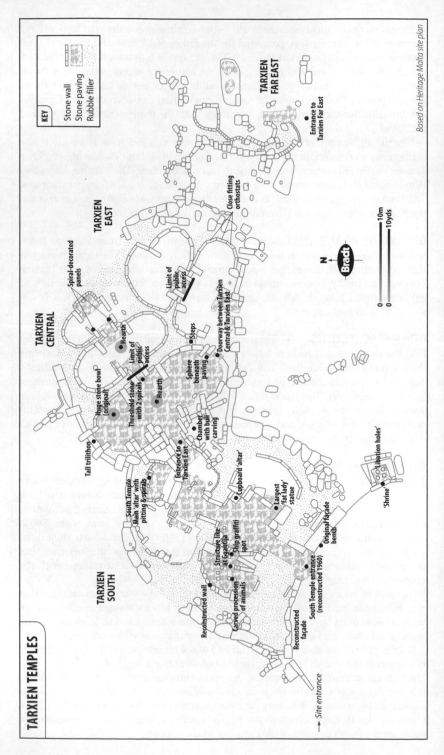

TARXIEN TEMPLES

KEY
Stone wall
Stone paving
Rubble filler

TARXIEN FAR EAST

Entrance to Tarxien Far East

TARXIEN EAST

Close fitting orthostats

Spiral-decorated panels

Limit of public access

Doorway between Tarxien Central & Tarxien East

TARXIEN CENTRAL

Hearth

Limit of public access

Hearth

Steps

Sphere beneath paving

Huge stone bowl (original)

Threshold stone with 2 spirals

Tall trilithon

Chamber with bull carving

Entrance to Tarxien East

South Temple Main 'altar' with pitting & spirals

Cupboard 'altar'

Largest 'fat lady' statue

'Shrine'

Libation holes

Structure like at Ġgantija

Ship graffiti spot

Original façade bench

TARXIEN SOUTH

Reconstructed wall

Carved procession of animals

South Temple entrance (reconstructed 1960)

Reconstructed façade

→ Site entrance

N

Bradt

0   10m
0   10yds

Based on Heritage Malta site plan

Going through the reconstructed doorway of the South Temple, you enter what was probably once the most elaborate area of any temple on the islands. In the right apse stood a **'fat lady' statue** more than 2m high, the largest known from Maltese prehistory. Only the lower half of the body – its conical thighs and pleated skirt – survives. A copy stands here now; the original is in the National Museum of Archaeology in Valletta. Ahead of you in this same apse is a very interesting **'altar'** (also a copy, the original is in the museum). It consists of a large block decorated with spirals with a flat table-like top on which stands a small shrine (or niche) made of cleanly cut rectangular stones. Look carefully at the front of the base block and you will see that there is a semicircular stone that is removable. The inside is in fact hollow. When first discovered by Temi Zammit the plug stone was held in place with two small wedges and within the **'cupboard'** were found a 4½-inch flint knife, oxen and sheep bones (both animals that appear on carvings in the temple), marine shells, a bone spatula and fragments of pottery. The knife and bones are the best evidence so far of animal sacrifice in the temples.

Other spiral stones decorate this apse and the one opposite it, where, on the floor, can be seen an oblong stone carved with a procession of domestic animals. The combination of a semicircular threshold stone, flanked by two spiral-decorated screens, that fronts this apse is almost identical to a structure in the first right apse of the South Temple at Ggantija on Gozo, attesting to close links between Malta and Gozo during the time of the temple culture. Next to this, a modern grey slab marks the position of an original stone slab that had ship graffiti on it. The slab is in the ticket office but it is impossible to make out the ships so content yourself with the picture here in the temple. It is not impossible that the ships are of the temple period, but it is much more likely that they are Bronze Age.

The back wall of this apse is partly reconstructed; the small stones are modern. Some believe this western wall may have been removed deliberately during prehistory. The first section of this temple is also where Bronze Age **cremation urns** were found.

In the doorway to the next apses are large hinge holes suggesting this was once a closable entrance. Similar arrangements can be seen on other doorways. The **inner apses** are less adorned than the first two, but the **central altar** is decorated with pitting, which has been partially replaced with spirals. This is now hard to see here, but is easily seen on the original preserved in the museum in Valletta. The right-hand apse was restructured in prehistory to give access to the next temple, Tarxien Central.

Tarxien Central The only surviving six-apse temple, the layout of Tarxien Central is quite hard to fathom on the ground so do take a look at the plan opposite or accept that it will be clearer when you view it from the perimeter walkway. Straight ahead of you, below the level of the walkway, is a **low bowl**, partly reddened by fire, probably a hearth. In the left apse is a **much larger and more impressive bowl** – an original – carved of globigerina limestone. This would not have withstood fire (and is not reddened) and its use is unknown. Also in this apse are a **porthole doorway** and a very **tall trilithon** (uprights with a top stone across them) that could possibly be a blocked doorway. The open doorway leads into a small room where animal bones and horns were found. The walls of large close-fitting stones (orthostats) in this apse are reddened by fire, which may date from the Bronze Age when the temple was a crematorium, or from an earlier destructive fire. The discolouring due to fire and the fact that the floor is paved with stone slabs may be evidence that this part of the temple was open to the sky.

Dr, later Sir, Themistocles 'Temi' Zammit (1864–1935) is known as the Father of Maltese Archaeology even though he was not by training an archaeologist. He was a distinguished professor of medicine, responsible, among other things, for the 1905 discovery of the cause of undulant fever or brucellosis, also called Malta fever (brucella bacteria transmitted directly from animals or via untreated milk).

Zammit brought to Maltese archaeology a more scientific and organised approach than his predecessors. He was appointed Director of the Valletta Museum (now the National Museum of Archaeology) in 1904 and went on to lead some of the most important early excavations of prehistoric sites including the hypogeum (1910), Tarxien (1915–19) and Ta' Ħaġrat (1920s), as well as various Punic and Roman sites.

He wrote up his findings at Tarxien in *Prehistoric Malta* (1930), bringing Maltese archaeology its first international recognition. Although he inevitably got some things wrong, Zammit's educated guess at a date for the temples – 3000BC – was remarkably close. Sir Temi was also Rector of Malta University and by the time he died in 1935 his son was already Curator of Archaeology at the National Museum and went on to become its Director.

The first apse on the right has a chamber off it containing original **carvings** of two bulls and a sow with piglets (more evidence of the importance of domesticated animals). They are badly weathered and hard to make out but the images are known from a plaster cast (now in the Museum of Archaeology, Valletta) taken in the 1950s before the carving became so faint. Their poor state makes clear the necessity for the canopy. There is also a well here, but it is not of the temple period: it is Byzantine.

The **innermost part of the temple** (beyond the hearth) is closed to the public but can be seen from the raised walkway as you circle the site. This part of the temple is separated from the first two apses by a vertical threshold stone, carved with two spirals. It has been suggested that this partial barrier marked the start of a more sacred area of the temple or a part with a different function.

The second two apses beyond this point were once screened by the large spiral-decorated slabs now in the front hall of the museum in Valletta. Copies now show where they stood. Here too is some remarkable temple furniture, stone shelving that looks rather like prehistoric IKEA storage. The topmost stones of these apses are modern reconstruction.

Back in the first right apse is the way out of Tarxien Central and into Tarxien East. Just to the left of this doorway (before going through) is a hole in the paving through which part of a stone sphere (like those at the front of the temple) can just be seen. One school of thought sees its presence here – tucked under one of the massive paving slabs – as evidence that it was used to roll the stone above it into place.

Tarxien East To the left just inside this temple is an unusual **flight of steps** which may have led to a second floor or perhaps to the roof. The flooring at ground level is of torba (ground limestone) rather than stone slabs so this temple would almost certainly have been roofed. In the right apse (opposite the steps), admire the way the huge vertical building blocks (orthostats) fit so closely together. The inner apses of this temple are not open to the public (but they look quite like the others and can be seen from the outer walkway).

Tarxien Far East Beyond and separate from the three linked temples is the earliest building on the site, a much less well-preserved five-apse temple. It was built of smaller, rougher 'found' blocks; less stable than the huge orthostats of the later temples and more easily carted off for other uses. From the raised walkway it is possible to make out the shape of the temple, including the threshold stone that was once the main entrance at the centre of a concave façade.

HAL SAFLIENI HYPOGEUM ✳

(Burial St, Paola, PLA 1116; ☎21805018/9; w heritagemalta.org; pre-booked tours only, on the hour 09.00–16.00; €35 adults, €20 over-60s/children aged 12–17/ students, €15 children aged 6–11. Children under 6 not admitted. Numbers are limited to 10/tour to protect this UNESCO World Heritage Site, so book well in advance (weeks ahead in peak season). Tickets available online. Tickets for the noon & 16.00 tours are not sold in advance but on a first-come-first-served basis at Fort St Elmo in Valletta & the Gozo Archaeological Museum in the Citadel. These last-minute tickets cost €40 each (for all ages). The essential audio guide is available in English, French, German, Italian, Japanese, Maltese & Spanish; for anyone unable to use the audio guide, the text is available by request in advance to Heritage Malta.) An unobtrusive doorway in a suburban street is the unlikely entrance to this extraordinary prehistoric site – a complex underground burial chamber, a temple of the dead that echoes the architecture of the above-ground temples. Built on three levels, the upper being the oldest (used from around 3800BC), the lower the latest (until about 2350BC), the hypogeum probably served the same community as the Tarxien Temples – and perhaps also the nearby Kordin Temples. Protected from weather and human interference, the hypogeum offers a unique insight into the art and culture of the temple people.

Discovered in 1899, the find was not reported until four years later when a workman digging a cistern broke through into the hypogeum again. The site was first examined by a Jesuit priest and historian of Maltese antiquity, Father Manwel Magri. Unfortunately, in 1907, he was called away to do missionary work in Tunisia, where he died, and the records of his excavation have never been found.

Temi Zammit (see box opposite) took over in 1910 and his report on the site is still a key document. It was he who estimated that the hypogeum once held some 7,000 bodies. This might seem a lot on an island whose entire prehistoric population was probably around that figure, but it is not excessive bearing in mind that the hypogeum was in use for over 1,000 years.

GETTING THERE AND AWAY Several buses stop at Paola parish church within 5 minutes' walk of the hypogeum, which is 10 minutes' walk from the Tarxien Temples. The ticket offices at both the temples and the hypogeum should be able to give you a little map showing how to get between the two. There is free parking on the street outside, although it can be difficult to find a space.

EXPLORING THE SITE The hypogeum tour starts with a short audiovisual presentation and a display of a few items from the burials. The most important finds, however, including the iconic Sleeping Lady, are in the National Museum of Archaeology in Valletta. You then descend into the maze of underground passages, halls and interconnecting chambers – particularly atmospheric because, for preservation reasons, lights only come on for a limited time at each stop.

The tour starts on the **upper (oldest) level**, which would once have had a monumental entrance and possibly been marked with a stone circle. As it sits at the edge of the Tarxien Plateau, this would have made it visible from the Grand Harbour. The people who dug this complex – particularly the later parts – were sophisticated geo-engineers, using natural fault lines to achieve the strongest and smoothest walls. And they carved and smoothed them further, creating illusions of architecture: pitted columns, windows and doors, benches and even – in the so-called Holy of Holies – a corbelled roof (excellent evidence that this system of roofing was used above ground). The corners and lines of these architectural features are as clean and sharp as if they had been machine-made yesterday, yet they were made entirely by hand some 5,000 years ago.

In a few places, painted decoration can be seen – red ochre spirals, a plant-like structure (a tree of life?) and something not seen above ground: a chequered pattern of black-and-white squares. In the **'oracle chamber'** a concave stone has a bizarre effect on the male voice. Low-pitched sounds are amplified, reverberating around the subterranean complex. Whether this is deliberate and perhaps used in ritual, or a chance effect, we can only guess.

There are also a few stone spheres of the type some experts believe were used to roll stones into place. The sceptical cite their presence underground – where the architecture is cut from the rock not built of blocks – as evidence that the balls were not rollers but had some other significance.

One other underground tomb complex has been found, the much smaller and rougher Xagħra Hypogeum on Gozo – it is possible there are others.

KORDIN III TEMPLES

(Next to the Capuchin church in Paola, which has a huge purple cross outside, & opposite the country's only mosque; ✆ 21695578; w heritagemalta.org; there are no facilities at this site) There were originally three temple complexes in this area (hence the name), but only this one survives. Remains here are sparse and difficult to interpret so this is only for the very interested. It will help a lot to have the **guidebook** (*The Prehistoric Temples at Kordin III* by Nicholas Vella, Insight Heritage Guides; €7.99) with its aerial photo and explanations. Better still is to visit in the company of a knowledgeable person who can point things out (ask when booking entry with Heritage Malta if this can be arranged).

GETTING THERE AND AWAY Buses stop outside this complex. If you have a **car**, you can park for free in the large church car park. The site is about 1km from the hypogeum. If asking for **directions**, or for the right bus stop, ask for the mosque. It is the only one on the islands so everyone knows it.

EXPLORING THE TEMPLES There are **two temples** on this site. The one to the **left** is the better preserved and here it should be possible to make out the line of the concave façade and the entrance with a sill, a raised threshold over which you must step to enter. It is a three-apse globigerina limestone temple built in the first phase of temple building. The apses have been walled off, probably during the later Tarxien phase about 3000BC – something that is also seen at the Skorba Temple site (page 236). Unusually, both the courtyard outside the temple and the inner court are paved (though this is sometimes covered by vegetation).

The most interesting (indeed unique) feature of this temple is a large **trough** made from a single piece of coralline limestone (probably hauled from an outcrop about a kilometre away near Żabbar) with seven compartments carved out of it, separated by narrow walls of stone. The trough lies across the threshold of part of the left apse and is thought to be a quern for grinding grain – evidence of at least some secular activity in the 'temple'.

The **right-hand temple** (closer to the entrance) is of a similar age but has just two apses. Behind it and often difficult to make out in the grass are traces of elliptical torba-floored huts (perhaps 3800BC), suggesting the presence here (again, as at Skorba) of a village before the temples were built.

ŻEJTUN

Originally the main village in the area, Żejtun has (by virtue of being further from the urban centres of Valletta, Sliema and the Three Cities) retained some integrity. Named for its production of olive oil (*żejt* means 'oil') Żejtun was right in the path of the invaders in 1565 at the start of the Great Siege. Fortunately Grand Master Jean Parisot de Valette had the foresight to evacuate the population and their livestock to within the fortifications of Birgu. The cavalry left to patrol the area were the first to engage the Turks. Two young Knights were captured and the lies they told under torture led the Turks to the wrong strategic conclusions and helped the order towards its eventual narrow victory. The two Knights paid with their lives.

At the centre of the town today is the fine Baroque **Parish Church of St Catherine** with Classical pilasters and an octagonal dome. It was designed by Lorenzo Gafà (architect of the cathedrals of Mdina and Gozo) and built between 1692 and 1728. The *festa* here is held in June.

The parish of Żejtun goes back long before this church was built and was one of the original ten Maltese parishes listed in 1436. At that time the parish church was the much smaller Old Church of St Catherine of Alexandria, usually known as the **Church of St Gregory** (San Girgor; St Gregory St; ☏ 21677187), which had just been built. Its low dome, now thought to be the oldest in Malta, was added in 1495. The Knights made their own alterations and additions but apart from the 16th-century Renaissance portal, the façade is 15th century. The interior frescoes, however, were lost when the Royal Engineers (who really ought to have known better!) whitewashed the church for use as a storeroom after World War II.

If you look at the main door you will see that it is off-centre. This was intended to prevent the devil – who apparently only walks in straight lines – from disrupting services! There is also a more macabre oddity: up a narrow stone spiral staircase are two secret passageways hidden between the inner and outer walls of the church. These passageways were discovered in 1969 and found to contain the bones of a few tens of people. Nobody knows who they were or how they got there. Some suggest they were locals who hid here during the Turkish raid of 1547 and were overpowered by smoke when the Turks set light to the inside of the church. Others, noting that the bones were neatly stacked when found, say they may have come from elsewhere. The passageways can be visited by arrangement with the church.

GETTING THERE AND AWAY **Parking** is possible on the streets, but beware of the usual range of restrictions. **Buses** also serve Żejtun.

MARSASKALA/MARSASCALA

This small harbour town (whose name is sometimes shortened to M'Skala) with a mix of traditional and modern small boats in the water has a pleasant-enough seafront promenade and plenty of rocky shore to swim off (though there are cleaner places). The rest of the town feels a bit run-down and the bars at the bus-station end of the seafront can be noisy. There are no sights within the town – though a few nearby (see below) – and a couple of popular restaurants.

GETTING THERE AND AWAY There is a bus station is in the middle of town on the seafront by Grabiel's restaurant. **Parking** is mostly free.

✖ WHERE TO EAT AND DRINK

✖ **Grabiel** Mifsud Bonnici Sq 1; ☎21634194, 21636368; w grabielrestaurant.com; ⏱ 09.00–22.30 daily. Traditional trattoria-style restaurant that you know is good the minute you enter just from the smells. A painting of the harbour on glass separates the entrance from the restaurant. Mainly Italian cuisine, specialising in fish. The kitchen separates Grabiel from Terrazza – the formica-table inexpensive café with the same owners. €€–€€€

✖ **La Favorita** Triq il-Gardiel; ☎21634113; f; ⏱ noon–14.30 Tue–Sun & 19.00–23.00 Mon–Sat. Almost next door to the more famous Tal-Familja, this restaurant is also family-run & although it looks less prepossessing, the food is at least as good & prices generally lower. Emphasis on fresh fish & seafood. Families welcome. €€

✖ **Nargile** Triq il-Gardiel; ☎21636734; m 99515883; w nargileloungemalta.com; ⏱ 12.30–14.30 Wed–Sun & 19.00–22.30 Mon & Wed–Sat. Tiny frontage. Fusion in both its food (Arab, Indian, Mediterranean & mixed) & its décor (terracotta walls, white sofas & African rugs). Meat is halal. Post-dinner shisha pipes in a covered outdoor lounge at the back. Occasional belly dancing. Take-away service. €€

✖ **Tal-Familja** Triq il-Gardiel; ☎21632161; w talfamiljarestaurant.com; ⏱11.00–23.00 Tue–Sun. Up a seedy road alongside a stagnant canal beyond the seafront. Popular family-run & family-friendly restaurant. Traditional décor, stylish – specialising in fish & Maltese food. Locals love to come here for long Sun lunches. Highchairs available. €€

WHAT TO SEE AND DO AROUND MARSASKALA

St Thomas's Tower On the Il-Gżira headland between Marsaskala Bay and St Thomas's Bay, this substantial tower was built after the last full-scale Turkish invasion of Malta which landed at Marsaskala in 1614. The 5,000-strong force was beaten back, but only when it reached Żejtun. St Thomas's Tower was part of Grand Master de Wignacourt's scheme to strengthen coastal defences that included the building of six new watchtowers. The exterior of this tower has been renovated and looks very fine. You can go inside by appointment with Fondazzjoni Wirt Artna (☎ 21800992; w wirtartna.org), but there isn't much in there – better to visit one of the towers that are regularly open to the public (page 86).

St Thomas's Bay Not especially picturesque, but if you are hot and need a cooling dip in the sea, this bay fits the bill. A narrow sandy beach edges a little harbour of small boats. Locals crowd in on summer weekends and there is a café-pizzeria next to the rocks. From here, it is possible to walk to the next bay, Xrobb I-Għaġin (page 187), in about half an hour.

Torri Mamo (Triq id-Damla Ta' San Tumas, about 10mins' walk from the Marsaskala bus station; restored & maintained by Din L-Art Ħelwa (Malta's National Trust): ☎21225952; w dinlarthelwa.org; ⏱ 09.30–noon Thu–Sun; admission free) A very unusual fortified home built by the Mamo family in 1657. The house is shaped like the cross of St Andrew, giving it 16 sides. Inside is a domed central room with four rooms off it (the arms of the cross). A staircase leads to the roof which has views as far as St Thomas's Bay – the most likely source of the pirates against whom the house was fortified. It originally had a drawbridge across the 2m ditch that runs right round the building and in the ditch is a 4th-century Roman tomb, possibly first used in Phoenician times.

MARSAXLOKK

A few of Malta's traditional brightly painted boats can be seen in many of the country's harbours, but the place to see them en masse is Marsaxlokk, a pleasant fishing village with a long harbourfront full of cafés and restaurants, mostly specialising in fish fresh off the boats.

At one end of the harbour is the village square with its parish church (*festa* at the beginning of August) and on the harbourside itself is a daily market – largest on Sundays – selling pungent fresh fish first thing in the morning then a mix of souvenirs, clothes and local foods until mid afternoon.

Marsaxlokk is a very pleasant place for a wander and there is a small tourist office in the car park with maps and information.

HISTORY Marsaxlokk has always had a good harbour. Prehistoric Maltese people almost certainly fished from here, and at the start of the Great Siege, 181 Turkish galleys sailed in with 35,000 of Mustapha Pasha's men on board (page 12). Over two centuries later, in 1798, this was one of five places where the French landed by night for their successful invasion (but short-lived occupation) of Malta. The British duly followed, using the bay to resupply their forces and repair their ships. In December 1989, in the midst of a wild winter storm, US president George Bush Sr and Soviet president Mikhail Gorbachev held their groundbreaking end-of-the-Cold War Malta Summit here on board Soviet cruise ship SS *Maxim Gorky*.

GETTING THERE AND AWAY Buses connect Marsaxlokk to Valletta and to Tarxien and Marsaskala. There is a large free car park on the harbourside near the parish square.

⌂ WHERE TO STAY

⌂ **Quayside Apartments** (5 units, rising to 11) Marsaxlokk quayside between the village square & the main car park (at the north end of the harbour); m 99478225; w quaysidemalta. com. A little row of brightly coloured front doors in a 19th-century limestone façade on the quayside makes this place easy to spot. 1 dbl room & 10 'apartments' each with 1 bedroom (plus sofa bed), kitchenette, TV, Wi-Fi, & its own or access to communal outside space with washing machine & barbecue. 1st-floor rooms have barbecue, 'penthouses' their own jacuzzi. All self-catering but cleaned daily. €–€€

⌂ **Duncan Guesthouse** (9 studios & a 2-bedroom apt) Rooms above Duncan bar & restaurant; ☏ 21657212; m 79863105;

w duncanmalta.com. Good-value, spacious, clean & modern studio rooms some with kitchenette, most with balcony, all with modern shower rooms, TV, fridge & microwave. Guests have use of a washing machine & the flat roof. Some rooms can sleep 4, even 5. Good discounts for children. Lift to rooms. AC & fan. B/fast & other meals available in the inexpensive café downstairs (page 187). €

⌂ **Port View B&B** (13 rooms) 18 Triq Il-Luzzu; m 99492961, 99076004; w portview.com. Run by a father & son, this modern B&B is up a side street about 25m from the waterfront. Dbls & quadruples. Fridge, AC & central heating, Wi-Fi. Chairlift up front steps & lift within. Terrace with panoramic views over the harbour (glass-walled & heated in winter). €

✕ WHERE TO EAT AND DRINK
Marsaxlokk is where the Maltese come to eat fresh fish (although restaurants elsewhere also do excellent fish). Many of the restaurants along the harbour here display whole fresh fish on trays or trolleys so you can

MALTESE BOATS

As Malta is an archipelago in the middle of the Mediterranean, boats have necessarily played a crucial role in both culture and survival. Even today, traditional boats find their place alongside modern yachts and motorboats. The old boats are easy to spot as they are made of wood and painted in bright colours, particularly blue, red, yellow and green and most have a black 'moustache' across the bow.

LUZZU An open, traditional fishing boat with a high, pointy prow and stern. Sea-going, but for day trips rather than lengthy voyages. Traditionally used to catch *lampuki*, the national fish, and sometimes sporting the 'eye of Osiris' on the prow to ward off evil and bring good luck. Traditional *luzzus* are no longer built but many survive.

KAJJIK (*caiques*) A smaller fishing boat with a high, pointy prow, but a flat stern. Traditionally only about 4m long and intended for coastal fishing; later versions were bigger and often went well out to sea. A popular fishing craft: in 1920, more than half of Malta's 760 registered fishing boats were *kajjiks*.

DGHAJSA A traditional harbour boat for transport rather than fishing. Originally rowed – from a standing position Venetian-style. Now most also have motors. A host of these boats used to ply the waters of the Grand Harbour. Most disappeared when the Royal Navy left and there were no longer sailors needing transport to and from their ships. A few survive as water taxis, mainly for tourists.

---

select your own (particularly in the evening when the temperature is lower). Fish is usually simply grilled or steamed but may come with lemon and capers or other Mediterranean flavourings. You have to take the whole fish so if you choose a big one you will need two (or more) people, or a large appetite and a deep pocket. What is on offer varies with the season. Malta's national fish – *lampuki* (dolphin fish) – is usually available mid-August until December. The price of a fish dish depends on the species and the weight. Most main courses come in at about €15–25 but do ask (the main course prices quoted below are necessarily for other main courses). All the places recommended here are on the road along the harbourfront, Xatt is-Sajjieda, so only building numbers are given in the individual entries.

✕ **La Capanna** No 60; ☎21657755; w lacapanna.com.mt; ⏰ 11.45–14.30 & 18.30–22.30 Tue–Sun. Pine & beamed interior & a few outside tables. This is an unpretentious, friendly place, much loved by the Maltese who come for *aljotta* – Maltese fish soup – as well as whole fresh fish. Service sometimes slow. Prefers children to be over 5. €€–€€€

✕ **Tartarun** No 29; ☎21658089; m 99177258; w tartarun.com; ⏰ noon–15.00 Tue–Sun & 19.30–22.30 Tue–Sat. No outside seating but excellent fresh fish & other dishes & interesting 'fish snacks'. €€–€€€

✕ **La Nostra Padrona** No 87; ☎27667720; m 99496184; ❚; ⏰ usually 11.00–23.00 Wed–Mon. Fresh modern interior & tables across the road right on the waterfront in good weather. €€
✕ **T'Annamari** No 28; ☎27446211; m 79499827; w tannamari.com. On the north side of the harbour between the square & the car park, this marine-themed Sicilian restaurant does a particularly good fish *meze*. Tasty fresh home-cooked bread too. €€
✕ **Three Sisters** (official name Ta' Frenċ Il-Koy) No 85; ☎27656501; ❚; ⏰ 10.00–16.00 Tue–Sun & 19.00–23.00 in summer, in winter the same

lunchtimes but only open in the evening on Sat. Pizza & local fresh fish – some of it caught by the sisters' husbands. A place for sitting out on the waterfront. €–€€

✗ **Duncan Bar & Restaurant** No 33; ☎21657212; m 79863105; ⏱ 10.00–16.00 daily & 19.00–22.00/23.00 Wed–Sun (summer), Fri–Sun (winter). Fresh fish isn't cheap so if you are on a tight budget, Duncan's, on the corner of Church Sq, is the place to get a filling pasta dish. Tables inside & out. €

✗ **Rising Sun** On the stretch of seafront the other side of Church Sq from the rest of the eateries. A small, nondescript-looking 'bus driver's' caff serving inexpensive fresh *kalminara* among other things. €

✗ **Ta' Victor** No 36, next to Duncan's on the village square; ☎21641033; m 99474249; w tavictorrestaurant.com; ⏱ 11.00–14.30 & 18.30 until everyone has left. In a simple interior & at tables on the square, Victor serves traditional Maltese food (& fish). Order a main & you also get a Maltese platter of bread, cheese & sausage; pasta of the day & pudding. €

DELIMARA PENINSULA AND SWIMMING

The Delimara Peninsula is a few kilometres outside Marsaxlokk. It is walking distance (30–40mins) to the swimming places below, but in summer it is a hot and not especially nice walk. Otherwise you need a car or taxi to get here.

On the Marsaxlokk side of the peninsula is Malta's largest power station. On the other side are some of the best swimming spots in the area. A single road runs the length of the peninsula. You can park almost anywhere along it.

PETER'S POOL A delightful spot to sit and to swim, Peter's Pool is signposted from the road but you cannot drive all the way to it – one reason it remains so nice! Walk 5 minutes through small agricultural fields and caper bushes then down some rough stone steps to reach this rocky cove. High sides block out views of the power station and the water is clear and inviting. It is rarely busy on spring and autumn weekdays, but has recently become more popular in the summer. Be warned: it is not safe to swim here if there is any swell or choppiness. It is blissfully free of any commercialisation so you will need to bring your own water and refreshments.

DELIMARA BAY (IL-QALA TAT-TAWWALIJA) Further along the peninsula towards the point is another set of stone steps down to a quiet rocky bay. A derelict restaurant mars the view but there are rocks to swim off and deep clear water. The huge chunks of rock in the water fell during winter storms, so beware overhangs.

DELIMARA POINT At the point is **Delimara Lighthouse** which has been renovated by Din L'Art Ħelwa – Malta's National Trust – and is now available as a holiday rental (☎ 21225952, 21220358; w dinlarthelwa.org). The views across Marsaxlokk Bay are somewhat marred by the massive **Malta Freeport** and there is a military communications post at the point too, but it is a pleasant spot to get away from it all. It is a good place for birdwatching during migration (though keep in mind that this means it's also a good place for bird hunting; pages 26 and 50).

On the Marsaxlokk side of the point is **Delimara Fort** built low into the rock by the British in 1881. It was used as a cowshed until about ten years ago and is now deserted and in a poor state.

RAS IL-FENEK AND XROBB I-GĦAĠIN At the base of the Delimara Peninsula on the opposite side from Marsaxlokk are two bays divided by Ras Il-Fenek (Rabbit's Headland). The rock of this peninsula has a picturesque hole in its tip that gained it its name, and in summer boats make the trip to the bays for **swimming** (it can get quite crowded). It is apparently also possible to walk through the hole in the rock (at your own risk!).

If you don't have access to a boat, you can drive round to Xrobb I-Għaġin, with a small bay, a few salt pans, deep clear water and rocks to swim off (in dead calm only). You can also walk down from here into the closest of the Rabbit's Head bays.

BIRŻEBBUĠA

This unattractive town is itself of little interest to the visitor and lies in the shadow of the vast industrialised area of the Malta Freeport to its south. On the north side is the headland separating Birżebbuġa from Marsaxlokk and here stands **St Lucian Tower**, built in 1610–11 as one of Grand Master de Wignacourt's six coastal defence towers (page 85). The British expanded it into a small Victorian fortress with a defensive ditch and a curved entranceway (allowing a clear line of fire on enemies attempting to enter). It now houses Malta's Centre for Fisheries Sciences.

The town has two bays: **St George's Bay** (not to be confused with the one near St Julian's) and **Pretty Bay**, which is moderately pretty, with its white sandy beach (topped up with imported sand), so long as you keep your eyes firmly turned away from the cranes and concrete of the Malta Freeport. Birżebbuġa is, however, worth a visit for the two prehistoric/ancient sites on the edge of town.

GĦAR DALAM (Birżebbuġa Rd, BBG 9014; ✆ 21657419; w heritagemalta.org; ⏲ 09.00–17.00 daily (last entry 16.30); €5 adult, €3.50 over-60s/children aged 12–17/students, €2.50 children aged 6–11, children under 6 free) This natural cave (pronounced *ar-dalam* and meaning the 'Cave of Darkness') was one of the first places in Malta to be inhabited by humans who arrived on the islands in the 6th millennium BC. The presence of these early people is known from human remains, animal bones in rubbish pits and pottery. The pots have simple geometric decoration made by etching into the wet clay and are of the same style seen in Sicily during this era, suggesting that the first Maltese came from the neighbouring island 93km away.

The cave has also revealed animal remains dating from 180,000 to 130,000 years ago – including bones of hippo, elephant, brown bear, fox and wolf as well as a giant dormouse. A **guidebook** by Nadia Fabri (Insight Heritage Guides; €7.99) is available from the ticket desk.

LAMPUKA – MALTA'S NATIONAL FISH

Given its position in the middle of the sea, it is hardly surprising that fish is an important part of Maltese cooking and the favourite fish is *lampuka* or (in English) dolphin fish. Known to the Spanish as *dorado* for its golden-silver colouring, the *lampuka* migrates past Malta between August and December and *lampuki* make up a full one-third (by weight) of Malta's annual catch.

The *lampuki* season begins with a blessing of the fishing boats by the local priest and the fish are still caught in a traditional way. Floats of palm fronds and cork are laid on the water, the shade they create attracting small fish. *Lampuki* are in turn attracted to feed on the small fish. The fishermen simply come along and gather up the *lampuki* periodically with their nets. So plentiful are the fish that *lampuka* is the cheapest fresh fish in Malta and much enjoyed grilled, fried or in *lampuki* pie.

Getting there and away The **bus** from Valletta (via Tarxien) stops just outside. If travelling by **car**, the site is on the main road into Birżebbuġa and is signposted. There is parking less than 100m from the main entrance.

Museum The 'Old Museum' to the right of the entrance is lined with traditional tall glass-fronted dark-wood 1930s-style cabinets packed full of Pleistocene hippo bones and prehistoric elephant molars. There are also slightly younger deer bones and antlers.

On the other side of the entrance is a modern museum explaining the significance of the cave and its contents. Most intriguing is the development of dwarfed and gigantic prehistoric animals. During the Pleistocene era (1.8 million years to 10,000 years ago), the last part of which is commonly known as the ice age, animals travelled south from continental Europe to Sicily and Malta (then linked, at least intermittently, by a land bridge) in search of warmer climes. At this latitude the 'ice age' was merely a rain age and some animals settled and thrived.

When sea levels rose again, the islands were cut off and these creatures evolved separately from their relatives in the rest of Europe, with some species changing quite dramatically in size. While the continental elephant stood 4m to the shoulder, the Maltese equivalent was a mere 1m tall. Hippo, deer, brown bear, fox and wolf all shrank. But some smaller animals grew, so Malta had tortoises nearly as big as today's Galápagos giants and dormice the size of modern guinea pigs.

Garden As you leave the museum building, on the ground to your left is a pair of Malta's ancient or prehistoric cart ruts (see box, page 204). Ahead, the long flight of shallow steps leading from the museum to the cave has been landscaped with native Maltese plants. Among them (on your left) is the national plant of Malta, the rare little bush, rock centaury (*widnet il-baħar; Cheirolophus crassifolius*), and to the right is the national tree, the sandarac gum tree (*siġra ta' l-għargħar; Tetraclinis articulata*), a member of the cypress family. Among many others are a carob tree (brought here in ancient times when the Phoenicians and Romans used the seed as a unit of weight), oleander, and a caper bush.

From the steps you can see across the valley to a microcosm of Malta's historical landscape: almost straight ahead is a Knights' watchtower and, just above it, a World War II pillbox. Above and to the right of the towers, next to a gate and an orangey limestone wall, stands Tal-Kaċċatur, the site of a Roman villa with the largest Roman cistern found on the island (not open to the public). To the left, a cross on the top of a hill marks the Bronze Age settlement of Borġ In-Nadur. There are plans to build a walkway across the valley and link all of these sites into a heritage trail.

Cave The triangular rock with a hole in it that stands at the entrance to the cave is a tethering stone from the days when the cave was used as a cattle pen, as indeed it was right up until the start of excavations in the 19th century. The cave also served as a World War II shelter in 1940 and then as a military fuel store. Fast minelayers would come into the nearby harbour under cover of night, offload fuel and other supplies and disappear again the following night.

The cave itself is a broad tunnel 145m long (though the far end is closed for safety reasons). It was formed by water percolating through the rocks. The river that flowed above it eventually deepened and broke through its roof (at the point at which we now enter), probably bringing with it the earliest animal bones found here. The walkway leads past still-forming stalactites, nests of Spanish sparrows in the cave walls, and the excavation pits. A mound and pillar have been left to show the various excavated layers and what was found in them.

Southeast Malta BIRŻEBBUĠA

8

BORĠ IN-NADUR (Birżebbuġa–Għar Dalam Rd; ⊕ most of the Bronze Age & modern parts of the site are always open; the few temple remains are open only by arrangement with Heritage Malta; ☏ 22954000; w heritagemalta.org) On a natural plateau above the surrounding countryside, Borġ In-Nadur is an interesting multi-period site, though not the easiest to interpret. It has sparse ruins of a Tarxien-phase prehistoric temple and the remains of a Bronze Age settlement, as well as being the centre of a small modern-day Christian cult.

Borġ In-Nadur gives its name to the Bronze Age phase of Maltese archaeology (mid 2nd millennium–700BC) and is also the site of some important cart ruts (see box, page 204). These ran right up to the village and led one of the experts in the field, Dr David Trump, to believe that the cart ruts originated in this period. Unfortunately these ruts are very difficult to find without help.

Getting there and away Borġ In-Nadur is on the main Birżebbuġa–Għar Dalam road on the edge of the town, about 1km south of Għar Dalam and it is not difficult to park. By **public transport**, buses towards Birżebbuġa stop nearby – ask the driver or another passenger to tell you which stop to get off at. The Bronze Age and modern parts of the site can be reached freely by following a path from the main road signed 'Il-Madonna ta' Lourdes'.

Temple The temple site is approached via a duck farm and a weird modern stone carving of a face – do not be put off. Large megaliths mark the unusual fact that this temple's forecourt was surrounded by a high wall. The rest is quite hard to make out but does in fact form the ground plan of a typical four-apse temple. There must have been a temple-period village in the area, from which people presumably fished in Marsaxlokk Bay, and there are known to have been other temples nearby at Tas Silġ and at Xrobb I-Għaġin. The Borġ In-Nadur temple was probably long abandoned by the time the Bronze Age settlers built their village here.

Bronze Age settlement At least 1,000 years after the temple people deserted this site, Bronze Age settlers developed a thriving community covering the whole of this rocky spur. A great deal of pottery has been found along with oval huts (now covered over again). Many more Bronze Age huts are assumed to lie below the modern fields.

The most notable feature today is the 4.5m Bronze Age stone wall. The plateau is naturally defended on three sides. This wall defended the fourth. The big stones are original while the smaller rubble is reconstruction.

The large mound outside the wall is spoil from the 1880s archaeological dig. On top of it stands a modern cross. Since 2006, a local man has claimed to see visions of the Madonna on this spot, starting a minor cult with worshippers regularly gathering here to pray.

Outside the site On the path down from the Bronze Age settlement to St George's Bay is a gate in the stone wall that takes you into a pretty little 'Garden of Peace' (which pre-dates the hilltop cult) with flowers, benches, shade and a little shrine.

St George's Bay At the bottom of the path is the head of St George's Bay with its own evidence of prehistoric activity. On the triangular terrace below the promenade you can see two covered raised stone circles, and on the rocky foreshore are several fair-sized holes, some plugged, some open and some flooded with seawater. All of these are probably **Bronze Age grain silos** linked to the Borġ In-Nadur community which may have used this bay as a harbour for overseas trade.

There is also a pair of **cart ruts** that runs into the water. This is most unlikely to be because the carts ran into the sea; more likely it is due to rising water levels. It is thought that these ruts are Bronze Age and may have been made by vehicles carrying grain to and from the silos.

For a bit of more recent history, turn your back to the water to see a **Knights-period redoubt** (mini fort) that defended the bay. It now has a chapel built onto it. These redoubts usually come in threes and you can see another (now a private home) on the other side of the bay. The third has been destroyed.

SEND US YOUR SNAPS!

We'd love to follow your adventures using our *Malta and Gozo* guide – why not tag us in your photos and stories via Twitter (🐦 @BradtGuides) and Instagram (📷 @bradtguides)? Alternatively, you can upload your photos directly to the gallery on the Malta and Gozo destination page via our website (w bradtguides.com/malta).

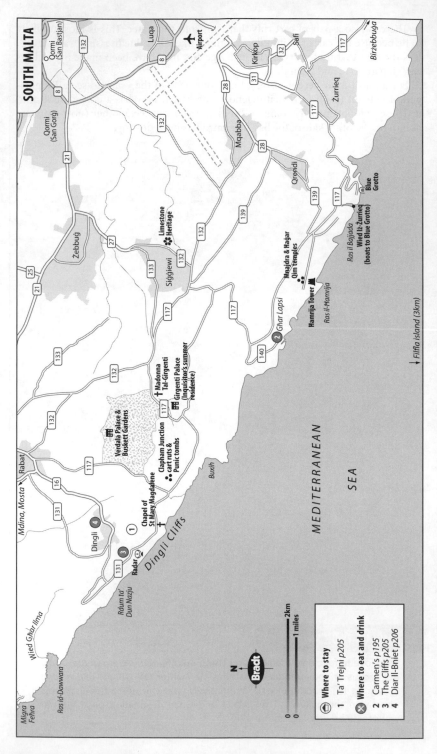

9

South Malta

This southern region is the heartland of traditional Malta. Villages like Żebbuġ and Siġġiewi are snapshots of what Malta used to be, with their church squares, band clubs, old limestone houses and little gaggles of elderly (and sometimes not-so-elderly) men sitting outside on benches or in the local café chatting the day away.

You won't find many tourists here; these villages are not on the main visitors' maps. Except Żurrieq, that is. Even here, though, most tourists simply pass through on their way to the Blue Grotto boat trip.

Beyond the villages, along the south coast, are two major sights – the prehistoric temples of Mnajdra and Ħaġar Qim and the Dingli Cliffs (with a variety of things to see) – as well as a popular rocky swimming spot.

GETTING THERE AND AWAY

Buses run to each of the villages. If you are driving, you should have no trouble parking.

ŻEBBUĠ *(NB: There is also a Żebbuġ on Gozo; page 293)*

This attractive peaceful village naturally centres around the church square, St Philip's Square (Misraħ San Filep), with its Baroque parish church. The **Church of St Philip** (1599–1659, with finishing touches added by Maltese architect Tommaso Dingli) has a double bell tower and ornate interior with a mass of golden arches above the altar. In the square, it is complemented by the colourful *gallariji* and traditional decorative wrought iron of the village's two band clubs. *Festa* is held quite early here – usually towards the end of April.

Żebbuġ was one of Malta's first ten parishes listed in 1436 and its name – which means 'olives' – goes back at least to the 14th century, although there have been olive groves here since Roman times. The British tried to replace this industry with cotton. They had limited success, but Żebbuġ did become a centre for the making of sailcloth and in the 19th century supplied the Royal Navy and other ships over in the Grand Harbour.

Żebbuġ is a traditional residential area, popular with wealthy Maltese. It was the birthplace of Dun Karm, Malta's national poet who wrote the words of the national anthem, and of Anthony Sciortino, Malta's most famous modern sculptor. Nowadays, it seems to be lawyers, doctors and the like who have the money to buy the beautiful centuries-old traditional stone houses. And the French government; its ambassador's residence sits on a quiet street just behind the church.

At the roundabout between Żebbuġ and Siġġiewi is the **de Rohan Arch** (1777), once the monumental entrance to Żebbuġ. Grand Master de Rohan visited the *festa* of St Philip in Żebbuġ in 1776 as part of his policy of re-engaging with the Maltese

The penultimate grand master of the Order of St John in Malta was, like many of his predecessors, a French aristocrat. Unlike some others, however, he was both clever and conscientious. By the second half of the 18th century, the order as a whole had slipped into self-satisfaction and self-gratification. Their monastic vows of poverty (not to mention chastity) had long been ignored and the order's relationship with the Maltese was at an all-time low. The Ottoman Empire was in decline so the order was no longer a crucial bulwark on the borders of Christendom. The Knights had run out of money and de Rohan was reduced to selling ships to the kings of Naples and Spain to raise cash.

The new grand master tried to reintroduce a moral and administrative structure. He took the fleet off a war footing and formalised its role in commerce. He reformed taxation and modernised the legal system, abolishing the worst forms of torture. The *Code de Rohan*, his two-volume constitutional law book, is still a part of Maltese law.

De Rohan was responsible for the building of the National Library in Valletta to house the Knights' archives, records and book collection. He also ordered the construction of Fort Tigné to pair with Fort St Elmo in defending Marsamxett Harbour.

In his efforts to improve relations with the local population he created ten new Maltese noble titles and visited villages around the country. The Maltese recognised his efforts and developed a great respect for him. For the order, though, it was too late and de Rohan didn't help matters with his politically ill-considered, though loyal and generous, support for his beleaguered monarch.

In 1791, de Rohan sold most of the order's silver to help fund Louis XVI's ill-fated flight from revolutionary Paris. When Napoleon arrived in Malta seven years later (a year after de Rohan's death), the order tried to claim it was a neutral religious community that should be left in peace. The French general reminded them of their grand master's actions, helped himself to what was left of their silver and kicked the Knights out of Malta.

population (see box above). The villagers asked to be given the status of a town and the grand master agreed. Żebbuġ gained the honorific Citta Rohan and built an arch to commemorate the event.

SIĠĠIEWI

A classic southern Maltese village, Siġġiewi was one of the first ten Maltese parishes listed in 1436 and is now a mix of long-time residents (mostly involved in local agriculture) and well-off families moving out of the urban sprawl. Tourists often make it to the edge of the village – to the Limestone Heritage centre – but rarely bother with the place itself.

Siġġiewi has a large double church square – an L-shape sloping down from the large highly decorated parish **Church of St Nicholas** (1675–93) whose *festa* is held towards the end of June. The tall, thin mid 19th-century dome of this church can be seen from miles around. The church's Baroque triple-arched façade (with angels keeping a watchful eye over the main entrance) is part of the original church designed by Lorenzo Gafà (architect of the Mdina and Gozo cathedrals).

Inside, the altarpiece of St Nicholas is thought to be Mattia Preti's last, and unfinished, work.

Below in the square, a tall statue of St Nicholas stands as if addressing a crowd, and at the head of the lower arm of the square – where the buses stop – is the much smaller **Church of St John the Baptist** (1730), also known as the Church of the Beheading of St John on account of a gory painting of this event inside.

LIMESTONE HERITAGE (Mgr M Azzopardi St, Siġġiewi, SGW 2050; ☎ 21464931, 21464437; w limestoneheritage.com; ⊕ 09.00–16.00 Mon–Fri, 09.00–noon Sat; €9/€6/€3 adults/children up to 12/students. A bus (from Valletta) stops here or it is a few minutes' walk from the centre of Siġġiewi. There is plenty of free parking on site.) Limestone really is a major part of Malta's heritage. The buildings – from the prehistoric temples, through the Knights' forts and churches to today's houses – are mostly built of limestone because, quite simply, it is what Malta is made of. This well-designed centre, created and run by a family of quarrymen and stonemasons in a disused quarry, sets out to show how limestone has been sourced and used over the years.

An 8-minute **film** introduces a short audio guide (both multi-lingual) which takes you round a series of **tableaux** of stone-working, tools and vehicles. The story starts 100 years ago (when techniques had in fact changed little for 1,000 years) and leads up to mechanisation, which only happened fully during the 1950s dash to rebuild after World War II. More stone was quarried in the 40 years after the war than in the previous 700. The **original quarry** wall can still be seen, and there are examples of different kinds of stone building from a *girna*, the ancient circular rubble-built farmer's hut (some of which are still in use today), to a traditional Maltese home. Inside are a geological map and some original Victorian tools.

You can also watch **stonemasons** at work or even have a go yourself. In the garden are peacocks, chickens and a donkey as well as a **Punic tomb** that has been re-used as a cistern.

As well as limestone carvings, the **souvenir shop** has a small but well-chosen selection of **books** including *Limestone Heritage* by Vincent Zammit (Insight Heritage Guides; €6.99) with lots more detail about stone working in Malta.

GĦAR LAPSI

(A bus stops here in summer; free parking although it gets busy on summer w/ ends) On the coast south of Siġġiewi is this popular place for **swimming** on windless summer days (it isn't safe when there are waves). The rocks here form protected little lidos and, despite the length of concrete shore, it is an inviting place to enter the clear blue water. It can get very crowded with locals (and a few tourists) on summer weekends.

Għar Lapsi is also a very popular place for **rock climbing**. Some 400m above the village is a great arc of cliffs where the intrepid (and properly equipped!) can be seen like little insects working their way up the rock face. (For more on rock climbing, see page 74.)

✕ **WHERE TO EAT AND DRINK** *Map, page 192*

✕ **Carmen's** Għar Lapsi; ☎ 21467305; m 99404121; f; ⊕ 11.30–17.00 & 19.00–23.00 Mon, Wed & Thu, 10.30–23.30 Fri, 09.00–23.00 Sat, 10.30–20.30 Sun. Small, unassuming place with views of the water & good Mediterranean food & fresh fish. Very popular on summer w/ends. €€

Żurrieq is the largest village in the south of Malta and, while vast numbers of tourists go through it en route to the Blue Grotto at Wied Iż-Żurrieq, few stop. There is not a vast amount to make them do so, except perhaps the **Church of St Catherine of Alexandria** (1634–59) containing six paintings by Mattia Preti, who lived in Żurrieq for a while, and the late 17th-century **Knights' Armoury** in Mattia Preti Square, although this is quite ordinary-looking. Żurrieq's *festa* is held in late July.

There are, however, a number of things to see around Żurrieq and there are several walks in the area detailed by the Malta Tourism Authority in free downloads (w visitmalta.com/en/walks) or in booklet form (available from the main tourist offices). These include the Ħal Millieri walk; Dingli, Fawwara, Wied Iż-Żurrieq; and particularly the Windmills Walk. There are several **windmills** around Żurrieq including the only functioning windmill on the island (Xarolla Windmill).

AROUND ŻURRIEQ
Ħal Millieri Chapel (⏰ 09.00–noon 1st Sun of each month or by appointment with Din L-Art Ħelwa (Malta's National Trust); ✆ 21225952, 21220358; w dinlarthelwa. org) Just north of Żurrieq is this wayside Chapel of the Annunciation. Ħal Millieri was a medieval settlement and this little church dates from about 1450. Inside is Malta's only surviving medieval church art – 14 frescoes (some damaged) of Byzantine saints. The paintings are somewhat old-fashioned even for their time and it has been suggested they may be copies of earlier local frescoes, created to provide continuity of devotional activity when, for whatever reason, the earlier frescoes disappeared.

Wied Iż-Żurrieq On the road from Żurrieq to Wied Iż-Żurrieq there is a viewpoint at the side of the road from where you can look down on the **Blue Grotto**, and, in the right light, see the luminous blue that gives the place its name. In decent weather, though, it is still worth taking the Blue Grotto boat trip to see it, and other caves, close up.

Wied Iż-Żurrieq lies 3km from Żurrieq and is a little fishing village-turned-tourist site. It has survived the transformation quite well with just a small street of souvenir shops and cafés leading down to the boats. On the other side of the road is an open 'garden' area with views out to sea towards the uninhabited island of **Filfla** (see box below) and a **Knights' watchtower** built under Grand Master Lascaris (1636–57).

FILFLA

An uninhabited island some 5km offshore, Filfla seems to have been named from *felfel*, the Arabic for 'pepper', though the reason isn't clear. The island is a mere 350m across, standing 60m out of the water at its highest point. A chapel was built here after a major storm in 1343 but was destroyed around 1575. The British and NATO used the island for bombing target practice. It is now more peacefully used by a breeding colony of storm petrels and, between February and October, a couple of hundred breeding pairs of Cory's shearwaters. There are also a number of yellow-legged gulls (which unfortunately feed on petrels). The island is a nature reserve with no access for people.

Blue Grotto boat trip (ticket booth: 21640058, additional numbers: 21685172, 21680660; m 79640058, 79680660; f Blue Grotto Boat Service Malta; ⊕ summer 09.00–17.00 daily, weather permitting, winter 09.00–15.30 daily; €8/4 adults/ children aged 3–10; price inc any commentary; boatmen should not ask for extra) Follow the road downhill to the ticket office and the landing stage in a protected inlet. From here an endless stream of colourful little boats (seating up to nine passengers) putters out around the coast to explore the caves and rock formations. The Blue Grotto is the largest and most impressive of these: a high double-arched cave with a pedestal/column between the arches. When the light is right – on sunny mornings – the sun bouncing off the white sandy seabed turns the water a bright luminous blue. Glimpses of this can also be seen in some of the other caves and even when the light is not right the trip is still enjoyable. At peak times of year, it can get horribly busy so try to arrive first thing.

MNAJDRA AND ĦAĠAR QIM ✷

(Triq Ħaġar Qim, Qrendi, QRD 2502; 21424231; w heritagemalta.org; ⊕ 09.00– 17.00 daily (last admission 16.30), 1hr later in summer; €10 adults, €7.50 over-60s/children 12–17/students, €5.50 children aged 5–11, under 5s free. Buses stop right at the temples' entrance. There is plenty of free parking.) Mnajdra and Ħaġar Qim are the most atmospheric temples to visit. They sit in an idyllic location well away from Malta's urban sprawl, surrounded by blue sea, grey rock and, in spring, greenery and flowers. The view from a distance is interrupted by the vast cream-coloured canopies that have been built to protect the temples from sun and rain. There can be no doubt that these are necessary, and in some ways they enhance the visitor experience (see box, page 199).

The visitor centre (well tucked into the landscape so that it does not intrude too much) contains an attractive but uninformative audiovisual presentation and a more informative exhibition focusing on the interpretation, construction and use of the temples. There are also loos here (but no café) and a children's room and free children's activity sheets. Mnajdra and Ħaġar Qim are neighbouring temple complexes 500m apart. It is not clear in what way they were originally connected (if at all) but we do know that they were used simultaneously and right up until the end of the temple period (mid 3rd millennium BC). They are, however, quite different from each other: the Mnajdra Temples show well-preserved examples of many of the common characteristics of Malta's temples, while Ħaġar Qim has some very unusual features. Mnajdra is usually less busy because coach parties often don't make it further than the ruins closest to the visitor centre.

For more information on the history of the temples and understanding what you see, see page 79.

MNAJDRA Three temples stand along one curved side of an oval forecourt or plaza 30m across. All three have outer walls of coralline limestone with inner parts in the smoother, more decorative (but more easily weathered) globigerina limestone.

First temple Up a few steps on your right, is the smallest and oldest (first half of the 4th millennium BC). It has an unusual **triple entrance** and a typical trefoil (three-lobed) design, although the central lobe is very shallow so it looks almost like a mere niche. The walls include a lot of 20th-century reconstruction (in limestone rubble).

The central **'altar'** has pitted decoration and on the inner face of the uprights (clearer on the right) are a few lines of dots. It has been speculated that these are

9

tally holes relating to the appearance of certain stars' constellations, perhaps making a crude calendar (though many, including one of the leading experts, are sceptical).

South temple The furthest temple (closest to the sea) was built by around 3000bc. It is much larger and more complex than the first temple, with a well-preserved **concave façade** that extends some way beyond the temple walls around the edge of the forecourt. The **'bench'** along the façade is clearly visible and wide enough here that it could have been a walkway. In front of the main doorway, on the ground, is a so-called **'tethering point'** (where animals may or may not have been tied up) and the threshold has a dark band across it – a natural feature of the stone, but clearly chosen as decoration for an important entrance.

Inside, look back at the **main entrance** – it has an architecturally sophisticated double trilithon construction (two uprights with a topstone repeated one inside the other; page 80), giving it extra strength. It is also a good place to compare the two limestones from which the temple is constructed. The inner trilithon of the doorway is of globigerina while the outer is coralline.

Turning back to look into the temple, the **left apse** is a good place to see how cleanly and tightly the stones of the walls are fitted together. There is also a framed **'porthole' stone** (with pitted decoration) through which you can see a large **pedestal altar** in a further 'room'.

The temple has an interesting alignment to the sun at sunrise. On the equinoxes (the first day of spring and autumn), sunlight beams straight through the front door of the temple and down its central axis. On the winter solstice (between 20 and 23 December) the light hits the outer edge of the pitted upright to the right of the inner doorway. On the summer solstice (Midsummer Day) the beam seems to strike a similar distance to the other side of the doorway just missing the now-damaged

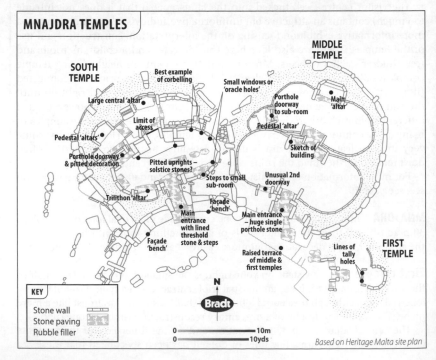

MNAJDRA TEMPLES

Based on Heritage Malta site plan

After 5,000 years, why should these temples suddenly require canopies to protect them? The answer is that for the first 1,000 years or so the temples had roofs and for most of the rest they were largely buried under soil. Ħaġar Qim was excavated in 1839, Mnajdra in 1840. Since then significant damage has been done by weathering (quite obvious when photos from the 1890s are compared with what is seen today). Action was necessary and urgent. A covering that protects the stones without affecting the integrity of the buildings seems an appropriate response. The canopies do not touch the temples and are completely removable. Mnajdra and Ħaġar Qim were the first to be covered because this was where there was the most to lose. They had been well preserved so far and were deteriorating fast. Ħaġar Qim is built entirely of soft, easily weathered, globigerina limestone, while Mnajdra is mainly globigerina with harder coralline limestone on the outside. Ġgantija (on Gozo), for instance, is of less concern as it is mostly made of the tougher coralline stone. The Tarxien Temples are also built of globigerina and so were next to receive a canopy.

Despite somewhat damaging the view from outside at Mnajdra and Ħaġar Qim, the canopies have a positive effect once you are inside the temples, making them feel more like the roofed buildings they once were (though without losing air or light as the canopy is high above you and open sided). They help you appreciate the internal structure of the temples, walking its 'corridors' and being in its 'rooms'. The canopies also protect visitors from rain and remove the glare of the sun, making it easier to see details on the stones and to take photographs.

The canopies' supporting structures are carefully positioned to ensure that the view from the front of the temples is not obscured and the line of the sun's rays at the solstices and equinoxes still fall where they were (probably) intended to fall.

upright. Perhaps it once just hit the stone, or maybe it was always intended to carry on through the small doorway to land on the pedestal altars.

The **right apse** has the best surviving example of corbelling with the stones leaning progressively inwards towards the top of the walls. There are a few 'oracle holes', like windows through the walls, and a porthole doorway up a small flight of steps leading to a chamber between the apse wall and the outer perimeter wall.

At the far end of the temple is a **central altar** with huge verticals. The **last pair of apses** is sometimes roped off, but if they are open, the right apse is quite plain while the left is filled with pedestal altars, which are also part of the structure of the temple. The large two-level ones look like vast shelves.

Middle temple The middle temple, tucked in between the other two, is the latest (3000–2350BC). It has a similar internal structure to the south temple with two pairs of apses, but its shape is simpler and its interior plainer. Entrance is from a raised terrace through a **large porthole doorway** (made of one massive stone, now broken) with an unusual extra door next to it.

Inside, to the left of the doorway leading to the second pair of apses, is a little engraved drawing of a temple with a triple entrance. As you pass through this central doorway, look back at its strong double trilithon or 'box-within-a-box' construction (page 80). You can see where the lintel was rebated into the outer uprights for extra strength. The temple people were really quite sophisticated builders!

BETWEEN AND AROUND MNAJDRA AND ḤAĠAR QIM The 500m path between the two temple sites is lined with wild fennel, looking like yellow cow parsley in summer and smelling of aniseed. Here are also the starting points for two trails, Trail A along the coast and Trail B up onto the rocky garigue inland.

On the garigue are several stone huts. These are trappers' hides where Maltese men traditionally hid to net finches during autumn and spring migration (page 26). Dotted around the landscape are a number of small quarries. These are mostly not prehistoric, but the *misqa* tanks (inland of Mnajdra and signed on Trail B) almost certainly are. They were probably built as water tanks – and still collect rainwater – but their exact use is uncertain.

Towards the sea is a small **cenotaph to Walter Norris Congreve** – a British World War I general and governor of Malta in the 1920s who died in office and is buried at sea halfway between here and the uninhabited island of Filfla (see box, page 196). The channel between the two islands is named the Congreve Channel after him.

Just beyond the cenotaph on the cliff edge is **Hamrija Tower**, built in 1659 as part of the chain of coastal defence and communications towers commissioned by Grand Master de Redin. It is not open to the public, but makes a good starting point for a wander along the coast. If you are nimble and have a head for heights, you can get down nearly to sea level here, and there is an attractive rock arch just offshore.

ḤAĠAR QIM Ḥaġar Qim is unusual. It sits on a kind of acropolis and seems to have no specific front. You approach a clear concave façade (like that at other temples), but if you walk around the building there is another on the other side along with a second monumental entrance, complete with 'libation holes'.

Exterior It is as if it looks out in all directions. The **'bench'** goes almost all the way round and there are doorways at both ends. There is also an external **'shrine'** – a semicircular recess in the outside wall that may have had a ritual use. To the left of the 'shrine' is one of the largest stones in the temple – a 20-ton megalith. Also visible from the outside, on the other side of the building, are the legs of two **'fat lady'** statues (signposted). Returning to the main entrance, you can see a large **'tethering point'** (which may alternatively have been where ropes were attached when transporting the stone) before entering through the tunnel-like entrance.

Interior The **main building** at Ḥaġar Qim has a confusing arrangement of rooms. It is as if a much smaller four-apse temple has had large rooms added onto one side (see site plan, opposite). The **first apses** are screened from the main passageway and each has a porthole doorway. The two doors are positioned such that from just inside each one you cannot see through the other. Copies of **decorated stones** can be seen (the originals are in the National Museum of Archaeology in Valletta) including 'the Ḥaġar Qim Altar' which looks like an ornate stone stool with leaf-like patterning up the pedestal. The second right apse shows evidence of corbelling and has a hole through which the sun beams on the summer solstice.

The apse on the left contains a complex assortment of **'altars'**. Some seem ill-suited to being altars (due to their shape and height). Two, however, are strong candidates for being sacrificial altars. They are mushroom-shaped and the round-top stones once had rims around the edge (now badly weathered), which would have controlled

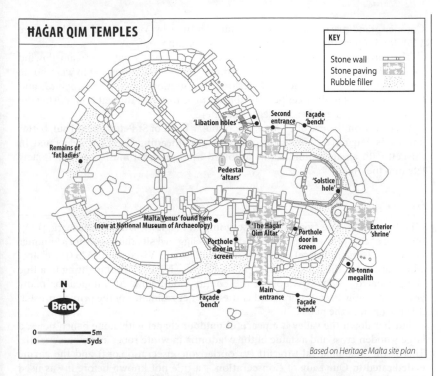

ḤAĠAR QIM TEMPLES

KEY
Stone wall
Stone paving
Rubble filler

'Libation holes'
Second entrance
Façade 'bench'
Remains of 'fat ladies'
Pedestal 'altars'
'Solstice hole'
'Malta Venus' found here (now at National Museum of Archaeology)
'The Ḥaġar Qim Altar'
Porthole door in screen
Exterior 'shrine'
Porthole door in screen
20-tonne megalith
N
Façade 'bench'
Main entrance
Façade 'bench'

0 ——— 5m
0 ——— 5yds

Based on Heritage Malta site plan

the flow of blood or other liquid on its surface. Four **'fat ladies'** (or possibly gents, now in the Valletta museum) were found here. Where you would normally expect the 'main altar', Ḥaġar Qim has its second entrance/exit and views to the world outside.

BUSKETT GARDENS (IL-BUSKETT) AND VERDALA PALACE

(The bus stops by Buskett and it is also walking distance from the Dingli Cliffs; if you are in a car you can drive into & through the gardens &/or park inside while you walk) Malta's only substantial patch of woodland was deliberately planted by the Knights in the 17th century and stocked as a private hunting forest. The deer are long gone, but this is a popular place for the Maltese to meet and picnic or eat in one of the two café-pizzerias.

By the main gate is a **milestone**, with its place name and distance scraped out – a wartime measure intended to hinder spies or invaders trying to find their way around the island. As you enter the gardens along a long driveway, you can see the castle-like **Verdala Palace**, perched above the gardens (there are even better views from the approach to Clapham Junction). Built in 1586 as a summer retreat and hunting lodge for French grand master Hugues Loubenx de Verdalle (the only grand master who also became a cardinal), it was designed by Girolamo Cassar, the military engineer who planned much of early Valletta. Despite its four turrets and dry moat, it was a place primarily for leisure rather than defence, although it was intended to be able to withstand 24 hours of siege in case senior Knights were caught out here during a corsair attack. Today it is the summer residence of Malta's president and is not normally open to the public, but there are occasional events here and a few tours offer a visit. The inside is painted by Florentine artist Philippo Paladini who escaped to Malta after misbehaving at home. The chapel was added in the 17th century by the

Cotoner grand masters and includes altar paintings by Mattia Preti (see box, page 126). If it is open, there are panoramic views from the roof.

The **gardens** are now a public park of trees and paths with a stream flowing through in winter. For visitors from northern Europe this is nothing to write home about, although it is good for **birdwatching** at migration times when songbirds and birds of prey rest in the trees here. Bird hunting is illegal in Buskett even during the open autumn season when it is legal elsewhere.

Each year on the eve of 29 June, the popular **Feast of St Peter and St Paul**, better known as Mnarja or Imnarja (from *luminarja* meaning 'light') is celebrated in Buskett with an agricultural show followed by traditional music and rabbit stew late into the night.

GIRGENTI

(The bus comes here from Rabat, also going to Siġġiewi, Dingli and Żurrieq) On the edge of this pretty valley about 4km from Siġġiewi sits the **Inquisitor's Summer Palace (the Girgenti Palace)** built by Inquisitor Horatus Visconti in 1625 (the chapel added in 1760). The palace is just one room deep, its seven rooms sitting in a line along a narrow ridge overlooking the countryside below. Abandoned for many years, it has now been restored and is the summer residence of the prime minister. It is not open to the public.

Further down the valley is a peaceful **outdoor chapel** with stone bench pews, a large wooden cross and a statue of the Madonna in white robes and a blue mantle. This is the **Madonna Tal-Girgenti** (w ourladyofconsecration.org) and the shrine is dedicated to Our Lady of Consecration – a title not known before it was used here. This Marian shrine was built in 1986 as a result of two visions claimed by a local woman, Guza Mifsud. She said she had been told by the Madonna to spread devotion to the new title, and also claimed that during a break from farming her family's land in the Girgenti Valley, the Madonna had appeared to her dressed in white with a blue mantle. The shrine is visited by pilgrims and is always open.

Another modern Christian landmark is the **Laferla Cross**, up on the Hill of the Cross (Tas Salib), 218m above sea level. Visible for miles around, it was erected in 1903 to celebrate the start of the 20th Christian century. It was destroyed in a storm, but replaced in 1963. While the cross itself is of no more interest close up than from a distance, the hill affords panoramic views of the surrounding area. On Maundy Thursday the cross is floodlit and crowds of people make their way up the rough track.

THE DINGLI CLIFFS AND CLAPHAM JUNCTION ✳

DINGLI CLIFFS (Buses stop here and there is free parking on the roads) The highest place in Malta, the Dingli Cliffs fall a sheer and impressive 250m into the sea. Their flat rocky top is a great place for **walking** (except in the midday heat) and there is usually a breeze up here. It is also possible to drive along the edge of the cliff for some distance. The views of the Mediterranean are spectacular and this is a popular spot from which to watch the sunset. In spring the area is covered in wild flowers. Even in summer wild fennel and caper bushes flourish, and the smell of thyme wafts up as you brush the greenery underfoot.

During migration these cliffs are the first land many migrating birds have seen for hundreds of miles so they are an ideal place for **birdwatching** if you aren't too offended by the occasional presence of bird hunters (more on pages 26 and 50).

The Cliffs restaurant (page 205) offers walks – self-guided with an informative map, or with a guide – highlighting the plants, geography, history and prehistory of the area. You'll discover all sorts of things you might otherwise have walked past, or even over. And you can then return to the restaurant and taste some of the edible ones! The restaurant generously welcomes any visitor to use their toilet facilities, whether eating there or not.

Alone on the edge of the cliff stands the little **Chapel of St Mary Magdalene** (1646), occasionally the target of vandals, but otherwise a peaceful spot from which to survey the sea and look out towards the uninhabited island of Filfla (see box, page 196). The chapel can also be reached by car. It is closed except on 22 July, when evening Mass is said here on St Mary's feast day.

CLAPHAM JUNCTION (Bus to Buskett & walk 500m following signs to cart ruts; free parking on the road) On the rocky plateau on top of the Dingli Cliffs is this bizarre sight: more than 40 pairs of **cart ruts** (see box, page 204) running along the rough rock, dividing and combining, parallel and criss-crossing, disappearing (where the surface of the rock has been eroded) and reappearing. Some can be followed for many metres. You can see how the place got its name.

Most of the ruts have a gauge of about 1.4m, although one pair is much wider. The most recent research suggests that these (though not all Malta's cart ruts) were probably made for, and further eroded by, vehicles carrying stone from the ancient Punic/Roman quarries (now masked by modern fields). The vehicles would have followed the ruts across the rocky plateau to a surfaced road. The depth of the channels varies enormously and debate still rages about what kind of vehicle ran in them.

Punic tombs There are three shaft-and-chamber tombs close to the cart ruts (one in fact is cut across by a pair of ruts, which has played a part in dating the ruts). The tombs are surrounded by little modern drystone walls and are found by walking from the (signed) cart ruts across the rock, up an incline going away from the sea, towards the (signed) troglodyte caves. The tombs are open squarish holes in the ground a couple of metres across and of a similar depth. They are obviously manmade and at the base of the main hole is the entrance to a chamber cut into the rock, which would have held the body (or bodies). Take a torch if you want to look in.

Għar il-Kbir Troglodyte Settlement A little further up the slope (going away from the sea) is a complex of natural caves extended by people, now partially collapsed. This was a troglodyte settlement from perhaps as early as the Bronze Age until possibly as late as the 19th century.

There is documentary evidence of an established community in the caves in 1536, and in 1647 27 families (117 people) are listed as living here. A description from 1637 tells how the caves were lit through shafts in the roof and how drystone walls were used to create façades across the cave entrances and to divide the caves internally between different families. There is still evidence of this and you can see how the inhabitants improved their subterranean homes with cupboards, alcoves and seats carved out of the rock walls.

In 1678, a Dutch visitor noted that the people living here were tall and healthy and the women remarkably good-looking. Keith Buhagiar (in his thesis on the settlement) describes how the people were vegetarian, raising animals only for dairy produce and for sale and how the community spoke a dialect closer to Arabic than is Maltese.

9

Malta's and Gozo's ancient (or prehistoric) 'cart ruts' are something of a mystery. Pairs of grooves cut and/or worn into the rocky ground can be seen at various locations across the islands. The most extensive set of ruts is on the Dingli Cliffs where so many tracks criss-cross one another that the place has become known as Clapham Junction. The ruts range from a few centimetres to 60cm deep and vary somewhat in width and shape as well. They have an average gauge of 1.4m, though one track at Clapham Junction is much wider. When and how the ruts were made is a source of endless debate, although recent research has added somewhat to our understanding and provided some tentative answers. Cart ruts of this sort are not unknown elsewhere in the world, but with 186 known sites (some still visible, some not) Malta has by far the greatest concentration.

DATING Cart ruts elsewhere in the world have been dated from the Bronze Age to the 19th century. In Malta, it had been suggested that the ruts dated to the temple period and were made during the transportation of stone, but this is not generally supported by their locations – none leads to a temple site. Dr David Trump, a leading authority on prehistoric Malta, plumps for the later Bronze Age with particular reference to ruts associated with the Bronze Age settlement at Borġ In-Nadur. Here the ruts lead to the settlement and to and from a series of silos by the coast. The latest research suggests that this dating is probably correct for these cart ruts, but that other ruts may be of a later date.

It is quite possible that the ruts date from a variety of periods – and some were perhaps used at more than one time. The cart ruts at Clapham Junction seem to be linked to Punic/Roman quarries and there are ruts near the Roman Domus in Rabat that are likely to date from a similar time to the building itself (1st century AD). Just to keep archaeologists on their toes, there is a set of cart ruts near St Paul's Bay that is known to have been created by a 20th-century mechanical harvester!

WHAT MADE THEM? In the past the suggestion has been made that these are not cart ruts at all but were created to collect rainwater. In some cases (including

There is some dispute over how the community disappeared. It is usually said that the British found the place unhygienic and in 1835 moved the reluctant population to Siġġiewi. Some even say that the troglodytes were so keen on their caves that they kept returning until the authorities deliberately collapsed the roof. Buhagiar, however, believes that the roof collapsed naturally after the people had drifted away.

THE COAST NORTHWEST OF DINGLI CLIFFS
Dingli is not the only place for walking. There are lovely **walks** along the coast to its northwest where the landscape is quite different from Dingli and where few people go. You will need your own transport. Try parking at **Migra Feħra** and walking south along the coast. There is a narrow path on the edge of the cliff (take care and don't bring young kids). Much of the rock here is weathered smooth, shining bright creamy-white in the sunshine, and in spring it is set off magnificently with greenery and wild flowers. The area teems with butterflies and the national bird, the blue rock thrush, is a not uncommon sight.

This place is good for **birdwatching** (and therefore also for bird hunting and trapping; page 26). There are lots of stone hides and cleared trapping areas.

the ruts at San Pawl Tat-Tarġa outside Naxxar), the channels have been used for this purpose but this is almost certainly a secondary use. It seems fairly clear that the cart ruts are just that – made by, or for, some sort of vehicle. One suggestion is that many of the ruts were first cut by hand, ie: that they were deliberately created to help a vehicle pass more easily over the rough rocky terrain. The ruts would then have been further carved out by use, and suffered additional natural erosion after they had been abandoned. Others, however, believe that wear and weathering are wholly responsible for the ruts.

So what sort of vehicle ran along these tracks? Sledges, wheeled carts and slide cars have all been proposed. Sledges seem least likely because straight runners would not have been able to take the sharp corners seen in several sets of ruts. A simple cart with wooden wheels is more likely. It would have had to have a loose axle in order to run in ruts whose distance apart varies significantly, and the wheels would have needed to be large to cope with the depth of some of the ruts. Slide cars fit the profile too. They are made of two long thin pieces of wood set diagonally along each side of a load-bearing platform. One end of the wooden poles would have been pulled by man or beast while the other – perhaps tipped with hard stone or metal – slid along the ground, a movement likely to create a clear line of wear in the rock. How and when the cart ruts were made remains the subject of research and heated debate.

BEST PLACES TO SEE THE CART RUTS See the map of prehistoric sites, page 82.

FURTHER INFORMATION A small gallery dedicated to the cart ruts in the National Museum of Archaeology in Valletta has a reconstruction of some ruts and an interesting video by world expert on prehistoric Malta, Dr David Trump. A recent compendium of research is to be found in *The Significance of Cart Ruts in Ancient Landscapes*, edited by Joseph Magro Conti and Paul C Saliba, published by Midsea Books and Heritage Malta. There are also lots of photos, locations and interesting speculations at **w** cartrutsmalta.com.

If you keep walking along here you will come to a bay, **Ras id-Dawwara**, at the head of which is a **small waterfall** – a real rarity in Malta – at Wied Għar Ilma. From about November to April (depending on rainfall) water flows over the edge of the cliff, plunging into the sea above a large sea cave.

WHERE TO STAY *Map, page 192*
There are a few self-catering properties in and around Dingli Village.

Ta' Trejni **m** 79533535; **f**. 3-bedroom detached villa/farmhouse with its own pool, close to the Dingli Cliffs. **€€€**

WHERE TO EAT AND DRINK *Map, page 192*
The Cliffs Triq Panoramika, Dingli Cliffs; ****21455470; **m** 79273747; **w** thecliffs.com.mt; **⏰** 11.30–16.00 Wed–Mon (full lunch service until 15.00), Jun–Sep 19.00–22.30 daily, Oct–May Fri & Sat. Built on brown-field ex-RAF land, this restaurant-cum-interpretation centre prides itself

on being environmentally friendly & utterly local. It buys cheese from the last Dingli goat herd & collects wild & semi-wild food (from herbs to quince) from the cliffs. Try the One Kilometre Platter – everything from within 1km – or the excellent salads & delicious borage ravioli (stuffed with local cheese as well as local borage). You can also buy Cliffs herbs & jams to take home. The Cliffs also run a programme of informative local walks with an introductory video, map & optional guide. €€

✕ **Diar Il-Bniet** Main St, Dingli; 27620727; m 77620002; w diarilbniet.com/the-restaurant; ◷ noon–15.00 daily & 18.30–21.30 exc Wed & Sun, also afternoon tea 16.30–19.00 Sun. In Dingli Village, this bright attractive restaurant serves fresh local food. 85% of it comes from their own farm & estate, including all the fruit & veg, chicken, rabbit, eggs, sheep's cheese & even the wine. Everything is homemade, from marinades to cakes. You can also buy their homemade jams (fig, quince, pomegranate) to take home. On Sun they do a Maltese buffet (do book). €€

10

Mdina and Rabat

In the centre of the island a natural ridge rises from the countryside and on top of it sits Mdina, the old capital of Malta. It is easy to see why this was the capital in the days when all danger of invasion came from the sea and natural defences were the starting point for manmade defences. Around Mdina lies the town of Rabat (meaning 'suburb'), missed by many tourists, but with some very interesting historical sites of its own from the late Roman and Knights' periods.

MDINA ✳

Mdina is a medieval walled town, but its history goes back far earlier. This was Malta's first capital, its main town from at least Roman times, when it was called Melite, until the arrival of the Order of St John in 1530. The Knights needed to be closer to their ships and so based themselves in Birgu (Vittoriosa) on the Grand Harbour. The Maltese aristocracy, however, remained in Mdina and it continued to be an important centre.

This is an extraordinary place. Strategically perched on the edge of a plateau 150m above the surrounding countryside, it is a striking sight as you approach by road: sitting on top of its rock, impenetrable, lording it over all it surveys. Within its fortified walls there are very few shops and offices; it is mainly *palazzi* (grand old houses) and religious buildings set in a labyrinth of narrow streets, many of them (wonderfully) too small to take a car. There are almost no vehicles by day and just a few in the early evening as some of Mdina's 400 residents (the only people allowed to drive here) come home from work. Mdina's nickname, the Silent City, remains well earned.

It is not so silent when the tourist groups are out in force, however, but you can always duck down a smaller alley to get away from the crowds. Alternatively, come back in the evening: take a stroll along the cobbles in the twilight, have a meal in one of several good restaurants, watch *festa* fireworks from the top of the bastion walls (on summer weekends), and return through peaceful darkness, back to the 21st century.

HISTORY With its obvious natural advantages, this site has been inhabited since at least the Bronze Age, becoming the main town and administrative centre of the island under Punic or Roman domination. The sizeable fortified Roman town of Melite spread into today's Rabat almost as far as St Paul's Church. Under Arab rule, in the late 9th or 10th century, the town was reduced to its present and more defensible size, fortifications were strengthened and the name changed to Mdina (Arabic, Medina).

As the Arabs gave way to the Normans and subsequent medieval rulers, Mdina was repeatedly remodelled and refortified, and became the place where noble families built their *palazzi*. The streets were deliberately kept narrow and angled

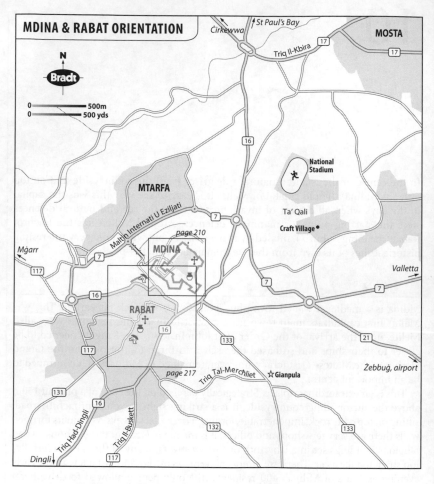

page 210

page 217

to protect against invasion. When in 1429 the Saracens attacked and laid siege, the population of Mdina held out, apparently inspired by a vision of St Paul riding a white stallion and waving a flaming sword. They earned the town the soubriquet Citta Notabile from its overlord of the time, Aragonese king Alfonso V.

When the Order of St John arrived in Malta in 1530, Mdina's role as the capital ended, although it initially remained important both in terms of defence and as the seat of the Maltese nobility. Whilst the Knights' first priority was to strengthen the fortifications of their harbourside capital Birgu (Vittoriosa), they also improved Mdina's defences. During the Great Siege of 1565, troops of the order made sorties from the safety of Mdina, helping to weaken the Turkish invaders.

After the building of Valletta, Mdina became known as Citta Vecchia ('The Old Town') and its influence waned. Its buildings fell into disrepair and in 1693, when a strong earthquake hit the central Mediterranean, Mdina was particularly badly damaged. Many houses and the cathedral had to be rebuilt and in the early 18th century, Grand Master de Vilhena commissioned a major refurbishment led by French military engineer Charles François de Mondion.

When the French arrived in 1798, Napoleon's troops looted Mdina's churches. Having already taken much of the treasure from the Carmelite priory church, the soldiers unwisely returned for more. This was the last straw and the local people ran riot. They threw the French commander out of a first-floor window and began the rebellion that eventually brought France's brief rule in Malta to an end and ushered in the British. The British naturally centred their administration in Valletta and Mdina retired gracefully to become the wonderful living museum that it is today.

GETTING THERE AND AWAY Multiple **buses** stop close to the Main Gate into Mdina. There is also a car park here, as well as some street **parking** in the area.

TOURIST INFORMATION There is a **tourist information office** (☏ 21454480; ⊕ 09.00–17.15 Mon–Sat, 09.00–13.00 Sun & public holidays) in the Torre dello Standardo, the tower on your left just inside the Main Gate of Mdina. The office has a good free map and helpful staff.

🏠 **WHERE TO STAY** *Map, page 210*
Note that there are also places to stay in Rabat that are only a few minutes' walk from Mdina.

🏠 **The Xara Palace Relais et Chateaux***** (17 rooms, mostly suites) Misraħ Il-Kunsill, MDN 1050; ☏ 21450560; e info@xarapalace.com; w xarapalace.com.mt. The only hotel within the walls of Mdina, this is a place of real character: a converted 17th-century *palazzo* with an air of calm. Furnished with antiques, original Maltese paintings & historic objects. Some suites have a terrace & outdoor jacuzzi. Past guests include Bruce Willis & family, Sharon Stone & Brad Pitt. €€€€

✕ **WHERE TO EAT AND DRINK** *Map, page 210*
✕ **De Mondion Restaurant** Xara Palace Hotel, see above for contact details; ⊕ 19.30–22.30 daily. This elegant establishment, the top-floor restaurant of the Xara Palace Hotel, has repeatedly come very high up in Malta's restaurant awards. It is genuine fine dining with a price to match. The excellent French/Mediterranean/Maltese food is beautifully presented & service is attentive without being intrusive. The narrow terrace has panoramic views, the interior an open fire in winter. Small menu. €€€€

✕ **Coogi's** 5 St Agatha Esplanade, MDN 1160; ☏ 21459987; m 77707240 (Olivier), 79072414 (Eric); w coogis.co; ⊕ 10.30–22.00 Mon–Sat, full food service noon–15.00 & 19.00–22.00. Tucked away in a quiet corner of Mdina, this very good restaurant is run by 2 Italian cousins & serves Maltese & Italian cuisine. There's a delightful courtyard, traditional stone interior & a back courtyard beneath the bastion walls, on top of which is a small terrace with panoramic views. Service can be slow, but this just means you have time to relax & enjoy. €€€

✕ **Medina** 7 Holy Cross St; ☏ 21454004; m 79490748; w medinarestaurantmalta.com; ⊕ 19.00–22.30 Mon–Sat & noon–15.00 Wed–Sun (may close at lunchtime in summer). Atmospheric setting in a lovely stone-vaulted medieval building in a quiet Mdina side alley just off St Paul's Sq. Sink into sofas in the bar for a Maltese aperitif & eat by an open fire in winter. In summer sit in the traditional (now covered) fan-cooled stone courtyard hung with oleander & vines. Mediterranean food attractively presented. €€€

✕ **Bacchus** Inguanez St; ☏ 21454981; w bacchus.com.mt; ⊕ 10.00–23.00 daily, main meals served 11.30–15.30 & 17.00–23.00. 2 vaulted stone chambers built as gunpowder magazines in 1658 & 1660 by Grand Master de Redin now serve as the atmospheric location for this sizeable restaurant that also has open-air tables (in summer) in a green & pleasant garden on Mdina's bastion walls. Large menu of very good Mediterranean & Maltese food, some available all day – & you can come in just for a drink or snack too. Families welcome. €€

✕ **Trattoria** AD**1530** Misraħ Il-Kunsill; ☏ 21450560; w xarapalace.com.mt; ⊕ noon–22.30 daily. Owned by the same people as the Xara Palace & De Mondion, this is the casual everyday

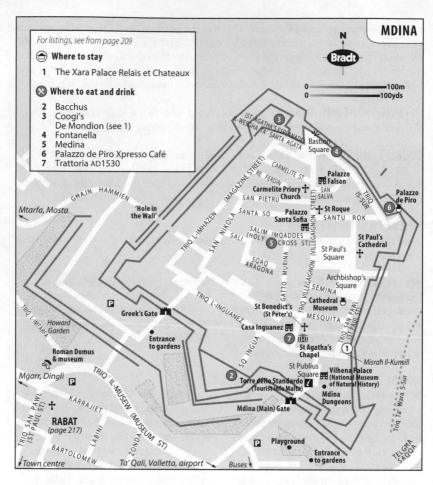

For listings, see from page 209

MDINA

Bradt

For listings, see from page 209

🏠 **Where to stay**

1 The Xara Palace Relais et Chateaux

❌ **Where to eat and drink**

2 Bacchus
3 Coogi's
  De Mondion (see 1)
4 Fontanella
5 Medina
6 Palazzo de Piro Xpresso Café
7 Trattoria AD1530

---

version. A welcoming vaulted interior & tables outside in the quiet little square. A mix of light meals, pizza, pasta, salads & vegetarian options. The substantial Maltese Platter makes a great local & inexpensive lunch. Families welcome (and plenty come). Highchairs available & crayons & colouring for kids. €€

🍴 **Palazzo de Piro Xpresso Café** 3 Triq Is-Sur; 20100560; w palazzodepiro.com; 09.30–17.00 Mon–Thu, 09.30–22.00 Fri & Sat, 09.30–17.30 Sun. Inside this 17th-century *palazzo* tucked into the bastion walls to the left of the cathedral is Xpresso Café. It has tables inside, out

in a shady courtyard, & on top of the bastion walls where you can have 180° panoramic views with your coffee. Drinks, snacks, lunches, & dinner at w/ends. €–€€€

🍴 **Fontanella** 1 Bastion St (just off Bastion Sq); 21454264, 21450208; w fontanellateagarden.com; 10.00–midnight daily. Famous for cakes & views. The terrace is on top of Mdina's bastions with a 180° panorama, & the chocolate cake is known countrywide. Some of the other cakes are just as good & there is a long list to choose from. Also serves sandwiches, pizzas, etc. €

WHAT TO SEE AND DO

The gates There are three ways of passing through Mdina's walls and into the town. The **Greek's Gate** (Porta Graecorum) is the oldest – the only complete medieval gateway left in Malta. It was always a secondary entrance, opening as it does into the front ditch, but it would once have had a wooden drawbridge. From the outside what you see is early 18th century, but from the inside you can see the typically medieval pointed horseshoe shape. The wooden doors are Knights-period, but the walls to either side are medieval ramparts some 3m thick and 10m high. It is possible to distinguish between the different aged walls: the purely vertical are usually medieval, while the slanted ones, which are reinforced at the base against cannon-fire, were built by the Knights.

The 'Hole in the Wall' (Magazine St) was created in the late 19th century so that residents of Mdina could get to the station of the Mdina–Valletta railway quickly. The railway closed in 1931 but the gate remained open.

The **Main Gate** is where most people first enter Mdina as it is closest to the bus stop and the car park. In the Knights' time, this was where a newly appointed grand master would formally meet the Università (the Maltese governing council) to guarantee their freedoms – at least in theory – and receive the key to the city. The present gate was built a few metres along the walls from its predecessor (whose outline is just visible to the right) in de Mondion's 1724 refurbishment. It is decorated with the coat of arms of the grand master of the day, Manoel de Vilhena, who also ordered the restructuring of the Grand Master's Palace, just inside the gate, that bears his name (see below).

St Publius Square

Looking back at the gate from inside the walls, you see (left to right) St Publius, St Paul and St Agatha, Mdina's three patron saints. The little square you are in is named after Publius (later St Publius; see box, page 7), the Roman governor of Malta at the time of St Paul's shipwreck here. The governor's residence was in Melite (Mdina).

On the left as you come through the gate is the **Torre dello Standardo** (Tower of the Standard), used by the Knights to flag up danger of corsairs or Turkish invasion to people living in the surrounding countryside and to communicate with other towers. The tower now contains a **tourist information office**. On the right are the Mdina Dungeons (page 212) and the Vilhena Palace.

Vilhena Palace and the National Museum of Natural History (St Publius

Sq; ☎ 21455951; w heritagemalta.org; ⏰ 09.00–17.00 daily (last entry 16.30); €5 adults, €3.50 over-60s/children 12–17/students, €2.50 children 6–11, children under 6 free) Just inside the main gate of Mdina to your right is this lovely Baroque building with its peaceful courtyard. It was commissioned by Grand Master de Vilhena and was the last of the island's grand masters' palaces to be built. Designed by de Mondion, it replaced the original building of the Maltese Università (governing council). Vilhena was not a modest man and his coat of arms tops the gate and his bust the door. He would come here particularly in summer when Mdina's altitude and narrow streets shadowed by buildings made it cooler than Valletta. During British times the palace became a military hospital, before being taken over by the Maltese government and turned into the National Museum of Natural History.

Museum The collections include 15,000 rocks and minerals, 4,000 birds and birds' eggs, a couple of hundred each of mammals and fish, thousands of insects and a few fossils. Some of the stuffed birds are a bit scruffy, but they do offer a close-up look at some of the birds that might be seen in Malta if habitats were protected and there were no hunting. The museum takes a very clear line against the killing of birds and other wildlife and is a useful educational resource in this respect. There are informative displays on Malta's geology, its minor islands and the Wignacourt Aqueduct (see box, page 226), as well as some attractive shells and polished stones.

Mdina Dungeons (St Publius Sq; ☏ 21450267; w dungeonsmalta.com; ☉ 10.00–16.15 daily; €5 adults, €2 students & children under 16) The underground prison cells of Vilhena Palace – some of which date back to the days of the Università when the palace was also the law courts – have been turned into the Mdina Dungeons 'attraction'. This revolting exhibition is a series of tableaux of waxworks being subjected to some of the hideous tortures that have been used here through the ages.

Villegaignon Street This is Mdina's main street, running the length of the town from just off St Publius Square to Bastion Square. Most of the key sights are on or very close to this street – but do stray off it at some stage in your wanderings (especially if there are crowds around) to get a real feel for Mdina. If you start up Villegaignon Street, you will come across the following sites before you reach Bastion Square.

St Agatha's Chapel (1st cnr Villegaignon St, coming from Publius Sq) This tiny, recently renovated chapel was first built in 1417 and reconstructed after the 1693 earthquake to a design by Lorenzo Gafà (who also rebuilt the cathedral). St Agatha is a patron saint of Mdina and regarded as protector of the city after the part she is meant to have played in repulsing a Turkish invasion force in 1551 (see box below).

Close to St Agatha's Chapel is the **Church of St Benedict** (also called St Peter's), first built in 1418 and reconstructed in 1625. It has an altarpiece by Mattia Preti (see box, page 126). Opposite is **Casa Inguanez**, the palace and private home of

---

THE LEGEND OF SAINT AGATHA

St Agatha was brought up in a wealthy family in Sicily under Roman rule. As a young woman she was asked to marry the Roman governor Quintianus. She refused, raising the wrath of both the governor and the Emperor Decius. She fled to Malta, arriving in AD249, and is said to have lived in Mdina and prayed at the site that is now St Agatha's Catacombs in Rabat. Her insistence that she would remain a virgin married to God and her attacks on Roman polytheism did little to improve her reputation back home. In AD251, she returned to Sicily where she was imprisoned and had her left breast (or some say both breasts) cut off, before being stripped naked and burnt to death.

Medieval Malta took this story to its heart. St Agatha became a patron saint of Mdina and is frequently depicted, usually either covering her left breast or holding a pair of shears. She became even more beloved of the people of Mdina after apparently seeing off a Turkish attack on the city – led by fearsome corsair Dragut Reis – in 1551. A nun had a vision telling her that the statue of St Agatha (which today still stands in the saint's church in Rabat; page 222) should be paraded by the population around the walls of the city. Whether due to St Agatha's intervention or because of the sight of so many people on the ramparts, the Turks turned tail and Mdina was saved. Unfortunately for Gozo, the Turkish force headed there instead and enslaved most of the smaller island's population!

above left The Maltese everlasting (*Helichrystum melitense*) is a rare bush that grows up to 1m high and flowers yellow (JS/W) page 24

above right The buds from the caper bush (*Capparis spinosa*) are harvested for use in cooking and salads (JR) page 24

right Maltese rock centaury (*Cheirolophus crassifolius*) is Malta's national plant, and the sandarac gum tree (*Tetraclinis articulata*) is its national tree (DB/W and C/W)

below Prickly pear (*Opuntia ficus-indica*) is found all over Malta and its fruit is used to make a local liqueur (SS) page 64

above left   The blue rock thrush (*Monticola solitarius*) is Malta's national bird (SS) page 25

above right   The European bee-eater (*Merops apiaster*) is one of the most brightly coloured European birds (SS) page 94

left   Little bittern (*Ixobrychus minutus*) have been known to nest at Is-Simar Nature Reserve (RC/FLPA) page 252

below   Scopoli's shearwater (left; PV/S) and the rare Yelkouan shearwater (right; SS) can be seen gathering at dusk off the coastal cliffs page 25

above   Lizards are an extremely common sight all over Malta (GL) page 24

right   Shark egg pouches collected from the fish market by conservation NGO Sharklab Malta are hatched at the National Aquarium – don't worry, not dangerous sharks (JR) page 78

below   Goats (and sheep) are kept to provide milk for the making of *gbejna*, traditional local cheese that comes in mini roundels (CC/VM) page 64

above   The Blue Grotto caves on Malta's south coast are famous for the luminous azure of their waters (MG/VM) page 196

left   Malta's mysterious ancient cart ruts criss-cross the limestone in key locations (JR) page 204

below   Għajn Tuffieħa is one of Malta's quieter beaches managed by an environmental NGO (P/S) page 239

above With a resident population of only three, Comino is the ultimate getaway in Malta (JR) page 257

right Comino has a dozen dive sites for beginners and experts alike (SB) page 261

below The Blue Lagoon on Comino is Malta's most popular swimming spot (VM) page 259

left   Gozo's charming little capital, Victoria, is officially named after Britain's Queen but known locally as Rabat (RS/S) page 279

below   Blue-flag Ramla Bay, with its distinctive red sand and no visible development, is Gozo's best beach (IS/S) page 301

bottom   The Church of the Visitation in Gharb's main square is modelled on Sant'Agnese in Rome (VM) page 289

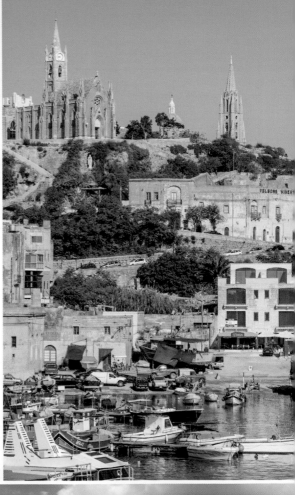

above   Ta' Kola is one of Malta's few remaining windmills; for centuries, the ability to mill grain was hugely important to the islands (GL) page 300

right   Almost everyone coming to Gozo arrives at Mġarr (GL) page 278

below   Ta' Pinu Sanctuary is Malta's most important pilgrimage site (a/S) page 291

The Dingli Cliffs offer spectacular sea views (VM) page 202

DESIGN SUITE

ST. JULIANS, MALTA

DESIGNER SUITE

HOTEL & RESTAURAN

LOBBY CAFE

JULIANI SUITE

PRIVATE POOL

ZEST RESTAURAN

Hotel *Juliani*

Malta's Top Boutique Hotel

The family-run Hotel Juliani is located within a meticulously converted historic townhouse in Spinola Bay—once a traditional fishing village that is now the centre of Malta's entertainment district. Like its surrounding neighbourhood, the Hotel Juliani effortlessly blends city style with seaside charm.

The Juliani's relaxing atmosphere owes to a combination of the hotel's elegant design approach and its welcoming team. With 65 rooms and boutique facilities, the Juliani's personalised approach guarantees a stay to remember.

SMALL | STYLISH | BOUTIQUE

2015 HALL of FAME
tripadvisor
CERTIFICATE of EXCELLENCE

25 St. George's Road
St Julians, Malta
www.hoteljuliani.com
tel: +356 2138 8000
connect: @hoteljuliani

the oldest titled Mdina family. Created barons in 1350 for putting down a Gozitan rebellion against the Aragonese king, the family led the Università until the arrival of the Knights. The *casa* was originally built in 1370 but most of what you see now is much later.

St Paul's Square (Misraħ San Pawl) This is Mdina's central square. The cathedral fills the far end of the square, while to the right is **Banca Giuratale**, the public records office where the Università met after Grand Master de Vilhena took over its previous base for his palace. In 1798, Banca Giuratale became the first headquarters of the rebellion against the French, and it was from here that the Maltese requested help from the British.

Mdina (St Paul's) Cathedral (St Paul's Sq; ↘ 21456620, 21454136, 21454697; w metropolitanchapter.com/mdina-metropolitan-cathedral; ⊕ 09.30–16.00 Mon– Sat (cathedral until 17.00), 15.00–17.00 Sun; tickets are bought from the museum to the right of the cathedral as you look at its façade & cover admission to the cathedral, the museum & the museum extension in the Palazzo de Piro: €5 adults, €3.50 students & older children, under-12s free; you can of course enter free for Mass; *festa* at the end of Jun/early Jul)

Exterior Designed by Lorenzo Gafà, Mdina's St Paul's Cathedral was completed in 1702 just before its architect died. The simple façade is set off by two bell towers and two clock faces – one telling the time, the other the date. The dome, visible across much of Malta, cannot be seen from directly in front of the church. The cathedral is dedicated to St Paul, and legend has it that it is built on the site of Roman governor Publius's house, where St Paul is said to have healed the governor's father and converted Publius to Christianity in AD60 (see box, page 7). St Publius, the story goes, is buried beneath the high altar.

The visitors' entrance to the cathedral is in the side wall to the right of the main door, in Archbishop's Square.

Interior The interior is the most impressive in Malta after St John's Co-Cathedral in Valletta. Here too the floor is a rich symphony of coloured marble tombs and memorials – and you can actually see more of them than at St John's because fewer are covered. One marble tomb on the floor just to the right of the main door is to Alyosius Deguara, a priest at the cathedral and author of its **guidebook**, *The Metropolitan Cathedral Mdina* (Insight Heritage Guides; €7.99). His birth date is there (1928) but his death date is absent. The reason is that (at the time of writing) he is still alive!

In the **Chapel of the Blessed Sacrament** to the left of the high altar is an **icon** of the Madonna and Child. This was long believed by locals to have been painted by St Luke when he was on Malta after being shipwrecked with St Paul; it is actually 13th century. To the right of the altar, beyond the organ loft, is a small **oval window** that allows the bishop, without leaving his palace, to keep an unseen eye on proceedings in the cathedral.

Looking at the **main altar**, the two oval pictures of St Peter (left) and St Paul may look like paintings, but they are actually mosaics (1873). The main altarpiece, the *Conversion of St Paul*, is by Mattia Preti (see box, page 126), as is the mural above it of St Paul's shipwreck. The other paintings in the choir are all by Preti and his studio – they survived the earthquake.

A few other items remain from the earlier (pre-earthquake) church. The heavy, early **16th-century carved timber door** to the sacristy was the main door of the old cathedral, and the **marble font**, supported by caryatids and topped with a highly decorated octagonal carved wooden lid with St Paul at its peak, is 15th century.

Museum This building was originally a Baroque seminary (1733–40) and was built on the site of the house where Cicero is believed to have stayed while writing his indictment of Gaius Verres, corrupt Roman governor of Sicily and Malta (see box, page 7).

There is a real mix of exhibits here, starting with some beautiful church silver, the oldest bell in Malta (1370) and a cask with a skull in it. This is said to be the skull of St Publius, 'first bishop of Malta' (see box, page 7). The excellent numismatic collection starts with some extraordinarily well-preserved 4th-century BC Carthaginian **coins** and has examples of currency from every subsequent administration on the islands right up to the 20th century.

Other displays include a room dedicated to Malta's **national poet**, Dun Karm Psaila (1871–1961), who wrote the words to the national anthem, and an impressive collection of **Maltese silverware**, vestments, **illuminated religious tracts** and grand masters' **swords**. The many pictures are of variable quality but include some by **Mattia Preti** and a collection of over 50 woodcuts and copperplates by **Albrecht Dürer** (1471–1528). Dürer never came to Malta and these are rather an incongruous thing to find here. The prints were given to the cathedral by an anonymous donor in the 18th century.

Interesting historic documents include a 1507 declaration from King Ferdinand II of Spain that Malta would remain 'attached to his crown' in perpetuity. This followed the leasing of Malta to a Spanish nobleman, Consalvo de Monroy, for 30,000 florins. De Monroy's imposition of excessive taxes on the Maltese led to an uprising. The population raised almost the full 30,000 florins and begged the king to let them buy Malta back. He eventually agreed and assured them in this document that 'any future deed of alienation or cession will be null and void'. This did not, of course, stop Charles V from handing Malta over to the Knights a mere 23 years later.

An extension to the museum is now housed in Palazzo de Piro.

Palazzo de Piro (3 Triq Is-Sur, MDN 1131; \ 21450560; w palazzodepiro.com; ⊕ 09.30–17.00 Mon–Thu, 09.30–22.00 Fri & Sat, 09.30–17.30 Sun, but exhibition times may be more limited; exhibition entry with cathedral ticket; page 213) This renovated 17th-century *palazzo* was the birthplace, in the 19th century, of one of Malta's most holy sons: Giuseppe (Joseph) de Piro, a relative of the family that still owns Casa Rocca Piccola in Valletta (page 131). Highly respected for his charitable work, he is currently a candidate for beatification. The *palazzo* was bought by the neighbouring cathedral and is managed by the Xara Palace Hotel. Palazzo de Piro now houses a café-restaurant (page 210) and a permanent exhibition, **Tools, Trades and Traditions**, displaying a private collection of lacemaking, wood-working and other traditional tools. The *palazzo* also hosts regular temporary exhibitions put on by the Cathedral Museum as well as occasional concerts and other events.

Palazzo Santa Sofia Back on Villegaignon Street, almost immediately on your left is Palazzo Santa Sofia, the ground floor of which is thought to be the oldest in Mdina and carries a date of 1233. The first floor, however, was built no earlier than 1938. You can only see this *palazzo* from the outside; it is not open to the public.

Carmelite Priory Church (⊕ usually in the mornings but opened by volunteers so times may vary) Built between 1660 and 1675, this was the first elliptical church and dome in Malta. The altarpiece is the original 1677 Annunciation by Stefano Erardi and there are several paintings – including the four Carmelite saints above the small chapels – by Giuseppe Calì (1910). The painted wooden processional statue of Our Lady of Mount Carmel dates from 1765. At *festa* time, on the feast of Our Lady of Mount Carmel (1st Sun after 16 Jul) it is apparently very amusing to watch the difficulty her bearers have manoeuvring her through Mdina's narrow streets!

This is the church the French sacked in 1798 shortly after their arrival in Malta. Having already stolen the silver, the troops returned for the rich red damask that covers the church during *festa*. The locals locked the church. Some boys ran up the belfry and rang the bells rallying the population who chased the French troops through Mdina, killing their commander and beginning the rebellion that eventually led to the defeat of the French in Malta (page 15). The damask, although rescued from the French, has sadly disappeared.

The church is attached to a priory next door.

Palazzo Falson (Villegaignon St; ☏ 21454512; e info@palazzofalson.com; w palazzofalson.com; ⊕ 10.00–17.00 Tue–Sun, last entry 16.00; €10 adults, €5 over-60s/children aged 12–17/students, children aged 6–12 free, no children under 6, admission fee inc informative 45min audio guide (in English, Italian, Spanish, French, German), which is necessary as there are few labels; free children's activity book; touch tours available for the blind) The second-oldest building in Mdina, dating in parts from the mid 13th century, Palazzo Falson is named after its early 16th-century owner, Vice Admiral Michele Falsone, but its eclectic contents come from the 45 collections of its last private owner, soldier, shipping magnate and philanthropist Captain Olof Gollcher (1889–1962).

Just inside the main entrance, to the right behind the door, is the original 700-year-old medieval lock that closed the door until less than a decade ago. In the basement is a **slave cell** surrounded by Gollcher's formidable collection of **weapons**. Here too is a **chastity belt** – either a medieval original or perhaps a Victorian model of what they thought a medieval chastity belt should look like!

There is an important 80-piece **oriental rug collection** and an extensive display of **silver**, including a couple of wonderful 19th-century wheeled galleons that carried cutlery and condiments along the dinner tables of the wealthy. The shipping theme continues upstairs with a collection of harbour- and sea-battle pictures and shipping ornaments. There is lots of **antique furniture** (some beautifully inlaid), **paintings** by significant artists including Mattia Preti, **jewellery** and **coins** (starting from the 3rd century BC). Amongst these smaller objects, the highlight is a 1791 **French 10-hour pocket watch**. French Revolutionary time divided the day into 10 hours, each of 100 minutes, but this didn't catch on and there are only three watches of this kind in the world.

On the roof of the building is the **museum café**, probably the highest coffee shop in Malta, with views over Mdina's roofs to the cathedral dome and across the countryside to the Mosta Dome and the sea. When open (which can be a bit variable) it serves drinks (including local beer), snacks and sandwiches.

Bastion Square At the top of Villegaignon Street is Bastion Square, from where you can look over the thick bastion walls and survey the surrounding countryside. On the plain below Mdina is the **Ta' Qali National Football Stadium** and Meridiana Winery's main **vineyard**. Straight ahead is **Mosta** with its prominent dome. **Valletta** can just about be picked out to the right by finding the distant (and hence tiny) tall dome of the Basilica of Our Lady of Mount Carmel, beyond the vast urban sprawl.

On a close hilltop (slightly left) is **Mtarfa** (or Imtarfa in British spelling), the former military town that housed troops patrolling the stretch of the Victoria Lines (see box, page 239) from here to Binġemma and the military hospital where British writer Vera Brittain spent several weeks recovering from a mystery illness before she could take up her World War I nursing duties (see box, page 16).

RABAT

Rabat is Arabic for 'suburb' and this is indeed Mdina's suburb, the undefended area outside the walls that could evacuate to Mdina in times of trouble. It is often overlooked in favour of its fortified neighbour but it has its own attractions and is also a pleasant place to wander. The town centres on Parish Square (Misraħ Il-Paroċċa) where St Paul's Church stands; everything is within walking distance from here.

Several of Rabat's sights are underground. The town sits on a honeycomb of tunnels and caverns. Most are catacombs – Romano-Christian tomb complexes dating from the late Roman or Byzantine period (4th–8th century AD). A few are natural caves, earlier burials (Phoenician/Punic) and tombs of other faiths, and there are also World War II shelters.

GETTING THERE AND AWAY The same **buses** come here as to Mdina; indeed the two are barely separable except by the bastion walls. There is a car park near Mdina's Main Gate and one close to the Roman Domus as well as some limited **parking** on the streets.

🏠 **WHERE TO STAY** *Map, opposite*

🏠 **Quaint Boutique Hotel** (12 rooms) 2 Republic St; 🌜21550899; **w** quainthotels.com. In a former cinema less than 5mins' walk from both Mdina's Main Gate & St Paul's Catacombs, this modern, minimalist-style hotel is quaint in location rather than décor. Good-sized rooms, roof terrace overlooking Rabat, & set-you-up-for-the-day full English b/fast. Pricier rooms are spacious with in-room jet baths & balcony. €€

🏠 **Villa Vittoria Guesthouse** 35 St Augustine St (Triq San Wistin); **m** 79230173; **e** borgbern@ gmail.com or via booking.com. Charming little guesthouse run by a local couple on a tiny Rabat alley. Good-value en-suite rooms. Discounts for longer stays. They also run Toffee & Co café next door. €

✕ **WHERE TO EAT AND DRINK** *Map, opposite*

✕ **Fork & Cork** 20 Telgha Tas-Saqqajja; 🌜21454432; **w** forkandcork.com.mt; ⏰ 18.30–22.30 Mon–Sat. Foodie contemporary Mediterranean/European dishes in a small limestone-walled restaurant & out on the little terrace. Very popular (booking essential). €€€

✕ **San Andrea, Palazzo Castelletti** St Paul St (Triq San Pawl); 🌜21452562; **w** palazzocastelletti. com/sanandrea; ⏰ 18.00–22.00 Mon–Thu, 19.00–22.30 Fri & Sat, noon–15.00 Sun. In a recently renovated *palazzo* that pre-dates the Knights & sits on Roman foundations, here you can dine beneath portraits of Knights of the Order or sit out in the peaceful limestone courtyard. Food is beautifully presented modern Mediterranean

& European fusion & very popular with locals. Families welcome. €€€

✕ **Red White** Details as for San Andrea; ⏰ 18.00–22.00 Mon–Thu, 18.00–22.30 Fri, noon–22.00 Sun. In the same historic *palazzo* as San Andrea & with the same owners, Red White occupies the balustraded stone roof terrace in summer & the cellar in winter. Relaxed casual trattoria serving tasty salads, pastas & pizza as well as mains. €€

✕ **Cosmana Navarra** 28 St Paul St (Triq San Pawl); 🌜21450638; 🅵; ⏰ noon–15.00/16.00 Tue–Sun & 18.00–22.00+ Tue–Sat but opening times may vary. This 16th-century building was once owned by the woman who paid for the

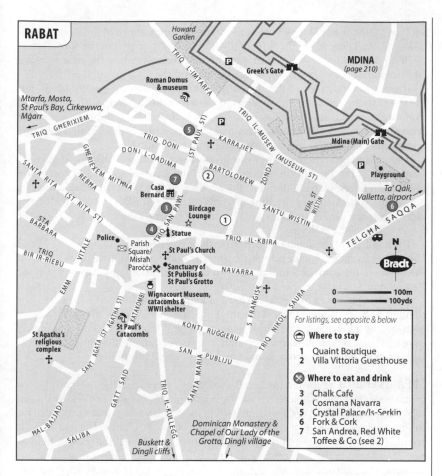

MDINA (page 210)

RABAT

For listings, see opposite & below

Where to stay

| 1 | Quaint Boutique |
| 2 | Villa Vittoria Guesthouse |

Where to eat and drink

3	Chalk Café
4	Cosmana Navarra
5	Crystal Palace/Is-Serkin
6	Fork & Cork
7	San Andrea, Red White
	Toffee & Co (see 2)

construction of St Paul's Church, opposite. Her pious-looking 17th-century portrait hangs on the stone staircase, & the place has been sensitively converted, retaining its historic (though not pious!) atmosphere. Stylish, but relaxed with some enjoyable nooks & corners. Homemade pasta, pizzas, mains. €–€€

Crystal Palace/Is-Serkin St Paul St (at the Mdina end near the Roman Domus). Inside, this café remains the tiny workmen's caff, Crystal Palace, that has been here for decades & is famous for its inexpensive puffy *pastizzi* straight from the

oven. Also milky tea & coffee Maltese-style out of a glass. Outside it now has a modern decked terrace with the title Is-Serkin, aimed more at tourists. €

Chalk Café 36 St Paul St; m 99456240; f; ☺ around 09.30–17.30/18.00 daily. Fun little café with a handful of tables upstairs, homemade cakes, Maltese salad, Maltese-style sandwiches. €

Toffee & Co Details as for Villa Vittoria Guesthouse; ☺ noon–17.00 Wed–Mon. Tiny interior & a few red-&-white check tables on a pedestrian alley just off the main street. Excellent homemade cakes. €

WHAT TO SEE AND DO

Roman Domus (Il-Wesgha Tal-Muzew, just outside Mdina's Greek's Gate; ☏21454125; w heritagemalta.org; ☺ 09.00–17.00 daily (last entry 16.30); €6 adults, €4.50 over-60s/children aged 12–17/students, €3.50 children aged 6–11, children under 6 free) This is the best-preserved and most excavated of Malta's Roman villas and houses – and the only one regularly open to the public. Standing just outside the walls of Mdina, it would have been well within the fortifications of the Roman town of Melite. We know where the Roman town ended because part of the surrounding ditch survives behind St Paul's Church and because we know where the catacombs are (Roman burials were always just outside the city walls).

There is not much left of the structure of this Roman townhouse (*domus*), but the foundations and some well-preserved mosaics remain, along with a variety of Roman artefacts: coins, bone hairpins, vessels, architectural fragments, and some remarkable examples of Roman glass including beautiful little coloured perfume bottles and (amazingly) an intact glass amphora some 50cm tall.

A few **Islamic gravestones**, with Kufic inscriptions, are also on display. They come from a few of the 245 Muslim graves found in the archaeological layer just above the Roman floors. Like the Romans, the Muslims bury their dead outside the city, but Mdina was smaller in the time of Arab rule. The Muslim graves yielded few objects but the display includes an 11th-century silver signet ring found on the finger of one of the skeletons.

The highlight of the *domus* is the Roman **floor mosaics**, dated to between 125 and 75BC. They include complex geometric patterns, some using optical illusion, and at the centre of the courtyard mosaic are two delightful 'drinking doves' – a popular Roman motif.

Interesting too are a finely **carved head of Emperor Claudius** and a toga-clad boy thought to be his adopted son (later the Emperor Nero). These, along with other high-quality 1st-century AD marble statuary suggest that by AD50 the house may have had some official function. Certainly, the *domus* did not stand alone. Remains have been found of numerous Roman buildings behind this house.

St Paul's Church

(Parish Sq (Misraħ Il-Paroċċa); ⊕ very variable; *festa* in early Jul; the grotto under the church is accessed via the Wignacourt Museum – see below) Known as St Paul's Outside the Walls, this church sits in the defensive ditch that surrounded the Roman walls of Melite, now in the central square of modern Rabat. The marvellously named Bishop Hilarius mentions the church as early as 1336, but the present building was constructed in the 16th century with funds from a local noblewoman, Cosmana Navarra, who lived on the corner opposite the church (page 216). It was completed with the addition of the dome by Lorenzo Gafà in 1683. This dome collapsed (fortunately during the night) in the early 20th century and was rebuilt in 1926.

The vast altarpiece is a highly regarded *Shipwreck of St Paul* by Stefano Erardi (1683) depicting dramatic seas and the newly shipwrecked St Paul miraculously unharmed by the viper that has just bitten him (see box, page 7).

Next to the church is the **Sanctuary of St Publius** built in 1617 through the efforts of a pious Spanish hermit of noble birth who also looked after the grotto beneath it (see opposite).

Wignacourt Museum

(cnr Parish Sq & College St across the road from St Paul's Church; ☏ 27494905; w wignacourtmuseum.com; ⊕ 09.30–17.00 daily, last admission 16.00; €5 adults, €3.50 seniors/students, €2.50 children, under 6 free, inc access to all parts of the site & St Paul's Grotto audio guide €2) The college was originally built at the start of the 17th century but reached its present form in 1749. It is now an interesting museum, with catacombs and underground World War II shelters, and access to St Paul's Grotto beneath the parish church.

Museum The museum's prize possessions include a very rare portable wooden **galley altar** used to celebrate Mass on the Knights' ships, and a giant wooden 'rattle' wheel (like a massive version of the rattles football fans used to wave around – but in the shape of a wheel). This was sounded instead of church bells during Holy Week.

In the **picture gallery** grand masters and saints in the robes of the order stare down from the walls, alongside paintings by **Mattia Preti**, including a touchingly beautiful *Madonna of the Sorrows* (probably 1690s) and a *Penitent St Peter*.

The **treasurer's room** still has its treasure chest, as well as the bed from which the treasurer was expected to guard the college's silver plate and money throughout the night. Just off this room don't miss an interesting little display of 17th-century **ex-voto paintings** (see box, page 291). These small pictures in oil of people in various forms of trouble were mostly given in thanks for what the giver believed was miraculous rescue.

Amongst the many pieces of antique furniture is a sedan chair (1770–80) with the coat of arms of the knight who had it made, Fra Giovanni Pellerano, Vice-Chancellor of the Order and Bishop of Malta (whose portrait can also be seen). Other exhibits include rare religious books, coins, Roman pottery and early maps of Malta.

Catacombs and World War II shelter Like much of Rabat, the museum sits on a labyrinth of underground tunnels. The extensive catacombs (most of which were once part of the St Paul's complex; see below) are only partially cleared of rubble. Often empty of other visitors, the place is very atmospheric, not to say a little spooky. The tombs are on several levels (possibly suggesting different periods) and of a wide variety of types (see box, page 220). There is one particularly open area with a well-preserved agape table (where funerary meals were taken) and just above a small staircase is a graffito of the tree of life.

At a lower level still is the World War II shelter: corridors totalling about 1km in length link some 50 rooms (not all open to the public and many unlit – take a torch). Some 400–450 people hid down here at the height of the bombing.

St Paul's Grotto Accessed via an underground passage that takes you beneath the road, this grotto beneath St Paul's Church is meant to be where St Paul spent most of his three months in Malta. He is variously described as imprisoned here (and it was used as a prison sometime during the Roman period), choosing to live in simplicity, or just coming here to preach. He may of course not have been here at all.

What is for sure is that the people of Malta had created a Pauline cult around this place even before the arrival of the Knights in Malta, and that Grand Master Wignacourt (1601–22) decided to tap into this belief and turn the grotto into a destination for international pilgrims. He succeeded, and even today the sanctuary and grotto are visited by both secular tourists and Catholic pilgrims.

The **grotto** is cut into the bedrock and because of the biblical story of St Paul's miraculous immunity to snake venom, the rock became regarded as an antidote to poison. Perhaps to assuage the guilt of those who chipped away at this sacred place, the legend grew up that however much stone was taken, the walls were never eroded. Today the grotto holds a **statue of St Paul** donated by Grand Master Pinto in 1748 and a **metal lantern** in the shape of a ship donated by the Order of St John in 1960 to mark the 1,900th anniversary of the shipwreck. Behind the statue is an opening in the wall, which takes you into a small **catacomb** (you'll need a torch) with window tombs and an agape table (see box, page 220) – a taster of what can be seen in Rabat's larger catacombs.

St Paul's Catacombs ✳ (St Agatha St (Triq Sant'Agata); ☏ 21454562; w heritagemalta. org; ⊕ 09.00–17.00 daily, last admission 16.30; €5 adults, €3.50 over-60s/children aged 12–17/students, €2.50 children aged 6–11, children under 6 free) The largest, most

impressive and most accessible of all Malta's catacombs, this place is a must-see, with over 2,000m² of Romano-Christian (Byzantine) tombs. There are also a few Jewish and pagan tombs amongst the smaller hypogea across the road from the visitors' centre. There is a wide variety of tomb types here, from simple loculi to once-extravagant canopied sarcophagi (see box below). The earliest is a small Phoenician burial, and the latest dates from shortly before the start of Arab rule in AD870. Most are 4th–8th-century AD. All sorts seem to have been buried here from tiny infants (see the little *loculi* in the walls) to important/wealthy adults.

The **visitors' centre** provides a good introduction to the site. There is a 35-minute audiovisual introduction as well as a sample tomb (complete with skeleton) and glass cases with a few finds from the catacombs. The tombs had been looted by the time they were excavated in the 19th century but a few terracotta statuettes and 'teardrop' bottles were found along with a substantial number of Aladdin-style oil lamps used to light the underground complex.

BURIAL AND TOMB TYPES IN MALTESE ROMAN/BYZANTINE CATACOMBS

The Romans buried their dead just outside the city walls, often, particularly in the case of Christians, in substantial catacomb complexes. Usually the shrouded body, perhaps treated with oils and perfumes, was placed directly in the tomb, its head in the rounded shape cut into a stone headrest for the purpose. These headrests allow us to know how many people were buried in each tomb – at least initially. Many tombs are designed for two, but they were often re-used with more bodies added at a later date.

After the body was interred and/or on anniversaries of the burial, family and friends would gather for a **funerary meal**, the *refrigerium*, in the catacomb. In Malta (and parts of North Africa), the tables at which they ate have survived because they are cut into the rock of the catacomb. There are no such tables in the catacombs of Rome itself but here there are very well-preserved examples of the agape table, *triclinium* or *stibadium*. These tables usually have a raised edge and a drainage hole (presumably for cleaning). Most are surrounded by a C-shape of rock-cut benches where the diners would recline.

The catacombs were lit partly by *luminaria*, occasional shafts cut through to the surface letting in a beam of natural light, but mainly by small Aladdin-style lamps burning olive oil, placed in the mini alcoves that can be seen along the walls in all the catacombs, and especially around the agape tables.

There are seven main types of tomb, the use of which seems to have depended primarily on wealth and social status. All types have headrests.

Loculus A simple rectangular recess cut into the wall. Would usually have had a stone or terracotta cover.

Forma or floor grave A rectangular pit cut into the ground rock. Also had a stone or terracotta lid.

Main catacombs As you descend into the catacombs, there is a wide open area with two large well-preserved agape tables (round stone tables for the funerary meal – see box below). Each is in a typical C-shaped enclosure that would once have been stuccoed and painted. On the other side of the entrance is a spacious rectangular room that seems to have been used as a chapel in the post-Arab Christian period. In its walls are perfect examples of children's *loculi*, and tombs are dug into its floor (both would have been lidded/covered). The rest of the catacombs is a fascinating maze of tombs and tunnels.

Smaller tombs Tomb number 3, next to the main catacomb, has two well-preserved agape tables and a remarkable heavy stone door plug carved with images of surgical instruments, perhaps connecting this little tomb complex with a medical guild. On the far side of the road are numerous small hypogea, of which numbers 10, 12, 13 and 14 contain Jewish tombs.

Window grave Unique to Malta, a grave cavity cut into the rock, accessed through a window that is sometimes arched.

Arcosolium An arched recess with rectangular grave or graves in the sill.

Table grave Looks like a stone box, but actually carved from solid rock.

Bench grave Also a box, but against the wall.

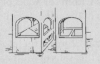

Baldacchino or canopied grave The most elaborate type of grave consisting of a rock-cut sarcophagus topped with a four-arched canopy. The grave may be covered with a vaulted ('saddle-back') or flat lid.

Some tombs were decorated with carvings or paint. Not all rock-cut tombs in Malta's catacombs are Christian. There are a few Jewish tombs, some of which can be seen at St Paul's Catacombs.

St Agatha's religious complex (St Agatha St (Triq Sant'Agata); ☏ 21454419, 21454503; w stagathamalta.com; ☉ 09.00–16.30 Mon–Fri, 09.00–13.30 Sat; 30min tours: €5 adults, €4 over-60s/students, €2 children under 12) Just up the road from St Paul's Catacombs is the second-largest tomb complex on the island along with a historic chapel/crypt and church.

Crypt Down a flight of 20 rock-cut steps is St Agatha's Crypt – an underground chapel to the saint who, legend has it, spent some time here around AD250 escaping persecution in her native Sicily. In St Agatha's time this was a small natural cave. It may have been expanded and embellished as early as the 4th century AD, although the current chapel is medieval. It is decorated with frescoes of saints. St Paul and St Agatha were painted around 1280, while the rest are 16th century. The saints have been defaced – probably by the Turks during the attack of 1551 as the Koran forbids the depiction of saints and prophets. For the legend of St Agatha and her part in the 1551 attack, see the box on page 212.

Catacombs The catacombs are low-ceilinged with narrow corridors (much more claustrophobic than St Paul's) with all the different tomb types in evidence. Several graves still contain skeletons, and two tombs are decorated with frescoes – one with a charming picture of a bird. Deep in the complex, the corridors open out into a room – a wealthier tomb chamber or chapel – with carved pillars. It originally had an agape table but this was removed when the Church apparently abolished their use. In the wall here is a semicircular alcove painted with a colourful little fresco of a scallop shell curving over two birds and various flowers, dated to the 4th century AD.

Museum The small museum is a real old-fashioned jumble of objects from Romano-Maltese coins and Egyptian-style amulets (possibly Phoenician) through medieval carved stone slabs to 19th-century Church ornaments. The highlight is the 1666 alabaster statue of St Agatha (with deliberately damaged breasts; see box, page 212) that used to be the altarpiece of the underground crypt.

Church Built at the very beginning of the 16th century, the church houses the statue of St Agatha (of a similar date) that was paraded around the ramparts of Mdina in 1551, purportedly saving the city from the Turks. This event is still remembered with a special procession every February.

Casa Bernard (46 St Paul St (Triq San Pawl); ☏ 21451888; m 99844343; w casabernard.eu; tours on the hour 10.00–16.00 Mon–Sat, or by appointment; €8 adults, €4 children up to age 12) A tour of this historic house, guided by its owner Georges, is a tour through the history of Mdina and Rabat. The 16th-century *palazzo* is built on the foundations of a Roman *domus* that was within the walls of Melite. The well (cistern) is Roman as are the walls and one arch of the cellar, which dates to the time of Cauis Verres and Cicero (see box, page 7).

The dining room is medieval, built around 1350 as part of a one-storey structure with a watchtower (still extant). By this time the site was outside the walls of Mdina, and even in 1580 when the simple pre-Baroque *palazzo* was built, the designer was concerned about defence: the windows are high and tapered towards the outside and the walls are very thick.

Dominican Monastery and Chapel of Our Lady of the Grotto (Ġorġ Borġ Olivier St (Triq Ġorġ Borġ Olivier); ☏ 21454592; w opmalta.org/content.

aspx?id=187638; ☉ 06.00–20.30, Mass usually 06.00, 07.30, 12.15, 18.30) This is a significant walk from the centre of Rabat but there is a bus. This is a functioning priory (with a handful of remaining friars) that opens its doors in daylight hours. The public can wander the peaceful high barrel-vaulted cloisters around a courtyard of citrus trees, and around Mass times (though not during), visit the church and chapels. If you are lucky, you will be welcomed by one of the friars who will show you round and open up the venerated and highly decorated underground grotto after which the chapel is named. If not, you can see into the grotto through a grille (surrounded by railings) in the floor of the church.

The story begins around 1400 when a hunter is said to have seen a vision of Our Lady in this cave. The grotto quickly became a place of prayer and by 1414 seems to have been established as a chapel devoted to Our Lady of the Grotto. In 1450, the Dominicans came to Malta from Sicily and (wisely) created their mission – and in due course this priory and church – around the sacred cave.

A variety of 'miraculous' events, from a flower that stayed fresh for months to cures for illness, kept the cult alive. In 1999, it received a further boost. The beautiful stone sculpture of Our Lady now in the grotto (which gives Mary a touchingly human look of love towards her son) was by 1980 becoming too delicate to be paraded around at *festa* time, so a copy in white marble was made. This is the one on the altar of the above-ground chapel. Shortly after the *festa* in 1999, the copy-statue was apparently seen – on two consecutive days – to cry a bloodstained tear. Photos were taken on both occasions and, on the second, the tear – which divided into two little streams – was left on her cheek. Look closely and you can still see it beneath the statue's left eye.

Men may also visit the priory upstairs (accompanied by a friar); women are not allowed.

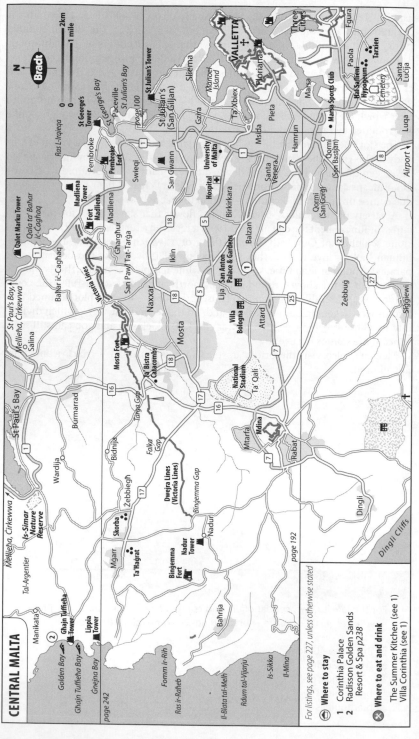

CENTRAL MALTA

N

Bradt

0   1 mile
0   2km

page 242

page 100

page 192

Golden Bay
Għajn Tuffieħa Bay
Gnejna Bay
Manikata
Għajn Tuffieħa Tower
Lippia Tower
Tal-Argentier
Mellieħa, Ċirkewwa
Is-Simar Nature Reserve
St Paul's Bay
Wardija
Burmarrad
Salina
St Paul's Bay
Mellieħa, Ċirkewwa
Baħar iċ-Ċagħaq
Qala tal Bahar iċ-Ċagħaq
Qalet Marku Tower
Madliena Tower
Fort Madliena
Madliena
Gharghur
San Pawl Tat-Targa
Victoria Lines
Naxxar
Mosta
Mosta Fort
Ta' Bistra Catacombs
Bidnija
Zebbiegh
Mġarr
Skorba
Ta'Ħagrat
Bingemma Fort
Nadur Tower
Dwejra Lines (Victoria Lines)
Bingemma Gap
Nadur
Falka Gap
Targa Gap
Mtarfa
Mdina
Rabat
National Stadium
Ta' Qali
Villa Bologna
Attard
Lija
Balzan
San Anton Palace & Gardens
Birkirkara
Santa Venera
Qormi (San Gorg)
Qormi (San Bastjan)
Zebbug
Siġġiewi
Dingli
Dingli Cliffs
Bahrija
Forrm ir-Rih
Ras ir-Raheb
Il-Blata tal-Melh
Rdum tal-Vijariju
Is-Sikka
Il-Mina
University of Malta
Hospital
San Gwann
Swieqi
Pembroke
Pembroke Fort
St George's Tower
St George's Bay
Paceville
St Julian's Bay
St Julian's Tower
St Julian's (San Ġiljan)
Gżira
Sliema
Manoel Island
Ta' Xbiex
Pieta
Msida
Hamrun
Floriana
VALLETTA
Marsa
Three Cities
Fgura
Paola
Tarxien
Santa Lucija
Ħal Saflieni Hypogeum
Cemetery
Marsa Sports Club
Luqa
Airport
Ras L-Irqieqa
Iklin
Mtarfa

For listings, see page 227, unless otherwise stated

Where to stay

1 Corinthia Palace
2 Radisson Golden Sands
   Resort & Spa *p228*

Where to eat and drink

The Summer Kitchen (see 1)
Villa Corinthia (see 1)

11

Central Malta

Several key areas of central Malta – the capital Valletta, the old capital of Mdina with its suburb Rabat, and the resort areas of Sliema, St Julian's and Paceville – have been covered in chapters of their own, so this chapter covers the rest of the region, predominantly urban and suburban districts dotted with historic and prehistoric sites. The boundary of the region to the northwest is the Victoria Lines, the defensive wall built by the British across the entire width of Malta, but for reasons of access to some tourist sites, Mġarr, to the north of the lines, is included here.

BIRKIRKARA AND THE THREE VILLAGES

BIRKIRKARA Part of the urban sprawl spreading inland from Sliema and Valletta, Birkirkara (often shortened to B'Kara) is the most populous town in Malta with over 21,500 residents. It is largely untouched by tourism (apart from through traffic) but hidden among its maze of streets is Malta's only sight for railway buffs, and the best close-up views of the early 17th-century arched **Wignacourt Aqueduct,** which once brought Valletta's water all the way from Mdina (see box, page 226). It runs along much of the length of St Joseph High Road/Triq Il-Kbira San Ġużepp, where in some places the arches now form rather grand dividers between the residents' off-road parking spaces.

There are also churches, of course, including the large parish **Church of St Helen** (built 1727–45) with a fine Baroque façade, as well as Malta's ugliest church, the flaking-concrete 20th-century flying saucer that is St Theresa's. On Wednesdays and Fridays, St Helen's is surrounded by a large local market selling just about everything. The **Sanctuary of Our Lady Tal-Ħerba (of Ruins)** – a chapel in the street of the same name – was built in 1610. Heavily remodelled in the 20th century, it contains the largest collection of **ex-voto paintings** in Malta (⊕ usually 06.00–10.00 & 16.15–19.00 Mon–Sat, but 06.00–11.00 Wed & Fri, 06.00–10.00 Sun). For more on ex-voto paintings, see the box on page 291.

In **Station Garden** (Ġnien L-Istazzjon), a little public park and children's playground, is what was once the Birkirkara Station on the British steam railway that ran from Valletta to Mdina from 1883 until 1931. A little green third-class carriage of the train known by the Maltese as Il-Vapur ta' L-Art ('The Land Steamer') sits next to the original station building, which has a sign spelling out the name of the town the British/Italian way, Birchircara. There are several metal plaques telling the story of the railway, its extension to Imtarfa (Mtarfa) to serve the newly built Victoria Lines (see box, page 239) and its final decline. The British had intended to create a railway network all over the island but, despite the popularity of the train, railways in Malta proved to be financially unviable and this was the only line ever built. For more information and lots of photos for railway buffs, check out *The Malta Railway* by Joseph Bonnici and Michael Cassar (BDL; €17.50).

On their very first visit to Malta, the Knights remarked that there was a shortage of fresh water in the country. The problem became more acute with the building of Valletta, which stands on a particularly dry peninsula and needed a good enough supply of water to be able to hold reserves in case of siege. The Order of St John ruled that every house built in Valletta had to have a system for collecting and storing rainwater. The old houses still have large cisterns beneath them (see one at Casa Rocca Piccola; page 131).

Yet, as the population of Valletta grew, the city's need for water outstripped what it could collect from winter rains so Grand Master Alof de Wignacourt (1601–22) commissioned an ambitious solution: a 15.7km channel to bring water from natural springs near Mdina all the way to Valletta. Begun in 1610, it took 600 men four years to build the aqueduct. Much of the channel is underground but in order for the water to flow most of the way under gravity, parts of it – mostly through Birkirkara, Santa Venera and Ħamrun – had to be raised and were built as a classic arched aqueduct. Stretches of this structure can still be seen, notably on the streets of Birkirkara.

The completion of the aqueduct was royally celebrated in Valletta as the water flowed into a fountain in the square outside the Grand Master's Palace. The fountain now stands in St Philip's Gardens in Floriana (page 143). Water from the aqueduct also ran to a fountain just outside Porta della Marina, today's Victoria Gate, on the Grand Harbour side of Valletta. Here, ships could fill up with water from a spout in the shape of a cannon barrel (now in the Malta Maritime Museum). Above the spout stood the statue of Neptune that now adorns the inner courtyard of the Grand Master's Palace.

The Wignacourt Aqueduct went a long way to solving Valletta's water problems but as the centuries passed and Malta's population continued to grow, the whole country was, by the 1970s, once again short of fresh water and new solutions had to be found (see box opposite).

Getting there and away Lots of **bus** routes run through Birkirkara. **Parking** is free but can be difficult, particularly during shopping hours.

THE THREE VILLAGES, AND ST ANTON PALACE AND GARDENS Birkirkara merges imperceptibly into **Balzan**, which itself merges into **Lija** and **Attard**. These three together are known to tourist guides as 'The Three Villages', though locals rarely refer to them as such. They are not villages anymore, of course, but nor are they bustling modern towns. They retain a certain traditional upmarket calm and charm – a taste of old Malta. There is little tourism here, just a very pleasant place to be with some fine buildings, including St Anton Palace and Gardens, which sit roughly on the border of Balzan and Attard. The villages have the usual church square at their centres, and each has a *festa* (Balzan in July, Attard on the Feast of the Seven Marys on 15 August and Lija earlier in the same month), with Lija's known for good fireworks. Attard's church square extends right round the church and includes a popular Maltese–British café with pleasant outside tables.

Getting there and away **Buses** go to all three of the Three Villages and it is possible to **park** around the Corinthia Palace Hotel. It can be difficult in other areas.

Where to stay

★ ⌂ **Corinthia Palace Hotel** [map, page 224] (150 rooms) De Paule Av, Attard, BZN 9023; ☎ 21440301; w corinthia.com. Opposite the entrance to San Anton Gardens & the summer palace of Malta's president, & far from the noise of the tourist areas. Calm & peaceful like the upmarket residential streets around it. Low-rise with attractively landscaped gardens, split-level outdoor pool (no inflatables), comfortable rooms, several cafés/restaurants including the poolside Summer Kitchen & fine dining Villa Corinthia in the original 19th-century villa around which the hotel is built. Well-run separate spa with good-sized indoor pool (age 16+), jacuzzi, etc (page 97). Helpful staff. Courtesy bus to Valletta & St Julian's. Close to a public bus stop, but own transport preferable. €€–€€€

⌂ **Hotel Kappara***** (28 rooms) Triq Wied Ghollieqa, Kappara, San Gwann; ☎ 27334462; w hotelkappara.com. Run by the University of Malta but open to all, this simple hotel is good value & while not close to sights it is only 50m from the bus stop & not far from Valletta. Swimming pool, bar & restaurant. All rooms twin, some have balcony. Kitchenette available. €

✗ Where to eat and drink
As well as the listings below, there is also a very good garden restaurant, The Summer Kitchen, and an elegant fine-dining restaurant, Villa Corinthia, both in the Corinthia Palace Hotel.

✗ **Bahia** 75 Triq Preziosi, Lija, LJA 1203; m 99991279; w bahia.com.mt; ⊕ 19.00–23.00 Tue–Sat, noon–15.00 Sun. In a bright conversion of a 200-year-old house in the heart of Lija. Small

A THIRSTY ISLAND? *Hilary Bradt*

How does a small, arid island like Malta provide enough fresh water for its population, and for the influx of tourists during the dry summer months? To find out I visited the Pembroke Reverse Osmosis plant on the northeast coast of the island.

In the old days, Stephen Zerafa (Head of Public Relations at the Water Services Corporation) told me, all Maltese houses had a well, and even rainwater mixed with seawater was drinkable because it was filtered through porous rock so lost its salinity. Indeed, until the 1980s the underground water table was sufficient for all Malta's needs, but the tripling of visitor numbers in three decades required additional supplies and the first reverse osmosis plant was built. There are now three such plants on the island, providing 57% of Malta's water. At maximum capacity, they can provide 94,000m³ of water, with the Pembroke plant doing the lion's share.

The technology is both simple and beautiful, with skeins of what looks like angel's hair – soft and golden – playing a major part. These are actually tiny tubes, through which seawater is forced at high pressure. Salt and other impurities stay behind and pure water passes through the semi-permeable walls. The salt is dumped back on the ocean and the pure water fed into pipes to supply Malta and Gozo.

Despite the recovering of 30% of the energy used, the electric motors needed to run the plant use the same amount of power as a small town. And there are six such motors. Solar power is the most promising source of sustainable energy, or offshore wind turbines. Meanwhile, as long as Malta has power it has sufficient water for islanders and visitors, and acts as a model for other islands or countries with a limitless supply of ocean, but dry summers.

seasonal menu of delicious & interesting foodie European dishes. In the courtyard is a *bahia* (navel orange) tree called Chloe. €€

✘ **Jalie's** Behind Attard Parish Church; 📞2143590; 🎫; ⏰ 10.00–22.00 Tue–Sun for food, until 23.00/midnight for drinks. Run by a Maltese man & his Yorkshire wife. Buzzy interior, roof terrace (with retractable roof) & pleasant seating outside opposite a garden square where children can play. Particularly popular for Sun roast

(with Yorkshire pud), plus excellent soups & cakes. €–€€

✘ **Kitchen Garden** San Anton, Attard; 📞21423371, 21226226; 🎫; ⏰ Jun–Oct 09.00–23.00 daily, Nov–May 09.00–19.00 daily. In the original kitchen gardens of San Anton Palace, this café is surrounded by veg beds, a kids' playground & a little zoo. Serves ice cream, cakes, sandwiches & *pastizzi*. €–€€

San Anton Palace and Gardens (⏰ Gardens summer 07.00–20.00 daily, at other times until roughly dusk daily; palace interior not open to the public unless there is a special event/exhibition; bus from Valletta stops at the gates) This is the largest and nicest of Malta's public gardens outside the capital, with mature trees (unusual in this dry country) offering shade over a maze of paths that pass colourful flowers and cooling fountains. Ducks, terrapins, fish ponds, peacocks and aviaries, along with a hedge maze, make this a good place for a break if you are touring with kids.

The palace was built as a private summer retreat for Fra Antoine de Paule – known for his unpriestly love of luxury and inattention to monastic vows – shortly before he became grand master in 1623. On his death in 1636, the estate passed to the Order of St John and successive grand masters found it a convenient place in which to escape the heat of Valletta.

In 1798, it became the headquarters of the Maltese resistance to French rule and in 1799, HQ for Alexander Ball, the British naval commander sent to help displace Napoleon's troops. It was here in September 1800 that the French capitulation was signed. Throughout British rule, the palace was home to the governor, and the gardens were opened to the public in 1882. When Malta became a republic in 1974, the palace became the official residence of the president.

Although the main building is not open to the public, you can walk through the palace precincts. Enter from the gardens beneath the clock and between two stone thrones, passing a plaque listing Malta's presidents to date and a little chapel. A covered stone walkway runs alongside the president's private garden then out onto St Anton Street (Triq San Anton). The President's Kitchen Garden opposite includes a large café, mini zoo and children's play area as well as remnants of the palace kitchen garden.

Villa Bologna (30 St Anthony St, Attard; 📞21417973; m 99537925; w villabologna. com; ⏰ 09.00–17.00 Mon–Sat; adults €6, seniors/students/children aged 12+ €4, under 12s free (self-guided); prices for private guided tours on request) Behind San Anton Gardens is a private villa with the largest historic gardens in Malta besides San Anton. Built in 1745 (still in the time of the Knights) by a Maltese nobleman, called Bologna, for his wife-to-be, it later passed (through the female line) to Lord Strickland, fourth prime minister of Malta, and MP in Malta and at Westminster simultaneously. He and his wife founded the *Times of Malta*, which was run for many decades, including throughout World War II, by his daughter Mabel Strickland. Villa Bologna was at the heart of Malta's cultural, social and political life for much of the early 20th century. Now owned, inhabited and run by Lord Strickland's great-grandson, Jasper de Trafford, it is not a museum but a home, a wedding venue and a place to visit, wander and sit in the gardens (18th-century Baroque and 1920s in origin) amid citrus orchards, limestone statuary, mature trees (not common in Malta), and fountains – including the elaborate 18th-century Four Seasons nymphaeum with

wrought-iron gates that represented Maltese craftsmanship at the British Empire Exhibition in London in 1924. The villa interior is viewable by appointment and includes Strickland's study, some beautiful 18th-century inlaid furniture, and family portraits. Beneath the gardens is the family's sizeable hand-cut World War II shelter (complete with stairs in Lady Strickland's favourite material – marble). Villa Bologna also has its own pottery making hand-painted dishes, lamps and figures.

NAXXAR

Naxxar is one of Malta's oldest 'villages'. The cart ruts (see box, page 204) just outside the modern town suggest there has been a settlement here since at least Roman times, quite probably earlier and Naxxar was among Malta's first ten parishes listed in 1436. It has now sprawled its way to meet neighbouring Mosta, but **Victory Square** still has a typical centre-of-the-village feel with its Baroque **Parish Church of the Nativity of the Virgin Mary** (1616–30, by Tumas Dingli, with side apses and façade added in the 20th century). If you are in the area over Easter, this is one of very few churches that still put up the black damask of mourning on Good Friday. The official line of today's Catholic Church is that Good Friday is not a time for mourning but for celebrating the gift of Christ the Saviour, but this parish has stuck with its traditions. The September *festa* (page 32) is also very popular.

Opposite the church is the deceptively simple façade of Palazzo Parisio, a late 19th-century confection that its owners like to describe as a mini Versailles.

GETTING THERE AND AWAY Several **buses** come to Naxxar. In theory you can **park** but narrow streets make this difficult.

WHERE TO STAY

Chapel 5 (10 rooms) 5 Alley 5, St Lucy St; ☎27577555. Family-run, arty B&B with eclectic décor, 2 plunge pools, roof terrace, b/fast room, courtyard & sitting room. Occasional complementary massage & yoga (Apr–Nov). On a typical Naxxar alley a few mins' walk from the main square. No children under 6. €€–€€€

Loggia Mariposa (8 rooms) 16 Alley 3, St Lucy St; m 99476261; w loggiamariposa.com. Stylish B&B with personal service, a small peaceful courtyard swimming pool, traditional b/fast room (& good b/fasts with homemade & local products) & roof terrace. Full of the owners' collected artefacts. €€

WHERE TO EAT AND DRINK

Luna at Palazzo Parisio See page 230 for contact details; ⊕ b/fast & lunch daily, dinner Thu–Sun. Enjoy fine dining & international cuisine either in the elegant pink-&-grey interior or eat out in the *palazzo's* lovely garden under cream canopies, fountains tinkling. The Mediterranean take on bread & butter pudding is superb. €€€€

Brass & Knuckle 5 Oratory St; ☎27222722; m 99222722; w brassandknuckle.com; ⊕ 10.00–22.30 daily (until 23.00 w/ends). Meat specialists. Choose your cut & the chef will cook it for you how you like it (or you can take it home & cook it yourself!). €€€

Ta' Stringi Victoria Hse A1, Triq Il-Labour; m 79660099; w tastringi.com; ⊕ 19.00–late

daily & 11.30–15.00 Fri–Sun. In a traditional limestone 450-year-old house. Seasonal Maltese & Mediterranean dishes, quality pizza, pasta & salads. €€

KefaKafe 2 St Lucy St; m 79955785; ▪; ⊕ 09.00–18.00 Mon–Fri, 09.00–15.00 Sat & Sun. The smell of freshly ground coffee permeates the street from this tiny artisan coffee shop opposite the parish church. Coffees from around the world. Friendly. Shabby chic. Crates to sit on outside. €

The Old Charm Alley 6, St Lucy St; m 77503087; ▪; ⊕ 19.00 onwards Tue–Sun. In a converted house on a tiny side street. Stop here for a glass of wine &, yes, a bit of old-style charm. Run by a couple of Brits. €

WHAT TO SEE AND DO
Palazzo Parisio (29 Victory Sq, NRX 1700; ℡ 21412461; w palazzoparisio.com; ⏱ 09.00–18.00 daily (last entry 17.30); prices, inc audio guide: €12 adults, €7 students/children over 16, €5 children aged 5–15, under 5 free; also available to hire for weddings (see box below) & corporate events) Originally built in 1733 as a country house for Grand Master Manoel de Vilhena (he of the Manoel Theatre), by the end of the 18th century it was in the hands of the Sicilian–Maltese aristocratic Parisio family (who also owned Palazzo Parisio in Valletta). The opulent *palazzo* you see today, however, was created by the grandfather of the family that still own it, Giuseppe Scicluna (nephew of the Scicluna who built the Dragonara Palace on Spinola Bay). One of the richest families in Malta, the Sciclunas founded the Scicluna Bank, now absorbed into the Bank of Valletta, and Giuseppe was a man of flamboyant taste. For eight years he imported designers and master craftsmen from Italy, to work on the house, and landscape gardeners to create a ½-mile-long formal garden (now much truncated but still attractive).

He died just a year after completing Palazzo Parisio in 1906, leaving it to his four-year-old son, John. In due course, John took over the family bank and under him it became the first bank in Malta to issue cheques, gaining its owner the nickname 'Cisk' (pronounced *chisk* – a mispronunciation of cheques). When he later opened a brewery, he called his beer Cisk – now the best-selling lager in the land.

The house is an exuberant celebration of excess with an eclectic mix of Roman-style wall painting, romanticised classical scenes, marble statues, armour, columns,

GETTING MARRIED IN MALTA

Malta markets itself as a place to get married – particularly for Roman Catholics and for those seeking a civil ceremony (heterosexual or same sex) in a different setting and/or a more amenable climate. There are over 300 Catholic churches on Malta and Gozo in a wide range of architectural styles as well as other wonderful settings. There are, of course, churches of other denominations too, as well as two registry offices – in Valletta and in Gozo's capital, Victoria. For a more interesting non-church setting (at an additional charge) you can choose to have your wedding almost anywhere on the islands, from a Knights-period *palazzo*, to the beach. Several historic buildings regularly host weddings and wedding receptions including Naxxar's Palazzo Parisio.

Several tour operators offer specific wedding packages, which may include a wedding organiser, hairdresser, photographer, flowers, cake, etc. You can even have your dress made locally. It is also possible to organise a wedding in Malta yourself. The **Malta Tourism Authority** (℡ (UK) 020 8877 6990; e office. uk@vistimalta.com) produces a weddings information pack.

THE LEGAL STUFF All the forms you need can be obtained from the MTA (as above). The request for the publication of banns (form RZ1) needs to reach the registry office in Malta at least six weeks before the wedding date, along with birth certificates of both bride and groom and the declaration of oath (RZ2). Each of the couple also needs to provide a 'free status certificate' to show they have never been married, otherwise documents are required showing that any previous marriage is legally over. Couples need to arrive in Malta in time to visit the registry office at least once before the wedding to finalise the arrangements.

patterned floors and rich textiles. The peak is reached in the ballroom where golden busts of grand masters are held up by white marble *putti*, and vast chandeliers light the gilded and mirrored walls.

The first-floor terrace looks out over the formal garden, a pleasant place to stroll with its trees, small lawns, fountains and over 60 species of hibiscus as well as bougainvilleas and citruses. The orangery is from the original 1733 house.

San Pawl Tat-Tarġa (St Paul of the Step)
About 10 minutes' walk or a very short drive from the centre of Naxxar towards St Paul's Bay is the collection of buildings known as San Pawl Tat-Tarġa, centred on a chapel but with several other historical curiosities too.

Chapel (☉ only for occasional Mass) Built in 1696 on a spot where St Paul is thought to have preached. The story goes that he could be heard all the way to Gozo. On a very clear day you can see Gozo from here (hearing is another matter). You can also see the statue of St Paul on St Paul's Island.

16th-century towers Behind the church in this pretty little square is **Torri Gauci (Gauci Tower)** built by the Gauci family in 1548 as a fortified residence. Several members of the family had already been captured by Turkish corsairs and sold into slavery so they weren't taking any more chances. Opposite (across the road) stands **Torri tal-Kaptan (the Captain's Tower)**, an early Knights' watchtower erected under Grand Master Jean Parisot de Valette in 1558 for the captain of the Maltese Cavalry. The tower looks north towards St Paul's Bay and Salina Bay.

Victorian and World War II fortifications A little further along the road towards St Paul's Bay are remains of the more recent fortifications of the **Victoria Lines** (see box, page 239), a British wall and military walkway that ran the width of Malta to prevent invaders landing in the north and travelling overland to the more populous parts of the island and the crucial harbours. (For a better-preserved stretch of the lines, see page 232.)

Just below the Victoria Lines is a **World War II pillbox**, the only one on the island that has been restored to look exactly as it did during the war, even down to the fake painted windows meant to make it look like an ordinary residence. At least some of the holes in the walls are shell damage.

Looking across the valley from the pillbox you should be able to see a modern satellite dish next to a curved red wall. The wall is a 1930s **early warning sound wall** designed to pick up the sound of aircraft flying out of Sicily. It dates originally from the Abyssinian Crisis of 1936 (when Mussolini invaded Ethiopia).

Cart ruts On open waste ground about 50m below the pillbox (still on the left of the road as you go from Naxxar towards St Paul's Bay) are pairs of ancient cart ruts (see box, page 204). They are a little tricky to spot, but once you spot them they are clearly cart ruts. This set of ruts includes a hairpin bend (not unlike that of the nearby modern road) and some of the deepest ruts in Malta, one of which has been re-used to channel rainwater to a cistern.

MOSTA

The second-largest town in Malta, with a population of around 19,000, Mosta was once part of the parish of Naxxar but has now far outstripped it both in size and in the number of tourist visitors. Mosta attracts some quarter of a million tourists a year, purely to see its vast domed parish church, although there are also a couple of little-known sights of interest on the outskirts.

GETTING THERE AND AWAY Buses stop directly outside the Mosta Dome. Other buses also come to Mosta but not necessarily to the dome so check with the driver before boarding. There is a **car park** right next to the Mosta Dome in the middle of town.

✗ WHERE TO EAT AND DRINK

✗ **The Lord Nelson** 278–80 Triq il-Kbira; m 79432590; w thelordnelsonrestaurant.com; ⏲ 18.30–22.30 Mon–Sat. This is a calm, elegant, intimate restaurant (especially good in winter). Set over 3 floors of a historic building. A tiny stone spiral staircase links the floors & there is a wonderful (& very popular) table in the 1st-floor *gallarija* with views of the Mosta Dome. The food is excellent modern European. €€€

✗ **Ta' Marija** Constitution St; ☎ 21434444; m 79573796; w tamarija.com; ⏲ 11.30–14.30 Tue–Sun & 18.30–22.30 daily. In complete contrast to the Lord Nelson, this Malta institution glories in its lace tablecloths, twinkly lights, guitars & tableside serenades (Wed & Fri evenings). This sort of kitsch would be tourists-only in many countries, but Ta' Marija is hugely popular with the Maltese & has won the award for best Maltese food in the country's top restaurant guide many times. Serves all the traditional dishes: *aljotta* (fish soup), *braġioli* (meat dish), snails, rabbit, quail & fresh fish. Maria & son Ben move among the diners like the proud host & hostess of a large party. Maltese-sized portions, so be hungry. Great for families, many of whom come for Sun lunch. €€€

WHAT TO SEE AND DO

Mosta Dome (Pjazza Rotunda; ⏲ usually 09.00–11.45 & 15.00–19.00; admission €2; *festa* 15 Aug, Feast of the Seven Marys) The 19th-century parish Church of Santa Marija Assunta (the Church of the Assumption) is known to all as Mosta Dome or, occasionally, the Rotunda. It dominates the town – and often the skyline of Malta – and is claimed to be the third-largest unsupported church dome in Europe. This all depends on what you measure. The Gozitans insist that theirs (the Xewkija Rotunda; page 306) is bigger. It is indeed taller, but at 60m across (45m inside), Mosta's dome is wider.

Partly inspired, it is said, by the Pantheon in Rome, the church was constructed, amid considerable controversy, between 1833 and 1860. First, money earmarked for the church was diverted to deal with a cholera epidemic, then the French architect, Georges Grognet de Vasse, became embroiled in a bizarre argument in which he insisted that Malta was the tip of the lost city of Atlantis. And finally, the bishop, unconvinced that a round church was really Christian, refused to lay the foundation stone.

The project did eventually get off the ground, however, and its towering neoclassical façade hides an impressive (and in summer, blissfully cool) interior. The inner surface of the dome is white, blue and gold and the floor is a geometric pattern of marble. The relatively plain walls are dotted with white marble tombs and there are eight murals by Giuseppe Calì.

In April 1942, as a congregation of around 300 attended afternoon Mass, a bomb broke through the dome, thudded to the ground and rolled across the floor. It failed to explode and no-one was hurt, a 'miracle' still celebrated in the sacristy museum where a large bomb (real, but not *the* bomb) takes pride of place in the small museum.

The Victoria Lines and Mosta Fort [map, page 224] Just above the town with views back over Mosta is the Ġnien L-Għarusa tal-Mosta public garden, a slightly faded place but with a well-preserved stretch of the British-built defensive wall and walkway, the Victoria Lines (see box, page 239), which runs along the natural ridge. The lines make a great walk with expansive views and an easy path underfoot.

Within the gardens is a milestone, defaced as they all were during World War II when the British feared invasion and wanted to be sure that no enemy would be helped by signposting. The low-lying 19th-century Fort Mosta, a little further along the Victoria Lines, was one of the three main forts linked by the lines. It is now an army and police base, not open to visitors.

Ta' Bistra Catacombs [map, page 224] (Triq il-Missjunarji Maltin; w heritagemalta. org; ⊕ 09.00–17.00 Tue, Thu, Sat; €5 adults, €3.50 seniors, students & children aged 12–17yrs, €2.50 children aged 6–11yrs, 5 & under free) Just outside Mosta, these are the largest set of visible catacombs not in Rabat. An interesting site of 4th–8th-century tombs starting beneath a 20th-century farmhouse. Some 57 tombs in 16 groups (not all of which are visible) are ranged along a limestone ridge which runs under the road and continues on the other side. Unlike the catacombs of Rabat, these are rural catacombs cut into the side of the rock. Many of them are visible from a covered walkway that isn't even underground and part of the site is accessible to wheelchair users, making this the only place where a wheelchair can get to the mouth of a tomb from this period. Most of the visible tombs are in a long row; walk along and peer inside to see some well-preserved window tombs and agape tables.

TA' QALI

Ta' Qali (pronounced *ta ahli* with a bit of a glottal stop for the 'q') is Malta's old airport, known by the British RAF as Takali. Built in 1938 as a civilian airfield it was rapidly taken over by the military after the outbreak of World War II and became the most bombed airfield in the world. It is now home to the National Football Stadium, a craft village and Malta's Aviation Museum.

GETTING THERE AND AWAY Several **buses** stop here and if coming by **car**, there is plenty of space to park and free parking at both the craft village and aviation museum.

CRAFT VILLAGE (Ta' Qali; ⊕ 09.00–16.00 Mon–Fri, 09.00–13.00 Sat) Rows of old Nissen huts have been taken over by craftspeople and retailers to demonstrate and sell Maltese crafts. You can watch glassblowing, pottery making, stone polishing, carpentry and filigree work, and buy a mix of tourist tat and genuine crafts.

MALTA AVIATION MUSEUM (Ta' Qali, RBT 13 (on the former RAF airfield, between the Craft Village & the National Stadium); ☏ 21416095, 21419374; w maltaaviationmuseum.com; ⊕ 09.00–17.00 daily (last entry 16.00) except Jun–Sep when Sun opening is 09.00–13.00; €7 adults, €6 concessions (inc seniors & students), €2 children aged 3–12) Two hangars full of Malta's aviation history. The museum started with one Spitfire – EN199 – that took part in the invasion of Sicily in 1943. The museum exists largely thanks to the energy and enthusiasm of Ray Polidano, who still runs it. Anybody with an interest in things aeronautical should definitely seek him out for a chat.

Apart from the Spitfire, highlights include a Hawker Hurricane discovered by a diver off the Blue Grotto in 1995 (now fully restored), an Aeritalia Fiat G91, a 1950s NATO plane of which there is no example in the UK, and one of only 12 Fairey Swordfish biplanes (nicknamed 'string bags') left in the world. There is also a diminutive forerunner of today's microlights, the Flying Flea (Le Pou du Ciel) built to 1930s designs, and a modern passenger jet cockpit you can climb into.

There is a detailed **guidebook** full of pictures and all the plane-buff facts you could want (by Anthony Spiteri; €4.70).

MĠARR

A very pleasant little inland village (not to be confused with Mġarr Harbour on Gozo), Mġarr centres (like any self-respecting Maltese settlement) on its church square, with the large silver-domed parish **Church of the Assumption** (*festa* in the third week of August) fronted by a broad raised terrace where a strawberry festival is held each April. The church was begun in 1898 when the people of Mġarr were granted their own parish, breaking away from Mosta, and finished in 1946. Its design is not noticeably modern, but with its neoclassical columns and plain interior it is an echo of the Mosta Dome. Opposite the church is the unprepossessing **Il-Barri** (The Bull) restaurant. Do not be fooled – this place is more than it looks both culinarily and historically.

GETTING THERE AND AWAY Several **buses** come here and it is possible to **park** too.

✗ WHERE TO EAT AND DRINK *Map, below*

✷ **✗ Il-Barri** See *Mġarr Shelter* (below); ⏱ 09.00–midnight Tue–Sun, 17.30–midnight Mon. Authentic & inexpensive Maltese home cooking. When you order a meal you may well get a pre-starter, most likely some excellent *bigilla* (bean & garlic paste) with *galletti* (crackers) & *ħobż biż żejt* (literally 'bread with oil', but actually also with tomatoes). Locals love this place for its rabbit (*fenek*): starter of spaghetti with rabbit sauce, followed by rabbit in wine, rabbit stew or the very tasty fried rabbit. Pasta dishes, pizza & burgers also available. Don't miss their delicious homemade puddings, & if you order rabbit, leave room for the peanuts in their shells that traditionally follow. Family-run & great for families. €–€€

WHAT TO SEE AND DO

Mġarr Shelter ✷ (Il-Barri restaurant, Church Sq; ☎ 215732355, 21574054; w il-barri.com.mt/world-war-2-shelter; ⏱ 09.00–13.00 Tue–Sat, 10.00–11.30 Sun; €3 adults, €1.50 children under 10) Behind a nondescript door in the basement of Il-Barri restaurant is a large World War II shelter (see box, page 151). Rediscovered

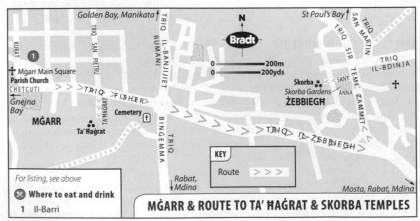

For listing, see above

⊗ Where to eat and drink
1   Il-Barri

MĠARR & ROUTE TO TA' ĦAĠRAT & SKORBA TEMPLES

less than two decades ago, the 125m hand-dug tunnel with numerous side rooms descends 12m below ground. Up to 400 people sheltered down here during the war including a member of the family who runs Il-Barri. Born in 1943, he was one of the last babies to occupy the newborns' nursery in the shelter, designed to keep the vulnerable babies away from the overcrowded corridors where disease spread quickly. His elder sister died as a result of scabies at the age of five months.

The shelter originally had no electricity (it does now) and would have been full of smoke from candles and oil lamps. It did, however, have a hygienically tiled hospital area where casualties – civilian and military – were taken, a birth room and even a small schoolroom. Also on show in the shelter is the wing of a Junkers 88 aircraft retrieved from a local field in 1941. It is cool and damp down here so you may need a sweatshirt.

Ta' Ħaġrat Temple (Triq Ta' Ħaġrat; ☏ 21239545; w heritagemalta.org; ☉ 09.00–17.00 daily, last admission 16.30; €3.50 adults, €3 over-60s/children aged 12–17, €2.50 children aged 6–11, children under 6 free; tickets are not available on site – buy them online, at another Heritage Malta site, from the local council (Konsul Lokali), Mġarr Snack Bar in Mġarr church square or Farmer's Bar in Żebbiegħ close to Skorba Temple) If you leave Church Square along Triq Fisher then turn right down Triq Ta' Ħaġrat and walk to the end, you will find the Ta' Ħaġrat prehistoric temple (see below for a locator map), built in the 4th millennium BC (see pages 4 and 79 for more on the temples). You can see a little through the wire fence, but this is just the side of the temple – the back wall of an apse – so it is worth coming when the site is open. At the front of the temple you can clearly see the concave façade, with a bit of bench at its base, facing out over the valley.

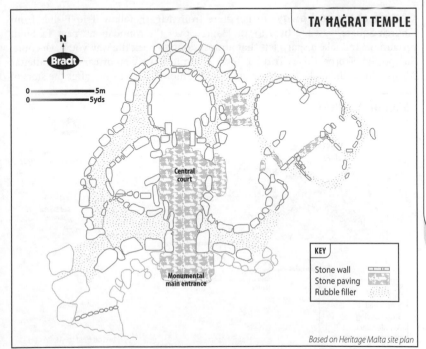

TA' ĦAĠRAT TEMPLE

N

Bradt

0 —— 5m
0 —— 5yds

Central court

Monumental main entrance

KEY
Stone wall
Stone paving
Rubble filler

Based on Heritage Malta site plan

11

The monumental entrance (partially restored, and with views of the Mġarr church dome behind it) leads into a paved central courtyard surrounded by three apses. The apses have been screened off, probably during a later phase of the temple period (ending 2350BC). No decorated stone was found here, but a little model of a temple was discovered (now in the National Museum of Archaeology in Valletta), which contributed to the debate about how the temples were roofed.

To the right and behind this temple are the remains of another, even smaller, irregular building joined to the first by a flight of steps of unknown date. This may have been a second tiny temple or perhaps used as priests' living quarters. The pottery found in excavations suggests that, like Skorba (see below), there was a village here for some time before the temple was built.

Skorba Temples (Żebbiegħ, near Mġarr, about 1.5km from Ta' Ħaġrat; other details as for Ta' Ħaġrat) Not as attractive as Ta' Ħaġrat and with much less left standing, Skorba yielded a great deal of archaeological information. This is largely because it was first excavated only in the 1960s when archaeology was more careful and more advanced than in the 19th century, the period in which most of the temples were unearthed.

Skorba began as a settlement before the temples were built in the 4th and 3rd millennia BC. East of the temple remains are foundations of two small buildings. Dr David Trump, who led the 1960s excavation, suggests that they are the foundations of a shrine or shrines pre-dating the temples. Foundations of oval huts were also found (now lost or very difficult to identify), one dating back further than any other unearthed on the islands. Two early types of pottery first identified on this site – the later of which is coloured with red ochre – have been used to name two pre-temple phases in Maltese archaeology – Grey Skorba and Red Skorba.

Getting there and away To get here from Mġarr, follow Triq Fisher from Church Square, past the turn to Ta' Ħaġrat, over the roundabout, past Ta' Soldi restaurant, and take a sharp left that almost doubles back the way you have come. Signposted 'Skorba', this is Triq Sir Temi Zammit. If arriving by car from Valletta/Mosta/Mdina then take the first right – a fork more than a turn – after the start of

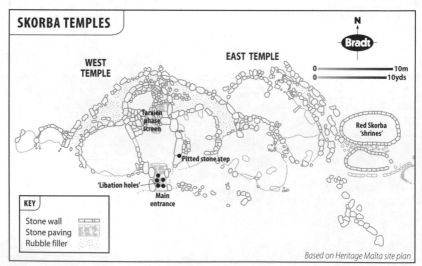

Based on Heritage Malta site plan

the buildings of Mġarr and carry on up the hill towards the children's playground; turn left and you are there. See page 236 for a locator map.

Exploring the site As you enter the enclosure, it is initially hard to make sense of the stones. There are sparse remains of two temples here, but only the west temple is comprehensible to the untrained eye. Built in the 4th millennium BC, only one megalith of the façade is left standing but you can identify the main doorway by the two standing stones with holes for door bars, the fallen topstone that lies in front of them and the paving either side of it. The paving contains five 'libation holes' (holes perhaps used for making liquid offerings).

You can see quite a bit of the wall of the left apse, while the right apse is barely more than a shape on the ground. There is a step to the right apse that has pitted decoration. This is thought to be a re-used stone from the later Tarxien phase (mid 3rd millennium BC), during which the apses here are thought to have been screened off from the central 'corridor'. Around this time too, part of the eastern wall of this temple was demolished and a second, four-apse, temple built. The second (east) temple is now hard to visualise.

AROUND MĠARR

Binġemma Gap A couple of kilometres south of Mġarr lies this wonderful little spot where several items of historic and natural interest come together in a small area. The **Chapel of Our Lady of the Way**, more often known locally as Il-Madonna ta' Ittria, built in 1680, marks the spot. There are panoramic views from here back towards Mġarr (with the shining silver dome of its parish church) and, on a clear day, all the way to Gozo.

During migration times (spring and autumn), birds – including raptors – pass through here, making it a good spot for **birdwatching** in the early morning and late afternoon. Inevitably this also makes it a good place for hunting and trapping of birds. If you stay around the chapel and the public road and paths you should not have any problems with hunters, who mostly patrol the rocky area behind the chapel (more on hunting and safety on pages 26 and 50 respectively).

Below the chapel is a cave that was once inhabited, and if you look across the small valley at the hillside opposite, you will see more caves – natural and manmade. These are in fact a **Punic/Roman/Byzantine necropolis**, which can be reached by following the little path through the vegetation – including fig, almond and carob trees, and wild fennel. (In spring, when vegetation is thickest, you may want long trousers.) Most of the tombs have some natural light but if you want to see into the depths you will need a torch. There are multiple entrances and everything from small individual tombs to complexes of burials with carved arches and square windows as well as typical stone headrests and little niches for oil lamps. Some of the complexes interconnect and this is a great place to explore (at your own risk, and with care so that nothing is damaged).

At the head of the little valley you will see an impressive defensive wall. This is a part of the **Victoria Lines** (see box, page 239) known as the **Dwejra Lines**. This stretch has been restored and is a great place for a **walk**. Cross the bridge over the little valley and you come to a corner which is another vantage point for surveying the landscape. From here you can walk along the Victoria Lines for more than a kilometre with panoramic views to the north, including of the Verdala Palace and Mdina.

Nadur Tower This 17th-century tower, one of eight built by Grand Master de Lascaris (1636–57), stands at the highest spot on the island after Dingli Cliffs, 242m above sea level. This makes it good for **birdwatching,** as well as offering dramatic **views** along the coast and as far as the Ta' Ċenċ cliffs of Gozo. The best views are from the road just before you reach the tower.

THE WEST COAST

Along the west coast of Malta, not far from Mġarr, lies a series of bays. All are good **swimming** places, and there are some attractive **walks** along the cliffs either side of the bays too (best outside the heat of the summer). Each bay is different in character.

🏠 **WHERE TO STAY**   *Map, page 224*

🏠 **Radisson Golden Sands Resort & Spa*****   (329 rooms) Golden Bay, MLH 5510; ✆23561000, 23560001; w radissonblu.com/ goldensandsresort-malta. A modern 5-star resort hotel right on the sandy beach at Golden Bay. Indoor swimming pool & outdoor pools (inc children's pool) on terrace overlooking the bay.

Relaxing spa (page 97) overlooking the sea. Lots of organised activities in summer from guided walks to yoga, table tennis to cocktail making as well as children's activities & kids' club. All rooms have balcony. 7 restaurants/bars from international buffet to fine dining. Games room, shop & watersports centre. Good for families. €€–€€€

✕ **WHERE TO EAT AND DRINK**   Besides the beach snack bars and the five-star hotel restaurants, there is **The Apple's Eye** (✆ 21573359, 21581042; w appleseyemalta.com; ⏲ summer 09.00–21.30+ Mon–Fri, 09.00–22.00+ Sat, 08.00–21.30+ Sun, winter 09.00–18.00 Mon–Fri, 09.00–20.00 Sat, 08.00–20.00 Sun; €) up the hill behind Golden Bay Beach. This café-bar-pizzeria has a terrace overlooking the beach and serves everything from drinks and ice creams to rabbit stew and pizza (eat-in or take-away).

THE BAYS
Fomm ir-Riħ Bay   A large beautiful bay, Fomm ir-Riħ ('mouth of the wind'), is surrounded by cliffs and completely undeveloped. A smooth slope of grey clay backs a pebbly beach from which it is possible to **swim** and **snorkel**. You can reach it by boat or by walking down a narrow rocky footpath (about 10mins from the nearest parking, which is down a small road to the left as you arrive at the bay from Baħrija). Because of the walk and its unsuitability for children this place gets relatively few visitors. Quite an isolated spot, it would be unwise to swim here alone, and it is unsafe in windy weather.

There is good **birdwatching** from the headlands on both sides of the bay during migration (spring and autumn). This inevitably also means there may be hunters around during the autumn season (pages 26 and 50).

Ġnejna Bay   Popular with locals, this red sandy beach with rocks to snorkel off has a car park right next to the water and buses stopping close by. Known as 'Mġarr's Beach', it is about 3km from the town (and a steep walk back!). There is a pretty row of boathouses (mostly now used as beach huts) cut into the base of the cliffs, and sometimes a not-so-pretty gaggle of caravans that aren't supposed to be there. Above the bay is the **Lippia Tower**, one of the watchtowers built by Grand Master Lascaris in 1636–57.

The water is lovely, although there can be litter on the shore and, more importantly, the cliffs are crumbling. A boy was killed here when loose clay was dislodged by a vehicle parked above, so beware of overhangs and think about where you sit.

The British were worried about enemies landing in the north of the island and travelling overland to attack the more populated Grand Harbour area and the British Mediterranean Fleet. They built a system of defences that spans the entire width of the island, 12km, along a natural ridge from Madliena to Fomm ir-Rih. Work began in the early 1870s with the building of a fort at either end and one in the middle at Mosta (none is open to the public). The forts were later joined together by a strong defensive wall, wide enough for infantry to march along. Complete with batteries, entrenchments, stop walls and emplacements for searchlights and howitzers, the whole system was officially inaugurated in 1897 and named the Victoria Lines after Queen Victoria's Diamond Jubilee.

No invader ever tried to cross the lines, and as early as 1907 military technology had overtaken these defences and they fell into disuse. Recent renovations have rescued several sections of the wall, some of which look very impressive viewed from the north and also make good walks. The wall is itself an excellent path and, being right on the edge of the ridge, affords panoramic views.

Għajn Tuffieħa Bay Although this bay is only just across the headland from Għnejna Bay, to get between them by car you have to go back into Mġarr and out by a different route. The road does, however, connect directly to Golden Bay and several **buses** come here. The long flight of steps that leads down from the car park to the bay means that this lovely narrow red sandy blue-flag beach does not get as crowded as Golden Bay or Għnejna Bay. There's a **snack bar** and small **watersports** and **sunlounger** outlets. It is not built up and is managed by the GAIA Foundation, a conservation NGO. This is a thoroughly pleasant place to relax and swim. Be aware that there can be a dangerous undertow a little way out from the beach during, or just after, rough weather.

On the tip of the headland by the car park is **Għajn Tuffieħa Tower** built by Grand Master Lascaris (1636–57) – part of the same defensive system as Nadur Tower and the Lippia Tower on Għnejna Bay. Għajn Tuffieħa Tower is open to the public at irregular times. Contact the GAIA Foundation (see below) for more information.

There are also Roman Baths near the bay. Long earmarked for restoration, these are still closed at the time of writing.

It is possible to walk from here across the headland to Golden Bay.

Golden Bay (Ramla tal-Mixquqa) (Buses stop metres from the beach) Dominated by the Radisson SAS Golden Sands Resort and Spa hotel, this broad yellow sandy beach is still a lovely place to sunbathe and swim, though it gets crowded at the height of summer. Like many of Malta's beaches there can be a dangerous undertow here, particularly during or after rough weather, so do keep an eye on the flags (when they fly in season) and take advice from locals. Don't stray too far from the shore out of season. In summer, stones are cleared from the water's edge but in spring you may want water shoes, especially for kids. There are plenty of **watersports** available here as well as two **snack bars** and all the facilities of the five-star hotel. There is good **walking** on the coastal cliff tops behind (north of) the hotel.

Up the hill from the beach just after the Apple's Eye café en route to Għajn Tuffieħa Bay is the **GAIA Foundation Centre** (Għajn Tuffieħa Rd, MLH 5510;

Central Malta THE WEST COAST

11

℡ 21584473/4; f; ⏱ 08.00–14.00 Mon–Sat), the headquarters of this conservation NGO. Among other projects, GAIA has responsibility for a couple of stretches of Malta's coastline including Ramla Beach on Gozo (where they are conserving the sand dunes) and Għajn Tuffieħa Bay just up the road from here. At the centre, you can visit their nursery where plants – native, and in some cases unique, to the Maltese islands – are propagated and nurtured, find out more about the conservation of Malta's coast or even volunteer some time and get directly involved (see page 27 for details). There is also a **shop** selling their own organic olive oil, honey and a few other local products.

12

North Malta

The north of Malta, divided from the south by rocky ridges, has many small bays, very accessible by sea (in summer). Historically, this made it vulnerable to corsair attack and few people chose to live here during the time of the Knights. The British built a defensive barrier – the Victoria Lines – across the entire width of the country cutting off the north to protect the south, although the Royal Navy also patrolled the northern coasts and as the danger of corsair attack waned, the population of the north began to grow. Come the late 1970s and 80s mass tourism added greatly to the numbers of people here, at least in summer, particularly as the Gozo ferry departs from Ċirkewwa on Malta's northwestern 'hammerhead' (the Marfa Peninsula). The area is still more sparsely populated than the rest of Malta, however, and there is much more countryside here than elsewhere.

The attractive area around Mġarr and the west coast is, for reasons of access to certain sites, included in *Chapter 11*. So this chapter begins north of there in Mellieħa, moving on to the peninsula that looks across to Gozo and Comino, before turning southeast to St Paul's Bay, the resort areas of Buġibba and Qawra, and the scenic North Coast Road leading back to Paceville and St Julian's.

MELLIEĦA

Mellieħa perches (in places precariously) on a ridge above the southern side of Mellieħa Bay (Għadira Bay) with **Mellieħa Beach** (Għadira Beach) to its northwest along the head of the bay. This is a classic white-sand beach, the longest in Malta (about 800m) with a lovely gentle slope into clear blue sea, making it great for families. There are sunbeds and umbrellas galore, snack bars and watersports facilities. It is a shame about the busy main road that runs its full length and the ugly buildings at either end, but this blue-flag beach has plenty going for it.

It is a steep uphill climb into the village. Just before the shops start, there is an unobtrusive stone doorway on the left, which leads down a long flight of stone steps to the underground chapel of **Our Lady of the Grotto** (Il Madonna Tal-Għar). This Madonna is believed to have special powers to help the very young and the grotto walls are hung with baby clothes and votive notes requesting intervention on behalf of sick children or showing gratitude for their recovery. Most of the letters are in Maltese but there are a few in English including one accompanied by a tiny Babygro giving thanks for the arrival of a much-wanted newborn. Heart-warmingly, there is also a photo, clearly added later, of a healthy young boy. Some locals have it that there is (miraculously) one fewer step going down to the grotto than there are climbed coming up – see what you think.

Mellieħa was one of the first ten parishes in Malta listed in 1436, but by the mid 16th century it had been abandoned due to the fear of corsair attack, only becoming a parish again in 1844. The present parish church (in the square up the steps opposite

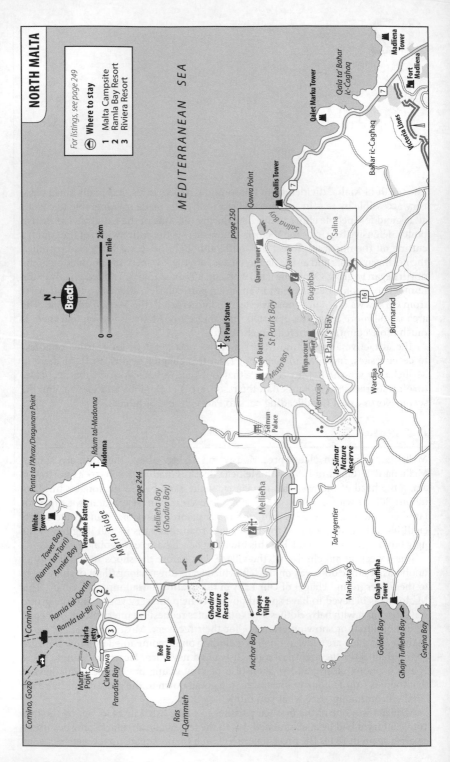

NORTH MALTA

For listings, see page 249

Where to stay
1 Malta Campsite
2 Ramla Bay Resort
3 Riviera Resort

MEDITERRANEAN SEA

Comino, Gozo

Comino

Ras il-Qammieh

Paradise Bay
Marfa Point
Ċirkewwa
Marfa jetty

Ramla tal-Bir
Ramla tal-Qortin

Red Tower

Anchor Bay

Popeye Village

page 244

Ponta ta' l-Aħrax/Dragunara Point

White Tower
Tower Bay (Ramla tat-Torri)
Armier Bay
Vendôme Battery

Marfa Ridge

Rdum tal-Madonna
Madonna

Ghadira Nature Reserve

Mellieħa Bay (Għadira Bay)

Mellieħa

Tal-Argentier

Manikata

Għajn Tuffieħa Tower

Golden Bay

Għajn Tuffieħa Bay

Gnejna Bay

St Paul Statue

Piniè Battery

St Paul's Bay

Mistra Bay

Selmun Palace

Wignacourt Tower

Xemxija

Is-Simar Nature Reserve

Wardija

Burmarrad

Qawra Point
Ghallis Tower

page 250

Qawra Tower
Qawra
Salina Bay
Salina
Buġibba
St Paul's Bay

Baħar iċ-Caghaq

Qalet Marku Tower
Qala ta' Baħar iċ-Caghaq

Victoria Lines

Fort Madliena
Madliena

Madliena Tower

0   1 mile
0   2km

N

Bradt

242

the entrance to the grotto), dedicated to the Nativity of Our Lady (*festa* 8 September), was built for the 'new' parish towards the end of the 19th century. The neighbouring **Sanctuary of Our Lady of Mellieħa** (*festa* in late September), however, is the oldest Marian shrine in Malta. It is surrounded by legend – including one relating a visit here by St Paul after his shipwreck on Malta in AD60 – and it is still a place of pilgrimage, with a large collection of ex-voto notes and offerings. This is due primarily to the chapel's rock painting of the Madonna and Child attributed by believers to Paul's companion St Luke, although its style dates it to the 13th or 14th century.

Back on the main street above Our Lady of the Grotto, if you look up to the left, there are several buildings perched on a rocky ridge looking distinctly unstable. They are in fact undermined by a series of **caves** whose openings you can see in the rock face beneath them. These are a combination of natural caves and manmade extensions. The smaller ones may have been Punic tombs, and several were once inhabited. One was a medieval troglodyte chapel and still contains a Madonna, and the cave with its mouth covered was occupied until very recently and may still be.

GETTING THERE AND AWAY Multiple buses stop both in Mellieħa village and by the beach. **Parking** is free in Mellieħa, but can be difficult in the narrow streets of the village. You can park along the road by the beach but it fills up fast on summer weekends.

TOURIST INFORMATION There is a helpful tourist information office (✆ 21524666; ⊕ 09.00–13.00 Mon–Sat) almost next to the police station (between Commando restaurant and the sanctuary) just off the main road up from the bay.

WHERE TO STAY *Map, page 244*
The Mellieħa hotels are mostly mass-tourism establishments, though generally with a calmer atmosphere than those in Buġibba and Qawra. Most are booked through package deals but they can be booked direct.

Seabank Hotel**** (540 rooms) Marfa Rd, MLH 9063; ✆ 22891000; w dbhotelsresorts. com/dbseabank. A cut above its competitors in the area, this all-inclusive hotel lies just across the road from the beach. Clean, fresh & airy with a natural look, it has excellent facilities including the largest hotel pool in Malta, plus an indoor pool with glass walls, lots of outside space, kids' club with its own building & fenced play area, kids' pool, gym, spa, & bowling alley. Choice of restaurants ranging from jungle-themed American (with kids' play area) to Italian buffet & Brazilian meat specialists. Full programme of activities & entertainment (especially in summer). €€–€€€

Pergola Club Hotel**** (91 apt rooms) Adenau St, MLH 2014; ✆ 21523912/3; w pergolahotel.com.mt. Up in the village, 20–30mins' walk (or a bus ride) from beach. Studios & apt rooms with twin/dbl bed(s), sofa bed (sleeping up to 2 extra), kitchenette, table & chairs; also hotel rooms. Small indoor pool, 2 outdoor pools & children's paddling pool. 4 restaurants/bars including 1 in a cave under the hotel. €–€€

Mellieħa Holiday Village*** (150 bungalows) Mellieħa Bay, MLH 9064; ✆ 22893000; w mhc.com.mt. Built by a Danish trade union for its workers, but open to all. A smaller & more basic early version of Center Parcs, with rows of fortress-like limestone bungalows, each with a walled patio & roof terrace. Shared facilities include gardens, terrapin pond, large outdoor pool, shaded kids' paddling pool, table tennis, supermarket & 2 restaurants. A tunnel under the road leads directly to the beach. Wheelchair accessible. €

WHERE TO EAT AND DRINK *Map, page 244*
The Arches Ġorġ Borg Olivier St; ✆ 21523460, 21520533; w thearchesmalta. com; ⊕ from 19.00 Tue–Sat. Innovative French–Mediterranean food in an award-winning smart

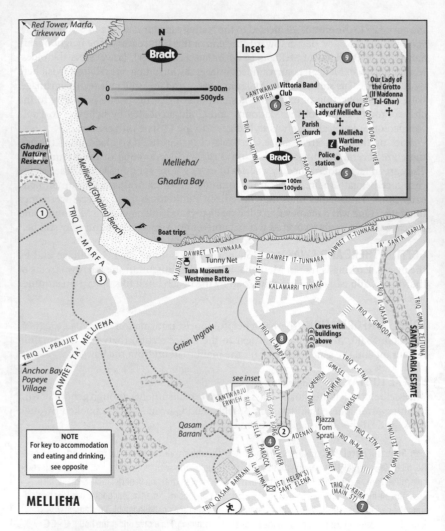

Red Tower, Marfa, Ċirkewwa

Inset

0   500m
0   500yds

Ghadira
Nature
Reserve

Melli012ħa/
Għadira Bay

Mellieħa (Għadira) Beach

TRIQ IL-MARFA

SAĠIEDA

Boat trips

DAWRET IT-TUNNARA

Tunny Net
**Tuna Museum &
Westreme Battery**

DAWRET IT-TUNNARA

DAWRET IT-TUNNARA

TA' SANTA MARIJA

TRIQ IT-TRILL

KALAMARRI TUNAĠĠ

TRIQ IL-QASAR

TRIQ GĦAJN ŻEJTUNA

SANTA MARIA ESTATE

Anchor Bay
Popeye
Village

ID-DAWRET TA' MELLIEĦA

TRIQ IL-PRAJJIET TA' MELLIEĦA

Gnien Ingraw

TRIQ IL-MARFA

**Caves with
buildings
above**

TRIQ IL-GĦAQDA

TRIQ L-ETNA

TRIQ L-GĦERIEN

GĦASEL

SAGĦTAR

GĦASEL

Pjazza
Tom
Sprati

TRIQ L-ETNA

TRIQ IN-NAĦAL

TRIQ IL-ĦOLLJIET

TRIQ GĦAJN ŻEJTUNA

Qasam
Barrani

SANTWARJU
ERWIEĦ

RIQ S VELLA

TRIQ GORĠ BORĠ OLIVER

ADENAU

TRIQ IL-MITĦNA

see inset

NOTE
For key to accommodation
and eating and drinking,
see opposite

TRIQ QASAM BARRANI

(ST HELEN'S)
SANT ELENA

TRIQ IL-KBIRA
(MAIN ST)

MELLIEĦA

Inset:

SANTWARJU
ERWIEĦ

**Vittoria Band
Club**

RIQ S VELLA

**Our Lady of
the Grotto
(Il Madonna
Tal-Għar)**

TRIQ IL-MITĦNA

**Sanctuary of Our
Lady of Mellieħa**

**Parish
church**

● **Mellieħa
Wartime
Shelter**

TRIQ GORĠ BORĠ OLIVER

**Police
station**

RIQ S VELLA

TRIQ PAROĊĊA

0   100m
0   100yds

---

modern restaurant. Children over 5 welcome.
€€€€

✖ **Commando** Misraħ Iz-Żjara tal-Papa;
📞 21523459; m 99498843; w commandorestaurant.
com; ⏱ summer 18.30–22.00 daily & noon–15.00
Sun, winter closed Mon & Sun nights. Excellent family-
run Mediterranean restaurant named by Royal Marine
Commandos during the war. Eat in the 300-year-
old house or out on the terrace. Seared scallops
recommended. €€€

✖ **Il-Mithna** (The Mill House) 58 Triq il-Kbira/
Main St; 📞 21520404; m 79478896; w mithna.
com; ⏱ 18.00–22.30 daily, exc Sun in winter
noon–15.00 only. Modern Mediterranean food
with an award-winning Maltese wine list in a

historic setting. Eat in this 17th-century windmill
built by the Knights of St John, or in summer on
the terrace or patio outside. Good-value early bird
set menu. Families welcome; highchairs available.
€€€

✖ **one80 Cafe at Loft** 30 Triq il-Wied ta'
Ruman, MLH 4023; 📞 21521637; w one80.com.
mt; ⏱ noon–22.30 Sun–Thu, noon–23.00 Fri &
Sat. Very good modern Mediterranean food. W/
day afternoons (15.00–18.00) menu is reduced
to bar food but this is interesting & various. Kids'
menu with drawing activities. Halfway up the
hill between beach & village. Excellent 180°
views (hence the name).
€€–€€€

ⓢ **Where to stay**
1 Mellieħa Holiday Village
2 Pergola Club
3 Seabank

ⓧ **Where to eat and drink**
4 The Arches
5 Commando
6 Il-Bottegin
7 Il-Mithna
8 one80 Cafe at Loft
9 Sea View Bar

✗ **Il-Bottegin** Misraħ Il-Paroċċa (Parish Sq); ☏21523248; w bottegin.com; ⏲ 08.00–23.00+ daily. In the Vittoria Band Club (the traditional parish band club) on the main square. Local food & drink with local people. Meaty menu plus pasta & pizza. €–€€

🍴 **Sea View Bar** Sanctuary St; ☏21524008; ⏲ summer 10.30–22.00/23.00 daily, winter 10.30–c18.00 daily. Hidden behind the church next to the cemetery, this tiny café selling snacks & drinks sits like an eyrie on the top of a cliff with stunning views over Mellieħa Bay. Plenty of space outside. €

WHAT TO SEE AND DO

Mellieħa Wartime Shelter [map, opposite] (Our Lady of the Grotto St, MLH 06; m 79521970; ⏲ 09.00–noon (may be open much later) Mon–Sat; €2.40 adults, €0.70 children up to 12) Halfway down the steps from the church square to Ġorġ Borġ Olivier Street is the little entrance to this extensive World War II shelter (for information on Malta's wartime shelters, see box, page 151). Dug entirely by hand into solid rock, 500m of corridors lead to private 'rooms', a tiled maternity area and a once-guarded treasure room where national treasures were stashed. Exhibits from Valletta museums were stored here until they became too damp and had to be moved. Many hundreds of people sheltered in these damp narrow spaces during the worst of the bombing in World War II (for more on which, see pages 17 and 132). The door is usually manned by one of two very well-informed men who are happy to answer your questions.

Tunnara (Tuna) Museum and Westreme Battery [map, opposite] (On Mellieħa Bay, at the bottom of the hill up to the village; m 99407704; ⏲ opened by a volunteer usually 10.00–noon Mon, Tue, Thu, Sat, & around 14.30–17.00 Tue, Wed, Fri; admission by donation) The Westreme Battery was built by the Knights in 1716 for coastal defence. A searchlight room was added next to it by the British during World War II. From as early as 1748 the battery was used as a tuna storehouse, which is why the small museum inside is dedicated largely to traditional tuna fishing. This used to take place during tuna migration in a massive netting operation across the whole of Mellieħa Bay. Tuna is still fished here (sometimes controversially). Nowadays, the fish are caught young and 'grown' in pens, mostly for the Japanese market.

Boat trips Boat trips depart from 'Tunny Net', Mellieħa Bay (by the Tuna Museum at the bottom of the hill up to the village). These include day trips to the Blue Lagoon on Comino, and rides along the coast to the Grand Harbour and neighbouring Marsamxett Harbour either side of Valletta (see box, page 114). Try English Rose Cruises (☏ 21550552; m 99495842; w englishrosecruises.com).

Għadira Nature Reserve [map, page 242] (BirdLife Malta; ☏ 21347646; w birdlifemalta.org; ⏲ Nov–May 10.00–16.00 w/ends or by arrangement with BirdLife Malta; admission free) Just across the road from the beach is one of two bird reserves run by BirdLife Malta (the other is on St Paul's Bay; page 252). It is tiny by British standards with one good-sized hide looking out over a few hectares of wetland and salt marsh, but it is an important place for Malta's birds. It provides a safe haven – a habitat that will not be overtaken by development, agriculture or pollution and where there are no hunters – as well as a source of education for Maltese children that may help them develop an interest in watching living birds.

Needless to say, the hunting lobby does not like this place. Hunters have occasionally broken into the site in order to shoot rare birds and the reserve has been damaged on more than one occasion including in an arson attack and by oil being thrown into the water. However, there have been no serious attacks in the last few years.

BirdLife has a very dedicated staff and the reserve feels very peaceful inside. Little ringed plover breed here (the only place in Malta where they do), along with warblers (Cetti's, fan-tailed, Sardinian), corn bunting and occasionally finches. You may also see Temminck's stint, little stint, turtle doves and a variety of waders (depending on the season). For more on birding in Malta, see pages 25, 72 and 93. For more on hunting, see pages 26 and 50.

From here it is walking distance up to the Red Tower on the Marfa Ridge.

Popeye Village [map, page 242] (Anchor Bay; ✎21524782/3/4; w popeyemalta. com; ☺ 09.30–16.30 daily, 09.30–17.30 late Apr–Jun, Sep & Oct, 09.30–19.00 Jul & Aug; €15 adults, €12 children aged 3–12, children under 3 free) If you have seen and enjoyed the film *Popeye* (the 1980 live-action one starring Robin Williams) or have young children who have had enough history, you might want to pop into the village of 'Sweethaven' – the original movie set for the film. It is a bit pricey, but the brightly coloured plasterboard buildings at zany angles linked by zigzagging wooden walkways are fun to run along if you are aged about five to nine. There is a little boat ride on the hour around the pretty bay, robotic scenes, a craftsman making filigree Maltese crosses, a fun pool, minigolf, a small playground and a terrace of fake grass and sunbeds. Outside the slightly tacky complex is a World War II pillbox (free!) and a little coarse-sand beach. You can also get a good view of the 'village' from the road on the other side of the bay for nothing.

Getting there Public **buses** stop right outside and there is a shuttle service from 'Tunny Net', Mellieħa Bay, on the hour, and a hotel pickup service from Valletta, Sliema, Buġibba/Qawra and Mellieħa (book ahead) for an all-day visit.

THE MARFA PENINSULA

The Marfa Ridge runs the length of the hammerhead (the Marfa Peninsula), commanding great views, both over the sea towards Comino and Gozo and back over the main island of Malta. You can walk an entire circuit of the hammerhead (about 11–12km; see the MTA's Watchtower's Walk, downloadable free at w visitmalta.com/en/walks or available as a leaflet from tourist offices). The road runs the length of the ridge so you can also take a scenic drive along here. Down by the water, however, you can only get directly from bay to bay on foot. By car you have to keep going back to the ridge road (not that the distances are very great).

GETTING THERE AND AWAY **Buses** do not run along the peninsula, just to it. They stop at, or just before, the Gozo ferry at Ċirkewwa. There should be no problem **parking** in this area.

WHAT TO SEE ON THE MARFA RIDGE
The Red Tower (It Torri L-Aħmar) [map, page 242] (Renovated & run by Din L-Art Ħelwa (Malta's National Trust); ✎ 21225952, 21220358; w dinlarthelwa.org,

redtowermalta.wordpress.com; ⊕ by volunteers, mid-Sep–mid-Jun 10.00–16.00, mid-Jun–mid-Sep 10.00–17.00; €2 pp, free to British National Trust members, although donations welcome to help with restoration/maintenance) Also known as St Agatha's Tower, the Red Tower was built in 1647–48 by Grand Master Lascaris to defend the Straits of Comino and communicate early warning of attack via other towers to Valletta. It was equipped with four or five cannons and, at times of trouble, up to 49 men. It isn't clear why it was painted red (perhaps to make it easier to see from other towers?), but this was the original colour and it has been retained.

Entrance to the tower is via an impressive flight of steps and a wooden bridge that would probably have been a drawbridge. Inside are two vaulted rooms which may once have been split horizontally to provide sleeping quarters. The roof – with its four corner towers – affords magnificent 360° **views** of most of northern Malta, Gozo, Comino, Mellieħa Bay, Għadira Nature Reserve and a fair chunk of the rest of Malta. The Santa Marija Tower on Comino and the White Tower at the other end of the 'hammerhead' are also easily seen. No wonder the Knights built their tower here. (If travelling with young children, be aware that the roof has only a low wall around it.)

Getting there The tower is **walking** distance (uphill) from Mellieħa Bay. By **bus,** take any bus going to the Gozo ferry and stopping at Mellieħa Bay and get off on the main road below the tower. If you have a **car,** you can park next to the tower as well as further along the headland.

Beyond the Red Tower

From the Red Tower you can walk or drive out over the garigue (limestone rock with low scrubby vegetation) to the tip of the headland at **Ras il-Qammieħ** from where there are **panoramic views** to the Ta' Ċenċ cliffs of Gozo in one direction and right along the west coast of Malta in the other. Keep your back to the (mercifully small) derelict NATO radar station. Sticking out to sea as it does, this headland is a good spot for **birdwatching** during spring and autumn migration. There are therefore hunters' and trappers' hides here and, in autumn in particular, you may come across men with guns (more on hunting on pages 26 and 50, and on birdwatching on pages 25, 72 and 93). From here, it is possible to walk down an old military path (now somewhat broken up) and stone steps cut by the British to reach **Paradise Bay** and its beach (page 248). From the beach, footpaths link each bay all the way along the coast facing Gozo and Comino to the far end of the hammerhead where the path leads back up onto the ridge.

By car you have no choice but to double back along the ridge road past the Red Tower to join or cross the main road leading from Mellieħa and the south to Ċirkewwa and the Gozo ferry.

If you cross the main road and keep travelling the **scenic route** along the top of the ridge, you will pass on your left a *girna*, a traditional circular drystone hut with a corbelled roof. This is a farmers' shelter often found in Malta's older agricultural landscapes and particularly in this area. Next you come to a small (planted) woodland, popular with hunters in season, before reaching the far end of the ridge at Rdum tal-Madonna.

Rdum tal-Madonna On this often windswept spot stands a little white statue of the Madonna (1870) and the **Chapel of the Immaculate Conception**, built in 1961 to replace a 19th-century chapel that had become too close to the cliff edge. The original chapel was built by a fisherman in votive thanks for his safe return as the only survivor of a fishing accident. The cliffs here are eroding fast and it is advisable not to go too close to the edge.

There are great views out to sea and over Mellieħa Bay. The circles in the water are fish farms. On the Mellieħa Bay side there is also a cliff path leading down to a small undisturbed bay, unattractively known as **Slugs Bay** (after a brown sea slug found in the area), with a few square metres of sandy beach. The rare Mediterranean sea daffodil (*Pancratium maritimum*) may be seen here in August. Rdum tal-Madonna is also of interest to birders as the rare **yelkouan shearwater** breeds in the cliffs (see box, page 251). A small number of the larger Scopoli's shearwater also breed here, as do short-toed larks and resident birds, including the blue rock thrush (Malta's national bird) and the spectacled warbler. Other birds are seen during migration (for more on birding in Malta, see pages 25, 72 and 93).

THE NORTHWEST COAST (FACING COMINO AND GOZO)
Dragunara Point (Ponta ta' l'Aħrax) [map, page 242] From Rdum tal-Madonna there is a scenic cliff path along the end of the hammerhead down to Dragunara Point. Alternatively, return to the road and walk or drive down to Daħlet ix-Xmajjar, turn right, leave the car by the campsite (see opposite) and walk a couple of hundred metres.

Dragunara Point is a barren promontory of rough rock with a large hole in it looking straight down into the sea. This is a cave whose roof has collapsed (which makes you wonder a little what you are walking on elsewhere!) and it is particularly impressive when the sea is choppy and waves crash within it (take care).

The White Tower (It-Torri L-Abjad) and Tower Bay (Ramla tat-Torri) [map, page 242] On the next mini headland is the White Tower (It-Torri L-Abjad). No longer white, it is for now best seen from a distance. The area around it has long been a grubby mess, though there are moves, led by Din L-Art Ħelwa (Malta's National Trust) to renovate the tower so this may improve. The White Tower is one of the de Redin towers (page 85), built in 1658 under Grand Master Martin de Redin (1657–60) as part of an early warning communication system that ran from one tower to another all the way down the coast. Straw was burnt to send a warning and a fire at this tower would certainly have been visible from the Red Tower, Selmun, and the tower on Comino. Neighbouring Ramla tat-Torri/Tower Bay has a rather uninviting, muddy sandy beach and a village of boathouses.

Bays and beaches [map, page 242] The small sandy beach (mixed with a bit of clay) of **Little Armier** offers watersports and a café-pizzeria that also hires out sunbeds. It is backed by an old defensive wall now surrounded by boathouses and a gaggle of caravans. A few minutes' walk (or a 10min drive) takes you to **Armier Bay** with a larger sandy beach (and less clay), a few food outlets and an unsightly derelict bar. There is a Knights-period redoubt just above the bay and on the headland is the 17th-century **Vendôme Battery**, named after the knight who commissioned it, the brother of Louis XIII of France.

Ramla tal-Bir is dominated by the Ramla Bay Resort which owns the small sandy beach. Another redoubt overlooks the bay. On the Ċirkewwa side is the **Red Palace (Il-Palazz l-Aħmar)**, originally a 1657 watchtower extended to its present form in the 20th century. Here too (opposite the Riviera hotel) is the departure point for most of the Comino ferries.

On the other side of Marfa Point (at the tip of which is the Gozo ferry terminal), lies **Paradise Bay**, accessed down a flight of stone steps. It is sandy with clear blue water and a thatched bar and restaurant – easily the nicest beach along this coast (1km from the bus stop – page 247).

All the beaches here become crowded on summer weekends, when the locals arrive to join the tourists.

WHERE TO STAY *Map, page 242*
Hotels

Ramla Bay Resort**** (263 rooms) Triq Ir-Ramla Tal-Bir, Marfa, MLH 7100; ☎22812281; w ramlabayresort.com. Family-friendly resort hotel with panoramic views across the water to Comino & Gozo. Thatched gazebos/umbrellas, 3 outdoor pools, spa & indoor pools, watersports, dive centre & small private sandy beach. New wing with especially spacious, bright rooms. Good range of restaurants. Offers all-inclusive in summer. Wheelchair-accessible rooms. €€

Riviera Resort**** (250 rooms) Marfa, MLH 9069; ☎21525900; w rivierahotelmalta. com. On a pleasant seafront promenade, next to the departure point for Comino ferries. Reception & 24hr bar with large windows looking out at the sea & Comino. Indoor pool, outdoor seawater

pools, children's paddling pool, 3 restaurants, functional spa, watersports; dive centre, seafront sunbeds & access to the sea. Helpful staff. Recently refurbished. All-inclusive. €€

Camping

Malta Campsite Daħlet ix-Xmajjar, Limiti tal-Mellieħa; ☎21521105; m 99496707; w maltacampsite.com. Not much shade, & a long way from public transport (bus stop a 1hr walk or camp taxi), Malta's only campsite is nonetheless a cheap accommodation option in a good location for walks. Small shop, café & above-ground swimming pool (surrounded by fake grass), clean (coin-op) showers. Caravans & little 'chalets' also available (but these can get unbearably hot in summer). €

ST PAUL'S BAY AREA

This large and beautiful bay, which was a quiet fishing area until the 20th century, is sadly now surrounded by ugly modern apartments and mass-tourism hotels. Buġibba and Qawra on the southern side are particularly unattractive. These are the areas that have given Malta a bad name as a styleless concrete package-holiday destination. There are, however, still a few pretty corners including around Wignacourt Tower and Tarragon Restaurant (page 251).

Out in the bay is **St Paul's Island** which dips in the middle, making it look like two islands. On it stands a tall 19th-century statue of the saint who is said to have been shipwrecked on these rocks in AD60 (see boxes, pages 7 and 140).

The bay played a bloody part in the end of the Great Siege of 1565. The Turkish fleet, having fled Marsamxett Harbour when fresh troops arrived from Sicily to relieve the Knights, returned, anchoring in St Paul's Bay. Here they faced a rout that some reports say turned the sea red.

The northern side of the bay, around **Xemxija**, is much quieter than Buġibba and Qawra and includes the secluded **Mistra Bay** where there is almost nothing but a sandy, seaweed-strewn and slightly grubby beach, a pizzeria (page 251) and, on the small **Ras il-Mignuna headland**, the **Pinto Battery**, an 18th-century redoubt built by Grand Master Manoel Pinto de Fonseca whose coat of arms can still be seen carved into the stone.

Also on the Xemxija side of the water is the **Selmun Palace**, an 18th-century fortified building that was the base of the Monte di Redenzione degli Schiavi, a foundation that raised money to pay ransoms to retrieve Christians taken into slavery by the Turks. There was always more demand than money so who was rescued was decided by lottery. The building became part of the Selmun Palace Hotel, now closed.

GETTING THERE AND AWAY Buses stop in St Paul's, Xemxija, Salina, Buġibba and Qawra where there is a small bus station.

Parking is free but spaces are at a premium at weekends.

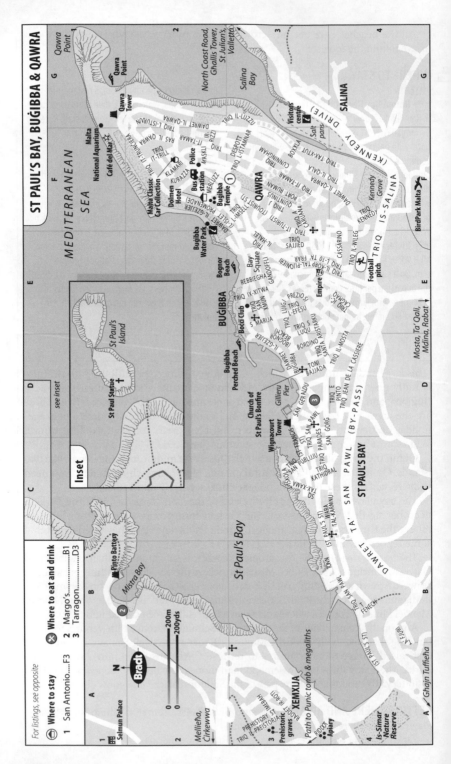

ST PAUL'S BAY, BUĠIBBA & QAWRA

For listings, see opposite

🏛 **Where to stay**
1 San Antonio.........F3

✕ **Where to eat and drink**
2 Margo's...................B1
3 Tarragon.................D3

Bradt

250

WHERE TO STAY

The best deals in this area are likely to be through package-holiday operators and unless you get a very cheap deal or actively like the sound of the area, you would be better off staying elsewhere. There is, however, one bright, good-value, all-inclusive resort hotel, part of the same group as the Seabank in Mellieħa Bay.

San Antonio [250 F3] (516 rooms) Triq it-Turisti, St Paul's Bay, SPB 1024; 21583434/5; w dbhotelsresorts.com/dbsanantonio. Bright airy modern all-inclusive hotel, inland but 1min walk from the seafront. Indoor & outdoor pools (inc 1 adults-only), sports & activities, evening shows, kids' & teens' clubs, decent food. All rooms have balcony, some sea view. Accessible rooms available. €€

WHERE TO EAT AND DRINK

Tarragon [250 D3] 21 Church St, St Paul's Bay; 21573759; m 99266999; w tarragonmalta.com; ⏰ 18.30–23.00 Mon–Sat, noon–15.30 Sun (Jul & Aug closed Sun). Won Malta's Best Restaurant award 2018. Excellent modern Mediterranean cuisine in a simple but elegant space with glass walls (open in summer) overlooking the sea. Lots of interesting meat dishes plus fresh fish. €€€

Margo's [250 B1] Mistra Bay; 21582736; w margosmalta.com; ⏰ in good weather 19.00–22.00 Fri, noon–15.00 & 19.00–22.00 Sat, noon–15.00 (until 16.00 Sun), closed in winter. In the attractive surroundings of what was once the summer house of a wealthy Maltese family home overlooking the bay. This is a 'gourmet' pizzeria that uses home-milled flour, organic water buffalo mozzarella, home-smoked sausage & fresh tuna. They also offer a fantasy pizza (let the chef's imagination run wild) & 'the world's most expensive pizza' with everything including gold leaf although it's not often ordered at €1,800. Apart from the latter… €

XEMXIJA Xemxija is largely made up of modern apartments, but on its rocky fringes are some minor but interesting unfenced prehistoric and ancient sites. The

YELKOUAN SHEARWATERS

Malta is home to about 10% of the world's population of the rare yelkouan shearwater (*Puffinus yelkouan*) and about a third of them breed in the cliffs of Rdum tal-Madonna. The birds, whose name means 'wind-chaser', arrive in Malta from October and breed in burrows in the cliffs. They usually lay a single egg at the end of February, which hatches around the second week in May. In July, when the chicks are old enough, almost all the birds leave the island and head east. Like many seabirds they do not make landfall again until the next breeding season and part of the project here is to tag the birds to find out where they fish and where they spend the winter.

Even when breeding, at least one parent spends the day at sea and in the late afternoon the birds gather in a 'raft' on the surface of the water before flying in to their nests just after dark. Their loud hoarse call (more high-pitched from the male than the female) can be heard, especially on moonless nights between February and April.

The LIFE Yelkouan Shearwater Project (w birdlifemalta.org/conservation/past-projects/yelkouan-shearwater-project), which, lasting four years, succeeded in reversing the decline in the species here by studying its habits and acting on threats including rats (so please don't leave any rubbish), hunting and disturbance by boats. It also created a blueprint for dealing with other sites of importance to birds.

local council has produced a booklet, **Xemxija Heritage Trail**, that leads you through this archaeological landscape. It is available free from the tourist office in Mellieħa.

Prehistoric graves [250 A3] On rocky ground next to Prehistory Street (Triq il-Preistorja) on the northwestern edge of Xemxija (the Mellieħa side), you will find a series of holes in the ground marked by cairns. There are six rock-cut tombs here, mostly smaller and less regular than the Punic tombs, consisting of a vertical shaft into the rock (occasionally with steps cut for easier access) and one or more kidney-shaped (or lobed) chambers. Tomb 5 (the one nearest the bottom of the slope) is the largest with five lobes and it was the shape of this tomb that prompted archaeologist John Evans, who led excavations here in 1955, to suggest that such tombs may be precursors to the design of the temples. Most of the artefacts found here date from the earliest temple period (Ġgantija phase 3600–3200BC) though some tombs seem to have been re-used in the Bronze Age before being lost to sight for 3,000 years. Take a strong torch if you want to see into the chambers.

There are also some **cart ruts** (see box, page 204) that run along the rock here. Others are (appropriately) covered by Prehistory Street.

Apiary, Punic tomb and megaliths [250 A3] Follow signposts to 'archaeological site' from Triq ir-Ridott on the edge of Xemxija to find this cave with its front covered by a stone wall cut through with a regular grid of arched holes. This is an apiary, claimed to date back to Roman times, but in fact used for beekeeping from early modern times until the 20th century.

If you walk up the steps to the right of the apiary you find yourself on what is dubiously regarded as a Roman path across high rocky scrubland. You will soon see a small sign painted on a cairn pointing right to a Punic tomb and left to 'prehistoric temple'. To the right there is indeed a rock-cut Punic tomb. Walking left, you follow a path through bushes and small trees. There are no further signposts but on your left a few large stones grouped together may once have been part of an apse of a prehistoric temple. There is little left and what remains is difficult to interpret, particularly because bird hunters have built a stone hide in the middle of it.

Heading straight on from the hand-painted sign, the path leads along a rocky ridge with sweeping views. If it's not too hot, this is a very pleasant place for a walk.

IS-SIMAR NATURE RESERVE [250 A4] (BirdLife Malta; ✆21347646; w birdlifemalta. org; ☼ Nov–May 10.00–16.00 Sun or by arrangement with BirdLife Malta) Just outside Xemxija at the head of St Paul's Bay is this tiny bird sanctuary run by BirdLife Malta. Even smaller than their other site at Għadira (Mellieħa Bay), it provides a little patch of wetland, reed bed and trees, where migrating birds can settle in safety and resident birds can breed. No hunting is allowed within 500m of the reserve. There are three hides along a little nature trail and a dedicated staff. Little bittern have nested here; rail, kingfisher and herons (including squacco) and the rare ferruginous duck may be seen; and regular breeding species include reed warbler, coot, moorhen and little salina grebe. To visiting birders these last may not sound very important but to the staff of BirdLife Malta, 'every new species breeding is a triumph' – a triumph of nature over development, modern agriculture and hunting.

ST PAUL'S BAY Confusingly, the narrow strip of buildings between Xemxija and Buġibba is, like the bay it sits on, known as St Paul's Bay, and this is far and away the nicest part of the area. Tarragon restaurant sits on a corner above the little harbour while a couple of hundred metres away is the oldest of the Knights' towers.

Born in 1547, Alof de Wignacourt was a member of the Knights' French *langue*. He enrolled as a knight in Malta in 1566 and was made captain of the new city of Valletta before becoming grand master in 1601. His legacy has been lasting: he built six watchtowers of which four remain; he commissioned the aqueduct that brought water from near Mdina to Valletta (see box, page 226) and still bears his name; he was patron to the painter Caravaggio (see box, page 125); and he expanded the cult of St Paul, particularly surrounding the grotto in Rabat (page 219), where he founded the neighbouring 'College' (for officiating priests) that now houses the Wignacourt Museum. He was also the first head of the Monte di Redenzione degli Schiavi, the foundation that raised money to ransom Christians taken into slavery by the Turks. He died in 1622 following a riding accident while hunting in the grounds of Verdala Palace (today's Buskett Gardens) and is buried in the crypt beneath the main altar of St John's Co-Cathedral in Valletta.

Wignacourt Tower [250 D3] (Din L-Art Ħelwa (Malta's National Trust); \ 21215222, 21225952, 21220358; w dinlarthelwa; ⊕ by volunteers, usually 10.00–13.00 Mon–Sat & 1st Sun of month but call ahead to check; €2 adults, children under 16 & National Trust members free, but donations always welcome for restoration/maintenance) The oldest surviving coastal defence tower in Malta, this was the first of the towers built by Grand Master Alof de Wignacourt (see box above). When it was finished in 1610, this tower was the only defensive outpost in the north. Three decades would pass before it was joined by the Red Tower (page 246).

The Wignacourt Tower was intended to protect the Order of St John's galleys when they were anchored in St Paul's Bay, as well as keeping an eye out for invaders. St Paul's Bay was a known weak point, prone to corsair attack. The tower had two cannons similar to that now displayed on its roof, which commands panoramic views over the bay and St Paul's Island (with the great advantage that Buġibba and Qawra are behind you!). In 1715, the coastal battery with three larger cannons was added.

The first floor (where you would originally have entered) has been restored as closely as possible to how it would have been when the master gunner was in charge here, with fireplace, cooking oven, stone latrine, pikes and muskets, and the original wooden main door. The well could also be accessed from here in case it was not safe to go outside.

BUĠIBBA, QAWRA AND SALINA BAY This is the mass-market tourism centre of Malta: sunnier than Blackpool, but without the sand (or the illuminations) though with much warmer, bluer water. Most of the 'beach' here is rock, though there is a small scruffy manmade patch of sand outside the Dolmen Hotel. There are a couple of paint-peeling lidos, but by far the best swimming here is off the rocks straight into deep water. Two of the rocky 'beaches' have blue-flag status: Qawra Point (near Qawra Tower) and Buġibba Perched Beach, on the main seafront, backed by a long parade of bars, dodgems and McDonald's.

This is the downmarket version of St Julian's. One stretch of waterfront is officially named Bognor Beach and the Bognor Bar offers a pint with a chip butty. I think you get the picture. The **National Aquarium** complex has brought a touch of modern design to the Qawra Waterfront and **Café del Mar** [250 B1] (\ 22588144;

w cafedelmar.com.mt; ⊕ 10.00–late daily) has established itself as quite a trendy place to be. It has a contemporary waterside lido and kids' pool, bar and restaurant while after dark it becomes a nightclub.

The opposite side of Qawra from St Paul's Bay looks over Salina Bay with a large swathe of historic salt pans and, on the far side of the water, a Knights' tower (page 256) and an odd-looking hill. The hill is in fact a vast rubbish dump that can get smelly when the weather is very hot and the wind is in the wrong direction. Efforts are under way to deal with this.

What to see and do

Church of St Paul's Bonfire [250 D3] At the St Paul's Bay end of Buġibba on Triq il-Plajja tal-Bognor (Bognor Beach Road) is St Paul's Church, generally known as the Church of St Paul's Bonfire (San Pawl tal-Ħġejjeġ), built on what is traditionally regarded as the spot where a fire was lit to warm St Paul, St Luke and their companions after they were shipwrecked in the bay in AD60. This is where he is said to have been bitten by a snake while collecting firewood and, showing no ill effects, been revealed as a saintly presence (see box, page 7).

This little church was originally built by Grand Master Wignacourt (replacing an earlier church which stood where the Wignacourt Tower now stands) and linked to St Paul's Grotto in Rabat. A bomb hit the church in 1943 and what you see today is a 1957 reconstruction.

Malta National Aquarium [250 G1] (Triq it-Trunciera, Qawra Point, SPB 1500; ☏ 22588100; w aquarium.com.mt; ⊕ 10.00–18.00 daily, last admission 30mins before closing; €13.90 adults, €11.90 seniors 60+, €7 children 12 & under, under 5s free) The aquarium's 26 display tanks house everything from Mediterranean sealife to tropical fish and small sharks. The largest tank, 12m in diameter, has a walk-through tunnel putting you in the midst of the marine action – including rays and sharks. Sharks can also be seen waiting to hatch. They are part of a conservation project with Sharklab-Malta (page 78). There's a large, airy café overlooking the sea, and outside a children's play area and waterside terrace accessible without charge.

Buġibba Temple [250 F2] (Inner courtyard of Dolmen Hotel; Triq Dolmen, Qawra, SPB 2402) The scant remains of this prehistoric temple have been swallowed up into the gardens of the large Dolmen Hotel but you can wander in and have a look. Incongruous among the sunbeds, the prehistoric stones are not a dolmen but the reconstructed monumental entrance to what was once a Tarxien-phase (3150–2500BC) temple. A few stones also remain from the façade and a couple of apses. Two decorated 'altar blocks' found here, one carved with fish, the other with spirals, are in the National Museum of Archaeology in Valletta. See also pages 4 and 79.

Salt pans [250 G3] Salina Bay's historic salt pans have been cleaned up and restored (though you might not know it from the occasional smell of rotting Neptune grass from a nearby stream). This area was Malta's main centre of salt production, producing at its height some 4,000 tons of coarse salt per year. *Salini* means 'salt' in Maltese, as does *melh* (probably where the name of nearby Mellieħa comes from). You can still see salt being produced in the traditional way in Xwejni Bay, Gozo and small-scale production is just getting going again at Salina too, using the salt-drying barn opposite the visitors' centre.

The salt pans area is also of ecological interest. A Natura 2000 site and SSSI (Site of Special Scientific Interest), it is home to an endemic killyfish (a pre-glacial species) and a favourite spot for wading birds in spring and autumn and a multitude of gulls in winter. The area is due to be handed over to BirdLife Malta to run as a reserve. At time of writing this has yet to happen but the visitors' centre (⊕ usually 09.00–15.00 Mon–Fri) is usually manned by an exceptionally well-informed young warden, Nimrod, a Maltese who has worked for the RSPB in the UK.

Boat trips Sea Adventure Excursions (✆ 27054344; w seaadventureexcursions.com) is an established family business running boat trips to Comino and Gozo, including swimming and snorkelling stops, with a sundeck onboard and a water slide from the boat.

Malta Classic Car Collection [250 F2] (Tourists St, Qawra (near the bus terminus); ✆ 21578885; w classiccarsmalta.com; ⊕ 09.00–18.00 Mon–Fri, 09.00–13.30 Sat; €10 adults, €4.50 children) One man's passion for motors turned into a museum: the display comprises more than 100 cars and motorbikes, from a 1932 Wolseley Hornet to a 2004 Mercedes SL55 AMG. There's also a cinema showing car-related documentaries and movies, plus a large collection of model cars.

Buġibba Boċċi Club [250 E3] (On the promenade next to McDonald's; ✆ 21577362; m 99442919) Boċċi is Malta's traditional game – a bit like boules or pétanque – and this club, unusually, organises games for tourists. Just give them a call or drop by. For more on the game and its rules, see box, page 305 (though note the rules vary from place to place).

BirdPark Malta [250 F4] (Imdawra Rd, SPB 6342, just inland of Salina Bay; m 99868608; w birdparkmalta.com; ⊕ 10.00–17.00 w/ends; €8 adults, €5 children under 13) Bird park full of feathered friends as diverse as owls, flamingos and parrots. Join a guided tour, help with feeding time, or just enjoy a wander around looking at the birds.

Buġibba Water Park [250 F2] (⊕ Jun–Sep 10.00–19.00 daily; free for 20mins) Splashing fun for kids on the waterfront. Some 800m² divided into three zones for children of different heights with a total of 17 water features that spray, drop, blast and squirt.

THE NORTH COAST ROAD

From the edge of Qawra at the head of Salina Bay, the main road runs along the coast as far as the Victoria Lines before turning a little inland en route to St Julian's. Once you leave Qawra behind, it is a scenic route and the only real coast road on Malta. There are sparkling sea views and a series of Knights' towers. You may even spot men bathing with their racehorses in the shallows. Bus 212 travels the length of the coast road.

KNIGHTS' TOWERS (Din L-Art Ħelwa (Malta's National Trust); ✆ 21225222; w dinlarthelwa.org) In 1658–59, Grand Master de Redin (1657–60) built a series of coastal watchtowers and incorporated earlier towers to create a warning system that ran along the coast from Gozo to Valletta. The towers communicated through flag signalling or by lighting warning fires on the roof. The North Coast Road is the perfect place to see how this worked.

The **Qawra Tower** [250 G1] on Qawra Point was built by the grand master before de Redin, Jean Paul de Lascaris Castellar in 1637, and linked into de Redin's coastal communication system when he built the **Ghallis Tower** [map, page 242] (1658–59, restored by Din L-Art Ħelwa, open by appointment) just the other side of Salina Bay. This tower in turn has a clear view of Qrejtan Point on the next bay where stands the **Qalet Marku Tower** or St Mark's Tower [map, page 242] (de Redin, 1658–59) (🕘 by appointment with Din L-Art Ħelwa). Looking along the coast from here, you can see the **Madliena Tower** [map, page 242] (de Redin, 1658–59) near the end of the Victoria Lines.

At this point the road leaves the coast, but the communication line of towers continues with **St George's Tower** (built by de Lascaris) on Paceville's St George's Bay and then **St Julian's Tower** (de Redin). Several of the towers, including Qalet Marku and Madliena, were re-used by the British.

13

Comino

Most people visit Comino (Maltese: Kemmuna) only on day trips and never get further than the Blue Lagoon, Malta's most popular swimming spot. In summer, however, this barren little island – just 2.5km long and with a resident population of just a single family – is a great place to chill out for a few days. Besides simply lazing around, it offers excellent snorkelling and swimming, some watersports (including a small dive centre), a bit of walking and a historic tower and chapel. There is just one hotel (open between April and October), no shops (except the small one in the hotel lobby), no real roads, only a handful of vehicles and a total ban on hunting (which, in such a small place, actually holds), making it a good place for birdwatching.

Malta Tourism Authority information on Comino can be found at w visitmalta. com/en/island-of-comino.

HISTORY

Comino may be named after the spice cumin or from the Arabic for 'sheltered place'. Unlike on Malta and Gozo, there is no evidence here of Neolithic settlement, or indeed of any settlement of any size, until the time of the Knights. Even then, a significant community was maintained only for a few decades. The island quickly reverted to its previous state – a state in which it has since remained: minimally populated except by visitors, whether they be pirates, Turkish raiders, smugglers, hunting Knights or, today, tourists.

In the 13th century, the island had one resident, Spanish Jewish ecstatic Kabbalistic philosopher and self-proclaimed messiah, Abraham ben Samuel Abulafia (1240–91), who spent the last years of his life in exile on Comino writing *The Book of the Sign* (*Sefer ha-Ot*). He had been driven from Italy after trying to convert Pope Nicholas II to his teachings. The Pope's response was, 'burn the fanatic', but it was the Pope who, within hours, died of an apoplectic fit.

Legend has it that Abulafia had one visitor, a Maltese hermit. Stoned out of Malta for trying to impose morality on his neighbours, the pious Kerrew sailed on his mantle over the sea to Comino to chat with Abulafia before continuing his unconventional journey to Gozo where he settled in a cave in Qala.

Through the next couple of centuries the island's caves and coves were the haunt of corsairs, pirates and smugglers – convenient places from which to attack passing sea traffic or make brief forays onto Gozo or northern Malta. There was an attempt in the 15th century to get a watchtower built here, but the money went astray and the project foundered. Even the arrival of the Knights in Malta in 1530 seems to have had little impact on Comino until finally, in 1618, Grand Master Alof de Wignacourt built a system of towers linking Gozo and Malta via Comino. The substantial Comino Tower still stands.

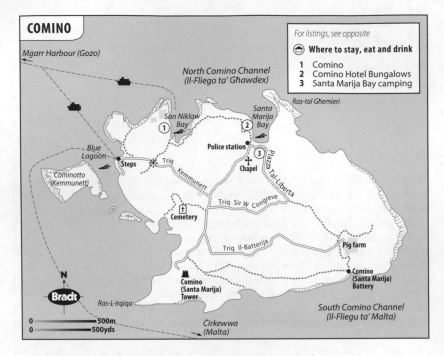

Mġarr Harbour (Gozo)

North Comino Channel
(Il-Fliego ta' Għawdex)

For listings, see opposite

Where to stay, eat and drink
1 Comino
2 Comino Hotel Bungalows
3 Santa Marija Bay camping

Ras-tal Ghemieri

Santa
Marija
Bay

San Niklaw
Bay

Police station

Blue
Lagoon

Cominotto
(Kemmunett)

Steps

Triq

Kemmunett

Chapel

Piazza Tal-Liberta

Triq Sir W Congreve

Cemetery

Triq Il-Batterija

Pig farm

N

Bradt

Ras-L-Irqiqa

Comino
(Santa Marija)
Tower

Comino
(Santa Marija)
Battery

South Comino Channel
(Il-Fliegu ta' Malta)

0   500m
0   500yds

Ċirkewwa
(Malta)

The grand master hoped that incorporating Comino into the defences of Malta and Gozo would encourage people to settle on the island. For a while it did and the population briefly rose to around 200, but by the end of the 17th century Comino was primarily a private playground for the Knights who came here to hunt wild boar and hare. Anyone caught poaching faced up to three years slaving in the order's galleys.

In 1800, after the British had helped the Maltese to chase the French out of Malta and Gozo, Comino was used as a holding camp for some 2,000 French soldiers waiting to be shipped back to France. It became a place of isolation again in World War I when a small quarantine hospital was built next to the tower and in the 1970s when foot and mouth disease hit Malta, a pig farm was opened on Comino to breed disease-free pigs.

GETTING THERE AND AWAY

Comino is reached from Malta by a small **ferry** taking about 25 minutes from Marfa jetty (near Ċirkewwa, opposite the Riviera Hotel). From Gozo, boats to Comino leave from Mġarr Harbour and take 15–20 minutes. You can now generally just turn up and hop on, although booking may be wise at peak times from Malta. In Gozo the boats have got together to allow you to take different companies out and back, providing greater flexibility. Alternatively you can take a day cruise from Ċirkewwa, Sliema or Mellieħa.

You will never have trouble finding a boat to Comino in summer and the tourist cruises are widely advertised. Most boats cater primarily for day trippers and run to the Blue Lagoon, but the Comino Hotel has its own boat which lands at San Niklaw Bay right next to the hotel. Hotel guests take precedence, but there is usually room for other passengers. It is a 10-minute walk between the hotel and the Blue Lagoon.

The ferries (including the hotel boat) almost all charge the same return fares: €10 for adults, €5 children aged five to ten. Under fives are usually free.

🛥 **Comino Ferries Co-op** m 99406529 (Mark), 99474142 (Lorrie), 99835766 (Joe), 99408294 (John); w cominoferries.com. Hourly departures between Ċirkewwa & the Blue Lagoon. Afternoon departures from the Blue Lagoon take you via some of Comino's caves.

🛥 **Comino Hotel Boat** ☎21529821; w cominohotel.com. Runs several times a day from Ċirkewwa & from Mgarr, Gozo.

🛥 **Ebson** m 79065669, 79204014, 79321518; w cominoferryservice.com. Well-established company offering hourly trips from Mġarr Harbour

& from Malta to the Blue Lagoon roughly 08.00–18.00. Extra €5 for cave tour.

🛥 **English Rose Cruises** m 99495842; w englishrosecruises.com; €13 adults, children under 11 half price, under 5s free. Day trips from Mellieħa, Apr–Oct.

🛥 **Sea Adventure Excursions** ☎27054344; w seaadventureexcursions.com. Established family business running boat trips from Buġibba. Boats with sun deck & waterslide. Cave visits usually include Comino day trip €20 adults, €15 children.

WHERE TO STAY, EAT AND DRINK *Map, opposite*

🏠 **Comino Hotel & Bungalows****** (95 rooms & 46 bungalows) San Niklaw Bay; ☎21529821; w cominohotel.com; ☺ Apr –Oct. The hotel is right on the edge of the bay. Small coarse-sand 'private' beach, large outdoor swimming pool & children's paddling pool, sand tennis courts (extra cost). This 1960s hotel is getting a bit tired & is quite basic for its 4-star rating, but it is clean & relaxed & the only hotel on Comino. Most guests are German. HB (with buffet dinner) essential – there is no other source of supper on the island. Lunch is buffet in the restaurant, light meal/snacks from the bar

or room service (not too expensive) or bring your own from Malta/Gozo. Watersports equipment for hire (windsurfing, water skiing, canoes, etc). Bungalows in Santa Marija Bay (10mlns' walk or hotel vehicle) are dbl room & sitting room. Own restaurant with pleasant terrace overlooking Santa Marija Bay & swimming pool. Cheaper if you stay more than 1 night & may cost less through a tour operator. €€

⚑ **Santa Marija Bay camping** There is a small dusty area used for camping next to Santa Marija Beach. No apparent supervision, small toilet block, hotel bungalows & restaurant/café 100m away.

WHAT TO SEE AND DO

BLUE LAGOON In summer (and even in spring and autumn) tourists flock to the Blue Lagoon (Maltese: Bejn il-Kmiemen, 'Between the Cominos'). It's a beautiful stretch of turquoise sea over perfect white sand and snorkel-friendly vegetation between Comino and the tiny islet of Cominotto (Kemmunett). The lagoon is surrounded by handsome **caves** and is genuinely a delightful place to explore. The tiny areas of beach and rocky shore can, however, become absurdly crowded, particularly on the Comino side, from about 10.30 until 16.00/17.00 (later at weekends) in summer. If you are coming on your own boat or intending to stay on the island, get here early or late for a glorious **swim**. Do be aware, though, if swimming at quiet times that, particularly during or after windy or stormy weather (unlikely in summer but very possible in spring and autumn), there can be dangerous currents here. Two British tourists sadly drowned in spring 2015.

There are **loos** and a few **kiosks** selling drinks and snacks, but there is no shade except for the umbrellas, which can be rented (if they haven't been already) and the caves. Be aware that cruise boats may not take you right up to the lagoon area (ask them) and boats that drop you off may leave you a bit stranded if you find you have had enough sun, the weather is bad (northwesterly winds have the most impact), or there are too many jellyfish for swimming. Check that you can get a boat back sooner rather than later should you want to. Some cruise-boat operators (but not ferries) will take you to another bay if the Blue Lagoon is not good for swimming. Most of the time, though, this is Malta's top swimming spot for a reason.

COMINO (SANTA MARIJA) TOWER (St Mary's Tower; maintained by Din L-Art Ħelwa (Malta's National Trust); ☎ 21225952 (or call HQ: 21220358); m 9905186; w dinlarthelwa.org; ⊕ by volunteers, Apr–Oct Tue, Wed, Fri–Sun when the flag is flying; about 20mins' walk from the hotel, 15mins from the Blue Lagoon) The tower has a marvellous dominant position some 80m above sea level with another 8m added by a manmade plinth on which you can walk right round the tower. Built by Grand Master Alof de Wignacourt in 1618, the tower's construction was partly financed by the sale of brushwood from the island. It was part of the Knights' earliest attempt at a national defence system, connecting the Gozo Citadel to Mdina. Being alone on the island, it had to be particularly strong and able to withstand attack for longer than most of the other towers. Its walls are 6m thick and its four corner turrets are topped by a battlement roof. Both the plinth and roof afford panoramic views of the Blue Lagoon, Cominotto, Gozo, northern Malta and Comino itself.

The tower was incorporated into later coastal defences (Lascaris, de Redin, Perellos; page 85) and has a clear line of sight to the Red Tower on Malta (which could send alarm signals all the way along the coast to Valletta), as well as to Fort Chambrai and other parts of Gozo. In 1714, the tower was joined by the battery (see below) built at the other end of the Malta-facing coast. Comino Tower was abandoned by the British in 1829, and the ground floor seems to have been used for animals, but it was brought back into service in World War II and more recently played the part of Château d'If in the 2002 film *The Count of Monte Cristo*.

COMINO (SANTA MARIJA) BATTERY (St Mary's Battery; contact details as for the tower; see above) From the tower you can walk right along the south coast of the island on a dirt track at the top of the cliffs with sea views to one side and open unspoilt garigue on the other. It is a lovely walk and leads directly to St Mary's Battery on the island's western tip. This semicircular gun platform with cannons facing out to sea was built in 1715–16 to defend the Gozo Channel, part of another round of major defensive upgrading (under Grand Master Ramon Perellos y Roccaful). The garrison slept in the blockhouse, which was also the ammunition store. From here you can turn inland, walking past the old pig farm, and carry on across the island to Santa Marija Bay and thence San Niklaw Bay. A full circuit of the island takes about 2 hours.

SANTA MARIJA BAY (ST MARY'S BAY) (10mins' walk from San Niklaw Bay or complimentary hotel transport) The hotel bungalows are to one side of this bay with their own café and outdoor pool. The **beach** here is larger than at San Niklaw and sandy – and it is where Brad Pitt (as Achilles) meets his mum in the 2004 film *Troy*. The sand and sea are, however, quite weedy and there are submerged rocks in the shallows (mind toes and shins). You may prefer to swim off the rocky shore straight into deeper water.

Set back from the beach are a few trees offering rare shade, and a small **camping area**. The pink building is 18th century and is now Comino's diminutive **police station**, manned in summer by two policemen from Gozo – a flag flies when a policeman is on duty. A short way inland is a charming little medieval-style **chapel** with a plain façade topped by bells. There has been a church of some kind on this site since the 12th century – documented by a very early navigational map in the British National Maritime Museum in Greenwich. The present **Chapel of Our Lady's Return from Egypt** was built in the same year as the tower, 1618, and enlarged in 1667 and 1716. Mass is held here – by a priest who visits from Gozo – every weekend in summer.

SAN NIKLAW BAY (ST NICHOLAS BAY) (10mins' walk from the Blue Lagoon) The Comino Hotel fills one side of this bay and its terrace and swimming pool overlook the sea. There are two small patches of coarse-sand beach, technically private to the hotel. The beaches are nothing to write home about, but there can be good snorkelling even just a few metres offshore and there is a buoyed-off swimming area to keep you safe from the small yachts and motorboats that moor in the bay.

DIVING Comino has some dozen dive sites around its coast, including caves, reefs, walls and a couple of wrecks. There is plenty for beginners as well as challenges for the more experienced. The dive centre is next to the hotel but independently run by Diveshack, which also has a centre on the main island. For more on diving, see pages 70 and 89.

Comino Dive Centre via the hotel on 21529821 or directly on 21345671; m 7993483; w divecomino.com. Courses from PADI Bubblemaker (age 8+) to Divemaster & specialist qualifications, as well as accompanied dives from shore & boat, & equipment hire.

BIRDWATCHING Comino, designated a bird reserve, is one of the best places in Malta to birdwatch simply because there is no hunting. This is particularly important in autumn when bird hunting is allowed across most of the rest of the country; Comino is an oasis from which to watch migrating species including passerines, which make landfall here.

In spring, common whitethroats, garden and icterine warblers, spotted and pied flycatchers and woodchat shrike are seen and semi-collared flycatcher, rufous bush robin and barred warbler have also been recorded in recent years. **BirdLife Malta** (21347646; w birdlifemalta.org) runs a ringing station and bird observatory on the island during migration periods. In summer, spectacled warblers can be seen on the garigue, along with short-toed larks, chukars (members of the partridge family), and Malta's national bird, the blue rock thrush.

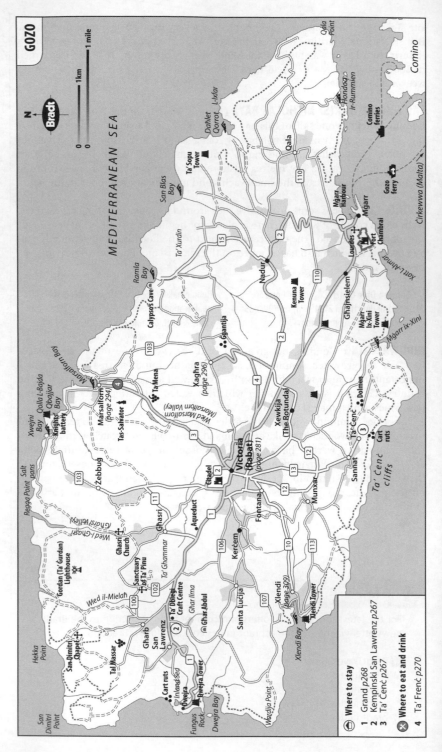

14

Gozo

Arriving in Gozo (Maltese: Għawdex, pronounced *owdesh*), you may find an involuntary sigh passing your lips as you leave the port and head for open country. For all its holiday reputation and patches of beautiful landscape, Malta is a busy place; Gozo is more rural and much more laid-back. Residents say it runs on GMT – Gozo Maybe Time – but in fact timekeeping is not significantly more wayward than on Malta. Gozo just feels so much more relaxed. The two islands may be part of the same country and a mere 6km apart, but their atmospheres are completely different.

The Maltese tell some of the same jokes about the Gozitans that the English tell about the Irish, and traditionally life has been tougher on Gozo. But plenty of Gozitans seem to do very well for themselves on Malta – returning at weekends to their lovely unspoilt island. Some Gozitans go further afield and you will find houses on Gozo called 'God Bless Australia', 'House of Canada' or 'Old Glory USA' – there is even a model kangaroo outside a house near Calypso's Cave – all in gratitude to the nations where the owner earned the money to build or buy the house.

Gozo is only 7km by 14km and has been largely bypassed by the rush to mass tourism that has blighted parts of Malta. There are a few patches of unrestrained building (particularly in Marsalforn) but there is plenty of Gozo that is unspoilt. It is more like Malta was a few decades ago – although the landscape is different. Gozo is made up of small flat-topped hills divided by fertile valleys – green even through most of the summer when Malta goes brown. Wild fennel (with its typical aniseed smell), caper bushes, carob and oleander are common sights along with the omnipresent prickly pear.

Church bells ring out over terraces of hillside agriculture and traditional limestone villages, at whose heart is usually an attractive square (sometimes actually a triangle). The square is dominated by an oversized church, often accompanied by a tiny police station marked with a traditional British blue lantern, a red phone box and sometimes an old-fashioned British red letterbox built into a yellow limestone wall. Many villages have a café and a village shop on or near the square and you may even see an elderly lady sitting on her doorstep making lace.

If you fly over Gozo (which some international flights do) it looks like a cardboard cut-out, so sharply defined are its sheer cliff edges, especially on the northern side. Edward Lear visited the island in 1866 and wrote, 'I drew every bit of it, walking fifteen or twenty miles a day – its coast scenery may truly be called pomskizillious and gromphiberous, being as no other words can describe its magnificence.' He also started a poem, 'Gozo my child is the isle of Calypso', referring to Gozo's identification with Homer's island where the hero of the *Odyssey* spends seven years under the spell of the loving sea nymph (see box, page 7).

Gozo has a couple of beautiful red-sand beaches and a multitude of rocky bays and inlets with inviting clear blue water for swimming and snorkelling, as well as some of Malta's (and even the Mediterranean's) best dive sites. And if the wind blows on one side of the island, ruining the swimming and diving, you can hop the few kilometres to the other – or find an inlet facing the other way – and you will probably find calm, welcoming waters.

There is history here too, of course. One of the oldest temple complexes, Ġgantija (after which the first temple phase is known) sits on a high plateau with commanding views of the Gozo countryside. The Citadel in the capital Rabat (or Victoria) is a mini Mdina, a tiny, impressively walled medieval city, first fortified in the Bronze Age and refortified by every occupier of Gozo since.

HISTORY

Much of Gozo's history is, of course, shared with Malta. Ever since prehistory the two islands have shared one culture. Since medieval times, Gozo has tended to receive less attention than its larger neighbour and so to be less developed. This may have been a disadvantage in times gone by, but in recent decades it is more of a happy escape.

Gozo was less protected than Malta at the time of the Knights and suffered even more from corsair attack. In 1551, the Turks, led by Sinam Pasha and Dragut Reis, captured the Citadel, destroyed much of Rabat and took almost the entire able-bodied population – nearly 5,000 people – into slavery. Some were ransomed or escaped and returned home, but it took over a century for pre-1551 population levels to be recorded again, and Turkish attacks continued until 1708. In the 17th century, the Knights belatedly strengthened the Citadel and built the defensive watchtowers that dot the coast, providing early warning of attack and defence against pirates and smugglers.

Napoleon's troops nonetheless overran Gozo (as they did Malta) in 1798, although once the Maltese rebellion began in Mdina the Gozitans took up the challenge with gusto and got rid of the invaders more quickly than their larger neighbour. The French holed up in Fort Chambrai (above Mġarr Harbour) and the Citadel and were ousted, with help from the British Royal Navy, by October 1798. Gozo then had almost a year as an independent nation until Malta was freed in September 1799. The two islands were reunited under the British (1800–1964).

In World War II when Malta suffered severely under Italian and German bombs, Gozo escaped almost unscathed. The Gozitan role in the war was to share its grain – a little reluctantly – with the larger island, helping to keep the population going during the crucial siege of 1942.

GETTING THERE AND AWAY

Despite being a separate island from Malta, it should take no more than about 3 hours to get from the airport to your accommodation on Gozo – and it can be a pleasant journey.

BY SEA
By ferry The Gozo ferry (Gozo Channel Head Office, Mġarr, Gozo; ☏ 22109000) runs every 45 minutes throughout the day (and less frequently throughout the night) making the crossing in under half an hour from Ċirkewwa in northern Malta to Mġarr in Gozo. You pay only on the leg from Gozo to Malta: €4.65 for adults, €1.15 for children under 12 and €15.70 for a car with driver. Should you find

yourself short of cash, there is an ATM at each side of the Gozo ferry – at Ċirkewwa and in the Mġarr ferry terminal on Gozo.

The ferry can get particularly busy around 09.00–11.00 and between 14.00 and 18.00, and Sunday evenings as people head back to Malta after a weekend in Gozo. There is no booking, so if you have a plane to catch be there early to be sure of getting on.

By boat via Comino See page 59 for details.

GETTING AROUND

You can get to most villages by bus, with services, at least hourly from early morning until well into the evening. A hire car does, however, still offer the greatest flexibility. See also from page 275, for information on cycling, walking and boats.

BY BUS There are buses to most places on Gozo. They tend to be less frequent than on Malta, particularly in winter. Many run once an hour. All the buses start/finish at Victoria/Rabat bus station on Main Gate Street/Triq Putrijal (a few minutes' walk from It-Tokk), with the exception of no. 322 which runs from Marsalforn to Mġarr.

Fares are the same as on Malta: €1.50 for a 2-hour pass in winter, €2 in summer. Purchase 12 2-hour tickets for €15 and a seven-day pass for €21.

Bus routes and timetables are available from the tourist information office in It-Tokk, online (**w** publictransport.com.mt), or by calling ✆ 21222000. There are also two companies running hop-on, hop-off open-topped tour buses that can be an excellent way to get around the island (see below).

CAR HIRE AND TAXIS As in Malta, some companies require you to be aged at least 25 to hire a car and may ask for a medical certificate if you are over 70. Some charge extra for a second driver. Check the insurance policy: the likelihood of having a serious accident here is lower than in Malta, but the chances of getting the car scratched are still relatively high. And make sure you are given a parking clock (page 260).

🚗 **Frank's Garage** ✆ 21556814, 21554591; **m** 99497565; **e** franksgaragegozo@gmail.com; **w** franksgarageltd.com. Taxis & hire cars, self-drive & with driver. They have some good drivers with excellent English & knowledge of the island. Child seats available.

🚗 **Mayjo** [281 E3] Fortunato Mizzi St, Victoria (opposite Arkadia); ✆ 21556678, 21551772; **m** 99802505, 99890600; 2nd branch at Marina St, Marsalforn (Apr–Oct); ✆ 21555650; **e** info@mayjo.com.mt; **w** mayjocarhire.com. Family firm with 40 years' experience. Usually 3-day min hire. Self-drive or with driver & 24hr taxi service.

🚗 **Sixt** [map, page 262] Kempinski Hotel, San Lawrenz (as well as at the airport on Malta); ✆ 27490500; **w** sixt.co.uk/car-hire/malta/gozo/malta-gozo-hotel-kempinski; ⏰ 08.00–noon with 24hr returns & out-of-hours pickup by arrangement (& extra fee).

🚗 **Trac Rental** Triq Patri A Debono, Victoria; ✆ 21563021; **m** 99826339; **w** tracgozo.com; car hire & airport transfers.

🚗 **Xlendi Tourist Services** Rabat Rd, Xlendi Bay; ✆ 21560683; **w** xlendi.com/car-hire-gozo-island. Min age 21. Also rents 50cc & 80cc scooters & baby seats. Book direct or through Europcar (**w** europcar.com).

GOZO TOURS

Bus tours Two companies offer hop-on, hop-off bus tours of Gozo: **City Sightseeing Gozo** (✆ 21569996; **m** 79569996; **w** citysightseeinggozo.com) and **Gozo Sightseeing** (✆ 21694967, 21677197; **w** maltasightseeing.com/bus-tours/gozo-hop-on-hop-off). Both have departures every 45 minutes starting from Mġarr and stopping at key sights including the Citadel, Ġgantija, Dwejra and the bays of Ramla, Marsalforn and Xlendi. Routes are slightly different. An all-day ticket costs €17–18 for adults, €10–11 for children.

Jeep tours If you fancy a private open-air tour, jeep tours cover the island fairly comprehensively. **Gozo Pride** (27 Anton Butigieg St, Qala; ☎27564776; m 99440845; e info@gozopridetours.com; w gozopridetours.com) offers full-day tours for around €60 per person including lunch and pickup from your accommodation.

Segway tours Quiet and solar-powered, these Segways are an eco-friendly way to tour Gozo. **Gozo Segway Tours** (m 99448901, 79778901; w gozosegway.com) offers six routes ranging from 1 hour (€15) to 6 hours (€60 inc lunch) covering some of Gozo's best scenery. Also e-bike tours and rental.

Driving If driving yourself, note that **petrol** is only available in Victoria, Xagħra, Mġarr, Għajnsielem and Xewkija. There is a petrol station just opposite Arkadia shopping centre at the Mġarr end of Victoria's main street. Most pumps are serviced by day and self-serve with €10 notes by night.

The **standard of driving** in Gozo is not dramatically better than in Malta – in that it remains unpredictable – but everything moves more slowly and drivers are generally more considerate, so it is an easier and safer place to drive. Road surfaces vary enormously. The few main roads are excellent but many of the side roads are very pot-holed. In the towns, **parking** is sometimes restricted. It does not cost anything but you need to have a parking clock and stays are limited. The cardboard clocks are available from the Gozo Channel Office at the ferry terminal or from the ADT office at the bus station, and one is usually provided with hire cars. Check local signs for what is allowed and when restrictions apply (usually mornings only), set your clock at your arrival time and do not overstay – the wardens are zealous! Parking in the villages is free and usually easy.

Finding your way Signposting is generally not bad, particularly to the main tourist sites, though it does sometimes peter out prematurely. You can always ask, however; Gozitans are extremely helpful. The answer may not always be as exact as you might wish, and watch the hand movements to confirm left and right. You may need to ask more than once, but you will be treated with patience and generosity and you will get there.

It is useful to have a decent **map**, especially if you are planning to drive yourself around or walk a lot. The free maps available from many tourist locations are good as far as they go but don't have many roads or any paths. Even the more detailed maps do not cover all minor roads and footpaths. For advice on which maps to buy and where to get them, see below and page 43.

TOURIST INFORMATION

Maps and books can be bought in the Agenda Bookshop on the Gozo ferry and at Bookworm [281 C2] (105 Republic St, next to the police station; ☎21556215, 21563328). For more on maps, see page 43.

🛈 **Gozo Tourism Association** 5 Ġorġ Borġ Olivier St (Triq Ġorġ Borġ Olivier), Victoria; ☎27551999, 27565171; w islandofgozo.org, blog. islandofgozo.org (blog offers more in-depth features)

ℹ Malta Tourism Authority [281 B2] It-Tokk, Victoria; w visitmalta.com/en/about-gozo; ☏22915452/3; ⏱ 09.00–17.30 Mon–Sat, 09.00–13.00 Sun & public holidays. The MTA's main Gozo office is in Victoria's main square, known as It-Tokk (officially 17 Independence Sq), next to St James's Church. There is also an MTA booth in the Gozo ferry terminal, Mġarr (☏ 21554538; ⏱ 09.00–14.00 daily). It is just inside the main entrance on the right (much easier to find as you leave than as you arrive!).

ℹ Ministry for Gozo St Francis St, Victoria; ☏ 21561482; w visitgozo.com. An interactive map & lots of online tourist information.

OTHER SOURCES OF INFORMATION
Gozo News w gozonews.com
Gozo Weather Page ⓕ gozoweatherpage
Gozo Weather Station w gozo.ws/forecast.php

⌂ WHERE TO STAY

Gozo has a wide range of accommodation from five-star hotels to bed and breakfasts and everything in between, as well as plenty of self-catering in both village farmhouses and seaside apartment blocks (concentrated in the two resorts of Marsalforn and Xlendi). The hotel star system can sometimes be a little misleading. Designations are rarely changed and Gozo's four stars, for instance, would often be three stars in the UK.

Farmhouses can be a great option, particularly for families, offering space, flexibility, privacy and in many cases your own pool. Most are away from the tourist centres, often in traditional residential village locations, so bear in mind that you may need a car. The word farmhouse has come to mean any stone-built rental house. Some are 400 years old, others closer to four, and there are a number of questions worth asking before booking a farmhouse: What is next door? Any potential noise problems? Does it have air conditioning/central heating? (Many do not.) Are there fans/heaters/large windows? How old is the building? Is it in a complex of rented houses? What are the dimensions of the pool? And of the garden/outside area?

Because Gozo is so small, accommodation is listed altogether here, according to price category. Where listings are mapped, we have included the relevant cross reference.

TOP END
⌂ **Kempinski San Lawrenz******* [map, page 262] (122 rooms) Triq ir-Rokon, San Lawrenz, SLZ 1040; ☏22110000; e reservations. sanlawrenz@kempinski.com, sales.sanlawrenz@kempinski.com; w kempinski-gozo.com. A low-rise hotel on the edge of countryside & a traditional Gozitan village. Set in its own landscaped gardens with outdoor pools (the nicest of which is reserved for people aged 13 & over) & paddling pool. The spa (page 97) has a large indoor pool, wonderfully warm in winter (children 2–13 allowed until 15.00, no children under 2). Also tennis, squash, indoor kids' club, & courtesy bus to the coast & Victoria. Room rates change constantly & winter rates are about half those in summer. €€€
⌂ **Ta' Ċenċ******* [map, page 262] (84 rooms) Sannat, SNT 9049; ☏22191000; w tacenc.com.

In a wonderful location opening onto the Ta' Ċenċ cliffs, this is an attractive hotel that blends into the landscape, with each room opening onto gardens, countryside or courtyards. The 8 corbell-roofed stone *trullos* are particularly fun. The Ta' Ċenċ has delightful gardens, 2 large outdoor swimming pools, a spa with heated indoor/outdoor pool & comfortable communal rooms. Service can be a little mixed. A courtesy bus runs to Victoria & to 'Kantra Beach' – a bar & sunbeds at a rocky inlet off Mġarr ix-Xini with steps into deep clear waters. €€€

MID-RANGE
⌂ **Cesca's** [map, page 309] (18 rooms) 2 Xlendi Rd, Munxar; m 79999984; ⓕ. Boutique hotel overlooking a steep green valley on the road out of Xlendi. Lovely rooftop infinity pool. Rooms with rural views. Restaurant serving b/fast & lunch. Run

by the same family as Ta' Karolina in Xlendi (page 273). €€€

🏠 **Cornucopia Hotel****** [map, page 296] (48 rooms & 11 bungalows) 10 Ġnien Imrik St, Xagħra, XRA 1521; ✆21556486, 21553866. A charming garden courtyard leads into this converted/extended farmhouse (part 18th century). Gardens with palms & flowers, 2 small pools & paddling pool, cosy traditional bar, all staff Gozitan. Pine & tiled rooms are now tired; bungalows across the road are fresher, with great views over valley & own pool. €€

🏠 **Dar Ta' Zeppi B&B** (5 rooms) 28th of April St, Qala (just off main square); ✆21555051; m 99297553 (Tanja), 99845538 (Vince); e info@ dartazeppi.com; w dartazeppi.com. Spacious, relaxed B&B in traditional Gozitan family house, full of cats, books, *objets d'art* & (in school hols) children, run by Belgian Tanja & her Gozitan husband, Vince. Art/craft workshops, yoga/ meditation; kids' art table, terrace & plunge pool. €€

🏠 **Dar Tal-Kaptan** (4 rooms) Lighthouse St, Ghasri; ✆21555647; m 99498095, 99829836; w dartalkaptan.com. Luxury B&B with 4 richly decorated, individually designed suites. Use of kitchen, sitting room, computer, sauna, garden & small pool. Attentive hosts full of local knowledge. Excellent b/fast. Some sexually explicit sculptures. No children. €€

🏠 **Grand Hotel****** [map, page 262] (105 rooms) 58 St Anthony St, Għajnsielem/Mġarr, GSM 9026; ✆21563840; e info@grandhotelmalta. com; w grandhotelmalta.com. Up on the hill overlooking the harbour & ferry terminal (nicer than that sounds). Inviting rooftop swimming pool with a view (no inflatables or balls). Helpful staff. Family rooms sleeping up to 5. €€

🏠 **Hotel Calypso****** [map, page 294] (100 rooms) Marina St, Marsalforn; ✆21562000, 21562012; w hotelcalypsogozo.com. Right on Marsalforn Bay, metres from the beach, bars & restaurants. The large, rather bare roof terrace has a small, shallow pool & rooftop restaurant with good views. Room quality is variable. Some are spacious & clean. Interconnecting family rooms available. Land-view rooms overlook a cul-de-sac so should not be too noisy. €€

🏠 **Quaint Hotels** w quainthotels.com; ✆22108500; e reservations@quainthotels.com. Small chain of little hotels in quaint locations

at the heart of Gozitan villages: **Quaint Nadur** (12 rooms; 13th December St); **Quaint Xewkija** (10 rooms; main village square dominated by the Xewkija Rotunda); **Quaint Sannat** (13 rooms; next to parish church in main village square). Urban minimalist contemporary interiors of concrete grey with splashes of colour & black-&-white photos, some rooms with in-room bath/ jacuzzi. €€

🏠 **Casa Gemelli** [281 C2] (9 rooms) 21 Republic St, Victoria; ✆21559067, 21553630; w tamariagozo.com/accommodations/ casagemelli. Truly Gozitan. Like walking into a houseproud Gozitan's traditional front room. Most rooms have view of the Citadel. Limestone courtyard. Full English b/fast with homemade jams & pancakes. Run by the same family as Maria Giovanna in Marsalforn (see below). No under-18s. €–€€

🏠 **Ferrieha Farmhouse B&B** (4 rooms) Tac-Cawl St, Qala, QLA 1503; ✆21553819; m 99055708; w ferriehafarmhouse.com. Luxury (but unpretentious) B&B run with great care by Swedish couple Eva & Hans. Peaceful roof terrace with good-sized swimming pool & sunbeds. Upper floors have stunning views. Mosquito screens & quality mattresses. €–€€

🏠 **Murella Living** [map, page 294] (24 rooms) Triq il-Forn, Marsalforn; ✆21550340; w murellaliving.com. Imaginative designer B&B just off the waterfront in former summer home of its Gozitan owner. Arty takes on Gozitan life, very comfortable beds & good b/fast on little terrace. 10% discount at Murella restaurant 5mins' walk away & at Jubilee Café & Jubilee Foods in Victoria (same owner). Good value. €

🏠 **San Andrea***** [map, page 309] (28 rooms) Xlendi Promenade, Xlendi, XLN 1302; ✆21565555, 21565400; e info@hotelsandandrea. com; w hotelsandandrea.com. Very pleasant, welcoming little hotel right on the Xlendi Waterfront. 5th-floor lounge with terrace overlooking the bay. Good food. All rooms twin, en suite, with balcony. AC & central heating throughout. €

BUDGET

🏠 **Maria Giovanna Guest House** [map, page 294] (15 rooms) 41 Rabat Rd, Marsalforn; ✆21553630; m 99821790; e info@tamariagozo. com; w tamariagozo.com. Very popular guesthouse set back from the seafront: friendly, basic, clean, traditional communal areas like a Gozo version of a 1950s British B&B – doilies & ornaments. A little dark perhaps (but therefore cooler in summer). 6 superior rooms are spacious & modern. Roof terrace & laundry room.

€–€€ 🏠 **Gallarija House** [281 A2] (3 rooms) 41 Archpriest Saver Cassar St, Victoria; m 99994689; e info@gallarijahouse.com; w gallerijahouse. com. On an atmospheric alley in the heart of Victoria, a couple of mins from the main square, this friendly little 'B&noB' offers excellent-value en-suite rooms in a restored traditional 250-year-old house. €

🏠 **Il-Wileg** (10 rooms) 54 Triq Il-Mithna, Qala; ☎21560750; m 99885482; w ilwileg.com. Colourful rooms in traditional limestone houses with rural village outlook & 2 pools. B&B, but owner is a chef so may be able to negotiate meals, especially if there is a group of you. €

🏠 **Lantern Guesthouse** [map, page 294] (15 rooms) Qbajjar Rd, Marsalforn; ☎21556285. Rooms above a little restaurant just off the waterfront. Sgls, dbls, trpls & quadruples. Book more than 2 nights & they offer a free transfer to/from the ferry. €

🏠 **Mariblu Guesthouse** [map, page 296] (8 rooms) Mġarr Rd, Xewkija; ☎21551315; m 99497757; e info@mariblugozo.com; w mariblugozo.com. Clean, friendly place that smells of home cooking. Cheerful, brightly painted wine bar & restaurant, small swimming pool. Simple rooms with kitchenette, 1 family room, 1 2-bedroom apt. Own transport helpful. €

🏠 **San Antonio Guesthouse** [map, page 309] (13 rooms) Tower St (Triq il-Torre), Xlendi, VCT 115; ☎21563555, 21555587; e cgmail@clubgozo.com. mt; w clubgozo.com.mt. Delightful guesthouse on a quiet residential street about 10mins' walk up the hill from the bay. Comfortable, airy communal rooms, chequered tablecloths in the dining room & a small swimming pool on a peaceful terrace with views over Xlendi Tower & the sea. Simple rooms, nicest upstairs. €

🏠 **Santa Martha Hostel** [map, page 294] (11 rooms) Qolla St, Marsalforn; ☎21551263, 21564868; m 79277022; e saliba.maria@gmail. com; w santamarthahostel.com. A few minutes' walk from the waterfront this very simple but clean & pleasant hostel offers sgl, dbl & trpl rooms

(with other configurations possible). Small shared kitchen. Low prices. €

🏠 **Ulysses Aparthotel** [map, page 309] (14 rooms) Triq il-Gostra (Gostra St), Xlendi, XLN 1404; ☎21551616; e info@mobydivesgozo.com; 📘. Functional clean rooms, studios & 1-bedroom apts above Moby Dives so frequented by divers. A few mins' walk from the waterfront. Rooms with AC & central heating. Wine bar & restaurant. 1 room adapted for wheelchair users. €

SELF-CATERING ACCOMMODATION

Also, **Cornucopia**, **Maria Giovanna** & **Mariblu** all rent out apts & farmhouses (see opposite and this page for their websites and contacts), as does the owner of Il-Wileg restaurant (see left). Farmhouses, villas & apts are also listed by location on the Ministry of Gozo's website (w visitgozo. com) & MTA-approved accommodation is featured on their Gozo website (w visitmalta.com/en/plan-trip-gozo).

🏠 **Baron Holiday Homes** Office at Karlu Galea St, Victoria [281 F3]; ☎21556600; w baronholidayhomes.com. A large selection of good-quality farmhouses across the island, all with pool. Includes some 'exclusive' properties with heated indoor as well as outdoor pool, jacuzzi, PlayStation, full AC & underfloor heating. €€–€€€€

🏠 **Abraham's Farmhouses** [map, page 296] Gajdoru St, Xagħra; ☎21563231; w abrahamgozofarmhouses.com. Farmhouses old & modern with private pools. €€

🏠 **Gozo Village Holidays** (48 maisonettes) ☎21557255/6; w gozovillageholidays.com. Villaġġ Tal-Fanal in Għasri is a pleasant complex of 26 newly built, but traditional-style limestone mini villas (maisonettes) around a landscaped swimming pool in a quiet residential area. Another 22 units share a 2nd pool across the road. Attractively furnished, sleep 2–8, fans (no AC), a heater in winter. Villaġġ Ta-Sbejħa is a similar complex in Għarb & the company also owns apts in Għasri as well as 8 individual houses (sleeping 2–8, own pools) & the Ta' Frenċ restaurant (page 270). €–€€

🏠 **Moby Dick Complex** [map, page 309] (6 apts) Xlendi Waterfront; ☎21561518; e mobydickcomplex@gmail.com; w mobydickxlendi.com. Modern apts above a good, no-frills restaurant overlooking the bay. Clean designer look, AC, fans, lift, backup generator, flat-screen TV. 1–2 bedrooms plus sofa bed & can interconnect 2 apts. €–€€

🏠 **Pergola Farmhouses** [map, page 296] Emerald Pearl Ville, Marsalforn Rd, Xagħra; 📞21557136; 📱 99433442; w pergolafarmhousesgozo.com. Farmhouses with 2–6 bedrooms, country/sea views & own pool. €–€€

🏠 **Unique Gozo Farmhouses** (12 farmhouses plus apts) 'Aldador', Daleland St, Qala; 📞21562957; 📱 99496975, 79562957; w uniquegozofarmhouses.com. Family business renting out farmhouses – old & new, with pools & views – & sea-view apts in Marsalforn. €–€€

🏠 **Bella Vista Farmhouses** [map, page 296] Srug St, Xagħra; 📞21561750; w bellavistafarmhousesgozo.com. A cluster of 21 2-, 3-, & 4-bedroom traditional-style houses

10mins' walk from main square of Xagħra with views, terrace, pool, barbecue & AC. 2-bedroom from €44/night (winter), €80/night (summer). €

🏠 **Gozo Farmhouses** (25 houses) 3 Mġarr Rd, Għajnsielem; 📞21561280/1; w gozofarmhouses.com. One of the first companies to convert traditional village houses into holiday lets. Houses with 1–4 bedrooms, all with washing machine, cable TV, most with pool & barbecue. Also estate agent for similar properties. €

🏠 **Villa Bronja & Villa Xemxija** [map, page 309] (2 + 7 apts) In Xlendi, Bronja: Triq It-Torri (Tower St), Xemxija Triq il Qsajjem & Triq il-Bizantin (cnr Triq il Qsajjem); 📞21551954; 📱 99462897, 79241958; w cometogozo.com. 2 little blocks of great-value apts (sleeping 2–5) just up the hill from the centre of Xlendi. Friendly, helpful owners who live in the top of Villa Bronja. Small rooftop pool at Villa Bronja, ground-level pool at Villa Xemxija. €

✕ WHERE TO EAT AND DRINK

When it comes to eating, Gozo is at least as well provided for in terms of good restaurants as Malta. It has everything from very inexpensive and delicious traditional Gozitan pizza (*ftira*) baked in a wood-fired oven (in Nadur) to some of Malta's top restaurants including excellent mid-priced chef-owned establishments like Beppe's (in Sannat), and not forgetting an old favourite like Ta' Rikardu (in the Victoria Citadel).

Gozo is not a big place, so if you have a car no restaurant is much more than a 20-minute drive away. But in case you are on public transport, don't fancy driving, or just want something close by, the restaurants described below are listed by location. Where listings are mapped, we have included the relevant cross reference.

DWEJRA
✕ **Azure Window Restaurant** Inland Sea, Dwejra; 📞21566560; 📱 79067196; e azurewindow.cassar@gmail.com; 🅵; ⊕ summer 09.30–late, winter: weather- & demand-dependent. Pleasant terrace above the Inland Sea. There are fans in summer, glass surround in winter. Specialises in fresh local fish & the rest of the food tastes very fresh too. Excellent Gozitan pizza & pastas. Families welcome. Can also just stop for a drink. €–€€

GĦAJNSIELEM
✕ **Ta' Philip** 24–26 St Anthony St; 📞21561965; 📱 79001965; w taphilip.com; 🅵; ⊕ 17.30–22.30 Tue–Sat, 17.30–22.00 Sun &

11.30–15.00 Sat & Sun. Seasonal menu of Maltese & Mediterranean food with an emphasis on local ingredients. Wood-burning oven. €€

✕ **Giuseppe's Cafe/Bistro** In the traditional village band club, Our Lady of Loreto Sq; 📞21563592; w giuseppecafebistro.com; 🅵; ⊕10.00–midnight daily. Good-value Mediterranean food (& pizza) in the heart of the village. €

MARSALFORN *Map, page 294, unless otherwise stated*
✕ **Ta' Frenċ** [map, page 262] Off Marsalforn–Victoria road, XRA 9010; 📞21553888; e info@tafrencrestaurant.com; w tafrencrestaurant.com; ⊕ Apr–Dec noon–13.30 & 19.00–21.30

Wed–Mon, Jan–Mar w/ends only (Fri dinner to Sun lunch). Gozo's top 'fine-dining' restaurant. Elegant, atmospheric & with excellent French & Maltese food. Specialists in *flambé* (try the crêpe suzette) & a wine book of 700 wines from 19 countries (€12–2,000+). Enter through the herb garden. The restaurant grows its own or sources locally wherever possible – salt is from Xwejni, honey from next door, quail, rabbit & chicken from down the road. Drink in the converted centuries-old farm building & eat on the covered terrace, or inside decorated with traditional Maltese clocks & modern art. Highchairs available at lunch. Booking advisable. Children's menu of pasta & steak, coeliac & veggie options available & a lunchtime set menu much cheaper than à la carte. €€€€

✗ Arzella   Triq Għar Qawqla or steps from the harbourside; ☎ 21554662; ⓕ; ◷ 11.00–15.00 daily & 18.00–23.00 Sat. Excellent fresh local fish, as well as other Mediterranean food on the Marsalforn seafront at the far end of the row of restaurants on the harbourside. 1st-floor sea-view terrace, open in summer, glassed in winter. €€

✗ Otters Bistro & Lounge   Seafront, St Mary St; ☎ 21556606; ⓕ; ◷ 11.00–23.00 daily for food, may be earlier & later for coffee/drinks. Modern bar-café-restaurant right on the water's edge. Pizza, pasta & fancy mains. €€

✗ Murella   Marina St; ☎ 21562473; m 79208903; ◷ winter 11.00–23.00 daily, summer 09.00–23.00 daily. Large, colourful, relaxed café-restaurant owned by the same people as the Jubilee Cafés. Good for salads & burgers. At the back is the Piano Bar nightclub (◷ winter 21.00–late) & next door is the **Candy Café** (waffles, pancakes) all under the same management. €

MĠARR

✗ Porto Vecchio   Martinu Garces St, Yacht Marina (walk right round the edge of the harbour at sea level until you reach it); ☎ 21563317; m 99444999; e portovecchiogozo@gmail.com; w portovecchiorestaurant.com; ◷ noon–15.00 & 19.00–22.00 Fri–Tue (sometimes also Thu in summer), closed Jan. Not cheap, but with good & interesting food, particularly seafood (fish in limoncello sauce for instance), a smart nautical-themed interior & pleasant terrace on the marina. The Bishop of Gozo wrote in its visitor book that the food was 'fantastically delicious'. €€–€€€

✗ Tmun Mġarr   Martinu Garces St; ☎ 21566276; m 79446832; e info@tmunmgarr. com; w tmunmgarr.com; ◷ noon–14.30 Wed–Mon & 18.30–22.30 daily. Leli Buttigieg has been running restaurants in Gozo for 30 years, always specialising in fresh fish (the roast beef ravioli & homemade ice creams are scrumptious too). Now his son Paolo is executive chef (his other son runs his own excellent restaurant, Patrick's, in Victoria specialising in meat; page 272). Dine outdoors amid the traditional boats pulled out of the water of Mġarr Harbour or in the maritime interior where you can watch the chefs at work in the open kitchen. €€

♀ Gleneagles Bar   Ix-Xatt St, just up from the ferry terminal on the right; ◷ 08.00–midnight. Mġarr's 'local', this is the place for a bottle of Cisk (Maltese lager), a snack & a chat among the fishing kit. €

MĠARR IX-XINI

✗ Mġarr ix-Xini   m 79854007; ◷ Mar–Nov 10.30–17.00 daily, lunch until 16.00, drinks & ice creams continue. Under tamarisk trees & umbrellas at the head of this picturesque rocky inlet, Noel & Sandra serve fresh fish caught by Noel's brothers & other local fishermen, & prepared in the tiny kitchen. Exactly what is on offer & the price depend on the day's catch. Ask Noel what is best today. The small interior is now brightly coloured having been painted by the crew of *By The Sea*, Angelina Jolie & Brad Pitt's 2015 movie in which Mġarr ix-Xini plays 1970s South of France & the restaurant the village shop. A few photos & props remain. For lunch, be sure to book during summer w/ends. This place is a little pricey, but very popular. €€€

NADUR

The last 2 are not strictly places to eat as both are take-aways but they deserve a mention nonetheless.

✗ Osteria Scottaditto   20 Triq Madre Gemma Camilleri; ☎ 27333000; m 77330009; w osteriascottadito.com; ◷ 19.00–23.00 Tue–Sun. Tasty Italian food all cooked fresh to order so can adapt to allergies & preferences (but don't be in too much of a hurry). €€

✗ Fliegu   Mġarr Rd (down the hill from the village, opposite Nadur football pitch); ☎ 21550055; w fliegugozo.com; ◷ noon–15.00

& 18.00–22.00 Wed–Mon. Food with a view. Over 180° panorama of the Gozo Channel (*fliegu* means 'channel'). Good salads & 38 different types of great wood-oven pizzas. Try the Fliegu al Tartufo. Gluten-free pizzas & take-away also available. €

✖ Maxokk Bakery St James St (Church Sq); ✆ 21550014; **w** maxokkbakery.com; ⊕ 10.30–19.00 Mon–Sat, 13.00–19.00 Sun. Small place baking pizza/*ftira* in a wood-burning oven. Far less traditional than nearby Mekren's (see below) and with more conventional 'modern' results. €

✖ Mekren's Bakery Hanaq St (signed to Ramla); ✆ 21552342; **m** 99858249; ⊕ 04.30–19.00 daily. Drop in for real Maltese bread in the morning or phone in your pizza order to collect later. A small, busy & totally traditional bakery making bread, *ftira* (Gozitan pizza) & pizzas. The traditional closed cheese *ftira* is especially delicious & the *ftira* & pizza are huge & cheap. €

QALA

✖ D Bar St Joseph's Sq ✆ 21556242; **f**; ⊕ 18.00–22.30 Tue–Fri, noon–14.30 Sat & Sun. Right on the main square of this attractive village, family-owned D Bar has particularly popular pizza & ribs. Also serves pasta & Maltese specialities. €–€€

☆ Xerri L-Bukkett Zewwieqa Rd; ✆ 21553500; **w** xerril-bukkett.com; ⊕ 11.00–22.00 Wed–Mon (until 23.00 Sat). A lovely place for a drink with fabulous views over the Gozo Channel. It used to be said that this was the place with the best views in Gozo & the worst food, but the food has improved greatly. €

SANNAT

✖ Beppe's Parish Sq (next to Quaint Hotel); ✆ 27500567; **f**; ⊕ 18.30–22.00 daily & noon–14.00 Sun. Probably safe to say this place has the best steaks in Gozo, possibly in Malta. Choose your cut of meat (plenty of choice) & have it cooked in a wood-burning oven in the open kitchen for exceptional flavour. Sauces on offer but you won't need them. €€–€€€

VICTORIA

✖ Patrick's [281 F2] Europe St, VCT 2735; ✆ 21566667; **e** info@patrickstmun.com; **w** patrickstmun.com; ⊕ for food 19.00–21.30 Mon–Thu, 19.00–22.00 Fri & Sat, winter also noon–14.00 Sun (closed Mon), for drinks & cocktails until late. Book, especially at w/ends. Multi-award-winning restaurant with a modern designer interior but relaxed, informal atmosphere. Excellent innovative European food, particularly meat dishes & a wine book of over 200 wines, majoring in Shiraz. Also wines by the glass from a special temperature-controlled unit. All very much the baby of patron Patrick Buttigieg, whose father runs the more traditional, seafood restaurant Tmun Mġarr. Mainly indoor with AC opening to a small roadside terrace. €€€

✖ Brookies [281 A1] 1/2 Wied Sara (Żebbuġ Rd); ✆ 21550924; **m** 77074215; **w** brookiesgozo. com; ⊕ 18.30–22.30 Mon–Sat, noon–14.30 Sun. Good Mediterranean & Maltese food made fresh to order (so be sure not to be in a hurry). Pleasant rural-outlook terrace on edge of Victoria. €–€€

✖ It-Tokk [281 B2] Pjazza Indipendenza (next to the tourist information office); ✆ 21551213; **w** it-tokkrestaurant.com; ⊕ kitchens 10.00–22.00 (sometimes longer depending on demand) Mon–Sat. In one of the oldest buildings outside the Citadel, this unpretentious café-bar-restaurant is right at the centre of things. Sit on the square or escape inside. The covered stone-arched restaurant terrace upstairs (cooled by fans) allows you to enjoy the hustle & bustle of It-Tokk from above at lunchtime or the calm of the city by night. Try the pasta dishes or the It-Tokk pizza with the works. €–€€

✖ Ta' Rikardu [map, page 283] 4 Triq Il Fosos, the Citadel; ✆ 21555953; ⊕ 09.00–18.00+ daily. This is the place for a traditional rural Gozitan lunch. Rikardu not only oversees the cooking of the food, he also produces many of the ingredients. He makes the cheeses himself each morning in his dairy round the corner from the restaurant, using milk from his own sheep & goats. The large Traditional Platter of cheeses, fresh tomatoes, sundried tomatoes, capers, onion & olives (with bread of course) is delicious & big enough to be a starter or a small lunch for 2. Wash down with one of Rikardu's own wines, made from grapes he grows on his own vines. Rikardu's ravioli – filled with his cheese – is the best I know, & he also makes traditional dishes of rabbit & sometimes goat. Rustic interior & roof terrace with panoramic views in the heart of the Gozo Citadel. Not to be missed. €–€€

✖ Green Mood [281 C2] 11A Republic St (next door to Astra Band Club); **m** 99746660; **f**; ◷ 08.30–16.30 Mon–Sat, 09.30–16.30 Sun. This is modern Gozo; a tiny vegan lunch place. Upcycled wood & almost no plastic. Great smoothies & juices (some interesting combos). Pick & mix food: choose your meal then add your own flavours – olive oils (plural), turmeric, chillis, cinnamon, herbs etc. Fun & healthy. €

✖ Tepie's [281 B2] St George Sq; **m** 79208903; **f**; ◷ 08.00–22.00 daily. Sit out on Victoria's 2nd square with a homemade burger, salad or local speciality (rabbit spaghetti?) – or just a coffee. €

☕ Bellusa [281 B2] 34 Independence Sq (It-Tokk); **m** 99407134; **f**; ◷ 07.00–18.00 daily. One of the longest serving cafés in Victoria – the owner has been making coffee here since he was 6. A real local. Ideal for a coffee & *pastizzi* break on Victoria's main square. €

☕ Café Jubilee [281 B2] & [map, page 283] 8 Pjazza Indipendenza; 21558921; **e** info@ cafejubilee.com; **w** cafejubilee.com; ◷ kitchen 08.00–22.30 daily (drinks may be served as late as 02.00 at w/ends). Café-bar with wooden tables, old posters & miscellaneous objects all over the walls. Cosy in winter, AC in summer. Good value. Food from b/fast (full English or filled croissants) to sandwiches, traditional homemade ravioli, soups & pies. They also have a food shop next door selling local foods including souvenir-sized pots. €

XAGĦRA *Map, page 296*
All 3 of these restaurants are on Xagħra's main square in front of the parish church.

✖ D Venue Bar & Restaurant 39 Victory Sq; 21566542; **m** 79557230; **w** dvenuerestaurant. com; ◷ noon–15.00 & 19.00–23.00 Tue–Sun. Traditional stone exterior belies shiny modern interior with red bar & chairs & modern art on the walls. Fri nights in winter are very popular late band nights with live music starting around 22.00. The upstairs restaurant is quieter & has 1 particularly desirable table on the stone balcony overlooking the square. €€

✖ Latini Victory Sq; 21550950; **f**; ◷ 10.00–14.00 & 18.30–22.00 daily. Very popular family-run restaurant serving attractively presented Mediterranean food. Sit inside or out on the square. €€

✖ Oleander Victory Sq; 21557230; **e** oleander@onvol.net; ◷ noon–15.00 & 19.00–22.00 Tue–Sun. The restaurant has a small interior, but it is much nicer outside on Xagħra's main square (with oleander blossom in summer). Mainly Maltese food. €€

XLENDI *Map, page 309*
✲ **✖ Ic-Ċima** St Simon St; 21558407; **m** 99558407, 99877510; **w** cimarestaurant. com; ◷ Easter–Nov noon–14.30 & 18.30–22.30 Wed–Mon, winter w/ends only Fri eve, Sat lunch & eve, Sun lunch. With a lovely roof terrace looking out over the bay, this restaurant is particularly wonderful at sunset in summer, but views are good all day & there is inside space too. Tasty Italian & Maltese dishes artistically presented. €€

✖ Zafiro Xlendi Waterfront, under San Andrea Hotel; 21565555; **m** 79604770; **w** hotelsanandrea.com/zafiro-restaurant; ◷ 08.00–10.00, 11.00–15.00 & 18.00–21.30 daily. Very good Mediterranean & local food including fresh fish, salads & homemade puds. Eat inside or on the waterfront looking out over Xlendi Bay. €€

✲ **✖ Ta' Karolina** Marina St; 21559675; **m** 79564769; **w** karolinarestaurant.com; ◷ noon–15.30 (Tue–Sun) & 18.30 onwards (closing time depends on diners). In the corner of Xlendi Bay, right on the water's edge, Ta' Karolina's tables are next to a tiny sandy beach & mini bay of shallow sea – perfect for young kids to paddle or splash about in while you sit over a good meal. Older children can climb the steps up to a path along the rocks leading to a bay once used by nuns to swim in seclusion. Very good Mediterranean/Maltese food, especially fresh fish. Pizzas too. Friendly, relaxed. Book for a table next to the water. €–€€

ŻEBBUĠ
✖ Francesco's Pizzeria In the village square; 21559568; ◷ evenings 18.00 until he chooses to close Mon–Fri, 11.00 onwards, Sat & Sun lunch & supper. Very simple village pizzeria; great, good-value pizzas & an outdoor terrace. People cross the island for Francesco's pizzas so if you want to eat in at w/ends it's worth booking. Take-away also available. €

SOUVENIRS Souvenirs from Gozo include **lace** – which you may still occasionally see elderly women sitting outside painstakingly making. Handmade lace is usually in small pieces, each slightly different, and expensive (though not if you price it by the hours required to make it!). There is also lots of machine-made lace around (not always labelled as such). One way to be sure you are getting the real thing is to contact Dr Consiglia Azzopardi (↘21553299; m 79270064; e consiglia@malteselace. eu), lace designer and lecturer in lacemaking at the University of Gozo, who heads a co-operative selling real handmade Gozitan lace. Meet her and see the lace by appointment in the village of Sannat. She also runs courses and takes commissions. **Silver filigree** is made on Gozo as on the main island. Traditional silversmiths as well as other craftspeople – including makers of Gozo's highly coloured glass – can often be seen at work at **Ta' Dbiegi Craft Village** [map, page 262] (near the Kempinski Hotel between the villages of San Lawrenz and Għarb). Here a range of crafts are sold alongside standard tourist souvenirs.

For more contemporary Gozitan arts and crafts, pick up a copy of the Victoria **Artisan's Trail** map from one of the participants named here. The map details six artists/craftspeople's studio-shops in the alleys behind Victoria's main square (around St George Sq). Along St George Street, for instance, you will find **Prickly Pear** [281 A3] (m 77156920; w pricklypeargozo.com; 10.00–14.00 Mon–Sat) selling work of local visual artist Bob Cardona and silversmith Rachel Robinson, and **Gallery 9** [281 A3] (**f**; ⊕ usually 09.30–15.30 daily) studio of Italian artist Emanuele Li Pira who produces beautiful and interesting modern prints inspired by Gozo.

Gozitan food is the other main souvenir. Local honey, carob syrup, prickly pear jam, and sea salt from the Gozo salt pans are just a few of the more portable specialities. You can even get Gozitan cheeses shrink-wrapped for travel (though they are often not as good as those not shrink-wrapped). Try **Gozo Traditions** by the Knights' wash house in Fontana, and **Savina** (↘ 21562236; m 79562236; w savina. com.mt), whose products tend to be their own combinations rather than classic versions and are sold at various locations including the international airport (after security) and at their production centre on Xewkija Industrial Estate. Here you can also watch work in progress and taste some of the goodies.

Perhaps most convenient, though, is **Jubilee Foods** [281 B2] (next to Jubilee Café on It-Tokk/Independence Sq, Victoria; ↘ 21558921; w jubileefoods.net), which does helpfully small, packable and inexpensive 100g pots of most of their excellent additive-free products and lets you taste them too.

SUPPLIES If you are staying in self-catering accommodation, there will probably be a village shop nearby and food vans are likely to visit. The following stores in Victoria are nonetheless useful for stocking up.

Arkadia shopping centre [281 E3] Fortunato Mizzi St (extension of Republic St); ↘22103000, 22103221, 22103316; ⊕ 09.00–19.00 (supermarket from 08.00), in winter closes 13.00–16.00. The largest supermarket on Gozo as well as a department store & other retail outlets. Parking outside (free with parking clock).
Bugeja's fish market GSM 9010, on the Mġarr rd in Għajnsielem; ↘21560686; m 99493661. If

you are into fish, this place has the works, from local fish straight out of the sea to all sorts of imports & home-smoked fish.
Jubilee Foods [281 B2] See page 67. For local specialities & their tasty & great-value range of local ready meals. *Lampuki* pie (in season) to chicken & mushroom or broad bean & cheese pies as well as risottos. Packs contain 400g or 1,400g.

OTHER PRACTICALITIES

Wi-Fi is now available in almost all accommodation (usually for free) and in most restaurants and cafés. There are even hotspots on a few waterfronts and street corners.

OUTDOOR ACTIVITIES

Gozo has a lot to offer outdoors – on land and sea. It's worth referring to *Part One* (from page 1) of this guide for more general information, as what follows is specific to Gozo. Excursions company **Gozo Adventures** (m 99994592, 99994689; e info@ gozoadventures.com; w gozoadventures.com), offers a range of activities including sea kayaking, mountain biking, rock climbing and abseiling, snorkelling and hiking. Full days cost €65 (including packed lunch and ferry pickup if necessary), half days €45. They also run an Eco Tour aiming to get you under the skin of Gozo with visits to locals and a 'farm-to-table' experience. A full day costs €75 per person including sit-down traditional Gozitan lunch.

BOAT TRIPS, SAILING AND FISHING Gozo is a great jumping-off point for boat trips, whether to circle the island for impressive views of the sheer cliffs, to swim and snorkel in harder-to-reach bays, to fish, birdwatch or to take a cruise over to Comino with its caves and the Blue Lagoon. A number of other boat companies run to Comino and the Blue Lagoon. See page 258 for details.

⚠ **Hey Lampuki Excursions** m 79253735; f. Sunset cruises & charters for sightseeing, swimming, snorkelling, diving. Licensed for up to 18 guests.

⚠ **Mariblu Excursions** Mġarr Rd, Xewkija (as in Mariblu Guesthouse); ☎ 21551315; m 99497757; e info@mariblugozo.com; w mariblugozo.com/ excursions.html. Wide range of trips & charters including on motor sailing yacht *Barbarossa*, or a standard motorboat. Trips around Gozo, Comino & the Blue Lagoon. Also traditional & game fishing, & combined boat & jeep tours.

⚠ **Sail Gozo** m 79561526; e bob@sailgozo. com; w sailgozo.com. Regular sunset sailing tours to Comino as well as yacht charter.

❋ ⚠ **Xlendi Cruises** 18 Bakery St, Marsalforn (also has a kiosk on Xlendi Bay); ☎ 21559967; m 99478119, 99427917; e info@xlendicruises. com; w xlendicruises.com. This established company runs regular boat trips as well as hiring out boats, self-drive or with a boatman & offering fishing trips. Regular half-day cruises do a full circuit of Gozo or Comino – or a full-day trip goes round both. There are always 2 or more swimming stops (snorkels & masks provided) & optional buffet lunch. Trips leave from Mġarr, but there is free transport from Xlendi & Marsalforn or hotel pickup & return for a small extra fee.

KAYAKING Gozo Adventures ❋ (see above) runs day and half-day kayaking trips to Comino or around the coast of Gozo. A wonderful way to see the coastal landscape from the sea, close-up and at your own speed. And you'll stop for a swim and snorkel too.

WALKING Gozo is a great place for walking, especially around the coast which, after walking it himself, Edward Lear described as 'pomskizillious and gromphiberous'. The ideal time for walking is spring but autumn is good too, as is very early on summer mornings before it gets too hot.

Bear in mind that in autumn, and for a brief period in spring, you may be sharing the countryside, and particularly the coast, with bird hunters (pages 25 and 50), especially first thing in the morning and in the late afternoon/early evening. In summer, the time between sunrise and about 08.30 can be an idyllic time to take a stroll if you can get yourself up that early. It is possible to walk most places on Gozo (despite some dead-end paths that lead only to fields). The views can be spectacular and the shape of the weathered landscape extraordinary.

Great **coastal (or part-coastal)** walks include Mġarr to Mġarr ix-Xini; Mġarr ix-Xini to Ta' Ċenċ cliffs; along the cliffs from Xlendi Tower (potentially all the way to Sannat); out beyond San Dimitri Chapel (page 290); and from Xwejni Bay past the salt pans and on to Żebbuġ or down into Wied il-Għasri or Wied il-Mielah (page 291).

Non-coastal walks include up Għammar Hill (with the Ta' Pinu Stations of the Cross); up Ta' Ġurdan Hill to the lighthouse; Santa Luċija to Dwejra via Għar Abdul (much of this can also be driven); and Santa Luċija out to Wardija Point (where there are coastal views and the option to continue walking to Dwejra).

The tourist board produces nine full-colour booklets, each containing a substantial walk with maps and information about what you will see along the way. These can be picked up free from the tourist office or downloaded from w visitmalta.com/en/walks. A walk making a full circuit of Gozo's coast is detailed by w greatwalksmalta.com which also publishes *Gozo: 10 Great Walks*. You can order the books from the website or download them. A few local companies organise guided walks – try **Gozo Adventures** (page 275) and British walking and cycling holiday specialists **Headwater** (\ 01606 720099 (UK); w headwater.com) offer a one-week self-guided walking holiday in Gozo (Sep–May) including detailed route notes.

CYCLING While I wouldn't advise cycling on Malta, Gozo is different. Traffic is much lighter and slower, and drivers more considerate. Manoeuvres can still be unpredictable, however, roads are narrow and you do need to keep a constant lookout for the many pot-holes.

Neat, pocket-sized book, *Cycle Malta & Gozo* (available from w cyclemaltaandgozo.com) describes three Gozo routes, all starting from the Mġarr ferry (making them easy to do on a day trip from Malta). Kindle book *Cycling Gozo* by Jonathan Henwood and Emmet McMahon offers lots of practical information, as well as mapped cycling routes including a route right round the coast.

For guided mountain biking, contact **Gozo Adventures** (page 275). British holiday operator **Headwater** (\ 01606 720099 (UK); w headwater.com) offers a one-week self-guided cycling tour of Gozo, September to May.

Bikes can be rented from:

&66 **On Two Wheels** [map, page 294] 36 Rabat Rd, Marsalforn; \ 21557104 ; m 79266879; e on2wheels@gozo.com; w on2wheelsgozo.com.

Bikes & motorbikes, delivered anywhere on the island. Mountain bikes cost €12.50 for 1 day or €7/day for 4 days or longer.

DIVING Gozo is one of the most popular places for diving in the Mediterranean and is good for beginners and old hands. It has some 14 dives accessible from the shore – ranging from Dwejra with the famous Blue Hole (caves, drop-offs, boulder slopes and a chimney) to Għasri Cave with its cathedral-like dome – as well as many boat-dives. For a guide to some of the top dive sites, see page 91.

There are more than a dozen legitimate dive companies on Gozo, listed at w visitmalta.com/en/dive-centres. For your own safety, be sure to use one of these. Four of the most established are listed below; for more on diving, see pages 70 and 89.

ᵏᵛ **Atlantis Diving Centre** [map, page 294] Qolla St, Marsalforn; \ 22190000; m 79710390;

e diving@atlantisgozo.com; w atlantisgozo.com. Well-established Gozitan company offering courses in several languages, accompanied dives & equipment hire & sale. Min age 10. Atlantis has its own accommodation close to the centre.

🤿 **Calypso Dive** [map, page 294] (est 1985) Marsalforn Bay seafront; ✆ 21561757; e info@calypsodivers.com; w calypsodivers.com. Calyspo runs courses, summer packages including accommodation & individual dive outings, as well as tailor-made programmes. Proud not to run on Gozo Maybe Time. Min age 12.

🤿 **Moby Dives** [map, page 309] (est more than 10 years) Gosta St, Xlendi Bay; ✆ 21564429, 21551616; m 99499596; e info@mobydivesgozo.com; w mobydivesgozo.com. This is the only centre with a training pool (helpful for beginners, though cold). They run all the PADI courses from

Bubblemaker (children aged 8+) & introductory adult dives in the pool via Open Water Diver to instructor & specialist qualifications. Also accompanied dives, boats & equipment. Their centre, 1 block back from the seafront, has its own accommodation (Ulysses Aparthotel; page 269) & inexpensive AC bar-restaurant, The Captain's Table.

🤿 **St Andrew's Divers Cove** [map, page 309] (est more than 20 years) St Simon St, Xlendi Bay; ✆ 21551301; e standrew@gozodive.com; w gozodive.com. Everything from adult beginner courses (in Xlendi Bay) to specialist qualifications (PADI, BSAC, CMAS), accompanied diving, & equipment hire & boat dives. Accommodation can also be arranged within 2mins of the centre.

SWIMMING AND SNORKELLING Gozo is a wonderful place for swimming and snorkelling with a good choice of bays, large and small, rocky and a few sandy, all with warm clear water. To find out which beach has the best conditions each day, check w whichbeach.com.mt. For more information on swimming and water safety, see pages 49 and 70.

ROCK CLIMBING Climbing is rapidly growing in Gozo which now has about 200 bolted sports routes in Mġarr ix-Xini, Munxar Valley, Xlendi, Wied il-Mielha and Dwejra. For the experienced there are many traditional climbs. The number for beginners is growing. Gozo Adventures (page 275) runs organised climbing trips and works closely with the Gozo Climbing Association (w gozo-climbing.com). See page 74 for more information on climbing.

BIRDWATCHING Gozo has some great places to birdwatch and, just as on Malta, you may have to share them with hunters during autumn migration, and possibly for a brief period in spring too (see page 50 for more information on safety and page 26 for information on hunting).

Ta' Ċenċ is probably Gozo's primary birding site, being high coastal garigue. Other good spots include **Dwejra** (coast, cliffs and garigue); the **Lunzjata Valley** (especially when northwesterly winds blow during migration), though be aware that much of the land here is private; **Xlendi Valley**; the **Citadel** in Victoria (during migration) because it is so high; and **Marsalforn Valley** (especially in migration time with southeasterly winds).

Boat trips are, of course, another way to see birds. The number of birds seen in spring and summer rose in 2009 after two years without spring hunting (since, unfortunately for birders, reopened) and the pallid swift, a newcomer to Malta, colonised several of Gozo's coastal caves. A boat trip is the best way to observe the dramatic sight of Scopoli's shearwaters rafting just off the coast in summer.

For more on birdwatching, see pages 72 and 93, and for the top birding locations, see page 95.

CULTURAL ACTIVITIES

The Ministry for Gozo produces an annual booklet of cultural events from *festas* to opera. It is available free from the tourist office.

ART Quite a few contemporary artists – local, foreign and long-time resident – work on Gozo. One of them, Jörg Bötcher, has turned his traditional Gozitan village home into the vibrant little **Farmhouse Gallery** (page 293). And six Victoria artists-craftspeople have put together an **Artisan's Trail** (page 274).

For those interested in being creative, Hermine Anna Sammut (✎ 21550545; m 79617746; w kreativurlaub-gozo.com) runs art and creativity courses for both adults and children.

PERFORMING ARTS There is just one commercial **cinema** in Gozo, the Citadel by It-Tokk [281 B2] (17 Castle Hill; ✎ 21559955; w citadelcinema.com), but two opera theatres (page 282)! An annual **opera festival** takes place each autumn and the villages make the most of their annual *festa* (page 32).

There are other free music festivals, too. June/July each year sees the **Victoria International Arts Festival** (VIA; w viaf.org.mt) – a month of daily concerts in St George's Basilica – while after Easter is the **Gaulitana Festival** (✎ 21560200; m 99258592; w gaulitanus.com) of concerts in the cathedral.

FOOD AND WINE Gozo has a small but growing number of artisan wineries and some have started to offer visits and tastings. **Tal Massar** winery just outside Għarb [map, page 262] (m 99288730 (Marisa Cauchi); w massarwinery.com) offers an interesting early evening talk beside the vines (while tasting the grapes) followed by an informed but relaxed wine tasting (and drinking) in their permanent gazebo (€25 pp). Alternatively **Ta Mena** [map, page 262] (on the Marsalforn–Victoria road near Ta' Frenċ restaurant, XRA 9010; ✎ 21564939, 21555699; m 99493842, 79555699; e info@tamena-gozo.com; w tamena-gozo.com) arranges tastings of their wine and olive oil as well as tours around the estate. Booking is necessary for all of these.

If you would like to learn about **Gozitan food**, contact Gozo Adventures (page 275) or Rikardu (page 272). **Rikardu** will show you round his small farm, introduce you to his goats and show you how he uses their milk (along with that of his sheep) to make typical Gozitan *gbejna* – cheeses – for his Citadel restaurant.

MĠARR

Almost everyone arriving in Gozo arrives at Mġarr Harbour (pronounced *imjar*, and not to be confused with the inland village of Mġarr on Malta). Now dominated by the modern ferry terminal, you can still see how pretty this village and its natural harbour once were. Traditional fishing boats bob on the water, and the road – edged with small bars and restaurants – sweeps round the bay up to the prominent little church and the Grand Hotel high above the sea. There are several good restaurants here (page 271).

WHAT TO SEE AND DO
Church of Our Lady of Lourdes This small Gothic-style church almost hangs off the edge of the rock above the town. It was built in the 1880s after a traveller commented that the rocks here looked like the grotto of Massabielle in Lourdes where a couple of decades earlier a young girl, Bernadette, had seen visions of Our Lady. This had turned Lourdes into one of the leading destinations for Christian pilgrims, and Gozo's little Lourdes Church, with its fairy-light Madonna, is visited by crowds of Gozitans on 11 February, the date when Bernadette saw her first apparition, with some pilgrims returning on the anniversaries of all 18 visions.

Fort Chambray (or Chambrai) On the sea cliffs above the town is this late attempt by the Knights to build an equivalent of Valletta for the smaller island. The idea had been around a long time but it was left to Jacques François de Chambray (Norman count and Lieutenant General of the Ships in the mid 18th century) to get around to implementing it. The city was intended to better protect the population and the Gozo Channel from invaders. But by the time the fortified walls were actually built and foundations laid in 1760 it was half a century since the last Turkish attack and the people of Gozo saw little point in purchasing plots and building afresh inside the new city walls.

Work stopped in 1788 with just a barracks and possibly a chapel completed. The fort held out briefly against the French invaders in 1798 but soon gave way, and the French were themselves ousted less than a year later.

The British used the fort as a garrison during the Crimean War and World War I and as a military rest home in World War II. It then became Gozo's mental hospital. Today the site is a partially occupied private housing estate. Only the outside can be seen by the public.

GĦAJNSIELEM

Mġarr blurs into Għajnsielem (pronounced *einseelem*) at the top of the hill. *Għajn* means 'spring', so the village name is 'Salem's Spring', 'Salem' being an Arab name, perhaps a landowner in Arab times or a Turkish corsair reputed to have regularly disembarked his galleys to replenish his water supply here.

The area was little occupied in the 16th century – being too close to possible corsair landings at Mġarr. As the threat diminished in the second half of the 17th century, however, a significant settlement grew up around this source of fresh water. The village once had a stone wash house like that in Fontana (page 286), but this was pulled down to make way for today's central square, **Pjazza Tad-Dehra (Apparition Square)**, where a local shepherd is said to have seen a vision of Our Lady, commemorated in a monument erected in the square in the 1990s. His vision resulted in the building of a shrine to Our Lady of Loreto, which soon became a chapel (1810–20) and is now known as the **Old Parish Church**. As the population grew, a larger church was built, the early 20th-century Gothic **Sanctuary of Our Lady of Loreto.**

Just off the main Mġarr–Victoria road is the oldest chapel in Gozo. **St Cecilia's Chapel**, thought to have been built in the 1540s though first documented in 1615, is a simple medieval-style aisleless stone chapel just 7m square. It has been restored and opened to the public by volunteers from Wirt Għawdex (Gozo Heritage NGO; ℡ 21563839; w wirtghawdex.org).

At Christmas Għajnsielem has the greatest nativity scene for many miles around. **Bethlehem f'Għajnsielem** (w ghajnsielem.com/bethlehem/index_frame.html) is a recreation of biblical Bethlehem over 20,000m² on the village outskirts complete with shops, craftsmen (blacksmith, carpenter, etc), houses with families in them, real animals, Roman legionaries, live Mary, Joseph and Baby Jesus and even an inn you can stay at. The spectacle runs from early December with the arrival of the Holy Family by donkey and ends with a re-enactment of the visit of the Magi on Epiphany.

VICTORIA/RABAT

Gozo's capital Rabat was renamed in honour of Britain's Queen Victoria in her Golden Jubilee year, 1887. It has been known by both names ever since, though locals more often refer to it as Rabat – from the Arabic for 'suburb'. The town is the suburb of the medieval walled Citadel (or Citadella or Il-Kastell) that sits on its northern flank. The impressive Citadel is a must-see and Victoria/Rabat is both pleasant to wander around and a good place to stock up on supplies, from food to petrol, a towel to a book. **Shops** are concentrated in the centre around the main square (It-Tokk; see below) and the bus station. There are two **banks** (HSBC and Bank of Valletta), both with ATMs and both on the main street (Republic St), where you will also find two **shopping centres**, Dukes [281 D2] and Arkadia [281 E3].

Victoria's bus station [281 C3] (Triq Putrjal, off Republic St), is Gozo's transport hub. You can get from here to most villages on the island and almost all bus routes come here. The main car park (free and unlimited but sometimes busy) is next to the bus station, although it is also possible to park on the street for shorter periods. You may need a parking clock (page 266).

WHAT TO SEE AND DO
It-Tokk/Independence Square (Pjazza Indipendenza) [281 B2] Rabat

centres on Pjazza Indipendenza, locally known as It-Tokk, meaning 'meeting place' – and it is. There is a market here each morning and open-air cafés in the afternoon – often overlapping. At one end is the semicircular Baroque **Banca Giuratale** [281 B2], built 1773–78 under Grand Master de Vilhena, and the seat of local government. It was designed by de Vilhena's French military engineer Charles François de Mondion, who was also responsible for all this grand master's restructuring of Mdina.

At the other end of the square is **St James's Church** [281 B2], a small recently built church on the site of earlier churches. It apparently took some time for the 20th-century congregation to get planning permission, because of their habit of using the church bells to drown out political speakers in the square!

Next to the church is Gozo's main tourist information office. Along the north side of the square runs the capital's main road, Republic Street. Along the other side spreads a little maze of narrow alleys (some of them medieval) full of small shops and a couple more church squares including St George Square.

St George Square (Pjazza San Ġorġ) [281 B2] This traffic-free square is an

agreeable place to sit for a cold Kinnie and a snack. The square is dominated by **St George's Basilica** [281 B2] (w stgeorge.org.mt), one of Victoria's two parish churches, the other being the cathedral in the Citadel. St George's was built 1672–78, with the façade added in 1818 and the dome, aisle and transepts in the 1930s. It is the most ornate church on the island (and there is plenty of competition), the interior a kaleidoscope of marble, paintings and gilded mouldings. The lavish black and bronze altar canopy is a scaled-down version of Bernini's in St Peter's, Rome. The altarpiece of St George with white charger and felled dragon in the left transept is a 1678 work by Mattia Preti (see box, page 126). The titular statue of St George was carved from a single log of wood in 1838 and was the first such statue in Gozo. It gets its annual outing at the head of the *festa* procession in the third week of July. The church also hosts the Victoria International Festival, a month of concerts in June/July.

Il-Ħaġar (Heart of Gozo) [281 B2] (Pjazza San Ġorġ, VCT 1101, to the left of the

church as you look at the façade; ☏21557504; w heartofgozo.org.mt; ⊕ 09.00–17.30 daily; admission free) This museum and cultural centre contains church treasures from Benedict XVI's *zucchetto* (skullcap) worn at Mass on the day he abdicated to silver, vestments and coins. There are also two interactive video presentations with interesting film introductions to Gozo's various villages and its historical and cultural institutions.

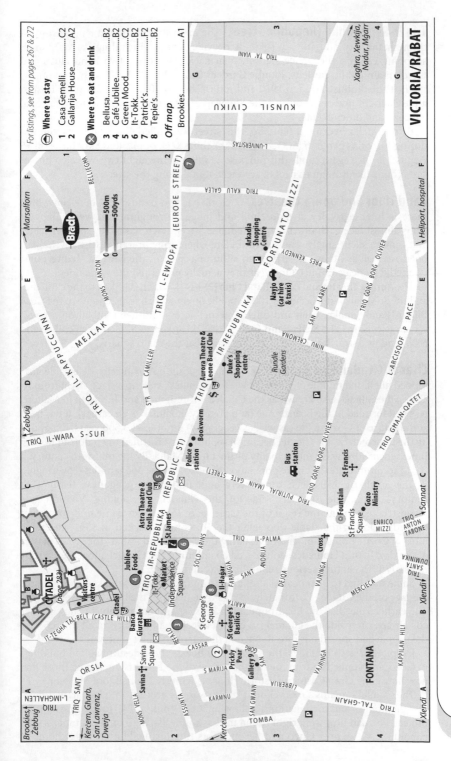

For listings, see from pages 267 & 272

Where to stay

1 Casa Gemelli........................C2
2 Gallarija House....................A2

Where to eat and drink

3 Bellusa................................B2
4 Café Jubilee.........................B2
5 Green Mood.........................C2
6 It-Tokk................................B2
7 Patrick's..............................F2
8 Tepie's................................B2

Off map

Brookies...............................A1

Triq ir-Repubblika (Republic Street) The main street of Rabat runs east–west through the city and into It-Tokk. It provides banks (including ATMs), small shopping centres, the police station, pharmacies, Victoria's two band clubs and Gozo's main public gardens, **Rundle Gardens (Ġnien Rundle)** [281 D3], laid out by the British administration in 1910 and refurbished in 2012. The park plays host to a busy agricultural show during the Sta Marija *festa* (mid-Aug) and to occasional concerts and other events.

Before Malta became a republic, this street was called Racecourse Street and during Victoria's two *festi* (St George's in the third week of July and Sta Marija on 15 August) it once again fulfils this purpose as *sulky*, lightweight two-wheeled horse-carts (quite like Roman chariots), are raced uphill along the street.

Band clubs and opera theatres Victoria has two band clubs, between which there is intense rivalry at *festa* time and indeed throughout the year. The two clubs almost face each other across Republic Street. Each has a bar, snooker tables and – more surprisingly – an opera theatre where they present a (usually Italian) opera, as well as other concerts, each autumn as part of the **Festival Mediterranea** (w mediterranea.com.mt). One year they actually presented the same opera.

The **Aurora Theatre and Leone Band Club** [281 D2], which is linked to the cathedral and the St Marija *festa*, occupies 100 Republic Street, which is also home to the **Gozo Billiards and Snooker Club** and offers internet access and live football on a large-screen television. The **Stella Band Club** [281 C2] (linked to St George's Basilica and *festa*) and its **Astra Theatre** are just up the hill near the main square.

Citadel/Citadella (Il Kastell) ✴ [map, opposite] A naturally defensible flat-topped hill in the middle of Gozo (now a few minutes' walk up a steep street from It-Tokk), the Citadel, also known as the Citadella from Italian and Il Kastell in Maltese, was first fortified in the Bronze Age (and possibly inhabited even earlier). It has been at the centre of Gozitan life (as well as geography) for at least 3,500 years. Expanded by the Phoenicians, the Citadel became a sophisticated fortified town during Roman times when Gozo was a municipality distinct from Malta. By the mid 13th century, it could accommodate the entire population of Gozo – some 366 families – overnight.

The northern walls seen today were built under the Aragonese (early 15th century) while the southern side of the Citadel overlooking Victoria was reconstructed during the reign of the Order of St John. They came to it somewhat belatedly, closing the stable door after the Turks had attacked in 1551, enslaving most of Gozo's population and devastating the Citadel and Rabat. The grand master of the day, Juan d'Homedes, considered abandoning the Citadel altogether, but by the early 17th century serious rebuilding was under way.

Some of it had to be repeated after the earthquake of 1693 wreaked considerable damage on the Citadel. Fortunately, by this time many of the buildings were empty. The earlier rule that the local population must spend each night in the summer corsair season inside the Citadel (in case of attack) had been revoked in 1637 and the people had spread out into Rabat and the surrounding countryside.

Despite these vicissitudes, the Citadel still boasts the oldest inhabited buildings in Gozo, and some date from before the arrival of the Knights, including those that now house the Gran Castello Historic House (formerly the Folklore Museum).

The Citadel remains a marvellous place to wander around with its narrow alleys, historic houses and fortifications. Following a €12 million EU-funded restoration project, you can now walk right round the bastion walls, high on the ramparts with panoramic views over Gozo and beyond. This tiny fortified city is today home to

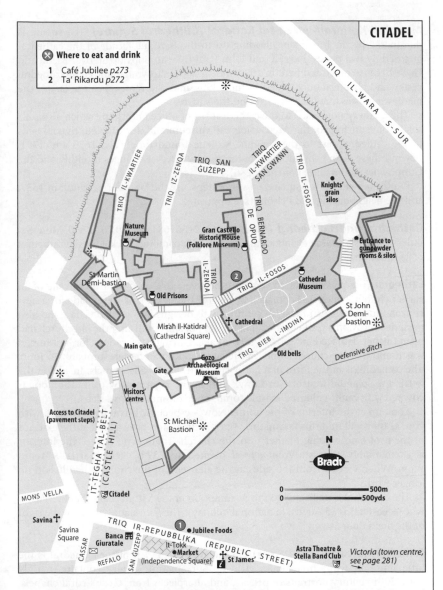

Where to eat and drink
1 Café Jubilee *p273*
2 Ta' Rikardu *p272*

TRIQ IL-WARA S-SUR

TRIQ IL-KWARTIER

TRIQ IZ-ZENQA

TRIQ SAN GUŻEPP

TRIQ IL-KWARTIER SAN GWANN

TRIQ BERNARDO DE OPUO

TRIQ IL-FOSOS

Knights' grain silos

Nature Museum

Gran Castello Historic House (Folklore Museum)

TRIQ IL-ZENQA

Entrance to gunpowder rooms & silos

St Martin Demi-bastion

Old Prisons

TRIQ IL-FOSOS

Cathedral Museum

St John Demi-bastion

Misħa Il-Katidral (Cathedral Square)

† Cathedral

TRIQ BIEB L-IMDINA

Old bells

Defensive ditch

Main gate

Gate

Gozo Archaeological Museum

Visitors' centre

St Michael Bastion

Access to Citadel (pavement steps)

IT-TEGHA TAL-BELT (CASTLE HILL)

N

Bradt

0 — 500m
0 — 500yds

MONS VELLA

🏰 Citadel

Savina †

Savina Square

CASSAR

REFALO

Banca Giuratale

SAN GUŻEPP

TRIQ IR-REPUBBLIKA (REPUBLIC STREET)

It-Tokk Market (Independence Square)

Jubilee Foods

† St James'

Astra Theatre & Stella Band Club

Victoria (town centre, see page 281)

just a handful of residents, five small museums/historic sites and the best traditional Gozitan lunch going (at Ta' Rikardu; page 272).

The Citadel is approached from Rabat via steps along It-Tegha tal-Belt (Castle Hill). The steps are limestone worn smooth by footfall and can be slippery when wet. To the right of the path is the Citadel visitors' centre, opened in 2017 on the site of a 19th-century British reservoir that once provided water for Victoria. Free to enter, it includes information panels and a loud but informative audiovisual presentation. There is a sometimes-functioning lift up to the entrance of the Citadel. Keep walking up the ramped road and you pass an obelisk celebrating the arrival of the first water at the reservoir, brought by an aqueduct, a fraction of which can still be seen on the Victoria–St Lawrence road (page 293).

Misraħ Il-Katidral/Pjazza tal-Katidral (Cathedral Square) The square is dominated by the broad steps leading up to the Baroque façade of the cathedral guarded by two popes: Pius IX and John Paul II (who pops up all over Malta and Gozo because he visited here in 1990 and in 2001). To your right is the cathedral vestry and chapter house added in the 1890s after the removal of the last of the medieval houses that used to surround the square.

The archway now leads to the cathedral ticket office and shop (which also sells some souvenir foods), the Archaeological Museum and, turning left, the old bells of the cathedral cast in the Knights' Valletta foundry between 1639 and 1791. Beyond these is an exhibition of contemporary art that changes monthly and the Gunpowder Room and Silos (page 286).

On the left side of the square, up some steps, are the law courts, rebuilt in 1687, and the neighbouring Old Prisons (see opposite).

Cathedral and Cathedral Museum (🕭 21563684; ⊕ 10.00–17.00 Mon–Sat unless there is a church event taking place; €3.50, combined ticket for the cathedral & its museum)

Cathedral The present church was built between 1697 and 1711 on the site of an earlier church, which was damaged in the 1551 attack. Plans were made for a new church much earlier in the 17th century with designs by Lorenzo Gafà (who also designed the Mdina Cathedral), but work did not start until after the old church had been further damaged in the 1693 earthquake. During preparations for building, it was found that the church stood on the site of a Roman temple, probably to Juno. The cathedral is in the form of a Latin cross with eight side chapels. Inside on the left is the splendid font of Gozo onyx and to the right a copy of it. The floor is covered with multi-coloured marble tombs and commemorative slabs.

Look up at the interior of the dome. Now – especially if you have childen with you, as they will find this fascinating – pop outside and have a look at the exterior of the roof before going further into the church. There is no dome. The interior is a remarkably successful *trompe l'oeil*, painted in 1739 by Sicilian artist Antonio Pippi. When viewed from the sides at the altar end of the church, the illusion no longer works.

The cathedral is dedicated to the Assumption of the Virgin Mary (Santa Marija) whose feast day is 15 August (a national holiday). The *festa* statue stands to the right of the main door as you leave.

Cathedral Museum (Triq il-Fosos) Up the alley to the left of the cathedral is the little museum with three floors. The upstairs picture gallery contains mainly 15th–20th-century portraits of priests, and altarpieces from Gozo's rural chapels. The basement silver vault has an impressive collection of ecclesiastical silver, including the vast *festa* candlesticks and the bishop's silver travelling box containing everything needed to celebrate the liturgy. The main hall is a jumble of all sorts of church objects from the bishop's 150-year-old landau, tapestries, mitres and masonry from the pre-1693 church, to a shoe belonging to Pope Pius VII (1800–23) and Pope John Paul II's hats and gloves.

Citadel museums (Heritage Malta, Gozo; 🕭 21564188; e info@heritagemalta. org; w heritagemalta.org; ⊕ 09.00–17.00 daily, last admission 16.30; joint ticket for the following 4 museums, €5 adult, €3.50 over-60s/students/children aged 12–17, €2.50 children aged 6–11, children under 6 free)

Gozo Archaeological Museum (↘ 21556144) This little museum occupies the 17th-century Casa Bondi (originally home to the Bondi family, whose Lou Bondi now anchors the main evening current affairs programme *Bondi Plus*). Glance up before you enter to see the attractive stone balcony above the door.

The museum houses information and a few items from the Neolithic period, but most of the best finds of this time are at the Ġgantija Temples.

The museum has some interesting Roman objects including a good-quality headless robed statue from around the 1st century AD, 5th-century BC jewellery, pottery from the Roman villa at Ramla Bay (page 302), and a stone olive press, as well as amphorae and a painted clay sarcophagus found in Victoria. A large Roman glass jar with two handles is remarkable for being in one unbroken piece despite dating from the 1st or 2nd century BC, and there is a bizarre sarcophagus found on Comino made of a vertically split amphora.

Near the exit is an intriguing Muslim tombstone of a girl buried between Xewkija and Sannat in 1174 (decades after Count Roger of Normandy took the island into Christian administration). The poetic Kufic inscription is translated into English.

Gran Castello Historic House (Folklore Museum) (Bernardo de Opuo St; ↘ 21562034) A maze of traditional small stone rooms and courtyards with Norman-style windows, this museum is worth a visit for the buildings alone. Originally four stone houses probably built in the very early 16th century before the arrival of the Knights, some rooms have been restored to this period with furnishing reminiscent of the way the place would have looked at a time when the Citadel was still Gozo's main city and night-time home to most of the population. The museum contains objects large and small related to farming, crafts and day-to-day life on Gozo through the ages. Among the collection is an early flour mill that would have been powered by donkey; a wide range of weights and measures; costumes; 'wells' (water tanks) – one of which has a lid that was the base of a Roman column; agricultural equipment; displays on local crafts including lacemaking and weaving, as well as on the cotton industry and fishing. There is a scale model of a traditional boat – an early ancestor of the Gozo ferry – and a room devoted to hunting.

Nature Museum (Triq il-Kwartieri ta' San Martin, behind the Law Courts; ↘ 21556153) In a group of early 17th-century houses, this museum focuses mainly on Gozo's natural resources, although it also includes a tiny piece of moon rock, along with a diminutive Maltese flag that went to the moon with *Apollo 11*. There is a geological map of Malta, fossils, minerals and stuffed birds (with a note deploring the killing of wild species), a few large shells and corals and a display of Maltese fish. There are small collections of Gozo's butterflies, moths and beetles and, in a room devoted to Maltese flora is a specimen of the plant (not actually a fungus) once so sought after on Fungus Rock in Dwejra.

Old Prisons (Cathedral Sq; ↘ 21565988) Built in 1548, these six old prison cells held errant Knights and locals; note the stocks outside! And Knights did err – usually by duelling or fighting. Even the grand master-to-be, Jean Parisot de Valette, was imprisoned on Gozo for four months in 1538 for attacking a layman. Other options for punishment included slaving on the order's galleys or, for lesser crimes, Knights and Malta residents were simply exiled to Gozo!

The six cells are full of graffiti: patterns, crosses and particularly ships. Most are of unknown date, though one is clearly marked 1809. Wrongdoers were sometimes sentenced to hard labour and prisoners from here were used in the 1920s to clear the Ġgantija site – not perhaps the help today's archaeologists would choose. The entrance hall to the museum served as a communal cell in Victorian times and this prison continued to be used into the 20th century.

Gunpowder Magazine, Low Battery and silos (Wirt Għawdex (Gozo Heritage), head office: Dar il-Lunzjata, Wied il-Lunzjata, Rabat, VCT 1680; m 79771981; e info@wirtghawdex.org; w wirtghawdex.org; ⊕ usually 10.30–approx 15.00 Mon–Fri, 11.00–13.30 Sat & Sun but run by volunteers, so may vary & often open less in winter; admission by donation – they need it for further restoration work) The Knights' gunpowder magazine was built here between 1599 and 1603. Until then specialist stores for gunpowder did not exist. It now serves as the starting point for an informal mini tour of a restored corner of the Knights' Citadel, including an unlikely visit to their extraordinary **grain silos**. (You may have seen such silos from the outside at Fort St Elmo and in Floriana.)

There may have been up to 100 such conical silos dug by hand in the Citadel to store the town's precious grain. Here it is possible to actually enter three large ones – about 10m deep. We can get into them because of a tunnel built by the British when they converted the silos into water tanks in 1887. Water was piped in (amazingly, under gravity alone) from Ta' Ċenċ and stored here. The big black valve you can see as you enter was turned to let water in by night, and to let it out to the town by day – an arrangement that continued until a few decades ago.

Next to the silos is a rock-cut corridor with a couple of rooms dug as World War II shelters (perhaps not the best place for them considering the possible effect of a bomb on a vast tank of water!) and a low hole leading to narrow steps. This is the entrance to a secret Knights-period tunnel connecting the Citadel with the town below. Beyond this is the **Low Battery**, a platform jutting out at the eastern corner of the Citadel. It has a stone sentry box and several cannons and overlooks the Citadel ditch and walls.

When you have finished the tour, walk up the steps onto the ramparts above. Here you can see three bumps in the stone floor – the tops of the silos. The plan is to cover these in Perspex to light the silos below and allow people to see in. The ramparts here are also the perfect place to walk along the walls and enjoy the views.

FONTANA A small village on the road to Xlendi that has become a suburb of Victoria, Fontana (meaning 'fountain') is so called because of its natural spring (L-Għajn il-Kbir – the 'Big Spring') that, most unusually in Malta, flows year-round. To make use of the water, the Knights built arched shelters over the spring on each side of the road. The larger **wash house** has two rows of stone basins for washing clothes with stone-carved coats of arms above. A couple of neighbouring buildings have become unobtrusive tourist shops.

KERĊEM AND SANTA LUĊIJA

Kerċem (pronounced *kerchem*) is a quiet village (apart from occasional motorbikes on its fringes) that has become an outer suburb of Victoria. It retains its own central square, however, with a church (late 19th/early 20th century) and well-stocked village shop. The church is the only one in Gozo dedicated to two saints, Pope St Gregory and Our Lady of Perpetual Help, so it has two *festi*: 12 March (St Gregory) and the second Sunday of July.

To the west of Kerċem is **St Luċija** (pronounced *santa loocheeya*), a tiny village of fewer than 400 people with (for once) an equally diminutive, pretty little church which is visited especially by those who have problems with their eyesight. *Festa* is celebrated in mid-December with a festival of light. This is an active village, which also organises other events (**w** santalucija.com; **f**).

From Santa Luċija you can walk through fertile land to **Wardija Point** (taking about an hour) for spectacular views of Dwejra and its famous rock formations. The energetic can continue to walk from here along the coast to Dwejra (approx 1¼hrs).

NEOLITHIC CAVES AND MODERN QUARRIES Beyond St Luċija is an area of fertile countryside that has been occupied since Neolithic times. It is from this area that water was carried along the British aqueduct to quench the thirst of the people of Rabat/Victoria.

From St Luċija follow signs down a drivable track to **Għar Abdul (Abdul Cave)**. When signs change to 'Dwejra & Quarries' stop and you should find to your right a flat-topped hill with a large cave in it. This is Għar Abdul, which was occupied at about the same time as Għar Dalam on Malta – around 5000BC, during the first human settlement of these islands.

You can climb up to the cave (at your own risk), which has clearly not been left unoccupied for the intervening 7,000 years and appears to be used by hunters in the migration season (pages 26 and 50). This is indeed a good spot for **birdwatching** – spectacled warblers and short-toed larks can be seen in summer as well as migratory species in spring (when EU law says there should be no hunting but Malta occasionally allows it for a brief period) and autumn (when hunting is allowed).

It is also possible to climb up onto the top of the hill. There are good views down to Dwejra and over to St Lawrence. Other caves in the area were also occupied in prehistoric times but these have been destroyed by quarrying.

To the left of the road is a large modern **quarry** where you can see how the globigerina limestone that is ubiquitous on the island is cut from the living rock. Little has really changed in thousands of years except that cutting the rock is quicker due to mechanisation and the blocks are more uniform.

From here the road leads into St Lawrence and down to Dwejra.

ST LAWRENCE (SAN LAWRENZ)

A traditional Gozitan village just above Dwejra. Centred on a large square with a domed 19th-century church (*festa* in the first week of Aug), San Lawrenz village square also has a small police station with blue lantern, a red phone box and letterbox, colourful oleander trees, a 'central stores' and a restaurant, not to mention the headquarters of St Lawrence Spurs FC!

A traditional **blacksmith** often works with his door open on Triq San Lawrenz, between the square and the **Kempinski Hotel** (page 267), which sits well disguised on the outskirts of the village 5 minutes' walk from the centre. Just beyond it, on the road towards Għarb, is the Ta' Dbiegi Craft Village.

Outside the heat of a summer day, it is very pleasant to **walk to Dwejra** from here. It can be made into a circular walk down the road (signed from between Church Square and the Kempinski) – about half an hour – and back up over the rocks behind the chapel (about 15mins). Go up the steps behind the chapel. You may pass cart ruts. Keep roughly above the Inland Sea (taking care not to go too close to the edge) until you reach a track. Turn right and you will join a minor road that leads up past a quarry to the village, entering behind and to the side of the church.

TA' DBIEGI CRAFT VILLAGE [map, page 262] (🕐 10.00–17.00 daily, though each studio/shop keeps its own hours so some may be open earlier/later in summer & fewer hours/days in winter) A collection of small buildings where craftspeople make and sell local products including lace; gold and silverwork; stone, onyx and alabaster; woollens and leather; and Gozo glass, which you can watch being blown. This is not a bad place to buy craft souvenirs with prices starting from a few euros.

DWEJRA

Dwejra (pronounced *dwayra*) has become a miniature tourist centre because of its **natural rocky features** and the Inland Sea. Unfortunately, a 2017 spring storm brought down its most famous sight, the Azure Window rock arch, which had become a symbol of Gozo. It had long been assumed that the top of the arch would eventually fall, but in the event the storm swept away the column first before the top piece followed, causing the arch to disappear completely.

Dwejra is, however, still a lovely place to explore, **swim**, **snorkel** and, for the experienced and well equipped, **dive**. It is considered to offer some of the best deep dives in the region, including the Blue Hole, underwater remains of the Azure Window, Fungus Rock and a variety of caves. For exploring the rocks and for swimming it is worth having appropriate footwear as the rock surfaces can be very sharp.

There are a few shack/van cafés and a good new restaurant, the Azure Window (page 270). A tiny **Gozo glass shop** sells local glassware and some other souvenirs, and a few other stalls sell clothes and other items in summer. Dwejra is a particularly pleasant place for a wander in the early evening after the groups and stallholders have gone.

Dwejra is a protected landscape subject to a project by Nature Trust Malta. Their website (w dwejra.org) has lots of information about the area. Dwejra has also been made a Marine Protected Area under a joint project with Sicily, known as PANACEA, and there is a small visitor centre beneath the Azure Window restaurant on the path to the Inland Sea. It has a few interesting displays about Dwejra's underwater landscape, flora and fauna.

FUNGUS ROCK [map, page 262] Just off the coast to the west of here, Fungus Rock is a great solid sentry post to **Dwejra Lagoon**, a lovely place for a deep-water swim or snorkel (especially off a boat). The rock is also called Il-Ġebla tal-Ġeneral, General's Rock, because 'Captain General' of the Knights' galleys was also responsible for coastal defences and hence for this rock. It stands 60m out of the water and is famous for having grown a rare plant, *Cynomorium coccineum* (also known as general's root), which was thought to be a fungus (hence Fungus Rock) but was in fact a parasite on salt-tolerant plants. Its red juice was treasured for its medicinal properties. So sought after was this plant that Grand Master Manoel Pinto de Fonseca (1741–73) found it necessary to smooth the sides of the rock to remove footholds, post a 24-hour guard and threaten unofficial pickers with a spell in the galleys. He also installed a basket on a 50m wire to transport legal pickers more easily.

The plant was presented to the monarchs of Europe as well as being used by the Knights against dysentery, bleeding and impotence. In 1800, the British forbade its collection and it has since been found in other locations around the Mediterranean and Asia as well as on Dingli Cliffs (Malta) and Ta' Ċenċ (Gozo).

INLAND SEA AND CAVES [map, page 262] Walk past the small white 1960s chapel of St Anne (the last rural chapel to be built in Gozo) down a long ramp to the Inland

Sea. This is a calm, shallow patch of clear seawater formed by the collapse of a vast cave. It is a pleasant place to swim, protected from the wind, and you can usually rent a sunbed and umbrella to make the rocky foreshore more comfortable if you want to settle in for a while.

The Inland Sea is connected to the open sea via a tall, narrow, Gothic-cathedral-like cave some 80m long. Local boatmen offer an enjoyable boat trip (€4 pp in boats carrying 6 people; weather permitting) through the cave tunnel and along the sheer cliffs the other side. There are a few caves here, some of which catch the sun in a way that produces luminous blue water and highlights the orange coral on the rocks beneath the surface of the water. The light is usually best in the morning.

CART RUTS [map, page 262] A set of Malta's mysterious cart ruts (see box, page 204) wind 350m down the rock face behind the chapel and the Inland Sea, descending from the top of the rocky hill almost to the cliff edge near the bottom. Some of the track has been weathered away and other parts are too tricky for the untrained eye to identify, but you can certainly find some of the ruts. Walk up the rock-cut path to the right of the chapel (possibly also very ancient and certainly here since the time of the Knights) to the right of the chapel.

At the top of the little flight of rock-cut steps turn 90° to your left and walk straight for about 25m. Here you should find yourself on a pair of cart ruts running away from you. Walk on up until you are close to the sign saying 'Danger: No Stone Throwing' which is close to the edge of the cliff. From here walk approximately 35m inland and uphill to find the clearest ruts in the area. From here, you can follow the ruts (allowing for patches of erosion) up towards the top of the plateau, from where there are also good views.

DWEJRA TOWER/QAWRA TOWER [map, page 262] (Din L-Art Ħelwa; ✆21225952, 21220358; w dinlarthelwa.org; ⊕ by volunteers, usually 09.00–15.00 Mon–Fri, 10.30–15.00 Sun, but you can tell it is open when the flag is flying) Up a short steep track from the Dwejra road is this 1652 coastal watchtower built under Grand Master Lascaris to guard Dwejra Bay from invaders. It was also later used to keep an eye on Fungus Rock and its precious plants.

Restored and run by Din L-Art Ħelwa (Maltese National Trust), steps lead up to the first-floor entrance. The interior has a well and a staircase to the roof, where the small room is a powder store. There are great views from here of the Crocodile Rock (flat in the sea, named for its shape), Fungus Rock and the rest of Dwejra. The bombardier in charge of the tower used to make a little extra income by collecting salt from the salt pans you can see in the rocks below.

The tower was manned until 1873 and used again as an observation post during World War II. From the base of the tower, paths lead off around the cliffs for good **walks** if it isn't too hot. You can walk all the way from here to Wardija Point or more inland to St Luċija, or up to San Lawrenz.

GĦARB

A particularly pretty village of yellow limestone and traditional stone balconies, Għarb (meaning 'west' in Arabic, pronounced *Arb*) is probably one of the oldest villages in Gozo, with evidence of settlement since Neolithic times. It is now home to quite a number of holiday lets (and with no apparent ill effect).

The attractive parish **Church of the Visitation** sits beautifully in the space of the charming central square (actually a triangle) alongside the diminutive police station (with blue lantern outside) and red phone box. The church was built in 1699, 20 years after Għarb became a parish, and was (very loosely) modelled on Francesco Borromini's Baroque church of Sant'Agnese in Piazza Navona in Rome. Its two bell towers each have a clock face. On one are the usual numbers, on the other, the words 'Ibni Għożż iż-Żmien', 'My Son, Value Time'.

The village has a very traditional feel and is famous for its craftspeople – blacksmiths, carpenters, lacemakers, weavers and makers of the Għarb blade (*sikkina ta'l-Għarb*), still considered an excellent knife. So it is an appropriate place for a folklore museum and for the **Ta' Dbiegi Craft Village** (on the road between here and San Lawrenz) selling local crafts including lace and blown glass.

WHAT TO SEE AND DO
Għarb Folklore Museum (99 Church Sq; ☎ 21561929; ⊕ usually 10.00–13.00 daily but phone ahead; €3.50 adults, children under 11 free) In a traditional early 18th-century stone house next to the church, this little museum has 28 small rooms set on two floors around a delightful little courtyard where you can sit and have a cold drink. The rooms are stuffed with objects relating to crafts and day-to-day life in Gozo: tools of the trade of the blacksmith, fisherman, quarryman, stonemason, winemaker, tinsmith, printer, weaver, candlemaker and baker; old water pumps; and small vehicles, including a splendidly painted horse-drawn child's hearse, a sedan chair and a sprinkler cart (for damping dusty roads) with beautifully decorated wheels. On the flat stone roof you can stand behind carvings of St Joseph and two lions and survey the square below.

San Dimitri Chapel [map, page 262] Down a narrow country road north of Għarb is a tiny chapel sitting in the middle of fields. The door is unlocked and you can see through an inner grille. The altarpiece is of St Demetrius riding a white horse. At his feet are a woman praying and a chained man. This painting depicts the legend attached to the chapel: one night, corsairs attacked the village, carrying off a local woman's only son, Matthew. The woman, Zgugina, ran despairing to the chapel to ask St Demetrius for help. She promised that if he intervened, she would keep an oil lamp alight for him at all times. As she wept and prayed, the saint rode out of the picture on his white horse, gave chase to the Turkish galley and returned with Matthew safe in his arms.

The chapel in which she prayed no longer exists. The story continues that it fell into the sea when the cliff under it collapsed in an earthquake. Sailors and fishermen are said to see the light still burning below the water. The present chapel was built in 1736 and a candle always burns in its front hall beneath a copy of a poem about the legend.

The coast beyond Drive or walk on along the rough country road beyond San Dimitri Chapel, then walk down a short track to your left and you come out onto layers of cliffs leading down to the sea, with views over countryside sprinkled with natural megaliths and trappers' huts (page 26). Continue towards the sea and there are some interesting (and attractive) effects of weathering including wave-shaped rocks and mini cliffs worn smooth and bright yellow like weird stone-hard sand dunes. This is a great place for a **walk**.

It is also a good spot for **birdwatching**, especially for short-toed larks and fan-tailed warbler (zitting cisticola) in summer and migratory birds in spring and autumn (though you may have to share the space with hunters – see pages 26 and 50).

Wied il-Mielah [map, page 262] The area north of Gharb has been cleaned up and a new route opened up along an attractive fertile valley to the coast and a formerly hard-to-reach rock window. A leaflet, 'Wied il-Mielah Country Walk' is available from tourist offices and provides a map and information on what you see along the way. The route can also be driven. The road is narrow, but smooth. To reach the start of the new route by road do not go through Gharb (there is a one-way system) but along the side road to the north of Ta' Pinu (this will make sense with the route map).

Sanctuary of Ta' Pinu [map, page 262] (Just outside Gharb; ⚲ 21556187; w tapinu.org; ⊕ 07.00–19.00 Mon–Sat, 06.00–12.15 & 13.30–19.00 Sun) Some 700m out of Gharb towards Victoria stands a substantial church, alone in open countryside. The Sanctuary of Ta' Pinu is Malta's most important pilgrimage site with a remarkable collection of ex-voto offerings, testament to local belief in the intercession of the Madonna Ta' Pinu. Pope John Paul II held Mass on its *parvis* (front terrace) during his visit to Gozo in 1990.

There has been a chapel on this site for centuries. In fact, in 1575, the little church here was so old and derelict it was condemned. The story goes, however, that when

---

EX-VOTO PAINTINGS AND OFFERINGS

There is a long tradition in Malta of ex-voto or votive offerings – paintings, models or objects left in a church requesting, or in thanks for, intercession by the Madonna (or occasionally some other divine figure) on behalf of a devotee in a time of trouble – illness, threat or, most frequently in Malta's history, peril at sea.

The earliest votive offerings here are maritime ex-votos, usually small naive oil paintings (usually less than 50cm across) made either by amateur individuals or specialist painters paid to produce them. The pictures are short on perspective and long on dramatic details of raging seas, figures and their plight. They tend to show a little picture of whichever Madonna has been appealed to (the Madonna comes in many forms in the Catholic Church) and often have the initials 'VFGA', 'Votum Fecit, Gratiam Acceptit' ('Vow Made, Grace Received') or simply 'EV' ('ex-voto', in fulfilment of a vow).

The tradition of ex-votos goes back to well before the arrival of the Knights, although they undoubtedly encouraged such shows of religious devotion and most surviving examples of the art are from post-1530. The oldest ex-voto in Malta with a date on it is a 1631 painting in Żabbar of the mutiny and escape of a group of Christians from slavery on a Tunisian ship.

Ex-votos are not always paintings. Some are small images or models in silver and, as the centuries have passed, real objects (such as crutches and baby clothes) and photographs have become increasingly common. The commissioning of artistic ex-votos came to an end around the middle of the 20th century apparently as a result of a liturgical directive, but the leaving of letters and relevant objects continues.

The best places to see ex-voto offerings include Ta' Pinu, Gozo (particularly modern ones); Żabbar Sanctuary Museum, Malta; Wignacourt Museum, Rabat, Malta; Senglea Parish Church Oratory of Christ the Redeemer; Malta Maritime Museum, Birgu; Sanctuary of Our Lady Tal-Ħerba, Birkirkara; and the Sanctuary of Our Lady of Mellieħa.

Among the votive pictures, letters and objects in the Ta' Pinu Sanctuary is this very modern tribute to Our Lady of Ta' Pinu:

My wife Carmen Gatt is from Victoria, Gozo. When we visited Malta and Gozo in the summer of 2000 we both went to the beautiful church of Ta' Pinu. I was struck by the beauty and story of Ta' Pinu. When I came back to America I put a magnet statue of her in my security office in World Trade Center Two, 30th floor. When the day of September 11 came I know Ta' Pinu was protecting me. I escaped out of the building just in time and she guided me with her voice out of the building. I pray and thank her.

the workman enlisted to demolish it struck the first blow, his arm broke. This was taken as a divine signal and the chapel was saved.

Three centuries later a local farm labourer used to stop to pray in the chapel on her way home to Għarb from the fields. One evening in 1883, Karmela Grima heard a female voice calling her from the chapel. Afraid, she nonetheless went in. Here the 'voice of Our Lady' came again telling her to say three Hail Marys, one for each day the Madonna's body lay in its tomb before her Assumption. The woman did as she was asked, then returned home where she became ill and was unable to return to the chapel for a year. When she recovered, she told a friend what had happened and he said that he too had heard voices there and prayed for his sick mother who was duly cured. Word spread and the chapel rapidly became a centre of pilgrimage and prayers for the sick.

So popular was it that the tiny chapel was overwhelmed and in the 1920s, on land donated by the de Piro family (who own Casa Rocca Piccola in Valletta), a grand neoromanesque church was built (completed 1931) in front of the old chapel, which is still intact behind the present altar. The arched interior is quite splendid. Note that the rosettes at the base of each arch are all different. All the pictures are mosaic or stonework, except the one in the old chapel, the 'miraculous' early 17th-century painting from which the voice is said to have come.

The narrow rooms either side of the altar, leading to the old chapel, are full of ex-voto offerings, from early naive paintings of ships at sea to crutches, children's clothes and photographs. There is even a letter from an American who worked in the Twin Towers (see box above).

Way of the Cross (Stations of the Cross) Opposite the church up Ta' Għammar Hill winds a peaceful Way of the Cross. The first station is by the church, the next 12, marked by life-size 3D white marble tableaux, sit alongside the path. The last station is a stone altar that stands in the middle of a hilltop amphitheatre. The walk is steep and can be a little dusty, but it is quiet even when the church is crowded. Lizards criss-cross your path, butterflies flutter in the bushes and the views from the top are spectacular. You can look across to the Ta' Ġurdan (Gordan) Lighthouse on the next hill (which can also be climbed) and down on everything else. There is a cold Kinnie machine at the bottom!

GĦASRI

Għasri (pronounced *asri*) is the smallest parish in Gozo, though you would not think it by looking at its huge domed church. The traditional church square has this area's usual trio of a little police station with blue lantern, a red British phone booth and an old-fashioned red letterbox in the wall. The church, dedicated to Christ the Saviour, does not look modern but was in fact built in the 20th century.

WHAT TO SEE AND DO

Gordan (Ta' Ġurdan) Lighthouse [map, page 262] On a flat-topped hill above

the village is the Gordan Lighthouse, built in 1853. Standing 180m above sea level, its beam was visible 50km away. You can walk up the hill for 360° views.

Aqueduct [map, page 262] Shortly after turning left onto the main road to Victoria from Għasri, you pass under one of the arches of an aqueduct, more of which can be seen on your right. Built by the British in 1839–43 it brought fresh water from Għar Ilma (between here and Dwejra near Għar Abdul) to the reservoirs in the Rabat/Victoria Citadel.

Għasri Valley (Wied il-Għasri) [map, page 262] A fertile valley runs from the village, between Żebbuġ and Gordan Hill, down to the sea, ending in a narrow inlet flanked by high cliffs. There is a tiny pebbly beach here and the place is popular with **divers** and those looking for a **secluded swim or snorkel** (though it is not as little visited as it used to be). A dirt track runs along the top of the eastern cliff and there is a steep flight of over 100 steps leading down to the 'beach'.

ŻEBBUĠ (NB: There is also a Żebbuġ on Malta; page 193)

Żebbuġ (which means 'olive'; pronounced *zeybooj*) is a traditional little village. It sits high between two valleys with commanding views over the surrounding countryside including the Gordan Lighthouse and Ta' Pinu. The pleasant central square (actually triangular) contains a small police station with an old-fashioned British blue police lantern, a damaged red phone booth and a red letterbox in the wall, as well as the dominating presence of the church. Next to the police station in the building of the traditional band club is the small and unpretentious Francesco's Pizzeria for whose pizzas people cross the island (page 273).

The parish **Church of St Mary**, with its plain façade guarded by two cannons, was built in the 1690s and it has been much embellished since. In fields facing the lighthouse, a deposit of onyx (sometimes called Gozo alabaster) was discovered in the 18th century. The locals kept it quiet until finally in 1980 the farmer sold the field to the diocese, the onyx was quarried and the church was given an onyx makeover. It now has an onyx altar, pulpit and font, as well as onyx chandeliers and even whole confessionals of onyx!

On a side road a couple of hundred metres behind the church is the **Farmhouse Gallery** (21 Skapuccina St; ☏ 21561434; m 99228770; w joergboettcher.com; ⏰ w/ends & when the key is in the lock – just knock & go in). Through the bright blue doors is a rainbow courtyard of brightly coloured paintings and photographs which spread into a smaller second courtyard and the traditional farmhouse home of the artist, Jörg Böttcher. A German resident in Gozo for 20 years, he is very welcoming and happy to chat about the island and his work.

MARSALFORN

Once a peaceful fishing village and quiet summer retreat, this is now Gozo's main resort town (though Gozo's largest is still pretty small). Slapdash, ill-judged development has done it no favours but this remains a popular place to **swim** and

293

hang out in summer and the only place in Gozo where anything much happens after 22.00. There is a small sandy beach (larger than at Xlendi, but shelving more steeply so less good for small children) as well as plenty of rocky and concrete shoreline from which to swim. **Water polo** is played on the western side of the bay.

Several of Gozo's **dive companies** are based here (page 276), including long-established Calypso Dives, and there are several dives in the area. **Xlendi Cruises** has its head office on the seafront at 18 Bakery Street, where you can book cruises and hire boats (page 275).

Marsalforn's church dates back to the 1730s and is dedicated to **St Paul Shipwrecked**. Local tradition has it that although wrecked on the main island, Paul

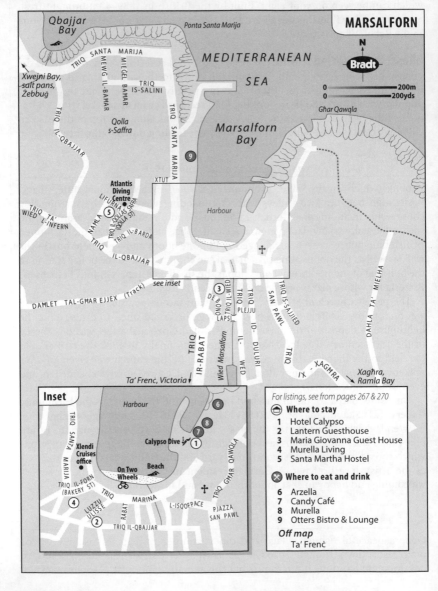

MARSALFORN

For listings, see from pages 267 & 270

Where to stay
1 Hotel Calypso
2 Lantern Guesthouse
3 Maria Giovanna Guest House
4 Murella Living
5 Santa Martha Hostel

Where to eat and drink
6 Arzella
7 Candy Café
8 Murella
9 Otters Bistro & Lounge

Off map
Ta' Frenċ

embarked for his onward voyage to Rome from Marsalforn (why this should be is not related!). The *festa* is celebrated on St Paul's feast day, 10 February.

Just outside Marsalforn on the road to Victoria is **Tas-Salvator** [map, page 262] (Christ the Redeemer). The statue of Christ, arms outstretched, on the peak of the hill is a copy of the statue that overlooks Rio de Janeiro. Also along this road is one of Gozo's (and Malta's) top-flight restaurants, Ta' Frenċ (page 270).

If you leave Marsalforn in the opposite direction and head north and west along the coast, you will find some very interesting coastal scenery.

XWEJNI BAY AND THE SALT PANS [map, page 262] Leaving Marsalforn Bay to the west you come to a small bay and popular summer swimming place, **Qbajjar Bay**, before you reach **Xwejni Bay** (pronounced *Shwaynee*) – which also fills with locals (and a few foreigners) swimming in hot weather. This bay lies next to an extraordinary clay rock formation, **Qolla L-Bajda**, with a cave beneath it and a late Knights-period battery (built in 1715–16) to its seaward side.

On the other side of Xwejni Bay stretch a couple of kilometres of **salt pans** ✳ below interestingly weathered cliffs of globigerina limestone. The salt pans are chequerboards of shallow rectangular pools cut into the rock, some white with dried salt, others dark with water. Seawater collects in them, either through waves in winter or by being deliberately filled, then as the sun shines the water evaporates, leaving the salt crystals, which are collected and stored in the rooms cut into the cliff faces before being sold as Gozo sea salt. Salt has been produced in this way here since Roman times and some of these salt pans certainly go back to the 19th century. They are fun to explore (but please don't tread *in* them or you may contaminate the salt). If you would like to know more about the salt pans contact Josephine Xuereb (☎ 21561184; m 99276948; e xwejnisalt@gmail.com), whose family has worked the salt pans for more than four decades and can usually be found there in summer.

You can **drive or walk** along the coast here all the way to Żebbuġ, although the road gets quite narrow and rough in places as you turn inland towards the village. Or you can keep going along the coast until the road turns to a track (still drivable), which leads you to the head of **Wied il-Għasri** (page 293).

XAGĦRA

Xagħra (pronounced *shara*) means 'wilderness' or 'scrubland'; though the town of this name is anything but. Gozo's largest town outside the capital is a very pleasant place with several visitor attractions. Its fine central square is dominated (of course) by the parish church, the **Basilica of the Nativity of Our Lady**, an early 19th-century building on the site of a much earlier church, with an ornate marble interior. The church is nicknamed Il-Bambina after its 19th-century French white marble statue of the Madonna. Also on the square are a couple of restaurants (page 273), a bank and a couple of petrol pumps.

WHAT TO SEE AND DO
Ġgantija Temples ✳ [map, page 298] (Heritage Malta; ☎ 21553194; e info@ heritagemalta.org; w heritagemalta.org; ⊕ Oct–May 09.00–17.00 daily (last entry 16.30), Jun–Sep 08.00–19.15; €9 adults, €7 over-60s/students/children aged 12–17, €5 children 6–11, children under 6 free; discounted entry after 16.30 in summer €6/4.50/3; ticket inc entry to Ta' Kola Windmill; for an introduction to the temples, see pages 4 & 79) Ġgantija (pronounced *jiganteeya*, meaning 'gigantic' or 'of the giants') is one of the oldest of Malta's extraordinary temple sites, giving its name to

14

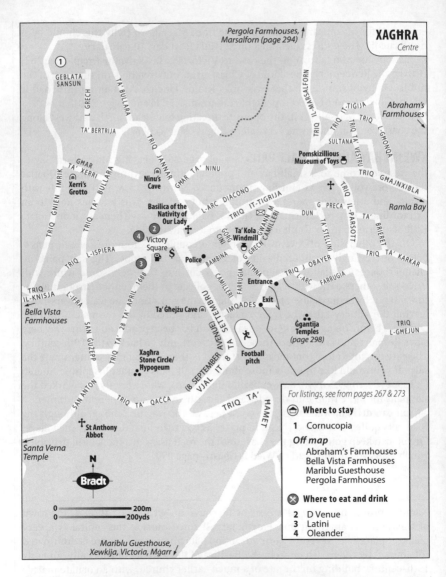

Pergola Farmhouses,
Marsalforn (page 294)

① GEBLATA
SANSUN

L-GREĊ

TA' BULLARA

TA' BERTRIJA

TRIQ JANNAR

GĦAR
TA' XERRI

Xerri's
Grotto

TRIQ GNIEN IMRIK

TRIQ TA' BULLARA

Ninu's
Cave

GĦAR TA' NINU

L-ARĊ DIACONO

Basilica of the
Nativity of
Our Lady

② ④ Victory
Square

③

L-ISPIERA

Police

TRIQ IL-MARSALFORN

TRIQ IT-TIGIJA

TRIQ IT-TIGIJA

TRIQ TA' L-GĦONQA

SULTANA

Pomskizillious
Museum of Toys

TRIQ GĦAJNXIBLA

G. PRECA

DUN

TA' STELLINI

IL-PARSOTT

TA'
BRIERET

TRIQ TA' KARKAR

Ta' Kola
Windmill

GORG CINI

G. GRECH CAMILLERI

GWANN M.

MITHNA

BAMBINA

TRIQ
IL-KNISJA

L-IFRA

TRIQ
IL-KNISJA

SAN GUŻEPP

TRIQ TA' 28 TA' APRIL 1688

Ta' Għejżu Cave

Xagħra
Stone Circle/
Hypogeum

(8 SEPTEMBER AVENUE)

VJAL IT 8 TA' SETTEMBRU

IMQADES

CAMILLERI

IBELLIETI

FARRUGIA

Entrance

Exit

TRIQ J. OBAYER

L-ARĊ FARRUGIA

Football
pitch

Ġgantija
Temples
(page 298)

TRIQ
L-GĦEJUN

Abraham's
Farmhouses

Ramla Bay

SAN ANTON

TRIQ TA' QAĊĊA

St Anthony
Abbot

Santa Verna
Temple

N

Bradt

0 ————— 200m
0 ————— 200yds

TRIQ TA'
HAMET

For listings, see from pages 267 & 273

🛏 **Where to stay**

1 Cornucopia

Off map
Abraham's Farmhouses
Bella Vista Farmhouses
Mariblu Guesthouse
Pergola Farmhouses

✖ **Where to eat and drink**

2 D Venue
3 Latini
4 Oleander

Bella Vista
Farmhouses

Maribu Guesthouse,
Xewkija, Victoria, Mgarr

the first phase of temple building in the 4th millennium BC. First excavated in 1827, two temples stand next to each other surrounded by one massive boundary wall. They also share a broad forecourt with panoramic views. As you stand with your back to the temples you have Xewkija and its Rotunda on your right, Nadur to the left and in between, Nuffara Hill, which was settled in the Bronze Age. The rural area around Ġgantija, Ta' Hamet, is one of the most fertile in Gozo. The farming people who built Ġgantija did not choose this spot for nothing.

The walls here have some of the biggest megaliths found on Malta. The largest are at the back of the temples, including one thought to weigh some 50 tons. Small wonder legend has it that the temples were built by a giantess. She is said to have eaten broad beans that (like Popeye with his spinach) made her so strong that she could carry her baby on one arm and a megalith on the other.

The outside of the temples is built of the darker, rougher and tougher coralline limestone, while decorative parts of the interiors are of the lighter, yellower, smoother but more easily weathered globigerina limestone (the one from which most domestic Maltese architecture is built). This had to be brought from about a kilometre away. No mean feat without machinery of any kind.

Visitor centre and museum You enter the site a little way away from the temples. The visitor centre contains an excellent introduction to the temple people and their culture as well as some of the most important finds from these temples and the surrounding area, which is dotted with (less well-preserved) Neolithic remains. There is an excellent video, the face of a temple woman reconstructed by a forensic scientist and intriguing information about what this community ate and wore and what diseases they suffered from.

The fascinating artefacts are all originals. Don't miss the little shard of pottery with beautiful pictures of birds on it in reception, nor the lifelike human heads carved of globigerina limestone and six amazingly well-preserved stone 'stick' figurines. These last were discovered at the nearby Xagħra Hypogeum, tightly packed together as if they had been in a (long-gone) container. They may have been 'in production' as some appear unfinished. The figures are like large carefully crafted pegs with the bottom end squared off and in two cases decorated like a skirt. The upper halves have heads, faces and, on some, styled hair or a headdress. The bottom half is the right size and shape for holding in your hand, leading to speculation that they may have been carried in some kind of ritual, although so far no others like them have been found. Accompanying them are three smaller models in a similar style, one with a dog-like head and another that might be a crawling baby.

The 'Fat Ladies' typical of the temple period statuary (page 5) are represented here by a beautifully crafted statuette of two 'fat ladies' sitting on a decorated couch. The couch is patterned not only on the top and sides but underneath too. The society that made this must have been quite sophisticated to have furniture, and representations of furniture, like this. Also from this period are two largish chunks of carved stone. One is a temple slab with a weathered snake carved up its side. This was found by the main 'altar' of the larger Ġgantija Temple. The other is a phallic pillar that once stood in the inner left apse of the same temple. Other items include cowry shell jewellery, carvings from cow toe bones and various small 'fat ladies' (some of which may in fact be men).

Passing some interesting information boards about early visitors to Ġgantija and what they saw, you exit the building onto a walkway that passes through a labelled collection of Gozo's native plants, down towards the temples. Your first view of the buildings themselves is from behind and slightly above. You should be able to spot the largest stone, estimated to weigh some 50 tons. Heading past these impressive walls you come to the front of the temples.

South Temple On your left, as you face the remains, is the South Temple. It is the larger and older of the two, having been built in the first half of the 4th millennium BC. If you look carefully at the remains of the façade you can see that it was typically concave. The left side of the façade, with large vertical stones (**orthostats**) topped with horizontal stones, stands over 6m tall, higher than any other surviving temple wall apart from a section of the wall of the inner (second) left apse of this same temple. These megaliths have not been rebuilt or repositioned. They have stood undisturbed at this height for more than 5,500 years. The ugly scaffolding is here to

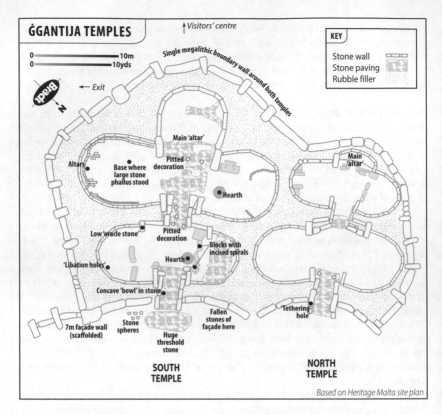

ĠGANTIJA TEMPLES

↑ *Visitors' centre*

KEY
Stone wall
Stone paving
Rubble filler

0 ————— 10m
0 ————— 10yds

Single megalithic boundary wall around both temples

← *Exit*

Bradt

N

Main 'altar'

Altars

Base where
large stone
phallus stood

Pitted
decoration

Hearth

Main
'altar'

Low 'oracle stone'

Pitted
decoration

'Libation holes'

Hearth

Blocks with
incised spirals

Concave 'bowl' in stone

7m façade wall
(scaffolded)

Stone
spheres

Huge
threshold
stone

Fallen
stones of
façade here

Tethering
hole

**SOUTH
TEMPLE**

**NORTH
TEMPLE**

Based on Heritage Malta site plan

ensure that this remains the case! A structural study is under way to assess whether a less intrusive form of support could be employed but it isn't straightforward. To the right of the temple doorway are the remains of the **façade 'bench'** (behind the large fallen stones) and to the left are a few **stone spheres** of the type some experts believe were used to roll the megaliths into place. The **entrance** itself is over a huge threshold stone (now mostly covered by the walkway) and is of the trilithon-within-a-trilithon type (page 80), as is the interior doorway. In the entranceway on the left is a **shallow bowl** (visible beneath the see-through section of walkway) which may have held liquid, perhaps for purification purposes.

At the far end of the entranceway, the upright stones on either side each have four holes in them, possibly for bars that could block the entrance, perhaps draped with an animal skin or other curtain. Inside, the passageway is paved with stone (reddened in places by fire) and the walls would once have been smoothed with plaster painted with red ochre. Bits of this plaster were found in the **first left apse** which has a round window or 'oracle hole' so close to the floor that it has been suggested the stone may have been re-used from a different position. The presence of the painted plaster suggests strongly that at least the main part of the temple was originally roofed; such decoration would not have survived being open to the elements.

In the **first right apse** is a pattern of construction and decoration very similar to that in the first left apse at Tarxien South – showing the close connections between the temple peoples of the two islands. A semicircular 'step' is flanked by two horizontal globigerina blocks decorated with spirals. These are now so weathered that the patterns can only be made out by looking very carefully or when the light is at the right angle, a clear demonstration of why most of the carvings have been taken inside.

You now come to another threshold stone (viewed through the see-through section of the walkway), the front of which has a pitted pattern on it – a common form of temple decoration. This divides the first pair of apses from the inner part of the temple.

Straight ahead of you now, behind the inner entranceway, you can see that the high step to the main central 'altar' is also pitted but less densely. It has been suggested this could be because it is of an earlier date. Here were found the two lifelike stone heads now in the visitor centre.

Above this 'altar', flanked by scaffolding, the stones of the main wall of the temple rise up. Those at the top are quite grey while those below more orangey. The grey parts were exposed before excavation in the 19th century, while the rest lay buried. The wooden walkway turns left here into an apse with a construction of three connected 'altars', originally three trilithons and four uprights. The additional supporting stones in the middle of two of the trilithons are modern additions needed to support the topstones. The snake pillar (now in the visitor centre) was found here, as was the large phallic pillar.

North Temple Sometime around 3000BC, part of the north wall of the South Temple was demolished to make way for a second smaller, simpler temple with four apses and a central niche. The boundary wall probably originally ran just around the South Temple and may have been broken and rebuilt to go around the new building. This would explain the kink that is still visible in the wall where the two temples meet.

The **entrance** to this temple, in a concave façade, has a clear threshold stone and a 'tethering point' hole through the corner of a low stone at the base of the left-hand upright. The **first two apses** are very plain but well preserved and where smaller blocks are seen here they are original, not reconstruction as they often are elsewhere. A step (now beneath the walkway) and inner doorway lead to two more apses and a central 'altar' with a broken topstone.

Xagħra Stone Circle/Hypogeum (Brochtorff/Brocktorff Circle) (Contact Heritage Malta; ☎22954000; w heritagemalta.org (where it is listed as a 'closed site'); ☺ by appointment; €5 adults, €3.50 over-60s/students/children aged 12–17, €2.50 children under 12 plus a significant administrative charge)

Getting there On the road out of Xagħra towards Xewkija/Victoria, past the children's playground, you follow a street to the right, Triq Ta' Qaċċa, signed to St Anthony Abbot. On the right is Razzett Xemxi farmhouse and down its right-hand side is a path. Walk round to the back of the house and turn left across a small field (taking care not to damage crops) and the wire gate of the 'circle' is ahead of you. A member of Heritage Malta staff will unlock the site for you.

Exploring the site 'Circle' is something of a misnomer. There was once a circle of stones here, actually the remains of a low perimeter wall, and it can be seen in an 1820s sketch by Charles Brochtorff, a copy of which is in the Gozo Archaeological Museum. This sketch gives the site its other name, the Brochtorff Circle. The stones were re-used in the building of neighbouring walls and houses later in the 19th century and what you see now is the excavated remains of a hypogeum, an underground burial complex that would once have been a smaller and rougher version of the Ħal Saflieni Hypogeum.

Made by extending natural caves, the Xagħra Hypogeum is of a similar date to Ħal Saflieni (4th and 3rd millennium BC). The site doesn't look like much at first, but look closely and you can spot an 'altar' arrangement in the middle. It was in this area that the remarkable group of 'stick' figurines now in the Gozo Archaeological Museum was found. The delicate double 'fat lady' statue in the museum was also found here. There are a few megaliths, and it is clear that there were once underground 'rooms'. Be aware that some of the stone-coloured lumps on the site are in fact sandbags holding up elements of the structure.

The Xagħra Hypogeum's main contribution to historical knowledge is not in what you can see here but in what was found during the excavations of 1987–94 and the fact that the items were undisturbed and could therefore be dated in a way that was not possible at the Ħal Saflieni Hypogeum. On the other hand, due to the fragile geology of the Xagħra Plateau, the Gozo site itself is in a much poorer state. The lead archaeologist on the excavations here, Prof Caroline Malone, is quoted as saying that while at Ħal Saflieni we have a well-preserved container that has lost most of its contents, at Xagħra most of the container has been lost while much of its contents remains.

Other prehistoric sites in and around Xagħra Although Ġgantija is the only temple on Gozo to have remained at all intact, there were once other temples on the island and there are little clumps of megaliths and individual standing stones, particularly on the Xagħra Plateau around the modern village. There seems to have been an extensive Neolithic settlement here around Ġgantija. Most of the sites are very small, difficult to identify and don't look like much. **Ta' Għejżu Cave** is marked with a sign on a piece of wasteland on the main road into Xagħra (8th September Avenue). It is on your left just after the right turn for Ġgantija. The hole in the ground that is the entrance to the cave is in the middle with a smaller secondary opening at the corner. Ġgantija-phase pottery was found here in 1936 and there was once a megalithic structure above it. The cave lies between Ġgantija and the Xagħra Stone Circle. Even closer to the Xagħra Circle is **Santa Verna Temple** where a fragment of megalithic wall remains in a field. It has recently been excavated by a British–Maltese team. To find it, pass St Anthony Abbot on your left then turn right up cul-de-sac Triq Santa Verna. At the end are a few houses and on your left, a path leading between small agricultural fields. The Neolithic stones are a short way along here to your right.

Ta' Kola Windmill (Contact Heritage Malta; ☏ 21561071; e info@heritagemalta. org; w heritagemalta.org; ⊕ 09.00–17.00 (last admission 16.30); admission with Ġgantija ticket – page 295) Built in 1725, this is one of very few remaining 18th-century windmills. The Knights, conscious of the importance of flour, had a special foundation for the building of windmills, which were then leased to millers. When the wind was strong enough, the miller would sound a *bronja* (a large shell) to let villagers know to bring their grain for milling. This windmill, used until about a century ago, is named after its last miller, Nikola (Kola) Grech. The lower floors are furnished to recreate the miller's spartan living quarters while the upper parts of the mill contain the working parts. Climb the narrowing spiral staircase to the top of the mill to see the mechanism, including the massive millstones. There are good views from the tiny window.

Xerri's Grotto (Triq l'Għar Ta' Xerri (Xerri's Grotto St) (from main square follow Church St which is to the right opposite the church, at crossroads turn right into Bullara St, then 1st left); ☏ 27552733; ⊕ 10.00–18.00 daily; €2.50) Ring the doorbell of this ordinary house near Xagħra's main square and follow the owner through her home and down a narrow stone spiral staircase 10m into the ground to visit the cave beneath. Discovered by the grandfather of the present owner in 1923 when he was digging a well, the Xerri's (pronounced *sherry's*) Grotto now has a little path and electric lights so you can see the stalagmites, stalactites, rock formations and coloured minerals. It isn't large, but it is quite fun. Nearby on Triq Jannar is another house with a cave beneath – **Ninu's Cave** – but this is less attractive.

Pomskizillious Museum of Toys (10 Ġnien Xibla St; ☎ 21562489; w gozotoymuseum.com; ⊕ May–Oct 10.30–13.00 Mon–Sat, Nov & Apr Thu–Sat, Dec, Feb & Mar Sat only, closed Jan; €2.80 adults, €1.50 over-60s, €1.20 children/ students) This tiny museum of 19th- and early 20th-century toys includes 'the world's smallest doll' – just a thumbnail long, made of wood with jointed limbs. There are also several doll's houses, one with wishbone furniture, an attractive Victorian découpage screen and a waxwork of Edward Lear at his desk. Lear visited Gozo in the 1860s and described its landscape as 'pomskizillious'; hence the museum's name.

Chapel of St Anthony Abbot There has been a chapel here since at least 1400 though it was rebuilt in 1601. It served as the first parish church of Xagħra until 1692. The 1816 painting (by Dun Salv Bondi) depicts St Anthony with the people of Xagħra living in tents during the plague of 1814, which killed 104 people and led to items from the church being burnt in an attempt at disinfection.

The chapel had to be extensively repaired after World War II and since 1948 its *festa* on 17 January, being the feast of St Anthony, patron saint of the animal kingdom, has included the blessing of pets and animals. At the end of the usual *festa* procession the priest blesses creatures from cattle to guinea pigs, giving each owner a souvenir picture of St Anthony, a bag of oats and a rusk.

RAMLA BAY ✳

This lovely red sandy bay is arguably Malta's nicest beach and unsurprisingly it's Gozo's most popular. Known locally as Ramla il-Hamra ('the red sandy beach'!), this blue-flag beach gets quite crowded on summer weekends but it is large enough to cope. There is a fairly gentle slope into clear blue water ideal for **swimming**, with rocks at the margins and further out for **snorkelling**. Much of the beach, like many in Malta, has stones at the water's edge so covering for the feet is helpful especially for kids. In summer there is a cleared area without stones and with a lifeguard and flags indicating the state of the water. A red flag (rip currents) or purple (jellyfish) means it is very inadvisable to swim. If these flags show, head for a bay on the other side of the island (eg: Xlendi or Mġarr ix-Xini).

You can **park** on the road leading up to the beach (the earlier you arrive the closer you get!). There is also a **bus** stop and **taxi** stand here. Two outdoor **cafés** (⊕ May–Oct) serve pizzas, snacks, basic meals and ice cream from Portakabins just off the road before the beach.

There is a **manmade reef** just out to sea built by the Knights to block invading fleets. This can be seen as a dark line from the viewing platform of Calypso's Cave. The Knights also drilled out large cone-shaped holes in boulders at either end of the beach to use as makeshift mortars called *fougasses*. The one at the far end of the beach from the road can still be clearly seen – and indeed explored (best done with something on your feet – the rocks are sharp).

The Knights also built a **battery** at the near end of the beach on top of the foundations of a **Roman villa**. The villa was excavated in 1910–12 by Temi Zammit (see box, page 180), revealing a once substantial structure of at least 19 rooms including marble floors and a heated bathing complex. There is nothing to see at the site now, but finds from here can be viewed in the Gozo Archaeological Museum in the Citadel.

The white **statue of the Madonna** that stands in the middle of the beach is an ex-voto offering from three 19th-century fishermen who, caught in a storm, promised to build a shrine if they returned safely to land.

CALYPSO'S CAVE [map, page 262] (Accessed by road from Xagħra (well signed) or on foot from Ramla Beach; admission free) High above Ramla Bay is 'Calypso's Cave'. Callimachus (310/5–240BC), Hellenistic writer-critic and librarian at Alexandria, identified Gozo as Homer's island of Ogygia where Odysseus (Ulysses) washed up on his way home from the Trojan War and spent seven years under the spell of the sea nymph Calypso. The Gozitans have taken up this identification with enthusiasm. Whether or not this cave has anything to do with the *Odyssey*, evidence has been found of Bronze Age occupation and it is worth a visit for the views. The cave has now collapsed so you can't go in but you can still stand on the viewing platform looking down over the sweep of Ramla Bay with the white Madonna shining against the red sand and the dark line of the Knights' defensive reef running through the blue sea.

NADUR

Sitting high on a rocky plateau, Nadur is appropriately named from the Maltese word *nadar* – 'to keep watch'. The Belvedere offers panoramic views over the countryside, Mġarr, the Gozo Channel, Comino and northern Malta. There are also swings-with-a-view – several pieces of children's play equipment along the promenade. The vast parish **Church of St Peter and St Paul**, with two cannons and two saints guarding its ornate marble-filled interior, was begun in 1760 though its aisle and façade are early 20th century. The *festa* is around 20 June. The church sits in a large traditional village square with its miniature police station (with blue lantern) and British red telephone box, as well as cafés, shops and an ATM, and around the corner, a small maritime museum. There is a second, smaller square behind the church which is home to the Quaint Hotel (page 268). Farmhouses are available to rent in the village and it is also home to two of Gozo's traditional bakeries.

WHAT TO SEE AND DO
Kelinu Grima Maritime Museum (Parish Priest St (Triq Il-Kapillan); ☏ 21551649; e jimmyxerri@tiscali.it; ⊕ usually in summer 10.00–14.00 Mon–Fri but may vary; in winter phone first; €2 adults, €1 children) One man's collection of maritime memorabilia gathered over 65 years. The collection was donated to the parish priest in 1999 and turned into a small museum. Among many photographs and model ships is a shoulder strap that belonged to Lord Mountbatten (worn in Malta in 1949), a 1942 letter from Churchill commending the bravery of one Joseph Grima, a small block of wood from HMS *Victory*, an 1803 letter ordering the burning of USS *Philadelphia* which had been taken by *The Pasha of Tripoli*, pictures of the Gozo ferry from when it was a wooden sailing boat to today, and an old canvas diving suit with lead boots.

Kenuna Tower and botanical garden [map, page 262] On the edge of town is a little botanical garden, recently created around the renovated Kenuna Tower. The tower was built by the British in 1848 when the telegraph arrived on the islands. This spot had long been used by the Knights to burn bonfires for communication with Comino and Malta and, after years of neglect, the tower is once again being used for communications and is topped with a metal triangle of ultra-modern equipment. As you might expect, the views from here are fabulous: Mġarr and its church, Fort Chambrai, Comino and Malta, Xagħra, and Xewkija with its Rotunda are all clearly seen.

Mekren's traditional bakery (Hanaq St (signed to Ramla); ✆ 21552342; f; ⏱ 09.00–19.00 Wed–Fri, Sun & Mon, 09.30–20.00 Sat, 09.30–15.00 Tue, but baking from the early hours) Whether you are hungry or not, take a look in here to see a truly traditional Maltese bakery at work. If you are hungry, order Malta's own version of pizza, *ftira*, or a normal pizza, in advance. Take a peep into the cavernous wood-burning oven into which the breads are placed with long wooden spatulas.

MALTESE BREAD AND THE MEDITERRANEAN STAPLE DIET

The Maltese are very proud of their bread. *Hobż Malti* is a crusty sourdough made of durum wheat with a soft inside. Traditionally, each village had a windmill and a baker who cooked the bread in a wood-burning oven. A few of these remain – including the Ta' Kola Windmill in Xagħra and Mekren's bakery, Nadur. Bread is increasingly produced with modern equipment but daily fresh bread is still regarded as a necessity by most Maltese and it is often delivered by van first thing in the morning.

Bread has been a staple in Malta since the Bronze Age when the Mediterranean triad – bread (grain), olive oil and wine – first became established. Archaeologist Reuben Grima, in his book *The Making of Malta*, points out that these products were probably favoured because the plants from which they are grown thrive in the Mediterranean climate, they ripen at different times of year so a small workforce could produce all three, they can be stored (in case of harvest failure the following year) and all are transportable.

This last was of great importance for Malta, whose population rapidly outstripped its ability to grow grain. Malta has not been self-sufficient for many centuries. Today, bread flour is bought by a central co-operative serving all bakers, and comes from as far afield as Iran and the USA. Even in Roman times grain was imported from Sicily, as it continued to be right through the time of the Knights and beyond.

So concerned were the order not to run out of grain in times of siege that they built huge underground granaries (*fossae* or grain silos) in their fortified cities. The round lids covering these can be seen outside Fort St Elmo in Valletta and in Floriana and you can now walk inside three of the silos in the Gozo Citadel. Those in Floriana were used until the 1980s when a modern grain terminal was built on the Kordin promontory on the Grand Harbour. Today most agriculture on the islands is concentrated on fruit and vegetable production and almost all cereals come from abroad. The bread itself, however, remains *hobż Malti*.

SAN BLAS

A short drive north from Nadur is this beautiful red-sandy bay at the end of one of the most fertile valleys in Gozo. A mini Ramla just along the coast from its larger neighbour, San Blas is more enclosed by cliffs and greenery. It used to be kept sparsely visited by the very steep (repeat, *very* steep) track you had to walk down (and then up!) to get to the beach. Now it is often possible in summer to get a jeep to take you back up. Like Ramla there can be rip currents here and there is no flag system to warn you so check with locals, especially if the weather has been windy, and keep young children and weaker swimmers in their depth. You can park at the top of the steep track and there is a small snack bar at the bottom. Along the coast, on the cliffs between here and Daħlet Qorrot (some 3km from Nadur) is the **Ta' Sopu Tower** [map, page 262] (It-Torri Isopu, also known as San Blas Tower and Torre Nuova). It was built in 1667 under Grand Master Nicolas Cotoner. The original staircase to the first-floor drawbridge has gone and the walls are quite weathered.

DAĦLET QORROT BAY

A popular swimming spot crowded with locals on summer weekends, Daħlet Qorrot (pronounced *darlet or-rot*) Bay is reached by road through a fertile valley to the northeast of Nadur. It is little visited by tourists and the small pebbly beach can be marred by quite a bit of dried seaweed. There is, however, good clear water, also accessible from the rocks and down steps from an area of concrete. Caves in the rock face have been extended and converted by local fishermen into a few boathouses. The steps beyond the boathouses give access to a pleasant stretch of coast – a good place for a short walk.

QALA

The village of Qala (pronounced *ahla* and meaning 'port', of which there was probably once one at nearby Ħondoq ir-Rummien) is high up to the northeast of Mġarr. It is Gozo's easternmost village with uninterrupted views over the channel to Malta. The little church, known as Il-Madonna tal-blat ('Madonna of the Rocks') faces Comino and tradition has it that this was so that the people of Comino could be involved in a Mass even when weather prevented a priest from reaching the smaller island.

High on the cliffs on the edge of Qala above Mġarr is a promenade commanding panoramic views across the channel to Comino and the Blue Lagoon, Cominotto and beyond, as well as down over Mġarr and the ferries coming and going. At Qala's high promenade there is a bar-pizzeria, Xerri il-Bukket that has its own *boċċi* pitch (see box opposite). Balls are provided and if nobody is playing you can help yourself and have a game.

In the main square is Zeppi's Pub, which often has locals playing live music on a Friday night, and in and around the square are a couple of restaurants (page 272) and bed and breakfasts (page 268).

ĦONDOQ IR-RUMMIEN BAY

A few minutes' drive from Qala (walkable in under an hour – but beware of the heat in summer) – is Ħondoq Bay (pronounced *hondok*). Directly opposite Comino's

A close relation of boules, bowls and pétanque, *boċċi* developed in Italy where it is called *bocce*, but the Maltese version is a little different. It is played by two teams of one, two or three players on a marked pitch of coarse sand (or a makeshift flat area of gravel, sand, soil or short-cut grass). Rules vary somewhat between clubs, but here is one version for example.

A team of one or two people has seven *boċċi* – three small round balls and four much larger cylinders. A team of three has 11 *boċċi* – three balls and eight cylinders. One team's *boċċi* are red (Team R), the other's green (Team G). There is also one very small marker ball – the jack.

The jack is thrown at the start of each frame and the aim of the game is to get your *boċċi* closest to the jack. This is done both by simply rolling the *boċċi* and by knocking the opposing team's *boċċi* out of the way – or indeed knocking the jack closer to your own *boċċi*. Balls and cylinders can be used interchangeably but the game usually starts with a ball and it is the cylinders – being larger and heavier – that are generally used for displacing opponents' *boċċi*.

HOW TO PLAY

1 Whichever team wins the toss of a coin – let's say Team R – starts.
2 Team R throws the jack. It must land between 15ft and 37ft away from the players. If the jack is thrown out of area twice then the other team gets to throw it and start the game. During the game the jack can be knocked anywhere on the pitch and the game continues, unless it lands less than 5ft from the players in which case play stops and the frame starts again.
3 Team R rolls a *boċċa* ball trying to get it as close as possible to the jack.
4 Team G takes a turn, trying to get a *boċċa* closer than Team R's. Team G continues to roll *boċċi* (balls or cylinders) until it gets one of its *boċċi* closer than Team R's (or runs out of *boċċi*). Play then passes back to Team R.
5 Teams take turns in this way, switching over each time a team gets a *boċċa* closer than the closest of its opponents' *boċċi*. This continues until both teams have run out of *boċċi*.

SCORING When all the *boċċi* have been used the team with the closest ball to the jack wins and gets a point for each *boċċa* (ball or cylinder) that is closer to the jack than the other team's closest ball. If each team's closest ball is the same distance from the jack no points are awarded. The winning team starts the next frame and play continues until one team reaches 12 points and wins the match.

WHERE TO PLAY Xerri Il-Bukket pitch, Qala on Gozo or games are organised for tourists at the **Buġibba Boċċi Club** on the promenade next to McDonald's; ask the barman (☏ 21577362; m 99442919) most days between 11.00 and 13.00.

Blue Lagoon, this bay is very popular with locals for summer **swimming**. It is easy to park here and there is a café, too. A small beach of coarse sand leads to smoother sand at the water's edge (so it is good for families) and there is also a concrete area with steps into the water and a jumping point much enjoyed by older children. It is not picturesque, but the water is crystal clear and the swimming good. It is also used by divers (especially the less experienced).

GOZO HONDOQ IR-RUMMIEN BAY

14

If you prefer something more secluded, walk a couple of hundred metres along the rocks to the west and you will round a corner to find a rocky inlet with steps into deep clear water and a small cave to explore.

XEWKIJA

The oldest parish in Gozo outside Victoria (1678), Xewkija (meaning 'thorny wasteland' in Arabic and pronounced *shewkeeya*) also has the most famous church in Gozo besides the Citadel cathedral: the parish **Church of St John the Baptist**, known to all as the **Rotunda**.

THE ROTUNDA (Church; ☏21556793; **f**; ⏰ 05.00–noon & 15.00–20.00 (approx), museum & lift 09.30–noon Mon–Sat – except if a Mass is in progress; admission free except lift) This huge church vies with Mosta to be the largest dome in Malta and both churches claim to have the third-largest unsupported dome in Europe (after St Peter's in Rome and St Paul's in London). For the record, Mosta Dome is wider, Xewkija is taller. The dome here is 27m in external diameter and 75m high and it can be seen from all over Gozo. Information leaflets in several languages are available inside the main door.

The smooth white limestone interior can accommodate three times the population of the village. It is dominated by vast Ionic columns, eight of which have ferroconcrete cores supporting the 45,000-ton dome. The church was built between 1951 and 1971 with contributions of money and labour from the people of the parish. It was constructed over the much smaller 17th-century Baroque parish church, which was only removed once the new building was complete. Many parts of the old church, including stone carvings, altars, altarpieces and marble tombs, can be seen in the **Sculpture Museum** (⏰ by volunteers c10.00–noon & 14.30–16.30) to the left of the modern altar. The coloured marble altar you pass here is the main altar of the old Baroque church.

Next to the museum is a **lift** (€2) up to a broad **balcony** that runs all the way round the base of the dome (older children should like this). Stand next to vast stone scrolls and above the main door and admire views of Gozo's other spires and domes, as well as the surrounding countryside.

The **feast of John the Baptist** is on 24 June and is celebrated on the nearest weekend.

MUNXAR

Munxar (pronounced *moonshar*) village is home to some 700 souls and is centred on a very open church square, with an unusually small Baroque-style, early 20th-century parish church. The last village in Gozo to become an autonomous parish, it lies just south of Rabat (Victoria) and beyond it is the scenic road to Xlendi. The church is dedicated to St Paul but Munxar does not celebrate its *festa* on his feast day in February, but at a time more conducive to outdoor entertainment, the third weekend of May.

SANNAT

An attractive little village with an early 18th-century parish **Church of St Margaret Martyr** (*festa* 20 July), Sannat is known as the gateway to the Ta' Ċenċ Plateau and cliffs. Billy Connolly has a house here and there is a congenial gathering place in Rosina's Bar. Quaint Hotel (page 268) and Beppe's Restaurant (page 272) are in the main square while on the outskirts of the village is the **Ta' Ċenċ Hotel** (page 267).

TA' ĊENĊ *

A marvellous place for a **walk**, the Ta' Ċenċ (pronounced *ta chench*) Plateau of rough rock and garigue is home to many of Gozo's most interesting flora and fauna as well as commanding views off the cliffs that plunge up to 145m into the sea. (Bits of them occasionally literally plunge, particularly in winter, so do not go too close to the edge!) If you walk off the tracks you will want closed shoes with a solid sole as the rocks are sharp and thorny plants common. Lizards are plentiful here and if you are lucky you might even see a black whip snake (the most common of Malta's snake species, none of which is dangerous).

This is also a good place for **birdwatching**. Scopoli's shearwaters nest in the cliffs and can be heard calling and seen through binoculars at dusk in summer. Also in summer there are short-toed larks, corn buntings, spectacled warblers, pallid swifts and Malta's national bird, the blue rock thrush. In spring and autumn, this is a great place to see migrating species as they fly over or make landfall for the first time in hundreds of miles. Be warned, however, that in autumn, and possibly even spring, you might find yourself sharing the cliffs with bird hunters even though the area is meant to be a hunting-free zone.

The hunters' stone huts make it difficult to differentiate the **prehistoric and ancient remains** that dot this rocky plateau from more modern construction in the same materials. However, a couple of sites can be identified. Follow the signs from Sannat to the cliffs and go down the track past some buildings, continuing for about 150m. To the left of the road on the edge looking out at panoramic views towards Xewkija (and the Rotunda) is a small low **dolmen** [map, page 262] – a horizontal capstone supported on other blocks. This was probably part of a Bronze Age tomb complex of which two or three other tombs survive.

The plateau is also criss-crossed with **cart ruts** [map, page 262]. Most are very hard to see, but if you walk towards the edge of the cliff along the back boundary wall of the hotel (past their limestone *trulli* – round huts) you will find a patch of open rock about 20m in from the cliff edge (best not to go any closer) with clear cart ruts running across it.

MĠARR IX-XINI *

Down a narrow, pot-holed road along a fertile valley leads from Sannat or Xewkija to this steep-sided rocky inlet (only attempt the final ramp if you are sure your car will make it up again!), Mġarr ix-Xini (pronounced *imjar ish shini*) is a lovely place for a swim, snorkel or dive. It is also the location used to represent the south of France in the 1970s in Angelina Jolie and Brad Pitt's 2015 film *By the Sea*. The tiny interior of the mainly outdoor fish restaurant at the head of the creek (page 271) was used as the village shop and the décor and a few props remain. Until recently right off the beaten track, Mġarr ix-Xini and its restaurant have recently become popular with main-island Maltese so this once-quiet inlet can get quite busy with boats and diners on summer weekends. There is a very small stony beach and rocks to swim and jump off. In summer, buoys mark two swimming areas, including a lengthy strip along one side of the rocky gorge. Boats are not allowed inside the buoys.

MĠARR IX-XINI TOWER [map, page 262] (Wirt Għawdex, Gozo Heritage, an NGO, head office: Dar il-Lunzjata, Wied il-Lunzjata, Rabat; ☎21562666; m 79771981; e info@wirtghawdex.org; w wirtghawdex.org; ⊕ Jul–Sep 11.00–13.30 Sat & when the flag is flying, otherwise by appointment) Climb up the rock-cut steps behind the beach on the opposite side from the road and follow the path – between wild fennel and thyme – along the rocky side of the inlet until you get to the tower looking out to open sea. Built in 1661 as part of Grand Master de Redin's coastal defence scheme, it also protected against smugglers (who may still use the inlet out of season). It was too late to prevent the enslavement of thousands of Gozitans apparently embarked onto Turkish ships hidden in this creek in 1551. The tower was re-used as a watchtower in World War II.

The little rock off the coast is **Ras in-Newwiela**. *Newwel* roughly translates as 'hand over, pass on', said to be the Turks' call as they loaded their newly captured Gozitan slaves from this rock onto their galleys.

The tower is entered by a stone staircase to a **first-floor drawbridge**. Inside is a **freshwater well** (to the left) and a **spiral staircase** in the thickness of the wall leading to the roof with two cannons (in a glass cupboard on the first floor is an 8cm limestone sphere that is probably a Knights' cannonball). Unusually there is also an armaments store and a guardroom on the roof, which may also have acted as a protective barrier in case of landward attack. There are great views here, including along the coast towards Mġarr. You can **walk** from here along the coast to Fort Chambrai (and thence Mġarr Harbour) in about 1¼ hours.

XLENDI

On the road down into Xlendi (pronounced *shlendi*) is **La Grotta** (✆ 21551149; m 99493748; f lagrottaleisure), one of Gozo's few nightclubs with a great location but otherwise not much to write home about. It is mercifully outside the village, which is a surprisingly peaceful place, much quieter than Gozo's other resort town, Marsalforn, on the north coast. Xlendi has a very pleasant waterfront full of cafés, restaurants and small hotels with the road and parking banished to behind the first row of buildings.

The bay ✳ is wonderful for **swimming** and popular for snorkelling and diving, too. There is a very small sand and pebble beach, offering a gently sloping entry into the water that is fine for all ages. There is also a long stretch of rocks down the western side of the bay where sunbathers lounge and from which you can swim straight into deep water. Buoys mark the swimming areas. Stay inside them and you do not run the risk of being run over by a boat.

Xlendi is home to several of the island's dive companies including two of the most established – Moby Dives and St Andrew's Divers Cove (page 277). The **Xlendi Cruises** kiosk organises all sorts of scheduled and tailor-made boat trips (page 275) and rents out pedaloes and simple canoes in summer.

You will find plenty of services in Xlendi including good restaurants (page 273), cafés, small fast-food outlets, agents ready to book you outings and an HSBC with ATM. If you are self-catering, there is a small grocery shop next to the San Andrea hotel, and shop vans (bakers, fruit and vegetables) also visit. The nearest supermarket is in Victoria, a 10–15-minute drive away.

XLENDI TOWER At the far end of the rock swimming area, you can walk out to Xlendi Tower, which is also very clearly seen on boat trips as it guards the entrance to the bay. Built in 1650 in the reign of Grand Master Lascaris, this is the oldest free-standing coastal watchtower on Gozo. It was intended to defend not only against the Turks but also against smugglers and quarantine evaders. It continued to be manned until the 1870s. It is due for restoration with a view to opening it to the

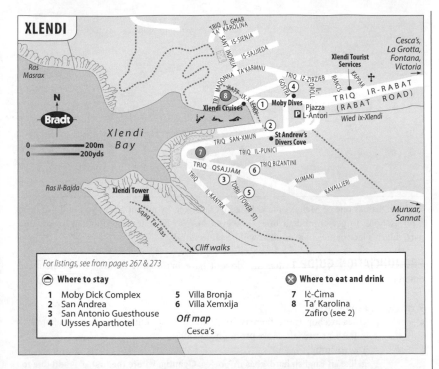

XLENDI

For listings, see from pages 267 & 273

Where to stay

1. Moby Dick Complex
2. San Andrea
3. San Antonio Guesthouse
4. Ulysses Aparthotel

5. Villa Bronja
6. Villa Xemxija

Off map
Cesca's

Where to eat and drink

7. Ić-Ćima
8. Ta' Karolina
Zafiro (see 2)

public, but for now can be seen only from the outside or by special arrangement with Munxar Council (℡ 21558755; e munxar.lc@gov.mt). The tower and its immediate surroundings offer a great **viewpoint** over the bay and along the cliffs, and a perfect place for **birders** to set up a telescope to see shearwaters rafting at dusk before they fly in to their nests in the cliffs.

Appendix 1

LANGUAGE

With English as one of Malta's official languages, spoken by all but a few, you will not need a phrasebook to get around. It does, however, help to be able to pronounce words and particularly place names in a way that will be understood.

PRONUNCIATION GUIDE Letters we do not have in English or that are pronounced differently:

Written	Pronounced
ċ	'ch' as in 'chop' (note: there is no 'c' without an accent so the accent is often left out. All 'c's in Maltese are pronounced 'ch')
ġ	'j' as in 'jump'
g	'g' like an English hard 'g', as in 'go' (eg: Ġgantija where the first 'g' is soft due to the accent, while the second 'g' is hard so the word is pronounced *jiganteeya*)
għ	Not sounded, eg: *għar* (meaning 'cave') is pronounced *are*
ħ	'h' as in 'house'
h	Hard as in 'ha!' – including when it comes at the end of a word. Or sometimes unsounded
j	'y' as in 'yam'
q	Not sounded when followed by a vowel although it does give the vowel a hard edge (it is as if you start to say 'k' but do not actually). Eg: Ta' Qali is pronounced Ta 'ali (or '*arli*) with a hard edge on the 'a'. At the end of a word or before a consonant it is pronounced a bit more like a 'k', eg: Ħondoq is pronounced *Hondok*. (Just to confuse things, the British colonials in Malta always pronounced 'q' as a 'k', so Ta' Qali was *Takali*.)
m	As in English, but when followed by another consonant at the start of a word can be more like 'im'. Eg: Mtarfa is said almost as *Imtarfa*.
r	May be a little rolled as in Italian
x	'sh' as in 'she'
ż	Soft, as in 'zoo' or 'buzz'
z	A 'ts' sound like in 'pants' (eg: 'pizza') or a 'ds' sound as in suds

The vowels

a	Can be long as in 'path', or shorter like 'u' in 'cut'
e	Short, as in 'egg' or longer like 'ai' in 'pair'
i	Mostly long like 'ee' but sometimes short as in 'pit'
o	Short as in 'pot', or long as in 'aw' in 'saw'
u	Like 'oo' as in 'pool' or 'u' in 'pull'

USEFUL WORDS AND PHRASES
Getting by

Good morning	*bonġu* (pronounced *bonjoo*)
Good evening	*bonswa*
Goodbye	*saħħa*
Thank you	*grazzi*
Please	*jekk jogħġox* (pronounced *yek yo-jbok*)
Yes	*iva* (pronounced *eeva*)
No	*le* (pronounced *lé*)

Places of interest

bay	*bajja* (pronounced *buya*)
beach	*plajja* (pronounced *playa*)
castle	*kastell*
cathedral	*katidral* (pronounced *kateedrahl*)
cave	*għar* (pronounced *are*)
cemetery	*ċimiterju* (pronounced *chimiteryu*)
cistern	*bir* (pronounced *beer*) (for water, usually translated in Malta as 'well' though it is more often a container for water than a source of groundwater)
city/urban area	*belt* (*Il-belt*)
cliffs	*rdum* (pronounced *ir doom*)
farmhouse	*razzett*
ferry	*vapur*
garden	*ġnien* (pronounced *Janine* – like the girl's name)
harbour	*marsa* (pronounced *marsa*) also *mġarr* (pronounced *imjar*)
inlet	*dahlet* (pronounced *darlet*)
neighbourhood	(like French *quartier*) *kwartier*
parish	*paroċċa* (pronounced *parocha*)
point/headland	*ras* (pronounced *rass*)
spring (of water)	*għajn* (pronounced *ine*)
square	*misrah* (pronounced *mizrah*)
street/road	*triq* (pronounced *treek*)
suburb	*rabat* (from the Arabic)
tower	*torri* (pronounced *tory*)
valley	*wied* (pronounced *weed*)
wharf	*xatt* (pronounced *shut*)
windmill	*mithna* (pronounced with the h lightly sounded). NB: *mitna* (pronounced as written) means 'we died'!

Signs

Closed	*magħluq* (pronounced *ma'look*)
Open	*miftuħ* (pronounced *miftoo*)
Private	*privat* (pronounced *preevat*)

And just to avoid misunderstanding ... *Ħaxix* pronounced *hashish* means 'vegetables' and *Xita* pronounced *shitter* means 'rain'!

Appendix 2

GLOSSARY

The following words are likely to come up in information available in Malta.

Agape table
Round table carved out of the rock in Roman/Byzantine catacombs, usually with benches cut around it. Used for family and friends of the dead to take a funerary meal. Malta is unusual in having well-preserved tables cut into the rock. Also called a *refrigerium* or *triclinium*.

Auberge
The inns or colleges (often translated in Malta as 'hostels') of the Knights where they lived and worked in communities of people speaking the same language (*langues*; see box, page 117).

Bastion
A projecting part of a fortified stone wall (in forts built after the advent of gunpowder, bastions are usually pentagonal).

Battery
In the context of fortifications this is an emplacement for heavy guns.

Cavalier
Part of a fortification that is higher than its surroundings, often built up from a bastion or similar, used as a gun platform (see *St James Cavalier*, page 118).

Corbelling
Where each layer of building material (in Malta, stone) projects in from the layer below so that a wall curves inwards at the top. In the case of a room (or a Maltese temple apse), this shrinks the space through which the sky can be seen and, if continued, eventually creates a domed roof.

Corsair
A sea pirate with some official backing.

Curtain
In the context of fortifications, this is the rampart wall joining two neighbouring bastions or towers.

Demi-bastion
A half-bastion, consisting of only one face and one flank.

Dolmen
A prehistoric structure of upright stones topped with a horizontal capstone. Usually a burial site.

E-boat
The Allies' name for small, fast, technically advanced gunboats developed by the Germans when they were forbidden, under the Versailles Treaty, to build large warships. Very effective at the start of World War II, they were copied by the Allies.

Enceinte
French word for a perimeter wall encircling any work of fortification around a town or castle.

Entrenchment
(noun) In the context of fortifications, this is an area protected by trenches or other field defences. In Malta it is also used to refer to solidly built sea walls that are part of the bastioned fortifications in some coastal areas.

Festa
Feast day. In Malta, it also means several days of religious and secular celebration surrounding a saint's day.

Fortizza	From the Italian, meaning fort.
Foss	Ditch.
Garigue	Sometimes spelt *garrigue*, this is open scrubland on limestone rock in the Mediterranean region.
Hornwork	A defensive structure outside the main fortification consisting of two demi-bastions linked by a curtain wall, usually very close to, or joined at the rear to, the main fortifications.
Langue	Literally, the French for 'tongue' (language), *langue* refers to one of the eight language groups into which the Knights divided themselves (see box, page 117).
Luzzu	Fishing boat (see box, page 186).
Megalith	A very large stone, particularly those found in prehistoric and ancient monuments/buildings (including Malta's temples).
Orthostat	One of a group of large stone slabs, lined up vertically to form the lower part of a wall in prehistoric and ancient megalithic construction, as in Malta's prehistoric temples.
Parapet	In the context of fortifications, this is an embankment or wall protecting soldiers from enemy fire.
Parvis	Large forecourt of a church, often a raised paved terrace.
Passeggiata (Italian) or *passiggatta* (Maltese)	Both used to describe a stroll or promenade, usually taken on summer evenings before it gets dark.
Pilier	A Knight of St John who heads one of the *langues*.
Ravelin	A V-shaped fortification outside the main fortifications, placed in front of a curtain wall.
Redoubt	A small defensive structure (or mini fort) generally for the use of infantry defending a position.
Refrigerium	See *Agape table*, opposite.
RTO	Abbreviation of the Italian *riservato*, but usually translated as 'Reserved To Owner', used to mark hunters' and trappers' hides and private land.
Torba	Crushed and pounded limestone often used for flooring of prehistoric buildings.
Triclinium	See *Agape table*, opposite.
Trilithon	A construction of three megaliths – two uprights supporting one placed horizontally across the top (to create something like a doorway).
UNESCO	United Nations Educational, Scientific, and Cultural Organization.

UPDATES WEBSITE

You can post your comments and recommendations, and read feedback and updates from other readers online at **w** bradtupdates.com/maltaandgozo.

Appendix 3

FURTHER INFORMATION

BOOKS
Prehistory and the temples

Bonanno, Anthony *The Archaeology of Malta & Gozo 5000BC–AD1091* Photos by Daniel Cilia, Heritage Malta, 2017. An excellent, clear, concise, academically sound and up-to-date introduction to Malta's pre- and early historical archaeological remains, with great photos.

Cilia, Daniel (ed.) *Malta before History* With photographs by Daniel Cilia, Miranda, 2004. Massive tome of 440 pages; hundreds of illustrations including marvellous colour photos as well as reconstructions of the temples and text by ten experts in the field.

Pace, Anthony *Maltese Prehistoric Art 5000–2500BC* Midsea Books, 2002.

Trump, David H *Malta: Prehistory and Temples* With photos by Daniel Cilia, Malta's Living Heritage series, Midsea Books, 2002. The key book on Malta's temples. Scholarly, but easy to read and with excellent photos. Includes a site-by-site guide. The author is a Cambridge archaeologist closely involved with excavations in Malta since 1954. This is the only one of these four books you would want to carry around (and much the least expensive!).

Vella, Godwin (ed.) *Ġgantija: The Oldest Freestanding Building in the World* Photos by Daniel Cilia, Heritage Malta, 2014. Coffee-table book with over 400 photos by the best photographer of the temples.

Vella, Godwin, Sagona, Nicoline and Cremona, John *The Ġgantija Temples: A History of Its Visitors and Views* Heritage Malta, 2011. Early pictures and descriptions of the temples by visitors in early modern times.

Vella Gregory, Isabelle *Human Form in Neolithic Malta* Photos by Daniel Cilia, Midsea Books, 2006. A large, expensive book with lots of photos as well as authoritative text.

Ancient history

Bonanno, Anthony *The Archaeology of Malta & Gozo 5000BC–AD1091* See above.

Bonnano, Anthony *Malta: Phoenician, Punic and Roman* With photos by Daniel Cilia, Malta's Living Heritage series, Midsea Books, 2005. The key book on this period. Beautifully produced, scholarly, but approachable with great illustrations. Includes a site-by-site guide.

Buhagiar, Mario (ed.) *Essays on the Archaeology and Ancient History of the Maltese Islands: Bronze Age to Byzantine* Midsea Books, 2014.

Weston, Gordon E *The Maltese Cart-Ruts: Unraveling an Enigma* Progress Press, 2010. Describes 50+ cart-rut sights, lots of photos and speculation.

Medieval Malta

Dalli, Charles *Malta: The Medieval Millennium* With photos by Daniel Cilia, Malta's Living Heritage series, Midsea Books, 2006. The latest in the excellent Living Heritage series. Expert text and excellent illustrations. Includes a site-by-site guide.

The Knights' period (including art)

Balbi di Correggio, Francisco *The Siege of Malta 1565* Translated from the Spanish edition of 1568 by Ernle Bradford, Boydell Press, 2005. Fascinating contemporary account of the Great Siege.

Bradford, Ernle *The Great Siege: Malta 1565* Open Road Media, 2014 (first published 1961). Well-written story of the 1565 siege by British historian and Malta expert.

Bradford, Ernle *The Shield and the Sword* Penguin, 2002. Well-written history of the Knights.

Cassar, Kenneth (ed.) *The Inquisitor's Palace: An Architectural Gem Spanning Centuries and Styles* Heritage Malta, 2013.

Clot, André *Suleiman the Magnificent* Saqi, 2012.

Crowley, Roger *Empires of the Sea: The Final Battle for the Mediterranean 1521–1580* Faber, 2009.

De Giorgio, Cynthia *Mattia Preti: Saints and Heroes for the Knights of Malta* Midsea Books, 2014. The curator of St John's Co-Cathedral uses Preti's work to explore the Knights' relationship to its saints. Lots of colour plates.

De Giorgio, Cynthia *Woven Splendour: The Tapestries of St John's* Midsea Books, 2017. A detailed look at these important tapestries by the curator of St John's.

De Giorgio, Cynthia and Guido, Sante *Mattia Preti: St Catherine of Alexandria* Midsea Books, 2005. Forty-eight pages on Malta's old master and one of his most important works.

Debono, Sandro *Understanding Caravaggio and His Art in Malta* Insight Heritage Guides, 2007. Short, accessible and copiously colour illustrated.

Freller, Thomas *The German Langue of the Order of Malta: A Concise History* Midsea Books, 2010.

Freller, Thomas *Malta: The Order of St John* With photos by Daniel Cilia, Midsea Books, 2010. Scholarly but accessible and with lots of good pictures, one of the best places to start for the story of the order during its time in Malta.

Freller, Thomas *The Palaces of the Grand Masters in Malta* Midsea Books, 2009.

Galea, Michael *The Grand Masters Series* PEG, 1990s–2000s. A book on each important grand master.

Gauci, Liam *In the Name of the Prince: Maltese Corsairs 1760–1798* Photos by Daniel Cilia, Heritage Malta, 2016. The result of ten years of research into newly found documents, interesting insights into 'legal, religious' Maltese plundering of the Mediterranean.

Grima, Joseph F *Legacy of the Order in Malta 360°* Photography by Enrico Formica, 2 volumes (1530–1680 & 1581–1798), Miranda, 2008. Large-format, beautifully produced, expensive hardback of photos.

Hughes, Quentin and Thake, Conrad *Malta: The Baroque Island* With photos by Daniel Cilia, Midsea Books, 2003. Large format with glossy photographs and an authoritative survey of the architecture of the Knights of St John in Malta.

Langdon, Helen *Caravaggio: A Life* Pimlico, 1999. An excellent biography including his time in Malta.

Mantella, Giuseppe and Guido, Sante *Mattia Preti: A Guide to His Paintings in the Churches of Malta & Gozo* Din L'Art Helwa (Malta's National Trust), 2014.

Masterpieces from the Armoury of Malta Between the Battlesword and the Cross Multiple authors, photos by Daniel Cilia, Heritage Malta, 2008.

Mercieca, Simon *The Knights of St John in Malta* Miller, 2005. Easy-to-read, colour-illustrated, short chronicle of the Knights in Malta by a Malta University historian.

Nicholson, Helen *The Knights Hospitaller* Boydell Press, 2001. Accessible history of the Knights from the beginning through to today.

O'Malley, Gregory *The Knights Hospitaller of the English Langue 1460–1565* Oxford, 2005.

Pickles, Tim *Malta 1565: Last Battle of the Crusades* Osprey, 1998. Short military history of the Great Siege.

Riley-Smith, Jonathan *Hospitallers: The History of the Order of St John* Hambledon, 2003. By a leading Cambridge University expert on the Crusades.

Sciberras, Keith *Caravaggio to Mattia Preti: Baroque Painting in Malta* Midsea Books, 2015.

Sciberras, Keith *Mattia Preti: The Triumphant Manner* Midsea Books, 2012. Pricey but beautiful book inlcuding a catalogue of the artist's work in Malta.

Sciberras, Keith and Stone, David M *Caravaggio: Art, Knighthood and Malta* Midsea Books, 2006.

Scicluna, Joe *By Order of Napoleon: The Taking of Malta* CreateSpace, 2015. Source book of the orders Napoleon issued in relation to the taking of Malta – from the orders to take Gozo to demanding the removal of silver from St John's.

Seward, Desmond *The Monks of War* Penguin, first published 1972. Covers all the military religious orders with plenty on the Knights of St John. The author has himself become a knight since the book was first published.

Sire, H J A *The Knights of Malta* Yale University Press, 1994. A thematic history of the Knights (not only in Malta). Well illustrated. Too heavy (literally, not literarily) for the luggage.

Spiteri, Stephen *Armoury of the Knights* Midsea Books, 2003. A comprehensive 400-page guide by the Armoury's one-time curator and leading expert in the field. Includes an annotated catalogue of the collection.

Spiteri, Stephen *The Art of Fortress Building in Hospitaller Malta* BDL, 2008. The key book on Malta's remarkable Knights-period fortifications. Spiteri is the top expert and this book is comprehensive and very well and informatively illustrated.

Spiteri, Stephen *Fortress Malta 360°* Photos by Enrico Formica, Miranda, 2007. Beautifully produced large-format expensive coffee-table book featuring images of Malta's fortifications with text by the leading expert.

Ware Allen, Bruce *The Great Siege of Malta: The Epic Battle between the Ottoman Empire and the Knights of St John* ForeEdge (University Press of New England), 2015.

Wettinger, Godfrey *Slavery in the Islands of Malta and Gozo 1000–1812* BDL, 2002. Some 700 pages on slavery (Muslim, Jewish and Christian).

The British and World War I

Bonnici, Joseph and Cassar, Michael *A Century of the Royal Navy in Malta* BDL, 1999.

Bonnici, Joseph and Cassar, Michael *The Malta Railway* Self-published, 1992. Detailed history with lots of photos.

Brittain, Vera *Because You Died: Poetry and Prose of the First World War and After* Edited by Mark Bostridge, Virago, 2008. Including several poems and photographs from her time during World War I nursing in Malta; see also *Testament of Youth*, below.

Brittain, Vera *Testament of Youth* Virago, 1978 and 2008. Memoir which includes her time nursing the wounded of World War I in Malta.

Elliot, Peter *The Cross and the Ensign: The Naval History of Malta 1798–1979* HarperCollins, 2009.

Grech, Jesmond *British Heritage in Malta* Miller, 2003. Ninety-five pages including lots of colour photos. Cross between a history and a guidebook.

MacGill, Thomas *Handbook, or Guide, for Strangers Visiting Malta 1839* Download free from w archive.org/details/ahandbookorguid00macggoog. An early 19th-century guidebook to Malta.

Manduca, John (ed.) *The Bonham-Carter Diaries 1936–1940* PEG, 2004. What the British governor thought of Malta and the Maltese.

Refalo, Michael *Slavery: Malta at the Crossroads* BDL 2015. Malta's role in slavery in the British period.

Rigby, B L *The Malta Railway* Oakwood Press, 2004.

Spiteri, Stephen *British Military Architecture in Malta* Self-published, 1996. Out of print but can still be found. The author is the leading expert on Malta's fortifications.

Stephenson, Charles *The Fortifications of Malta 1530–1945* Osprey, 2004. Short illustrated military history, particularly good on the British fortifications.

Warlow, Ben *The Royal Navy at Malta 1900–2000* Maritime Books, 2002. A book of black-and-white photos of the ships and life of the Royal Navy in Malta.

World War II

More books on World War II in Malta can be found at w pen-and-sword. co.uk (search 'Malta'). There is also an excellent selection at the Malta at War Museum in Birgu/Vittoriosa (page 149).

Austin, Douglas *Churchill & Malta: A Special Relationship* Spellmount Publishing, 2006. As First Lord of the Admiralty at the outbreak of both World Wars I and II, Churchill had a particular impact on Malta's wars.

Austin, Douglas *Churchill & Malta's War 1939–1943* Amberley, 2010.

Barnham, Denis *Malta Spitfire Pilot: Ten Weeks of Terror April–June 1942* Grub Street, 2013.

Bradford, Ernle *Siege: Malta 1940–1943* Pen & Sword Military Classics, 2003. Authoritative and gripping history by a man who himself served with the Royal Navy in Malta during the war.

Buerling, George F *Malta Spitfire: Diary of an Ace Fighter Pilot* Grub Street, 2011. First published in 1943.

Cassar, Kevin and Farrugia, Mario *Christmas in Wartime Malta 1939–1945* Fondazzjoni Wirt Artna, 2014. Small book/booklet with photos.

Douglas-Hamilton, Lord James *The Air Battle for Malta* Pen & Sword Books, 2007. A history based on the diaries of the author's uncle, Lord David Douglas-Hamilton, leader of Spitfire squadron in Malta.

Galea, Frederick R *Women of Malta: True Wartime Stories of Christina Ratcliffe and Tamara Marks* Wise Owl Publications, 2008. Christina Ratcliffe stayed on in Malta after Warburton's death and lived until 1988.

Gibbs, Patrick, Wing Commander *Tornado Leader on Malta* Grub Street, 1992/2002. Written in 1942, before the end of the war, this personal account of flying in World War II – mainly in Malta – is detailed and interesting for not having the benefit of hindsight.

Grech, Charles *Raiders Passed: Wartime Recollections of a Maltese Youngster* Translated by Joseph Galea Debono, Midsea Books, 1998. Malta's war from a child's perspective.

Gull, Brian and Galea, Frederick *Gladiators over Malta: The Story of Faith, Hope and Charity* Wise Owl, 2008.

Holland, James *Fortress Malta: An Island under Siege 1940–1943* Phoenix, 2004. A very human history of World War II in Malta, using survivors' tales and diaries to follow a wide variety of people through the war.

Lucas, Laddie *Malta: Thorn in Rommel's Side: Six Months That Turned the War* Penguin, 1993. The author was the commanding officer of Malta's top-scoring Spitfire squadron so he is writing about people and situations he knew well.

Pearson, Michael *The Ohio & Malta: The Legendary Tanker That Refused to Die* Leo Cooper Ltd, 2003. The story of the ship *Ohio* that limped into Malta at the end of Operation Pedestal still miraculously full of fuel.

Poolman, Kenneth *Faith, Hope and Charity: The Defence of Malta* Witness to War series, Crécy 2004.

Smith, Peter C *Pedestal: The Convoy that Saved Malta* Goodall Publications, 2002.

Spooner, Tony *Faith, Hope & Malta GC: Ground & Air Heroes of the George Cross Island* Witness to War series, Crecy 2008 (first published Newton 1992).

Spooner, Tony *Warburton's War: The Life of Maverick Flying Ace Adrian Warburton* Goodall Publications, 2003. English misfit, 'Warby', became one of the most decorated pilots of World War II and, along with his glamorous girlfriend, Christina Ratcliffe, part of Malta's wartime legend. He died mysteriously in 1944.

Sutherland, Jon *Air War Malta* Pen & Sword Books, 2008. The story of the RAF in Malta in World War II.

Sutherland, Jon and Canwell, Diane *Malta GC: Rare Images from Wartime Archives* Images of War Series, Pen & Sword Books, 2009. Many unseen photos of Malta under siege.

Williams, Paul *Malta: Island under Siege* Pen & Sword Books, 2009. Military history with lots of background. Includes a detailed guide to Malta's World War II locations.

Williamson, David G *The Siege of Malta 1940–42* Pen & Sword, 2007. Very clear, month-by-month account.

General history

Abela, Joseph S *Malta: A Panoramic History – A Narrative History of the Maltese Islands* PEG, 2002.

Blouet, Brian *The Story of Malta* Progress Press, 2004. Accessible history of Malta.

Cassar, Carmel *A Concise History of Malta* Mireva Publications, 2002. An interesting and unusual account of Malta's history focusing strongly on social history and, although for general readers, often giving documentary detail.

Grima, Reuben *The Making of Malta* With photos by Daniel Cilia, Midsea Books, 2008. A glossy, beautiful and also authoritative and informative book looking at Malta through seven themes: sea, rock, water, food, faith, war and celebration.

Manley, Deborah (ed.) *Malta: A Traveller's Anthology* Signal Books, 2010. A very enjoyable collection of travellers' comments about Malta from 1st century AD onwards.

Schofield, John and Morrissey, Emily *Strait Street: Malta's 'Red-Light District' Revealed* Midsea Books, 2013.

Zammit, Vincent *Malta: History & Traditions* With photos by Daniel Cilia, BDL, 2007. A glossy guide to Malta's history with lots of excellent and informative pictures.

360° Collection
A series of large-format, beautifully produced and expensive photographic books (weighing over 2kg each) of excellent photos published by Miranda. Some are listed in relevant history sections.

Gozo and Comino, text by Joseph Bezzina, photography by Attilio Boccazzi and Daniel Cilia, 1992.

Malta 360° by Geoffrey Aquilina Ross, photography by Enrico Formica, 2003.

Malta by Night by Geoffrey Aqulina Ross, photography by Enrico Formica, 2003.

World Heritage Sites in Malta 360° by Reuben Grima, photography by Enrico Formica, 2003. Authoritative text and excellent photos of the temples and Valletta.

Underground Malta 360° volume 1, by Geoffrey Aquilina Ross and Fiona Galea Debono, photography by Enrico Formica, 2004. Includes places not open to the public.

Underground Malta volume 2, by Edward Said, photography by Enrico Formica, 2005.

Fortress Malta 360° by Stephen Spiteri, photography by Enrico Formica, 2007.

Arts, crafts, special interest and miscellaneous
Note that books that cover a specific period are listed under that period.

Aquilina Ross, Geoffrey *At Home in Malta* Miranda Books, 2005. Coffee-table book about Malta's homes and gardens.

Attard, Robert and Azzopardi, Romina *Antique Collecting in Malta* Midsea Books, 2008. A guide to Malta's collections.

Azzopardi, Consiglia *Gozo Lace: An Introduction to Lace Making in the Maltese Islands* Gozo Press, 1999/2005. One of very few pieces of writing on Maltese lace. Includes some lace patterns.

Azzopardi, Emmanuel *The Coinage of the Crusaders and the World of Islam* With photos by Daniel Cilia, Midsea Books, 2006

Bologna, Alaine Apap *The Silver of Malta* Midsea Books, 1995. Catalogue to an exhibition featuring nearly 1,000 items of Maltese silver dating from the mid 16th to the 19th century.

Bonnici, Joseph and Cassar, Michael *The Malta Buses* BDL, 1989. The Maltese bus-lover's bible. A history and photographic catalogue of Malta's buses from 1905 to the late 1980s.

Bugelli, Martin (ed.) *Valletta, A Personal City Guide (by 8 tourist guides from Malta)* Midsea Books, 2018. Essays on different aspects of Valletta.

Cutaja, Dominic *Malta: The History and Works of Art of St John's Church, Valletta* M J Publications, 1999.

de Piro, Nicholas (ed.) *Costume in Malta: A History of Fabric, Form and Fashion* Midsea Books, 1998. A large, authoritative account by 21 authors with 300 illustrations.

de Piro, Nicholas *The National Portrait Gallery of Malta* Miller, 2015. The book is the gallery – some 2,000 portraits of all kinds connected with Malta.

Debono, Sandro *Understanding Caravaggio and His Art in Malta* Insight Heritage Guides, 2007. Short, accessible and copiously colour illustrated.

Ellul-Micallef, Roger *Zammit of Malta* Allied Publication, 2013. A life of Dr Thermistocles Zammit, leading Maltese medic of the early 20th century and 'father of Maltese Archaeology'.

Field, Brett B *Malta's Barrier of Beauty* CreateSpace, 2015. An art photographer's pictures of the doors of Malta.

Freller, Thomas *Gozo & The Grand Tour* Midsea Books, 2017.

Galea-Nandi, Joseph and Micallef, Denise *Guide to Maltese Furniture (1700–1900)* RBIT, 1993.

Hoe, Susanna *Malta: Women, History, Books & Places* Holo Books, The Women's History Press, 2015. Prominent women in Malta, what they did and where.

Kilin [sic] *A Hundred Wayside Chapels in Malta and Gozo* Midsea Books, 2000. The most authoritative guide to Malta's tiniest churches.

Manduca, John *Antique Furniture in Malta* Midsea Books, 2002.

Teatru Manoel: The National Theatre of Malta Midsea Books, 2016.

Thake, Conrad and Hughes, Quentin *Malta War & Peace – An Architectural Chronicle 1800–2000* Midsea Books, 2005. Pricey but beautifully illustrated architectural survey.

Wildlife, landscape and the great outdoors

Bonett, Guido *The Natural History of the Maltese Islands (through a Photographer's Lens)* BDL, 2011.

Borg, John J, Lanfranco, Edwin and Sultana, Joe *Nature in Gozo* BirdLife Malta, 2007. A guide to Gozo's landscape and habitats, flora and fauna with lots of colour photos.

Casha, Alex *Where to Watch Birds and Other Wildlife in Malta* BirdLife Malta, 2004. Short paperback with basic advice on what to see and where.

Dillon, Paddy *Walking in Malta: 33 Routes on Malta, Gozo and Comino* Cicerone, 2004. Clear, well-produced little book full of information.

Lanfranco, Edwin and Bonett, Guido *Wild Flowers of the Maltese Islands* BDL, 2015. Lovely field guide with excellent colour photos. English, Latin, Maltese and colloquial names. Nearly 300 species illustrated.

Pedley, Martyn, Hughes-Clarke, Michael and Abela, Pauline *Limestone Isles in a Crystal Sea: The Geology of the Maltese Islands* PEG, 2002. Summarises decades of research on Maltese geology with colour illustrations and a booklet of geological walks.

Raine, André, Sultana, Joe and Gillings, Simon *Malta Breeding Bird Atlas* BirdLife Malta, 2009. Full-colour guide. The first comprehensive atlas of its kind with a double-page spread of photos, maps and information on each of 32 birds.

Sultana, Joe and Falzon, Victor (eds) *Wildlife of the Maltese Islands* BirdLife Malta and Nature Trust, 2002. Nine expert authors cover some 1,000 species of flora and fauna with colour plates and hundreds of line drawings.

Weber, Hans Christian *Wild Plants of Malta* PEG, 2004. Colour-illustrated guide to Malta's rich flora.

Weber, Hans Christian and Kendzior, Bernd *Flora of the Maltese Islands: A Field Guide* Margraf, 2006.

Food and cooking

Caruana Galizia, Anne and Caruana Galizia, Helen *The Food and Cookery of Malta* Pax Books, 2001. No pictures but over 200 pages of highly informed writing and recipes.

Francis, Darmanin *A Guide to Maltese Cooking* Jumbo Publications, 1997. Traditions, anecdotes and recipes.

Mattei, Pippa *25 Years in a Maltese Kitchen* Miranda, 2003. Cookbook, including recipes for many traditional Maltese dishes.

Language

Bugeja, Paul *English–Maltese Pocket Dictionary and Phrasebook* (with pronunciation) Bay Foreign Language Books, 2004. Easy to use and reliable.

Fiction

Ball, David *The Sword and the Scimitar* Arrow Books, 2004. American historical adventure story set at the time of the Knights' rule in Malta. A Maltese brother and sister are separated when he is taken into slavery by the Ottoman Turks.

Barnard, Frank *Band of Eagles over Malta* Headline Review, 2007. A novel about fighter pilots on Malta in World War II.

Bianchi, Petra *Family Photos* Midsea Books, 1998. A Maltese author writes the story of a Maltese–Italian family in Valletta and Sliema across a century.

Cussler, Clive and Brown, Graham *Pharaoh's Secret* Michael Joseph, 2015. Thirteenth book in the bestselling NUMA Files adventure series.

Dingli, Rosanne *Death in Malta* BeWrite Books, 2005. A writer arrives in Malta to escape home and seek inspiration and becomes embroiled in local life and intrigue. The author was born in Malta but now lives in Australia.

Friggieri, Oliver *Koranta and Other Stories from Malta* Mireva, first published 1994. Malta's leading contemporary writer, writing in English.

Holland, James *A Pair of Silver Wings* William Heinemann, 2006. The tale of a World War II vet facing up to his experiences as a young spitfire pilot in Malta and Italy. By the author of the non-fiction *Fortress Malta* (page 317).

Kilin [sic] *Angelo's Eyes and Other Stories* Midsea Books, 2003. A collection of stories by Malta's best-selling author.

Mills, Mark *The Information Officer* Harper, 2009. Thriller set in World War II Malta by best-selling author of *The Savage Garden*.

Montsarrat, Nicholas *The Kappillan of Malta* Various publishers, first published 1973. A remarkable book both as a novel and as a history of Malta. Set in wartime Malta, the central character is a priest trying to care for his flock but it ranges across the full 7,000 years of Maltese history. Montsarrat, a former British naval officer, lived on Gozo from 1959 until his death in 1979.

O'Brien, Patrick *Treason's Harbour* (book 9 of the Aubrey/Maturin series) Harper, 2010. One of O'Brien's famous naval historical novels partly set in Malta.

Rinaldi, Nicholas *The Jukebox Queen of Malta* Bantam, 1999 or Black Swan, 2000. American author's novel set in Malta during World War II.

Trollope, Joanna (writing as Caroline Harvey) *The Brass Dolphin* Corgi, 1998. A romantic novel set in wartime Malta.

Other Europe guides For a full list of Bradt's Europe guides, see w bradtguides.com/shop.

Bird, Angela and Stewart, Murray *The Vendée and Surrounding Area* (1st edition) Bradt Travel Guides, 2018.
Bostock, Andrew *Greece: The Peloponnese with Athens, Delphi and Kythira* (4th edition) Bradt Travel Guides, 2019.
Darke, Diana, with Stewart, Murray *North Cyprus* (8th edition) Bradt Travel Guides, 2015.
Di Gregorio, Luciano *Italy: Abruzzo* (3rd edition) Bradt Travel Guides, 2017.
Facaros, Dana and Pauls, Michael *Northern Italy: Emilia-Romagna including Bologna* (1st edition) Bradt Travel Guides, 2018.
Robinson, Alex *Alentejo* (2nd edition) Bradt Travel Guides, 2019.
Sayers, David, with Stewart, Murray *Azores* (6th edition) Bradt Travel Guides, 2016.
Stewart, Murray *The Basque Country and Navarre* (2nd edition) Bradt Travel Guides, 2019.
Whitehouse, Rosie *Liguria* (3rd edition) Bradt Travel Guides, 2019.

WEBSITES
Newspaper websites
w independent.com.mt
w maltatoday.com.mt
w timesofmalta.com

Tourism, sights and events listings
w heritagemalta.org Lots of information, including practical details for visitors, for all Heritage Malta's sites, covering many of the islands' main historic and prehistoric sights.
w visitgozo.com Official tourism site for Gozo.
w visitmalta.com The main website of the Malta Tourism Authority with lots of useful information.
w whatson.com.mt

Transport
w maltaairport.com
w publictransport.com.mt

Weather
w maltairport.com/weather
w maltaweather.com

FOLLOW BRADT

For the latest news, special offers and competitions, subscribe to the Bradt newsletter via the website w bradtguides.com and follow Bradt on:

 BradtTravelGuides
 @BradtGuides
 @bradtguides
 bradtguides
 bradtguides

NOTES

Index

Page numbers in **bold** indicate major entries; those in *italics* indicate maps

INDEX OF ADVERTISERS